M

DATE DUE

withglam

We are shaped and fashioned by what we love.
Johann Wolfgang von Goethe

TO KNOW HISTORY
IS TO
LOVE HISTORY

Welcome to Prentice Hall's **T.L.C. Edition**.
That's **T**eaching and **L**earning **C**lassroom Edition.

Dear Student,

Your instructor already knows—and loves—history. *Do you?* **Welcome to the new and exciting T.L.C. Edition—**

this is the book that will change the way you feel about history. Prentice Hall developed this text to bring history to you with more visual appeal than ever. This is the book that you will want to read because it is interesting. You will think about what you're reading because it has relevance to your life. With this book and the multimedia tools we crafted to accompany it, you will truly experience history's dramatic trials and passionate triumphs in a way that adds meaning to your own life. And you will score better on tests because preparation will be easier and less time consuming than you ever dreamed possible.

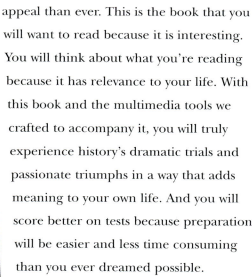

Read on and find out why this book is just the T.L.C. you need to say "I DO" know—and love—history.

TO KNOW HISTORY
IS TO LOVE HISTORY

Imagine if you could make sense of all the names, dates, events, and people who made history?
Imagine putting it all into a context that made you rethink your world, your life, yourself—
with the fascinating perspective that only history provides? All it takes is the T.L.C. you are now holding in your hand.

Here's what makes this T.L.C. Edition different...

- You will be compelled to READ this dramatically different, vividly illustrated, less dense textbook because it is not at all overwhelming

- You will be inspired to THINK about *what* you are reading *as* you are reading.

- You will come to class READY to take notes with your automatically bundled, portable, and easy-to-use *HistoryNotes*.

THE OUTBREAK OF WAR
AND THE DECLARATION OF INDEPENDENCE,
1774–1776

WHAT DEVELOPMENTS led to mounting tensions between the colonies and Britain?

After the Boston Tea Party, both the British and the Americans knew that they were approaching a crisis. A British officer in Massachusetts com-

independent States." Postponing a vote on the issue. Congress appointed a committee to draw up a declaration of independence. The committee turned to a young Virginian named Thomas Jefferson to compose the first draft. "You can write ten times better than I," John Adams supposedly told Jefferson. When the committee presented the document to Congress and it became clear that the majority favored independence, the Pennsylvania and South Carolina delegations switched sides in favor of it, and the New York delegation decided to abstain. Thus when Congress voted on the resolution for independence on July 2, 1776, it was approved unanimously by all voting delegations. After further tinkering with the wording, Congress officially approved the **Declaration of Independence** on July 4, 1776.

Congress intended the declaration to be a justification for America's secession from the British Empire. Jefferson later maintained that he did not write any more than what everyone was thinking. The political theory that lies behind the declaration is known as the **contract theory of government**. Developed by the late seventeenth-century English philosopher John Locke and others, the contract theory maintains that legitimate government rests on an agreement between the people and their rulers. The people are bound to obey their rulers only so long as the rulers offer them protection. Jefferson's prose, however, transformed what might have been a bland statement into one of history's great assertions of human rights.

The Declaration of Independence consists of a magnificently stated opening assumption, two premises, and a powerful conclusion. The opening assumption is that all men are created equal, that they therefore have equal rights, and that they can neither give up these rights nor allow them to be taken away. The first premise—that people establish governments to protect their fundamental rights to life, liberty, and property—is a restatement of contract theory. (With a wonderful flourish reflecting the Enlightenment's optimism about human potential, Jefferson changed "property" to "the pursuit of happiness.") The second premise is a long list of charges meant to justify the Americans' rejection of their hitherto legitimate ruler. Then follows the dramatic conclusion: Americans can rightfully overthrow King George's rule and replace it with something more satisfactory.

Historians have spilled oceans of ink debating Jefferson's use of the expression "all men." Almost certainly he was thinking in the abstract and meant "hu-

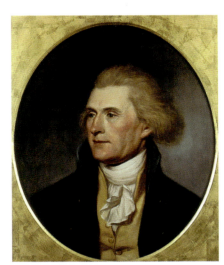

Thomas Jefferson, author of the Declaration of Independence and future president of the United States. Mather Brown, an American artist living in England, painted this picture of Jefferson for John Adams while the two men were in London on diplomatic missions in 1786. A companion portrait of Adams that Jefferson ordered for himself also survives. Brown's sensitive portrait of a thoughtful Jefferson is the earliest known likeness of him.

Declaration of Independence
The document by which the Second Continental Congress announced and justified its decision to re-

CHRONOLOGY

1775 April 19: Battles of Lexington and Concord.	**July 4:** George Rogers Clark captures British post in the Mississippi Valley.
May 10: Second Continental Congress meets.	**December 29:** British capture Savannah.
June 17: Battle of Bunker Hill.	**1779** **June 21:** Spain declares war on Britain.
December 31: American attack on Quebec.	Americans devastate the Iroquois country.
1776 **January 9:** Thomas Paine's *Common Sense*.	**September 23:** John Paul Jones captures the British ship *Serapis*.
July 4: Declaration of Independence.	
September 15: British take New York City.	

*To be able to be caught up into
the world of thought—that is to be educated.*
Edith Hamilton

Headquarters, Valley Forge
January 14, 1778

    I barely hinted to you my dearest Father my desire to augment the Continental Forces from an untried Source. . . . I would solicit you to cede me a number of your able bodied men Slaves, instead of leaving me a fortune. I would bring about a twofold good, first I would advance those who are unjustly deprived of the Rights of Mankind to a State which would be a proper Gradation between abject Slavery and perfect Liberty and besides I would reinforce the Defenders of Liberty with a number of gallant Soldiers. . . . If I could obtain authority for the purpose I would have a Corps of such men trained, uniformly clad, equip'd and ready in every respect to act at the opening of the next Campaign.

February 2, 1778

My dear Father,

    The more I reflect upon the difficulties and delays which are likely to attend the completing our Continental Regiments, the more anxiously is my mind

---

■ **You will EXPERIENCE history in class—with your instructor's lectures, enhanced by totally dramatic, multimedia representation of significant historical events.**

■ **You will make sense of it all by tying together everything you learned by DOING review and assessment activities in the text and with One Key.**

...and finally, you will begin to realize that *to know history is to love history.*

REVIEW QUESTIONS

1. Who were the loyalists and how many of them were there? Why did British and American attempts in 1775 to avert war fail?

2. What actions did the Second Continental Congress take in 1775 and 1776? Why did it choose George Washington to command its army? Why was he a good choice?

3. Why did Congress declare independence in July 1776? How did Americans justify their claim to independence?

4. What was republicanism, and why was the enthusiasm that it inspired insufficient to win the war?

5. Why did the British not crush the Americans immediately? Why did France decide to enter the war as an ally of the United States?

6. Why did the United States ultimately win? What were the immediate results of the American victory?

KEY TERMS

Battles of Lexington and Concord   Contract theory of government   Olive Branch Petition (p. 7)

With T.L.C. comes all the FREE resources you need to succeed in History.

Q: Wondering why *HistoryNotes* was bound free with your text?
A: BETTER TEST SCORES!

Having read and thought about the material in your text, you will come to class ready to take notes with *HistoryNotes*. This new tool replaces your traditional study guide, and offers you an incredible, portable system for taking and organizing notes, and for doing practice activities. Take *HistoryNotes* with you to class, and keep all of your notes in one place. *HistoryNotes* provides for every section of every chapter of this T.L.C. text:

- Map exercises for you to complete during or after class.
- Review/study activities for classroom collaboration or for individual review at home.
- Practice tests to reinforce what you've learned in class.
- Perforated pages with space on each page for note taking.

Map Exercise 15-B

Outline and label the following areas or places:

1. independent republic of Texas, 1836
2. Gadsden Purchase, 1853
3. Mexico after 1853
4. ceded to Texas 1845
5. ceded by Treaty of Guadelupe Hidalgo 1848

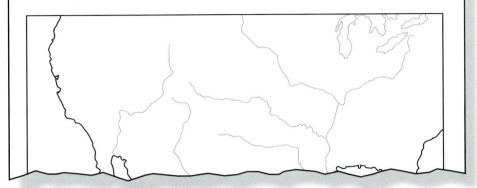

OneKey is your free, all-inclusive online resource for review and application of what you learn in this text and in class—and it is designed to simplify your test preparation so that your test performance will be better than ever. Think of **OneKey** as everything you need to succeed—all in one place—all designed to accompany this text, by chapter, including:

WEB-BASED ACTIVITIES

- Automatically graded quizzes and essay questions that can be emailed to your professor
- An online version of this text that automatically brings you to the page where you'll find the correct answers to any questions you may have answered incorrectly
- Chat rooms, message boards, and dynamic Web links for further exploration
- Interactive versions of the maps from your text

DRAMATIC MULTIMEDIA

- Authentic Primary and Secondary Source Documents
- Lively maps to illustrate the importance of the relationship between what happened and where it happened
- Biographies of the people who had influence on the development of distinctively American character
- Authentic live audio and video clips to animate key events throughout history.

RESEARCH MADE SIMPLE

OneKey offers you extensive help on finding and citing research with **Research Navigator**™ and its three exclusive databases of relevant, reliable source material including: EBSCO's *ContentSelect* Academic Journal Database; *The New York Times* Search by Subject Archive; and Best of the Web Link Library.

The American Journey

A HISTORY OF THE UNITED STATES

TEACHING AND LEARNING CLASSROOM EDITION

BRIEF THIRD EDITION

VOLUME TWO

David Goldfield

Carl Abbott

Virginia DeJohn Anderson

Jo Ann E. Argersinger

Peter H. Argersinger

William L. Barney

Robert M. Weir

PEARSON

Prentice
Hall

Upper Saddle River, New Jersey 07458

Library of Congress Cataloging-in-Publication Data

The American Journey: a history of the United States / David Goldfield ... [et al.],—Brief 3rd ed.
    p. cm.
    "Combined volume."
    Includes bibliographical references and index.
    ISBN 0-13-150093-7
    1. United States   History.   I. Goldfield, David R., 1944–
    E178.1.A4925   2004
    973—dc22   2003066029

VP, Editorial Director: Charlyce Jones Owen
Executive Editor: Charles Cavaliere
Associate Editor: Emsal Hasan
Editorial Assistant: Shannon Corliss
Editor-in-Chief, Development: Rochelle Diogenes
Senior Media Editor: Deborah O'Connell
Senior Development Editors: Roberta Meyer, Gerald Lombardi
**AVP, Director of Production
   and Manufacturing:** Barbara Kittle
Managing Editor: Joanne Riker
Production Editor: Randy Pettit
Production Assistant: Marlene Gassler
Prepress and Manufacturing Manager: Nick Sklitsis
Prepress and Manufacturing Buyer: Tricia Kenny
Director of Marketing: Beth Mejia
Executive Marketing Manager: Heather Shelstad
Creative Design Director: Leslie Osher

Interior and Cover Designer: Anne DeMarinis
Manager, Production, Formatting and Art: Guy Ruggiero
Cartographer: CartoGraphics
Electronic Artists: Maria Piper, Mirella Signoretto,
   Rosemary Ross, Bruce Killmer, Carey Davies
Director, Image Resource Center: Melinda Reo
Interior Image Specialist: Beth Boyd Brenzel
Color Scanning Services: Joe Conti, Cory Skidds,
   Greg Harrison, Rob Uibelhoer, Ron Walko
Cover Image Specialist: Karen Sanatar
Image Permission Coordinator: Craig Jones
Photo Researcher: Kathy Ringrose
Compositor: Preparé, Inc.
Printer/Binder: Von Hoffmann Corporation
Cover Printer: The Lehigh Press, Inc.
Cover Art: Amelia Earhart - Underwood & Underwood/
   Corbis/Bettmann

Credits and acknowledgments borrowed from other sources and reproduced, with permission, in this textbook appear on appropiate page within text (or on page C-1)

Pearson Education Ltd., London
Pearson Education Australia Pty., Limited, Sydney
Pearson Education Singapore, Pte., Ltd.
Pearson Education North Asia Ltd., Hong Kong

Pearson Education Canada, Ltd., Toronto
Pearson Educación de Mexico, S.A. de C.V.
Pearson Education — Japan, Tokyo
Pearson Education Malaysia, Pte., Ltd.

10 9 8 7 6 5 4 3 2 1

ISBN 0-13-1501046

BRIEF CONTENTS

CONTENTS

1

WORLDS APART   2

Voices from the American Journey:
Moctezuma   4

2

TRANSPLANTATION, 1600–1685   30

Voices from the American Journey:
Thomas Dudley   32

3

THE CREATION OF NEW WORLDS   56

Voices from the American Journey:
Olaudah Equiano   58

4

CONVERGENCE AND CONFLICT   80

5

IMPERIAL BREAKDOWN, 1763–1774   108

6

THE WAR FOR INDEPENDENCE, 1774–1783   132

VISUALIZING THE PAST
The Rattlesnake as a National Symbol   164

7

THE FIRST REPUBLIC, 1776–1789   166

Voices from the American Journey:
William Shepard   168

8

A NEW REPUBLIC AND THE RISE OF PARTIES, 1789–1800   194

Voices from the American Journey:
William Maclay   196

9

THE TRIUMPH AND COLLAPSE OF JEFFERSONIAN REPUBLICANISM, 1800–1824 216

10

THE JACKSONIAN ERA, 1824–1845 240

11

SLAVERY AND THE OLD SOUTH, 1800–1860 264

15

BATTLE CRIES AND FREEDOM SONGS: THE CIVIL WAR, 1861–1865   378

VISUALIZING THE PAST
The Civil War   412

16

RECONSTRUCTION, 1865–1877   414

17

A NEW SOUTH: ECONOMIC PROGRESSION AND SOCIAL TRADITION, 1877–1900   439

18

INDUSTRY, IMMIGRANTS, AND CITIES, 1870–1900   468

19

TRANSFORMING THE WEST, 1865–1890   496

VISUALIZING THE PAST
Mythologizing the "Wild West"   520

20

POLITICS AND GOVERNMENT, 1877–1900   522

21

THE PROGRESSIVE ERA, 1900–1917   546

Voices from the American Journey:
Inez Milholland   548

22

CREATING AN EMPIRE, 1865–1917   578

Voices from the American Journey:
Major-General Leonard Wood   580

23

AMERICA AND THE GREAT WAR, 1914–1920   602

24

TOWARD A MODERN AMERICA, THE 1920S   628

VISUALIZING THE PAST
Advertising and the Modern Woman   652

25

THE GREAT DEPRESSION AND THE NEW DEAL, 1929–1939   654

26

WORLD WAR II, 1939–1945   684

27

THE COLD WAR AT HOME AND ABROAD, 1946–1952   712

28

THE CONFIDENT YEARS, 1953–1964   736

*Voices from the American Journey:
Melba Pattillo*   738

29

SHAKEN TO THE ROOTS, 1965–1980   760

*Voices from the American Journey:
Buzz Aldrin and Neil Armstrong*   762

AMERICAN VIEWS

FROM THEN TO NOW

MAPS

*Denotes Interactive Map Explorations

OVERVIEW TABLES

PREFACE

The path that led us to *The American Journey* began in the classroom with our students. Our goal is to make American history accessible to students. The key to that goal—the core of the book—is a strong clear narrative. American history is a compelling story and we seek to tell it in an engaging, forthright way. But we also provide students with an abundance of tools to help them absorb that story and put it in context. We introduce them to the concerns of the participants in America's history with primary source documents. The voices of contemporaries open each chapter, describing their own personal journeys toward fulfilling their dreams, hopes, and ambitions as part of the broader American journey. These voices provide a personal window on our nation's history, and the themes they express resonate throughout the narrative.

But if we wrote this book to appeal to our students, we also wrote it to engage their minds. We wanted to avoid academic trendiness, particularly the restricting categories that have divided the discipline of history over the last twenty years or so. We believe that the distinctions involved in the debates about multiculturalism and identity, between social and political history, between the history of the common people and the history of the elite, are unnecessarily confusing.

What we seek is integration—to combine political and social history, to fit the experience of particular groups into the broader perspective of the American past, to give voice to minor and major players alike because of their role in the story we have to tell.

APPROACH

In telling our story, we had some definite ideas about what we might include and emphasize that other texts do not—information we felt that the current and next generations of students will need to know about our past to function best in a new society.

Chronological Organization A strong chronological backbone supports the book. We have found that the jumping back and forth in time characteristic of some American history textbooks confuses students. They abhor dates but need to know the sequence of events in history. A chronological presentation is the best way to be sure they do.

Geographical Literacy We also want students to be geographically literate. We expect them not only to know what happened in American history, but where it happened as well. Physical locations and spatial relationships were often important in shaping historical events. The abundant maps in The American Journey—all numbered and called out in the text—are an integral part of our story.

Regional Balance *The American Journey* presents balanced coverage of all regions of the country. In keeping with this balance, the South and the West receive more coverage in this text than in comparable books.

Point of View *The American Journey* presents a balanced overview of the American past. But "balanced" does not mean bland. We do not shy away from definite positions on controversial issues, such as the nature of early contacts between Native Americans and Europeans, why the political crisis of the 1850s ended in a bloody Civil War, and how Populism and its followers fit into the American political spectrum. If students and instructors disagree, that's great; discussion and dissent are important catalysts for understanding and learning.

Religion Nor do we shy away from some topics that play relatively minor roles in other texts, like religion. Historians are often uncomfortable writing about religion and tend to slight its influence. This text stresses the importance of religion in American society both as a source of strength and a reflection of some its more troubling aspects.

Historians mostly write for each other. That's too bad. We need to reach out and expand our audience. An American history text is a good place to start. Our students are not only our future historians, but more important, our future. Let their American journey begin.

FEATURES OF THE TEXT

The American Journey Teaching and Learning Classroom Edition includes an array of features designed to make American history accessible to students. It provides more learning tools than any other U.S. history text.

- The **Student Tool Kit** that follows this preface helps students get the most out of the text and its features. It introduces students to key conventions of historical writing and it explains how to work with maps, documents, and visuals.

- **Single-Column Design** allows for a clean, easy-to-read narrative. Ample space in the margins allows for strategic placement of pedagogy.

- A new feature, **Voices from the American Journey**, opens each chapter. Consisting of letters, diary entries, and other first-hand accounts, these voices highlight the personal dimension of the American journey and show students the wealth and variety of experiences that make up this country's history. From Olaudah Equiano's narrative of his forced journey to Virginia as a slave, to the ultimate journey Sullivan Ballou made during the Civil War defending the Union, to Cambodian refugee Celia Noup's harrowing journey to California where she took her place as one of the thousands of new immigrants who are reshaping the face of our nation, "Voices from the American Journey" set the stage for the key themes that are explored in each chapter.

- **Visualizing the Past** essays, found at the end of selected chapters, analyze important aspects of U.S. History through photographs, fine art, sculpture, woodcuts, and advertisements. Focus questions and a running narrative guide students through a careful examination of the historical implication of each topic in question.

- The **American Views** box in each chapter contains a relevant primary source document. Taken from letters, diaries, newspapers, government papers, and other sources, these bring the people of the past and their concerns vividly alive. An introduction and prereading questions relate the documents to the text and direct students' attention to important issues. New "American Views" include the internment of Japanese Americans in Chapter 26 and working in the New Economy in Chapter 31.

- **America's Journey: From Then to Now**, found in more than half the chapters, relates important issues and events in each chapter to the issues and events of today, letting students see the relevance of history to their lives. Several are new to this edition. Examples include, "The Disappearance of Cod off the Grand Banks" (Chapter 1) and "Loyalty in 2001 and 1917" (Chapter 31).

- **Chapter-opening Questions** ask students to consider carefully the main issues addressed in the narrative.

- **Overview Tables** summarize complex issues.

- **Quick Reviews**, found at key places in the margins of each chapter, encourage students to review important concepts before moving on.

- Chapter **Chronologies** help students build a framework of key events.

- **Third-level subheads**, new to the Third Edition, highlight key topics in the narrative and make them more accessible for study and review. In the sections on social history,

for example, these headings help highlight the roles of women and minorities in the American journey.

- **Key Terms** are highlighted within each chapter and defined in a running marginal **Glossary**. The end of each chapter includes a list of key terms and relevant page numbers.

- Chapter **Review Questions,** organized by key subtopics in each chapter, help students review material and relate it to broader themes.

- A **Bibliography** at the end of the text directs interested students to further information about the subject of the chapter.

- **Where To Learn More** sections, found at relevant places in the margin, and listed at the end of each chapter, describe important historical sites (both real and virtual) that students can visit to gain a deeper understanding of the events discussed in the chapter.

- Abundant **maps** help students understand the spatial dimension of history. The topographical detail in many of the maps helps students understand the influence of geography on history.

- **Illustrations** and **photographs**—tied to the text with detailed captions—provide a visual dimension to history.

CHANGES TO THE THIRD EDITION
ORGANIZATION

- To make the text even more accessible to students—and to better match the teaching calendars of many institutions—the number of chapters in the Third Edition has been reduced from thirty-three to thirty-one.

- The chapters on urbanization and social change and reform movements in the antebellum period have been combined into a new chapter, "The Market Revolution and Social Reform" (Chapter 12). The chapter focuses on economic changes and industrialization as well as the connections between these forces and reform movements. Chapter 11, "Slavery and the Old South," now precedes this chapter.

- The Civil War is now treated in a single chapter (Chapter 15).

- The Eighties is now examined in an entirely revamped Chapter 30, "The Reagan Revolution and a Changing World."

- An all-new final chapter "Complacency and Crisis," examines America at the millennium and after September 11, 2001.

Taken together, these organizational changes make *The American Journey* an even more effective textbook for both students and instructors.

SUPPLEMENTARY INSTRUCTIONAL MATERIALS

The American Journey comes with an extensive package of supplementary print and multimedia materials for both instructors and students.

PRINT SUPPLEMENTS

Instructor's Resource Binder

This innovative, all-in-one resource organizes the instructor's manual, the Test-Item File, and the transparency pack by each chapter of *The American Journey* to facilitate class preparation. The Instructor's Resource Binder also includes an **Instructor's Resource CD-ROM**, which contains all of the maps, graphs, and illustrations from the text in easily downloadable electronic files.

Prentice Hall Test Generator

Suitable for both Windows and Macintosh environments, this commerical-quality, computerized test-management program allows instructors to select items from the test-item file and design their own exams.

History Notes (Volumes I and II)

Replacing a traditional study guide, History Notes provides students with practice tests, map exercises, and How? When? Where? Questions for each chapter of *The American Journey*. Each copy of the T.L.C. edition comes bundled with History Notes.

Retrieving the American Past: A Customized U.S. History Reader, 2004 Edition

This collection of documents is an on-demand history database written and developed by leading historians and educators. It offers eighty-six compelling modules on topics in American history, such as "Women on the Frontier," "The Salem Witchcraft Scare," "The Age of Industrial Violence," and "Native American Societies, 1870–1995." Approximately thirty-five pages in length, each module includes an introduction, several primary documents and secondary sources, follow-up questions, and recommendations for further reading. Instructor-originated material, including other readings and exercises, can be incorporated. Contact your local Prentice Hall representative for more information about this exciting custom-publishing option.

American Stories: Biographies in United States History

This two-volume collection of sixty-two biographies in United States history is free when packaged with *The American Journey*. Introductions, pre-reading questions, and suggested resources enrich this new supplement.

Prentice Hall and Penguin Bundle Program

Prentice Hall is pleased to provide adopters of *The American Journey* with an opportunity to receive significant discounts when copies of the text are bundled with Penguin titles in American history. Contact your local Prentice Hall representative for details.

MULTIMEDIA SUPPLEMENTS

Companion Website

Available at **http://www.prenhall.com/goldfield** *The American Journey Companion Website* offers students multiple choice, true-false, essay, identification, map labeling, and document questions based on material from the text, organized by the primary subtopics in each chapter. Additionally, the *Companion Website* provides numerous interactive maps tied to the text, source documents, and other interactive modules related to the content in each chapter. The Faculty Module contains materials for instructors, including the entire instructor's manual in PDF file, and downloadable presentations with maps, charts, graphs, summary tables, and illustrations.

U.S. History Documents CD-ROM

Bound in every new copy of *The American Journey*, and organized according to the main periods in American history, the U.S. History Documents CD-ROM contains over 300 primary sources in an easily-navigable PDF file. Each document is accompanied by essay questions that allow students to read important sources in U.S. history via the CD-ROM and respond online via a dedicated website.

Exploring America CD-ROM

The new *Exloring America CD-ROM* features thirty-one interactive learning activities that drill down to explore the impact of key episodes and developments in United States history, including such topics as industrialization, immigration, the women's suffrage movement, the Harlem Renaissance, the American Indian Movement, and globalization.

Evaluating Online Sources with Research Navigator, 2003 Edition

This brief guide focuses on developing critical thinking skills necessary to evaluate and use online sources. It provides a brief introduction to navigating the Internet with comprehensive references to History web sites. It also provides an access code and instruction on using Research Navigator, a powerful research tool that provides access to three exclusive databases of reliable source material: ContentSelect Academic Journal Database, *The New York Times* Search by Subject Archive, and Link Library.

OneKey

OneKey lets you in to the best teaching and learning resources all in one place. OneKey for *The American Journey* is all your students need for out-of-class work conveniently organized by chapter to reinforce and apply what they've learned in class and from the text. Among the resources available for each chapter are: a complete media-rich, interactive e-book version of *The American Journey*, quizzes organized by the main topics of each chapter, primary source documents, map labeling and interactive map quizzes. OneKey is all you need to plan and administer your course. All your instructor resources are in one place to maximize your effectiveness and minimize your time and effort. Instructor material includes: images and maps from *The American Journey*, hundreds of documents, video and audio clips, interactive learning activities, and PowerPoint presentations.

Prentice Hall History Resource Center

This site offers a rich array of hundreds of historical sources in textual, visual, or audio-visual format. All were carefully selected by history professors as particularly relevant to the United States survey course. Interactive Maps present historical transformations in a clear and compelling way. Learning Activities offer in-depth explorations of important topics. The Prentice Hall History Resource Center also includes a comprehensive glossary of terms and Best of the Web links for additional study.

ACKNOWLEDGMENTS

We would like to thank the reviewers whose thoughtful and often detailed comments helped shape this and the previous editions of *The American Journey*:

Joseph Adams, *Saint Louis Community College*
David Aldstadt, *Houston Community College*
William Allison, *Weber State University*
Janet Allured, *McNeese State University*
Tyler Anbinder, *George Washington University*
Michael Batinski, *Southern Illinois University*
Michael Bellesiles, *Emory University*
Eugene Berwanger, *Colorado State University*
Terry Bilhartz, *Sam Houston State University*
Fred Blue, *Youngstown State University*
Eric J. Bolsteri, *University of Texas at Arlington*
Charles Bolton, *University of Arkansas at Little Rock*
James Bradford, *Texas A&M University*
Michael Bradley, *Motlow State Community College*
Henry William Brands, *Texas A&M University*
Neal Brooks, *Essex Community College*
Richard Brown, *University of Connecticut*
Tom Bryan, *Alvin Community College*
Randolph Campbell, *University of North Texas*

Dale Carnagey, *Blinn College*
E. Wayne Carp, *Pacific Lutheran University*
JoAnn Carpenter, *Florida Community College*
David Castle, *Ohio University, Eastern Campus*
Andrew Cayton, *Miami University*
Bill Cecil-Fronsman, *Washburn University*
John Chalberg, *Normandale Community College*
Myles Clowers, *San Diego City College*
David Conrad, *Southern Illinois University*
William Corbett, *Northeastern State University*
Robert Cray, *Montclair State College*
Richard Crepeau, *University of Central Florida*
Samuel Crompton, *Holyoke Community College*
Gilbert Cruz, *Glendale Community College*
Light T. Cummins, *Austin College*
Paul K. Davis, *University of Texas at San Antonio*
Eugene Demody, *Cerritos College*
Joseph Devine, *Stephen F. Austin State University*
Donald Dewey, *California State University*
Leonard Dinnerstein, *University of Arizona*
Dean Dunlap, *Rose State College*
Marvin Dulaney, *University of Texas at Arlington*
Jonathan Earle, *University of Kansas*
Leflett Easley, *Campbell University*
Iris Engstrand, *University of San Diego*
Robin Fabel, *Auburn University*
Jay Fell, *University of Colorado*
Nancy Gabin, *Purdue University*
Scott Garrett, *Paducah Community College*
Marilyn Geiger, *Washburn University*
George Gerdow, *Northeastern Illinois University*
Gerald Ghelfi, *Rancho Santiago College*
Louis Gimelli, *Eastern Michigan University*
James Goode, *Grand Valley State University*
Gregory Goodwin, *Bakersfield College*
Laura Graves, *South Plains College*
Ralph Goodwin, *East Texas State University*
Robert Greene, *Morgan State University*
Mark Grimsley, *Ohio State University*
Ira Gruber, *U.S. Military Academy*
Harland Hagler, *University of North Texas*
Steve Haley, *Shelby State Community College*
Gwendolyn Hall, *Rutgers University*
Timothy D. Hall, *Central Michigan University*
David Hamilton, *University of Kentucky*
Joe Hapak, *Moraine Valley Community College*
Ronald Hatzenbuchler, *Idaho State University*
David G. Hogan, *Heidelberg College*
Alfred Hunt, *SUNY Purchase*
John Ingham, *University of Toronto*
Priscilla Jackson-Evans, *Longview Community College*
Donald Jacobs, *Northeastern University*

Frederick Jaher, *University of Illinois*
John Johnson, *University of Northern Iowa*
Wilbur Johnson, *Rock Valley College*
Juli Jones, *St. Charles Community College*
Yvonne Johnson, *Central Missouri State University*
Yasuhide Kawashima, *University of Texas at El Paso*
Joseph E. King, *Texas Tech University*
Gene Kirkpatrick, *Tyler Junior College*
Lawrence Kohl, *University of Alabama at Tuscaloosa*
Michael Krenn, *University of Miami*
Michael Krutz, *Southeastern Louisiana University*
Robert LaPorte, *North Texas University*
Armand LaPotin, *SUNY Oneonta*
John LaSaine, *University of Georgia*
Bryan LeBeau, *Creighton University*
J. Edward Lee, *Winthrop University*
Mark Leff, *University of Illinois, Urbana-Champaign*
Richard Lowe, *University of North Texas*
Ed Lukes, *Hillsborough Community College*
Leo Lyman, *Victor Valley College*
Scott Martin, *Bowling Green State University*
Ronald McArthur, *Atlantic Community College*
Donald McCoy, *University of Kansas*
David McFadden, *Fairfield University*
Gerald MacFarland, *University of Massachusetts*
Thomas McLuen, *Spokane Falls Community College*
Peter C. Mancell, *University of Kansas*
Norman Markowitz, *Rutgers University*
Frank Marmolejo, *Irvine Valley College*
James Matray, *New Mexico State University*
Karen Miller, *Oakland University*
Otis Miller, *Belleville Area College*
Nancy Smith Midgette, *Elon College*
Worth Robert Miller, *Southwest Missouri State University*
Timothy Morgan, *Christopher Newport University*
Christopher Moss, *University of Texas at Arlington*
Harmon Mothershead, *Northwest Missouri State University*
Benjamin Newcomb, *Texas Technological University*
Elizabeth Nybakken, *Mississippi State University*
Colleen O'Connor, *San Diego Mesa College*
William Paquette, *Tidewater Community College*
Chris Padgett, *Weber State University*
David Parker, *Kennesaw State College*
Peggy Pascoe, *University of Utah*
Christopher Phillips, *Emporia State University*
Thomas L. Powers, *University of South Carolina, Sumter*
Kay Pulley, *Trinity Valley Community College*
Norman Raiford, *Greenville Technical College*
John Rector, *Western Oregon State University*
Thomas C. Reeves, *University of Wisconsin, Parkside*
Gary Reichard, *Florida Atlantic University*
Joseph Reidy, *Howard University*

Ronald Reitvald, *California State University, Fullerton*
Howard Rock, *Florida International University*
Hal Rothman, *University of Nevada, Las Vegas*
Richard Sadler, *Weber State University*
Henry Sage, *Northern Virginia Community College, Alexandria*
Bufford Satcher, *University of Arkansas at Pine Bluff*
Sandra Schackel, *Boise State University*
Michael Schaller, *University of Arizona*
Dale Schmitt, *East Tennessee State University*
Ronald Schultz, *University of Wyoming*
Nancy Shoemaker, *University of Connecticut*
Rebecca Shoemaker, *Indiana State University*
Frank Siltman, *U.S. Military Academy*
David Sloan, *University of Arkansas*
J.B. Smallwood, *University of North Texas*
Sherry Smith, *University of Texas at El Paso*
Kenneth Stevens, *Texas Christian University*
William Stockton, *Johnson County Community College*
Mark Summers, *University of Kentucky*
William Tanner, *Humbolt State University*
Quintard Taylor, *University of Oregon*
Emily Teipe, *Fullerton College*
Frank Towers, *Clarion University*
Paula Trekel, *Allegheny College*
Stanley Underal, *San Jose University*
Andrew Wallace, *Northern Arizona University*
Harry Ward, *University of Richmond*
Ken Weatherbie, *Del Mar College*
Stephen Webre, *Louisiana Tech University*
Edward Weller, *San Jacinto College, South*
Michael Welsh, *University of Northern Colorado*
James Whittenberg, *College of William and Mary*
Brian Wills, *Clinch Valley Community College*
John Wiseman, *Frostburg State University*
James Woods, *Georgia Southern University*
Mark Wyman, *Illinois State University*
Neil York, *Brigham Young University*
William Young, *Johnson County Community College*
Nancy Zen, *Central Oregon Community College*

All of us are grateful to our families, friends, and colleagues for their support and encouragement. Jo Ann and Peter Argersinger would like in particular to thank Anna Champe, Linda Hatmaker, and John Willits; William Barney thanks Pamela Fesmire and Rosalie Radcliffe; Virginia Anderson thanks Fred Anderson, Kim Gruenwald, Ruth Helm, Eric Hinderaker, and Chidiebere Nwaubani; and David Goldfield thanks Frances Glenn and Jason Moscato. Jim Miller, Sylvia Mallory, and Sally Constable played key roles in the book's inception and initial development.

Finally, we would like to acknowledge the members of our Prentice Hall family. They are not only highly competent professionals but also pleasant people. We regard them with affection and appreciation. None of us would hesitate to work with this fine group again. We would especially like to thank our editorial team: Charles Cavaliere, executive editor, and Roberta Meyer, senior development editor, for their creativity and skill in crafting the plan for the fourth edition, and for helping us to execute it. Charlyce Jones Owen, vice president and editorial director for the Humanities, who organized her team flawlessly; Heather Shelstad, executive marketing manager, and Beth Meija, marketing director, whose creative and informed marketing strategies demonstrated a unique insight into the textbook market; Anne DeMaranis, designer, and Leslie Osher, creative design director; Joanne Riker and Randy Pettit for keeping the production on schedule; Rochelle Diogenes, editor in chief for development, for ensuring that the book had the developmental resources it needed; Nick Sklitsis, manufacturing manager, Tricia Kenny, manufacturing buyer, and Yolanda deRooy, president of Prentice Hall's Humanities and Social Sciences division, who had the good sense to let her staff run with this book.

DG
CA
VDJA
JEA
PHA
WLB
RMW

STUDENT TOOL KIT

When writing history, historians use maps, tables, graphs, and visuals to help their readers understand the past. What follows is an explanation of how to use the historian's tools that are contained in this book.

TEXT

Whether it is a biography of George Washington, an article on the Civil War, or a survey of American history such as this one, the text is the historian's basic tool for discussing the past. Historians write about the past using narration and analysis. Narration is the story line of history. It describes what happened in the past, who did it, and where and when it occurred. Narration is also used to describe how people in the past lived, how they passed their daily lives and even, when the historical evidence makes it possible for us to know, what they thought, felt, feared, or desired. Using analysis, historians explain why they think events in the past happened the way they did and offer an explanation for the story of history. In this book, narration and analysis are interwoven in each chapter.

STUDY AIDS

A number of features in this book are designed to aid in the study of history. Each chapter begins with **Questions**, organized by the main subtopics of each chapter, that encourage careful consideration of important themes and developments. Each question is repeated at the appropriate place in the margin of the text (see example below). A **Conclusion** and **Summary** at the end of each chapter puts the subject of the chapter in the broader perspective of U.S. history. All of these study aids can be used to review important concepts.

PROBLEMS AT HOME

Neither prosperity nor political stability accompanied the return of peace in 1783. The national government struggled to avoid bankruptcy, and in 1784, an economic depression struck the country. As fiscal problems deepened, creditor and debtor groups clashed angrily in state legislatures. The only solid accomplishment of the Confederation Congress during this troubled period was to formulate an orderly and democratic plan for the settlement of the West.

WHAT WERE the weaknesses of the United States after the Revolution?

MAPS

Maps are important historical tools. They show how geography has affected history and concisely summarize complex relationships and events. Knowing how to read and interpret a map is important to understanding history. Map 5–1 from Chapter 5 shows the British colonies on the eastern seaboard of North America in 1763, about twelve years before the American Revolution. It has three features to help you read it: a **caption**, a legend, and a scale. The caption explains the historical significance of the map. Here the caption tells us that in 1763 the British government sought to restrict colonial settlement west of the Appalachian Mountains to prevent conflict between colonists and Indians. Colonial frustration with this policy contributed to the outbreak of the American Revolution.

The **legend** and the **scale** appear in the lower right corner of the map. The legend provides a key to what the symbols on the map mean. The solid line stretching along the Appalachian Mountains from Maine to Georgia represents the Proclamation Line of 1763. Cities are marked with a dot, capitals with a star, and forts by a black square. Spanish territory west of the Mississippi River is represented in blue; territory settled by Europeans is represented in green. The scale tells us that 7/8ths of an inch on the map represents 300 miles (about 480 kilometers) on the ground. With this information, estimates of the distance between points on the map are easily made.

The map also shows the topography of the region—its mountains, rivers, and lakes. This helps us understand how geography influenced history in this case. For example, the Appalachian Mountains divide the eastern seaboard from the rest of the continent. The mountains obstructed colonial migration to the west for a long time. By running the Proclamation Line along the Appalachians, the British hoped to use this natural barrier to separate Indians and colonists.

A **critical-thinking** question asks for careful consideration of the spatial connections between geography and history.

MAP EXPLORATION
To explore an interactive version of this map, go to
http://www.prenhall.com/goldfield/map5.1

MAP 5–1

Colonial Settlement and the Proclamation Line of 1763   This map depicts the regions claimed and settled by the major groups competing for territory in eastern North America. With the Proclamation Line of 1763, positioned along the crest of the Appalachian Mountains, the British government tried to stop the westward migration of settlers under its jurisdiction and thereby limit conflict with the Indians. The result, however, was frustration and anger on the part of land-hungry settlers.

WHY DO you suppose the Proclamation Line of 1763 was positioned along the crest of the Appalachian Mountains?

MAP EXPLORATIONS

Many of the maps in each chapter are provided in a useful interactive version on the text's Companion Website. These maps are easily identified by a bar along the top that reads "Map Explorations." An interactive version of Colonial Settlements and the Proclamation Line of 1763 can be found at **www.prenhall.com/goldfield/map5.1**. The interactive version of this particular map provides an opportunity to pan over an enlarged version of the territory in question. Cities, forts, settlements, and terrain are shown in detail. By moving the cursor north, south, east, or west one can gain a bird's-eye view of the entire region.

ANALYZING VISUALS

Visual images embedded thoughout the text can provide as much insight into our nation's history as the written word. Within photographs and pieces of fine art lies emotional and historical meaning. Captions also provide valuable information, such as in the example below. When studying the image, consider questions such as: "Who are these people?"; "How were they feeling?"; "What event motivated this photograph or painting?"; and "What can be learned from the backdrop surrounding the focal point?" Such analysis allows for a fuller understanding of the people who lived the American journey.

VISUALIZING THE PAST

These essays, found at the end of selected chapters, analyze important aspects of U.S. history through photographs, fine art, sculpture, woodcuts, and advertisements. Focus questions and a running narrative provide a careful examination of the historical implications of each topic in question.

OVERVIEWS

The Overview tables in this text are a special feature designed to highlight and summarize important topics within a chapter. The Overview table shown here, for example, summarizes the purpose and significance of the major laws and constitutional amendments passed during the Progressive Era.

VISUALIZING THE PAST . . .

The Rattlesnake as a National Symbol

One of the tasks facing the Revolutionary generation was to create symbols around which to rally. There was no official flag, no anthem, no Uncle Sam. Benjamin Franklin made perhaps the earliest attempt to create a visual symbol for the prospective nation when he drew "Join, Or Die" to accompany his 1754 Plan of Union. He pictured the colonies as a snake cut into pieces. Why a snake? In mythology, snakes can reattach themselves. Twenty years later, Paul Revere used the snake for the masthead of the revolutionary newspaper, the *Massachusetts Spy*. Once war began, military units adopted the snake as their battle flag. The most famous of these is the Gadsden flag. Christopher Gadsden was a delegate to the Second Continental Congress from South Carolina who played a leading role in creating the U.S. Navy and in appointing Esek Hopkins of Rhode Island as its first commander. He gave the Gadsden flag to Hopkins for his personal standard.

In 1775, pleased with the popular adoption of the snake as a national symbol, Benjamin Franklin noted, that:

As if anxious to prevent all pretentions of quarrelling with her, the weapons with which nature has furnished her, she conceals in the roof of her mouth, so that, to those who are unacquainted with her, she appears to be a most defenceless animal; and even when those weapons are shewn and extended for her defence, they appear weak and contemptible; but their wounds however small, are decisive and fatal: — Conscious of this, she never wounds till she has generously given notice, even to her enemy, and cautioned him against the danger of treading on her.—Was I wrong, Sir, in thinking this a strong picture of the temper and conduct of America?

What other characteristics of snakes in general, and rattlesnakes in particular, might have appealed to Revolutionary Era Americans in choosing a national symbol?

◀ The Gadsden flag, used initially by the U.S. Navy. By 1775 the lines indicating the divisions among the colonies have disappeared. The snake has become the rattlesnake, a reptile unique to North America, and one with a highly poisonous venom. "Don't Tread On Me" captured the revolutionaries' insistence that they fought only to defend their liberties.

164

OVERVIEW

MAJOR LAWS AND CONSTITUTIONAL AMENDMENTS OF THE PROGRESSIVE ERA

Legislation	Effect
New York Tenement House Law (1901)	Established a model housing code for safety and sanitation
Newlands Act (1902)	Provided for federal irrigation projects
Hepburn Act (1906)	Strengthened authority of the Interstate Commerce Commission

QUICK REVIEWS

The quick reviews, placed at key locations in the margins of each chapter, provide pinpoint summaries of important concepts.

QUICK REVIEW

The Fur Trade
◆ Fur traders were critical to New France's success.
◆ New France was ruled by royal appointees.
◆ *Coureurs de bois*: independent fur traders living among the Indians.

CHRONOLOGIES

Each chapter includes a Chronology, a list of the key events discussed in the chapter arranged in chronological order. The chronology for Chapter 16 lists the dates of key events during the Reconstruction era from 1865 to 1877. Chronologies provide a review of important events and their relationship to one another.

CHRONOLOGY

1863	Lincoln proposes his Ten Percent Plan.		**1871**	Congress passes Ku Klux Klan Act.
1864	Congress proposes the Wade Davis Bill.		**1872**	Freedmen's Bureau closes down. Liberal Republicans emerge as a separate party. Ulysses S. Grant is reelected.
1865	Sherman issues Field Order No. 15. Freedmen's Bureau is established. Andrew Johnson succeeds to the presidency, unveils his Reconstruction plan. Massachusetts desegregates all public facilities. Black people in several Southern cities organize Union Leagues. Former Confederate states begin to pass black codes.		**1873**	Severe depression begins. Colfax Massacre occurs. U.S. Supreme Court's decision in the *Slaughter-house* cases weakens the intent of the Fourteenth Amendment. Texas falls to the Democrats in the fall elections.

PRIMARY SOURCE DOCUMENTS

Historians find most of their information in written records and original documents that have survived from the past. These include government publications, letters, diaries, newspapers—whatever people wrote or printed, including many private documents never intended for publication. Each chapter in the book contains a feature called American Views—a selection from a primary source document. The example shown here is a letter from a Union soldier fighting during the Civil War. Each American Views feature begins with a brief introduction followed by several questions—for discussion or written response—on what the document reveals about key issues and events.

In addition, each chapter begins with Voices from the American Journey, a brief firsthand account from an individual that powerfully recounts the personal journey he or she took in their lives. Each of these "voices" relates to the themes that follow in the chapter. For example, in Chapter 18 is an excerpt from a letter written by Mary Antin, a Russian-Jewish immigrant who came to America at the turn of the last century.

◆ AMERICAN VIEWS ◆

A SOLDIER PROMOTES THE UNION CAUSE

S oldiers wrote their thoughts down in diaries, in letters to their families, and, as in the case here of D. Beardsley, from Tompkins County, New York, to newspapers. Morale faltered in both the civilian and military ranks on both sides during the Civil War as this excerpt indicates. At the same time, Beardsley is buoyed by the sense of mission brought about by Abraham Lincoln's Emancipation Proclamation, which took effect one month before this letter.

DEMOCRATIC SOCIETIES have to balance civil liberties with the necessity of carrying on a war. What does this soldier think about where the balance ought to occur? The writer refers to "desertion" in the ranks. Why was there a morale problem in the Union armies in February 1863? How does this soldier hope the Emancipation Proclamation will affect the war effort in the North?

I having the honor of being a volunteer from old Tompkins County, and also fighting under the same banner and for the same principles that Washington did—still holding to my priviledges [sic] as a citizen of the United States, I think it will not be out of place for me to speak a few words through your columns, to the good people of my native county. . . .

If our Government would have no rebellion, she must pluck the tares of rebellion from the heart of the nation; and if we would have this rebellion crushed, we must cease to have traitors in power. Let that class in the Northern States, who would kiss the red hand of treason for a momentary peace, remember that the hand will be no less red by the kiss, or the blow no less sure by the pause; and I would humbly beg the people of the North, in the name of a soldier for the Union, that they will, in this dark and trying hour of our country's history, give us their undivided support, first, by stripping all power from the traitors at home, and then by their repentant prayers for our success in battles. . . . A few have deserted, and may God have mercy upon them. Let them go, their *blood* is altogether too poor to enrich the soil of worn out Virginia. We want the blood of patriots to make it bring forth the fruits of freedom. . . . We hope that in future the people and the army will become more pure, and work with a nobler purpose of heart. The first step toward this reformation has already been taken. We begin to see that all men have rights, whether white or black, and we hope that when the smoke of battle shall have cleared away, that the bright sun of peace will shine upon a truly free people.

Source: D. Beardsley, "Co. K, 137th Reg't, N.Y. Vols" that appeared in the *Ithaca Journal*, March 3, 1863; dated February 16, 1863 and written from Acquia Landing, Virginia.

18–5
Address by George Engel,
Condemned Haymarket
Anarchist (1886)

UNITED STATES HISTORY DOCUMENTS CD-ROM

Bound into every new copy of this textbook is a free U.S. History Documents CD-ROM. This is a powerful resource for research and additional reading that contains more than 300 primary source documents central to U.S. History. Each document provides essay questions that are linked directly to a website where short-essay answers can be submitted online or printed out. Particularly relevant or interesting documents are called out at appropriate places in the margin of each chapter. A complete list of documents on the CD-ROM is found at the end of the text.

FROM THEN TO NOW
Women and Work in American Offices

At the end of the twentieth century, women filled the majority of America's office-based jobs. More women than men worked as office managers, receptionists, library administrators, bank tellers, travel agents, administrative assistants, insurance agents, bookkeepers, and other desk-and-computer occupations.

In 1997, women made up 46 percent of the American labor force. Seven out of ten of these women worked in professional, managerial, technical, administrative support, and sales positions. They ranged from corporate CEOs and college professors to clerks in state motor vehicle offices and the voices that take your orders and reservations when you dial 800.

This employment pattern, which most Americans now take for granted, is the product of 140 years of gradual change that began with, and was triggered by, the Civil War. Before the Civil War, American women found employment as domestic servants, sometimes as mill operatives, and increasingly as schoolteachers, but not as office workers. Clerks were men—sometimes settled into lower-status white-collar careers and sometimes learning a business from the inside before rising into management. Their jobs consisted of copying letters and documents by hand, tracing orders and correspondence, and keeping financial records.

The Civil War, however, sharply increased the flow of government paperwork while diverting young men into military service. The U.S. Treasury Department in Washington responded in 1862 by hiring women to sort and package federal bonds and currency. Treasury officials fretted about the moral implications of mixing men and women in offices but overcame these concerns when they found that women were both cheap and reliable workers. By 1870, several hundred women worked in Washington's federal offices, enough for a character in a novel about the Hayes administration (1877–1881) to comment that he could learn from a glance to "single out the young woman who supported her family upon her salary and the young woman who bought her ribbons with it; the widow who fed half-a-dozen children."

As the national economy grew in the late nineteenth century, it generated ever-increasing flows of information. New technologies such as telephones and typewriters routinized clerical work. These trends increased the need for desk workers, a need largely filled by middle-class women, whose literacy was often guaranteed by the high school diplomas that went disproportionately to women in the later nineteenth century. As women workers filled new downtown skyscrapers, the central districts of large cities lost some of their rough edges and grew more respectable as centers of shopping and entertainment.

By 1900, the division of labor that would characterize the first half of the twentieth century was in place. Women comprised 76 percent of the nation's stenographers and typists and 29 percent of its cashiers, bookkeepers, and accountants. For the most part, however, they occupied the lower echelons of the office hierarchy. It was men who determined what was to be said; women who transcribed, transmitted, recorded, and filed their messages. Only in recent decades have women begun successfully to challenge that established order.

FROM THEN TO NOW

The feature called From Then to Now connects events and trends in the past to issues that confront Americans today, illustrating the value a historical perspective can contribute to our understanding of the world we live in. The example here, from Chapter 30, compares the roles of women in the American workforce today to those before the Civil War and at the turn of the century.

REVIEW QUESTIONS, WHERE TO LEARN MORE, AND ADDITIONAL STUDY RESOURCES

At the end of each chapter review questions reconsider the main topics. The section called Where to Learn More lists important historical sites and museums and related Websites (which are also found at appropriate places in the margins of the text) that provide first-hand exposure to historical artifacts and settings. The URL for the Companion Website ™ is also found at the end of each chapter; this is an excellent resource for additional study aids.

W WHERE TO LEARN MORE

The Underground Railroad
Freedom Center, Cincinnati, Ohio
www.undergroundrailroad.org

REVIEW QUESTIONS

1. What do Eliza Farmar's letters tell us about the crisis over dutied tea in 1773 and 1774? What makes her increasingly sympathetic to the colonial position?

2. How did the British victory in the French and Indian War affect the relations between Native Americans and white settlers? Between British authorities and Americans?

3. How did the expectations of American and British authorities differ in 1763? Why were new policies offensive to Americans?

4. How was stationing British troops in America related to British taxation of the colonists? Why did the colonists object to taxation by Parliament?

5. How did Americans oppose the new measures? Who participated in the various forms of resistance? How effective were the different kinds of resistance?

6. What led to the meeting of the First Continental Congress? What did the Congress achieve?

WHERE TO LEARN MORE

Charleston, South Carolina. Many buildings date from the eighteenth century. Officials stored tea in one of them—the Exchange—to prevent a local version of the Boston Tea Party. The website for Historic Charleston, **http://www.cr.nps.gov/nr/ travel/charleston**, provides a map, a list of buildings, and information about them.

GLOSSARY/KEY TERMS

Significant historical terms are called out in heavy type throughout the text, defined in the margin, and listed at the end of each chapter with appropriate page numbers. These are listed alphabetically and defined in a glossary at the end of the book.

KEY TERMS

Boston Massacre (p. 122)	**Declaratory Act** (p. 119)	**Sons of Liberty** (p. 118)
Boston Tea Party (p. 124)	**First Continental Congress** (p. 125)	**Stamp Act** (p. 116)
British Constitution (p. 117)	**Intolerable Acts** (p. 125)	**Stamp Act Congress** (p. 119)
Cherokee War (p. 114)	**Nonimportation movement** (p. 118)	**Sugar Act** (p. 116)
Coercive Acts (p. 125)	**Parson's Cause** (p. 115)	**Suffolk Resolves** (p. 127)
Committees of correspondence (p. 124)	**Pontiac's Rebellion** (p. 114)	**Tea Act of 1773** (p. 124)
Continental Association (p. 127)	**Proclamation Line** (p. 113)	**Tories** (p. 128)
Currency Act (p. 116)	**Proclamation of 1763** (p. 112)	**Townshend Duty Act** (p. 121)
Declaration of Rights and Grievances (p. 119)	**Quartering Acts** (p. 113)	**Whigs** (p. 128)
	Quebec Act (p. 125)	**Writs of assistance** (p. 117)
	Regulators (p. 120)	

The war passed from words to stones which the white children began to hurl at the colored. Several colored children were hurt and, as they had not resented the rock throwing . . . , the white children became more aggressive and abusive.

Edmund Commander, after your boxes came;

Mississippi Freedman School, 1866. Noon at the primary school for Freedmen at Vicksburg, Mississippi.

16

RECONSTRUCTION
1865–1877

WHY DID Southerner's remember the Civil War as a Lost Cause?

WHAT WERE African-American aspirations in 1865?

HOW DID Presidential Reconstruction differ from Congressional Reconstruction?

WHAT ROLE did the Ku Klux Klan play in Counter-Reconstruction?

WHAT WERE the effects of the Civil Rights Act of 1875 and the Compromise of 1877?

WHY AND HOW did Reconstruction end, and what were its failed promises?

Marianna, Florida 1866

The white academy opened about the same time the church opened the school for the Negro children. As the colored children had to pass the academy to reach the church it was easy for the white children to annoy them with taunts and jeers. The war passed from words to stones which the white children began to hurl at the colored. Several colored children were hurt and, as they had not resented the rock-throwing in kind because they were timid about going that far, the white children became more aggressive and abusive.

One morning the colored children armed themselves with stones and determined to fight their way past the academy to their school. [They] approached the academy in formation whereas in the past they had been going in pairs or small groups. When they reached hailing distance, a half dozen white boys rushed out and hurled their missiles. Instead of scampering away, the colored children not only stood their ground and hurled their missiles but maintained a solemn silence. The white children, seeing there was no backing down as they expected, came rushing out of the academy and charged the colored children.

During some fifteen minutes it was a real tug of war. In the close fighting the colored children got the advantage gradually and began to shove the white children back. As they pressed the advantage the white children broke away and ran for the academy. The colored fighters did not follow them but made it hot for the laggards until they also took to their heels. There were many bruises on both sides, but it taught the white youngsters to leave the colored ones alone thereafter.

—*T. Thomas Fortune,*
Norfolk Journal and Guide

T. Thomas Fortune, "Norfolk Journal and Guide," August 20, 1927, reprinted in Dorothy Sterling, ed., *The Trouble They Seen: Black People Tell the Story of Reconstruction* (Garden City, NY: Doubleday & Co., 1976): 22–24.

IMAGE KEY
for pages 414–415

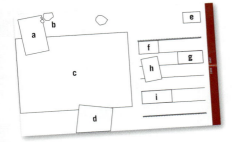

a. A young African American boy with new clothes and a book provided by the Freedman Bureau.

b. Rocks and stones like those used to hurl at former slaves.

c. Noon at the primary school for Freedmen at Vicksburg, Mississippi: colored engraving, 1866.

d. Two members of the Ku Klux Clan holding guns and wearing hoods and long robes, pictured in Harper's Weekly.

e. Pages from the New England Primer; primers such as this one were used to educate former slaves.

f. A dead Confederate soldier lies prostrate beneath his rifle in an earthen trench on the battlefield at Petersburg, Virginia during the Civil War, April 3, 1865.

g. Freedmen (freed black slaves) wait to vote in 1867.

h. Three white men decry the Reconstruction Acts of Congress as "usurpations and unconstitutional, revolutionary, and void" while clasping hands above the fallen body of a black man.

i. African American worshippers during a tumultuous church service on New Year's Eve. Sketch by Joseph Becker.

T. THOMAS FORTUNE, a New York newspaper editor, recalled this battle between black and white schoolchildren sixty years earlier, at the beginning of the Reconstruction era. In the scheme of things, it did not amount to much. However, for ten-year-old Thomas, born a slave in Marianna, the incident encapsulated the dilemma of Reconstruction. In the journey from slavery to freedom, education was an important element of full citizenship for African Americans. The eagerness with which black children (and adults) flooded schools was matched by the hostility of the white community who resented any pretense of equality that education implied.

Reconstruction was not merely a series of white aggressions against African-American aspirations, followed by black retreats. The violence and disorder that punctuated Southern society after the Civil War was due in part to the refusal of black people to relinquish their dreams of equal citizenship, including the right to a decent education.

Young Thomas did not back down, though by 1878 he felt that the journey from slavery to freedom would always be incomplete in the South. Together with his young bride, Carrie Smiley of Jacksonville, Florida, Thomas left for New York City, where he obtained a job as a printer for the *New York Sun*. He died there in 1928. New York's gain was the South's loss, a process repeated many times over after the Civil War as talented young black men and women left the region of their birth and their ancestors. It was a double tragedy for the South: losing people who could have rebuilt a shattered region, and missing the opportunity to create a society based on racial equality.

The position of African Americans in American society and how to reform the Former Confederate states were the two great issues of the Reconstruction era. Americans disagreed about both of them. The formation of a national consensus on freedom and reunification began with the demands and hopes of three broad groups: the Republican party, the more than 4 million former slaves, and white Southerners.

Between 1865 and 1867, under President Andrew Johnson's Reconstruction plan, white Southerners pretty much had their way with the former slaves and with their own state governments. Congressional action between 1867 and 1870 attempted to balance black rights and home rule, with mixed results. After 1870, white Southerners regained control, denying black Southerners their political gains while Republicans in Washington lost interest in policing their former enemies.

WHITE SOUTHERNERS AND THE GHOSTS OF THE CONFEDERACY, 1865

Confederate soldiers—generals and troops alike—returned to devastated homes they could scarcely recognize. Their cause lost and their society reviled, white Southerners lived through the summer and fall of 1865 surrounded by ghosts—the ghosts of lost loved ones, joyful times, bountiful harvests, self-assurance, and slavery. Defeat shook the basic tenets of their religious beliefs. But many other white Southerners refused to accept their defeat as a divine judgment. Instead, they insisted, God had spared the South for a greater purpose. Robert E. Lee became the patron saint of this cause, his poignant nobility a contrast to the crassness of the Yankee warlords. Some white Southerners would not allow the memory of the bloody struggle to die, transforming it into the **Lost Cause**, a symbol of courage against great odds. The Old South was transformed into a stainless civilization, worth fighting and dying for, and the Civil War became not a savage conflict, but a romantic and chivalrous contest.

Fifteen years after the war, Mark Twain traveled the length of the East Coast. After visiting a gentlemen's club in Boston, he recalled that the conversation had covered a variety of topics, none of which included the Civil War. Northerners had relegated that conflict to history books and moved on. In the South, on the other hand, defeat and destruction demanded rationalization and remembrance.

Most white Southerners approached the great issues of freedom and reunification with unyielding views. They saw African Americans as adversaries whose attempts at self-improvement were a direct challenge to white people's beliefs in their own racial superiority. They also saw outside assistance to black Southerners as another invasion.

WHY DID Southerners remember the Civil War as a Lost Cause?

Lost Cause   The phrase many white Southerners applied to their Civil War defeat. They viewed the war as a noble cause and only a temporary setback in the South's ultimate vindication.

MORE THAN FREEDOM: AFRICAN-AMERICAN ASPIRATIONS IN 1865

WHERE TO LEARN MORE

★ Penn Center Historic District,
St. Helena Island, South Carolina
www.penncenter.com

Freedmen's Bureau   Agency established by Congress in March 1865 to provide social, educational, and economic services, advice, and protection to former slaves and destitute whites; lasted seven years.

The engraving shows Southerners decorating the graves of rebel soldiers at Hollywood Memorial Cemetery in Virginia, 1867. Northerners and Southerners alike honored their war dead. But in the South, the practice of commemorating fallen soldiers became an important element in maintaining the myth of the Lost Cause that colored white Southerners' view of the war.

The Granger Collection, New York

I f black people could have peered into the minds of white Southerners, they would have been stunned. The former slaves did not initially even dream of social equality; far less did they plot the kind of vengeful murder and mayhem white people feared. They did harbor two potentially contradictory aspirations. The first was to be left alone, free of white supervision. The second was land, voting and civil rights, and education. To secure these, they needed the intervention and support of the white power structure.

The first step Congress took beyond emancipation was to establish the Bureau of Refugees, Freedmen, and Abandoned Lands in March 1865. Congress envisioned the **Freedmen's Bureau**, as it came to be called, as a multipurpose agency to provide social, educational, and economic services, advice, and protection to former slaves and destitute whites. The Bureau marked the federal government's first foray into social welfare legislation. Congress also authorized the bureau to rent confiscated and abandoned farmland to freedmen in 40-acre plots with an option to buy. This auspicious beginning to realizing African-American aspirations belied the great disappointments that lay ahead.

EDUCATION

The greatest success of the Freedmen's Bureau was in education. The bureau coordinated more than fifty northern philanthropic and religious groups, which in turn established three thousand freedmen's schools in the South serving 150,000 men, women, and children.

Initially, single young women from the Northeast comprised much of the teaching force. One of them, a 26-year-old Quaker named Martha Schofield, came to Aiken, South Carolina, from rural Pennsylvania in 1865. The school she founded has been part of Aiken's public school system since 1953.

By the time Schofield opened her own school in 1871, black teachers outnumbered white teachers in the "colored" schools. Support for them came from black churches, especially the African Methodist Episcopal (AME) Church. The former slaves crowded into basements, shacks, and churches to attend school. At the end of the Civil War, only about 10 percent of black Southerners were literate, compared with more than 70 percent of the white Southerners. Within a decade, the freedmen's schools had reduced illiteracy among the former slaves to below 70 percent.

Some black Southerners went on to one of the thirteen colleges established by the American Missionary Association and black and white churches. Between 1860 and 1880 more than one thousand black Southerners earned college degrees at institutions still serving students today such as Howard University in Washington, D.C., Fisk University in Nashville, and Biddle Institute (now Johnson C. Smith University) in Charlotte.

Pursuing freedom of the mind involved challenges beyond those of learning to read and write. Many white Southerners condemned efforts at "Negro improvement." They viewed the time spent on education as wasted, forcing the former slaves to catch their lessons in bits and pieces between work, often by candlelight or on Sundays. After the Freedmen's Bureau folded in 1872, education for black Southerners became more haphazard.

"FORTY ACRES AND A MULE"

Although education was important to the freed slaves in their quest for civic equality, land ownership offered them the promise of economic independence.

Even before the war's end, rumors circulated through black communities in the South that the government would provide each black family with 40 acres and a mule. These rumors were fueled by General William T. Sherman's **Field Order No. 15** in January 1865, which set aside a vast swath of abandoned land along the South Atlantic coast from the Charleston area to northern Florida for grants of up to 40 acres. The Freedmen's Bureau likewise raised expectations when it was initially authorized to rent 40-acre plots of confiscated or abandoned land to freedmen.

By June 1865, about forty thousand former slaves had settled on "Sherman land" along the southeastern coast. In 1866, Congress passed the **Southern Homestead Act**, giving black people preferential access to public lands in five southern states. By the late 1870s, more than fourteen thousand African-American families had taken advantage of a program to finance land purchases with state-funded, long-term, low-interest loans.

Land ownership did not ensure financial success. Most black-owned farms were small and on marginal land. Black farmers also had trouble obtaining credit to purchase or expand their holdings. A lifetime of field work left some freedmen without the managerial skills to operate a farm.

The vast majority of former slaves, especially those in the Lower South, never fulfilled their dreams of land ownership. Rumors to the contrary, the federal government never intended to implement a land redistribution program in the South. General Sherman viewed his field order as a temporary measure to support freedmen for the remainder of the war. President Andrew Johnson nullified the order in September 1865, returning confiscated lands to their former owners. Even Republican supporters of black land ownership questioned the constitutionality of seizing privately owned real estate. They envisioned former slaves assuming the status of free laborers, not necessarily of independent landowners.

For most officials of the Freedmen's Bureau, who shared these views, reviving the southern economy was a higher priority than helping former slaves acquire farms. They wanted both to get the crop in the field and start the South on the road to a free labor system. They thus encouraged freedmen to work for their former masters under contract and postpone their quest for land.

At first, agents of the Freedmen's Bureau supervised labor contracts between former slaves and masters. But after 1867, bureau surveillance declined. Agents assumed that both black laborers and white landowners had become accustomed to the mutual obligations of contracts. The bureau, however, underestimated the power of white landowners to coerce favorable terms or to ignore those they did not like.

MIGRATION TO CITIES

While some black Southerners asserted their rights as workers on southern farms, others affirmed their freedom by moving to towns and cities. Even before the war, the city had offered slaves and free black people a measure of freedom unknown in the rural South. After the war, African Americans moved to cities to find families, seek work, escape the tedium and supervision of farm life, or simply test their right to move about. Between 1860 and 1870, the official African American population in every major Southern city rose significantly.

WHERE TO LEARN MORE

Hampton University Museum,
Hampton, Virginia
www.hamptonu.edu/museum

Field Order No. 15   Order by General William T. Sherman in January 1865 to set aside abandoned land along the southern Atlantic coast for forty-acre grants to freedmen, rescinded by President Andrew Johnson later that year.

Southern Homestead Act   Largely unsuccessful law passed in 1866 that gave black people preferential access to public lands in five southern states.

Milk sampling at Hampton Institute. Hampton, which opened in Virginia in 1868, was one of the first of several schools established with the help of Northern philanthropic and missionary societies to allow freedmen to pursue a college education. Hampton stressed agricultural and vocational training. The military uniforms were typical for male students, black and white, at agricultural and mechanical schools.

Courtesy of Hampton University Archives

Once in the city, freedmen had to find a home and a job. They usually settled for the cheapest accommodations in low-lying areas or on the outskirts of town where building codes did not apply. Rather than developing one large ghetto, as in many Northern cities, black Southerners lived in several concentrations in and around cities.

Sometimes armed with a letter of reference from their former masters, black people went door to door to seek employment. Many found work serving white families—as guards, laundresses, maids—for very low wages. Both skilled and unskilled laborers found work rebuilding war-torn cities like Atlanta. Most rural black Southerners, however, arrived in cities untrained in the kinds of skills sought in an urban work force and so worked as unskilled laborers. In both Atlanta and Nashville, black people comprised more than 75 percent of the unskilled work force in 1870.

FAITH AND FREEDOM

Religious faith framed and inspired the efforts of African Americans to test their freedom on the farm and in the city. White Southerners used religion to transform the Lost Cause from a shattering defeat to a premonition of a greater destiny. Black Southerners, in contrast, saw emancipation in biblical terms as the beginning of an exodus from bondage to the Promised Land.

Some black churches in the postwar South originated in the slavery era, but most split from white-dominated congregations after the war. The church became a primary focus of African-American life. It gave black people the opportunity to hone skills in self-government and administration that white-dominated society denied them. Within the supportive confines of the congregation, they could assume leadership positions, render important decisions, deal with financial matters, and engage in politics. The church also operated as an educational institution.

The church spawned other organizations that served the black community over the next century. Burial societies, Masonic lodges, temperance groups, trade unions, and drama clubs originated in churches. By the 1870s, African Americans in Memphis had more than two hundred such organizations.

African Americans took great pride in their churches, which became visible measures of their progress. In Charleston, the first building erected after the war was a black church. Black people donated a greater proportion of their earnings to their churches than white people did. The church and the congregation were a cohesive force in black communities. They supported families under stress from discrimination and poverty. Most black churches looked inward to strengthen their members against the harsh realities of postbellum Southern society. Few ministers dared to engage in or even support protest activities. Some, especially those in the Colored Methodist Episcopal Church, counseled congregants to abide by the rules of second-class citizenship and to trust in God's will to right the wrongs of racism.

Northern-based denominations, however, notably the AME Church, were more aggressive advocates of black rights. AME ministers stressed the responsibility of individual black people to realize God's will of racial equality. Henry McNeal Turner, probably the most influential AME minister of his day, helped expand the denomination into the South from its small primarily northern base at the end of the Civil War. His church elevated him to bishop in 1880.

Turner's career and the efforts of former slaves in the classroom, on the farm, in cities, and in the churches reflect the enthusiasm and expectations with which black Southerners greeted freedom. But the majority of white Southerners were unwilling to see those expectations fulfilled. For this reason, African Americans could not secure the fruits of their emancipation without the support and

The black church was the center of African American life in the postwar urban South. Most black churches formed after the Civil War, but some, such as the first African Baptist Church in Richmond, shown here in an 1874 engraving, traced their origins to before 1861.

The Granger Collection, New York

CHRONOLOGY

1863	Lincoln proposes his Ten Percent Plan.	**1871**	Congress passes Ku Klux Klan Act.
1864	Congress proposes the Wade Davis Bill.	**1872**	Freedmen's Bureau closes down. Liberal Republicans emerge as a separate party. Ulysses S. Grant is reelected.
1865	Sherman issues Field Order No. 15. Freedmen's Bureau is established. Andrew Johnson succeeds to the presidency, unveils his Reconstruction plan. Massachusetts desegregates all public facilities. Black people in several Southern cities organize Union Leagues. Former Confederate states begin to pass black codes.	**1873**	Severe depression begins. Colfax Massacre occurs. U.S. Supreme Court's decision in the *Slaughter-house* cases weakens the intent of the Fourteenth Amendment. Texas falls to the Democrats in the fall elections.
1866	Congress passes Southern Homestead Act, Civil Rights Act of 1866. Ku Klux Klan is founded. Fourteenth Amendment to the Constitution is passed (ratified in 1868). President Johnson goes on a speaking tour.	**1874**	White Leaguers attempt a coup against the Republican government of New Orleans. Democrats win off year elections across the South amid widespread fraud and violence.
1867	Congress passes Military Reconstruction Acts, Tenure of Office Act.	**1875**	Congress passes Civil Rights Act of 1875.
1868	President Johnson is impeached and tried in the Senate for defying the Tenure of Office Act. Republican Ulysses S. Grant is elected president.	**1876**	Supreme Court's decision in *United States* v. *Cruikshank* nullifies Enforcement Act of 1870. Outcome of the presidential election between Republican Rutherford B. Hayes and Democrat Samuel J. Tilden is contested.
1869	Fifteenth Amendment passed (ratified 1870).	**1877**	Compromise of 1877 makes Hayes president and ends Reconstruction.
1870	Congress passes Enforcement Act. Republican regimes topple in North Carolina and Georgia.		

protection of the federal government, and the issue of freedom was therefore inextricably linked to that of the rejoining of the Confederacy to the Union, as expressed in federal Reconstruction policy.

FEDERAL RECONSTRUCTION, 1865–1870

When the Civil War ended in 1865, no acceptable blueprint existed for reconstituting the Union. In 1863, Lincoln proposed to readmit a seceding state if 10 percent of its prewar voters took an oath of loyalty to the Union and it prohibited slavery in a new state constitution. But this Ten Percent Plan did not require states to grant equal civil and political rights to former slaves, and many Republicans in Congress thought it was not stringent enough. In 1864, a group of them responded with the Wade-Davis Bill, which required a *majority* of a state's prewar voters to pledge their loyalty to the Union and demanded guarantees of black equality before the law. The bill was passed, but Lincoln kept it from becoming law by refusing to sign it (an action known as a pocket veto).

The controversy over these plans reflected two obstacles to Reconstruction that would continue to plague the ruling Republicans after the war. First, neither the Constitution nor legal precedent offered any guidance on whether the president or Congress should take the lead on Reconstruction policy. Second, there was no agreement on what that policy should be.

HOW DID Presidential Reconstruction differ from Congressional Reconstruction?

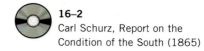

16–2
Carl Schurz, Report on the Condition of the South (1865)

President Andrew Johnson, some conservative Republicans, and most Democrats believed that because the Constitution made no mention of secession, the Southern states never left the Union, so there was no need for a formal process to readmit them. Moderate and radical Republicans disagreed, arguing that the defeated states had forfeited their rights. Moderates and radicals parted company, however, on the conditions necessary for readmission to the Union. No group held a majority in Congress, and legislators sometimes changed their positions (see the overview table "Contrasting Views of Reconstruction").

PRESIDENTIAL RECONSTRUCTION, 1865–1867

When the Civil War ended in April 1865, Congress was not in session and would not reconvene until December. Thus the responsibility for developing a Reconstruction policy initially fell on Andrew Johnson, who succeeded to the presidency upon Lincoln's assassination. Johnson seemed well suited to the difficult task. Johnson was the only Southern senator to remain in the U.S. Senate after secession. This defiant Unionism won him popular acclaim in the North and credibility among Republican leaders.

Most Northerners and many Republicans approved Johnson's Reconstruction plan when he unveiled it in May 1865. Johnson extended pardons and restored property rights, except in slaves, to Southerners who swore an oath of allegiance to the Union and the Constitution. The plan had nothing to say about the voting rights and civil rights of former slaves.

Northern Democrats applauded the plan's silence on these issues and its promise of a quick restoration of the Southern states to the Union. They expected the Southern states to favor their party and expand its political power. White Southerners, however, were not so favorably impressed, and their response turned Northern public opinion against the president. On the two great issues of freedom and reunion, white Southerners quickly demonstrated their eagerness to reverse the results of the Civil War. Although most states accepted President Johnson's modest requirements, several objected to one or more provisions. Mississippi and Texas refused to ratify the Thirteenth Amendment, which abolished slavery. South Carolina declined to nullify its secession ordinance. No Southern state authorized black voting. When Johnson ordered special congressional elections in the South in the fall of 1865, the all-white electorate returned many prominent Confederate leaders to office.

In late 1865, the newly elected Southern state legislatures revised their antebellum slave codes. The updated and renamed **black codes** allowed local officials to arrest black people who could not document employment and residence, or who were "disorderly," and sentence them to forced labor on farms or road construction crews. The codes also restricted black people to certain occupations, barred them from jury duty, and forbade them to possess firearms. (see American Views: "Mississippi's 1865 Black Codes"). President Johnson did not seem perturbed about this turn of events.

The Republican-dominated Congress reconvened in December 1865 in a belligerent mood. A consensus formed among radical Republicans, who comprised nearly half of the party's strength in Congress, that to gain readmission, a state would have to extend suffrage to black citizens, protect freedmen's civil rights, and have its white citizens officially acknowledge these rights. Some radicals also supported the redistribution of land to former slaves, but few pressed for social equality.

Thaddeus Stevens of Pennsylvania led the radical forces in the House of Representatives, while abolitionist veteran Charles Sumner of Massachusetts rallied radicals in the Senate. Stevens dreamed of a South populated by white and black yeoman farmers. With no large plantations and few landless farmers, the

Black codes Laws passed by states and municipalities denying many rights of citizenship to free blacks after the Civil War.

• AMERICAN VIEWS •

MISSISSIPPI'S 1865 BLACK CODES

White Southerners feared emancipation would produce a labor crisis; freedmen, they expected, would either refuse to work or strike hard bargains with their former masters. White Southerners also recoiled from having to treat former slaves as social equals. Thus, beginning in late 1865, several Southern states, including Mississippi, enacted laws to control black labor, mobility, and social status. Northerners saw the codes as a bold move to deny the result of the war and its consequences.

HOW DID the black codes fit into President Andrew Johnson's Reconstruction program? Some Northerners charged that the black codes were a backdoor attempt at reestablishing slavery. Do you agree?

From an Act to Confer Civil Rights on Freedmen, and for other Purposes

Section 1.   All freedmen, free negroes and mulattoes may sue and be sued, implead and be impleaded, in all the courts of law and equity of this State, and may acquire personal property, and choose in action, by descent or purchase, and may dispose of the same in the same manner and to the same extent that white persons may: Provided, That the provisions of this section shall not be so construed as to allow any freedman, free negro or mulatto to rent or lease any lands or tenements except in incorporated cities or towns, in which places the corporate authorities shall control the same.

From an Act to Amend the Vagrant Laws of the State

Section 2.   All freedmen, free negroes and mulattoes in this State, over the age of eighteen years, found on the second Monday in January, 1866, or thereafter, with no lawful employment or business, or found unlawful assembling themselves together, either in the day or night time, and all white persons assembling themselves with freedmen, Free negroes or mulattoes, or usually associating with freedmen, free negroes or mulattoes, on terms of equality, or living in adultery or fornication with a freed woman, freed negro or mulatto, shall be deemed vagrants, and on conviction thereof shall be fined in a sum not exceeding, in the case of a freedman, free negro or mulatto, fifty dollars, and a white man two hundred dollars, and imprisonment at the discretion of the court, the free negro not exceeding ten days, and the white man not exceeding six months.

Source: "Laws in Relation to Freedmen," 39 Congress, 2 Session, Senate Executive Document 6, Freedmen's Affairs, 182–86.

South would become an ideal republic, a boon to the rest of the nation instead of a burden. Few shared his vision, and when he died in 1868, a reporter noted that "no man was oftener outvoted."

Charles Sumner was among the foremost abolitionist politicians before the Civil War. His combative nature won him few friends, even within his own party. As fierce as Stevens was in the promotion of black civil and political rights after the war, he also believed that the Reconstruction era offered a "golden moment" to remake the South into an egalitarian region. Sumner died in 1874 as his dream was fading.

But the radicals could not unite behind a program, and it fell to their moderate colleagues to take the first steps toward a Congressional Reconstruction plan. The moderates shared the radicals' desire to protect the former slaves' civil and voting rights, but they would not support land redistribution schemes or punitive measures against prominent Confederates. The Civil Rights Act of 1866 was a direct response to the black codes. The act specified the civil rights to which all U.S. citizens were entitled. In creating a category of national citizenship with rights that superseded state laws restricting them, the act changed federal–state relations (and in the process overturned the *Dred Scott* decision). President Johnson

QUICK REVIEW

Thaddeus Stevens
- Stevens of Pennsylvania led the radical forces in the House of Representatives.
- Stevens envisioned a South with no large plantations and few landless farmers.
- Stevens found few supporters for his ideas.

OVERVIEW

CONTRASTING VIEWS OF RECONSTRUCTION: PRESIDENT AND CONGRESS

Politician or Group	Policy on Former Slaves	Policy on Readmission of Former Confederate States
President Johnson	Opposed to black suffrage Silent on protection of black civil rights Opposed to land redistribution	Maintained that rebellious states were already readmitted Granted pardons and restoration of property to all who swore allegiance to the United States
Radical Republicans	Favored black suffrage Favored protection of black civil rights Favored land redistribution	Favored treating rebellious states as territories and establishing military districts* Favored limiting franchise to black people and loyal white people
Moderate Republicans	Favored black suffrage Favored protection of civil rights Opposed land redistribution	Favored some restrictions on white suffrage* Favored requiring states to meet various requirements before being readmitted* Split on military rule

* True of most but not all members of the group.

vetoed the act, but it became law when Congress mustered a two-thirds majority to override his veto, the first time in American history that Congress passed major legislation over a president's veto.

Andrew Johnson's position reflected both his view of government and his racial attitudes. The Republican president remained a Democrat in spirit. Like most Democrats, he favored a balance between federal and state power. He also shared with many of his white Southern neighbors a belief in black inferiority.

To keep freedmen's rights safe from presidential vetoes, state legislatures, and federal courts, the Republican-dominated Congress moved to incorporate some of the provisions of the 1866 Civil Rights Act into the Constitution with an amendment. The **Fourteenth Amendment**, which Congress passed in June 1866, addressed the issues of civil and voting rights. It guaranteed every citizen equality before the law. The two key sections of the amendment prohibited states from violating the civil rights of their citizens, thus outlawing the black codes, and gave states the choice of enfranchising black people or losing representation in Congress.

The amendment disappointed advocates of woman suffrage, because for the first time the word *male* in the Constitution was used to define who could vote. Susan B. Anthony, who had campaigned for the abolition of slavery before the war and helped mount a petition drive that collected 400,000 signatures for the Thirteenth Amendment, formed the American Equal Rights Association in 1866 with her colleagues to push for woman suffrage at the state level.

The amendment had little immediate impact on the South. Although enforcement of black codes diminished, white violence against blacks increased. In the 1870s, several decisions by the U.S. Supreme Court would weaken the amendment's provisions. Eventually, however, the Fourteenth Amendment would play a major role in securing the civil rights of African Americans when the issue reemerged in the 1950s.

President Johnson seemed to encourage white intransigence by openly denouncing the Fourteenth Amendment. The president's diatribes against the Republican Congress won him followers in those Northern states with a reservoir of opposition

Fourteenth Amendment Passed by Congress in 1866, guaranteed every citizen equality before the law by prohibiting states from violating the civil rights of their citizens, thus outlawing the black codes.

to black suffrage. But the tone and manner of his campaign offended many as undignified. In the November elections, Republicans managed better than two-thirds majorities in both the House and Senate, sufficient to override presidential vetoes. Radical Republicans, joined by moderate colleagues buoyed by the election results and revolted by the president's and the South's intransigence, seized the initiative.

CONGRESSIONAL RECONSTRUCTION, 1867–1870

The radicals' first salvo in their attempt to take control over Reconstruction occurred with the passage over President Johnson's veto of the Military Reconstruction Acts. The measures, passed in March 1867, inaugurated a period known as **Congressional Reconstruction** or Radical Reconstruction. They generally divided the ex-Confederate states into five military districts (see Map 16–1) and provided for elections to a state constitutional convention guaranteeing universal manhood suffrage.

The Reconstruction Acts fulfilled the radicals' three major objectives. First, they secured the freedmen's right to vote. Second, they made it likely that Southern states would be run by Republican regimes that would enforce the new constitutions, protect former slaves' rights, and maintain the Republican majority in Congress. Finally, the acts set standards for readmission that required the South to accept the consequences of defeat: the preeminence of the federal government and the end of involuntary servitude.

To limit presidential interference with their policies, Republicans passed the Tenure of Office Act, prohibiting the president from removing certain officeholders without the Senate's consent. Johnson, angered at what he believed was an unconstitutional attack on presidential authority, deliberately violated the act in February 1868. He fired Secretary of War Edwin M. Stanton, a leading radical. The House responded to this defiance of congressional authority by approving, for the first time in American history, articles of impeachment against the president. The Senate voted thirty-five to nineteen to convict, one vote short of the two-thirds necessary to remove Johnson. The outcome weakened the radicals' clout in Congress and eased the way for moderate Republican Ulysses S. Grant to gain the party's nomination for president in 1868.

The Republicans viewed the 1868 presidential election as a referendum on Congressional Reconstruction. Grant won the election, but his margin of victory was uncomfortably narrow.

The Republicans retained a strong majority in both houses of Congress and managed to pass another major piece of Reconstruction legislation, the **Fifteenth Amendment**, in February 1869. In response to growing concerns about voter fraud and violence against freedmen, the amendment guaranteed the right of American men to vote, regardless of race. Although the amendment provided a loophole allowing states to impose restrictions on the right to vote based on literacy requirements or property qualifications, it was nonetheless a milestone. It made the right to vote perhaps the most distinguishing characteristic of American citizenship.

The Fifteenth Amendment allowed states to keep the franchise a male prerogative. Susan B. Anthony now broke with her abolitionist colleagues and opposed the amendment. Fellow abolitionist and woman suffragist Elizabeth Cady Stanton warned

MAP EXPLORATION

To explore an interactive version of this map, go to
http://www.prenhall.com/goldfield2/map16.1

MAP 16–1

Congressional Reconstruction, 1865–1877   When Congress wrested control of Reconstruction policy from President Andrew Johnson, it divided the South into the five military districts depicted here. The commanding generals for each district held the authority both to hold elections and decide who could vote.

WHAT DID each of the former Confederate states have to do to be eligible for readmission to the Union?

Congressional Reconstruction   Name given to the period 1867–1870 when the Republican-dominated Congress controlled Reconstruction era policy.

Fifteenth Amendment   Passed by Congress in 1869, guaranteed the right of American men to vote, regardless of race.

Casting a ballot. Black voters in Richmond vote on a state constitutional conventions in 1867. A key objective of Congressional Reconstruction was to secure the voting rights of freedman.

The Granger Collection, New York

WHERE TO LEARN MORE

★ Beauvoir, Biloxi, Mississippi
www.beauvoir.org

Scalawags Southern whites, mainly small landowning farmers and well-off merchants and planters, who supported the Southern Republican party during Reconstruction.

Carpetbaggers Northern transplants to the South, many of whom were Union soldiers who stayed in the South after the war.

Union Leagues Republican party organizations in Northern cities that became an important organizing device among freedmen in Southern cities after 1865.

that "if you do not wish the lower orders of Chinese, African, Germans and Irish, with their low ideas of womanhood to make laws for you and your daughters . . . awake to the danger . . . and demand that woman, too, shall be represented in the government!" Such ethnic and racial animosity created a major rift in the nascent women's movement. Women who supported the amendment formed the New England Woman Suffrage Association, challenging Anthony's American Equal Rights Association.

SOUTHERN REPUBLICAN GOVERNMENTS, 1867–1870

Away from Washington, the first order of business was to draft state constitutions. The documents embodied progressive principles new to the former Confederacy. They mandated the election of numerous local and state offices. Self-perpetuating local elites could no longer appoint themselves or cronies to powerful positions. The constitutions committed Southern states, many for the first time, to public education. Lawmakers enacted a variety of reforms, including social welfare, penal reform, legislative reapportionment, and universal manhood suffrage.

The Republican regimes that gained control in Southern states promoted vigorous state government and the protection of civil and voting rights. Three diverse Republican constituencies supported these governments. One consisted of white natives, most of them yeomen farmers, who resided mainly in the upland regions of the South and long ignored by lowland planters and merchants in state government. The conflict had left many of them devastated. They struggled to keep their land and hoped for an easing of credit and for debt-stay laws to help them escape foreclosure. They wanted public schools for their children and good roads to get their crops to market. Collectively, these native white Southerners were called **scalawags**, a derogatory term derived from the name of the district of Scalloway, on Scotland's Shetland Islands, known for its scraggly livestock. The term was first applied in western New York before the Civil War to an idle person and then to a mischievous one. Although their opponents may have perceived them as a unified group, scalawags in fact held a variety of views.

Northern transplants, or **carpetbaggers**, as their opponents called them, constituted a second group of Southern Republicans. The term also had antebellum origins, referring to a suspicious stranger. Cartoonists depicted carpetbaggers as shoddily dressed and poorly groomed men, their worldly possessions in a ratty cloth satchel, slinking into a town and swindling the locals before departing with their ill-gotten gains. The reality was far different from the caricature. Many were Union soldiers who simply enjoyed the climate and perhaps married a local woman. Most were drawn by economic opportunity. Land was cheap and the price of cotton high. Some also hoped to aid the freedmen.

Carpetbaggers never comprised more than 2 percent of any state's population. Most white Southerners viewed them as an alien presence, instruments of a hated occupying force. They provoked resentment because they seemed to prosper while most Southerners struggled in poverty.

African Americans constituted the Republican party's largest Southern constituency. In three states—South Carolina, Mississippi, and Louisiana—they also formed the majority of eligible voters. They viewed the franchise as the key to civic equality and economic opportunity and demanded an active role in party and government affairs. In February 1865, black people in Norfolk, Virginia, gathered to demand a say in the new government that Union supporters were forming in that portion of the state. In April, they created the Colored Monitor Union club, modeled after Republican party organizations in northern cities, called **Union Leagues**. They demanded "the right of *universal* suffrage" for "*all* loyal men, without distinction of color." Despite white threats, black people thronged to Union League meetings in 1867, even forging interracial alliances in states such as North Carolina and Alabama. Focusing on political education and recruitment, the leagues successfully mobilized black voters.

Black Southerners were not content just to vote; they also demanded political office. The number of Southern black congressmen in the U.S. House of Representatives increased from two in 1869 to seven in 1873, and more than six hundred African Americans, most of them former slaves from plantation counties, were elected to Southern state legislatures between 1867 and 1877.

White fears that black officeholders would enact vengeful legislation proved unfounded. African Americans generally did not promote race-specific legislation. Rather, they supported measures such as debt relief and state funding for education that benefited all poor and working-class people. Like all politicians, however, black officials in Southern cities sought to enact measures beneficial to their constituents.

Republicans gained support by expanding the role of state government to a degree unprecedented in the South. Southern Republican administrations appealed to hard-pressed upland whites by prohibiting foreclosure and passing stay laws that allowed farm owners extra time to repay debts. They undertook building programs that benefited both blacks and whites, erecting hospitals, schools, and orphanages. Stepping further into social policy than most Northern states at the time, Republican governments in the South expanded women's property rights, enacted legislation against child abuse, and required child support from fathers of mulatto children. In South Carolina, the Republican government provided medical care for the poor; in Alabama, it provided free legal aid for needy defendants.

Despite these impressive policies, southern Republicans were unable to hold their diverse constituency together. The high costs of their activist policies further undermined the Republicans by forcing them to raise state taxes. Small property holders, already reeling from declining staple prices, found the taxes especially burdensome, despite liberal stay laws. Revenues nonetheless could not keep pace with expenditures. The expenditures and the liberal use of patronage sometimes resulted in waste and corruption.

COUNTER-RECONSTRUCTION, 1870–1874

Republicans might have survived battles over patronage, differences over policy, and the resentment provoked by extravagant expenditures and high taxes; but they could not overcome racism. Racism killed Republican rule in the South because it deepened divisions within the party, encouraged white violence, and eroded support in the North. Southern Democrats discovered that they could use race baiting and racial violence to create racial solidarity among white people that overrode their economic and class differences. Unity translated into election victories.

Northerners responded to the persistent violence in the South not with outrage but with a growing sense of tedium. Racism became respectable. Noted intellectuals and journalists espoused "scientific" theories that claimed to demonstrate the natural superiority of white people over black people. These theories influenced the Liberal Republicans, followers of a new political movement that splintered the Republican party, further weakening its will to pursue Reconstruction policy.

By 1874, Americans were concerned with an array of domestic problems that overshadowed Reconstruction. With the rest of the nation thus distracted and weary, white Southerners reclaimed control of the South.

THE USES OF VIOLENCE

Racial violence preceded Republican rule. As African Americans moved about, attempted to vote, haggled over labor contracts, and carried arms as part of occupying Union forces, they tested the patience of white Southerners.

WHAT ROLE did the Ku Klux Klan play in Counter-Reconstruction?

16–8
Albion W. Tourgee, Letter on Ku Klux Klan Activities (1870)

The Klan directed violence at African Americans primarily for political activity. Here, a black man, John Campbell, vainly begs for mercy in Moore County, North Carolina, in August 1871.

The Granger Collection, New York

Cities, where black and white people competed for jobs and where black political influence was most visible, became flashpoints for interracial violence.

White paramilitary groups flourished in the South during the Reconstruction era and were responsible for much of the violence directed against African Americans. Probably the best known of these groups was the **Ku Klux Klan**. Founded in Tennessee by six Confederate veterans in 1866, the Klan was initially a social club that soon assumed a political purpose. Klan night riders in ghostlike disguises intimidated black communities. The Klan directed much of its violence toward subverting the electoral process. One historian has estimated that roughly 10 percent of all black delegates to the 1867 state constitutional conventions in the South became victims of political violence during the next decade. The most serious example of political violence occurred in Colfax, Louisiana, in 1873 when a white Democratic mob attempted to wrest control of local government from Republicans. For three weeks, black defenders held the town against the white onslaught. When the white mob finally broke through, they massacred the remaining black people, including those who had surrendered and laid down their weapons.

Racial violence and the combative reaction it provoked both among black people and Republican administrations energized white voters. Democrats regained power in North Carolina during the election of 1870, and that same year, the Republican regime in Georgia fell as well.

The federal government responded with a variety of legislation. One example was the Fifteenth Amendment, ratified in 1869, which guaranteed the right to vote. Another was the Enforcement Act of 1870, which enabled the federal government to appoint supervisors in states that failed to protect citizens' voting rights. A more sweeping measure was the Ku Klux Klan Act of 1871, which permitted federal authorities, with military assistance, if necessary, to arrest and prosecute members of groups that denied a citizen's civil rights if state authorities failed to do so and established a new precedent in federal–state relations.

THE FAILURE OF NORTHERN WILL

The success of political violence after 1871 reflected less the inadequacy of congressional legislation than the failure of will on the part of Northern Republicans to follow through on commitments to Southern Republican administrations. The commitment to voting rights for black Southerners, widespread among Republicans in 1865 and affirmed in the Fifteenth Amendment passed in 1869, faded as well. American politics in the 1870s seemed increasingly corrupt and irresponsible. Scandal abounded. Democratic boss William M. Tweed and his associates transformed Tammany Hall, a Democratic club, into a full-fledged political machine that robbed New York City of an astounding $100 million. Federal officials allowed private individuals to manipulate the stock market for spectacular gains. Several members of Congress and President Grant's vice president exchanged government favors for railroad stock.

Racism gained an aura of scientific respectability in the late nineteenth century. Science was held in high esteem at the time, helping assure public acceptance of the putatively scientific views of the racial theorists. According to those views, some peoples are inherently inferior to others, a natural state of affairs that no government interference can change.

Concerns about the quality of the electorate, also tinged with racism, reflected the rising stakes of public office in post–Civil War America. The urban industrial economy boomed in the five years after the war. Engineers flung railroads across the continent. Steam propelled factories to unprecedented levels of productivity and ships to new speed records. Discoveries of rich natural resources such as oil and iron presaged a new age of industrial might. Republicans promoted and ben-

QUICK REVIEW

Tammany Hall and Corruption

◆ William Tweed transformed Tammany Hall into a political machine.

◆ Tammany Hall facilitated widespread corruption.

◆ Corruption in American government extended to the federal level.

Ku Klux Klan Perhaps the most prominent of the vigilante groups that terrorized black people in the South during Reconstruction era, founded by Confederate veterans in 1866.

efited from the boom, and it influenced their priorities. Railroad, mining, and lumber lobbyists crowded Washington and state capitals begging for financial subsidies and favorable legislation. In an era before conflict-of-interest laws, leading Republicans sat on the boards of railroads, land development companies, and industrial corporations. While the federal government denied land to the freedmen, it doled out millions of acres to corporations.

Not all Republicans approved the party's promotion of economic development. Some questioned the prudence of government intervention in the "natural" operation of the nation's economy. The emerging scandals of the Grant administration led to calls for reform. Republican governments, North and South, were condemned for their lavish spending and high taxes. The time had come to restore good government.

LIBERAL REPUBLICANS AND THE ELECTION OF 1872

Liberal Republicans put forward an array of suggestions to improve government and save the Republican party. They advocated civil service reform to reduce reliance on patronage and the abuses that accompanied office seeking. To limit government and reduce artificial economic stimuli, the reformers called for tariff reduction and an end to federal land grants to railroads. For the South, they recommended a general amnesty for white people and a return to "local self-government" by men of "property and enterprise."

When the Liberals failed to convince other Republicans to adopt their program, they broke with the party. Taking advantage of this split, the Democrats forged an alliance with the Liberals. Together, the Democrats and Liberals nominated journalist Horace Greeley to challenge Ulysses S. Grant for the presidency in the election of 1872. Grant won resoundingly, helped by high turnout among black voters in the South. The election suggested that the excesses of the Grant administration had not yet exceeded public tolerance and that the Republican experiment in the South retained some public support. But within a year, an economic depression, continued violence in the South, and the persistent corruption of the Grant administration would turn public opinion against the Republicans. With this shift, support for Reconstruction and black rights would also fade.

REDEMPTION, 1874–1877

For Southern Democrats, the Republican victory in 1872 underscored the importance of turning out larger numbers of white voters and restricting the black vote. They accomplished these goals over the next four years with a surge in political violence. Preoccupied with corruption and economic crisis and increasingly indifferent, if not hostile, to African-American aspirations, most Americans looked the other way. The elections of 1876—on the local, state, and national levels—affirmed the triumph of white Southerners. Reconstruction did not end; it was overthrown. Southern Democrats called their victory "Redemption," and this interpretation of the Reconstruction era would affect race relations for nearly a century.

THE DEMOCRATS' VIOLENT RESURGENCE

The violence between 1874 and 1876 differed in several respects from earlier attempts to restore white government by force. Attackers operated more openly and more closely identified themselves with the Democratic party. Mounted, gray-clad ex-Confederate soldiers flanked Democratic candidates at campaign rallies and "visited" black neighborhoods afterward to discourage black people from voting. With black people intimidated and white people already prepared to vote, election days were typically quiet.

WHAT WERE the effects of the Civil Rights Act of 1875 and the Compromise of 1877?

Democrats swept to victory across the South in the 1874 elections. "A perfect reign of terror" redeemed Alabama for the Democrats. In Louisiana, a group of elite Democrats in New Orleans organized a military organization known as the *White League* in 1874 to challenge the state's Republican government. In September 1874, more than eight thousand White Leaguers staged a coup to overthrow the Republican government of New Orleans.

THE WEAK FEDERAL RESPONSE

Unrest like that in Louisiana also plagued Mississippi and South Carolina. When South Carolina governor Daniel H. Chamberlain could no longer contain the violence in his state in 1876, he asked the president for help. Although President Grant acknowledged the gravity of Chamberlain's situation, the president would only offer the governor the lame hope that South Carolinians would exercise "better judgment and cooperation" and assist the governor in bringing offenders to justice "without aid from the federal Government."

Congress responded to the violence with the Civil Rights Act of 1875. Introduced by Charles Sumner, the bill finally passed in a watered-down version after Sumner's death. The act prohibited discrimination against black people in public accommodations such as theaters, parks, and trains and guaranteed freedmen's rights to serve on juries. It had no provision for voting rights, which Congress presumed the Fifteenth Amendment protected. The only way to enforce the law was for individuals to bring grievances related to it before federal courts in the South.

When black people tested the law by trying to make free use of public accommodations, they were almost always turned away. In 1883, the U.S. Supreme Court overturned the act declaring that only the states, not Congress, could redress "a private wrong, or a crime of the individual."

THE ELECTION OF 1876 AND THE COMPROMISE OF 1877

Reconstruction officially ended with the presidential election of 1876 in which Democrat Samuel J. Tilden ran against Republican Rutherford B. Hayes. When the ballots were counted, it appeared that Tilden, a conservative New Yorker respectable enough for Northern voters and Democratic enough for white Southerners, had won. But despite a majority in the popular vote, disputed returns in three Southern states left him with 184 of the 185 electoral votes needed to win. The three states—Florida, South Carolina, and Louisiana—were the last in the South still to have Republican adminstrations.

Both camps maneuvered intensively in the months following the election to claim the disputed votes. Congress appointed a fifteen-member commission to settle the issue. Eventually the so-called **Compromise of 1877** installed Hayes in the White House and gave Democrats control of all state governments in the South.

Southern Democrats emerged the major winners of the Compromise of 1877. President Hayes and his successors into the next century left the South alone. In practical terms, the Compromise of 1877 signaled the revocation of civil rights and voting rights for black Southerners. The Fourteenth and Fifteenth Amendments would be dead letters in the South until well into the twentieth century. On the two great issues confronting the nation at the end of the Civil War, reunion and freedom, the white South had won. It reentered the Union largely on its own terms with the freedom to pursue a racial agenda consistent with its political, economic, and social interests.

THE MEMORY OF RECONSTRUCTION

Southern Democrats used the memory of Reconstruction to help maintain themselves in power. As white Southerners elevated Civil War heroes into saints, and battles into holy struggles, Reconstruction became the Redemption. Whenever Southern

Compromise of 1877 The Congressional settling of the 1876 election which installed Republican Rutherford B. Hayes in the White House and gave Democrats control of all state governments in the South.

Democrats felt threatened over the next century, they reminded their white constituents of the "horrors of Reconstruction," the menace of black rule, and the cruelty of Yankee occupiers. The Southern view of Reconstruction permeated textbooks, films, and standard accounts of the period. By the early 1900s, professional historians at the nation's finest institutions concurred in this view, and most Americans believed that the policies of Reconstruction had been misguided and had brought great suffering to the white South. This view allowed the South to maintain its system of racial segregation and exclusion without interference from the federal government.

Not all memories of Reconstruction conformed to this thesis. In 1913, John R. Lynch, a former black Republican congressman from Mississippi, published *The Facts of Reconstruction* to "present the other side." But most Americans ignored his book. Two decades later, W.E.B. Du Bois's *Black Reconstruction* (1935) met a similar fate.

The national historical consensus grew out of a growing national reconciliation concerning the war, a mutual agreement that it was time to move on. Lost in all the good will was the tacit agreement among both Southern and Northern whites that the South was free to work out its own resolution to race relations.

There is much to be said in favor of sectional reconciliation as opposed to persistent animosity. There are enough examples in the world today of antagonists in the same country never forgetting or never forgiving their bloody histories. Ideally, Americans could have had *both* healing and justice, but instead, they settled for the former. Frederick Douglass worried about what the peace that followed the Civil War would mean for race relations: "If war among the whites brought peace and liberty to the blacks, what will peace among the whites bring?" But white Americans seemed intent on shaking hands and getting on with their lives.

THE FAILED PROMISE OF RECONSTRUCTION

Most black people and white people in 1877 would have agreed on one point: Reconstruction had failed. If the demise of Reconstruction elicited a sigh of relief from most white Americans, black Americans greeted it with frustration. Their dreams of land ownership faded as a new labor system relegated them to a lowly position in Southern agriculture. Redemption reversed their economic and political gains and deprived them of most of the civil rights they had enjoyed under Congressional Reconstruction.

The former slaves were certainly better off in 1877 than in 1865. They were free, however limited their freedom. Some owned land; some held jobs in cities. But by 1877, the "golden moment"—an unprecedented opportunity for the nation to live up to its ideals by extending equal rights to all its citizens, black and white alike—had passed.

SHARECROPPING

When they lost political power, black Southerners also lost economic independence. As the Freedmen's Bureau retreated from supervising farm labor contracts and opportunities for black people to possess their own land dried up, the bargaining power of black farm laborers decreased, and the power of white landlords increased.

The upshot was that by the late 1870s, most former slaves in the rural South had been drawn into a subservient position in a new labor system called **sharecropping**. The premise of this system was relatively simple: The landlord furnished the sharecroppers a house, a plot of land to work, seed, some farm animals and farm implements and advanced them credit at a store the landlord typically owned. In exchange, the sharecroppers promised the landlord a share of their crop, usually one-half. The croppers kept the proceeds from the sale of the other half to pay off their debts at the store and save or spend as they and their families saw fit. In theory, a sharecropper could save enough to secure economic independence.

WHY AND how did Reconstruction end, and what were its failed promises?

WHERE TO LEARN MORE W

Levi Jordan Plantation, Brazoria County, Texas
www.webarchaeology.com

16–12
A Sharecrop Contract (1882)

Sharecropping Labor system that evolved during and after Reconstruction whereby landowners furnished laborers with a house, farm animals, and tools and advanced credit in exchange for a share of the laborers' crop.

As this Thomas Nast cartoon makes clear, the paramilitary violence against black Southerners in the early 1870s threatened not only the voting rights of freedmen, but also their dreams of education, prosperity, and family life as well. In this context, the slogan, "The Union As It Was" is highly ironic.

Courtesy of Library of Congress

With landlords holding the accounts at the store, black sharecroppers found that the proceeds from their share of the crop never left them very far ahead. In exchange for extending credit to sharecroppers, store owners felt justified in requiring collateral. But sharecroppers had no assets other than the cotton they grew. So Southern states passed crop lien laws, which gave the store owner the right to the next year's crop in exchange for this year's credit. The sharecropper sank deeper into dependence.

Sharecropping represented a significant step down from tenancy. Tenants owned their own draft animals, farm implements, and seed. Once they negotiated with a land owner for a fixed rent, they kept whatever profits they earned. Eventually, they could hope to purchase some land and move into the landlord class themselves.

Historians have often depicted the sharecropping system as a compromise between white landlord and black laborer. But compromise implies a give-and-take between relatively equal negotiators. As Northern and federal support for Reconstruction waned after 1870 and Southern Democrats regained political control, white power over black labor increased. Black people had no recourse to federal and state authorities or, increasingly, to the polls as a white reign of terror stripped them of their political rights.

The only difference between Northern and Southern employers' outlook on labor was that Southerners exercised more control over their workers. What had been a triangular debate—among white Northerners, white Southerners, and freedmen—had become a lopsided discourse divided along racial rather than sectional lines.

MODEST GAINS AND FUTURE VICTORIES

Black Southerners experienced some advances in the decade after the Civil War, but these owed little to Reconstruction. Black families functioned as economic and psychological buffers against unemployment and prejudice. Black churches played crucial roles in their communities. Self-help and labor organizations offered mutual friendship and financial assistance. All of these institutions had existed in the slavery era, although on a smaller scale. And some of them, such as black labor groups, schools, and social welfare associations, endured because comparable white institutions excluded black people. Black people also scored some modest economic successes during the Reconstruction era, mainly from their own pluck.

The Fourteenth and Fifteenth Amendments to the Constitution are among the few bright spots in Reconstruction's otherwise dismal legacy. The Fourteenth Amendment guaranteed former slaves equality before the law; the Fifteenth Amendment protected their right to vote. Both amendments elevated the federal government over the states by protecting freedmen from state attempts to deny them their rights. But the benefits of these two landmark amendments did not accrue to African Americans until well into the twentieth century. In the *Slaughterhouse cases* (1873), the Supreme Court contradicted the intent of the Fourteenth Amendment by decreeing that most citizenship rights remained under state, not federal, control. In *United States v. Cruikshank* (1876), the Court overturned the convictions of some of those responsible for the Colfax Massacre, ruling that the Enforcement Act applied only to violations of black rights by states, not individuals. Within the next two decades, the Supreme Court would uphold the legality of racial segregation and black disfranchisement, in effect declaring that the Fourteenth and Fifteenth Amendments did not apply to African Americans. The Civil War had killed secession forever, but states' rights enjoyed a remarkable revival.

As historian John Hope Franklin accurately concluded, Reconstruction "had no significant or permanent effect on the status of the black in American life. . . . [Black people] made no meaningful steps toward economic independence or even stability."

QUICK REVIEW

Advances
◆ Black families and institutions played a crucial role in Reconstruction Era.
◆ Fourteenth Amendment guaranteed equality before the law.
◆ Fifteenth Amendment protected the right to vote.

Slaughterhouse **cases** Group of cases resulting in one sweeping decision by the U.S. Supreme Court in 1873 that contradicted the intent of the Fourteenth Amendment by decreeing that most citizenship rights remained under state, not federal, control.

United States v. *Cruikshank* Supreme Court ruling of 1876 that overturned the convictions of some of those responsible for the Colfax Massacre, ruling that the Enforcement Act applied only to violations of black rights by states, not individuals.

FROM THEN TO NOW
African-American Voting Rights in the South

Right from the end of the Civil War, white Southerners resisted African-American voting rights. Black people, with equal determination, used the franchise to assert their equal right to participate in the political process. Black voting rights proved so contentious that Congress sought to secure them with the Fourteenth and Fifteenth Amendments to the U.S. Constitution. But U.S. Supreme Court decisions in *United States* v. *Cruikshank* (1876) and in the *Civil Rights Cases* (1883) undermined federal authority to protect the rights of freedmen, including voting rights. A combination of violence, intimidation, and legislation effectively disfranchised black Southerners by the early twentieth century.

During the 1960s, Congress passed legislation designed to override state prohibitions and earlier court decisions limiting African-American voting rights. The key measure, the 1965 Voting Rights Act, not only guaranteed black Southerners (and later, other minorities) the right to register and vote but protected them from procedural subterfuges, many of which dated from the first Reconstruction era; that would dilute their votes. These protections proved necessary because of the extreme racial polarization of Southern elections: White people rarely voted for black candidates.

To ensure African-American candidates an opportunity to win elections, the federal government after 1965 insisted that states and localities establish procedures to increase the likelihood of such a result. As part of this process, the federal government also monitored state redistricting for Congressional elections, which occurs every decade in response to population shifts recorded in the national census.

By the early 1990s, states were being directed to draw districts with majority-black voting populations to ensure African-American representation in the Congress and state legislatures. The federal government cited the South's history of racial discrimination and racially polarized voting to justify these districts. But white Southerners challenged such claims.

In 1993, the U.S. Supreme Court issued a decision in a North Carolina redistricting case, *Shaw* v. *Reno*, that struck down a majority-black Congressional district in that state. Subsequent decisions in other southern districts produced similar rulings. The general principle followed by the Court has been that if race is a key justification for drawing these districts, then they violate the Fourteenth Amendment, which, according to the Court majority, demands color-blind electoral procedures. But, as the late Supreme Court Justice William Brennan noted, "to read the Fourteenth Amendment to state an abstract principle of color-blindness is itself to be blind to history." The framers of the Reconstruction Amendments had the protection of the rights of the freedmen (including and especially voting rights) in mind when they wrote those measures. One voting rights expert has charged that the Court rulings have ushered in a "Second Redemption."

CONCLUSION

Formerly enslaved black Southerners had entered freedom with many hopes, among the most prominent of which was to be let alone. White Southerners, after four bloody years of unwanted attention from the federal government, also longed to be left alone. But they did not include their ex-slaves as equal partners in their vision of solitude. Northerners, too, began to seek escape from the issues and consequences of the war, eventually abandoning their commitment to secure civil and voting rights for black Southerners.

White Southerners robbed blacks of their gains and sought to reduce them again to servitude and dependence, if not to slavery. But in the process, the majority of white people lost as well. Yeoman farmers missed an opportunity to break cleanly from the Old South and establish a more equitable society. Instead, they allowed the old elites to regain power and gradually ignore their needs. They preserved the social benefit of a white skin at the cost of almost everything else. Many lost their farms and sank into tenancy, leasing land from others. Fewer had a voice in state legislatures or Congress. A new South, rid of slavery and sectional antagonism, had indeed emerged, redeemed, regenerated, and disenthralled. But the old South lingered on in the new like Spanish moss on live oaks.

As Federal troops left the South to be redeployed restraining striking workers in the North and suppressing Native Americans on the Great Plains, an era of possibility for American society ended and a new era began. "The southern question is dead," a Charleston newspaper proclaimed in 1877. "The question of labor and capital, work and wages" had moved to the forefront. The chance to redeem the sacrifice of a bloody civil war with a society that fulfilled the promise of the Declaration of Independence and the Constitution for all citizens slipped away. It would take a new generation of African Americans a long century later to revive it.

Summary

White Southerners and the Ghosts of the Confederacy, 1865. While some white Southerners saw the destruction of the Confederacy as punishment, others came to view the war as the "Lost Cause" and would not allow the memory of the Civil War to die. The myth of the Lost Cause was a need to rationalize and justify the devastation and loss of life; the Reconstruction era became the Redemption and forged community in a time of uncertainty about the future. In this mythology, African Americans were cast in the role of adversaries who challenged whites' belief of their own racial superiority.

More than Freedom: African-American Aspirations in 1865 Former slaves wanted to be free of white supervision; they also desired land, voting and civil rights, and education. At the end of the Civil War, African Americans had reason to hope their dreams might be achieved through such actions as the establishment of the Freedmen's Bureau. The vast majority of former slaves was never able to realize their dreams of independent land ownership and continued to work as farm laborers; others migrated to cities. Their religious faith inspired them; they saw their emancipation in biblical terms and the church became the primary focus of the African-American community.

Federal Reconstruction, 1865–1870 The federal government had two great challenges following the Civil War; supporting the freedom of former slaves and rejoining the Confederacy to the Union. No blueprint for Reconstruction existed; the Constitution was silent on the issue and there was no agreement on policy. Presidential Reconstruction and Congressional Reconstruction brought mixed results. The Civil Rights Act and the Fourteenth and Fifteenth Amendments were key legislative acts during this period; however, by 1870, white Southerners were gradually regaining control of their states and using violence and intimidation to erode gains made by African Americans.

Counter-Reconstruction, 1870–1874 While most of the nation was distracted by political scandals and a serious economic depression, white Southerners regained control of the South. Racial violence through groups like the Ku Klux Klan subverted the electoral process; the success of political violence reflected the erosion of Northern support for Congressional Reconstruction.

Redemption, 1874–1877 After more than fifteen years of Reconstruction, Republicans lost interest in policing their former enemies. By 1877 the Redeemers had triumphed, and all the former Confederate states had returned to the Union in the Compromise of 1877 following the disputed 1876 presidential election. Southern states now had all of their rights and many of their leaders restored to pre-Civil War conditions. Freed slaves remained in mostly subservient positions with few of the rights and privileges enjoyed by other Americans.

The Failed Promise of Reconstruction The tacit agreement between Southern and Northern whites was that the South was now free to work out its own resolution to race relations. The price of sectional reconciliation was that the dream that former slaves held of economic independence and equality would not materialize.

The Fourteenth and Fifteenth Amendments were bright spots in the legacy of Reconstruction; the overwhelming majority of African Americans had become landless agricultural workers, eking out a meager income that merchants and landlords often snatched to cover debts. For most, Reconstruction was a failed promise.

REVIEW QUESTIONS

1. Do you think white Southerners should have supported black people's aspirations for civil rights, land, and suffrage? How differently would things had turned out if they had?

2. Is it fair to blame Reconstruction's failures on Southern Republicans? Explain your response.

3. What gains did black people achieve during Reconstruction, despite its overall failure?

4. In T. Thomas Fortune's recollection of a boyhood incident, why was it important for him and his friends to fight back?

KEY TERMS

Black codes   (p. 422)
Carpetbaggers   (p. 426)
Compromise of 1877   (p. 430)
Congressional Reconstruction   (p. 425)
Field Order No. 15   (p. 419)
Fifteenth Amendment   (p. 425)

Fourteenth Amendment   (p. 424)
Freedmen's Bureau   (p. 418)
Ku Klux Klan   (p. 428)
Lost Cause   (p. 417)
Scalawags   (p. 426)
Sharecropping   (p. 431)

Slaughterhouse **cases**   (p. 432)
Southern Homestead Act   (p. 419)
Union Leagues   (p. 427)
United States **v.** *Cruikshank*   (p. 432)

WHERE TO LEARN MORE

Penn Center Historic District, St. Helena Island, South Carolina. The Penn School was a sea-island experiment in the education of free black people established by northern missionaries Laura Towne and Ellen Murray in 1862 that they operated until their deaths in the early 1900s. The Penn School became Penn Community Services in 1948, serving as an educational institution, health clinic, and a social service agency. **www.penncenter.com**

Hampton University Museum, Hampton, Virginia. Hampton University was founded by the Freedmen's Bureau in 1868 to provide "practical" training in the agricultural and mechanical fields for former slaves. In addition to a history of the institution, the museum includes one of the oldest collections of African art in the United States. **www.hamptonu.edu/museum**

Beauvoir, Biloxi, Mississippi. The exhibits at Beauvoir, the home of Jefferson Davis, evoke the importance of the Lost Cause for the white survivors of the Confederacy. Especially interesting is the Jefferson Davis Soldiers Home on the premises and the Confederate Veterans Cemetery. Davis spent his retirement in Beauvoir. **www.beauvoir.org**

Levi Jordan Plantation, Brazoria County, Texas. This site provides an excellent depiction and interpretation of the lives of sharecroppers and tenants during and immediately after the Reconstruction era. The site is especially valuable for demonstrating the transition from slavery to sharecropping. **www.webarchaeology.com**

 For additional study resources for this chapter, go to:
www.prenhall.com/goldfield/chapter16

The colored woman of to-day
occupies a unique position in this country . . .

Teaching a laboratory class at the Tuskegee Institute, c. 1900.

17

A NEW SOUTH
PROGRESS AND SOCIAL TRADITION
1877–1900

WHAT CHANGED in the New South between 1870 and 1900, and what stayed the same?

WHAT WERE the origins and nature of Southern Populism?

WHAT WERE women's roles in the New South?

HOW DID segregation and disfranchisement change race relations in the South?

Ida B. Wells

Black Heritage USA **25**

The colored woman of to-day occupies . . . a unique position in this country. . . . She is confronted by both a woman question and a race problem. . . . While the women of the white race can with calm assurance enter upon the work they feel by nature appointed to do [including reform efforts both inside and outside the home], while their men give loyal support and appreciative countenance to [these] efforts, recognizing in most avenues of usefulness the propriety and the need of woman's distinctive co-operation, the colored woman too often finds herself hampered and shamed by a less liberal sentiment . . . on the part of those for whose opinion she cares most. . . .

You do not find the colored woman selling her birthright for a mess of pottage. . . . It is largely our women in the South to-day who keep the black men solid in the Republican party. The black woman can never forget—however lukewarm the party may to-day appear—that it was a Republican president who struck the manacles from her own wrists and gave the possibilities of manhood to her helpless little ones; and to her mind a Democratic Negro is a traitor and a time-server.

To be a woman in a . . . [new] age carries with it a privilege and an opportunity never implied before. But to be a woman of the Negro race in America, and to be able to grasp the deep significance of the possibilities of the crisis, is to have a heritage, it seems to me, unique in the ages. In the first place, the race is young and full of the elasticity and hopefulness of youth. All its achievements are before it. . . . Everything to this race is new and strange and inspiring. There is a quickening of its pulses and a glowing of its self-consciousness. Aha, I can rival that! I can aspire to that! I can honor my name and vindicate my race! Something like this, it strikes me, is the enthusiasm which stirs the genius of young Africa in America; and the memory of past oppression and the fact of present attempted repression only serve to gather momentum for its irrepressible power. . . . What a responsibility then to have the sole management of the primal lights and shadows! Such is the colored woman's office. She must stamp weal or woe on the coming history of this people. May she see her opportunity and vindicate her high prerogative.

Anna J. Cooper,
—*A Voice from the South*, 1892

Anna Julia Cooper, *A Voice from the South* (Xenia, OH: The Aldine Printing House, 1892): 134–135, 138–140, 142–145. The book may be accessed from the Internet: **http://docsouth.unc.edu/church/cooper/cooper.html**

IMAGE KEY
for pages 436–437

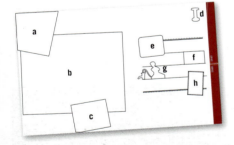

a. Texas and Pacific Railway and its map showing the connections.
b. Students and a teacher work in a laboratory at the Tuskegee Institute in Alabama., c. 1900.
c. An ad for Juliet chewing tobacco.
d. Thread on a large spool.
e. E. A. Overstreet and members of the class of 1900 of the Georgia State Independent College.
f. Women spin yarn and tend children on the porch of a log cabin in North Carolina in 1907.
g. A woman in a hoop skirt grips gently the handle of an old-fashioned water pump next to an antebellum house in Natchez, Mississippi.
h. Ida B. Wells (1862–1931) pictured on a United States postage stamp from 1989.

ANNA J. COOPER undertook an incredible journey that took her from slavery at her birth in Raleigh, North Carolina, in 1858 to a doctoral degree at the Sorbonne in Paris, France, and to a prominent career as an educator. She was a firm believer in the role women, especially black women, should play in striking down both white supremacy and male domination. In 1892, Cooper published *A Voice from the South*, excerpted here. The book appeared when the first African-American generation raised in freedom had generated a relatively prosperous, educated middle-class intent on challenging the limits of race in the New South. This assertiveness alarmed white Southerners who responded with a campaign of violent repression.

Despite these threats, Cooper's tone reflects the optimism of the New South and an enthusiasm for the expanding public role of women. Though Cooper overestimated white women's freedom of choice outside the home, she believed that black men, unlike their white counterparts, held black women back. She also suggests that black men share the blame for the white assault on their political rights. Her solution for racial advancement was to increase the public profile of black women. But, traditional views of Southern whites on race and gender rendered that solution untenable.

Cooper lived to see the dawn of a new racial and gender era in the South and in America, but that journey took many years and many lives. She died at the age of 106 in 1964.

Solid South   The one-party (Democratic) political system that dominated the South from the 1890s to the 1950s.

THE NEWNESS OF THE NEW SOUTH

Southerners of both races and genders shared Anna J. Cooper's optimism in the decades after Reconstruction. They did what other Americans were doing between 1877 and 1900—they built railroads and factories and moved to towns and cities, only on a smaller scale and with more modest results. The factories did not dramatically alter the South's rural economy, and the towns and cities did not make it an urban region. The changes, nonetheless, brought political and social turmoil, emboldening black people, like Cooper, to assert their rights, encouraging women to work outside the home and pursue public careers, and frightening some white men.

By 1900, however, Southern white leaders had used the banner of white supremacy to stifle dissent. They removed African Americans from political life and constricted their social and economic role.

The New South's "newness" was thus to be found primarily in its economy, not in its social relations, though the two were complementary. After Reconstruction, new industries absorbed tens of thousands of first-time industrial workers from impoverished rural areas. Southern cities grew faster than those in any other region of the country. Railroad construction linked these cities to one another and to the rest of the country, giving them increased commercial prominence. Cities extended their influence into the countryside with newspapers, consumer products, and new values. But this urban influence had limits. It did not bring electricity, telephones, public health services, or public schools to the rural South. It did not greatly broaden the rural economy with new jobs. And it left the countryside without the daily contact with the outside world that fostered a broader perspective.

The Democratic party dominated Southern politics after 1877. Democrats purged most black people and some white people from the electoral process and suppressed challenges to their leadership. The result was the emergence by 1900 of the **Solid South**, a period of white Democratic party rule that lasted into the 1950s.

Although most Southern women remained at home or on the farm, some enjoyed new options after 1877. Middle-class women in the cities, both white and black, became increasingly active in civic work and reform. They organized clubs, preserved and promoted the memories

WHAT CHANGED in the New South between 1870 and 1900, and what stayed the same?

The pride of accomplishment is evident in this photograph of the Georgia State College class of 1900. By this time, black institutions of higher education in the South were turning out ambitious and talented graduates who faced an increasingly grim future in their native region.

Shivery Family Photograph Collection, Photographs and Prints Division, Schomburg Center of Research in Black Culture, The New York Public Library, Astor, Lenox, and Tilden Foundations

QUICK REVIEW

Southern Women: 1877–1900

◆ Most Southern women remained at home or on the farm.

◆ Middle-class women increasingly active in civic work and reform.

◆ Young white women found work in mills, factories, and as servants.

WHERE TO LEARN MORE

W

★ Levine Museum of the New South, Charlotte, North Carolina
www.museumofthenewsouth.org

of war, lobbied for various causes, and assumed regional leadership on important issues. Many young white women from impoverished rural areas found work in textile mills, in city factories, or as servants. These new options challenged prevailing views about the role of women but ultimately did not change them.

The status of black Southerners changed significantly between 1877 and 1900. The members of the first generation born after Emancipation sought more than just freedom. They also expected self-respect and the right to work, vote, go to school, and travel freely. White Southerners responded with the equivalent of a second Civil War—and they won. By 1900, black Southerners where more isolated from white Southerners and had less political power than at any time since 1865. Despite these setbacks, they built, especially in the cities, a rich community life and spawned a vibrant middle class.

AN INDUSTRIAL AND URBAN SOUTH

Since the 1850s, public speakers calling for economic reform in the South had been rousing audiences with the tale of the burial of a southern compatriot whose headstone, clothes, and coffin, as well as the grave-diggers' tools all came from the North. The speakers urged their listeners to found industries, build railroads, and grow great cities so that the South could make its own goods and no one in the future would have to suffer the indignity of journeying to the next world accompanied by Yankee artifacts.

Certainly, Southerners manufactured little in 1877, less than 10 percent of the national total. By 1900, however, they boasted a growing iron and steel industry, textile mills that rivaled those of New England, a world-dominant tobacco industry, a timber-processing industry that helped make the South a leading furniture-manufacturing center, and prominent regional enterprises, including Coca-Cola.

Birmingham, barely a scratch in the forest in 1870, exemplified one aspect of what was new about the New South. By 1889, Birmingham was preparing to challenge Pittsburgh, the nation's preeminent steelmaking city.

The Southern textile industry also expanded during the 1880s. Several factors drew local investors into textile enterprises, including low farm income. The entrepreneurs located their mills mostly in rural areas, not in cities. The center of the industry was in the Carolina Piedmont, a region with good railroads, plentiful labor, and cheap energy. By 1900, the South had surpassed New England to become the nation's foremost textile-manufacturing center.

Virginia was the dominant tobacco producer, and its main product was chewing tobacco. The discovery of bright-leaf tobacco, a strain suitable for smoking in the form of cigarettes, changed Americans' tobacco habits. In 1884, James B. Duke installed the first cigarette-making machine in his Durham, North Carolina, plant. By 1900, Duke's American Tobacco Company controlled 80 percent of all tobacco manufacturing in the United States.

Atlanta pharmacist Dr. John Pemberton developed a soft drink—a mixture of oils, caffeine, coca leaves, and cola nuts—in his backyard in an effort to find a good-tasting cure for headaches. He called it Coca-Cola. Pemberton, short of cash, sold the rights to it to another Atlantan, Asa Candler, in 1889. Candler improved the taste and marketed the product heavily. By the mid-1890s, Coca-Cola enjoyed a national market.

Southern track mileage doubled between 1880 and 1890, with the greatest increases in Texas and Georgia. By 1890, nine out of ten Southerners lived in a county with a railroad running through it. In 1886, the Southern railroads agreed to conform to a national standard for track width, linking the region into a national transportation network and ensuring access for Southern products to the booming markets of the Northeast.

The railroads connected formerly isolated small Southern farmers to national and international markets and gave them access to new products, from fertilizers to fashions.

The railroad also opened new areas of the South to settlement and economic development. In 1892, according to one guidebook, Florida was "in the main inaccessible to the ordinary tourist, and unopened to the average settler." By 1912, there were tourist hotels as far south as Key West. Railroads also opened the Appalachian Mountains to timber and coal-mining interests.

The railroad increased the prominence of interior cities at the expense of older cities along the southern Atlantic and Gulf Coasts. Antebellum ports such as New Orleans, Charleston, and Savannah declined as commerce rode the rails more than the water. Cities such as Dallas, Atlanta, Nashville, and Charlotte, astride great railroad trunk lines, emerged to lead Southern urban growth. Five major rail lines converged on Atlanta by the 1870s. As early as 1866, it had become "the radiating point for Northern and Western trade coming Southward, and . . . the gate through which passes Southern trade and travel going northward." When the Texas and Pacific Railway linked Dallas to Eastern markets in 1872, it was a small town of three thousand people. Eight years later, its population had grown to more than ten thousand, and within thirty years it had become the South's twelfth largest city. By 1920, New Orleans and Norfolk were the only coastal ports still among the ten most populous southern cities.

A town on a rail line that invested in a cotton press and a cottonseed oil mill would become a marketing hub for the surrounding countryside within a day's wagon ride away. Local merchants would stock the latest fashions from New York, canned foods, and current issues of popular magazines such as *Atlantic* or *Harper's*. The number of towns with fewer than five thousand people doubled between 1870 and 1880 and had doubled again by 1900.

By the 1890s, textile mills were a common sight in towns throughout the South. The mills provided employment for impoverished rural families, especially women and children.

T.E. Armistead Collection, University of South Alabama Archives

QUICK REVIEW

Railroads and the South

♦ Connected small Southern farmers to national and international markets.

♦ Opened new areas in the South to settlement and development.

♦ Increased the importance of interior cities at the expense of older cities.

THE LIMITS OF INDUSTRIAL AND URBAN GROWTH

Rapid as it was, urban and industrial growth in the South barely kept pace with that of the booming North (see Chapter 18). Between 1860 and 1900, the South's share of the nation's manufacturing increased only marginally from 10.3 percent to 10.5 percent, and its share of the nation's capital declined slightly from 11.5 percent to 11 percent. About the same percentage of people worked in manufacturing in the Southern states east of the Mississippi in 1900 as in 1850. Between 1860 and 1880, the per capita income of the South declined from 72 percent of the national average to 51 percent and by 1920 had recovered to only 62 percent (see Figure 17–1).

Southern industrial workers earned roughly half the national average manufacturing wage during the late nineteenth century. Business leaders promoted the advantages of this cheap labor to Northern investors. In 1904, a Memphis businessman boasted that his city "can save the northern manufacturer . . . who employs 400 hands, $50,000 a year on his labor bill."

Despite their attractiveness to industrialists, low wages undermined the Southern economy in several ways. Poorly paid workers didn't buy much, lim-

CHRONOLOGY

1872	Texas and Pacific Railway connects Dallas to Eastern markets.
1880	First Southern local of the Women's Christian Temperance Union is formed in Atlanta.
1881	Booker T. Washington establishes Tuskegee Institute.
1882	Agricultural Wheel is formed in Arkansas.
1883	Laura Haygood founds the home mission movement in Atlanta.
1884	James B. Duke automates his cigarette factory.
1886	Dr. John Pemberton creates Coca-Cola.
	Southern railroads conform to national track gauge standards.
1887	Charles W. Macune expands the Southern Farmer's Alliance from its Texas base to the rest of the South.
1888	The Southern Farmers' Alliance initiates a successful boycott of jute manufacturers.
1890	Mississippi becomes the first state to restrict black suffrage with literacy tests.
1892	The Populist party forms.
1894	United Daughters of the Confederacy is founded. Populist and Republican fusion candidates win control of North Carolina.
1895	Booker T. Washington delivers his "Atlanta Compromise" address.
1896	Populists endorse the Democratic presidential candidate and fade as a national force.
	In *Plessy* v. *Ferguson*, the Supreme Court permits segregation by law.
1898	North Carolina Mutual Life Insurance is founded. Democrats regain control of North Carolina.
1903	W.E.B. Du Bois publishes *The Souls of Black Folk*.
1905	James B. Duke forms the Southern Power Company. Thomas Dixon publishes *The Clansman*.
1906	Bloody race riots break out in Atlanta.
1907	Pittsburgh-based U.S. Steel takes over Birmingham's largest steel producer.

FIGURE 17–1

Per Capita Income in the South as a Percentage of the U.S. Average, 1860–1920
This graph illustrates the devastating effect of the Civil War on the Southern economy. Southerners began a slow recovery during the 1880s that accelerated after 1900. But even as late as 1920, per capita income in the South was still lower relative to the country as a whole than it had been before the Civil War.

Data Source: *Richard A. Easterlin, "Regional Economic Trends, 1840–1950," in* American Economic History. ed. Seymour E. Harris (1961).

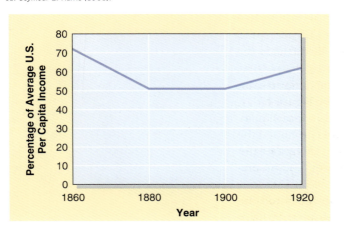

iting the market for Southern manufactured goods. They kept tax revenue low, restricting the states' ability to fund services like public education. Birmingham, Alabama, probably spent more on public education than any other Southern city, but the skilled workers in its steel mills tended to leave as soon as they could for higher-wage opportunities in Northern cities like Pittsburgh and Cleveland. Investment in education lagged in the South. Per-pupil expenditure in the region was at least 50 percent below that of the rest of the nation in 1900.

Low wages kept immigrants—and the skills and energy they brought with them—out of the South. With steady work available at higher wages north of the Mason-Dixon line, only a scattering of Italian farm laborers, Chinese railroad workers, and Jewish peddlers ventured below it. Between 1860 and 1900—during one of the greatest waves of immigration the United States has yet experienced— the foreign-born population of the South actually declined from about 10 percent to less than 2 percent.

Why didn't the South benefit more from the rapid expansion of the national economy in the last three decades of the nineteenth century? The simple answer is that the Civil War had wiped out the South's capital resources. Northern goods flowed into the South, but Northern capital, technology, and people did not. Northern-based national banks emerged in the wake of the Civil War to fund Northern economic expansion. The South, in contrast, had few banks, and those lacked sufficient capital reserves to fuel an equivalent expansion there.

Northern banks imposed higher interest rates and shorter terms on loans to Southerners than on loans to their northern customers. When Southern rail lines failed during a depression in the 1870s, Northern financiers purchased the companies at bargain prices. By the 1890s, Northern firms owned the five major rail lines serving the South.

With limited access to other sources of capital, the South's textile industry depended on thousands of small investors in towns and cities. These investors avoided risk, shunned innovation, and remained small-scale.

The lumber industry, the South's largest, typified the shortcomings of Southern economic development in the late nineteenth century. It required little capital, relied on unskilled labor, and processed its raw materials on site. After clear-cutting—felling all the trees—in one region, sawmills moved quickly to the next stand of timber, leaving behind a bare landscape, rusting machinery, and a work force no better off than before.

Birmingham's iron and steel industry also suffered from financial weakness. Mill owners relied on cheap black labor rather than investing in expensive technology. Another problem was the limited market for steel in the mostly agricultural South. Pittsburgh-based U.S. Steel took over Birmingham's largest steel producer in 1907. Thereafter, pricing policies favoring Pittsburgh plants limited Birmingham's growth.

The tobacco industry, however, avoided the problems that plagued other Southern enterprises. James B. Duke's American Tobacco Company was so immensely profitable that he became, in effect, his own bank. With more than enough capital to install the latest technology in his plants, Duke bought out his competitors. He then diversified into electric power generation and endowed what became Duke University.

Southern industry fit into a narrow niche of late-nineteenth-century American industrialization. With an unskilled and uneducated work force, poor access to capital and technology, and a weak consumer base, the South processed raw agricultural products, and produced cheap textiles, cheap lumber products, and cheap cigarettes. "Made in the South" became synonymous with bottom-of-the-line goods.

In the South most textile mills were typically located in the countryside, often in mill villages, where employers could easily recruit families and keep them isolated from the distractions and employment alternatives of the cities. The timber industry similarly remained a rural-based enterprise. Tobacco manufacturing helped Durham and Winston, North Carolina, grow, but they remained small compared to Northern industrial cities. Duke moved his corporate headquarters to New York to be near that city's financial, advertising, and communications services.

FARMS TO CITIES: IMPACT ON SOUTHERNERS

If industrialization in the South was limited compared to the North, it nonetheless had an enormous impact on Southern society. In the southern Piedmont, for example, failed farmers moved to textile villages to earn a living. Entire families secured employment and often a house in exchange for their labor. Widows and single young men also moved to the mills, usually the only option outside farm work in the South. Nearly one-third of the textile mill labor force by 1900 consisted of children under the age of 14 and women. They worked twelve hours a day, six days a week, although some firms allowed a half-day off on Saturday.

Southern urban growth, which also paled in comparison with that of the North, had a similarly disproportionate impact on Southern society. One observer noted the changes in a North Carolina town between 1880 and 1890. The town in 1880 presented a sorry aspect: rutted roads, a shanty for a school, a few forlorn churches, and perhaps three families of prominence. Twenty years later, another

WHERE TO LEARN MORE

Sloss Furnaces National Historical Landmark, Birmingham, Alabama
www.slossfurnaces.com

QUICK REVIEW

Southern Industry
◆ Textile industry depended on thousands of small investors.
◆ Lumber industry typified the shortcomings of Southern industry.
◆ Tobacco industry avoided problems that plagued other Southern enterprises.

MAP EXPLORATION

To explore an interactive version of this map, go to **http://www.prenhall.com/goldfield2/map17.1a**

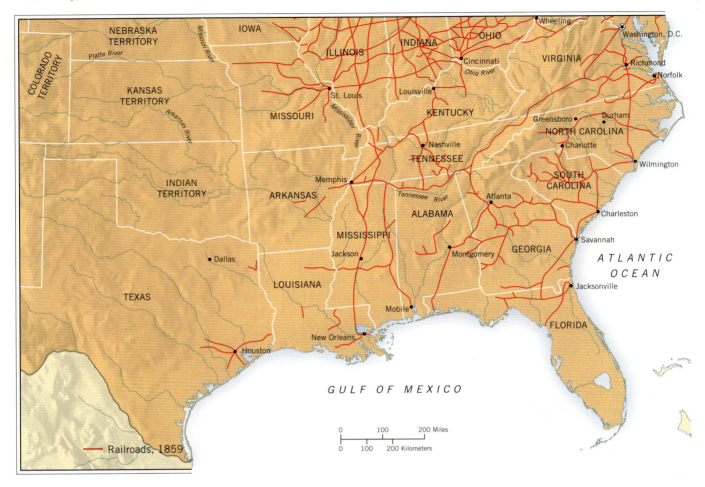

MAP 17–1A

Railroads in the South, 1859 and 1899   A postwar railroad construction boom promoted commercial agriculture and industry in the South. Unlike the railroads of the prewar South, uniform gauges and connections to major trunk lines in the North linked Southerners to the rest of the nation. Northern interests, however, owned the major southern railroads in 1899, and most of the products flowing northward were raw materials to be processed by northern industry or shipped elsewhere by northern merchants.

railroad, bustling commerce, and textile mills had produced a new scene: paved streets, two public schools—one for blacks, one for whites—and a cosmopolitan frame of mind among its residents. "The men have a wider range of activities and the women have more clothes." In another twenty years, the observer predicted, it will be "very like hundreds of towns in the Middle West."

By 1900, a town in the New South would boast a business district and more elegant residences than before. Its influence would extend into the countryside. Farm families visited nearby towns and cities more often. A South Carolina writer related in 1900 that "Country people who . . . went to town annually or semiannually, can now go quickly, safely, pleasantly, and cheaply several times a day." Many never returned to the farm. "Cheap coal, cheap lights, convenient water supply offer inducements; society and amusements draw the young; the chance to speculate, to make a sudden rise in fortunes, to get in the swim attracts others."

MAP EXPLORATION

To explore an interactive version of this map, go to **http://www.prenhall.com/goldfield2/map17.1b**

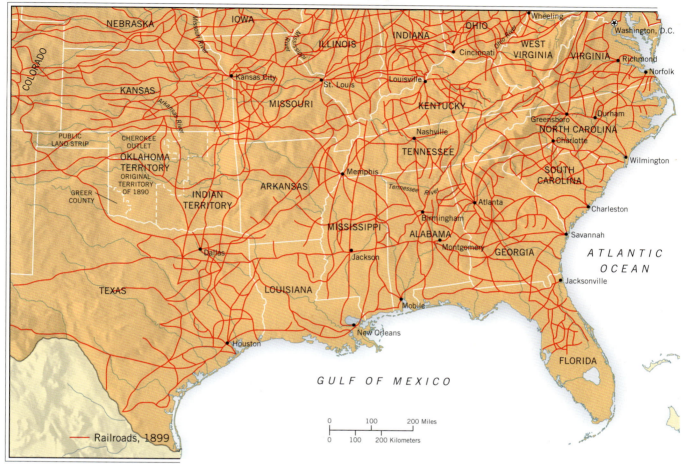

Railroads, 1899

MAP 17–1B

WHAT EFFECT did railroads have on the Southern workforce?

The urban South drew the region's talented and ambitious young people. White men like William Henry Belk moved to cities to open shops or take jobs as bank clerks, bookkeepers, merchants, and salesmen. White women worked as retail clerks, telephone operators, and office personnel. Black women filled the growing demand for laundresses and domestic servants. And black men also found prospects better in towns than on the farm, despite a narrow and uncertain range of occupations available to them.

To some Southerners, urbanization and the emphasis on wealth, new technology, and display represented a second Yankee conquest. Ministers warned against traffic with the urban devil, whose temptations could overcome even the most devout individual. Evangelist Sam Jones, a reformed alcoholic, chose Atlanta for his largest revivals in the 1890s, challenging its residents to keep the Sabbath holy, reject alcohol, and obey the Golden Rule.

White Southerners in town and country, who not long ago had lived similar lives, grew distant. White farmers and their families had fallen on hard times. The market that lured them into commercial agriculture threatened to take away their independence. They faced the loss of their land and livelihood. Their way of life was no longer the standard for the South. New South spokesmen promoted cities and industries and ordered farmers to get on board the train of progress before it left the station without them.

THE SOUTHERN AGRARIAN REVOLT

WHAT WERE the origins and nature of Southern Populism?

Even more than before the Civil War, cotton dominated Southern agriculture between 1877 and 1900. And the economics of cotton brought despair to cotton farmers. Rice and tobacco production increased, and Louisiana and Arkansas overtook South Carolina in rice production. Steady demand, however, allowed rice and tobacco growers to maintain a decent standard of living. Cotton was another matter. The size of the cotton crop continued to set annual records after 1877. The railroad opened new areas for cultivation in Mississippi and eastern Texas. But the price of cotton fell while the price of fertilizers, agricultural tools, food, and most other necessities went up. As a result, the more cotton the farmers grew, the less money they made.

Before the Civil War, the South fed itself. After the war, with railroads providing direct access to major cotton-marketing centers, the South became an importer of food. As a common lament went in 1890, "Five-cent cotton, forty-cent meat, how in the world can a poor man eat?"

COTTON AND CREDIT

The solution to this agrarian dilemma seemed simple: Grow less cotton. But in a cash-poor economy, credit ruled. Food crops generated less income per acre than cotton, even in the worst years. Local merchants, themselves bound in a web of credit to merchants in larger cities, accepted cotton as collateral. "No cotton, no credit" became a standard refrain throughout the South after 1877.

Trapped in debt by low cotton prices and high interest rates, small landowning farmers lost their land in record numbers. Less than one-third of white farmers in the South were tenants or sharecroppers just after the Civil War. By the 1890s, nearly half were.

Some areas did diversify. Good rail connections in Georgia, for example, made peach farming profitable for some farmers. Cattle ranching spread in Texas. But few crops or animals had the geographical range of cotton. Soil type, rainfall, animal parasites, and frost made alternatives unfeasible for many farmers. Cotton required no machinery or irrigation system. James Barrett, a farmer outside Augusta, Georgia, said of his experiment with diversification in 1900: "I have diversified, and I have not made any money by diversification. . . . I grow green peas and everything I know of. I have raised horses, cows, and hogs, and I have diversified it for the last three years and have not been able to make a dollar."

SOUTHERN FARMERS ORGANIZE, 1877–1892

As their circumstances deteriorated, farmers lobbied for debt-stay laws and formed organizations to widen the circle of their community to include other farmers sharing their plight. They wanted to make the market fairer, to lower interest rates and ease credit, to regulate railroad freight rates, and to keep the prices of necessities in check.

These goals required legislation. But presidential administrations between 1877 and 1900, Republican or Democrat, did not favor debt relief or extensive regulation of business. And the Redeemer Democrats who gained control of the Southern state governments after Reconstruction represented large landowners and merchants, not poor farmers.

To strengthen their authority and suppress dissent, the Redeemer Democrats portrayed themselves as having saved the South from the rule of black people and Republicans. Insurgent farmers who challenged this leadership risked being branded as disloyal.

The Democrats nonetheless faced some opposition. In some states, like North Carolina, the Republicans retained support in mountain areas and among black voters. In addition, disaffected white farmers mounted independent political campaigns against the Redeemers in several states in the late 1870s and early 1880s to demand currency reform and the easing of credit. But the Democrats, in firm control of the election machinery throughout the South, turned back these challenges. Although Independents at one point succeeded in gaining control of the Virginia legislature, their few other victories were confined to the local level. Hard-pressed farmers began to organize on a broader scale.

By 1875, nearly 250,000 Southern landowners had joined the National Grange of the Patrons of Husbandry, more popularly known as the **Grange** (see Chapter 22). The leaders of the Grange, however, were large landowners. Their interests were not the same as the small farmers who made up the organization's rank and file. The Grange leadership in the South, for example, favored fence laws, limited government assistance, controls on farm labor, and other policies that hurt small farmers. The rank-and-file members, in contrast, pushed a more radical agenda including establishing community stores, cotton gins, and warehouses to bypass the prevailing credit system.

The Grange failed to stem the reverses of small Southern farmers. In 1882 a group of farmers in Arkansas formed an organization called the **Agricultural Wheel** that had attracted more than 500,000 Southern farmers by 1887. Wheelers tried to purchase farm equipment directly from manufacturers, avoiding merchant middlemen. Unlike the Grange, they called for an array of federal programs to ease the credit and cash burdens of farmers, including a graduated income tax and the printing and distribution of more paper money.

The most potent agricultural reform organization, the **Southern Farmers' Alliance**, originated in Texas in the late 1870s. Alliance-sponsored farmers' cooperatives provided their members with discounts on supplies and credit. Members also benefited from marketing their cotton crops collectively. Although it endorsed some candidates for office, the Alliance was not a political party and did not challenge Democratic domination of the South.

The Alliance was still very much a Texas organization in 1887 when Charles W. Macune, a Wisconsin native, became its driving force. Macune sent a corps of speakers to create a network of Southern cooperatives. Within two years, the Alliance had spread throughout the South and into the North and West. By 1890, it claimed more than a million members. Almost all were small farmers who owned their own land. The success of the Alliance reflected both the desperate struggle of these small farmers to keep their land and the failure of other organizations to help them.

The Alliance operated like a religious denomination. Its leaders preached a message of salvation through cooperation to as many as twenty thousand people at huge revival-like rallies. Qualifications for membership included a belief in the divinity of Christ and the literal truth of the Bible. Alliance speakers, many of them rural ministers, often held meetings in churches, combining biblical nostrums with economic policy. They urged members to visit "the homes where lacerated hearts are bleeding, to assuage the suffering of a brother or a sister, bury the dead, care for the widows and educate the orphans." The Alliance lobbied state legislatures to fund rural public schools. To increase the sense of community, the Alliance sponsored picnics, baseball games, and concerts.

Grange   The National Grange of the Patrons of Husbandry, a national organization of farm owners formed after the Civil War.

Agricultural Wheel   One of several farmer organizations that emerged in the South during the 1880s. It sought federal legislation to deal with credit and currency issues.

Southern Farmer's Alliance   The largest of several organizations that formed in the post-Reconstruction South to advance the interests of beleaguered small farmers.

The faces of this white sharecropper family in North Carolina reflect the harshness of farm life in the late nineteenth- and early twentieth-century South, a period when thousands of Southerners, white and black alike, slipped from land ownership to sharecropping.

Courtesy of the North Carolina Division of Archives and History

Colored Farmer's Alliance An organization of Southern black farmers formed in Texas in 1886 in response to the Southern Farmer's Alliance, which did not accept black people as members.

Subtreasury plan A program promoted by the Southern Farmer's Alliance in response to low cotton prices and tight credit. Farmers would store their crop in a warehouse until prices rose, in the meantime borrowing up to 80 percent of the value of the stored crops from the government at a low interest rate.

The Alliance imposed strict morality on its members, prohibiting drinking, gambling, and sexual misconduct. Alliance leaders criticized many Baptist, Methodist, and Presbyterian ministers for straying from the traditional emphasis on individual salvation and for defending a status quo that benefited large planters and towns. Cyrus Thompson, North Carolina Alliance president and a prominent Methodist, declared in 1889 that "the church today stands where it has always stood, on the side of human slavery."

Some Alliance members left their churches for new religious groups. Holiness movement disciples advocated simple dress, avoided coffee and pork, and swore off all worldly amusements. The members of the Church of God, which formed in the mountains of Tennessee and North Carolina in 1886, similarly sought to cleanse themselves of secular evils. The new churches promoted a vision of an egalitarian South. They accepted women on an equal basis and occasionally black people as well. As many as a third of Holiness preachers were women.

Women also found an active role as officers and speakers in the Alliance. As a Texas woman declared, "The Alliance has come to redeem woman from her enslaved condition. She is admitted into the organization as the equal of her brother, and the ostracism which has impeded her intellectual progress in the past is not met with."

However, the Alliance did not accept black members. Black farmers formed the first **Colored Farmers' Alliance** in Texas in 1886, which had fewer landowners and more tenants and sharecroppers in its ranks than the white organization. It concerned itself with issues relevant to this constituency, such as higher wages for cotton pickers. In 1891, the Colored Alliance attempted a regionwide strike over farm wages but was unable to enforce it in the worsening Southern economy.

The white Alliance had better results with a protest over price fixing. To protect cotton shipped to market, farmers wrapped it in a burlaplike material called jute. In 1888, jute manufacturers combined to raise the price from 7 cents to as much as 14 cents a yard. The Alliance initiated a jute boycott throughout the South, telling farmers to use cotton bagging as an alternative. The protest worked, forcing the chastened jute manufacturers to offer farmers their product at a mere 5 cents per yard.

This success encouraged Macune to propose his **subtreasury plan**. Alliance members were to store their crops in a subtreasury (a warehouse), keeping their cotton off the market until the price rose. In the meantime, the government would loan the farmers up to 80 percent of the value of the stored crops at a low interest rate of 2 percent per year. This arrangement would free farmers from merchants' high interest rates and crop liens.

Macune urged Alliance members to endorse political candidates who supported the subtreasury scheme. Many Democratic candidates for state legislatures throughout the South did endorse it and were elected with Alliance backing in 1890. Once in office, however, they failed to deliver.

The failure of the subtreasury plan combined with a steep drop in cotton prices after 1890 undermined the Alliance. Its cooperatives collapsed as crop liens cut down small landowners as though with scythes. A Georgia Allianceman wrote in 1891 that "Hundreds of farmers will be turned adrift, and thousands of acres of our best land allowed to grow up in weeds through lack of necessary capital to work them." Alliance membership declined by two-thirds in Georgia that year. Desperate Alliance leaders merged their organization with a new national political party in 1892, the People's or **Populist party**. Populists appropriated the Alliance program and challenged Democrats in the South and Republicans in the West. The merger reflected desperation more than calculation.

SOUTHERN POPULISTS

Northern farmers, like their Southern counterparts, faced growing financial pressure in the 1880s that by the early 1890s had led them too to join the Alliance. Just as Southern farmers had turned to the Democratic party to redress their grievances, Northern farmers turned to the dominant party in the Northern farming states—the Republican party—to redress theirs. Like the Democrats, the Republicans failed to respond. Beginning in Kansas in 1890, disillusioned farmers formed the People's party, soon called the Populist party.

The Populists supported a wide range of reforms, many adopted from the Alliance, including the direct election of United States senators by popular vote rather than by state legislatures, an income tax, woman suffrage, government ownership of railroads, and various proposals to ease credit. In the South, they challenged the Democratic party, sometimes courting the votes of Republicans, including black voters.

Southern Populists were ambivalent about African Americans. On the one hand, black people constituted a potential voting bloc the Populists could ill afford to ignore. On the other hand, appealing to blacks would expose Populists to demagogic attacks from Democrats for undermining white supremacy, frightening away potential white backers. The *Baton Rouge Daily Advocate*, for example, informed its readers in 1892 that the Populist party was "the most dangerous and insidious foe of white supremacy."

Despite the risks, in Texas, black Populist John B. Rayner, the "silver-tongued orator of the colored race," spoke to racially mixed audiences around the state. The Texas Populist platform called for "equal justice and protection under the law to all citizens without reference to race, color or nationality." In Georgia, Populist leader Tom Watson supported a biracial party organization and counseled white people to accept black people as partners in their common crusade. "You are kept apart," Watson told black and white Georgians, "that you may be separately fleeced of your earnings. You are made to hate each other because upon that hatred is rested the keystone of the arch of financial despotism which enslaves you both."

Despite Rayner's and Watson's efforts, most black people remained loyal to the Republican party for its role in abolishing slavery and for the few patronage crumbs the party still threw their way. Black people also suspected Populists' motives. The party appealed mainly to small, landowning farmers, not, as most black Southerners were, propertyless tenants and sharecroppers. And even the Texas Populists opposed black officeholding and jury service.

The Populists finished a distant third in the 1892 presidential election. In the South, their only significant inroads were in the state legislatures of Texas, Alabama, and Georgia. Even in these states, widespread voter fraud among Democrats undermined Populist strength.

Despite a deepening economic depression, the Populists had only a few additional successes in the South after 1892. Adopting a fusion strategy, the Populists ran candidates on a combined ticket with Republicans in North Carolina. The fusion candidates captured the governorship and state legislature.

Higher cotton prices and returning prosperity in the late 1890s, however, undermined Populist support in North Carolina, as in the rest of the South. In 1896,

17–9
The Omaha Platform of the Populist Party (1892)

QUICK REVIEW

Political Affiliation of African Americans

◆ Some populists made appeals to African Americans.

◆ Most African Americans remained loyal to the Republican party.

◆ Many blacks were suspicious of the populists' motives.

Populist party   A major third party of the 1890s formed on the basis of the Southern Farmer's Alliance and other reform organizations.

the Populists assisted in their own nationwide demise by merging with the Democrats for the presidential election of 1896. In 1898, Democrats surged back into office in North Carolina on the strength of a virulent white supremacy campaign and promptly undid the work of the fusionists.

WOMEN IN THE NEW SOUTH

Just as farm women found their voices in the Alliance movement of the 1880s, a growing group of middle-class white and black urban women entered the public realm and engaged in policy issues. In the late-nineteenth-century North, women became increasingly active in reform movements, including woman suffrage, labor legislation, social welfare, and city planning. Building on their antebellum activist traditions, Northern women, sometimes acting in concert with men, sought to improve the status of women in society.

Southern women had a meager reform tradition to build on. The war also left them ambivalent about independence. With male family members dead or incapacitated, some determined never again to depend on men. Others, responding to the stress of running a farm or business, would have preferred less independence.

Southern men had been shaken by defeat. They had lost the war and placed their families in peril. Many responded with alcoholism and violence. To regain their self-esteem, they recast the war as a noble crusade and imagined Southern white women as paragons of virtue and purity who required men to defend them. Even small changes in traditional gender roles would threaten this image. Southern women never mounted an extensive reform campaign like their sisters in the North.

Urban middle-class Southern women found opportunities to broaden their social role and enter the public sphere in the two decades after 1880 when servants, stores, and schools freed them of many of the productive functions—like making clothing, cooking, and child care—that burdened their sisters in the country and kept them tied to the home.

CHURCH WORK AND PRESERVING MEMORIES

Southern women waded warily into the public arena. The movement to found home mission societies, for example, was led by single white women in the Methodist church to promote industrial education among the poor and help working-class women become self-sufficient. Laura Haygood, an Atlantan who had served as a missionary in China, founded a home mission in Atlanta when she returned in 1883. Lily Hammond, another Atlantan, extended the mission concept when she opened settlement houses in black and white city neighborhoods in Atlanta in the 1890s. Settlement houses, pioneered in New York in the 1880s, promoted middle-class values in poor neighborhoods and provided them with a permanent source of services. In the South, they were supported by the Methodist church and known as *Wesley Houses*, after John Wesley, the founder of Methodism.

Religion also prompted Southern white women to join the **Women's Christian Temperance Union (WCTU)**. The first Southern local formed in Lucy Haygood's church in Atlanta in 1880. WCTU members visited schools to educate children about the evils of alcohol, addressed prisoners, and blanketed men's meetings with literature. As a result, they became familiar with the South's abysmal school system and its archaic criminal justice system. They thus began advocating education and prison reform as well as legislation against alcohol.

By the 1890s, many WCTU members realized that they couldn't achieve their goals unless women had the vote. Rebecca Latimer Felton, an Atlanta suffragist and

QUICK REVIEW

Southern Women and Reform
- Southern women played an active role in the public arena.
- Laura Haygood started the movement to found home mission societies.
- Lily Hammond opened settlement houses in Atlanta in the 1890s.

Women's Christian Temperance Union (WCTU) Women's organization whose members visited schools to educate children about the evils of alcohol, addressed prisoners, and blanketed men's meetings with literature.

WCTU member, reflected the frustration of her generation of Southern women in an address to working women in 1892:

> But some will say—you women might be quiet—you can't vote, you can't do anything! Exactly so—we have kept quiet for nearly a hundred years hoping to see relief come to the women of this country—and it hasn't come. How long must our children be slain? If a mad dog should come into my yard, and attempt to bite my child or myself—would you think me out of my place, if I killed him with a dull meat axe? . . . [You] would call that woman a brave woman . . . and yet are we to sit by while drink ruins our homes?

WCTU rhetoric implied a veiled attack on men. Felton, for example, often referred to men who drank as "beasts." When the WCTU held its national convention in Atlanta in 1890, local Baptist and Methodist ministers launched a bitter attack against the organization, claiming that it drew women into activities contrary to the Scriptures and that its endorsement of woman suffrage subverted traditional family values.

Few women, however, had such radical objectives in mind. Rebecca Felton and her husband Dr. William H. Felton, a physician and minister, eked out a modest living teaching school and working a small farm during the Civil War and its aftermath. Four of their five children died. Seeing Southern families worse off than her own, Felton threw herself into a variety of reform activities, ranging from woman suffrage to campaigns against drinking, smoking, and Coca-Cola. She fought for child-care facilities, sex education, and compulsory school attendance and pushed for the admission of women to the University of Georgia. But she had no qualms about the **lynching** of black men—executing them without trial—"a thousand times a week if necessary" to preserve the purity of white women. In 1922, she became the first woman member of the U.S. Senate.

The dedication of Southern women to commemorating the memory of the Confederate cause also suggested the conservative nature of middle-class women's reform in the New South. Ladies' Memorial Associations formed after the war to ensure the proper burial of Confederate soldiers and suitable markings for their graves. These activities reinforced white solidarity and constructed a common heritage for all white Southerners regardless of class or location. A new organization, the United Daughters of the Confederacy (UDC), appeared in 1894 to preserve Southern history and honor its heroes.

WOMEN'S CLUBS

A broader spectrum of Southern middle-class women joined women's clubs than joined church-sponsored organizations or memorial associations. By 1890, some clubs and their members had begun to discuss political issues such as child labor reform, educational improvement, and prison reform. The Lone Star (Texas) Federation scrutinized public hospitals, almshouses, and orphanages at the turn of the century. Its president asserted, "The Lone Star Federation stands for the highest and truest type of womanhood—that which lends her voice as well as her hand." Southern women's club members sought out their sisters in the North. As Georgia's federated club president, Mrs. A. O. Granger, wrote in 1906, "Women of intellectual keenness in the South could not be left out of the awakening of the women of the whole country to a realization of the responsibility which they properly had in the condition of their fellow-women and of the children."

The activities of black women's clubs paralleled those of white women's clubs. Only rarely, however—as at some meetings of the Young Women's Christian Association (YWCA) or occasional meetings in support of prohibition—did black and white club members interact.

The Confederate battle flag on this parade float reflects its emerging status as an icon of the Lost Cause in the late nineteenth century.

Courtsy of Library of Congress

Lynching   Execution, usually by a mob, without trial.

Most white clubwomen were unwilling to sacrifice their own reform agenda to the cause of racial reconciliation. Some women suffragists in the South argued that the combined vote of white men and women would further white interests.

The primary interest of most Southern white women's clubs was the plight of young white working-class and farm women. Single and adrift in the city, many worked for low wages, and some slipped into prostitution. The clubs sought to help them make the transition from rural to urban life or to improve their lives on the farm. To this end, they focused on child labor reform and on upgrading public education.

SETTLING THE RACE ISSUE

HOW DID segregation and disfranchisement change race relations in the South?

To counter black aspirations, white leaders enlisted the support of young white men. African Americans resisted the resulting efforts to deprive them of their remaining freedoms. Though some left the South, many more built new lives and communities within the restricted framework white Southerners allowed them.

THE FLUIDITY OF SOUTHERN RACE RELATIONS, 1877–1890

Race relations remained remarkably fluid in the South between the end of Reconstruction and the early 1890s. Despite the departure of Federal troops and the end of Republican rule, many black people continued to vote and hold office. Some Democrats even courted the black electorate.

In 1885, T. McCants Stewart, a black newspaperman from New York, traveled to his native South Carolina expecting a rough reception once his train headed south from Washington, D.C. To his surprise, the conductor allowed him to remain in his seat while white riders sat on baggage or stood. He provoked little reaction among white passengers when he entered the dining car. Some of them struck up a conversation with him. Stewart, who admitted he had begun his journey with "a chip on my shoulder . . . [daring] any man to knock it off," now observed that "the whites of the South are really less afraid to [have] contact with colored people than the whites of the North." In Columbia, South Carolina, Stewart found that he could move about with no restrictions. "I can ride in first-class cars. . . . I can go into saloons and get refreshments even as in New York. I can stop in and drink a glass of soda and be more politely waited upon than in some parts of New England."

To be sure, black people faced discrimination in employment and voting and random retaliation for perceived violations of racial barriers. But those barriers were by no means fixed.

THE WHITE BACKLASH

The black generation that came of age in this environment demanded full participation in American society. As the young black editor of Nashville's *Fisk Herald* proclaimed in 1889, "We are not the Negro from whom the chains of slavery fell a quarter of a century ago. . . . We are now qualified, and being the equal of whites, should be treated as such." Charles Price, an educator from North Carolina, admonished colleagues in 1890, "If we do not possess the manhood and patriotism to stand up in the defense of . . . constitutional rights and protest long, loud and unitedly against their continual infringements, we are unworthy of heritage as American citizens and deserve to have fastened on us the wrongs of which many are disposed to complain."

Many young white Southerners, raised on the myth of the Lost Cause, were continually reminded of the heroism and sacrifice of their fathers during the Civil War. For many, conditions were worse than their families had enjoyed before the war, and they resented the changed status of black people. David Schenck, a Greensboro,

North Carolina, businessman wrote in 1890 that "the breach between the races widens as the young free negroes grow up and intrude themselves on white society and nothing prevents the white people of the South from annihilating the negro race but the military power of the United States Government." Using the Darwinian language popular among educated white people at the time, Schenck concluded, "I pity the Negro, but the struggle is for the survival of the fittest race."

The South's deteriorating rural economy and the volatile politics of the late 1880s and early 1890s exacerbated the growing tensions between assertive black people and threatened white people. In the cities, black and white people came in close contact, competing for jobs and jostling each other for seats on streetcars and trains. Racist rhetoric and violence against black people accelerated in the 1890s.

Lynching became a public spectacle, a ritual designed to reinforce white supremacy. Note the matter-of-fact satisfaction of the spectators to this gruesome murder of a black man.

Courtesy Library of Congress

LYNCH LAW

In 1892, three prominent black men, Tom Moss, Calvin McDowell, and William Stewart, opened a grocery on the south side of Memphis, an area with a large African-American population. The People's Grocery prospered while a white-owned store across the street struggled. The proprietor of the white-owned store, W. H. Barrett, secured an indictment against Moss, McDowell, and Stewart for maintaining a public nuisance. Outraged black community leaders called a protest meeting at the grocery during which two people made threats against Barrett. Barrett learned of the threats, notified the police, and warned the gathering at the People's Grocery that white people planned to attack and destroy the store. Nine sheriff's deputies, all white, approached the store to arrest the men who had threatened Barrett. Fearing Barrett's threatened white assault, the people in the grocery fired on the deputies, unaware who they were, and wounded three. When the deputies identified themselves, thirty black people surrendered, including Moss, McDowell, and Stewart, and were imprisoned. Four days later, deputies removed the three owners from jail, took them to a deserted area, and shot them dead.

The men at the People's Grocery had violated two of the unspoken rules that white Southerners imposed on black Southerners to maintain racial barriers: They had prospered, and they had forcefully challenged white authority. White mobs lynched nearly two thousand black Southerners between 1882 and 1903. Most lynchers were working-class white people with rural roots who were struggling in the depressed economy of the 1890s and enraged at the fluidity of urban race relations.

The substitution of lynch law for a court of law seemed a cheap price to pay for white solidarity at a time when political and economic pressures threatened entrenched white leaders. In 1893, Atlanta's Methodist bishop, Atticus G. Haygood, typically a spokesman for racial moderation, objected to the torture some white lynchers inflicted on their victims but added, "Unless assaults by Negroes on white women and little girls come to an end, there will most probably be still further displays of vengeance that will shock the world."

Haygood's comments reflect the most common justification for lynching—the presumed threat posed by black men to the sexual virtue of white women. Sexual "crimes" could include remarks, glances, and gestures. Yet only 25 percent of the

Ida B. Wells, an outspoken critic of lynching, fled to Chigago following the People's Grocery lynchings in Memphis in 1892 and became a national civil-rights leader

The Granger Collection, New York

Segregation   A system of racial control that separated the races, initially by custom but increasingly by law during and after Reconstruction.

Disfranchisement   The use of legal means to bar individuals or groups from voting.

Plessy* v. *Ferguson   Supreme Court decision holding that Louisiana's railroad segregation law did not violate the Constitution as long as the railroads or the state provided equal accommodations.

lynchings that took place in the thirty years after 1890 had some alleged sexual connection. Certainly, the men of the People's Grocery had committed no sex crime.

Ida B. Wells, who owned a black newspaper in Memphis, used her columns to publicize the People's Grocery lynchings. The great casualty of the lynchings, she noted, was her faith that education, wealth, and upright living guaranteed black people the equality and justice they had long sought. The reverse was true. The more black people succeeded, the greater was their threat to white people. She investigated other lynchings, countering the claim that they were the result of assaults on white women. When she suggested that, on the contrary, perhaps some white women were attracted to black men, she enraged the white citizens of Memphis, who destroyed her press and office. Exiled to Chicago, Wells devoted herself to the struggle for racial justice.

SEGREGATION BY LAW

Southern white lawmakers sought to cement white solidarity and ensure black subservience in the 1890s by instituting **segregation** by law and the **disfranchisement** of black voters. Racial segregation restricting black Americans to separate and rarely equal public facilities had prevailed nationwide before the Civil War. After 1870, the custom spread rapidly in southern cities. In Richmond by the early 1870s, segregation laws required black people registering to vote to enter through separate doors, and registrars to count their ballots separately. The city's prisons and hospitals were segregated. So too were its horse-drawn railways, its schools, and most of its restaurants, hotels, and theaters.

During the same period, many Northern cities and states, often in response to protests by African Americans, were ending segregation. Massachusetts, for example, passed the nation's first public accommodations law in May 1865, desegregating all public facilities. Cities such as New York, Cleveland, and Cincinnati desegregated their streetcars. Chicago, Cleveland, Milwaukee, and the entire state of Michigan desegregated their public school systems. Roughly 95 percent of the nation's black population, however, lived in the South. In reality, integration in the North consequently required white people to give up very little to black people. And as African-American aspirations increased in the South during the 1890s as their political power waned, they became more vulnerable to segregation by law at the state level. At the same time, migration to cities, industrial development, and technologies such as railroads and elevators increased the opportunities for racial contact and muddled the rules of racial interaction.

White passengers objected to black passengers' implied assertion of economic and social equality when they sat with them in dining cars and first-class compartments. Black Southerners, in contrast, viewed equal access to railroad facilities as a sign of respectability and acceptance. When Southern state legislatures required railroads to provide segregated facilities, black people protested.

In 1890, Homer Plessy, a Louisiana black man, refused to leave the first-class car of a railroad traveling through the state. Arrested, he filed suit, arguing that his payment of the first-class fare entitled him to sit in the same first-class accommodations as white passengers. He claimed that under his right of citizenship guaranteed by the Fourteenth Amendment, neither the state of Louisiana nor the railroad could discriminate against him on the basis of color. The Constitution, he claimed, was colorblind.

The U.S. Supreme Court ruled on the case, ***Plessy* v. *Ferguson***, in 1896. In a seven-to-one decision, the Court held that Louisiana's railroad segregation law did not violate the Constitution as long as the railroads or the state provided equal accommodations. The decision left unclear what "equal" meant. In the Court's view, "Legislation is powerless to eradicate racial instincts," meaning that segregation of the races was natural and transcended constitutional considerations. The only justice to vote against the decision was John Marshall Harlan, a Kentuckian and former slave owner. In a stinging dissent, he predicted that the decision would result in an all-out assault on black rights. "The destinies of the two races . . . are indissolubly linked together," Harlan declared, "and the interests of both require that the common government of all shall not permit the seeds of race hate to be planted under the sanction of law."

Both Northern and Southern states enacted new segregation laws in the wake of *Plessy* v. *Ferguson.* In practice, the separate facilities for black people these laws required, if provided at all, were rarely equal. By 1900, segregation by law extended to public conveyances, theaters, hotels, restaurants, parks, and schools.

The segregation statutes came to be known collectively as **Jim Crow laws**, after the blackface stage persona of Thomas Rice, a white Northern minstrel show performer in the 1820s. Reflecting white stereo-types of African Americans, Rice caricatured "Jim Crow" as a foolish, elderly, lame slave who spoke in an exaggerated dialect.

Economic segregation followed social segregation. Before the Civil War, black men had dominated crafts such as carpentry and masonry. By the 1890s, white men were replacing them in these trades and excluding them from new trades such as plumbing and electrical work. Trade unions, composed primarily of craftworkers, began systematically to exclude African Americans. Confined increasingly to low or unskilled positions in railroad construction, the timber industry, and agriculture, black workers underwent *deskilling*—a decline in work force expertise—after 1890. With lower incomes from unskilled labor, they faced reduced opportunities for better housing and education.

DISFRANCHISEMENT

Following the political instability of the late 1880s and the 1890s, white leaders determined to disfranchise black people altogether, thereby reinforcing white solidarity and eliminating the need to consider black interests. Obstacles loomed—the Fifteenth Amendment, which guaranteed freedmen the right to vote, and a Republican-dominated Congress—but with a national consensus emerging in support of white supremacy, they proved easy to circumvent.

Support for disfranchisement was especially strong among large landowners in the South's plantation districts, where heavy concentrations of black people threatened their political domination. Urban leaders, especially after the turmoil of the 1890s, looked on disfranchisement as a way to stabilize politics and make elections more predictable.

Democrats enacted a variety of measures to attain their objectives without violating the letter of the Fifteenth Amendment. States enacted **poll taxes**, requiring citizens to pay to vote. They adopted the secret ballot, which confused and intimidated illiterate black voters accustomed to using ballots with colors to identify parties. States set literacy and educational qualifications for voting or required prospective registrants to "interpret" a section of the state constitution. To avoid disfranchising poor, illiterate white voters with these measures, states enacted **grandfather clauses** granting the vote automatically to anyone whose grandfather could have voted prior to 1867 (the year Congressional Reconstruction began). The grandfathers of most black men in the 1890s had been slaves, ineligible to vote.

Tennessee was the first state to pass disfranchising legislation. A year later, Mississippi amended its constitution to require voters to pass a literacy test and prove they "understood" the state constitution. When a journalist asked an Alabama lawmaker if Jesus Christ could pass his state's "understanding" test, the legislator replied, "That would depend entirely on which way he was going to vote."

Alarmed by the Populist uprising, Democratic leaders also used disfranchisement to gut dissenting parties. During the 1880s, minority parties in the

17–10
From *Plessy* v. *Ferguson*
(1896)

WHERE TO LEARN MORE

Atlanta History Center,
Atlanta, Georgia
**www.atlhist.org/exhibitions/html/
metropolitan_frontiers.htm**

Jim Crow laws   Segregation laws that became widespread in the South during the 1890s.

Poll taxes   Taxes imposed on voters as a requirement for voting.

Grandfather clause   Rule that required potential voters to demonstrate that their grandfathers had been eligible to vote; used in some Southern states after 1890 to limit the black electorate.

South consistently polled an average of 40 percent of the statewide vote; by the mid-1890s, that figure had diminished to 30 percent, despite the Populist insurgency. Turnout dropped even more dramatically. In Mississippi, for example, voter turnout in gubernatorial races during the 1880s averaged 51 percent; during the 1890s, it was 21 percent. Black turnout in Mississippi, which averaged 39 percent in the 1880s, plummeted to near zero in the 1890s. Overall turnout, which averaged 64 percent during the 1880s, fell to only 30 percent by 1910.

When 160 South Carolina delegates gathered to amend the state constitution in 1895, the six black delegates among them mounted a passionate but futile defense of their right to vote. Black delegate W.J. Whipper noted the irony of white people clamoring for supremacy when they already held the vast majority of the state's elected offices. Robert Smalls, the state's leading black politician, urged delegates not to turn their backs on the state's black population. Such pleas fell on deaf ears. (See American Views: "Robert Smalls Argues against Disfranchisement.")

A NATIONAL CONSENSUS ON RACE

How could the South get away with it? How could Southerners openly segregate, disfranchise, and lynch African Americans without a national outcry? Apparently, most Americans in the 1890s believed that black people were inferior to white people and deserved to be treated as second-class citizens. Contemporary depictions of black people show scarcely human stereotypes: black men with bulbous lips and bulging eyes, fat black women wearing turbans and smiling vacuously, and black children contentedly eating watermelon or romping with jungle animals. These images appeared on cereal boxes, in advertisements, in children's books, in newspaper cartoons, and as lawn ornaments. The widely read book *The Clansman* by Thomas Dixon, a North Carolinian living in New York City and an ardent white supremacist, glorified the rise of the Ku Klux Klan. D. W. Griffith transformed *The Clansman* into an immensely popular film under the title *Birth of a Nation*.

So-called scientific racism purported to establish white superiority and black inferiority on biological grounds. Northern-born professional historians reinterpreted the Civil War and Reconstruction in the white South's favor. Historian William A. Dunning, the generation's leading authority on Reconstruction, wrote in 1901 that the North's "views as to the political capacity of the blacks had been irrational." The progressive journal *Outlook* hailed disfranchisement because it made it "impossible in the future for ignorant, shiftless, and corrupt negroes to misrepresent their race in political action." Harvard's Charles Francis Adams Jr. chided colleagues who disregarded the "fundamental, scientific facts" he claimed demonstrated black inferiority. The *New York Times*, summarizing this national consensus in 1903, noted that "practically the whole country" supported the "southern solution" to the race issue, since "there was no other possible settlement."

Congress and the courts upheld discriminatory legislation. As a delegate at the Alabama disfranchisement convention of 1901 noted, "The race problem is no longer confined to the States of the South, [and] we have the sympathy instead of the hostility of the North."

By the mid-1890s, Republicans were so entrenched in the North and West that they did not need Southern votes to win presidential elections

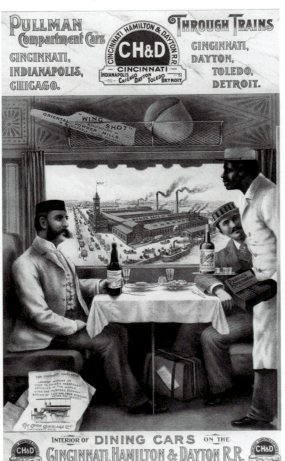

Racial stereotypes permeated American popular culture by the turn of the twentieth century. Images like this advertisement for Pullman railroad cars, which depicts a deferential black porter attending to white passengers, reinforced racist beliefs that black people belonged in servile roles. Immersed in such images, white people assumed they depicted the natural order of things.

Cincinnati, Hamilton & Dayton Railroad Advertisement, lithographic poster, 1894, Strobridge Lithographic Company, from the Bella C. Landauer Collection, negative number 51391. Collection of the New York Historical Society

• AMERICAN VIEWS •

ROBERT SMALLS ARGUES AGAINST DISFRANCHISEMENT

Born in Beaufort, South Carolina, in 1839, Robert Smalls served as a slave pilot in Charleston Harbor. In 1862, he emancipated himself, with his family and friends, when he delivered a Confederate steamer to a Union blockading fleet. He entered politics in 1864 as a delegate from his state to the Republican National Convention. He helped write South Carolina's Reconstruction constitution, which guaranteed the right of former slaves to vote and hold office. Smalls won election to the state legislature in 1869, and the U.S. House of Representatives in 1875. With opportunities for African Americans to hold public office declining following Reconstruction, Smalls was appointed collector of the Port of Beaufort, a federal post he occupied until his death in 1915. In the speech excerpted here—delivered to the South Carolina Constitutional Convention of 1895—he assails the state's plan to disfranchise black voters.

FROM THE white perspective, what is Smalls's most telling argument against the disfranchisement and the planned strategies to implement it? How does Smalls depict the black citizens of South Carolina? Why were white political leaders unmoved by Small's plea?

Mr. President, this convention has been called for no other purpose than the disfranchisement of the negro. . . .

The negroes are paying taxes in the south on $263,000,000 worth of property. In South Carolina, according to the census, the negroes pay tax on $12,500,000 worth of property. That was in 1890. You voted down without discussion . . . a proposition for a simple property and education qualification [for voting]. What do you want? . . . In behalf of the 600,000 negroes in the State and the 132,000 negro voters all that I demand is that a fair and honest election law be passed. We care not what the qualifications imposed are, all that we ask is that they be fair and honest, and honorable, and with these provisos we will stand or fall

by it. You have 102,000 white men over 21 years of age, 13,000 of these cannot read nor write. You dare not disfranchise them, and you know that the man who proposes it will never be elected to another office in the State of South Carolina. . . . Fifty-eight thousand negroes cannot read nor write. This leaves a majority of 14,000 white men who can read and write over the same class of negroes in this State. We are willing to accept a scheme that provides that no man who cannot read nor write can vote, if you dare pass it. How can you expect an ordinary man to "understand and explain" any section of the Constitution, to correspond to the interpretation put upon it by the manager of election, when by a very recent decision of the supreme court, composed of the most learned men in State, two of them put one construction upon a section, and the other justice put an entirely different construction upon it. To embody such a provision in the election law would be to mean that every white man would interpret it aright and every negro would interpret it wrong. . . . Some morning you may wake up to find that the bone and sinew of your country is gone. The negro is needed in the cotton fields and in the low country rice fields, and if you impose too hard conditions upon the negro in this State there will be nothing else for him to do but to leave. What then will you do about your phosphate works? No one but a negro can work them; the mines that pay the interest on your State debt. I tell you the negro is the bone and sinew of your country and you cannot do without him. I do not believe you want to get rid of the negro, else why did you impose a high tax on immigration agents who might come here to get him to leave?

Now, Mr. President we should not talk one thing and mean another. We should not deceive ourselves. Let us make a Constitution that is fair, honest and just. Let us make a Constitution for all the people, one we will be proud of and our children will receive with delight.

Source: The Columbia State, October 27, 1895.

or to control Congress. Besides, business-oriented Republicans found common ground with conservative Southern Democrats on fiscal policy and foreign affairs.

Although no Northern states threatened to deny black citizens the right to vote, they did increase segregation. The booming industries of the North generally did not hire black workers. Antidiscrimination laws on the books since the Civil War went unenforced. In 1904, 1906, and 1908, race riots erupted in Springfield, Ohio, Greensburg, Indiana, and Springfield, Illinois, matching similar disturbances in Wilmington, North Carolina, and Atlanta, Georgia.

RESPONSE OF THE BLACK COMMUNITY

African Americans organized more than a dozen boycotts of streetcar systems in the urban South between 1896 and 1908 in an effort to desegregate them, but not one succeeded. The Afro-American Council, formed in 1890 to protest the deteriorating conditions of black life, accomplished little and disbanded in 1908. W. E. B. Du Bois organized an annual Conference on Negro Problems at Atlanta University beginning in 1896, but it produced no effective plan of action.

A few black people chose to leave the South. Henry McNeal Turner of Georgia, an African Methodist Episcopal (AME) bishop, promoted migration to Liberia, but only a few hundred made the trip in the late 1870s, Turner not included, and most of those returned disappointed. Most black people who moved in the 1890s stayed within the South.

More commonly, black people withdrew to develop their own rich community life. Particularly in the cities of the South, they could live relatively free of white surveillance and even white contact. In 1890, fully 70 percent of black city dwellers lived in the South; and between 1860 and 1900, the proportion of black people in the cities of the South rose from one in six to more than one in three.

By the 1880s, a new black middle class had emerged in the South. Urban-based, professional, business-oriented, and serving a primarily black clientele, its members fashioned an interconnected web of churches, fraternal and self-help organizations, families, and businesses. Black Baptists, AME, and AME Zion churches led reform efforts in the black community, seeking to eliminate drinking, prostitution, and other vices in black neighborhoods.

African-American fraternal and self-help groups, led by middle-class black people, functioned as surrogate welfare organizations for the poor. Some groups, such as the Colored Masons and the Colored Odd Fellows, paralleled white organizations. Black membership rates usually exceeded those in the white community. More than 50 percent of Nashville's black men, for example, belonged to various fraternal associations in the city. Fraternal orders also served as the seedbed for such business ventures as the North Carolina Mutual Life Insurance Company, founded in Durham in 1898. Within two decades, North Carolina Mutual became the largest black-owned business in the nation and helped transform Durham into the "capital of the black middle class." Most Southern cities boasted active black business districts by the 1890s.

Nashville's J. C. Napier typified the activism of the African-American urban middle class in the New South era. He belonged to two of the city's prominent black churches, was active in Republican politics, played an important role in several temperance and fraternal societies, served as president of the local black YMCA chapter, and as an attorney helped his fellow African Americans with numerous legal matters.

The African-American middle class worked especially hard to improve black education. Black students in cities had only makeshift facilities; those in the countryside had almost no facilities. To improve these conditions, black middle-class leaders solicited educational funds from Northern philanthropic organizations.

QUICK REVIEW

Responses

◆ Desegregation efforts in the South failed.

◆ A few black people chose to leave the South.

◆ Most black people withdrew into their own communities.

Black women played an increasingly active and prominent role in African-American communities after 1877, especially in cities. Ida B. Wells moved to Memphis from Mississippi in 1884. In 1886, she attended a lecture at an interracial Knights of Labor meeting and witnessed a religious revival conducted by the nation's leading evangelist, Dwight Moody. The following year, Wells began her journalism career and soon purchased a one-third interest in a local black newspaper.

Black women's clubs supported day-care facilities for working mothers and settlement houses in poor black neighborhoods modeled after those in northern cities. Atlanta's Neighborhood Union, founded by Lugenia Burns Hope in 1908, provided playgrounds and a health center and secured a grant from a New York foundation to improve black education in the city. Black women's clubs also established homes for single black working women to protect them from sexual exploitation, and they worked for woman suffrage "to reckon with men who place no value on her [black woman's] virtue," as Nannie H. Burroughs of the National Association of Colored Women argued at the turn of the century.

Anna J. Cooper, a Nashville clubwoman, wrote in 1892 that to be a member of this generation was "to have a heritage unique in the ages." Assertive black women did not arouse the same degree of white antagonism as assertive black men. They could operate in a broader public arena than men and speak out more forcefully.

After disfranchisement, middle-class black women assumed an even more pivotal role in the black community. They often used their relations with prominent white women and organizations such as the WCTU and the YWCA to press for public commitments to improve the health and education of African Americans. Absent political pressure from black men, as well as the danger of African-American males asserting themselves in the tense racial climate after 1890, black women became critical spokespersons for their race.

The extension of black club work into rural areas of the South, where the majority of the African-American population lived, to educate families about hygiene, nutrition, and child care, anticipated similar efforts among white women after 1900. But unlike their white counterparts, these middle-class black women worked with limited resources in a context of simmering racial hostility and political and economic impotence. In response, they nurtured a self-help strategy to improve the conditions of the people they sought to help. One of the most prominent African-American leaders of the late nineteenth and early twentieth centuries, Booker T. Washington, adopted a similar approach to racial uplift.

Born a slave in Virginia in 1856, Washington and his family worked in the salt and coal mines of West Virginia after the Civil War. Ambitious and flushed with the postwar enthusiasm for advancement that gripped freedmen, he worked his way through Hampton Normal and Agricultural Institute, the premier black educational institution in the South at that time. In 1881, he founded the Tuskegee Institute for black students in rural Alabama. By learning industrial skills, Washington maintained, black people could secure self-respect and economic independence. Tuskegee emphasized vocational training over the liberal arts.

At an Atlanta exposition in 1895, Washington argued that African Americans should accommodate themselves to segregation and disfranchisement until they could prove their economic worth to American society. In exchange, white people should help provide black people with the education and job training they would need to gain their independence. This position was known as the **Atlanta Compromise**. Despite his conciliatory public stance, Washington secretly helped finance legal challenges to segregation and disfranchisement. But increasingly, black people were shut out of the kinds of jobs for which Washington hoped to train them. Facing a depressed rural economy and growing racial violence, they had little prospect of advancement.

17–11
W.E.B. Du Bois, from "Of Mr. Booker T. Washington and Others"

Atlanta Compromise   Booker T. Washington's policy accepting segregation and disfranchisement for African Americans in exchange for white assistance in education and job training.

FROM THEN TO NOW
The Confederate Battle Flag

Memories of the Civil War and Reconstruction formed a crucial part of southern civic and religious culture from the late nineteenth century onward. Southerners perceived themselves and the rest of the nation through the lens of the heroic Lost Cause and the alleged abuses of Reconstruction, and the symbols associated with those events took on the status of icons. During the 1890s, the memory industry that white political and religious leaders had promoted since the end of the war became institutionalized. Organizations such as the United Daughters of the Confederacy and the Sons of Confederate Veterans strove to educate a new generation of white Southerners on the meanings of the sacrifices of the war generation, bolstering the imposition of white supremacy through racial segregation and disfranchisement.

The Confederate battle flag emerged from this process as an icon of the Lost Cause and a symbol of white supremacy. Alabama, for example, redesigned its state flag in the 1890s to resemble more closely the battle flag. Its red St. Andrews cross on a white background symbolized the blood spilled in defense of the Southern homeland and the supremacy of the white race.

Still, the Confederate battle flag itself was displayed mostly at veterans' reunions and only rarely at other public occasions—until the late 1940s, that is, when civil rights for African Americans emerged as a national issue for the first time since the Reconstruction era. In 1948, Mississippians waved the flag at Ole Miss football games for the first time. In 1956, as the civil rights struggle in the South gained momentum, the state of Georgia incorporated the battle flag into its state flag. And, in 1962, as sit-ins and Freedom Riders spread throughout the South, officials in South Carolina—claiming to be commemorating the Civil War centennial—hoisted the battle flag above the State House in Columbia.

Long after the centennial celebration concluded, the battle flag continued to fly in Columbia. This official display became a focus of heated controversy. Proponents argued that the battle flag represents heritage, not hate. Opponents denounced it as a symbol of white supremacy. In the mid-1990s, South Carolina's Republican Governor David Beasley, seeking to defuse the issue, proposed removing the flag from atop the Capitol and installing it at a nearby history museum. The resulting firestorm of protest from some of the Governor's white constituents forced him to reverse himself, however, and contributed to his defeat in his bid for reelection.

The flag controversy erupted again in 1999, when South Carolina's state Democratic Party chairman urged voters to return a Democratic legislature that would, once and for all, remove the flag from the State Capitol. The angry response from both Republicans and some Democrats forced the new Democratic governor to quickly distance himself from the proposal. Then, in July 1999, the National Association for the Advancement of Colored People (NAACP) announced a national boycott of South Carolina, beginning in January 2000. Facing the loss of convention and tourist revenues, business groups pleaded with lawmakers to lower the flag, which they did in July 2000. But the flag's new home, near a monument on the Capitol grounds, is even more visible to the public, prompting the continuation of the NAACP boycott.

In 2001, Mississippians voted overwhelmingly to keep their state flag which includes the battle flag. That same year, an interracial group of Georgia legislators agreed to remove the battle flag from the state banner; the new design includes the Confederate emblem, but only as part of a ribbon that includes all of the flags that have flown over Georgia through its history. Legislators did not submit the new design to a referendum, though in 2003, Georgia's recently-elected Republican Governor Sonny Perdue reversed that decision.

When people in other parts of the country sometimes remark that white Southerners are still fighting the Civil War, it is controversies like the one over the battle flag that they have in mind. But the controversy is less about the past than it is about the way we use history to shape our understanding of the society we live in and our vision of its future. At issue is not just history, but whose history. In that sense the flag controversy, as much as it picks at wounds more than a century old, can at least generate positive dialogue. Even so, in the interests of reconciliation, it may be time for Southerners to follow Robert E. Lee's final order to his men and "Furl the flag, boys."

Another prominent African-American leader, W. E. B. Du Bois, challenged Washington's acceptance of black social inequality. Du Bois, the first African American to earn a doctorate at Harvard, promoted self-help, education, and black pride. A gifted teacher and writer, he taught at Atlanta University and wrote eighteen books on black life in America. Du Bois was a cofounder, in 1910, of the **National Association for the Advancement of Colored People (NAACP)**, an interracial organization dedicated to restoring African-American political and social rights.

Despite their differences, which reflected their divergent backgrounds, Washington and Du Bois agreed on many issues. Both believed that black success in the South required some white assistance. As Du Bois wrote in *The Souls of Black Folk*, "Any movement for the elevation of the Southern Negro needs the cooperation, the sympathy, and the support of the best white people in order to succeed." But "the best white people" did not care to elevate black Southerners. In 1906, after a bloody race riot in Atlanta, Du Bois left the South, a decision millions of black Southerners would make over the next two decades.

As long as it provided the raw materials for the North's new urban industrial economy and maintained the peace, the South could count on the rest of the country not to interfere in its solution to race relations. Indeed, to the extent that most white Americans concerned themselves with race, they agreed with the Southern solution.

National Association for the Advancement of Colored People (NAACP) Interracial organization co-founded by W. E. B. DuBois in 1910 dedicated to restoring African-American political and social rights.

CONCLUSION

In many respects, the South was more like the rest of the nation in 1900 than at any other time since 1860. Young men and women migrated to Southern cities to pursue opportunities unavailable to their parents. Advances in the production and marketing of cigarettes and soft drinks would soon make Southern entrepreneurs and their products household names. Southerners ordered fashions from Sears, Roebuck catalogs and enjoyed electric lights, electric trolleys, and indoor plumbing as much as other urban Americans.

Americans idealized a mythical South of rural grace and hospitality, a land of moonlight and magnolias, offering it as a counterpoint to the crowded, immigrant-infested, factory-fouled, money-grubbing North. Northern journalists offered admiring portraits of southern heroes like Robert E. Lee, of whom one declared in 1906, "the nation has a hero to place beside her greatest."

White Southerners cultivated national reconciliation but remained fiercely dedicated to preserving the peculiarities of their region: a one-party political system, disfranchisement, and segregation by law. The region's urban and industrial growth, impressive from the vantage of 1865, paled before that of the North. The South remained a colonial economy characterized more by deep rural poverty than urban prosperity.

Middle-class white people in the urban South enjoyed the benefits of a national economy and a secure social position. Middle-class women enjoyed increased influence in the public realm, but not to the extent of their Northern sisters. And the institutionalization of white supremacy gave even poor white farmers and factory workers a place in the social hierarchy a rung or two above the bottom.

For black people, the New South proved a crueler ruse than Reconstruction. No one now stepped forward to support their cause and stem the erosion of their economic independence, political freedom, and civil rights. They built communities and worked as best they could to challenge restrictions on their freedom.

The New South was thus both American and Southern. It shared with the rest of the country a period of rapid urban and industrial growth. But the legacy of war and slavery still lay heavily on the South, manifesting itself in rural poverty, segregation, and black disfranchisement.

Booker T. Washington counseled acquiescence to segregation, maintaining that black people could ultimately gain the acceptance of white society through self-improvement and hard work.

The Granger Collection, New York

SUMMARY

The Newness of the New South The "newness" of the New South was to be found primarily in its economic shift toward industrialization and urbanization rather than its social relations. Urban and rural white leaders had used the banner of white supremacy to constrict African-American social and economic roles; the Solid South, a white Democratic voting bloc emerged. Industry from textiles to steel dotted the Southern landscape, young men and women migrated to cities, and railroads connected the growing urban centers. Economically, the South remained behind the booming North; a weak agricultural economy, high birthrate, and low wages were some of the undermining factors.

The Southern Agrarian Revolt More than even before the Civil War, cotton dominated Southern agriculture; the price of cotton was low, and the prices of fertilizer, tools and necessities rose. Curtailing production to raise prices was not an option; the credit-based economy of the South was dependent upon cotton. Black and white sharecroppers and tenant farmers fought back by organizing, scoring limited successes; it took higher cotton prices and returning prosperity in the late 1890s to bring relief to farmers.

Women in the New South White women in the South were cast in the roles of paragons of virtue and purity who needed men to defend them. With these limitations, middle-class women entered the public arena slowly. Women's involvement in church organizations, temperance, and as protectors of Southern history allowed them involvement without challenging the class and racial inequalities of the New South, while women's club activities addressed their self-improvement and allowed them to help other women.

Settling the Race Issue The generation of black people who had come of age by the 1890s demanded full participation; white Southerners raised on the myth of the Lost Cause resented the changed status of black people. Economic and political violence worsened the tensions, and violence, including lynchings, accelerated. Segregation and disfranchisement laws were passed; the U.S. Supreme Court condoned separate accommodations in the case *Plessy* v. *Ferguson*. The majority of white Americans, North and South, ascribed to the notion of black inferiority; no national debate resulted in response to the new restrictions. African Americans responded by creating their own community life within these new confines. Booker T. Washington and W.E.B. DuBois differed on the approaches black people should take to accommodate and improve themselves.

REVIEW QUESTIONS

1. How did the activism of white middle-class women affect the politics of the South in the late 1880s and early 1890s?

2. How did the assertiveness of young urban black people affect the politics of the South in the late 1880s and early 1890s?

3. Why did white people believe that segregation and disfranchisement were reforms?

4. How did black Southerners respond to decreasing economic and political opportunities in the New South?

5. Why was Anna J. Cooper optimistic for African-American women in the South?

KEY TERMS

Agricultural Wheel   (p. 447)
Atlanta Compromise   (p. 459)
Colored Farmer's Alliance   (p. 448)
Disfranchisement   (p. 454)
Grandfather clause   (p. 455)
Grange   (p. 447)
Jim Crow laws   (p. 455)

Lynching   (p. 451)
National Association for the Advancement of Colored people (NAACP)   (p. 461)
Plessy v. *Ferguson*   (p. 454)
Poll taxes   (p. 455)
Populist party   (p. 449)

Segregation   (p. 454)
Solid South   (p. 439)
Southern Farmers' Alliance   (p. 447)
Subtreasuray Plan   (p. 448)
Women's Christian Temperance Union (WCTU)   (p. 450)

WHERE TO LEARN MORE

🛡 **Levine Museum of the New South, Charlotte, North Carolina.** The museum has exhibits on various New South themes and a permanent exhibit on the history of Charlotte and the Carolina Piedmont. **www.museumofthenewsouth.org**

🛡 **Atlanta History Center, Atlanta, Georgia.** The major exhibit, "Metropolitan Frontiers, 1835–2000," includes a strong segment on the New South era, including the development of separate black and white economies in Atlanta. The Herndon home, also on the grounds of the center, has an exhibit on black upper-class life in Atlanta from 1880 to 1930. **www.atlhist.org/exhibitions/html/metropolitan_frontiers.htm**

🛡 **Sloss Furnaces National Historical Landmark, Birmingham, Alabama.** The site recalls the time when Birmingham challenged Pittsburgh as the nation's primary steel-producing center. **www.slossfurnaces.com**

For additional study resources for this chapter, go to:
www.prenhall.com/goldfield/chapter17

Chinese Primary Public School, 920 Clay St., Chinatown, San Francisco

*Here we had been taken to a lonely place;
. . . our things were taken away, our friends
separated from us; a man came to inspect us,
as if to ascertain our full value . . .*

Noted urban photographer Lewis Hines captures the cramped working conditions
and child labor in this late nineteenth-century canning factory. Women and children
provided a cheap and efficient work force for labor-intensive industries.

18

INDUSTRY, IMMIGRANTS, AND CITIES
1870–1900

WHAT CHANGES did the American workforce experience in the late nineteenth century?

WHAT IMPACT did new immigration have on cities in the North?

WHO MADE up the new middle class?

ATLANTIC CITY, N.J.   Easter Sunday on the Boardwalk.
A display of fashions on the Boardwalk. J.H.M.

We were homeless, houseless, and friendless in a strange place. We had hardly money enough to last us through the voyage for which we had hoped and waited for three long years. We had suffered much that the reunion we longed for might come about; we had prepared ourselves to suffer more in order to bring it about, and had parted with those we loved, with places that were dear to us in spite of what we passed through in them, never again to see them, as we were convinced—all for the same dear end. With strong hopes and high spirits that hid the sad parting, we had started on our long journey. And now we were checked so unexpectedly but surely . . . When my mother had recovered enough to speak, she began to argue with the gendarme, telling him our story and begging him to be kind. The children were frightened and all but I cried. I was only wondering what would happen. . . .

Here we had been taken to a lonely place; . . . our things were taken away, our friends separated from us; a man came to inspect us, as if to ascertain our full value; strange-looking people driving us about like dumb animals, helpless and unresisting; children we could not see crying in a way that suggested terrible things; ourselves driven into a little room where a great kettle was boiling on a little stove; our clothes taken off, our bodies rubbed with a slippery substance that might be any bad thing; a shower of warm water let down on us without warning. . . . We are forced to pick out our clothes from among all the others, with the steam blinding us; we choke, cough, entreat the women to give us time; they persist, "Quick! Quick!—or you'll miss the train!"—Oh, so we really won't be murdered! They are only making us ready for the continuing of our journey, cleaning us of all suspicions of dangerous sickness. Thank God! . . .

Oh, what solemn thoughts I had! How deeply I felt the greatness, the power of the scene! The immeasurable distance from horizon; . . . the absence of any object besides the one ship; . . . I was conscious only of sea and sky and something I did not understand. And as I listened to its solemn voice, I felt as if I had found a friend, and knew that I loved the ocean.

—Mary Antin

Mary Antin, *The Promised Land* (Boston: Houghton Mifflin Company, 1912), Chapter VIII.

IMAGE KEY
for pages 464–465

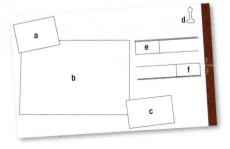

a. A classroom at work in the Chinese Public Primary School in Chinatown, San Francisco, with a Caucasian teacher.

b. A crowd of children at work in a 19th century canning factory. The children sit on overturned baskets while poring over their work under the gaze of an adult male supervisor in their midst.

c. Fashionable people crowded the Boardwalk in Atlantic City each Easter Sunday in the early 20th Century to see and be seen.

d. A replica of the first light bulb.

e. The Sixth Maryland militia in Baltimore fires into a hostile crowd of laborers chucking rocks during the Great Railroad Strike of 1877.

f. A family rides in a historic Ford Model T automobile.

MARY ANTIN, a thirteen-year old Jewish girl from Russia, describes her family's journey in 1884 from the persecution of Jews in tsarist Russia to the ship that sailed from Hamburg, Germany, that would take her to join her father in Boston.

Millions of European and Asian immigrants made similar journeys across the Atlantic and the Pacific, fraught with danger, heartbreak, fear and the sundering of family ties. So powerful was the promise of American life that the immigrant willingly risked these obstacles to come to the United States. Mary's letter to her uncle, was both a way of recounting her family's exodus and of maintaining contact with a world and a family she had left behind.

For Mary, America did indeed prove to be *The Promised Land*, as she entitled a memoir, published in 1912. After attending Barnard College in New York City, she wrote on immigrant issues, lectured widely, and worked for Theodore Roosevelt's Progressive Party. Her life shows how a teenage girl moved from a medieval life in tsarist Russia to a career as a writer in the United States.

Mary and her family were part of a major demographic and economic transformation in the United States between 1870 and 1900. Rapid industrial development changed the nature of the work force and the workplace. Large factories staffed by semiskilled laborers displaced the skilled artisans and small shops that had dominated American industry before 1870. Industrial development also accelerated urbanization. Between the Civil War and 1900, the proportion of the nation's population living in cities increased from 20 to 40 percent.

New opportunities opened as old opportunities disappeared. Vast new wealth was created, but poverty increased. New technologies eased life for some but left others untouched. The great dilemma of early-twentieth-century America was to reconcile these contradictions and provide a decent life for all.

Few locations encapsulated this dilemma better than Philadelphia during the Centennial Exposition of 1876, marking the nation's hundredth birthday. Its millions of visitors witnessed the ingenuity of the world's newest industrial power. Thomas Edison explained his new automatic telegraph, and Alexander Graham Bell demonstrated his telephone to the wonder of onlookers. A giant Corliss steam engine loomed over the entrance to Machinery Hall, dwarfing the other exhibits and providing them with power. "Yes," a visitor concluded, "it is in these things of iron and steel that the national genius most freely speaks."

For many Americans, however, the fanfare of the exposition rang hollow. The country was in the midst of a depression. Thousands were out of work, and others had lost their savings in bank failures and sour investments. With the typical daily wage a dollar, most Philadelphians could not afford the exposition's 50-cent admission price. They celebrated instead at "Centennial City," a ragtag collection of cheap bars, seedy hotels, small restaurants, and sideshows hurriedly constructed of wood and tin across the street from the imposing exposition.

This small area of Philadelphia reflected the promise and failure of the **Gilded Age**. The term is taken from the title of a novel by Mark Twain that satirizes the materialistic excesses of his day. It reflects the period's shallow worship of wealth—and its veneer of respectability and prosperity covering deep economic and social divisions.

Gilded Age   Term applied to late-nineteenth-century America that refers to the shallow display and worship of wealth characteristic of that period.

New Industry

Between 1870 and 1900, the United States transformed itself from an agricultural nation—a nation of farmers, merchants, and artisans—into the world's foremost industrial power, producing more than one-third of the world's manufactured goods. By the early twentieth century, factory workers made up one-fourth of the work force, and agricultural workers had dropped from a half to less than a third (see Figure 18.1). A factory with a few dozen employees would have been judged fair-sized in 1870. By the early twentieth century, many industries employed thousands of workers in a single plant. Some industries—petroleum, steel, and meatpacking, for example—had been unknown before the Civil War.

Although the size of the industrial work force increased dramatically, the number of firms in a given industry shrank. Mergers, changes in corporate management and the organization of the work force, and a compliant government left a few companies in control of vast segments of the American economy. Workers, reformers, and eventually government challenged this concentration of economic power.

WHAT CHANGES did the American workforce experience in the late nineteenth century, and what was the reaction of organized labor?

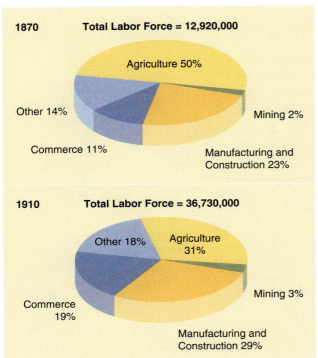

1870   **Total Labor Force = 12,920,000**

- Agriculture 50%
- Mining 2%
- Manufacturing and Construction 23%
- Commerce 11%
- Other 14%

1910   **Total Labor Force = 36,730,000**

- Other 18%
- Agriculture 31%
- Mining 3%
- Manufacturing and Construction 29%
- Commerce 19%

Figure 18–1   Changes in the American Labor Force, 1870–1910
The transformation of the American economy in the late nineteenth century changed the nature and type of work. By 1910 the United States was an urban, industrial nation with a matching work force that toiled in factories and for commercial establishments (including railroads), and less frequently on farms.

WHERE TO LEARN MORE

★ Edison National Historic Site, West Orange, New Jersey
www.nps.gov/edis

INVENTING TECHNOLOGY: THE ELECTRIC AGE

Technology transformed factory work and increased the scale of production. Steam engines and, later, electricity, freed manufacturers from dependence on water power. Factories could now be built anywhere accessible to the transportation system and a concentration of labor. Managers could substitute machines for workers, skewing the balance of power in the workplace toward employers. Technology also transformed city life. By the early twentieth century, electric lights, appliances, ready-made clothing, and store-bought food eased middle-class life. Electric trolleys whisked clerks, salespeople, bureaucrats, and bankers to new urban and suburban subdivisions. Electric street-lights lit up city streets at night. Movies entertained the masses. As the historian and novelist Henry Adams put it, "In the essentials of life . . . the boy of 1854 stood nearer [to] the year one than to the year 1900."

For much of the nineteenth century, the United States was dependent on the industrial nations of Europe for technological innovation. American engineers often went to England and Germany for training, and industries and railroads benefited from Europeans inventions.

In the late nineteenth century, the United States changed from a technological borrower to a technological innovator. By 1910, a million patents had been issued in the United States, 900,000 of them after 1870. Nothing represented this shift better than Thomas A. Edison's electric light bulb and electric generating system, which transformed electricity into a new and versatile form of industrial energy. Until the late nineteenth century, advances in scientific theory usually followed technological innovation. Techniques for making steel, for example, developed before scientific theories explained how they worked. Textile machinery and railroad technology developed similarly. In contrast, a theoretical understanding of electricity preceded its practical use as a source of energy. Scientists had been experimenting with electricity for half a century before Edison unveiled his light bulb in 1879. Edison's research laboratory at Menlo Park, New Jersey, also established a model for corporate-sponsored research and development that would rapidly increase the pace of technological innovation.

In 1876, Edison established his research laboratory at Menlo Park and turned his attention to the electric light. Scientists had already discovered that passing an electric current through a filament in a vacuum produced light. They had not yet found a filament, however, that could last for more than a few minutes. Edison tried a variety of materials, from grass to hair from a colleague's beard, before succeeding with charred sewing thread. In 1879, he produced a bulb that burned for an astounding forty-five hours. Then he devised a circuit that provided an even flow of current through the filament. After thrilling a crowd with the spectacle of five hundred lights ablaze on New Year's Eve in 1879, Edison went on to build a power station in New York City to serve businesses and homes by 1882. The electric age had begun.

Edison's initial success touched off a wave of research and development in Germany, Austria, Great Britain, France, and the United States. Whoever could light the world cheaply and efficiently held the key to an enormous fortune. Ultimately the prize fell not to Edison but to Elihu Thomson, a high school chemistry teacher in Philadelphia. Leaving teaching to devote himself to research full time, Thomson founded his own company and in 1883 moved to Connecticut. Thomson

CHRONOLOGY

1869   The Knights of Labor is founded in Philadelphia.

1870   John D. Rockefeller forms the Standard Oil Company.
Congress passes the Naturalization Act barring Asians from citizenship.

1876   The Centennial Exposition opens in Philadelphia.

1877   The Great Uprising railroad strike, the first nationwide work stoppage in the United States, provokes violent clashes between workers and federal troops.

1879   Thomas Edison unveils the electric light bulb.

1880   Founding of the League of American Wheelmen in 1880 helps establish bicycling as one of urban American's favorite recreational activities.

1881   Assassination of Russian Tsar Alexander II begins a series of pogroms that triggers a wave of Russian Jewish immigration to the United States.

1882   Congress passes the Chinese Exclusion Act.
First country club in the United States founded in Brookline, Massachusetts.

1883   National League merges with the American Association and opens baseball to working-class fans.

1886   The Neighborhood Guild, the nation's first settlement house, opens in New York City.
Riot in Chicago's Haymarket Square breaks the

Knights of Labor.
American Federation of Labor is formed.

1887   Anti-Catholic American Protective Association is formed.

1888   Wanamaker's department store introduces a "bargain room," and competitors follow suit.

1889   Jane Addams opens Hull House, the nation's most celebrated settlement house, in Chicago.

1890   Jacob A. Riis publishes *How the Other Half Lives.*

1891   African-American Chicago physician Daniel Hale Williams establishes Provident Hospital, the nation's first interracially staffed hospital.

1892   General Electric opens the first corporate research and development division in the United States.
Strike at Andrew Carnegie's Homestead steel works fails.

1894   Pullman Sleeping Car Company strike fails.
Immigration Restriction League is formed.

1895   American-born Chinese in California form the Native Sons of the Golden State to counter nativism.

1897   George C. Tilyou opens Steeplechase Park on Coney Island in Brooklyn, New York.

1898   Congress passes the Erdman Act to provide for voluntary mediation of railroad labor disputes.

purchased Edison's General Electric Company in 1892 and established the country's first corporate research and development division. By 1914, General Electric was producing 85 percent of the world's light bulbs.

Other major American companies now established research and development laboratories. Standard Oil, U.S. Rubber, the chemical giant Du Pont, and the photographic company Kodak all became world leaders in their respective industries because of innovations their laboratories developed.

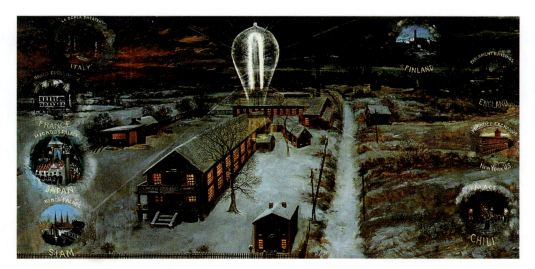

A humorous view of Thomas Edison's laboratories in Menlo Park, New Jersey, around 1880. There was no joking, however, about the potential of Edison's incandescent bulb and his other practical adaptations of electricity for everyday use. Electricity would soon transform life for millions of people. Edison's methods set the precedent for corporate research and development that would accelerate the pace of new discoveries with practical applications.

National Park Service, Edison National Historic Site

The modernization of industry that made the United States the world's foremost industrial nation after 1900 reflected organizational as well as technological innovation. As industries applied new technology and expanded their markets within and beyond national borders, their work forces expanded and their need for capital expenditures mounted. Coping with these changes required significant changes in corporate management.

THE CORPORATION AND ITS IMPACT

A corporation is an association of individuals with legal rights and liabilities separate from those of its members. This form of business organization had existed since colonial times but became a significant factor in the American economy with the growth of railroad companies in the 1850s. A key feature of a corporation is the separation of ownership from management. A corporation can raise capital by selling stock—ownership shares—to shareholders who may have no direct role in running it. The shareholders benefit from dividends drawn on the profits and, if the corporation thrives, from the rising value of its stock.

The corporation had two major advantages over other forms of business organization that made it attractive to investors. First, unlike a partnership, which can dissolve when a partner dies, a corporation can outlive its founders. This organizational stability permits long-term planning. Second, corporations enjoy limited liability. That means officials and shareholders are not personally liable for a corporation's debts. If it goes bankrupt, they stand to lose only what they have invested in it.

As large corporations emerged in major American industries, they had a ripple effect throughout the economy. Large corporations needed huge supplies of capital. They turned to the banks to help meet those needs, and the banks grew in response. The corporations stimulated technological change as they looked for ways to speed production, improve products, and lower costs. As they grew, they generated jobs throughout the economy.

By the early twentieth century, control of the workplace was shifting from well-paid, skilled artisans to managers, and semiskilled and unskilled workers were replacing skilled artisans. These new workers, often foreign-born, performed repetitive tasks for low wages.

Because the large industrial corporations usually located factories in cities, they stimulated urban growth. Large industrial districts sprawled along urban rivers and near urban rail lines, attracting thousands of workers. There were exceptions. Southern textile manufacturers tended to locate plants in villages and small towns and on the outskirts of larger cities. A few Northern entrepreneurs also constructed industrial communities outside major cities to save on land costs and ensure control over labor. Nonetheless, by 1900, fully 90 percent of all manufacturing occurred in cities.

Two organizational strategies—vertical integration and horizontal integration—helped successful corporations reduce competition and gain dominance in their industries. **Vertical integration** involved the consolidation of all functions related to a particular industry, from the extraction and transport of raw materials to the manufacture of products to finished-product distribution and sales. Geographical dispersal went hand in hand with vertical integration. Different functions—a factory and its source of raw materials, for example—were likely to be in different places, a development made possible by advances in communication like the telephone. The multiplication of functions also prompted the growth of corporate bureaucracy.

A good example of vertical integration occurred in the meatpacking industry under the influence of Gustavus Swift. Swift, a Boston native who moved to Chicago

Vertical integration   The consolidation of numerous production functions, from the extraction of the raw materials to the distribution and marketing of the finished products, under the direction of one firm.

in 1875, realized that refrigerated railway cars would make it possible to ship butchered meat from Western ranges to Eastern markets, eliminating the need to transport live cattle. When he invented a refrigerated car, however, he could not sell it to the major railroads. They feared losing the heavy investment they had already made in cattle cars and pens. Swift had the cars built himself and convinced a Canadian railroad with only a small stake in cattle shipping to haul them to Eastern markets. He established packing houses in Omaha and Kansas City, near the largest cattle markets; built refrigerated warehouses at key distribution points to store beef for transport or sale; and hired a sales force to convince Eastern butchers of the quality of his product. He now controlled the production, transportation, and distribution of his product, the essence of vertical integration. By 1881, he was shipping $200,000 worth of beef a week. Competitors soon followed his example.

Horizontal integration involved the merger of competitors in the same industry. John D. Rockefeller's Standard Oil Company pioneered horizontal integration in the 1880s. Born in western New York State, the son of a traveling patent medicine salesman, Rockefeller moved to Ohio at the age of 14 in 1853. He began investing in Cleveland oil refineries by his mid-twenties and formed Standard Oil in 1870. Using a variety of tactics—including threats, deceit, and price wars—Rockefeller rapidly acquired most of his competitors. Supported by investment bankers like J.P. Morgan, Standard Oil controlled 90 percent of the nation's oil refining by 1890. Acquiring oil fields and pipelines as well as refineries, Standard Oil achieved both vertical and horizontal integration. Rockefeller's dominant position allowed him to impose order and predictability in what had been an often chaotic industry, ensuring a continuous flow of profits. He closed inefficient refineries, opened new ones, and kept his operations up-to-date with the latest technologies.

Other entrepreneurs achieved similar dominance in other major industries and amassed similarly enormous personal fortunes. James B. Duke, who automated cigarette manufacturing, gained control of most of the tobacco industry. Andrew Carnegie consolidated much of the U.S. steel industry within his Carnegie Steel Company (later U.S. Steel). By 1900, Carnegie's company was producing one-quarter of the country's steel.

The giant corporations threatened to restrict opportunities for small entrepreneurs like the shopkeepers, farmers, and artisans who abounded at midcentury. In the words of one historian, the corporations "seemed to signal the end of an open, promising America and the beginning of a closed, unhappier society." Impersonal and governed by the profit margin, the modern corporation challenged the ideal of the self-made man and the belief that success and advancement would reward hard work.

Tabloid newspapers reinforced distrust of the corporations with exposés of the sharp business practices of corporate barons like Rockefeller and Carnegie and accounts of the sumptuous lifestyles of the corporate elite. Public concern notwithstanding, however, the giant corporations helped increase the efficiency of the American economy, raise the national standard of living, and transform the United States into a major world power. Corporate expansion generated jobs that attracted rural migrants and immigrants by the millions from Europe and Asia to American cities.

THE CHANGING NATURE OF WORK

The corporations provided abundant jobs, but they firmly controlled working conditions. A Pennsylvania coal miner spoke for many of his fellows in the 1890s when he remarked: "The working people of this country . . . find monopolies as strong as government itself. They find capital as rigid as absolute monarchy. They find their so-called independence a myth."

WHERE TO LEARN MORE

Senator John Heinz Pittsburgh Regional History Center, Pittsburgh, Pennsylvania
www.pghhistory.org

Horizontal integration   The merger of competitors in the same industry.

The deskilling process accelerated in the 1890s in response to new technologies, new workers, and workplace reorganization. By 1906, according to a U.S. Department of Labor report, industrial labor had been reduced to minute, low-skilled operations, making skilled artisans obsolete.

On the other hand, the birth of whole new industries—steel, automobiles, electrical equipment, cigarettes, food canning, and machine tools—created a huge demand for workers. Innovations in existing industries, like railroads, similarly spurred job growth. The number of people working for U.S. railroads increased from eighty thousand to more than 1 million between 1860 and 1910.

With massive waves of immigrants arriving from Europe and Asia between 1880 and 1920 (joined after 1910 by migrants from the American South), the supply of unskilled workers seemed limitless. The new workers, however, shared little of the wealth generated by industrial expansion and enjoyed few of the gadgets and products generated by the new manufacturing. The eastern European immigrants who comprised three-quarters of U.S. Steel's work force during the first decade of the twentieth century received less than $12.50 a week, significantly less than the $15.00 a week a federal government survey in 1910 said an urban family needed to subsist.

Nor did large corporations put profits into improved working conditions. In 1881, on-the-job accidents maimed or killed thirty thousand railroad workers. At a U.S. Steel plant in Pittsburgh, injuries or death claimed one out of every four workers between 1907 and 1910. In Chicago's meat plants, workers grew careless from fatigue and long-term exposure to the extreme temperatures of the workplace. Meat cutters working rapidly with sharp knives often sliced fingers off their numb hands. Upton Sinclair wrote in his novel *The Jungle* (1906), a chronicle of the killing floors of meatpacking plants in Chicago, "It was to be counted as a wonder that there were not more men slaughtered than cattle."

Factory workers typically worked ten hours a day, six days a week in the 1880s. Steel workers put in twelve hours a day. Because the mills operated around the clock, once every two weeks, when the workers changed shifts, one group took a "long turn" and stayed on the job for twenty-four hours.

Long hours affected family life. By Sunday, most factory workers were too tired to do more than sit around home. During the week, they had time only to eat and sleep. As one machinist testified before a U.S. Senate investigative committee in 1883:

> They were pretty well played out when they come home, and the first thing they think of is having something to eat and sitting down, and resting, and then of striking a bed. Of course when a man is dragged out in that way he is naturally cranky, and he makes all around him cranky . . . and staring starvation in the face makes him feel sad, and the head of the house being sad, of course the whole family are the same, so the house looks like a dull prison.

Workers lived as close to the factory as possible to reduce the time spent going to and from work and to save transportation expenses. The environment around many factories, however, was almost as unwholesome as the conditions inside. A visitor to Pittsburgh in 1884 noticed "a drab twilight" hanging over the areas around the steel mills, where "gas-lights, which are left burning at mid-day, shine out of the murkiness with a dull, reddish glare." Industrial wastes fouled streams and rivers around many plants.

In some industries, like the "needle," or garment, trade, operations remained small-scale. But salaries and working conditions in these industries were, if anything, worse than in the big factories. The garment industry was dominated by small manufacturers who contracted to assemble clothing for retailers from cloth provided by textile manufacturers. The manufacturers squeezed workers into small, cramped, poorly ventilated **sweatshops**. The workers pieced together garments on the manufacturer's sewing machines. A government investigator in Chicago in the 1890s described one sweatshop in a three-room tenement where the workers—a family of eight—both lived and worked: "The father, mother, two daughters, and a cousin work together making trousers at seventy-five cents a dozen pairs. . . . They work seven days a week. . . . Their destitution is very great."

Sweatshops   Small, poorly ventilated shops or apartments crammed with workers, often family members, who pieced together garments.

CHILD LABOR

Child labor was common in the garment trade and other industries. Shocked reformers in the 1890s told of the devastating effect of factory labor on children's lives. The legs of a 7-year-old girl were paralyzed and deformed because she toiled "day after day with little legs crossed, pulling out bastings from garments."

In the gritty coal mines of Pennsylvania, breaker boys, youths who stood on ladders to pluck waste matter from coal tumbling down long chutes, breathed harmful coal dust all day. Girls under sixteen made up half the work force in the

Noted urban photographer Lewis Hine captures the cramped working conditions and chid labor in this late nineteenth-century canning factory. Women and children provided a cheap and efficient work force for labor-intensive industries.

George Eastman House

silk mills of Scranton and Wilkes-Barre, Pennsylvania. Girls with missing fingers from mill accidents were a common sight in those towns.

By 1900, Pennsylvania and a few other states had passed legislation regulating child labor, but enforcement of these laws was lax. Parents desperate for income often lied about their children's age, and authorities were often sympathetic toward mill or mine owners, who paid taxes and provided other civic benefits.

WORKING WOMEN

The head of the Massachusetts Bureau of Labor Statistics observed in 1882, "A family of workers can always live well, but the man with a family of small children to support, unless his wife works also, has a small chance of living properly." Between 1870 and 1920, the number of women and children in the work force more than doubled.

Middle-class reformers worried about the impact on family life and on the women themselves. Employers paid them less than they paid men. A U.S. Department of Labor commissioner asserted that women worked only for "dress or pleasure." In one St. Louis factory in 1896, women received $4 a week for work for which men were paid $16 a week. An Iowa shoe saleswoman complained in 1886, "I don't get the salary the men clerks do, although this day I am 600 sales ahead! Call this justice? But I have to grin and bear it, because I am so unfortunate as to be a woman."

In 1900, fully 85 percent of wage-earning women were unmarried and under the age of 25. They supported siblings and contributed to their parents' income. A typical female factory worker earned $6 a week in 1900. On this wage, a married woman might help pull her family up to subsistence level. For a single woman on her own, however, it allowed little more, in writer O. Henry's words, "than marshmallows and tea."

Some working-class women turned to prostitution. The income from prostitution could exceed factory work by four or five times. "So is it any wonder," asked the Chicago Vice Commission in 1894, "that a tempted girl who receives only six dollars per week working with her hands sells her body for twenty-five dollars per week . . . ?" As much as 10 percent of New York City's female working-age population worked in the sex business in the 1890s. During depression years, the percentage was probably higher.

Victorian America condemned anyone guilty of even the most trivial moral transgression to social ostracism and treated the prostitute as a social outcast. Even those who urged understanding for women who violated convention faced exclusion. Kate Chopin, a New Orleans novelist, caused a tremendous uproar in the 1890s with stories that took a compassionate view of women involved in adultery, alcoholism, and divorce. Booksellers boycotted Theodore Dreiser's 1900 novel *Sister Carrie*, whose title character lived with a succession of men, one of them married.

Over time, more work options opened to women, but low wages and poor working conditions persisted. Women entered the needle trades after widespread introduction of the sewing machine in the 1870s. Factories gradually replaced sweatshops in the garment industry after 1900, but working conditions improved little.

The introduction of the typewriter transformed clerical office work, dominated by men until the 1870s, into a female preserve. Women were alleged to have the greater dexterity and tolerance for repetition that the new technology required. But they earned only half the salary of the men they replaced. Middle-class parents saw office work as clean and honorable compared with factory or

The new industrial age created great wealth and abject poverty, and the city became the stage upon which these hard economic lessons played out. Here, a "modest" Fifth Avenue mansion in turn-of-the-century New York City; further downtown, Jacob Riis found this tenement courtyard.

Getty Images Inc. Hutton Archive Photos

Photograph by Jacob A. Riis, The Jacob A. Riis Collection, Museum of the City of New York

sales work. Consequently, clerical positions drew growing numbers of native-born women into the urban work force after 1890. A top-paid office worker in the 1890s earned as much as $900 a year. Teaching, another acceptable occupation for middle-class women, typically paid only $500 a year.

By the turn of the century, women were gaining increased access to higher education. Coeducational colleges were rare, but by 1900 there were many women-only institutions. By 1910, women comprised 40 percent of all American college students, compared to 20 percent in 1870. Despite these gains, many professions—including those of physician and attorney—remained closed to women. Men still accounted for more than 95 percent of all doctors in 1900. Women also were rarely permitted to pursue doctoral degrees.

Women college graduates mostly found employment in such "nurturing" professions as nursing, teaching, and library work. Between 1900 and 1910, the number of trained women nurses increased sevenfold. In response to the growing problems of urban society, a relatively new occupation, social work, opened to women. Reflecting new theories on the nurturing role of women, school boards after 1900 turned exclusively to female teachers for the elementary grades.

Despite these gains, women's work remained segregated. Some reforms meant to improve working conditions for women reinforced this state of affairs. Protective legislation restricted women to "clean" occupations and limited their ability to compete with men in other jobs. As an economist explained in 1901,

"The wage bargaining power of men is weakened by the competition of women and children, hence a law restricting the hours of women and children may also be looked upon as a law to protect men in their bargaining power."

Women also confronted negative stereotypes. Most Americans in 1900 believed a woman's proper role was to care for home and family. The system of "treating" on dates reinforced stories about loose sales-girls, flirtatious secretaries, and easy factory workers. Newspapers and magazines published exposés of working girls descending into prostitution. These images encouraged sexual harassment at work, which was rarely punished.

Working women faced a difficult dilemma. To justify their desire for education and training, they had to argue that it would enhance their roles as wives and mothers. To gain improved wages and working conditions, they increasingly supported protective legislation that restricted their opportunities in the workplace.

RESPONSES TO POVERTY AND WEALTH

While industrial magnates flaunted their fabulous wealth, working men and women led hard lives on meager salaries and in crowded dwellings. In his exposé of poverty in New York, *How the Other Half Lives* (1890), Danish-born urban reformer Jacob Riis wrote that "the half that is on top cares little for the struggles, and less for the fate of those who are underneath so long as it is able to hold them there and keep its own seat." (See American Views: "Tenement Life" p. 477)

The industrial economy strained working-class family life. Workplace accidents and deaths left many families with only one parent. Infant mortality among the working poor in New York was nearly twice the citywide norm in 1900. Epidemic diseases, especially typhoid, an illness spread by impure water, devastated crowded working-class districts.

Inadequate housing was the most visible badge of poverty. Crammed into four- to six-story buildings on tiny lots, **tenement** apartments in urban slums were notorious for their lack of ventilation and light.

Authorities did nothing to enforce laws prohibiting overcrowding for fear of leaving people homeless. The population density of New York's tenement district in 1894 was 986.4 people per acre, the highest in the world at the time. (Today, the densest areas of American cities rarely exceed 400 people per acre, and only Calcutta, India, and Lagos, Nigeria, approach the crowding of turn-of-the-century New York; today Manhattan has 84 residents per acre).

The settlement house movement, which originated in England, sought to moderate the effects of poverty through neighborhood reconstruction. New York's Neighborhood Guild, established in 1886, was the first settlement house in the country; Chicago's **Hull House**, founded in 1889 by Jane Addams, a young Rockford (Illinois) College graduate, became the most famous.

The settlement house provided the working poor with facilities and education to help them improve their environment and, eventually, to escape it. By 1900, there were more than one hundred settlement houses throughout the country.

At Hull House, a rambling old residence in a working-class immigrant neighborhood, Italian immigrants and their families came to settle legal disputes and formed the Young Citizens' Club to discuss municipal issues. Addams renovated an adjacent saloon and transformed it into a gym. She began a day nursery as well. When workers at a nearby knitting factory went on strike, Addams arbitrated the conflict.

Settlement house gyms like the one Addams built for Hull-House provided them with much-needed recreational space. So too did the athletic fields and playgrounds built adjacent to public schools after 1900.

Tenements Four- to six-story residential dwellings, once common in New York, built on tiny lots without regard to providing ventilation or light.

Hull House Chicago settlement house that became part of a broader neighborhood revitalization project led by Jane Addams.

• AMERICAN VIEWS •

TENEMENT LIFE

In 1890, the Danish immigrant Jacob A. Riis published How the Other Half Lives, *an exposé of conditions among immigrants in New York City's Lower East Side. Riis's gruesome depictions, complete with vivid photographs, shocked readers and provided an impetus for housing reform in New York and other cities. His scientific tone, devoid of sensationalism, rendered the scenes that much more dramatic. For a nation that valued family life and the sanctity of childhood, Riis's accounts of how the environment, inside and outside the tenement, destroyed young lives provided moving testimony that for some, and perhaps many immigrants, the "promise" had been taken out of the Promised Land.*

WHAT IS Jacob Riis's attitude toward the tenement dwellers? Considering the destitute character of the family Riis describes, what sort of assistance do you think they receive? Why do you suppose the authorities were reluctant to enforce sanitary, capacity, and building regulations in these neighborhoods?

Look into any of these houses, everywhere the same piles of rags, of malodorous bones and musty paper all of which the sanitary police flatter themselves they have banished. . . . Here is a "parlor" and two pitch-dark coops called bedrooms. Truly, the bed is all there is room for. The family teakettle is on the stove, doing duty for the time being as a wash-boiler. By night it will have returned to its proper use again, a practical illustration of how poverty . . . makes both ends meet. One, two, three beds are there, if the old boxes and heaps of foul straw can be called by that name; a broken stove with crazy pipe from which the smoke leaks at every joint, a table of rough boards propped up on boxes, piles of rubbish in the corner. The closeness and smell are appalling. . . .

Well do I recollect the visit of a health inspector to one of these tenements on a July day when the thermometer outside was climbing high in the nineties; but inside, in that awful room, with half a dozen persons washing, cooking, and sorting rags, lay the dying baby alongside the stove, where the doctor's thermometer ran up to 115 degrees! Perishing for the want of a breath of fresh air in this city of untold charities! . . .

A message came one day last spring summoning me to a Mott Street tenement in which lay a child dying from some unknown disease. With the "charity doctor" I found the patient on the top floor, stretched upon two chairs in a dreadfully stifling room. She was gasping in the agony of peritonitis [abdominal infection] that had already written its death-sentence on her wan and pinched face. The whole family, father, mother, and four ragged children, sat around looking on with the stony resignation of helpless despair that had long since given up the fight against fate as useless. A glance around the wretched room left no doubt as to the cause of the children's condition. "Improper nourishment," said the doctor, which translated to suit the place, meant starvation. The father's hands were crippled from lead poisoning. He had not been able to work for a year. A contagious disease of the eyes, too long neglected, had made the mother and one of the boys nearly blind. The children cried with hunger. . . . For months the family had subsisted on two dollars a week from the priest, and a few loaves and a piece of corned beef which the sisters sent them on Saturday. The doctor gave direction for the treatment of the child, knowing that it was possible only to alleviate its sufferings until death should end them, and left some money for food for the rest. An hour later, when I returned, I found them feeding the dying child with ginger ale, bought for two cents a bottle at the pedlar's cart down the street. A pitying neighbor had proposed it as the one thing she could think of as likely to make the child forget its misery.

According to the **Gospel of Wealth**, a theory popular among industrialists, intellectuals, and some politicians, any intervention on behalf of the poor was of doubtful benefit. Hard work and perseverance, in this view, led to wealth. Poverty, by implication, resulted from the flawed character of the poor. Steel tycoon Andrew Carnegie sought to soften this doctrine by stressing the responsibility of the affluent to set an example for the working class and to return some of their wealth to the communities in which they lived. Carnegie accordingly endowed libraries, cultural institutions, and schools throughout the country. Beneficial as they might be, however, these philanthropic efforts scarcely addressed the causes of poverty, and few industrialists followed Carnegie's example.

Social Darwinism, a flawed attempt to apply Charles Darwin's theory of biological evolution to human society, emerged as a more common justification than the Gospel of Wealth for the growing gap between rich and poor. According to social Darwinism, the human race evolves only through competition. The fit survive, the weak perish, and humanity moves forward. Wealth reflects fitness; poverty, weakness. For governments or private agencies to interfere with this natural process is futile. Thus Columbia University president Nicholas Murray Butler, claiming that "nature's cure for most social and political diseases is better than man's," warned against charity for the poor in 1900. Standard Oil's John D. Rockefeller concurred, asserting that the survival of the fittest is "the working out of a law of nature and a law of God."

WORKERS ORGANIZE

The growing power of industrial corporations and the declining power of workers generated social tensions reminiscent of the sectional crisis that triggered the Civil War. Two prolonged depressions, one beginning in 1873 and the other in 1893—threw as many as 2 million laborers out of work. Skilled workers, their security undermined by deskilling and their hopes of becoming managers or starting their own businesses disappearing, saw the nation "drifting," as a carpenter put it in 1870, "to that condition of society where a few were rich, and the many very poor."

Beginning after the depression of 1873 and continuing through World War I, workers fought their loss of independence to industrial capital by organizing and striking (see the overview table "Workers Organize" p. 479). The first episode in this conflict was the railroad strike of 1877, sometimes referred to as the **Great Uprising**. When Baltimore & Ohio Railroad workers struck in July to protest another series of pay cuts, President Rutherford B. Hayes dispatched federal troops to protect the line's property. The use of federal troops infuriated railroad workers throughout the East and Midwest, and they stopped work as well. Violence erupted in Pittsburgh when the state militia opened fire on strikers and their families, killing twenty-five, including a woman and three children. As news of the violence spread, so did the strike, as far as Galveston, Texas, and San Francisco. Over the next two weeks, police and federal troops continued to clash with strikers. By the time this first nationwide work stoppage in American history ended, more than one hundred had been killed. The wage cuts remained.

The **Knights of Labor**, a union of craft workers founded in Philadelphia in 1869, grew dramatically after the Great Uprising under the leadership of Terence V. Powderly. The Knights saw "an inevitable . . . conflict between the wage system of labor and [the] republican system of government." Remarkably inclusive for its time, the Knights welcomed black workers and women to its ranks. Victories in several small railroad strikes in 1884 and 1885 boosted its membership to nearly one million workers by 1886.

In that year, the Knights led a movement for an eight-hour workday. Ignoring the advice of the national leadership to avoid strikes, local chapters staged more than 1,500 strikes involving more than 340,000 workers. Workers also organized boycotts against manufacturers and ran candidates for local elections. Social

Gospel of Wealth   Thesis that hard work and perseverance lead to wealth, implying that poverty is a character flaw.

Social Darwinism   The application of Charles Darwin's theory of biological evolution to society, holding that the fittest and wealthiest survive, the weak and the poor perish, and government action is unable to alter this "natural" process.

Great Uprising   Unsuccessful railroad strike of 1877 to protest wage cuts and the use of federal troops against strikers; the first nationwide work stoppage in American history.

Knights of Labor   Labor union founded in 1869 that included skilled and unskilled workers irrespective of race or gender.

OVERVIEW

WORKERS ORGANIZE

Organization	History	Strategies
Knights of Labor	Founded in 1869; open to all workers; declined after 1886	Disapproved of strikes; supported a broad array of labor reforms, including cooperatives; favored political involvement
American Federation of Labor	Founded in 1886; open to craft-workers only, and organized by craft; hostile to black workers and women; became the major U.S. labor organization after 1880s	Opposed political involvement; supported a limited number of labor reforms; approved of strikes
Industrial Workers of the World	Founded in 1905; consisted mainly of semiskilled and unskilled immigrant workers; represented a small portion of the work force; disappeared after World War I	Highly political; supported socialist programs; approved of strikes and even violence to achieve ends

reformer Henry George made a strong, though losing, effort in the New York City mayoral race, and labor candidates won several local offices in Chicago.

Employers convinced the courts to order strikers back to work and used local authorities to arrest strikers for trespassing or obstructing traffic. In early May 1886, police killed four unarmed workers during a skirmish with strikers in Chicago. A bomb exploded at a meeting to protest the slayings in the city's Haymarket Square, killing seven policemen and four strikers and wounding one hundred. Eight strike leaders were tried for the deaths, and despite a lack of evidence linking them to the bomb, four were executed.

The Haymarket Square incident and a series of disastrous walkouts that followed it weakened the Knights of Labor. By 1890, it had shrunk to less than 100,000 members. Thereafter, the **American Federation of Labor (AFL)**, formed in 1886, became the major organizing body for skilled workers.

The AFL, led by British immigrant Samuel Gompers, emphasized **collective bargaining**—negotiations between management and union representatives—to secure workplace concessions. The AFL also discouraged political activism among its members. With this business unionism, the AFL proved more effective than the Knights of Labor at meeting the needs of skilled workers, but it left out the growing numbers of unskilled workers, black workers, and women to whom the Knights had given a glimmer of hope.

The AFL organized skilled workers by craft and focused on a few basic workplace issues important to each craft. The result was greater cohesion and discipline. In 1889 and 1890, more than 60 percent of AFL-sponsored strikes were successful. A series of work stoppages in the building trades between 1888 and 1891, for example, won an eight-hour day and a national agreement with builders.

In 1892, Andrew Carnegie dealt the steelworkers' union a major setback in the Homestead strike. Carnegie's manager, Henry Clay Frick, announced that he would negotiate only with workers individually at Homestead and not renew the union's collective bargaining contract. Frick locked the union workers

18–5
Address by George Engel, Condemned Haymarket Anarchist (1886)

American Federation of Labor (AFL)
Union formed in 1886 that organized skilled workers along craft lines and emphasized a few workplace issues rather than a broad social program.

Collective bargaining
Representatives of a union negotiating with management on behalf of all members.

out of the plant and hired three hundred armed guards to protect the nonunion ("scab") workers he planned to hire in their place. Union workers, with the help of their families and unskilled workers, seized control of Homestead's roads and utilities. In a bloody confrontation, they drove back Frick's forces. Nine strikers and seven guards died. But Pennsylvania's governor called out the state militia to open the plant and protect the nonunion workers. After four months, the union capitulated. With the defeat of the union, skilled steelworkers lost their power on the shop floor. Eventually, mechanization cost them their jobs.

In 1894, workers suffered another setback in the Pullman strike, against George Pullman's Palace Sleeping Car Company. When the company cut wages for workers at its plant in the "model" suburb it built outside Chicago without a corresponding cut in the rent it charged workers for their company-owned housing, the workers appealed for support to the American Railway Union (ARU), led by Eugene V. Debs. The membership of the ARU, an independent union not affiliated with the AFL, had swelled to more than 150,000 workers after it won a strike earlier in 1894 against the Great Northern Railroad. Debs ordered a boycott of any trains with Pullman cars. The railroads fired workers who refused to handle trains with Pullman cars. Debs called for all ARU members to walk off the job, crippling rail travel nationwide. When Debs refused to honor a federal court injunction against the strike, President Cleveland, at the railroads' request, ordered federal troops to enforce it. Debs was arrested, and the strike and the union were broken.

These setbacks and the depression that began in 1893 left workers and their unions facing an uncertain future. But, growing public opposition to the use of troops, the high-handed tactics of industrialists, and the rising concerns of Americans about the power of big business sustained the unions. Workers would call more than 22,000 strikes over the next decade, the majority of them union-sponsored. Still, no more than 7 percent of the American work force was organized by 1900.

New Immigrants

The late-nineteenth-century was a period of unprecedented worldwide population movements. The United States was not the only New World destination for the migrants of this period. Many also found their way to Brazil, Argentina, and Canada.

The scale of overseas migration to the United States after 1870 dwarfed all that preceded it. Between 1870 and 1910, the country received more than 20 million immigrants. Before the Civil War, most immigrants came from northern Europe. Most of the new immigrants, in contrast, came from southern and eastern Europe. Swelling their ranks were migrants from Mexico and Asia, as well as internal migrants moving from the countryside to American cities (see Map 18–1).

By that time, the industrial work force was charging. As the large factories installed labor- and time-saving machinery, unskilled foreign-born labor flooded onto the shop floor. For many reasons, not least of which were the adjustments required for life in a new country, labor radicalism was not a high priority for many of the newcomers. Immigrants transformed not only the workplace, but the cities where they settled and the nation itself. In the process, they changed themselves.

OLD WORLD BACKGROUNDS

A growing rural population combined with unequal land distribution to create economic distress in late-nineteenth-century Europe. More and more people found themselves working ever-smaller plots as laborers rather than owners. In Poland, laborers accounted for 80 percent of the agricultural population in the

WHAT IMPACT did new immigration and migration have on cities in the North?

MAP EXPLORATION

To explore an interactive version of this map, go to **http://www.prenhall.com/goldfield2/map18.1**

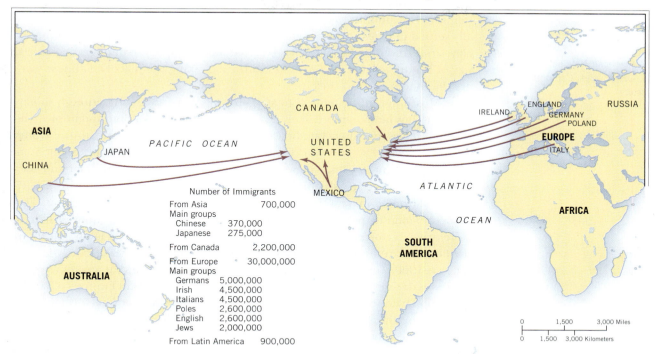

Number of Immigrants

From Asia	700,000
Main groups	
Chinese	370,000
Japanese	275,000
From Canada	2,200,000
From Europe	30,000,000
Main groups	
Germans	5,000,000
Irish	4,500,000
Italians	4,500,000
Poles	2,600,000
English	2,600,000
Jews	2,000,000
From Latin America	900,000

MAP 18–1

Patterns of Immigration, 1820–1914   The migration to the United States was part of a worldwide transfer of population that accelerated with the industrial revolution and the accompanying improvements in transportation.

WHAT FORCES propelled so many people to emigrate from European countries?

1860s. Similar conditions prevailed in the Mezzogiorno region of southern Italy, home of three out of four Italian emigrants to America.

For Russian Jews, religious persecution compounded economic hardship. In tsarist Russia, Jews could not own real estate and were barred from work in farming, teaching, the civil service, and the law. Confined to designated cities, they struggled to support themselves. After the assassination of Tsar Alexander II in 1881, which some leaders falsely blamed on Jews, the government sanctioned a series of violent attacks on Jewish settlements known as **pogroms**. At the same time, the government forced Jews into fewer towns, deepening their poverty and making them easier targets for violence.

The late-nineteenth-century transportation technologies permitted people to leave Europe. Railroad construction boomed in Europe during the 1870s and 1880s, and steamship companies in several European countries built giant vessels to transport passengers quickly and safely across the Atlantic. The companies sent agents into Russia, Poland, Italy, and the Austro-Hungarian empire to solicit business.

Sometime during the 1880s, an agent from the Hamburg-American Line (HAPAG), a German steamship company, visited a village in the Russian Ukraine where the great grandparents of one of this book's authors lived. Shortly after his visit, they boarded a train to Austrian-occupied Poland and Hamburg. There they boarded a HAPAG steamer emblazoned with a large banner proclaiming "Willkommen" ("Welcome"). Just boarding that ship they felt they were entering the United States. Millions of others like them sailed on ocean liners from Germany, Italy, and Great Britain over the next thirty years.

WHERE TO LEARN MORE

Strawbery Banke,
Portsmouth,
New Hampshire
www.strawberybanke.org

Pogroms   Government-directed attacks against Jewish citizens, property, and villages in tsarist Russia beginning in the 1880s; a primary reason for Russian Jewish migration to the United States.

WHERE TO LEARN MORE

★ Japanese American National
Museum, Los Angeles, California
www.janm.org

19–12
Mary Antin, *The Promise Land*
(1912)

Chain migration Process common
to many immigrant groups whereby
one family member brings over
other family members, who in turn
bring other relatives and friends and
occasionally entire villages.

Chinese and Japanese immigrants also came to the United States in appreciable numbers for the first time during the late nineteenth century. Most Chinese immigrants came from Canton in South China and worked on railroads and in mines throughout the West and as farm laborers in California. Many eventually settled in cities such as San Francisco where they established residential enclaves referred to as Chinatowns. The first wave of Japanese immigrants came by way of Hawaii to work on farms in California, taking the place of Chinese workers who had moved to the cities.

Most migrants intended to stay only a year or two, long enough to earn money to buy land or, more likely, to enter a business back home and improve life for themselves and their families. Roughly half of all immigrants to the United States between 1880 and World War I returned to their country of origin. Some made several round trips. As Jews were unwelcome in the lands they left, no more than 10 percent of Jewish immigrants returned to Europe.

Most newcomers were young men. (Jews again were the exception: They tended to migrate permanently in families.) Immigrants easily found work in the large urban factories with their voracious demands for unskilled labor. Except for the Japanese, few immigrants came to work on farms after 1880.

By 1900, women began to equal men among all immigrant groups as young men who decided to stay sent for their families. The success of Francesco Barone, a Buffalo tavern owner, convinced eight thousand residents of his former village in Sicily to migrate to that city, many arriving on tickets Barone purchased, a process called **chain migration**.

Immigrants tended to live in neighborhoods among people from the same homeland and preserve key aspects of their Old World culture. For Italians from the Mezzogiorno, for example, the family was the basic institution for obtaining work and securing assistance in times of stress, death, or sickness.

The desire of the new immigrants to retain their cultural traditions led contemporary observers to doubt their ability to assimilate into American society. Even sympathetic observers, such as social workers, marveled at the utterly foreign character of immigrant districts. In 1900, Philadelphia social worker Emily Dinwiddie visited an Italian neighborhood and described "black-eyed children, rolling and tumbling together, the gaily colored dresses of the women and the crowds of street vendors, that give the neighborhood a wholly foreign appearance."

THE NEIGHBORHOOD

Rarely did a particular ethnic group comprise more than 50 percent of a neighborhood. Chinese were the exception, but even the borders of Chinatowns usually overlapped with other neighborhoods.

In smaller cities and in the urban South, where foreign-born populations were smaller, ethnic groups were more geographically dispersed, though occasionally they might inhabit the same neighborhood. In turn-of-the-century Memphis, for example, Irish, Italian, and Jewish immigrants lived cheek by jowl in a single immigrant district (called the "Pinch"), sharing schools and recreational space even as they led their singular institutional, religious, and family lives.

Immigrants maintained their cultural traditions through the establishment of religious and communal institutions. The church or synagogue became the focal point for immigrant neighborhood life. Much more than a place of worship, it was a school for transmitting Old World values and language to American-born children and a recreational facility and a gathering place for community leaders. Jewish associations called *landsmanshaften* arranged for burials, jobs, housing, and support for the sick, poor, and elderly.

Religious institutions played a less formal role among Chinese and Japanese neighborhoods. For them, the family functioned as the source of religious activity and communal organization. Chinatowns were organized in clans of people with the same surname. An umbrella organization called the Chinese Consolidated Benevolent Association emerged; it functioned like the Jewish *landsmanshaften*. Perhaps most important, the association shipped the bones of deceased members back to China for burial in ancestral cemeteries. A similar association, the Japanese Association of America, governed the Japanese community in the United States. This organization was sponsored by the Japanese government, which was sensitive to mistreatment of its citizens abroad and anxious that immigrants set a good example. The Japanese Association, unlike other ethnic organizations, actively encouraged assimilation and stressed the importance of Western dress and learning English.

Ethnic newspapers, theaters, and schools supplemented associational life for immigrants. The Jewish *Daily Forward,* first published in New York in 1897, reminded readers of the importance of keeping the Sabbath while admonishing them to adopt American customs.

THE JOB

All immigrants perceived the job as the way to independence and as a way out, either back to the Old World or into the larger American society. Immigrants typically received their first job with the help of a countryman. Italian, Chinese, Japanese, and Mexican newcomers worked with contractors who placed them in jobs. They exacted a fee, sometimes extortionate, for their services. Other immigrant groups, such as Poles and Russian Jews, often secured work through their ethnic associations or village or family connections. Family members sometimes exchanged jobs with one another.

The type of work available to immigrants depended on their skills, the local economy, and local discrimination. Mexican migrants to southern California, for example, concentrated in railroad construction, replacing Chinese laborers when the federal government excluded Chinese immigration after 1882. Mexicans built the interurban rail lines of Los Angeles in 1900 and established communities at their construction camps. Los Angeles businessmen barred Mexicans from other occupations. Similarly, Chinese immigrants were confined to work in laundries and restaurants within the boundaries of Los Angeles's Chinatown. The Japanese who came to Los Angeles around 1900 were forced into sectors of the economy native-born whites had either shunned or failed to exploit. The Japanese turned this discrimination to their benefit when they transformed the cultivation of market garden crops into a major agricultural enterprise. By 1904, Japanese farmers owned more than 50,000 acres in California. George Shima, who came to California from Japan in 1889 with a little capital, made himself the "Potato King" of the Sacramento Delta. By 1913, Shima owned 28,000 acres of farmland.

Stereotypes also channeled immigrants' work options, sometimes benefiting one group at the expense of another. Jewish textile entrepreneurs, for example, sometimes hired only Italians because they thought them less prone to unionization than Jewish workers. Pittsburgh steelmakers preferred Polish workers to the black workers who began arriving in northern cities in appreciable numbers after 1900. This began the decades-long tradition of handing down steel mill jobs through the generations in Polish families.

Jews, alone among European ethnic groups, found work almost exclusively with one another. Jews comprised three-quarters of the more than half-million workers in New York's City's garment industry in 1910. Jews were also heavily concentrated in the retail trade.

QUICK REVIEW

Maintenance of Cultural Traditions
- Religious and communal institutions played a key role in maintaining immigrants' cultural traditions.
- Churches were often the focal point of immigrant life.
- The family was the most important institution in Chinese and Japanese communities.

WHERE TO LEARN MORE

Pasa al Norte, El Paso, Texas
www.utminers.utep.edu/panihm/
default.htm

Like their native-born counterparts, few married immigrant women worked outside the home, but unlike the native-born, many Italian and Jewish women did piecework for the garment industry in their apartments. Unmarried Polish women often worked in factories or as domestic servants. Japanese women, married and single, worked with their families on farms. Until revolution in China in 1911 began to erode traditional gender roles, married Chinese immigrant women typically remained home.

The paramount goal for many immigrants was to work for themselves rather than someone else. Most new arrivals, however, had few skills and no resources beyond their wits with which to realize their dreams. Major banks at the time were unlikely to extend even a small business loan to a budding ethnic entrepreneur. Family members and small ethnic-based community banks provided the initial stake for most immigrant businesses. Many of these banks failed, but a few survived and prospered. For example, the Bank of Italy, established by Amadeo Pietro Giannini in San Francisco in 1904, eventually grew into the Bank of America, one of the nation's largest financial institutions today.

Immigrants could not fully control their own destinies in the United States any more than native-born Americans could. Hard work did not always ensure success. Almost all immigrants, however, faced the antiforeign prejudice of American **nativism**.

NATIVISM

Immigrants have not always received a warm reception. Ben Franklin groused about the "foreignness" of German immigrants during the colonial era. From the 1830s to 1860, nativist sentiment, directed mainly at Irish Catholic immigrants, expressed itself in occasional violence and job discrimination.

When immigration revived after the Civil War, so did antiforeign sentiment. But late-nineteenth-century nativism differed in two ways from its antebellum predecessor. First, the target was no longer Irish Catholics but the even more numerous Catholics and Jews of southern and eastern Europe, people whose language and usually darker complexions set them apart from the native-born majority. Second, late-nineteenth-century nativism maintained that there was a natural hierarchy of race. At the top, with the exception of the Irish, were northern European whites, especially those of Anglo-Saxon descent. Following below them were French, Slavs, Poles, Italians, Jews, Asians, and Africans. Social Darwinism, which justified the class hierarchy, reinforced scientific racism.

When the "inferior" races arrived in the United States in significant numbers after 1880, a prominent Columbia University professor wrote in 1887 that Hungarians and Italians were "of such a character as to endanger our civilization." Nine years later, the director of the U.S. census warned that eastern and southern Europeans were "beaten men from beaten races. They have none of the ideas and aptitudes which fit men to take up readily and easily the problem of self-care and self-government." The result of unfettered migration would be "race suicide."

In the mid-1870s, a Chicago newspaper described recently arrived Bohemian immigrants (from the present-day Czech Republic) as "depraved beasts, harpies, decayed physically and spiritually, mentally and morally, thievish and licentious." A decade later, with eastern Europeans still pouring into Chicago, another newspaper suggested: "Let us whip these slavic wolves back to the European dens from which they issue, or in some way exterminate them." The *New York Times* concluded that Americans "pretty well agreed" that these foreigners were "of a kind which we are better without." *Scientific American* warned immigrants to "assimilate" quickly or "share the fate of the native Indians" and face "a quiet but sure extermination."

Nativism Favoring the interests and culture of native-born inhabitants over those of immigrants.

Such sentiments generated proposals to restrict foreign immigration. Chinese immigrants' different culture and their willingness to accept low wages in mining and railroad construction provoked resentment among native- and European-born workers. In 1870, the Republican-dominated Congress passed the Naturalization Act, which limited citizenship to "white persons and persons of African descent." The act was specifically intended to prevent Chinese from becoming citizens—a ban not lifted until 1943—but it affected other Asian groups also. The Chinese Exclusion Act of 1882 made the Chinese the only ethnic group in the world that could not emigrate freely to the United States. Anti-Asian violence raced through mining communities in the West for the next two years.

Labor competition also contributed to the rise of another anti-immigrant organization. A group of skilled workers and small businessmen formed the American Protective Association (APA) in 1887 and claimed half a million members a year later. The APA sought to limit Catholic civil rights in the United States to protect the jobs of Protestant workingmen.

The Immigration Restriction League (IRL), formed in 1894, proposed to require prospective immigrants to pass a literacy test that they presumed most southern and eastern Europeans would fail. The IRL vowed that its legislation would protect "the wages of our workingmen against the fatal competition of low-price labor."

The IRL ultimately failed to have its literacy requirement enacted. The return of prosperity and the growing preference of industrialists for immigrant labor put an end to calls for formal restrictions on immigration for the time being.

Immigrants and their communal associations fought attempts to impede free access of their countrymen to the United States. The Japanese government even hinted at violent retaliation if Congress ever enacted restrictive legislation similar to that imposed on the Chinese. But most immigrants believed that the more "American" they became, the less prejudice they would encounter.

In 1895, a group of American-born Chinese in California formed a communal association called the Native Sons of the Golden State (a deliberate response to a nativist organization that called itself the Native Sons of the Golden West). The association's constitution declared, "It is imperative that no members shall have sectional, clannish, Tong [a secret fraternal organization] or party prejudices against each other. . . . Whoever violates this provision shall be expelled." A guidebook written at the same time for immigrant Jews recommended that they "hold fast," calling that attitude "most necessary in America. Forget your past, your customs, and your ideals." Although it is doubtful whether most Jewish immigrants followed this advice whole, it nonetheless reflects the way the pressure to conform modified the cultures of all immigrant groups.

Assimilation connotes the loss of one culture in favor of another. The immigrant experience of the late nineteenth and early twentieth centuries might better be described as a process of adjustment between old ways and new, which resulted in entirely new cultural forms. The Japanese, for example, had not gone to Los Angeles to become truck farmers, but circumstances led them to that occupation. Sometimes economics and the availability of alternatives resulted in cultural modifications. In the old country, Portuguese held *festas* every Sunday honoring a patron saint. In New England towns, they confined the tradition to their churches instead of parading through the streets.

In a few cases, the New World offered greater opportunities to follow cultural traditions than the Old. Young women who migrated from Italy's Abruzzi region to Rochester, New York, found that it was easier to retain their Old World moral code and marry earlier in late-nineteenth-century Rochester, where young men outnumbered them significantly. In a similar way, Sicilians who migrated to lower

QUICK REVIEW

The Naturalization Act of 1870

◆ Limited citizenship to "white persons and persons of African descent."

◆ Act intended to bar Chinese from becoming citizens.

◆ Chinese Exclusion Act of 1882 made Chinese the only group that could not emigrate freely to the United States.

WHERE TO LEARN MORE W

Angel Island State Park, San Francisco Bay, California
www.angelisland.org

African Americans gather for a religious service at night in the streets of New York City near the turn of the century.

Brown Brothers

Manhattan discovered that ready access to work and relatively high geographical mobility permitted them to live near and among their extended families much more easily than in Sicily.

Despite native-born whites' antagonism toward recent immigrants, the greatest racial divide in America remained that between black and white. New-comers viewed their "whiteness" as both a common bond with other European immigrant groups and a badge of acceptance into the larger society.

ROOTS OF THE GREAT MIGRATION

Nearly 90 percent of African Americans still lived in the South in 1900, most in rural areas. Between 1880 and 1900 black families began to move into the great industrial cities of the Northeast and Midwest. They were drawn by the same economic promise that attracted overseas migrants and were pushed by growing persecution in the South. They were also responding to the appeals of black Northerners. As a leading black newspaper, the *Chicago Defender* argued in the early 1900s, "To die from the bite of frost is far more glorious than at the hands of a mob. I beg you, my brother, to leave the benighted land." Job opportunities probably outweighed all other factors in motivating what became known as the **Great Migration.**

In most northern cities in 1900, black people typically worked as common laborers or domestic servants. They competed with immigrants for jobs, and in most cases they lost. Immigrants even claimed jobs that black workers had once dominated, like barbering and service work in hotels, restaurants, and transportation. Fannie Barrier Williams, a turn-of-the-century black activist in Chicago, complained that between 1895 and 1905, "the colored people of Chicago have lost . . . nearly every occupation of which they once had almost a monopoly."

Black women had particularly few options in the northern urban labor force. The retail and clerical jobs that attracted young working-class white women remained closed to black women. As one historian concluded, advertisers and corporate executives demanded "a pleasing physical appearance (or voice)—one that conformed to a native-born white American standard of female beauty [and served] as an important consideration in hiring office receptionists, secretaries, department store clerks, and telephone operators." Addie W. Hunter, who qualified for a civil service clerical position in Boston, could not find work to match her training. She concluded in 1916, "For the way things stand at present, it is useless to have the requirements. Color . . . will always be in the way."

Black migrants confronted similar frustrations in their quest for a place to live. They were restricted to segregated urban ghettos. In 1860, four out of every five black people in Detroit lived in a clearly defined district, for example. The black

---

WHERE TO LEARN MORE

Statue of Liberty National Monument and Ellis Island, New York, New York
www.nps.gov/stli

Great Migration The mass movement of African Americans from the rural South to the urban North.

districts in Northern cities were more diverse than those of Southern cities. Migration brought rural Southerners, urban Southerners, and West Indians (especially in New York) together with the black Northerners already living there. People of all social classes lived in these districts.

The difficulties that black families faced to make ends meet paralleled in some ways those of immigrant working-class families. Restricted job options, however, limited the income of black families, even with black married women five times more likely to work than married white women. In black families, moreover, working teenage children were less likely to stay home and contribute their paychecks to the family income.

Popular culture reinforced the marginalization of African Americans, belittling black people and black characters with names like "Useless Peabody" and "Moses Abraham Highbrow." Immigrants frequented vaudeville and minstrel shows and absorbed the culture of racism from them. The new medium of film perpetuated the negative stereotypes.

An emerging middle-class leadership—including Robert Abbott, publisher of the *Chicago Defender*—sought to develop black businesses. But chronic lack of capital kept black businesses mostly small and confined to the ghetto. Black businesses failed at a high rate. Most black people worked outside the ghetto for white employers. Economic marginalization often attracted unsavory businesses to black neighborhoods. One recently arrived migrant from the South complained that in his Cleveland neighborhood, his family was surrounded by loafers, "gamblers [and] pocket pickers; I can not raise my children here like they should be. This is one of the worst places in principle you ever looked on in your life."

Other black institutions proved more lasting than black businesses. In Chicago in 1891, black physician Daniel Hale Williams established Provident Hospital, the nation's first interracially staffed hospital, with the financial help of wealthy white Chicagoans. Although it failed as an interracial experiment, the hospital thrived, providing an important training ground for black physicians and nurses.

The organization of black branches of the Young Men's and Young Women's Christian Association provided living accommodations, social facilities, and employment information for young black people. By 1910, black settlement houses modeled after white versions appeared in several cities.

NEW CITIES

Despite the hardships associated with urban life for both immigrants and black people, the American city continued to act, in the words of contemporary novelist Theodore Dreiser, as a "giant magnet." Immigration from abroad and migration from American farms to the cities resulted in an urban explosion during the late nineteenth century (see Map 18–2). The nation's population tripled between 1860 and 1920, but the urban population increased ninefold. Of the 1,700 cities listed in the 1900 census, only a handful—less than 2 percent—even existed in 1800.

In Europe, a few principal cities like Paris and Berlin absorbed most of the urban growth during this period. In the United States, in contrast, growth was more evenly distributed among many cities.

Despite the relative evenness of growth, a distinctive urban system had emerged by 1900, with New York and Chicago anchoring an urban-industrial core extending

WHO MADE up the new middle class?

MAP EXPLORATION

To explore an interactive version of this map, go to **http://www.prenhall.com/goldfield2/map18.2**

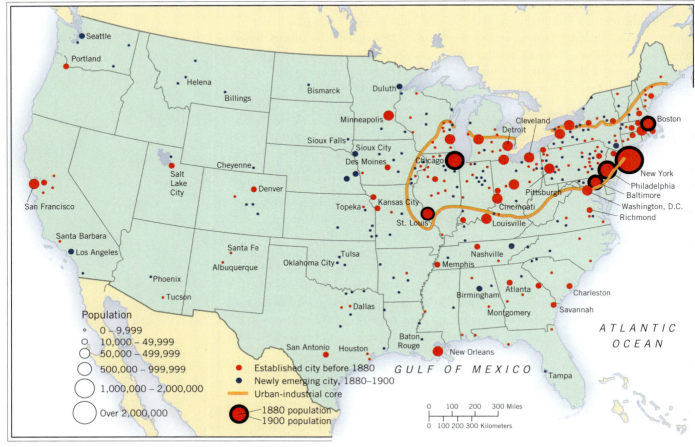

MAP 18–2

The Growth of America's Cities, 1880–1900   Several significant trends stand out on this map. First is the development of an urban-industrial core stretching from New England to the Midwest where the largest cities were located. And second is the emergence of relatively new cities in the South and West, reflecting the national dimensions of innovations in industry and transportation.

WHAT WERE the economic forces that contributed to the growth of some cities and the decline of others?

in a crescent from New England to the cities bordering the Great Lakes. This region included nine of the nation's ten largest cities in 1920. Western cities such as Denver, San Francisco, and Los Angeles emerged as dominant urban places in their respective regions but did not challenge the urban core for supremacy. Southern cities, limited in growth by low consumer demand, low wages, and weak capital formation, were drawn into the orbit of the urban core. Atlanta, an offspring of the railroad, prospered as the region's major way station for funneling wealth into the urban North. Dallas emerged as Atlanta's counterpart in the western South (see Chapter 19).

The crush of people and the emergence of new technologies expanded the city outward and upward as urban dwellers sorted themselves by social class and ethnic group. While the new infrastructure of water and sewer systems, bridges, and trolley tracks kept steel mills busy, it also fragmented the urban population by allowing settlements well beyond existing urban boundaries.

CENTERS AND SUBURBS

The centers of the country's great cities changed in scale and function in this era, achieving a prominence they would eventually lose in the twentieth century. Downtowns expanded up and out as tall buildings arose—monuments to business and finance—creating urban skylines. Residential neighborhoods were pushed out, leaving the center dominated by corporate headquarters and retail and entertainment districts.

Corporate heads administered their empires from downtown, even if their factories were located on the urban periphery or in other towns and cities. Banks and insurance companies clustered in financial centers like Atlanta's Five Points district to service the corporations. Department stores and shops clustered in retail districts in strategic locations along electric trolley lines. It was to these areas that urban residents usually referred when they talked about going "downtown." In the entertainment district, electric lights lit up theaters, dance halls, and restaurants into the night.

As retail and office uses crowded out residential dwellings from the city center, a new phenomenon emerged: the residential neighborhood. Advances in transportation technology, first the horse-drawn railway and, by the 1890s, the electric trolley, eased commuting for office workers. Some in the growing and increasingly affluent middle class left the crowded, polluted city altogether to live in new residential suburbs, leaving it to the growing ranks of working-class immigrants and African Americans.

The suburb emerged as the preferred residence for the urban middle class after 1870. The ideals that had promoted modest suburban growth earlier in the nineteenth century—privacy, aesthetics, and home ownership—became increasingly important for the growing numbers of middle-class families after 1880.

Consider the Russells of Short Hills, New Jersey. Short Hills lay 18 miles by railroad from New York City. William Russell, his wife, Ella Gibson Russell, and their six children moved there from Brooklyn in the late 1880s, seeking a "pleasant, cultured people whose society we could enjoy" and a cure for Russell's rheumatism. Russell owned and managed a small metal brokerage in New York and enjoyed gardening, reading, and socializing with his new neighbors. Ella Russell cared for the six children with the help of a servant and also belonged to several clubs and charities.

The design of the Russells's home reflected the principles Catherine Beecher and Harriet Beecher Stowe outlined in their suburban home Bible, *American Woman's Home* (1869). The new technology of central heating made it unnecessary to divide a house into many small rooms, each with its own fireplace or stove. Beecher and Stowe recommended that a home's ground floor have fewer but larger rooms to encourage the family to pursue their individual activities in a common space.

The entire Russell family was to be found enjoying the tennis, swimming, and skating facilities on the grounds of the Short Hills Athletic Club.

The emphasis on family togetherness also reflected the changing role of men in late-nineteenth-century society. Beecher and Stowe praised fathers who took active roles in child rearing and participated fully in the family's leisure activities. Women's roles also broadened, as Ella Russell's club work attested.

With the growth after 1890 of the electric trolley, elevated rail lines, and other relatively inexpensive forms of commuter travel, suburbs became accessible to a broader spectrum of the middle class. The social structure, architecture, and amenities of suburbs varied, depending on the rail service and distance from the city. The trolley and elevated railroads generated modest middle-class urban

WHERE TO LEARN MORE

Missouri Historical Society,
St. Louis, Missouri
www.mohistory.org

neighborhoods and suburbs, with densities decreasing and income increasing toward the ends of the lines. But for the working class—even skilled artisans—suburban living remained out of reach.

Residence, consumer habits, and leisure activities reflected growing social and class divisions. Yet, at the same time, the growing materialism of American society promised a common ground for its disparate ethnic, racial, and social groups.

THE NEW MIDDLE CLASS

From the colonial era, America's urban middle class had included professionals—physicians, lawyers, ministers, educators, editors—as well as merchants, shopkeepers, and skilled artisans (until they dropped from the middle class in the late nineteenth century). In the late nineteenth century, industrial technology and urban growth expanded the urban middle class to include salespeople, factory supervisors, managers, civil servants, technicians, and a broad range of "white-collar" office workers like insurance agents, bank tellers, and legal assistants. This newer middle class set national trends in residential patterns, consumption, and leisure.

The more affluent members of the new middle class repaired to new subdivisions within and outside the city limits. Simple row houses sheltered the growing numbers of clerks and civil servants who remained in the city. These dwellings contrasted sharply with the crowded one- or two-room apartments that confined the working class. Rents for these apartments ran as much as $3 a week at a time when few workers made more than $9 or $10.

The new middle class was a class of consumers. In earlier times, land had been a symbol of prestige. Now it was things. And the new industries obliged with a dazzling array of goods and technologies to make life easier and allow more time for family and leisure.

By 1910, the new middle class lived in all-electric homes, with indoor plumbing and appliances that eased food preparation. The modern city dweller worked by the clock, not by the sun. Eating patterns changed: cold, packaged cereals replaced hot meats at breakfast; fast lunches of Campbell's soup—"a meal in itself"—or canned stews weaned Americans from the heavy lunch. In Nashville Joel Cheek ground and blended coffee beans in his store for customers' convenience. He convinced the city's Maxwell House Hotel to serve his new concoction, and in 1907, when President Theodore Roosevelt visited the hotel and drained his cup, he declared that the coffee was "good to the very last drop." A slogan and Maxwell House coffee were born.

Advertisers now told Americans what they wanted; they created demand and developed loyalty for brand-name products. In early-twentieth-century New York, a six-story-high Heinz electric sign was a sensation, especially the 40-foot-long pickle at its top.

The middle class liked anything that saved time: trolleys, trains, electric razors, vacuum cleaners. By 1900, some 1.4 million telephones were in service, and many middle-class homes had one.

The middle class liked its news in an easy-to-read form. Urban tabloids multiplied after 1880, led by Joseph Pulitzer's *New York World* and William Randolph Hearst's *New York Journal*. The newspapers organized the news into topical sections, used bold headlines and graphics to catch the eye, ran human interest stories to capture the imagination, inaugurated sports pages to attract male readers, and offered advice columns for women.

As the visual crowded out the printed in advertising, newspapers, and magazines, these materials became more accessible to a wider urban audience. The tabloid press drew urban society together with new features such as the comic strip, and heartrending personal sagas drawn from real life. Immigrants received their initiation into the mainstream of American society through the tabloids.

Originating in the 1850s and 1860s with the construction of retail palaces such as Boston's Jordan Marsh, Philadelphia's Wanamaker & Brown, New York's Lord & Taylor, and Chicago's Marshall Field, the department store came to epitomize the bounty of the new industrial capitalism. The department store exuded limitless abundance with its extensive inventories, items for every budget, sumptuous surroundings, and efficient, trained personnel.

At first, most department store customers were middle-class married women. Industry churned out uniform, high-quality products in abundance, and middle-class salaries absorbed them. Department stores maintained consumers' interest with advertising campaigns arranged around holidays such as Easter and Christmas, the seasons, and the school calendar. Each event required new clothing and accessories, and the ready-made clothing industry changed fashions accordingly.

Soon the spectacle and merchandise of the department store attracted shoppers from all social strata, not just the middle class. "The principal cause of the stores' success," one shopper explained in 1892, "is the fact that their founders have understood the necessity of offering a new democracy whose needs and habits" are satisfied "in the cheapest possible way," providing "a taste for elegance and comfort unknown to previous generations." After 1890, department stores increasingly hired young immigrant women to cater to their growing foreign-born clientele. Mary Antin recalled how she and her teenage friends and sister would spend their Saturday nights in 1898 patrolling "a dazzlingly beautiful palace called a 'department store.'" It was there that Mary and her sister "exchanged our hateful home-made European costumes . . . for real American machine-made garments, and issued forth glorified in each other's eyes."

By 1900, department stores had added sporting goods and hardware sections and were attracting male as well as female customers from a wide social spectrum.

The expanding floor space devoted to sporting goods reflected the growth of leisure in urban society. And like other aspects of that society, leisure and recreation both separated and cut across social classes. As sports like football became important extracurricular activities at Harvard, Yale, and other elite universities, intercollegiate games became popular occasions for the upper class to congregate, renew school ties, and, not incidentally, discuss business. The first country club in the United States was founded in Brookline, Massachusetts, a Boston suburb, in 1882. Country clubs built golf courses for men and tennis courts primarily for women. The clubs offered a suburban retreat, away from the diverse middle- and working-class populations, where the elite could play in privacy.

Middle-class urban residents rode electric trolleys to suburban parks and bicycle and skating clubs. Both middle-class men and women participated in these sports, especially bicycling. New bikes cost at least $50, putting them beyond the reach of the working class.

Baseball was the leading spectator sport among the middle class. Baseball epitomized the nation's transition from a rural to an urban industrial society. Reflecting industrial society, baseball had clearly defined rules and was organized into leagues. Professional leagues were profit-making enterprises, and like other enterprises of the time, they frequently merged. Initially, most professional baseball games were played on weekday afternoons, making it hard for working-class

Thomas Eakins created this painting of baseball players practicing in 1875. Originating as a sport of urban gentlemen, baseball eventually broadened its appeal, drawing fans from all spectrums of city life.

Eakins, Thomas, *Baseball Players Practicing*, 1875. Watercolor; 10 7/8″ × 12 7/8″. Museum of Art, Rhode Island School of Design, Jesse Metcalf and Walter H. Kimball Funds. Photography by Cathy Carver

spectators to attend. After merging with the American Association (AA) in 1883, the National League adopted some of the AA's innovations to attract more fans, including beer sales, cheap admission, and, over the objections of Protestant churches, began playing Sunday games.

The tavern, or saloon, was the workingman's club. Typically an all-male preserve, the saloon provided drink, cheap food, and a place for workingmen to read a newspaper, socialize, and learn about job opportunities.

The amusement park, with its mechanical wonders, was another hallmark of the industrial city. Declining trolley fares made them accessible to the working class around 1900. Unlike taverns, they provided a place for working-class men and women to meet and date.

The most renowned of these parks was Brooklyn's Coney Island. In 1897, George C. Tilyou opened Steeplechase Park on Coney Island. He brought an invention by George Washington Ferris—a giant rotating vertical wheel equipped with swinging carriages—to the park from Chicago, and the Ferris Wheel quickly became a Coney Island signature. Together with such attractions as mechanical horses and 250,000 of Thomas Edison's light bulbs, Steeplechase dazzled patrons with its technological wonders. Steeplechase Park was quickly followed by Luna Park and Dreamland, and the Coney Island attractions became collectively known as "the poor man's paradise." One German immigrant opened a small café serving sausages that he named "frankfurters" after his native Frankfurt.

After 1900, the wonders of Coney Island began to lure people from all segments of an increasingly diverse city. Sightseers came from around the world. Notables such as Herman Melville, Mark Twain, and even Sigmund Freud (what did he think of Dreamland?) rubbed shoulders with factory workers, domestics, and department store clerks. Baseball was also becoming a national pastime as games attracted a disparate crowd of people who might have little in common but their devotion to the home team.

Increasing materialism had revealed great fissures in American urban society by 1900. Yet places like department stores, baseball parks, and amusement parks provided democratic spaces for some interaction. Newspapers and schools also indirectly offered diverse groups the opportunity to share similar experiences.

18–4
Richard K. Fox,
from *Coney Island Frolics*
(1883)

CONCLUSION

By 1900, the factory worker and the department store clerk were more representative of the new America than the farmer and small shopkeeper. Industry and technology had created thousands of new jobs, but they also eliminated the autonomy many workers had enjoyed and limited their opportunities to advance.

Immigrants thronged to the United States to realize their dreams of economic and religious freedom. They found both to varying degrees but also discovered a darker side to the promise of American life. The great cities thrilled newcomers with their possibilities and their abundance of goods and activities. But the cities also bore witness to the growing divisions in American society. As the new century dawned, the prospects for urban industrial America seemed limitless, yet the stark contrasts that had appeared so vividly inside and outside the Centennial Exposition persisted and deepened.

Labor unions, ethnic organizations, government legislation, and new urban institutions promised ways to remedy the worst abuses of the new urban, industrial economy.

SUMMARY

New Industry The Gilded Age of the late 1800s saw America transformed into the world's foremost industrial power. Technological and scientific advances, the modernization of industry, and the development of the modern corporation created changes in work life and urban living. The demand for workers drew immigrants to America and women and children into the work place. In the new urban landscape poverty abounded; the growing gap between rich and poor was seen as a result of Social Darwinism and survival of the fittest. Industrial tensions resulted in workers organizing into unions, and labor strikes, some violent, resulted as employers fought back to break the power of the unions.

New Immigrants The period saw a dramatic rise in immigration to the United States, as the number of people moving to America from northern and western Europe slackened, the numbers from southern and eastern Europe, Latin America, and Asia increased. Work, and the resulting independence it would bring, was the goal; immigrants maintained their religious and cultural traditions while some Americans attempted to restrict their numbers through legislation. African Americans moved into the industrial cities of the North and Midwest drawn by the same promise that attracted overseas immigrants.

New Cities Cities acted like giant magnets; an urban-industrial core extended from New England to the Great Lakes; the crush of people and the emergence of new technologies expanded the city outward and upward. Urban dwellers sorted themselves by social class and ethnic groups; residential neighborhoods, downtowns, and suburbs became fixtures of the modern city. The new middle class transformed America into a consumer society and leisure activities, spectator sports, and amusement parks became hallmarks of urban life.

REVIEW QUESTIONS

1. Could the benefits of industrialization have been achieved without its social costs? Explain your answer.

2. How did working-class women respond to the new economy? How did their participation and responses differ from those of working-class men?

3. Why is it said that immigrant groups adjusted to, rather than assimilated, American society?

4. Would individuals from other immigrant groups likely have expressed sentiments similar to those of Mary Antin about the adjustment to American life, or is Mary's reaction specific to her Jewish background?

KEY TERMS

American Federation of Labor (p. 479)
Chain migration (p. 482)
Collective bargaining (p. 479)
Gilded Age (p. 467)
Gospel of Wealth (p. 478)

Great Migration (p. 486)
Great Uprising (p. 478)
Horizontal integration (p. 471)
Hull House (p. 476)
Knights of Labor (p. 478)
Nativism (p. 484)

Pogroms (p. 481)
Social Darwinism (p. 478)
Sweatshops (p. 473)
Tenements (p. 476)
Vertical integration (p. 470)

WHERE TO LEARN MORE

Edison National Historic Site, West Orange, New Jersey. The site contains the Edison archives, including photographs, sound recordings, and industrial and scientific machinery. Its twenty historic structures dating from the 1880–1887 period include Edison's home and laboratory. **www.nps.gov/edis**

Japanese American National Museum, Los Angeles, California. Housed in a converted Buddhist temple, this museum includes artifacts and photographs of early Japanese immigration and settlement. The core exhibit is "Issei Pioneers: Japanese Immigration to Hawaii and the Mainland from 1885 to 1924." **www.janm.org**

Pasa al Norte. This museum, located in El Paso, Texas, serves as the Mexico-United States International Immigration History Center. Its exhibits focus on the importance of El Paso ("the Southwest Ellis Island") as a port-of-entry between the United States and Mexico from the late sixteenth century to the present. **utminers.utep.edu/panihm/default.htm**

Missouri Historical Society, St. Louis, Missouri. The Society displays a long-term exhibition accompanied by public programs called, "St. Louis in the Gilded Age," which focuses on the changes generated by industrialization and urban development in St. Louis from 1865 to 1900. **www.mohistory.org**

Senator John Heinz Pittsburgh Regional History Center, Pittsburgh, Pennsylvania. Through its long-term exhibition, "Points in Time: Building a Life in Western Pennsylvania, 1750–Today," the Center explores the growth of the Pittsburgh metropolitan area, especially its expansion during the great industrial boom at the turn of the twentieth century. **www.pghhistory.org**

Angel Island State Park, San Francisco Bay. Angel Island served as a detention center from 1910 to 1940 for Asian immigrants who were kept there for days, months, and, in some cases, years, while immigration officials attempted to ferret out illegal entries. Exhibits depict the era through pictures and artifacts. **www.angelisland.org**

Strawbery Banke, Portsmouth, New Hampshire. This museum includes an exhibit and audiovisual presentations on the adjustment of one immigrant family to American life: "Becoming Americans: The Shapiro Story, 1898–1929," presents the story of an immigrant Jewish family in the context of immigration to the small, coastal city of Portsmouth at the turn of the twentieth century. **www.strawberybanke.org**

Statue of Liberty National Monument and Ellis Island, New York, New York. More than 12 million immigrants were processed at Ellis Island between 1892 and 1954. The exhibits provide a fine overview of American immigration history during this period. There is an ongoing oral history program as well. **www.nps.gov/stli**

For additional study resources for this chapter, go to:
www.prenhall.com/goldfield/chapter18

The two locomotives then moved up until they touched each other, . . .and at one p.m., under an almost cloudless sky, and in the presence of about one thousand one hundred people, the completion of the greatest railroad on earth was announced.

This engraving, showing passengers shooting buffalo from a train crossing the plains, suggests the often casual approach Americans took toward the Western Environment. The destruction of the buffalo herds, for both profit and "sport," also destroyed the basis of the Plains Indians' economy and culture.

19

TRANSFORMING THE WEST
1865–1890

WHAT WAS the federal government's policy toward Indians in the late nineteenth century?

HOW DID Western railroads shape the West and affect the East?

WHAT BROUGHT the flood of migrants to the West in the late nineteenth century?

HOW WAS the environment transformed by Westward expansion?

After a pleasant ride of about six miles we attained a very high eleva-tion, and, passing through a gorge of the mountains, we entered a level, cir-cular valley, about three miles in diameter, surrounded on every side by mountains. The track is on the eastern side of the plain, and at the point of junction extends in nearly a southwest and northeast direction. Two lengths of rails are left for today's work. . . . At a quarter to nine A.M. the whistle of the C.P. [Central Pacific Railroad] is heard, and soon arrives, bringing a number of passengers. . . . Two additional trains arrive from the East. At a quarter to eleven the Chinese workmen commenced leveling the bed of the road with picks and shovels, preparatory to placing the ties. . . . At a quarter past eleven the Governor's train arrived. The engine was gayly decorated with little flags and ribbons, the red, white, and blue. At 12 M. the rails were laid, and the iron spikes driven. The last tie that was laid is 8 feet long, 8 inches wide, and 6 inches thick. It is of California laurel, finely polished, and is orna-mented with a silver escutcheon bearing the following inscription: "The last tie laid on the Pacific Railroad, May 10th, 1869." . . .

The point of contact is 1,085 4/5 miles from Omaha, leaving 690 miles for the C.P. portion of the work. The engine Jupiter, of the C.P., and en-gine 119, of the U.P.R.R. [Union Pacific Railroad] moved up within thirty feet of each other. . . . Three cheers were given for the Government of the Unit-ed States, for the railroad, for the President, for the Star Spangled Banner, for the laborers, and for those who furnished the means respectively. The four spikes—two gold and two silver—were furnished by Montana, Idaho, Cali-fornia, and Nevada. They were about seven inches long, and a little larger than the iron spike. Dr. Harkness, of Sacramento, on presenting to Governor Stanford a spike of pure gold, delivered a short and appropriate speech. The Hon. F.A. Tuttle, of Nevada, presented Dr. Durant with a spike of silver, say-ing: 'To the iron of the East, and the gold of the West, Nevada adds her link of silver to span the continent and wed the oceans'. . . . The two locomotives then moved up until they touched each other, . . . and at one P.M., under an almost cloudless sky, and in the presence of about one thousand one hundred people, the completion of the greatest railroad on earth was announced.

Andrew J. Russell, "The Completion of the Pacific Railroad," *Frank Leslie's Illustrated Newspaper,* June 5, 1869.

W WHERE TO LEARN MORE

★ Golden Spike National Historic Site, near Promontory, Utah
www.nps./gov/gosp

IMAGE KEY

for pages 496–497

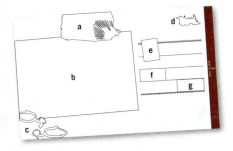

a. A feather fan carried by Yuchi dancers. American Museum of Natural History
b. Passengers and the train crew shooting buffalo on the line of the Kansas-Pacific Railroad: color line engraving, 1871.
c. Confederate cavalry spurs from the American Civil War.
d. An old fashioned steam locomotive engine with an attached coal car.
e. Chief Wooly Head's Wife and Child.
f. A Chinese mine worker steadies a water cannon in a shallow riverbed in Idaho with a fellow laborer standing nearby.
g. Thirty-three horse team harvester, cutting, threshing and sacking wheat, c. 1902.

ANDREW J. RUSSELL'S short journey on the morning of May 10, 1869, from Ogden to Promontory Summit, Utah, enabled him to document what he called "the completion of the greatest work of the age, by which this vast continent is spanned, from ocean to ocean, by the iron path of travel and commerce." The transcontinental railroad symbolized the classic American journey, a people and a nation moving westward.

Its construction also set a precedent for western development. The two railroads that met in a desolate sagebrush basin were huge corporate enterprises, not individual efforts, and corporations dominated-Western growth as much as they did Eastern industrialization. The federal government also played a crucial role. Congress had authorized the Union Pacific and Central Pacific to build the railroad link, given them the right-of-way for their tracks, and provided huge land grants and financial subsidies.

The railroads' dependence on capital investment, engineering knowledge, technological innovations, and labor skills also typified Western development. Their labor forces both reflected and reinforced the region's racial and ethnic diversity. European immigrants, Mexicans, Paiute Indians, both male and female, and especially Chinese, recruited in California and Asia, chiseled the tunnels through the mountains, built the bridges over the gulches, and laid the ties and rails across the plains. But Russell kept the Chinese out of the famous photographs he took at Promontory, an indication of the racism that marred so many Western achievements.

Laying track as quickly as possible to collect the subsidies awarded by the mile, the railroad corporations adopted callous and reckless construction tactics, resulting in waste, deaths (perhaps as many as a thousand Chinese), and environmental destruction—consequences that would also characterize other forms of economic development in the West. And as with most other American undertakings in the West, the construction provoked conflict with the Cheyenne, Sioux, and other tribes.

The most important feature of the railroad, however, was that traffic moved in both directions. The railroads not only helped move soldiers and settlers into the West, but they also moved western products to the growing markets in the East. Thus the railroad both integrated the West into the rest of the nation and made it a crucial part of the larger economic revolution that transformed America after the Civil War.

This photograph, taken by A.J. Russell, records the celebration at the joining of the Central Pacific and Union Pacific railroads on May 10, 1869, at Promontory Summit, Utah. Railroads transformed the American West, linking the region to outside markets, spurring rapid settlement, and threatening Indian survival.

Union Pacific Historical Collection

17–3
Horace Greeley, An Overland Journey (1860)

SUBJUGATING NATIVE AMERICANS

T he initial obstacle to exploiting the West was the people already living there, for despite Easterners' image of the West as an unsettled wilderness, Native Americans had long inhabited it and had developed a variety of economies and cultures. As white people pressed westward, they attempted to subjugate the Indians, displace them from their lands, and strip them of their culture. Conquest forced Indians onto desolate reservations, but efforts to destroy their beliefs and transform their way of life were less successful.

WHAT WAS the federal government's policy toward Indians in the late nineteenth century?

TRIBES AND CULTURES

Throughout the West, Indians had adapted to their environment. Each activity encouraged their sensitivity to the natural world, and each had social and political implications.

In the Northwest, abundant food from rich waters and dense forests gave rise to complex and stable Indian societies. During summer fishing runs, the Tillamooks, Chinooks, and other tribes caught salmon, which sustained them

WHERE TO LEARN MORE

National Museum of the American Indian, New York, New York
www.nmai.si.edu/index.asp

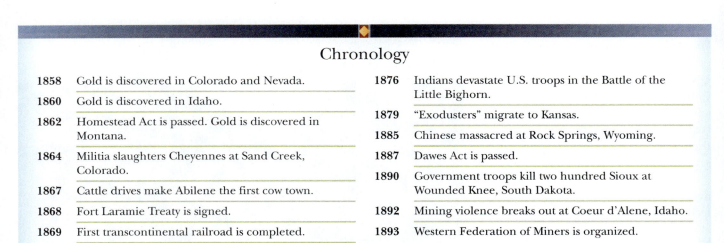

Chronology

1858	Gold is discovered in Colorado and Nevada.
1860	Gold is discovered in Idaho.
1862	Homestead Act is passed. Gold is discovered in Montana.
1864	Militia slaughters Cheyennes at Sand Creek, Colorado.
1867	Cattle drives make Abilene the first cow town.
1868	Fort Laramie Treaty is signed.
1869	First transcontinental railroad is completed.
1874	Gold is discovered in the Black Hills. Turkey Red wheat is introduced to Kansas. Barbed wire is patented.
1876	Indians devastate U.S. troops in the Battle of the Little Bighorn.
1879	"Exodusters" migrate to Kansas.
1885	Chinese massacred at Rock Springs, Wyoming.
1887	Dawes Act is passed.
1890	Government troops kill two hundred Sioux at Wounded Knee, South Dakota.
1892	Mining violence breaks out at Coeur d'Alene, Idaho.
1893	Western Federation of Miners is organized.

QUICK REVIEW

Indians in the West
- Desert tribes had to contend with a harsh environment.
- The cultures of many Southwest tribes emphasized communal solidarity.
- The most numerous Indian groups in the West lived on the Great Plains.

throughout the year. During the mild winters, they developed artistic handicrafts, elaborate social institutions, and a satisfying religious life.

The Cahuillas of the southern California desert survived only through their ability to extract food and medicines from desert plants. In the dry and barren Great Basin of Utah and Nevada, Shoshones and Paiutes ate grasshoppers and other insects to supplement their diet of rabbits, mice, and other small animals. Such harsh environments restricted the size, strength, and organizational complexity of societies.

In the Southwest, the Pueblos dwelled in permanent towns of adobe buildings and practiced intensive agriculture. Because tribal welfare depended on maintaining complex irrigation systems, the Zunis, Hopis, and other Pueblos emphasized community solidarity rather than individual ambition. Town living encouraged social stability and the development of effective governments, elaborate religious ceremonies, and creative arts.

The most numerous Indian groups in the West lived on the Great Plains. The largest of these tribes included the Lakotas or Sioux, who roamed from western Minnesota through the Dakotas; the Cheyennes and Arapahos, who controlled much of the central plains between the Platte and Arkansas Rivers; and the Comanches, predominant on the southern plains.

Despite their diversity, all tribes emphasized community welfare over individual interest. Their economies were based on subsistence rather than profit. They tried to live in harmony with nature to ward off sickness, injury, death, or misfortune. And they were absorbed with the need to establish proper relations with supernatural forces that linked human beings with all other living things. These connections also shaped Indians' attitude toward land, which they regarded—like air and water—as part of nature to be held and used communally.

Disdaining Native Americans and their religion, white people condemned them as "savages" to be converted or exterminated. Rejecting the concept of communal property, most white people demanded land for the exclusive use of ambitious individuals.

Perhaps no one expressed these cultural differences better than the great Sioux leader Sitting Bull. Referring to the forces of the spirit world, he declared:

> It is through this mysterious power that we too have our being and we therefore yield to our neighbors, even our animal neighbors, the same

right as ourselves, to inhabit this land. Yet, hear me, people. We have now to deal with another race. . . . Possession is a disease with them. These people have made many rules that the rich may break but the poor may not. . . . They claim this mother of ours, the earth, for their own and fence their neighbors away; they deface her with their buildings. . . . That nation is like a spring freshet that overruns its banks and destroys all who are in its path. We cannot dwell side by side.

FEDERAL INDIAN POLICY

The government had in the 1830s adopted the policy of separating white people and Indians. Eastern tribes were moved west of Missouri and resettled on land then scorned as "the Great American Desert," unsuitable for white habitation and development. This division collapsed in the 1840s when the United States acquired Texas, California, and Oregon. Mormons developed a trail through Indian country in 1847 and settled on Indian lands; gold and silver discoveries beginning in 1848 prompted miners to migrate across Indian lands. Rather than curbing white settler entry into Indian country, the government built forts along the overland trails and ordered the army to punish Indians who threatened travelers.

White migration devastated the Plains Indians. Livestock destroyed timber and pastures along streams in the semiarid region; trails eliminated buffalo from tribal hunting ranges. The Pawnees in particular suffered from the violation of their hunting grounds. One observer reported that "their trail could be followed by the dead bodies of those who starved to death." The Plains Indians also suffered from the white migrants' diseases for which Indians had no natural immunity. Cholera killed more than half of the Comanches and Kiowas, and most other tribes lost up to 40 percent of their population from the new diseases. Emigrants along the Platte River routes came across "villages of the dead."

Recognizing that the Great American Desert could support agriculture, white settlers pressed on the eastern edge of the plains and demanded the removal of the Indians. Simultaneously, railroad companies developed plans to lay tracks across the plains. The federal government decided to relocate the tribes to separate and specific reserves. In exchange for accepting such restrictions, the government would provide the tribes with annual payments of livestock, clothing, and other materials. To implement this policy, the government negotiated treaties, extinguishing Indian rights to millions of acres, and ordered the army to keep Indians on their assigned reservations.

The commissioner of Indian affairs aptly described the Indians' lot: "By alternate persuasion and force these tribes have been removed, step by step, from mountain to valley, and from river to plain, until they have been pushed halfway across the continent. They can go no further; on the ground they now occupy the crisis must be met, and their future determined."

QUICK REVIEW

White Migration and the Plains Indians
- Livestock destroyed timber and pastures.
- Buffalo were eliminated from tribal hunting grounds.
- New diseases killed as much as 40 percent of some Indian groups.

WARFARE AND DISPOSSESSION

From the 1850s to the 1880s, warfare engulfed the advancing frontier. Invading Americans bore ultimate responsibility for these wars. Even the men who led the white military assault conceded as much. General Philip Sheridan, for example, declared of the Indians: "We took away their country and their means of support, broke up their mode of living, their habits of life, introduced disease and decay among them, and it was for this and against this that they made war. Could anyone expect less?"

One notorious example of white aggression occurred in 1864 at Sand Creek, Colorado. When gold was discovered on land only recently guaranteed to the Cheyennes and Arapahos, white settlers wanted to eliminate the Indian presence altogether. John Chivington, a Methodist minister, led a militia force to the Sand Creek camp of a band of Cheyennes under Black Kettle, an advocate of peace and accommodation. An American flag flew over the Indian camp. Under Chivington's orders to "kill and scalp all, big and little," the militia attacked Black Kettle's sleeping camp without warning. One white trader later described the helpless Indians: "They were scalped, their brains knocked out; the [white] men used their knives, ripped open women, clubbed little children, knocked them in the head with their guns, beat their brains out, mutilated their bodies in every sense of the word."

The **Sand Creek Massacre** appalled many Easterners. The Cheyennes, protested the commissioner of Indian affairs, were "butchered in cold blood by troops in the service of the United States." A congressional investigating committee denounced Chivington for "a foul and dastardly massacre which would have disgraced the veriest savage among those who were the victims of his cruelty." Westerners, however, justified the brutality as a means to secure their own opportunities. One Western newspaper demanded, "Kill all the Indians that can be killed. Complete extermination is our motto."

Other tribes were more formidable. None was more powerful than the Sioux, whose military skills had been honed in conflicts with other tribes. On the Bozeman Trail, in what the Lakotas called the Battle of One Hundred Slain, the Sioux wiped out an army detachment led by a captain who had boasted that he would destroy the Sioux nation. General William T. Sherman, who had marched through Georgia against Confederates, knew that the odds were different in the West. Fifty Plains Indians, he declared, could "checkmate" three thousand soldiers. General Philip Sheridan calculated that the army suffered proportionately greater losses fighting Indians than either the Union or the Confederacy had suffered in the Civil War.

Describing white actions as "uniformly unjust," a federal peace commission in 1868 negotiated the **Second Treaty of Fort Laramie**, in which the United States abandoned the Bozeman Trail and other routes and military posts on Sioux territory—one of the few times Indians forced the advancing whites to retreat. The United States also guaranteed the Sioux permanent ownership of the western half of South Dakota and the right to inhabit and hunt in the Powder River country in Wyoming and Montana, an area to be henceforth closed to all whites.

For several years, peace prevailed on the northern plains, but in 1872, the Northern Pacific Railroad began to build westward on a route that would violate Sioux territory. Rather than stopping the railroad, the government sent an army to protect the surveyors. Sherman regarded railroad expansion as the most important factor in defeating the Indians, for it would allow troops to travel as far in a day as they could march in weeks. Other technological developments, from the telegraph to rapid-fire weapons, also undercut the skills of the Indian warrior.

The white people's destruction of the buffalo also threatened Native Americans. From 1872 to 1874, white hunters killed 4 million buffalo. Railroad construction disrupted grazing areas, and hunters working for the railroads killed hordes of buffalo, both to feed construction crews and to prevent the animals from obstructing rail traffic. Hide hunters slaughtered even more of the beasts for their skins, leaving the bodies to rot. Reporters found vast areas covered with "decaying, putrid, stinking remains" of buffalo. Federal officials encouraged the buffalo's extermination because it would destroy the Indians' basis for survival.

The climactic provocation of the Sioux began in 1874 when Colonel George A. Custer led an invasion to survey the Black Hills for a military post and confirm

WHERE TO LEARN MORE

Fort Laramie National Historic Site, near Guernsey, Wyoming
www.nps.gov/fola/

Sand Creek Massacre The near annihilation in 1864 of Black Kettle's Cheyenne band by Colorado troops under Colonel John Chivington's orders to "kill and scalp all, big and little."

Second Treaty of Fort Laramie The treaty acknowledging U.S. defeat in the Great Sioux War in 1868 and supposedly guaranteeing the Sioux perpetual land and hunting rights in South Dakota, Wyoming, and Montana.

the presence of gold. Thousands of white miners then illegally poured onto Sioux land. The army insisted that the Sioux leave their Powder River hunting grounds. When the Sioux refused, the army attacked. The Oglala Sioux under Crazy Horse checked one prong of this offensive at the Battle of the Rosebud in June 1876 and then joined a larger body of Sioux under Sitting Bull and their Cheyenne and Arapaho allies to overwhelm a second American column, under Custer, at the **Battle of the Little Bighorn**.

But the Indians had to divide their forces to find fresh grass for their horses and to hunt for their own food. "We have been running up and down in this country, but they follow us from one place to another," lamented Sitting Bull about the Army's pursuit. He led his followers to Canada, but the other bands capitulated in the winter of 1876–1877. The conquest of the northern plains came through attrition and the inability of the traditional Indian economy to support resistance to the technologically and numerically superior white forces.

The defeat of the Sioux nearly completed the Indian Wars. Smaller tribes, among them the Kiowas, Modocs, and Utes, had been overrun earlier. In the Northwest, the Nez Percé had outwitted and outfought the larger forces of the U.S. Army over a 1,500-mile retreat toward Canada. The exhausted Nez Percé surrendered after being promised a return to their own land, but the government refused to honor that pledge too and imprisoned the tribe in Oklahoma, where more than a third perished within a few years.

In the Southwest, the Navajos and the Comanches were subdued as the Sioux had been—by persistent pursuit that prevented them from obtaining food. The last to abandon resistance were the Apaches, under Geronimo. In 1886, he and thirty-six followers, facing five thousand U.S. troops, finally surrendered. Geronimo and other Apaches were sent to a military prison in Florida; the tribes were herded onto reservations. The Oglala chief Red Cloud concluded of the white invasion: "They made us many promises, more than I can remember, but they never kept but one. They promised to take our land, and they took it."

LIFE ON THE RESERVATION: AMERICANIZATION

The next objective of government policy was to require Indians to adopt white peoples' ways. This goal did not involve assimilation but merely "Americanization," an expression of cultural conquest.

The government received aid from many Christian denominations, which had long proposed nonviolent methods of controlling Indians. Beginning in the 1860s, they gained influence in reaction to the military's brutality. Religious groups helped staff the reservations as agents, missionaries, or civilian employees. Reformers wanted to change Indian religious and family life, train Indian children in Protestant beliefs, and force Indians to accept private ownership and market capitalism.

Confined on reservations and dependent on government rations, Indians were a captive audience for white reformers. White administrators sought to destroy traditional Indian government by prohibiting tribal councils from meeting and imprisoning tribal leaders.

Protestant religious groups persuaded the Bureau of Indian Affairs to frame a criminal code prohibiting and penalizing tribal religious practices. Established in 1884, the code remained in effect until 1933. It was first invoked to ban the Sun Dance, the chief expression of Plains Indian religion. To enforce the ban, the government withheld rations and disrupted the religious ceremonies that transmitted traditional values. In 1890, the army even used machine guns to suppress the Ghost Dance religion, killing at least two hundred Sioux men, women, and children at **Wounded Knee**, South Dakota.

WHERE TO LEARN MORE

★ Little Bighorn Battlefield National Monument. Crow Agency, Montana
www.nps.gov/libi/home.htm

17–7
Tragedy at Wounded Knee
(1890)

Battle of the Little Bighorn   Battle in which Colonel George A. Custer and the Seventh Cavalry were defeated by the Sioux and Cheyennes under Sitting Bull and Crazy Horse in Montana in 1876.

Wounded Knee Massacre   The U.S. Army's brutal winter massacre in 1890 of at least two hundred Sioux men, women, and children as part of the government's assault on the tribe's Ghost Dance religion.

·AMERICAN VIEWS·

Zitkala-Sa's View of Americanization

itkala-Sa, or Red Bird, was an 8-year-old Sioux girl when she was taken from her South Dakota reservation in 1884 and placed in a Midwestern missionary school, where she encountered what she called the "iron routine" of the "civilizing machine." Here she recalls her first day at the school.

WHAT LESSONS were the missionaries trying to teach Zitkala-Sa? What lessons did Zitkala-Sa learn?

Soon we were being drawn rapidly away by the white man's horses. When I saw the lonely figure of my mother vanish in the distance, a sense of regret settled heavily upon me. . . . I no longer felt free to be myself, or to voice my own feelings. The tears trickled down my cheeks, and I buried my face in the folds of my blanket. Now the first step, parting me from my mother, was taken, and all my belated tears availed nothing. . . . Trembling with fear and distrust of the palefaces . . . I was as frightened and bewildered as the captured young of a wild creature. . . .

[At the missionary school,] the constant clash of harsh noises, with an undercurrent of many voices murmuring an unknown tongue, made a bedlam within which I was securely tied. And though my spirit tore itself in struggling for its lost freedom, all was useless. . . .

We were placed in a line of girls who were marching into the dining room. . . . A small bell was tapped, and each of the pupils drew a chair from under the table. Supposing this act meant they were to be seated, I pulled out mine and at once slipped into it from one side. But when I turned my head, I saw that I was the only one seated, and all the rest at our table remained standing. Just as I began to rise, looking shyly around to see how chairs were to be used, a second bell was sounded. All were seated at last, and I had to crawl back into my chair again. I heard a man's voice at one end of the hall, and I looked around to see him. But all others hung their heads over their plates. As I glanced at the long chain of tables, I caught the eyes of a pale-face woman upon me. Immediately I dropped my eyes, wondering why I was so keenly watched by the strange woman. The man ceased his mutterings, and then a third bell was tapped. Every one picked up his

knife and fork and began eating. I began crying instead, for by this time I was afraid to venture anything more.

But this eating by formula was not the hardest trial in that first day. Late in the morning, my friend Judewin gave me a terrible warning. Judewin knew a few words of English; and she had overhead the paleface woman talk about cutting our long, heavy hair. Our mothers had taught us that only unskilled warriors who were captured had their hair shingled by the enemy. Among our people, short hair was worn by mourners, and shingled hair by cowards!

. . . I remember being dragged out, though I resisted by kicking and scratching wildly. In spite of myself, I was carried downstairs and tied fast in a chair. I cried aloud, shaking my head all the while until I felt the cold blades of the scissors against my neck, and heard them gnaw off one of my thick braids. Then I lost my spirit. . . . My long hair was shingled like a coward's. In my anguish I moaned for my mother, but no one came to comfort me. Not a soul reasoned quietly with me, as my own mother used to do; for now I was only one of many little animals driven by a herder. . . .

I blamed the hard-working, well-meaning, ignorant [missionary] woman who was inculcating in our hearts her superstitious ideas. Though I was sullen in all my little troubles, as soon as I felt better I was . . . again actively testing the chains which tightly bound my individuality like a mummy for burial. . . .

Many specimens of civilized peoples visited the Indian school. The city folks with canes and eyeglasses, the countrymen with sunburnt cheeks and clumsy feet, forgot their relative social ranks in an ignorant curiosity. Both sorts of these Christian palefaces were alike astounded at seeing the children of savage warriors so docile and industrious. . . .

In this fashion many [whites] have passed idly through the Indian schools during the last decade, afterward to boast of their charity to the North American Indian. But few there are who have paused to question whether real life or long-lasting death lies beneath this semblance of civilization.

Source: Zitkala-Sa, "The School Days of an Indian Girl" (1900). Reprinted in *American Indian Stories* (Glorieta, NM: Rio Grande Press, 1976).

FROM THEN TO NOW
The Legacy of Indian Americanization

The assumptions, objectives, and failures of the Americanization policies of the nineteenth century continue to affect American Indians more than a century later. Although periodically modified (see Chapter 27), these policies long persisted, as did their consequences. In the 1970s official investigations reported that the continuing attempts of the Bureau of Indian Affairs to use education to force Indians into an Anglo-American mold "have been marked by near total failure, haunted by prejudice and ignorance."

Similarly, the economic problems on reservations in the nineteenth century foreshadowed conditions a century later. Today Indians rank at the bottom of almost all measures of economic well-being. Lack of economic opportunity leaves isolated reservations with unemployment rates averaging 40 percent. Off the reservation, discrimination, limited skills, and inadequate capital further restrict Indians' job prospects.

Indians also continue to suffer from poor health standards. They have the highest rates of infant mortality, pneumonia, hepatitis, tuberculosis, and suicide in the nation and a life expectancy twenty-five years less than the national average.

Indian culture, however, did not succumb to the pressure to Americanize. In the words of a Shoshone writer, "Indian history didn't end in the 1800s. Indian cultures . . . evolve, grow, and continually try to renew themselves."

In recent decades, Indian peoples have begun to reclaim their past and assert control over their future. Dramatic protests—most notably a confrontation in 1973 between Indian activists and the FBI at Wounded Knee, the site of the notorious 1890 massacre—have called attention to Indian grievances. But Indians have also moved effectively to regain control of the institutions that define their cultural identity. They have established community schools and tribal community colleges that provide a bilingual, bicultural education, seeking to preserve traditions while opening new opportunities. They have built tribal museums and visitor centers in order to shape the presentation of their histories and cultures. By the late 1990s there were more than 200 such institutions, from the Seneca-Iroquois Museum in upstate New York to the Makah Tribal Museum on the Olympic peninsula.

Indians have also secured legal recognition of their right to their cultural patrimony. The Native American Graves Protection and Repatriation Act of 1990 gives Indian communities the right to reclaim, or "repatriate," material artifacts and skeletal remains from museums and historical societies. The Native American Religious Freedom Act of 1978 affirmed their right to practice their traditional religions and have access to sacred sites. Indian dance—once suppressed by white authorities—has revived, and the powwow has become a national Indian institution and symbol of Indian identity.

With the help of historians and lawyers, Indians are also winning enforcement of long-ignored treaty provisions guaranteeing them land ownership and water, hunting, and fishing rights. Court decisions have recognized the right of tribes to permit gambling on their reservations, and some tribes have built profitable casinos, attracting economic development that creates new job opportunities for their people and permits them to stay on their land.

Indians still confront hostility and condescension reminiscent of attitudes a century ago. A white museum official, for example—seeking to prevent the repatriation of Pawnee artifacts—claimed recently that Indians do not have a real religion. But Indians have proved resilient in preserving their cultural heritage and keeping it vibrant for future generations.

The government and religious groups also used education to eliminate Indian values and traditions. They isolated Indian children from tribal influences at off-reservation boarding schools. Troops often seized Indian children for these schools, where they were confined until after adolescence. The schoolchildren were forced to speak English, attend Christian services, and profess white American values. (American Views: "Zitkala-Sa's View of Americanization.")

Finally, government agents taught Indian men how to farm and distributed agricultural implements; Indian women were taught household tasks. These tactics reduced the status of Indian women, whose traditional responsibility for agriculture had guaranteed them respect and authority. Nor could men farm successfully on reservation lands, which white settlers had already rejected as unproductive. White people, however, believed that the real obstacle to economic prosperity for the Indians was their rejection of private property. As one Bureau of Indian Affairs official declared, Indians must be taught to be more "mercenary and ambitious to obtain riches." Congress in 1887 passed the **Dawes Act**, which divided tribal lands among individual Indians. Western settlers and developers who had no interest in the Indians supported the law because it provided that reservation lands not allocated to individual Indians should be sold to white people. Under this "reform," the amount of land held by Indians declined by more than half by 1900.

White acquisition and exploitation of Indian land seemed to be the only constant in the nation's treatment of Native Americans. Assimilation itself failed because most Indians clung to their own values and rejected as selfish, dishonorable, and obsessively materialistic those favored by white people. But if it was not yet clear what place Native Americans would have in America, it was at least clear by 1900 that they would no longer stand in the way of Western development.

Dawes Act   An 1887 law terminating tribal ownership of land and allotting some parcels of land to individual Indians with the remainder opened for white settlement.

HOW DID Western railroads shape the West and affect the East?

WHERE TO LEARN MORE

W

Bodie State Historic Park,
Bodie, California
www.bodie.net/

EXPLOITING THE MOUNTAINS: THE MINING BONANZA

Migrants to the American West exploited the region's natural resources in pursuit of wealth and success. Promoters, artists, and novelists developed images of the West as a land of adventure, opportunity, and freedom; pioneers as self-reliant individuals. All too often, however, reality differed from legend.

In the later nineteenth century, the West experienced several stages of economic development, but all of them transformed the environment, produced economic and social conflict, and integrated the region into the modern national economy. The first stage of development centered on mining, which attracted swarms of eager prospectors into the mountains and deserts in search of gold and silver. They founded vital communities, stimulated the railroad construction that brought further development, and contributed to the disorderly heritage of the frontier (see Map 19–1). But few gained the wealth they had expected.

RUSHES AND MINING CAMPS

The first important gold rush in the Rocky Mountains came in Colorado in 1859. More than 100,000 prospectors crowded into Denver and the nearby mining camps. Simultaneously, the discovery of the famous Comstock Lode in Nevada produced an eastward rush of miners from California. Some 17,000 claims were made around Virginia City, Nevada, the main mining camp. Strikes in the northern Rockies followed in the 1860s. Boise City and Lewiston in Idaho and Helena in Montana became major mining centers, and other camps prospered briefly before fading into ghost towns. Later, other minerals shaped frontier development: silver in Nevada, silver and lead in Colorado and Idaho, silver and in Arizona and Montana.

Mining camps were often isolated by both distance and terrain. They frequently consisted of only flimsy shanties, saloons, crude stores, dance halls, and brothels, all hastily built by entrepreneurs. Such towns reflected the speculative, exploitive, and transitory character of mining itself. And yet they did contribute to permanent settlement by encouraging agriculture, industry, and transportation in the surrounding areas.

MAP EXPLORATION

To explore an interactive version of this map, go to **http://www.prenhall.com/goldfield2/map19.1**

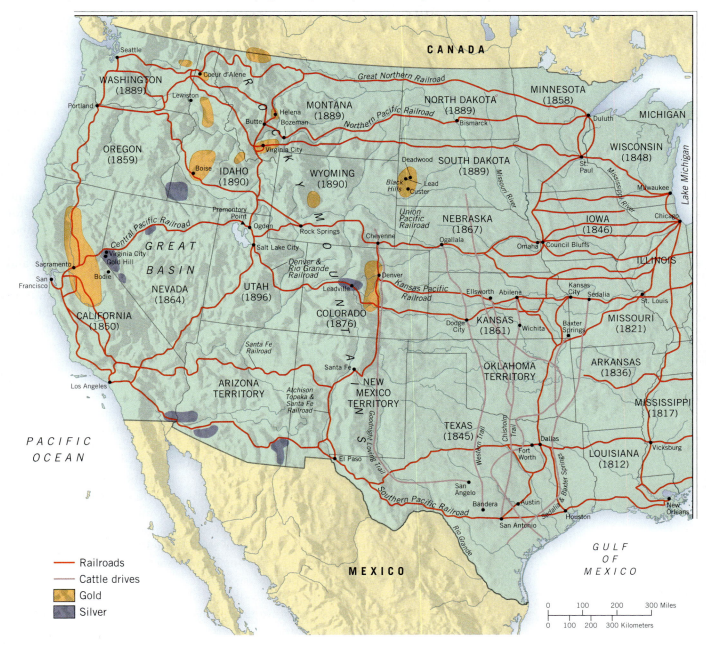

MAP 19–1

Economic Development of the West: Railroads, Mining, and Cattle, 1860–1900   The spread of the railroad network across the West promoted economic development by providing access to outside markets for its resources. The discovery of precious metals often attracted the railroads, but stockraisers had to open cattle trails to reach the railheads.

WHICH CITIES were most affected by the growth of railroads in the West?

The camps had an unusual social and economic structure. The population was overwhelmingly male. In 1860, for example, about 2,300 men and only thirty women resided in the Nevada mining camps of Virginia City and Gold Hill. Women found far fewer economic opportunities than men did on the mining frontier. Several opened hotels. Those with less capital worked as seamstresses and cooks and took in washing. The few married women often earned more than their husbands by boarding other miners willing to pay for the trappings of family life.

But the largest source of paid employment for women was prostitution. Mary Josephine Welch, an entrepreneurial Irish immigrant, settled in Helena in 1867 and soon established the Red Light Saloon, the first of many saloons, dance halls, and brothels that she owned and operated. Most women who engaged in such activities, however, were far less successful, and they entered brothels because they already suffered from economic hardship or a broken family. But prostitution usually only worsened their distress. By the 1890s, as men gained control of the vice trade, violence, suicide, alcoholism, disease, drug addiction, and poverty overcame most prostitutes. Public authorities showed little concern for the abuse and even murder of prostitutes, although they used "sporting women" to raise revenue by fining or taxing them. Protestant women in Denver and other cities established "rescue homes" to protect or rehabilitate prostitutes and dance hall girls from male vice and violence.

The gender imbalance in mining camps also made saloons prevalent among local businesses. An 1879 business census of Leadville, Colorado, reported 10 dry goods stores, 4 banks, and 4 churches, but 120 saloons, 19 beer halls, and 118 gambling houses. Saloons were social centers in towns where most miners lived in crowded and dirty tents and rooming houses. As Mark Twain wrote in *Roughing It* (1872), his account of Virginia City, "The cheapest and easiest way to become an influential man and be looked up to by the community at large, was to stand behind a bar, wear a cluster-diamond pin, and sell whiskey." One observer of the Montana camps reported that men, "unburdened by families, drink whenever they feel like it, whenever they have money to pay for it, and whenever there is nothing else to do. . . . Bad manners follow, profanity becomes a matter of course. . . . Excitability and nervousness brought on by rum help these tendencies along, and then to correct this state of things the pistol comes into play." Disputes over mining claims could become violent, adding to the disorder. The California mining town of Bodie experienced twenty-nine killings between 1877 and 1883. But such killings occurred only within a small group of males who were known as the Badmen of Bodie. Daily life for most people was safe.

Indeed, personal and criminal violence, which remains popularly associated with the West, was less pervasive than collective violence. White men often drove Mexicans and Chinese from their claims or refused to let them work in higher paid occupations in the mining camps. The Chinese had originally migrated to the California gold fields and thereafter spread to the new mining areas of the Rockies and the Great Basin, where they worked in mining when possible, operated laundries and restaurants, and held menial jobs like hauling water and chopping wood. In 1870, more than a quarter of Idaho's population and nearly 10 percent of Montana's was Chinese. Where they were numerous, the Chinese built their own communities and maintained their customs.

But racism and fear of economic competition sparked hostility and violence against the Chinese almost everywhere. The worst anti-Chinese violence occurred in Rock Springs, Wyoming, in 1885 when white miners killed twenty-eight unresisting Chinese miners and drove away all seven hundred residents from the local

QUICK REVIEW

Prostitution

◆ Largest source of paid employment for women in the West.

◆ Most women entered prostitution as a result of economic or familial hardship.

◆ Authorities showed little interest in welfare of prostitutes.

Chinatown. Although the members of the mob were well known, the grand jury, speaking for the white majority, found no cause for legal action: "Though we have examined a large number of witnesses, no one has been able to testify to a single criminal act committed by any known white person." There was community sanction for violence against racial minorities.

LABOR AND CAPITAL

New technology had dramatic consequences for both miners and the mining industry. Initially, mining was an individual enterprise in which miners used simple tools, such as picks and shovels, wash pans, and rockers, to work shallow surface deposits known as placers. More expensive operations were needed to reach the precious metal buried in the earth.

Hydraulic mining, for example, required massive capital investment to build reservoirs, ditches, and troughs to power high-pressure water cannons that would pulverize hillsides and uncover the mineral deposits. Still more expensive and complex was quartz, or lode, mining, sometimes called hard rock mining. Time, money, and technology were required to sink a shaft into the earth. Timber was needed for underground chambers and tunnels. Pumps were installed to remove underground water, and hoists were constructed to lower men and lift out rock. Stamp mills and smelters were built to treat the ore.

Such complex, expensive, and permanent operations necessarily came under corporate control. Often financed with Eastern or British capital, new corporations integrated the mining industry into the larger economy. Hard rock mining produced more complex ores than could be treated in remote mining towns, but with the new railroad network, they were shipped to smelting plants as far away as Kansas City and St. Louis and then to refineries in Eastern cities. Western ores thus became part of national and international business. The mining industry's increasing development of lower grade deposits led to greater capital investment and larger operations employing more workers and machinery.

But the new corporate mining had many disturbing effects. Hydraulic mining washed away hillsides, depositing debris in canyons and valleys to a depth of 100 feet or more, clogging rivers and causing floods, and burying thousands of acres of farmland. Such damage provoked an outcry and eventually led to government regulation.

Corporate mining also transformed prospectors into wage workers with restricted opportunities. Miners' status declined as new machinery like power drills reduced the need for skilled laborers and prompted employers to hire cheaper workers from eastern and southern Europe. Moreover, mining corporations did little to protect miners' health or safety. Miners died in cave-ins, explosions, and fires or from the great heat and poisonous gases in underground mines. Miners called the power hoists "man killers" because they frequently crushed and dismembered workers. In 1889, a Montana inspector of mines concluded that "death lurks even in the things which are designed as benefits."

To protect their interests, miners organized unions. These functioned as benevolent societies, using members' dues to pay benefits to injured miners or their survivors. Several unions established hospitals. Union halls offered an alternative to the saloons by serving as social and educational centers. The Miners' Union Library in Virginia City was the largest library in Nevada. Unions also promoted miners' interests on the job. They persuaded governments to adopt mine safety legislation and, beginning in the 1880s, to appoint mine inspectors. The chief role of these state officials was to answer the question posed by the Colorado mining inspector: "How far should an industry be permitted to advance its material welfare at the expense of human life?"

A Chinese mine worker steadies a water cannon in a shallow riverbed in Idaho with a fellow laborer standing nearby.

Chinese mining laborers, Idaho, 76-119.2/A, Idaho State Historical Society

But mining companies frequently controlled state power and used it to crush unions. Thus in 1892, in the Coeur d' Alene district of Idaho, mining companies locked out strikers and imported a private army, which battled miners in a bloody gunfight. Management next persuaded the governor and the president to send in the state militia and the U.S. Army. State officials then suppressed the strike and the union by confining all union members and their sympathizers in stockades. When mining companies in Utah, Colorado, and Montana pursued the same aggressive tactics, the local miners' unions in the West united for strength and self-protection. In 1893, they formed one of the nation's largest and most militant unions, the Western Federation of Miners.

As the law grew stronger and the owners adopted "legalized violence" as a repressive tool, miners turned to extralegal violence. In the Western mines, then, both management's tactics—blacklisting union members, locking out strikers, obtaining court injunctions against unions, and using soldiers against workers—and labor's response mirrored conditions in the industrial East. In sum, reflecting the industrialization of the national economy, Western mining had been transformed from a small-scale prospecting enterprise characterized by individual initiative and simple tools into a large-scale corporate business characterized by impersonal management, outside capital, advanced technology, and wage labor.

EXPLOITING THE GRASS: THE CATTLE KINGDOM

The development of the range cattle industry reflected the needs of an emerging Eastern urban society, the economic possibilities of the grasslands of the Great Plains, the technology of the expanding railroad network, and the requirements of corporations and capital. It also brought "cow towns" and urban development to the West.

CATTLE DRIVES AND COW TOWNS

The cattle industry originated in southern Texas, where the Spanish had introduced cattle in the eighteenth century. Developed by Mexican ranchers, "Texas longhorns" proved well adapted to the plains grasslands.

Following the Civil War, industrial expansion in the East and Midwest enlarged the urban market for food and increased the potential value of Texas steers. The extension of the railroad network into the West, moreover, opened the possibility of tapping that market. The key was to establish a shipping point on the railroads west of the settled farming regions, a step first taken in 1867 by Joseph McCoy, an Illinois cattle shipper. McCoy selected Abilene, Kansas, in his words "a very small, dead place, consisting of about one dozen log huts, low, small, rude affairs." But Abilene was also the Western railhead of the Kansas Pacific Railroad and was ringed by lush grasslands for cattle. McCoy bought 250 acres for a stockyard and imported lumber for stock pens, loading facilities, stables, and a hotel for cowhands. Texans opened the **Chisholm Trail** through Indian Territory to drive their cattle northward to Abilene. Within three years, a million and a half cattle arrived in Abilene, divided into herds of several thousand, each directed by a dozen cowhands on a "long drive" taking two to three months. With the arrival of the cattle trade, other entrepreneurs created a bustling town. As both railroads and settlement advanced westward, a series of other cow towns—Ellsworth, Wichita, Dodge City, Cheyenne—attracted the long drives, cattle herds, and urban development.

WHAT BROUGHT the flood of migrants to the West in the late nineteenth century?

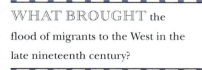

WHERE TO LEARN MORE

National Cowboy Hall of Fame, Oklahoma City, Oklahoma
www.cowboyhalloffame.org/index2.html

Chisholm Trail The route followed by Texas cattle raisers driving their herds north to markets at Kansas railheads.

As with the mining camps, the cow towns' reputation for violence was exaggerated. They adopted gun control laws, prohibiting the carrying of handguns within city limits, and established police forces to maintain order. The towns taxed prostitutes and gamblers and charged high fees for liquor licenses. By collecting such "sin taxes," Wichita was able to forgo general business taxes, thereby increasing its appeal to prospective settlers.

Most cow towns, like Abilene, dwindled into small towns serving farm populations, but like mining camps, cow towns contributed to the growth of an urban frontier. Railroads often determined the location and growth of Western cities, providing access to markets for local products, transporting supplies and machinery for residents, and attracting capital for commercial and industrial development. The West, in fact, had become the most urban region in the nation by 1890, with two-thirds of its population living in communities of at least 2,500 people.

RISE AND FALL OF OPEN-RANGE RANCHING

Indian removal and the extension of the railroad network opened land for ranching in Kansas, Nebraska, Wyoming, Colorado, Montana, and the Dakotas. Cattle reaching Kansas were increasingly sold to stock these northern ranges rather than for shipment to the packing houses. Ranches soon spread across the Great Plains and into the Great Basin, the Southwest, and even eastern Oregon and Washington. Calves were cheap, and ranchers did not buy, but merely used, the grazing lands of the open range, which was public land. It sufficed to acquire title to the site for a ranch house and a water source because controlling access to water in semiarid lands gave effective control of the surrounding public domain "the same as though I owned it," as one rancher explained. Ranchers thus needed to invest only in horses, primitive corrals, and bunkhouses. Their labor costs were minimal: They paid cowboys in the spring to round up new calves for branding and in the fall to herd steers to market.

By the early 1880s, the high profits from this enterprise and an expanding market for beef attracted speculative capital and reshaped the industry. Eastern and European capital flooded the West, with British investors particularly prominent. British and American corporations acquired, expanded, and managed huge ranches.

Large companies soon dominated the industry, just as they had gained control of mining. Some large companies illegally began to enclose the open range, building fences to exclude newcomers and minimize labor costs by reducing the number of cowboys needed to control the cattle. One Wyoming newspaper complained that "some morning we will wake up to find that a corporation has run a wire fence about the boundary lines of Wyoming, and all within the same have been notified to move." And a Coloradan wondered, "Will the government protect us if we poor unite and cut down their fences and let our stock have some of Uncle Sam's feed as well as them?"

The industry eventually collapsed in an economic and ecological disaster. Overgrazing replaced nutritious grasses with sagebrush, Russian thistle, and other plants that livestock found unpalatable. Ten times as much land was required to support a steer by the 1880s. Droughts in the mid-1880s further withered vegetation and enfeebled the animals. Millions of cattle starved or froze to death in terrible blizzards in 1886 and 1887.

The surviving ranchers reduced their operations, restricted the size of their herds, and tried to ensure adequate winter feed by growing hay. To decrease their dependence on natural vegetation even further, they introduced drought-resistant sorghum and new grasses; to reduce their dependence on rainfall, they drilled wells and installed windmills to pump water.

17–4
Joseph G. McCoy, Historic Sketches of the Cattle Trade of the West and Southwest (1874)

QUICK REVIEW

Cattle Ranching

♦ Indian removal and the arrival of the railroad opened land for ranching.

♦ High profits in the industry attracted speculative capital and large companies.

♦ The industry collapsed in the 1880s due to overgrazing.

Employees of the Prairie Cattle Company at the ranch headquarters in Dry Cimarron, New Mexico, in 1888. This company, a British corporation, held 8,000 square miles of land.

The Denver Public Library, Western History Department

COWHANDS AND CAPITALISTS

Cowboys' work was hard, dirty, seasonal, tedious, sometimes dangerous, and poorly paid. Many early cowboys were white Southerners unwilling or unable to return home after the Civil War. Black cowhands made up perhaps 25 percent of the trail-herd outfits. Mexican cowboys developed most of the tools, techniques, and trappings that characterized the cattle industry: from boots, chaps, and the "western" saddle to roundups and roping. Black and Mexican cowboys were often relegated to the more lowly jobs, such as wrangler, a "dust-eater" who herded horses for others to use, but most were ordinary hands on ranch or trail. Except in the few all-black outfits, they were rarely ranch or trail bosses. As the industry expanded northward, more cowboys came from rural Kansas, Nebraska, and neighboring states.

Initially, in the frontier-ranching phase dominated by the long drive, cowboys were seasonal employees who worked closely with owners. They frequently expected to become independent stock raisers themselves and typically enjoyed the right to "maverick" cattle, or put their own brand on unmarked cattle. These informal rights provided opportunities to acquire property and move up the social ladder.

With the appearance of large, corporate enterprises, the traditional rights of cowboys disappeared. Employers now prohibited cowhands from running a brand of their own. One cowboy complained that these restrictions deprived a cowhand of his one way "to get on in the world." To increase labor efficiency, some companies prohibited their cowboys from drinking, gambling, and carrying guns.

Cowboy strikes broke out where corporate ranching was most advanced. The first such strike occurred in Texas in 1883 when the Panhandle Stock Association, representing large operators, prohibited ranch hands from owning their own cattle and imposed a standard wage. More than three hundred cowboys struck seven large ranches for higher wages—$50 rather than $30 per month—and the right to brand mavericks for themselves and to run small herds on the public domain. Ranchers evicted the cowboys, hired scabs, and brought in the Texas Rangers for assistance. The strikers were forced to leave the region.

Other strikes also failed because corporate ranches and their stock associations had the power and cowhands faced long odds in their efforts to organize. They were isolated across vast spaces and had little leverage in the industry. Members of the Northern New Mexico Cowboys Union, formed in 1886, recognized their weakness. After asking employers for "what we are worth after many years' experience," they conceded, "We are dependent on you."

The transformation of the Western cattle industry and its integration into a national economy dominated by corporations thus made the cherished image of cowboy independence and rugged individualism more myth than reality. One visitor to America in the late 1880s commented: "Out in the fabled West, the life of the 'free' cowboy is as much that of a slave as is the life of his Eastern brother, the Massachusetts mill-hand. And the slave-owner is in both cases the same—the capitalist."

OVERVIEW

GOVERNMENT LAND POLICY

Legislation	Result
Railroad land grants (1850–1871)	Granted 181 million acres to railroads to encourage construction and development
Homestead Act (1862)	Gave 80 million acres to settlers to encourage settlement
Morrill Act (1862)	Granted 11 million acres to states to sell to fund public agricultural colleges
Other grants	Granted 129 million acres to states to sell for other educational and related purposes
Dawes Act (1887)	Allotted some reservation lands to individual Indians to promote private property and weaken tribal values among Indians and offered remaining reservation lands for sale to white settlers (by 1906, some 75 million acres had been acquired by white people)
Various laws	Permitted direct sales of 100 million acres by the Land Office

EXPLOITING THE EARTH: HOMESTEADERS AND AGRICULTURAL EXPANSION

Even more than ranching and mining, agricultural growth boosted the Western economy and bound it tightly to national and world markets. In this process, the government played a significant role, as did the railroads, science and technology, Eastern and foreign capital, and the dreams and hard work of millions of rural settlers. The development of farming produced remarkable economic growth, but it left the dreams of many unfulfilled.

HOW WAS the environment transformed by Westward expansion?

SETTLING THE LAND

To stimulate agricultural settlement, Congress passed the most famous land law, the Homestead Act of 1862 (see the overview table "Government Land Policy"). The measure offered 160 acres of free land to anyone who would live on the plot and farm it for five years. The governor of Nebraska exclaimed, "What a blessing this wise and humane legislation will bring to many a poor but honest and industrious family."

However, prospective settlers found less land open to public entry than they expected. Federal land laws did not apply in much of California and the Southwest, where Spain and Mexico had previously transferred land to private owners, or in all of Texas. Elsewhere, the government had given away millions of acres to railroads, or authorized selling millions more for educational and other purposes.

Settlers in Kansas, Nebraska, Minnesota, and the Dakotas in the late 1860s and early 1870s often found most of the best land unavailable for homesteading and much of the rest remote from transportation facilities and markets. Forty percent of the land in Kansas, for example, was closed to homesteading, which prompted the editor of the *Kansas Farmer* to complain that "the settlement of the state is retarded by land monopolists, corporate and individual." Although 375,000 farms were claimed by 1890 through the Homestead Act—a success by any measure—most settlers had to purchase their land.

The Homestead Act also reflected traditional Eastern conceptions of the family farm, which were inappropriate in the West. Here larger-scale farming was

WHERE TO LEARN MORE

★ American Historical Society of Germans from Russia Museum, Lincoln, Nebraska

necessary. And the law ignored the need for capital—for machinery, buildings, livestock, and fencing—that was required for successful farming on the Great Plains.

Other forces stimulated and promoted settlement. Newspaper editors trumpeted the prospects of their region. Land companies, eager to sell their speculative holdings, sent agents through the Midwest and Europe to encourage migration. Steamship companies, interested in selling transatlantic tickets, advertised the opportunities in the American West across Europe. The Scandinavian Immigration Society generated both publicity and settlers for Minnesota; the Hebrew Emigrant Aid Society established Jewish agricultural colonies in Kansas and North Dakota. The Mormons organized the Perpetual Emigrating Fund Company, which helped more than 100,000 European immigrants settle in Utah and Idaho. Their agricultural communities, relying on communal cooperation under church supervision, succeeded where individual efforts often failed in developing this region.

Most important, railroad advertising and promotional campaigns attracted people to the West. In 1882 alone, the Northern Pacific distributed more than 630,000 pieces of promotional literature in English, Swedish, Dutch, Danish, and Norwegian. "The glowing accounts of the golden west sent out by the R.R. companies," one pioneer later recalled, had convinced her that "they were doing a noble work to let poor people know there was such a grand haven they could reach." Only later did she realize that not only would the railroads profit from selling their huge land reserves to settlers, but also a successful agricultural economy would produce crops to be shipped East and a demand for manufactured goods to be shipped West on their lines. The railroads therefore advanced credit to prospective farmers, provided transportation assistance, and extended technical and agricultural advice.

Migrants poured into the West, occupying and farming more acres between 1870 and 1900 than Americans had in the previous 250 years. Farmers settled in every region. But most streamed into the Great Plains states, from the Dakotas to Texas. Much of Oklahoma was settled in virtually a single day in 1889 when the government opened up lands previously reserved for Indians. A reporter described the wild land rush that created Oklahoma City in hours and claimed 2 million acres of land by nightfall: "With a shout and a yell the swift riders shot out, then followed the light buggies or wagons and last the lumbering prairie schooners and freighters' wagons, with here and there even a man on a bicycle and many too on foot—above all a great cloud of dust hovering."

White migrants predominated in the mass migration, but African Americans initiated one of its most dramatic episodes, a millenarian folk movement they called the Exodus, which established several black communities in Kansas and Nebraska. Many settlers came from Europe, sometimes in a chain migration of entire villages, bringing with them not only their own attitudes toward the land but also special crops, skills, settlement patterns, and agricultural practices. By 1890, the foreign-born population of North Dakota exceeded 40 percent, and nonnatives made up much of the population in California and other Western states.

Migrants moved into the West in search of opportunity, which they sometimes seized at the expense of others already there. In the Southwest, Hispanics had long lived in village communities largely outside a commercial economy, farming small tracts of irrigated land and herding sheep on communal pastures. But as more Anglos, or white Americans, arrived, their political and economic influence undermined traditional Hispanic society. Congress restricted the original Hispanic land grants to only the villagers' home lots and irrigated fields, throwing open most of their common lands to newcomers. The notorious Santa Fe Ring, a group of lawyers and land speculators, seized millions of acres through fraud and legal chicanery.

QUICK REVIEW

Westward Migration

◆ The Homestead Act, promoters, and the railroad prompted migration.

◆ Migrants poured into the West between 1870 and 1900.

◆ Most migrants were whites, but African-American communities were established in Kansas and Nebraska.

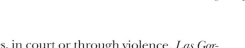

Spanish Americans resisted these losses, in court or through violence. *Las Gorras Blancas* (the White Caps) staged night raids to cut fences erected by Anglo ranchers and farmers and to attack the property of railroads, the symbol of the encroaching new order. "Our purpose," they announced, "is to protect the rights of the people in general and especially those of the helpless classes." Such resistance, however, had little success.

As their landholdings shrank, Hispanic villagers could not maintain their pastoral economy. Many became seasonal wage laborers in the Anglo-dominated economy, sometimes working as stoop labor in the commercial sugar beet fields that emerged in the 1890s, sometimes working on the railroads or in the mines. Women also participated in this new labor market. Previously crucial to the subsistence village economy, they now sought wage labor as cooks and domestic servants in railroad towns and mining camps. Hispanics retained some cultural autonomy, but they had little influence over the larger processes of settlement and development.

HOME ON THE RANGE

Farmers and their families encountered many difficulties, especially on the Great Plains, where they had to adapt to a radically new environment. The scarcity of trees on the plains meant that there was little wood for housing, fuel, and fencing. Until they had reaped several harvests and could afford to import lumber, pioneer families lived in dark and dirty sod houses. One Nebraska homesteader recalled that her first sight of a sod house "sickened me."

For fuel, settlers often had to rely on buffalo or cattle "chips"—dried dung. One farmer reported in 1879 that "it was comical to see how gingerly our wives handled these chips at first. They commenced by picking them up between two sticks, or with a poker. Soon they used a rag, and then a corner of their apron. Finally, growing hardened, a wash after handling them was sufficient. And now? Now it is out of the bread, into the chips and back again—and not even a dust of the hands!"

The scarcity of water also complicated women's domestic labor. They often transported water over long distances, pulling barrels on "water sleds" or carrying pails on neck yokes. Where possible, they also helped dig wells by hand.

Some women farmed the land themselves. Single women could claim land under the Homestead Act, and in some areas, women claimants made up 18 percent of the total and succeeded more frequently than men in gaining final title. At times, married women operated the family farm while their husbands worked elsewhere to earn money. In the 1870s, one Dakota woman recounted the demands women faced: "I had lived on a homestead long enough to learn some fundamental things: that while a woman had more independence here than in any other part of the world, she was expected to contribute as much as a man—that people who fought the frontier had to be prepared to meet any emergency; that the person who wasn't willing to try anything once wasn't equipped to be a settler."

Women especially suffered from isolation and loneliness on the plains because they frequently had less contact with others than the farm men. One farm woman complained that "being cut off from everybody is almost too much for me." Luna Kellie recalled that from her Nebraska farm "there were no houses in sight and it seemed like the end of the world." To break the silence, to provide some music and color, many homesteading families kept canaries among their few belongings.

FARMING THE LAND

Pioneer settlers had to make daunting adjustments to develop the agricultural potential of their new land. Advances in science, technology, and industry made such adjustments possible. The changes would not only reshape the agricultural

Each of the four Chrisman sisters claimed a homestead and built a sodhouse near Goheen, Nebraska. Farming on the Great Plains was typically a family operation, with all members of the family having important tasks.

Corbis/Bettmann

economy but also bring their own great challenges to traditional rural values and expectations.

Fencing was an immediate problem on the treeless plains. Barbed wire, developed in the mid-1870s, solved the problem. By 1900, farmers were importing nearly 300 million pounds of barbed wire each year from Eastern and Midwestern factories.

The aridity of most of the West also posed difficulties. In California, Colorado, and a few other areas, settlers used streams fed by mountain snowpacks to irrigate land. Elsewhere, enterprising farmers developed variants of the "dry farming" practices that the Mormons had introduced in Utah, attempting to preserve and maximize the limited rainfall. Some farmers erected windmills to pump underground water. The scarce rainfall also encouraged farmers to specialize in a single cash crop for market. Many plains farmers turned from corn to wheat, especially the drought-resistant Turkey Red variety of hard winter wheat that German Mennonites had introduced into Kansas from Russia. Related technological advancements included grain elevators that would store grain for shipment and load it into rail cars mechanically and mills that used corrugated, chilled-iron rollers rather than millstones to process the new varieties of wheat.

In semiarid regions, farmers required special plows to break the tough sod, new harrows to prepare the soil for cultivation, grain drills to plant the crop, and harvesting and threshing machines to bring it in. Thanks to more and better machines, agricultural efficiency and productivity shot up. By the 1890s, machinery permitted the farmer to produce eighteen times more wheat than hand methods had.

These developments reflected both the expansion of agriculture and its increasing dependence on the larger society. The rail network provided essential transportation for crops; the nation's industrial sector produced necessary agricultural machinery. Banks and loan companies extended the credit and capital that allowed farmers to take advantage of mechanization and other new advances; and many other businesses graded, stored, processed, and sold their crops. In short, because of its market orientation, mechanization, and specialization, Western agriculture relied on other people or impersonal forces as it was incorporated into the national and international economy.

When conditions were favorable—good weather, good crops, and good prices—Western farmers prospered. Too often, however, they faced adversity. In the late 1880s, drought coincided with a slump in crop prices. Expanding production in Argentina, Canada, Australia, and Russia helped create a world surplus of grain that drove prices steadily downward. Prices for other farm commodities also declined.

Squeezed between high costs for credit, transportation, and manufactured goods and falling agricultural prices, Western farmers faced disaster. They responded by lashing back at their points of contact with the new system. They especially condemned the railroads. Luna Kellie complained, "The minute you crossed the Missouri River your fate both soul and body was in their hands. What you should eat and drink, what you should wear, everything was in their hands and they robbed us of all we produced except enough to keep body and soul together and many many times not that."

Farmers censured the grain elevators in the local buying centers that were often owned by Eastern corporations, including the railroads themselves. A Minnesota state investigation found systematic fraud by elevators, which collectively cost farmers a massive sum.

Farmers also denounced the many Eastern bankers and mortgage lenders who had provided the credit for them to acquire land, equipment, and machinery. With failing crops and falling prices, many Western farms were foreclosed.

Stunned and bitter, Western farmers concluded that their problems arose because they had been incorporated into the new system, an integrated economy directed by forces beyond their control. And it was a system that did not work well. "There is," one of them charged, "something radically wrong in our industrial system. There is a screw loose."

CONCLUSION

With determination, ingenuity, and hard work millions of people settled vast areas, made farms and ranches, built villages and cities, brought forth mineral wealth, and imposed their values on the land. These achievements were tempered by a shameful treatment of Indians and an often destructive exploitation of natural resources. But if most Westerners took pride in their accomplishments, and a few enjoyed wealth and power, many also grew discontented with the new conditions they encountered as the "Wild" West receded.

Railroad expansion, population movements, Eastern investment, corporate control, technological innovations, and government policies had incorporated the region fully into the larger society. Indians experienced this incorporation most thoroughly and most tragically, losing their lands, their traditions, and often their lives; the survivors were dependent on the decisions and actions of interlopers. Cowboys and miners also learned that the frontier merely marked the cutting edge of Eastern industrial society; neither could escape integration into the national economy by managerial decisions, transportation links, and market forces. Most settlers in the West were farmers, but they too learned that their distinctive environment did not insulate them from assimilation into larger productive, financial, and marketing structures.

SUMMARY

Subjugating Native Americans As white people pressed westward, the initial obstacle to exploiting the West was the people who already lived there. The native peoples used the land in their own way, had different concepts of progress and civilization, and had developed a variety of economies and cultures. From the 1850s to the 1880s, warfare engulfed the advancing frontier; railroad expansion, the destruction of the buffalo, and technological development undercut the ability of the Native Americans to resist. The conquest gradually forced Indians onto reservations, but efforts to "Americanize" the Indian way of life were less successful.

Exploiting the Mountains: The Mining Bonanza The first stage of the economic development of the West centered on mining as swarms of eager prospectors were attracted into the mountains and deserts in search of gold and silver.

The male-dominated saloon society of the mining camps generated violence and social conflicts. Mining was transformed from an individual effort into a corporate one; as minerals became more difficult to uncover, mining became technologically complex and expensive. Corporate mining permanently changed the landscape of the West through its environmental impact.

Exploiting the Grass: The Cattle Kingdom The development of the range cattle industry opened a second stage in the exploitation of the West. It reflected the needs of the Eastern urban society for food and the ability of the expanding rail network to deliver it. The cattle kingdom spread from Texas into the Great Plains; after the era of the long drives, cattle ranching became an increasingly corporate endeavor. While the romantic image of the cowboy is one of a rugged individualist freed of societal constraints, the actual work was hard, dirty, seasonal, dangerous, and poorly paid.

Exploiting the Earth: Homesteaders and Agricultural Expansion Even more than ranching and mining, agricultural growth boosted the West's economy and bound it to national and world markets. Government played a significant role in the expansion of farming, as did railroads, science and technology, Eastern capital, and hard work. The Homestead Act, along with land, railroad, and steamship companies, encouraged Western migration. Settlers encountered many difficulties: a radically new environment, the need for new farming techniques, weather conditions, loneliness, and isolation. These were combined with farmers being part of a global economic system; farmers reached the conclusion that something was terribly wrong with the system, and that bankers, grain elevator operators, and the railroads were to blame.

REVIEW QUESTIONS

1. Why was the completion of the first transcontinental railroad so celebrated?

2. What factors most influenced the subjugation of American Indians?

3. What were the major goals of federal Indian policy, and how did they change?

4. How did technological developments affect Indians, miners, and farmers in the West?

5. How did the federal government help transform the West?

KEY TERMS

Battle of the Little Bighorn (p. 503)
Chisholm Trail (p. 510)
Dawes Act (p. 505)
Sand Creek Massacre (p. 502)

Second Treaty of Fort Laramie (p. 502)
Wounded Knee Massacre (p. 503)

WHERE TO LEARN MORE

Bodie State Historic Park, Bodie, California. The largest authentic ghost town in the West, Bodie was an important mining center from the 1860s to the 1880s. About 170 buildings remain, including a museum with mining equipment and artifacts of everyday life. **www.bodie.net/**

Little Bighorn Battlefield National Monument, Crow Agency, Montana. The site of Custer's crushing defeat includes a monument to the Seventh Cavalry atop Last Stand Hill. A new authorized Indian Memorial will include sacred texts, artifacts, and pictographs of the Plains Indians. **www.nps.gov/libi/home.htm**

American Historical Society of Germans from Russia Museum, Lincoln, Nebraska. This unique museum, consisting of a complex of restored homes, exhibitions, and archives, preserves the history and culture of Germans who emigrated to Russia and then to the American Great Plains, where they contributed importantly to the development of a multicultural society and an agricultural economy.

National Museum of the American Indian, New York, New York. Part of the Smithsonian Institution, this museum has a collection of artifacts illustrative of more than ten thousand years of the Native American culture. **www.nmai.si.edu/index.asp**

National Cowboy Hall of Fame, Oklahoma City, Oklahoma. This large institution contains an outstanding collection of Western art, displays of cowboy and Indian artifacts, and both kitschy exhibitions of the mythic, Hollywood West and serious galleries depicting the often hard realities of the cattle industry. Its many public programs also successfully combine fun with learning. **www.cowboyhalloffame.org/index2.html**

Golden Spike National Historic Site, near Promontory, Utah. The completion of the transcontinental railroad here in 1869 is reenacted from May to October, using reproductions of the original locomotives. Visitors can drive the route of the railroad, now a National Backway Byway through abandoned mining and railroad towns, from Promontory to Nevada. Virtual tour, history, and tourist links on: **www.nps./gov/gosp**

Fort Laramie, National Historic Site, near Guernsey, Wyoming. A fur-trading post, stop on the Oregon Trail, site of treaty negotiations with the Plains Indians, and staging area for military campaigns, Fort Laramie is now a living history museum with many original buildings. For a virtual tour of the fort and information about visiting see: **www.nps.gov/fola/**

 For additional study resources for this chapter, go to:
www.prenhall.com/goldfield/chapter19

Mythologizing the "Wild West"

WHAT ELEMENTS do the Remington sculptures, the Curtis photograph, and the "dime novel" illustrations have in common? What, to judge from these images, made the West "wild"? How much do you think these images match up with reality?

One artist, Frederic Remington, deserves much of the credit for creating the West of our imagination. In Montana in 1881 an "old-timer" told him that "there is no more West." Remington decided to "try to record some facts around me." He recorded them first in a series of illustrations, then in paintings, and then in sculpture. Another who determined to "record some facts" was Edward S. Curtis who produced the twenty volume collection, *The North American Indian*, between 1906 and 1930. Curtis persuaded Native American peoples to reenact traditional practices, such as hunting or war parties. Often there was a twenty to fifty year gap between the reenactment and the practice itself. In contrast to Remington and Curtis who sought to (re)capture the truth about the West, "dime novels" sought simply to provide thrills. The "Wild West" is still part of our imaginative landscape.

Edward S. Curtis, "On the Warpath — Atsina," from The North American Indian, v.04; Curtis notes: "These grim-visaged old warriors made a thrilling picture as they rode along, breaking out now and then into wild song of the chase or raid." The image recreates a raiding party. Note the headdress on the party's leader, fourth from left. The photograph was taken in 1908.

▼

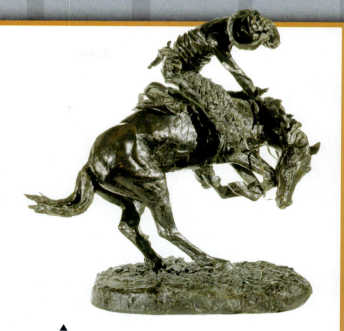

Frederick Remington, "The Cheyenne," a 1901 bronze statue, now at the Amon Carter Museum, Fort Worth, Texas. Remington loved to portray action; here a warrior is galloping on his pony into battle.

Frederick S. Remington, "The Cheyenne," 1901, cast 1904. Amon Carter Museum

http://memory.loc.gov/ammem/award98/ienhtml/curthome.html

Frederick Remington, "The Rattlesnake," (1905) Bronze (Height 23 7/8 inches), now at Amon Carter Museum, Fort Worth, Texas. Note how the rattlesnake has reverted from national symbol to natural menace as the cowboy's horse rears up and threatens to throw its rider.

Frederick S. Remington, "The Rattlesnake," 1905. Amon Carter Museum

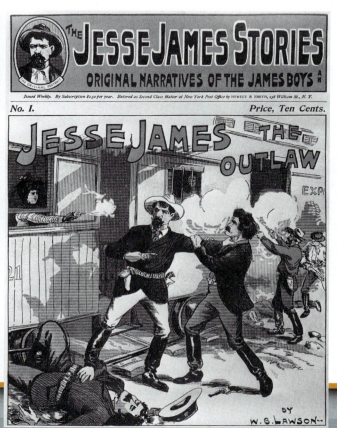

◄ **"Dime novels" purported to tell true tales of western adventure.** Jesse James was an historical figure, even if the stories in this "Log Cabin Library" edition bore no resemblance to his actual deeds. "The King of the Wild West" was a purely fictional creation.

From the Library of Congress's American Memory site
http://www.loc.gov/exhibits/treasures/tri015.html

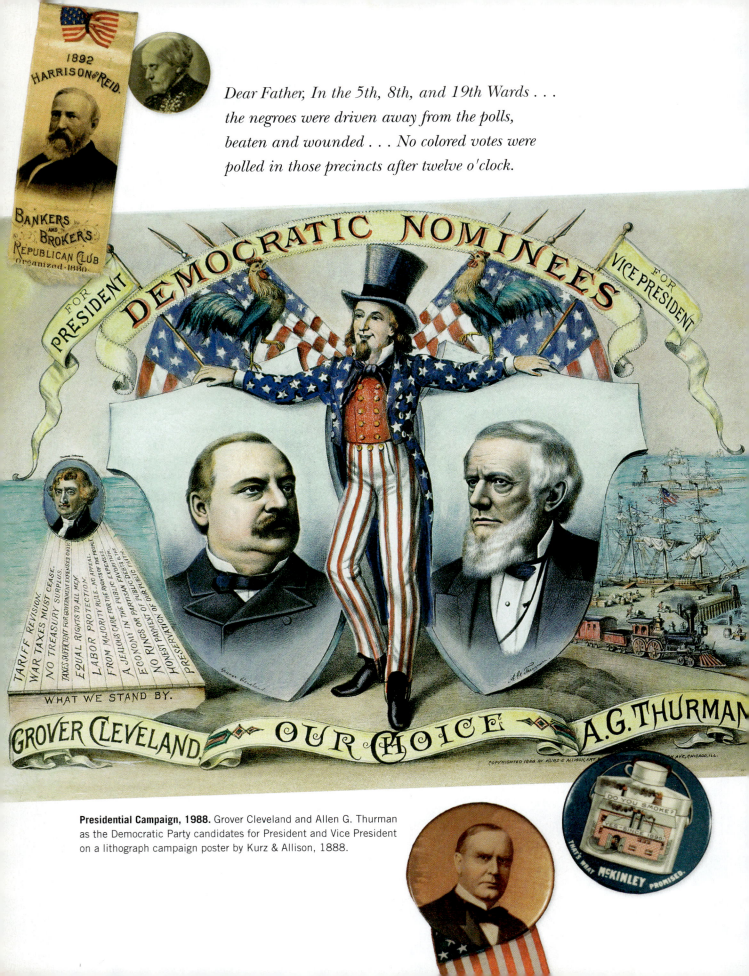

*Dear Father, In the 5th, 8th, and 19th Wards . . .
the negroes were driven away from the polls,
beaten and wounded . . . No colored votes were
polled in those precincts after twelve o'clock.*

Presidential Campaign, 1988. Grover Cleveland and Allen G. Thurman
as the Democratic Party candidates for President and Vice President
on a lithograph campaign poster by Kurz & Allison, 1888.

20

POLITICS AND GOVERNMENT
1877–1900

HOW WERE the campaigns run in the late 1800s, and what role did partisan politics play?

HOW EFFECTIVE was the federal government in addressing the problems of America's industrializing economy?

WHAT WERE the main policy issues of the 1880s and the 1890s?

WHAT WAS the platform of the Populist Party?

IMAGE KEY

for pages 522–523

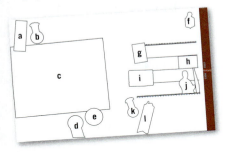

a. 1892 Benjamin Harrison presidential campaign poster sponsored by the Republican Club.

b. Susan B. Anthony medal. It was for the 1906 NY State Suffrage Association Convention, honoring Susan B Anthony in the year of her death.

c. Presidential Campaign, 1888. Grover Cleveland and Allen G. Thurman as the Democratic party candidates for President and Vice President on a lithograph campaign poster by Kurz & Allison, 1888.

d. Campaign buttons for William McKinley, 1896.

e. McKinley-Roosevelt campaign paraphernalia.

f. Benjamin Harrison 1888 Presidential campaign paraphernalia.

g. New Yorkers outside the Madison Square Garden during the Democratic National Convention of 1888, engraving from a contemporary American newspaper.

h. Coxey's Army with band passing a lumber yard.

i. Bosses of the Senate by Joseph Keppler. Giant corpulent (steel, copper, oil, sugar) trust figures loom over the deliberations of the US Senate in a 19th century political cartoon.

j. William Jennings Bryan (1860–1925)-Democratic Convention, 1896, in which he made the "Cross of Gold" speech.

k. Campaign button for William McKinley, 1896.

l. "Tilden and Hendricks have been elected" ribbon.

Cincinnati, Ohio
September 28, 1884

Dear Fanny,

    Will has been appointed chief supervisor and so has to take means to prevent fraud at the election. He must appoint assistants for each ward.

—Horace

October 12, 1884

Dear Father,

    Will has no time for anything but the election and his duties as chief supervisor. . . . I am afraid the election will be a stormy one & violence will not surprise me. I am one of a citizens' committee of the 18th ward and we propose to be on hand from 6 in the morning till the votes are counted at night.

—Horace

October 22, 1884

Dear Mother,

    We had an exciting time election day. The Democrats tried to introduce their Southern methods into northern elections and succeeded in one or two wards, but in general the U.S. Deputy Marshals managed to keep the scoundrels quiet. The negroes in many precincts voted at the risk of their lives. I saw a man shot & killed about fifteen feet from me at our polling place. . . . He drew a pistol on a Deputy Marshal but the Deputy was too quick for him.

—Horace

October 22, 1884

Dear Father,

    In the 5th, 8th, and 19th Wards the marshals were utterly useless and were soon overpowered. The police did nothing except to set on [incite] the crowd. . . . The negroes were driven away from the polls, beaten and wounded and exposed to as much abuse as they could have been south of Mason's and Dixon's line. No colored votes were polled in those precincts after twelve o'clock.

—Will

William H. Taft Papers, Manuscript Division, Library of Congress.

HORACE AND WILL TAFT kept their parents and sister Fanny informed of the 1884 congressional election in their hometown of Cincinnati. Alphonso, Louise, and Fanny Taft, all staunch Republicans, were desperate for such political news. Alphonso had served in President Ulysses S. Grant's cabinet and was now American minister to Austria. In Vienna, they eagerly awaited news of their party's success.

    As the Taft brothers reported, Cincinnati voters had a difficult journey to the polls. Rabid partisans had staged competing torchlight parades, with thousands of uniformed marchers; orators had stirred the huge crowds for hours with patriotic, religious, and cultural bombast. And the election itself produced the violence Horace had expected. The Republican brothers condemned the Democrats for intimidating African Americans and others likely to vote Republican, "importing" Democratic voters from other states, and using the local police to frighten or arrest Republicans.

But the Democrats also complained. The U.S. marshals so praised by Horace had been appointed by Republican federal officials under Will's supervision, and many of those marshals were merely thugs, paid and armed by local Republicans to improve Republican election prospects. As Will conceded, they first "drove from the city the night before election" hundreds of Democrats they alleged might commit election fraud. On election day itself they sought to incite violence in the city's Irish wards to keep other Democratic voters from the polls, and they made mass arrests of others trying to vote, often claiming that they were Kentucky Democrats who had crossed the Ohio River to "colonize" Cincinnati's election. Some deputies fired point-blank into Democratic crowds. As Will admitted to his father about those deputies, "it is attended with risk to furnish revolvers to men who are close to or belong to the criminal class."

"The Democrats are so mad at not being able to perpetrate these frauds," Will concluded with unwitting irony, "that they are trying to get even by crying fraud at us."

Not all American elections in the late nineteenth century were as riotous as this Cincinnati contest, but it suggests much about American politics at the time. From the military-style campaign to the rough act of voting itself, elections were a masculine business—although women were intensely interested. Campaigns attracted mass participation but often avoided substantive issues. The two major political parties shaped campaigns and controlled elections, which were tumultuous if not always violent. Partisan divisions overlapped with ethnic, racial, and other social divisions, and suffrage was a contested issue. Partisanship often determined both the membership and the activities of government agencies, even those charged with maintaining order. Local concerns took precedence over national concerns.

While these features of late-nineteenth century politics endured, they shaped not only campaigns and elections but the form and role of government as well. William Howard Taft eventually became president of the United States. His success, he explained, stemmed from his father's reputation, his own loyalty to his party, and keeping his "plate the right side up when offices were falling."

THE STRUCTURE AND STYLE OF POLITICS

Political parties dominated political life. They organized campaigns, controlled balloting, and held the unswerving loyalty of most of the electorate. While the major parties worked to maintain a sense of unity and tradition among their followers, third parties sought the support of those the major parties left unserved. Other Americans looked outside the electoral arena to fulfill their political goals.

HOW WERE campaigns run in the late 1800s, and what role did partisan politics play?

CAMPAIGNS AND ELECTIONS

Campaign pageantry absorbed communities large and small. The town of Emporia, Kansas, once witnessed a campaign rally of twenty thousand people, several times its population. A parade of wagons stretched 5 miles, reported the proud local newspaper. "When the head of the procession was under the equator the tail was coming around the north pole."

WHERE TO LEARN MORE

★ Rest Cottage, Evanston, Illinois
www.wctu.org/house.html

The excitement of political contests prompted the wife of Chief Justice Morrison Waite to write longingly on election day, 1876, "I should want to vote all day." But women could not vote at all. Justice Waite himself had just a year earlier written the unanimous opinion of the Supreme Court (in *Minor* v. *Happersett*) that the Constitution did not confer suffrage on women.

But turnout among male voters was remarkably high, averaging nearly 80 percent in presidential elections between 1876 and 1900, a figure far greater than ever achieved thereafter. In many states, even immigrants not yet citizens were eligible to vote and flocked to the polls. African Americans voted regularly in the North and irregularly in the South before being disfranchised at the end of the century.

Political parties kept detailed records of voters, transported them to the polls, saw that they were registered where necessary, and sometimes even paid their poll taxes or naturalization fees to make them eligible. With legal regulations and public machinery for elections negligible, parties dominated the campaigns and elections. Election clerks and judges were not public officials but partisans chosen by the political parties. Until the 1890s, most states had no laws to ensure secrecy in voting, and ballots were printed by the parties. Because they had only the names of the candidates of the party issuing them and often varied in size and color, ballots revealed the voters' party allegiance.

Paid party workers known as peddlers or hawkers stationed themselves near the polls, each trying to force his party ticket on prospective voters. Fighting and intimidation were so commonplace at the polls that one state supreme court ruled in 1887 that they were "acceptable" features of elections.

As the court recognized, the open and partisan aspects of the electoral process did not necessarily lead to election fraud, however much they shaped the nature of political participation.

MAP EXPLORATION

To explore an interactive version of this map, go to
http://www.prenhall.com/goldfield2/map20.1

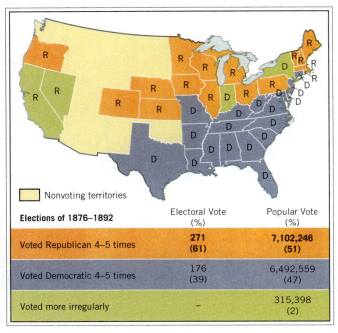

Elections of 1876–1892	Electoral Vote (%)	Popular Vote (%)
Voted Republican 4–5 times	**271 (61)**	**7,102,246 (51)**
Voted Democratic 4–5 times	176 (39)	6,492,559 (47)
Voted more irregularly	–	315,398 (2)

Nonvoting territories

MAP 20–1

The Two-Party Stalemate of the Late Nineteenth Century Strong parties, staunch loyalties, and an evenly divided electorate made for exciting politics but often stalemated government in the late nineteenth century. Most states voted consistently for one of the major parties, leaving the few swing states like New York and Indiana the scenes of fierce partisan battles.

WHAT WAS the geographical pattern of Republican versus Democratic voting during this time period?

PARTISAN POLITICS

Democrats and Republicans had virtually the same level of electoral support, so they worked hard to get out the vote (see Map 20–1). Rarely did either party control both the presidency and Congress at once. The party balance also gave great influence to New York, New Jersey, Ohio, and Indiana, whose evenly divided voters could swing an election either way. Both parties concentrated campaign funds and strategy on the swing states. Thus Republican presidential candidate James Garfield of Ohio commented during the election campaign in 1880: "Nothing is wanting except an immediate and liberal supply of money for campaign expenses to make Indiana certain. With a victory there, the rest is easy." Garfield carried Indiana by six thousand votes and the nation by nine thousand out of 9.2 million cast.

Interrelated regional, ethnic, religious, and local factors determined the party affiliations of most Americans. Economic issues generally did not decide party ties. Like religious belief and ethnic identity, partisan loyalty was largely a cultural trait passed from father to son, which helps explain the electoral stability of most communities.

Republicans were strongest in the North and Midwest, where they benefited from their party's role as the defender of the Union in the Civil War. The Republican party appealed primarily to old-stock Americans and other Protestants, including those of German and Scandinavian descent. African Americans, loyal to the party that had emancipated and enfranchised the slaves of the South, also supported the Grand Old Party, or GOP, where they could vote. Democrats were strongest in the South, where they stood as the defenders of the traditions of the region's white population. But Democrats also drew support in the urban Northeast, especially from Catholics and recent immigrants.

Each major party thus consisted of a complex coalition of groups with differing traditions and interests. One observer described the Democratic party in California as "a sort of Democratic happy family, like we see in the prairie-dog villages, where owls, rattlesnakes, prairie dogs, and lizards all live in the same hole."

Republicans identified their party with nationalism and national unity and attacked the Democrats as an "alliance between the embittered South and the slums of the Northern cities." They combined a "bloody shirt" appeal to the memories of the Civil War with campaigns for immigration restriction and cultural uniformity. Republican legislatures in several Eastern and Midwestern states in the 1880s and 1890s enacted laws regulating parochial schools, the use of foreign languages, and alcohol consumption.

Democrats portrayed themselves as the party of limited government and "personal liberties," a theme that appealed both to the racism of white Southerners and the resentment immigrants felt about the nativist meddling the Republicans favored. The Democrats' commitment to personal liberties had limits. They supported the disfranchisement of African Americans, the exclusion of Chinese immigrants, and the dispossession of American Indians from their lands. Nevertheless, their emphasis on traditional individualism and localism proved popular.

Both major parties had party machines, especially at the local level, led by powerful bosses like Democrat Richard Croker of New York or Republican George Cox of Cincinnati. These machines not only controlled city politics but also municipal government. Well-organized ward clubs mobilized working-class voters, who were rewarded by municipal jobs and baskets of food or coal doled out by the machine. Such assistance was often necessary given the lack of public welfare systems, but to buy votes the machine also sold favors. Public contracts and franchises were peddled to businesses whose high bids covered kickbacks to the machine.

Third parties organized around specific issues or groups. The **Prohibition party** championed the abolition of alcohol but also introduced many important reform ideas into American politics. Some farmers and workers formed larger but shorter lived third parties, charging that Republicans and Democrats had failed to respond to economic problems caused by industrialization or, worse still, had deliberately promoted powerful business interests at the expense of ordinary Americans. The **Greenback party** of the 1870s denounced "the infamous financial legislation which takes all from the many to enrich the few." Its policies of labor reform and currency inflation (to stimulate and democratize the economy) attracted supporters from Maine to Texas. The most significant third party was the **People's** or **Populist party** of the 1890s.

ASSOCIATIONAL POLITICS

Associations of like-minded citizens, operating outside the electoral arena, worked to achieve public policies beneficial to their members. Farmers organized the Patrons of Husbandry, known familiarly as the Grange (see Chapter 19). Its campaign for public regulation to control the rates charged by railroads and grain elevators helped convince Midwestern states to pass the so-called **Granger laws**. The Grange also sought reforms in the nation's financial system.

To the Grangers' dismay, industrialists also formed pressure groups. Organizations such as the American Iron and Steel Association and the American Protective Tariff League lobbied Congress for high tariff laws and made campaign

Prohibition party   A venerable third party still in existence that has persistently campaigned for the abolition of alcohol but has also introduced many important reform ideas into American politics.

Greenback party   A third party of the 1870s and 1880s that garnered temporary support by advocating currency inflation to expand the economy and assist debtors.

Populist party   A major third party of the 1890s, formed on the basis of the Southern Farmers' Alliance and other organizations, mounting electoral challenges against Democrats in the South and the Republicans in the West.

Granger Laws   State laws enacted in the Midwest in the 1870s that regulated rates charged by railroads, grain elevator operators, and other middlemen.

FROM THEN TO NOW
Political Parties

Few things in contemporary American politics present a sharper contrast to the nineteenth century than the role of political parties. In the late nineteenth century, parties dominated politics. They commanded the allegiance of Americans, controlled the selection of candidates, mobilized voters, shaped voting behavior, provided ballots, and ran elections. They also shaped public policies and, through patronage, staffed government positions. At the beginning of the twenty-first century, parties do virtually none of these things.

This transformation began at the end of the nineteenth century. Extreme partisanship prompted states to assert control over elections. The corruption attributed to party machines led gradually to such changes as nonpartisan municipal elections and increased public control over parties. Restrictions on campaign expenditures reduced the party hoopla that had made politics so exciting and voter turnout so high. The connection between parties and voters declined further as new voters unfamiliar with the passions and loyalties of the past joined the electorate.

The inability of the major parties to deal effectively with important national problems, so evident in the depression of the 1890s, prompted Americans to find other ways to influence public policy. Associational groups that had acted outside the partisan arena evolved into effective special-interest lobbying groups. Civil service reform, beginning with the Pendleton Act, steadily reduced party influence in government. So did the growing reliance in the twentieth century on independent regulatory commissions, rather than partisan legislative committees, to make and implement policies.

In recent decades, party decline has accelerated. The introduction and spread of primary elections have stripped parties of their control over nominations. Individual candidates have come increasingly to rely more on personal organizations than party apparatus to manage campaigns. Candidates often appeal for votes as individuals rather than as party members and communicate directly to voters through the mass media, relying less on the old door-to-door personal campaign requiring party workers. Television, in particular, with its focus on dramatic and personal sound bites, is better at promoting individual candidates than abstract entities like parties.

Campaign finance reform laws have reduced party control over the funding of campaigns. So too has the rise of political action committees (PACs) as an important source of support for candidates. PACs represent particular interests, not a collection of interests the way parties do. Candidates dependent on specific interests find it harder to make broader partisan appeals.

Polls show fewer and fewer Americans identifying with a particular party and indicate that partisanship has greatly declined as a factor in voting decisions. Americans increasingly regard parties as neither meaningful nor even useful, let alone essential to democratic government. Nearly half of the electorate favors making all elections nonpartisan or even abolishing parties. More and more people believe that interest groups better represent their political needs than parties. At the same time, fewer and fewer Americans bother to vote. Those who do are much more likely than before to split their ticket, voting for candidates of different parties for different offices. This often results in divided government—with the presidency controlled by one party and Congress by the other. The resulting stalemate increases public cynicism about parties.

Of course, parties endure and retain some importance. Election laws favor the two established parties and obstruct independent candidacies. Public funds subsidize party activities, and party coffers harvest unregulated "soft money" campaign contributions. Congress and state legislatures continue to rely on party divisions to organize their leadership and committee structures, and party discipline still influences the way legislators vote. But while such institutional factors guarantee the continued presence of a two-party system, the parties themselves no longer enjoy the influence they had in the nineteenth century.

CHRONOLOGY

1867	Patrons of Husbandry (the Grange) is founded.
1869	Massachusetts establishes the first state regulatory commission.
1873	Silver is demonetized in the "Crime of '73."
1874	Woman's Christian Temperance Union is organized.
1875	U.S. Supreme Court, in *Minor* v. *Happersett*, upholds denial of suffrage to women.
1876	Greenback party runs presidential candidate.
1877	Rutherford B. Hayes becomes president after disputed election. Farmers' Alliance is founded. Supreme Court, in *Munn* v. *Illinois*, upholds state regulatory authority over private property.
1878	Bland-Allison Act obliges the government to buy silver.
1880	James A. Garfield is elected president.
1881	Garfield is assassinated; Chester A. Arthur becomes president.
1883	Pendleton Civil Service Act is passed.
1884	Grover Cleveland is elected president.
1886	Supreme Court, in *Wabash* v. *Illinois*, rules that only the federal government, not the states, can regulate interstate commerce.

1887	Interstate Commerce Act is passed.
1888	Benjamin Harrison is elected president.
1890	Sherman Antitrust Act is passed. McKinley Tariff Act is passed. Sherman Silver Purchase Act is passed. National American Woman Suffrage Association is organized. Wyoming enters the Union as the first state with woman suffrage.
1892	People's party is organized. Cleveland is elected to his second term as president.
1893	Depression begins. Sherman Silver Purchase Act is repealed.
1894	Coxey's Army marches to Washington. Pullman strike ends in violence.
1895	Supreme Court, in *Pollock* v. *Farmers' Loan and Trust Company*, invalidates the federal income tax. Supreme Court, in *United States* v. *E. C. Knight Company*, limits the Sherman Antitrust law to commerce, excluding industrial monopolies.
1896	William Jennings Bryan is nominated for president by Democrats and Populists. William McKinley is elected president.
1900	Currency Act puts U.S. currency on the gold standard.

contributions to friendly politicians of both parties. A small group of conservative reformers known derisively as **Mugwumps** (the term derives from the Algonquian word for *chief*) devoted most of their efforts to campaigning for honest and efficient government through civil service reform. They organized the National Civil Service Reform League to publicize their plans, lobby Congress and state legislatures, and endorse sympathetic candidates.

Women were also active in associational politics. Susan B. Anthony and others formed groups to lobby Congress and state legislatures for constitutional amendments extending the right to vote to women. The leading organizations merged in 1890 as the **National American Woman Suffrage Association.** Despite the opposition of male politicians of both major parties, suffragists had succeeded by the mid-1890s in gaining full woman suffrage in four western states—Wyoming, Colorado, Idaho, and Utah—and partial suffrage (the right to vote in school elections) in several other states, East and West.

With petition campaigns, demonstrations, and lobbying, women's social service organizations sought to remedy poverty and disease, improve education and recreation, and provide day nurseries for the children of workingwomen. The Illinois Woman's Alliance, organized in 1888 by suffragists, women assemblies of the Knights of Labor, and middle-class women's clubs, investigated the conditions of women and children in workshops and factories and campaigned for protective labor legislation and compulsory school attendance laws.

The Woman's Christian Temperance Union (WCTU) gained a massive membership campaigning for restrictive liquor laws. Under the leadership of Frances

WHERE TO LEARN MORE W

Susan B. Anthony House National Historic Landmark, Rochester, New York
www.susanbanthonyhouse.org/main.html

Mugwumps   Elitist and conservative reformers who favored sound money and limited government and opposed tariffs and the spoils system.

National American Woman Suffrage Association   The organization, formed in 1890, that coordinated the ultimately successful campaign to achieve women's right to vote.

Willard, however, it inserted domestic issues into the political sphere with a campaign for social and economic reforms far beyond temperance. It particularly sought to strengthen and enforce laws against rape. Willard bitterly noted that twenty states fixed the age of consent at ten and that "in Massachusetts and Vermont it is a greater crime to steal a cow" than to rape a woman. The WCTU also pushed for improved health conditions and workplace and housing reforms.

A meeting in 1880 of the National Woman Suffrage Association protested the exclusion of women from electoral politics. Susan B. Anthony noted with regret that "to all men woman suffrage is only a side issue."

The Granger Collection, New York

HOW EFFECTIVE was the federal government in addressing the problems of America's industrializing economy?

QUICK REVIEW

The Late Nineteenth-Century Presidency

◆ Weak and subordinated to legislature.

◆ Presidents between 1877 and 1897 were conservative and offered few initiatives.

◆ Presidents of this era made little effort to reach out to public.

18–3
The Gilded Age (1880)

THE LIMITS OF GOVERNMENT

Despite enthusiasm for politics and the activity of associations, government in the late nineteenth century was neither active nor productive by present standards. The receding government activism of the Civil War and Reconstruction years coincided with a resurgent belief in localism and laissez-faire policies. In addition, a Congress and presidency divided between the two major parties, a small and inefficient bureaucracy, and judicial restraints joined powerful private interests to limit the size and objectives of the federal government.

THE WEAK PRESIDENCY

The presidency was a weak and restricted institution. The impeachment of President Johnson at the outset of Reconstruction had undermined the office. Then President Grant subordinated it to the legislative branch by deferring to Congress on appointments and legislation. And the presidents between 1877 and 1897—Republicans Rutherford B. Hayes (1877–1881), James A. Garfield (1881), and Chester A. Arthur (1881–1885), Democrat Grover Cleveland (1885–1889 and 1893–1897), and Republican Benjamin Harrison (1889–1893)—were all conservatives who proposed few initiatives. The most aggressive of them, Cleveland, vetoed two-thirds of all the bills Congress passed, more than all his predecessors combined. Vetoing relief for drought-stricken Texas farmers, Cleveland stated, "though the people support the Government, the Government should not support the people."

The presidents of this era made little effort to reach out to the public or to exert legislative leadership. In 1885, Woodrow Wilson, at the time a professor of history and government, described "the business of the president" as "not much above routine" and concluded that the office might be made purely administrative, its occupant a sort of tenured civil servant. (Wilson took a different view when he became president himself in 1913.) Benjamin Harrison spent six hours a day dealing with office seekers, and Garfield lamented, "My day is frittered away by the personal seeking of people, when it ought to be given to the great problems which concern the whole country."

The presidency was also hampered by its limited control over bureaus and departments and by its small staff, which consisted of half a dozen secretaries, clerks, and telegraphers. As Cleveland complained, "If the President has any great policy in mind or on hand he has no one to help him work it out."

THE INEFFICIENT CONGRESS

Congress exercised authority over the federal budget, oversaw the cabinet, debated public issues, and controlled legislation. Its members, as one senator conceded, "tolerated no intrusion from the President or from anybody else."

But Congress was inefficient. Its chambers were chaotic, and members rarely paid attention to the business at hand. Instead they played cards, read newspapers, or sent a page to get fruit or tobacco from the vendors who lined the hallways of the capitol. The repeated shifts in party control of Congress also impeded effective action. So too did the loss of experienced legislators to rapid turnover. In some Congresses, most members were first-termers.

Procedural rules often kept Congress from acting. The most notorious rule required that a quorum be not only present but also voting. When the House was narrowly divided along party lines, the minority could block all business by refusing to answer when the roll was called.

But as a nationalizing economy required more national legislation, business before Congress grew relentlessly (see Figure 20–1). The expanding scale of congressional work prompted a gradual reform of procedures and the centralization of power in the speaker of the House and the leading committees. These changes did not, however, create a coherent program for government action.

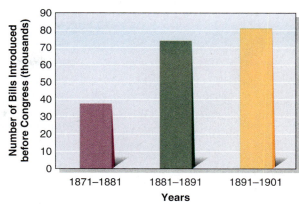

Figure 20–1 Increase in Congressional Business, 1871–1901
Industrialization, urbanization, and western expansion brought increased demands for government action, but the party stalemate, laissez-faire attitudes, and inefficient public institutions often blocked effective responses.

THE FEDERAL BUREAUCRACY AND THE SPOILS SYSTEM

The federal bureaucracy remained small and limited in the late nineteenth century. There were little more than fifty thousand government employees in 1871, and three-fourths of them were local postmasters scattered across the nation. Only six thousand, from President Grant to janitors, worked in Washington.

Most federal employees were selected under the so-called spoils system. Its basic principle was that victorious politicians awarded government jobs to party workers, with little regard for qualifications, and ousted the previous employees. Appointees then typically promised part of their salary and time to the political interests of their patron or party. The spoils system enabled party leaders to strengthen their organizations, reward loyal party service, and attract the political workers that parties needed to mobilize the electorate.

Critics charged that the system was riddled with corruption, abuse, and inefficiency. Rapid turnover bred instability; political favoritism bred incompetence. One secretary of the navy, appointed at the behest of Indiana's Republican machine, was said to have exclaimed during his first official inspection of a ship: "Why, the thing's hollow!" Certainly the spoils system was ineffective for filling positions that required special skills. More serious, the spoils system also absorbed the president and Congress in unproductive conflicts over patronage.

QUICK REVIEW

The Spoils System
- Fifty thousand federal employees in 1871.
- Politicians awarded government jobs to party workers.
- Critics charged that the system was corrupt.

INCONSISTENT STATE GOVERNMENT

Considered closer and more responsible to the people, state governments had long exercised police power and regulatory authority. They collected taxes for education and public works, and they promoted private enterprise and public health. Still, they did little by today's standards. Few people thought it appropriate for government at any level to offer direct help to particular social groups, and state constitutions often restricted the scope of public authority.

But state governments gradually expanded their role in response to the stresses produced by industrialization. Following the lead of Massachusetts in

1869, a majority of states had by the turn of the century created commissions to investigate and regulate industry. One observer noted in 1887 that state governments enacted many laws and established numerous state agencies in "utter disregard of the *laissez-faire* principle." In Minnesota, for example, the state helped dairy farmers by establishing a dairy commission, prohibiting the manufacture or sale of margarine, creating a bureau of animal industry, and employing state veterinarians. Other laws regulated railroads, telegraphs, and dangerous occupations, prohibited racial discrimination in inns, and otherwise protected the public welfare.

Not all such agencies and laws were effective. Southern states especially lagged, and one Midwesterner complained that his legislature merely "meets in ignorance, sits in corruption, and dissolves in disgrace every two years." Still, the widening scope of state action represented a growing acceptance of public responsibility for social welfare and economic life.

PUBLIC POLICIES AND NATIONAL ELECTIONS

Several great issues dominated the national political arena in the late nineteenth century, including civil service reform, tariffs, and business and financial regulation. Rarely, however, did these issues clearly and consistently separate the major political parties. Instead they divided each party into factions along regional, interest, and economic lines. As a consequence, these leading issues often played only a small role in determining elections and were seldom resolved by government action.

CIVIL SERVICE REFORM

Reform of the spoils system emerged as a prominent issue during the Hayes administration. Reformers like the Mugwumps wanted a professional civil service based on merit and divorced from politics. They wanted officeholders to be selected on the basis of competitive written examinations and protected from removal on political grounds. They expected such a system to promote efficiency, economy, and honesty in government. But they also expected it to increase their own influence and minimize that of "mere politicians." As one Baltimore Mugwump said, civil service reform would replace ignorant and corrupt officeholders with "gentlemen . . . who need nothing and want nothing from government except the satisfaction of using their talents."

President Hayes favored civil service reform. He struck a blow for change when he fired Chester A. Arthur from his post as New York customs house collector after an investigation pronounced Arthur's patronage system to be "unsound in principle, dangerous in practice, . . . and calculated to encourage and perpetuate the official ignorance, inefficiency, and corruption . . ."

The weakness of the civil service reformers was dramatically underscored in 1880 when the Republicans, to improve their chances of carrying the crucial state of New York, nominated Arthur for vice president on a presidential slate headed by James A. Garfield of Ohio. They won, and Garfield immediately found himself enmeshed in the demands of the unreformed spoils system. He once complained to his wife, "I had hardly arrived before the door-bell began to ring and the old stream of office-seekers began to pour in. They had scented my coming and were lying in wait for me like vultures for a wounded bison. All day long it has been a

WHAT WERE the main public policy issues of the 1880s and 1890s?

WHERE TO LEARN MORE

Rutherford B. Hayes Presidential Center, Fremont, Ohio
www.rbhayes.org/

WHERE TO LEARN MORE

James A Garfield Home, Mentor, Ohio
www.nps.gov/jaga/index.htm

steeple chase, I fleeing and they pursuing." Within a few months of his inauguration in 1881, Garfield was assassinated by a disappointed and crazed office seek-
er, and Arthur became president.

Public dismay over this tragedy finally spurred changes in the spoils system.
Arthur himself urged Congress to act, and in 1883, it passed the **Pendleton Civil
Service Act**. This measure prohibited federal employees from soliciting or receiving political contributions from government workers and created the Civil
Service Commission to administer competitive examinations to applicants for government jobs. A professional civil service free from partisan politics gradually
emerged, strengthening the executive branch's ability to handle its increasing administrative responsibilities.

The new emphasis on merit and skill rather than party ties opened new opportunities to women. By the early 1890s, women held a third of the clerical positions in the executive departments in Washington. Their work in public life
challenged the conventional belief that a woman's ability and personality limited
her to the domestic sphere. Julia Henderson described her work as an examiner
of accounts in the Interior Department in 1893 as "brain work of a character that
requires a knowledge not only of the rulings of this Department, but also those of
the Treasury, Second Auditor, Second Comptroller, and Revised Statutes; demanding the closest and most critical attention, together with a great deal of legal
and business knowledge."

THE POLITICAL LIFE OF THE TARIFF

Tariffs on imported goods provided revenue for the federal government and protected American industry from European competition. They promoted industrial growth but often allowed favored industries to garner high profits. By the 1880s,
separate tariffs covered more than four thousand items and generated more revenue than the government needed to carry on its limited operations.

Reflecting its commitment to industry, the Republican party vigorously championed protective tariffs. Party leaders also claimed that American labor benefited from tariff protection. "Reduce the tariff, and labor is the first to suffer," declared
William McKinley of Ohio. Most Democrats, by contrast, favored tariff reduction.
They argued that lower tariffs would encourage foreign trade and, by reducing the
treasury surplus, minimize the temptation for the government to pursue activist
policies. (See the overview table "Arguments in the Tariff Debates.")

Regardless of party position, congressmen of both parties voted for tariffs that
would benefit their districts. California Democrats called for protective duties on
wool and raisins, products produced in California; Massachusetts Republicans, to
aid their state's shoe manufacturers, supported tariffs on shoes but opposed tariffs on leather. A Democratic senator from Indiana, elected on a campaign pledge
to reduce tariffs, summed up the prevailing rule succinctly: "I am a protectionist
for every interest which I am sent here by my constituents to protect."

In the 1884 campaign, Republican presidential candidate James G. Blaine
maintained that prosperity and high employment depended on high duties. The
Democrats' platform endorsed a lowered tariff, but their candidate, Grover Cleveland, generally ignored the issue, and both parties turned to scandalmongering.
The Democrats exploited Blaine's image as a beneficiary of the spoils system. Republicans responded by exposing Cleveland as the father of an illegitimate child.

Cleveland continued to avoid the tariff issue for three years after his election,
until the growing treasury surplus and rising popular pressure for tariff reduction
prompted him to act. He devoted his entire 1887 annual message to attacking the
"vicious, inequitable, and illogical" tariff, apparently making it the dominant issue

18–7
The Assassination of President
Garfield (1889)

QUICK REVIEW

Tariffs and Politics

◆ Tariffs provided revenues and
protected American industries
from competition.

◆ Republicans were strong
supporters of protective tariffs.

◆ Congressmen voted for tariffs that
benefited their home districts.

Pendleton Civil Service Act   A law of
1883 that reformed the spoils system
by prohibiting government workers
from making political contributions
and creating the Civil Service
Commission to oversee their
appointment on the basis of merit
rather than politics.

OVERVIEW

ARGUMENTS IN THE TARIFF DEBATES

Area Affected	High-Tariff Advocates	Low-Tariff Advocates
Industry	Tariffs promote industrial growth.	Tariffs inflate corporate profits.
Employment	Tariffs stimulate job growth.	Tariffs restrict competition.
Wages and prices	Tariffs permit higher wages.	Tariffs increase consumer prices.
Government	Tariffs provide government revenue.	Tariffs violate the principle of laissez-faire and produce revenues that tempt the government to activism.
Trade	Tariffs protect the domestic market.	Tariffs restrict foreign trade.

WHERE TO LEARN MORE

President Benjamin Harrison's Home, Indianapolis, Indiana
www.presidentbenjaminharrison.org/

Interstate Commerce Act The 1887 law that expanded federal power over business by prohibiting pooling and discriminatory rates by railroads and establishing the first federal regulatory agency, the Interstate Commerce Commission.

Sherman Antitrust Act The first federal antitrust measure, passed in 1890; sought to promote economic competition by prohibiting business combinations in restraint of trade or commerce.

of his 1888 reelection campaign. However, Cleveland then proposed a Democratic platform that ignored his recent message and did not even use the word *tariff*. When the party convention adopted a tariff reduction plank, Cleveland named high-tariff advocates to manage his campaign. "What a predicament the party is placed in," lamented one Texas Democrat, with tariff reform "for its battle cry and with a known protectionist . . . as our chairman." Cleveland won slightly more popular votes than his Republican opponent, Benjamin Harrison of Indiana, but Harrison carried the electoral college, indicating the decisive importance of strategic campaigning, local issues, and large campaign funds rather than great national issues.

The triumphant Republicans raised tariffs to unprecedented levels with the McKinley Tariff Act of 1890. The law provoked a popular backlash that helped return the Democrats to power. Still, the Democrats made little effort to push tariff reform. The *Atlanta Constitution* mused about such tariff politics in a bit of doggerel:

> It's funny 'bout this tariff—how they've lost it or forgot;
> They were rushing it to Congress once; their collars were so hot;
> They could hardly wait to fix it 'till we harvested a crop;
> Was it such a burnin' question that they had to let it drop?

THE BEGINNINGS OF FEDERAL REGULATION

Popular pressure compelled Congress to take the first steps toward the regulation of business with the passage of the **Interstate Commerce Act** in 1887 and the **Sherman Antitrust Act** in 1890.

Farmers condemned the power of corporations over transportation facilities and their monopolization of industries affecting agriculture, from those that manufactured farm machinery to those that ran flour mills. Small business owners suffered from the destructive competition of corporations, workers were exploited by the corporations' control of the labor market, and consumers felt victimized by high prices. The result was a growing clamor to rein in the corporations.

The first target of this concern was the nation's railroads, the preeminent symbol of big business. Both farm groups and businesses complained of discriminatory shipping rates levied by railroads. Consumers condemned the railroads' use of pooling arrangements to suppress competition and raise rates. The resulting pressure was responsible for the Granger laws enacted in several Midwestern states in the 1870s to regulate railroad freight and storage rates.

In 1886, the Supreme Court ruled in *Wabash, St. Louis, and Pacific Railway Company* v. *Illinois* that only the federal government could regulate interstate commerce. This decision effectively ended state regulation of railroads but simultaneously increased popular pressure for congressional action. "Upon no public question are the people so nearly unanimous as upon the proposition that Congress should undertake in some way the regulation of interstate business," concluded a Senate committee. With the support of both major parties, Congress in 1887 passed the Interstate Commerce Act.

The act prohibited rebates, discriminatory rates, and pooling and established the Interstate Commerce Commission (ICC) to investigate and prosecute violations. The ICC was the first federal regulatory agency, but its powers were too limited to be effective. Senator Nelson Aldrich of Rhode Island, a leading spokesman for business interests, described the law as an "empty menace to great interests, made to answer the clamor of the ignorant." The railroads continued their objectionable practices. In its first fifteen years, only one court case was decided in favor of the ICC. Not surprisingly, then, popular dissatisfaction with the railroads continued into the twentieth century.

As with railroad regulation, the first antitrust laws—laws intended to break up or regulate corporate monopolies—were passed by states. Exposés of the monopolistic practices of such corporations as Standard Oil forced both major parties to endorse national antitrust legislation. In 1890, Congress enacted the Sherman Antitrust Act with only a single vote in opposition. Although it emphatically prohibited any combination in restraint of trade (any attempt to restrict competition), it was otherwise vaguely written and hence weak in its ability to prevent abuses. The courts further weakened it, and presidents of both parties made little effort to enforce it. Large corporations remained an ominous threat in the eyes of many Americans.

THE MONEY QUESTION

Persistent wrangling over questions of currency and coinage made monetary policy the most divisive political issue in the late nineteenth century. President Garfield hinted at the complexities of this subject when he wryly suggested that a member of Congress had been committed to an asylum after "he devoted himself almost exclusively to the study of the currency, became fully entangled with the theories of the subject, and became insane."

Creditors, especially bankers, as well as conservative economists and many business leaders favored limiting the money supply. They called this a **sound money** policy and insisted that it would ensure economic stability, maintain property values, and retain investor confidence. Farmers and other debtors feared this would depress already low crop prices, drive debtors further into debt, and restrict economic opportunities. They favored expanding the money supply to match the country's growing population and economy. They expected this inflationary policy to raise prices, stimulate the economy, reduce debt burdens, and increase opportunities.

The conservative leadership of both major parties supported the sound money policy, but their rank-and-file membership, especially in the West and the South, included many inflationists. As a result, the parties avoided confronting each other on the money issue.

The conflict between advocates of sound money and inflation centered on the use of paper money—"greenbacks"—and silver coinage. To meet its expenses during the Civil War, the federal government issued $450 million in greenbacks— paper money backed only by the credit of the United States, not by gold or silver, the traditional basis of currency. After the war, creditors demanded that these greenbacks be withdrawn from circulation. Debtors and other Americans caught

Sound money Misleading slogan that referred to a conservative policy of restricting the money supply and adhering to the gold standard.

up in a postwar depression favored retaining the greenbacks and even expanding their use.

In 1875 sound money advocates in Congress enacted a deflationary law that withdrew some greenbacks from circulation and required that the remainder be convertible into gold after 1878. Outraged inflationists organized the Greenback party. The Greenbackers polled more than a million votes in 1878 and elected fourteen members of Congress, nearly gaining the balance of power in the House. As the depression faded, however, so did interest in the greenback issue, and the party soon withered.

Inflationists then turned their attention to the silver issue, which would prove more enduring and disruptive. Historically, the United States had used both gold and silver as the basis of its currency, but in 1873, Congress passed a law "demonetizing" silver, making gold the only standard for American currency. Gold standard supporters hoped the law would promote international trade by aligning U.S. financial policy with that of Great Britain, which insisted on gold-based currency. But they also wanted to prevent new silver discoveries in the American West from expanding the money supply.

Indeed, silver production soon boomed, flooding the commercial market and dropping the value of the metal. Dismayed miners wanted the Treasury Department to purchase their surplus silver on the old terms and demanded a return to the bimetallic system. More important, the rural debtor groups seeking currency inflation joined in this demand. Many passionately denounced the "Crime of '73" as a conspiracy of Eastern bankers and foreign interests to control the money system to the detriment of ordinary Americans.

Eastern conservatives of both parties denounced silver; Southerners and Westerners demanded **free silver**, which meant unlimited silver coinage. By 1878, a bipartisan coalition succeeded in passing the Bland-Allison Act. This compromise measure required the government to buy at least $2 million of silver a month. However, the government never exceeded the minimum, and the law had little inflationary effect.

As hard times hit rural regions in the late 1880s, inflationists secured the passage of the Sherman Silver Purchase Act of 1890. The Treasury now had to buy more silver and pay for it with Treasury notes redeemable in either gold or silver, but this too produced little inflation because the government did not coin the silver it purchased, redeemed the notes only with gold, and, as Western silver production increased further, had to spend less and less to buy the stipulated amount of silver. Debtors of both parties remained convinced that the government favored the "classes rather than the masses." Gold standard advocates (again of both parties) were even less happy with the law and planned to repeal it at their first opportunity.

Free Silver Philosophy that the government should expand the money supply by purchasing and coining all the silver offered to it.

WHAT WAS the platform of the Populist party?

THE CRISIS OF THE 1890S

In the 1890s, a third-party political challenge generated by agricultural discontent disrupted traditional party politics. A devastating depression spawned social misery and labor violence. Changing public attitudes led to new demands on the government and a realignment of parties and voters.

AGRICULTURAL PROTEST

In the late 1880s, falling crop prices and rising debt overwhelmed many people already exhausted from overwork and alarmed by the new corporate order. "At the age of 52 years, after a long life of toil, economy, and self-denial, I find myself and family virtual paupers," lamented one Kansan. Their farm, rather than being "a house of refuge for our declining years, by a few turns of the monopolistic crank has been rendered valueless." To a large extent, the farmers' plight was the result of bad weather and an international overproduction of farm products. Looking for remedies, however, the farmers focused on the inequities of railroad discrimination, tariff favoritism, a restrictive financial system, and apparently indifferent political parties.

Angry farmers particularly singled out the systems of money and credit that worked so completely against agricultural interests. Government rules for national banks directed credit into the urbanized areas of the North and East at the expense of the rural South and West and prohibited banks from making loans on farm property and real estate. In the West, farmers borrowed money from mortgage companies to buy land and machinery. In hard times, mortgage foreclosures crushed the hopes of many farmers. In the South, the credit shortage interacted with the practices of cotton marketing and retail trade to create the sharecropping system, which trapped more and more farmers, black and white, in a vicious pattern of exploitation. The government's policies of monetary deflation worsened the debt burden for all farmers.

Farmers also protested railroad freight rates that were two or three times higher in the West and South than in the North and East. The near-monopolistic control of grain elevators and cotton brokerages left farmers feeling exploited. Protective tariff rates on agricultural machinery and other manufactured goods further raised their costs. The failure of the government to correct these inequities capped their anger.

In response, farmers turned to the **Farmers' Alliance**, the era's greatest popular movement of protest and reform. Originating in Texas, the Southern Farmers' Alliance spread throughout the South and across the Great Plains to the Pacific coast. By 1890, it had 1.2 million members. African-American farmers organized the Colored Farmers' Alliance. The Northwestern Farmers' Alliance spread westward and northward from Illinois to Nebraska and Minnesota. In combination, these groups constituted a massive grass-roots movement committed to an agenda of economic and ultimately political reform.

The Farmers' Alliance restricted its membership to men and women of the "producing class" and urged them to stand "against the encroachments of monopolies and in opposition to the growing corruption of wealth and power." The Alliance attempted to establish farmers' cooperatives to market crops and purchase supplies. It also developed ingenious proposals to remedy rural credit and currency problems. In the South, the Alliance pushed the subtreasury system, which called on the government to warehouse farmers' cotton and advance them credit based on its value (see Chapter 19). In the West, the Alliance proposed a system of federal loans to farmers using land as security. These proposals were immensely popular among farmers, but the major parties and Congress rejected them. The Alliance also took up earlier calls for free silver, government control of railroads, and banking reform, again to no avail. William A. Peffer, the influential editor of the Alliance newspaper the *Kansas Farmer*, declared that the "time has come for action. The people will not consent to wait longer. . . . The future is full of retribution for delinquents."

THE PEOPLE'S PARTY

In the West, discontented agrarians organized independent third parties, which eventually adopted the labels "People's" or "Populist." The founders of the Kansas People's Party, including members of the Farmers' Alliance, the Knights of Labor, the Grange, and the old Greenback party, launched a campaign marked by grim determination and fierce rhetoric. These people, women as well as men, were earnest organizers and powerful orators. One was *Kansas Farmer* editor Peffer. Others included "Sockless Jerry" Simpson, Annie Diggs, and Mary E. Lease. When hostile

Farmers' Alliance A broad mass movement in the rural South and West during the late nineteenth century, encompassing several organizations and demanding economic and political reforms.

A PARTY OF PATCHES.
Grand Balloon Ascension—Cincinnati, May 20th, 1891.

Established interests ridiculed the Populists unmercifully. This hostile cartoon depicts the People's party as an odd assortment of radical dissidents committed to a "Platform of Lunacy."
Kansas City Historical Society

19–5
The People's Party Platform (1892)

Omaha Platform   The 1892 platform of the Populist party repudiating laissez-faire and demanding economic and political reforms to aid distressed farmers and workers.

business and political leaders attacked the Populist plans as socialistic, Lease retorted, "You may call me an anarchist, a socialist, or a communist. I care not, but I hold to the theory that if one man has not enough to eat three times a day and another has $25,000,000, that last man has something that belongs to the first." Lease spoke as clearly against the colonial status experienced by the South and West: "The great common people of this country are slaves, and monopoly is the master. The West and South are bound and prostrate before the manufacturing East."

The Populist parties gained control of the legislatures of Kansas and Nebraska and won congressional elections in Kansas, Nebraska, and Minnesota. Their victories contributed to a massive defeat of the GOP in the 1890 midterm elections after the passage of the McKinley Tariff and the Sherman Silver Purchase Act. Thereafter, Populists gained further victories throughout the West. In the mountain states, where their support came more from miners than farmers, they won governorships in Colorado and Montana. On the Pacific coast, angry farmers found allies among urban workers and the Populists elected a governor in Washington, congressmen in California, and legislators in both states.

In Oklahoma, the Populist party drew support from homesteaders and tenant farmers, in Arizona, from miners and railroad workers. In New Mexico, the Southern Alliance established itself among small ranchers who felt threatened by corporate ranchers and land companies. The fear of corporate expansion even united usually antagonistic Anglo New Mexicans and poor Hispanics. One Alliance paper wrote of the need to defend Hispanics from the "mighty land monopoly which is surely grinding their bones into flour that it may make its bread." In the 1890 election, Populists gained the balance of power in the New Mexico legislature.

In the South, the Alliance did not initially form third parties but instead swept "Alliance Democrats" into office, electing four governors, several dozen members of Congress, and a majority of legislators in eight states.

With their new political power, farmers enacted reform legislation in many Western states. New laws regulated banks and railroads and protected poor debtors by capping interest rates and restricting mortgage foreclosures. Others protected unions and mandated improved workplace conditions. Populists were also instrumental in winning woman suffrage in Colorado and Idaho, although the united opposition of Democrats and Republicans blocked their efforts to win it in other states. In the South, however, the Democratic party frustrated reform, and most Alliance Democrats abandoned their promise to support Alliance goals in favor of loyalty to their party and its traditional opposition to governmental activism.

Populists met in Omaha, Nebraska, on July 4, 1892, to organize a national party and nominated former Greenbacker James B. Weaver for president. The party platform, known as the **Omaha Platform**, rejected the *laissez-faire* policies of the old parties and declared: "We believe that the powers of government—in other words, of the people, should be expanded . . . to the end that oppression, injustice, and poverty shall eventually cease in the land." The platform demanded government ownership of the railroads and the telegraph and telephone systems; a national currency issued by the government rather than private banks; the sub-treasury system; free and unlimited silver coinage; a graduated income tax; and the redistribution to settlers of land held by railroads and speculative corporations. Accompanying resolutions endorsed the direct popular election of senators, the secret ballot, and other electoral reforms to make government more democratic and responsive to popular wishes. When the platform was adopted, "cheers and yells," one reporter wrote, "rose like a tornado from four thousand throats and raged without cessation for 34 minutes, during which women shrieked and wept, men embraced and kissed their neighbors . . . in the ecstasy of their delirium."

The Populists left Omaha to begin an energetic campaign. Southern Democrats, however, used violence and fraud to intimidate Populist voters and cheat Populist candidates out of office. Some local Populist leaders were murdered. One Democrat confessed that Alabama's Populist gubernatorial candidate "carried the state, but was swindled out of his victory . . . with unblushing trickery and corruption." Southern Democrats also appealed effectively to white supremacy, which undermined the Populist effort to build a biracial reform coalition.

Midwestern farmers unfamiliar with Alliance ideas and organization ignored Populist appeals and stood by their traditional political allegiances. So did most Eastern working-class voters, who learned little of the Populist program beyond its demand for inflation, which they feared would hurt them.

The Populists lost the election but got more than a million votes (one out of every twelve votes cast). Populist leaders began immediately working to expand their support, to the alarm of both Southern Democrats and Northern Republicans.

THE CHALLENGE OF THE DEPRESSION

A harsh and lengthy depression began in 1893, worsening conditions for farmers and most other Americans. Labor unrest and violence engulfed the nation, reflecting workers' distress but frightening more comfortable Americans. The failure of the major parties to respond to serious problems swelled popular discontent.

Although the Populists had not triumphed in 1892, the election nonetheless reflected the nation's spreading dissatisfaction. Voters decisively rejected President Harrison and the incumbent Republicans in Congress. Turning again to the other major party, they placed Grover Cleveland and the Democrats in control. But almost oblivious to the mounting demand for reform, Cleveland delivered an inaugural address championing the doctrine of laissez-faire and rejecting government action to solve social or economic problems.

The economy collapsed in the spring of 1893. Railroad overexpansion, a weak banking system, tight credit, and plunging agricultural prices all contributed to the disaster. A depression in Europe reduced American export markets and prompted British investors to sell their American investments for gold. Hundreds of banks closed, and thousands of businesses, including the nation's major railroads, went bankrupt. By winter, 20 percent of the labor force was unemployed, and the jobless scavenged for food in a country that had no public unemployment or welfare programs. "Never within memory," said one New York minister, "have so many people literally starved to death as in the past few months."

Most state governments offered little relief beyond encouraging private charity to the homeless. In Kansas, however, the Populist governor insisted that traditional laissez-faire policies were inadequate. (See American Views, "A Populist views American Government.") Cleveland disagreed. The functions of the government, he said in 1893, "do not include the support of the people."

Jacob Coxey, a Populist businessman from Ohio, proposed a government public works program for the unemployed to be financed with paper money. This plan would improve the nation's infrastructure, create jobs for the unemployed, and provide an inflationary stimulus to counteract the depression's deflationary effects. In short, Coxey was advocating positive government action to combat the depression.

Coxey organized a march of the unemployed to Washington as "a petition with boots on" to support his ideas. **Coxey's Army** of the unemployed, as the excited press

---

QUICK REVIEW

The Depression of 1893

◆ Harsh and lengthy depression began in 1893.

◆ By winter 1893, 20 percent of the labor force was unemployed.

◆ Most state governments offered little relief.

Coxey's Army   A protest march of unemployed workers, led by Populist businessman Jacob Coxey, demanding inflation and a public works program during the depression of the 1890s.

• AMERICAN VIEWS •

A POPULIST VIEWS AMERICAN GOVERNMENT

 n educator, merchant, and former editor, Loren- zo D. Lewelling became an articulate champion of the Populist party. Elected governor of Kansas in 1892, he headed what was heralded as "The First People's Party Government on Earth." The following pas- sages from his inaugural address sketch out both Lewelling's views of the 1890s and his "dream of the future."

HOW DOES Lewelling's rhetoric reflect the deep di- visions of the 1890s? What is Lewelling's view of the prop- er role of government? Why does Lewelling criticize the government of the 1890s? What does Lewelling mean by his statement that "the rich have no right to the prop- erty of the poor"?

The survival of the fittest is the government of brutes and reptiles, and such philosophy must give place to a government which recognizes human brotherhood. It is the province of government to protect the weak, but the government today is resolved into a struggle of the masses with the classes for supremacy and bread, until business, home, and personal integity are trembling in the face of possible want in the family. Feed a tiger reg- ularly and you tame and make him harmless, but hunger makes tigers of men. If it be true that the poor have no right to the property of the rich let it also be declared that the rich have no right to the property of the poor.

It is the mission of Kansas to protect and advance the moral and material interests of all its citizens. It is its especial duty at the present time to protect the produc- er from the ravages of combined wealth. National legis- lation has for twenty years fostered and protected the interests of the few, while it has left the South and West to supply the products with which to feed and clothe the world, and thus to become the servants of wealth.

The demand for free coinage has been refused. The national banks have been permitted to withdraw their cir- culation, and thus the interests of the East and West have been diverged until the passage of the McKinley bill cul- minated in their diversement. The purchasing power of the dollar has become so great [that] corn, wheat, beef, pork, and cotton have scarcely commanded a price equal to the cost of production.

The instincts of patriotism have naturally rebelled against these unwarranted encroachments of the power of money. Sectional hatred has also been kept alive by the old powers, the better to enable them to control the products

dubbed it, marched through the industrial towns of Ohio and Pennsylvania and into Maryland, attracting attention and support. Other armies formed in Eastern cities from Boston to Baltimore and set out for the capital. Some of the largest armies organized in the Western cities of Denver, San Francisco, and Seattle. Three hundred men in an army from Oakland elected as their commander Anna Smith, who promised to "land my men on the steps of the Capitol at Washington." "I am a San Francisco woman, a woman who has been brought up on this coast, and I'm not afraid of any- thing," Smith explained. "I have a woman's heart and a woman's sympathy, and these lead me to do what I have done for these men, even though it may not be just what a woman is expected to do."

Despite public sympathy for Coxey, the government acted to suppress him. When he reached Washington with 600 marchers, police and soldiers arrested him and his aides, beat sympathetic bystanders in a crowd of twenty thousand, and herded the marchers into detention camps. Unlike the lobbyists for business and finance, Coxey was not permitted to reach Congress to deliver his statement, urging the government to assist "the poor and oppressed."

The depression also provoked labor turmoil. There were some 1,400 in- dustrial strikes involving nearly 700,000 workers in 1894. One result was the gov- ernment's violent suppression of the Pullman strike (see Chapter 18).

and make the producer contribute to the millionaire; and thus, while the producer labors in the field, the shop, and the factory, the millionaire usurps his earnings and rides in gilded carriages with liveried servants. . . .

The problem of today is how to make the State subservient to the individual, rather than to become his master. Government is a voluntary union for the common good. It guarantees to the individual life, liberty, and the pursuit of happiness. The government then must make it possible for the citizen to enjoy liberty and pursue happiness. If the government fails of these things, it fails in its mission. . . . If old men go to the poor-house and young men go to prison, something is wrong with the economic system of the government.

What is the State to him who toils, if labor is denied him and his children cry for bread? What is the State to the farmer who wearily drags himself from dawn till dark to meet the stern necessities of the mortgage on the farm? What is the State to him if it sanctions usury and other legal forms by which his home is destroyed and his innocent ones become a prey to the fiends who lurk in the shadow of civilization? What is the State to the business man, early grown gray, broken in health and spirit by successive failures; anxiety like a boding owl his constant companion by day and the disturber of his dreams by night? How is life to be sustained, how is liberty to be enjoyed, how is happiness to be pursued under such adverse conditions as the State permits if it does not sanction? Is the State powerless against these conditions?

This is the generation which has come to the rescue. Those in distress who cry out from the darkness shall not be heard in vain. Conscience is in the saddle. We have leaped the bloody chasm and entered a contest for the protection of home, humanity, and the dignity of labor.

The grandeur of civilization shall be emphasized by the dawn of a new era in which the people shall reign, and if found necessary they will "expand the powers of government to solve the enigmas of the times." The people are greater than the law or the statutes, and when a nation sets its heart on doing a great and good thing it can find a legal way to do it.

I have a dream of the future. I have the evolution of an abiding faith in human government, and in the beautiful vision of a coming time I behold the abolition of poverty. A time is foreshadowed when the withered hand of want shall not be outstretched for charity; when liberty, equality, and justice shall have permanent abiding places in the republic.

Source: *People's Party Paper* (Atlanta), January 20, 1893.

In a series of decisions in 1895, the Supreme Court strengthened the bonds between business and government. First, it upheld the use of a court-ordered injunction to break the Pullman strike. As a result, injunctions became a major weapon for courts and corporations against labor unions until Congress finally limited their use in 1932. In *United States* v. *E. C. Knight Company*, the Court gutted the Sherman Antitrust Act by ruling that manufacturing, as opposed to commerce, was beyond the reach of federal regulation. The Court thus allowed the American Sugar Refining Company, a trust controlling 90 percent of the nation's sugar, to retain its great power. Finally, the court invalidated an income tax that agrarian Democrats and Populists had maneuvered through Congress as an "assault upon capital." Not until 1913, and then only with an amendment to the Constitution, would it be possible to adopt an equitable system of taxation.

Cleveland's financial policies stirred further discontent. Cleveland blamed the economic collapse on the Sherman Silver Purchase Act, which he regarded as detrimental to business confidence and a threat to the nation's gold reserve. He persuaded Congress in 1893 to repeal the law but thereby enraged Southern and Western members of his own party, including William Jennings Bryan of Nebraska, who saw the silver issue in the context of a struggle between "the corporate interests of the United States, the moneyed interests, aggregated wealth

William Jennings Bryan (1860–1925) at the Democratic Convention, 1896, in which he made the "Cross of Gold" speech.

Culver Pictures, Inc.

and capital, imperious, arrogant, compassionless" and "an unnumbered throng . . . work-worn and dust-begrimed."

By 1894, the Treasury had begun borrowing money from Wall Street to bolster the gold reserve. These transactions benefited a syndicate of bankers headed by J. P. Morgan. It seemed to critics that an indifferent Cleveland was helping rich bankers profit from the nation's economic agony. "A set of vampires headed by a financial trust has control of our destiny," cried one rural newspaper.

THE BATTLE OF THE STANDARDS AND THE ELECTION OF 1896

These unpopular actions, coupled with the unrelenting depression, alienated workers and farmers from the Cleveland administration and the Democratic party. In the off-year elections of 1894, the Democrats suffered the greatest loss of congressional seats in American history. Populists increased their vote by 42 percent, making especially significant gains in the South, but the real beneficiaries of Cleveland's unpopularity were the Republicans, who gained solid control of Congress as well as state governments across the North and West. All three parties began to plan for the presidential election of 1896.

The silver issue came to overshadow all others. Populist Weaver declared the silver issue "the line upon which the battle should be fought. It is the line of least resistance and we should hurl our forces against it at every point." Both to undercut the Populists and to distance themselves and their party from the despised Cleveland, leading Democrats began using the silver issue to reorganize their party.

William McKinley, governor of Ohio and author of the McKinley Tariff Act of 1890, emerged as the leader of a crowd of hopeful Republican presidential candidates. His candidacy benefited particularly from the financial backing and political management of Marcus A. Hanna, a wealthy Ohio industrialist. Hanna thought McKinley's passion for high tariffs as the key to revived prosperity would appeal to workers as well as industry and business. Republicans nominated McKinley on the first ballot at their 1896 convention. Their platform called for high tariffs but also endorsed the gold standard, placating Eastern delegates but prompting several Western Silver Republicans to withdraw from the party.

The Democratic convention met shortly thereafter. With a fervor that conservatives likened to "scenes of the French Revolution," the Silver Democrats revolutionized their party. They adopted a platform that repudiated the Cleveland administration and its policies and endorsed free silver, the income tax, and tighter regulation of trusts and railroads. A magnificent speech supporting this platform by William Jennings Bryan helped convince the delegates to nominate him for president.

Holding their convention last, the Populists now faced a terrible dilemma. The Democratic nomination of Bryan on a silver platform undercut their hopes of attracting into their own ranks disappointed reformers from the major parties. Some Populists urged the party to endorse Bryan rather than split the silver vote and ensure the victory of McKinley and the gold standard. Others argued that fusing—joining with the Democrats—would cost the Populists their separate identity and subordinate their larger political principles to the issue of free silver. After anguished discussion, the Populists nominated Bryan.

The campaign was intense and dramatic, with each side demonizing the other. Eastern financial and business interests contributed millions of dollars to Hanna's campaign for McKinley. Standard Oil alone provided $250,000, about the same amount as the Democrats' total national expenses. Hanna used these funds to organize an unprecedented campaign. Republicans issued 250 million campaign documents, printed in a dozen languages. Many newspapers not only shaped their editorials but also distorted their news stories to Bryan's disadvantage.

The Democrats relied on Bryan's superb voice, oratorical virtuosity, and youthful energy. Bryan was the first presidential candidate to campaign systematically for election, speaking hundreds of times to millions of voters. McKinley stayed home in Canton, Ohio, where he conducted a "front porch" campaign. Explaining his refusal to campaign outside Canton, McKinley said, "I might just as well put up a trapeze . . . and compete with some professional athlete as go out speaking against Bryan." But Hanna brought groups of Republicans from all over the country to visit McKinley every day, and McKinley reiterated his simple promise to restore prosperity.

In the depression, that appeal proved enough. As the Democratic candidate, Bryan was ironically burdened with the legacy of the hated Cleveland administration. The intense campaign brought a record voter turnout. McKinley won decisively by capturing the East and Midwest as well as Oregon and California (see Map 20–2). Bryan carried the traditionally Democratic South and the mountain and plains states where Populists and silverites dominated. He failed to gain support in either the Granger states of the Midwest or the cities of the East. His silver campaign had little appeal to industrial workers. Hanna realized that Bryan was making a mistake in subordinating other popular grievances to silver: "He's talking silver all the time, and that's where we've got him."

The elections of 1894 and 1896 ended the close balance between the major parties. Cleveland's failures, coupled with an economic recovery in the wake of the election of 1896, gained the Republicans a reputation as the party of prosperity and industrial progress, firmly establishing them in power for years to come. By contrast, the Democratic party receded into an ineffectual sectional minority dominated by Southern conservatives, despite Bryan's liberal views. The People's party simply dissolved.

McKinley plunged into his presidency. Unlike his predecessors, he had a definite, if limited, program, consisting of tariff protection, sound money, and overseas expansion. He worked actively to see it through Congress and to shape public opinion, thereby helping establish the model of the modern presidency. He had promised prosperity, and it returned, although not because of the record high tariff his party enacted in 1897 or the Currency Act of 1900, which firmly established the gold standard. Prosperity returned instead because of reviving markets and a monetary inflation that resulted from the discovery of vast new deposits of gold in Alaska, Australia, and South Africa. The silverites had recognized that an expanding industrial economy required an expanding money supply. Ironically, the new inflation was greater than would have resulted from free silver. With the return of prosperity and the decline of social tensions, McKinley easily won reelection in 1900, defeating Bryan a second time.

MAP EXPLORATION

To explore an interactive version of this map, go to
http://www.prenhall.com/goldfield2/map20.2

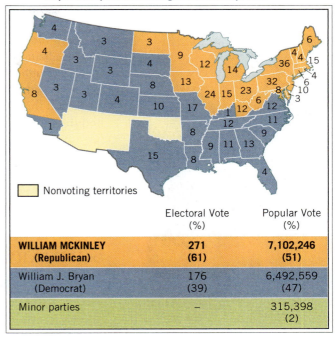

Nonvoting territories

	Electoral Vote (%)	Popular Vote (%)
WILLIAM MCKINLEY (Republican)	**271 (61)**	**7,102,246 (51)**
William J. Bryan (Democrat)	176 (39)	6,492,559 (47)
Minor parties	–	315,398 (2)

MAP 20–2

The Election of 1896   William Jennings Bryan carried most of the rural South and West, but his free silver campaign had little appeal to more urban and industrial regions, which swung strongly to Republican candidate William McKinley.

WAS THE election of 1896 closer than the electoral vote would suggest?

CONCLUSION

In late-nineteenth-century America, politics and government often seemed at cross-purposes. Closely balanced political parties commanded the zealous support of their constituents and wielded power and influence. The institutions of government, by contrast, were limited in size, scope, and responsibility. A weakened presidency and an inefficient Congress, hampered by

WHERE TO LEARN MORE

Fairview, Lincoln, Nebraska
www.bryanlgh.org/aboutus/
fairviewhistory.htm

a restrictive judiciary, were often unable to resolve the very issues that were so dramatically raised in the political arena. The issue that most reflected this impasse was civil service reform. The patronage system provided the lifeblood of politics but also disrupted government business.

The localism, laissez-faire, and other traditional principles that shaped both politics and government were becoming increasingly inappropriate for America's industrializing society. The national nature of the railroad network, for example, finally brought the federal government into the regulatory arena, however imperfectly, with the Interstate Commerce Act of 1887. Both the depression of the 1890s and the popular discontent underscored the need for change and discredited the limited government of the Cleveland administration.

By the end of the decade, the Republicans had emerged as the dominant party, ending the two-party stalemate of previous decades. Campaign hoopla in local communities had given way to information-based campaigns directed by and through national organizations. A new activist presidency was emerging, and the disruptive currency issue faded with the hard times that had brought it forth.

SUMMARY

The Structure and Style of Politics Politics in the late nineteenth century expressed social values as they determined who held the reins of government. While the two major political parties dominated, third parties sought to activate those the Democrats and Republicans left unserved. Virtually all men participated in politics; the voter turnout of that era has never been equaled. Religious, ethnic, and regional factors determined party ties, but third parties, such as the Populists, emerged around issues. Women also participated in politics and some states now allowed full or partial suffrage.

The Limits of Government Government in the late nineteenth century was neither active nor productive by present standards; localism and laissez-faire policies were resurgent. Congress and a presidency divided between the two political parties, a small and inefficient federal bureaucracy, and judicial restraints joined powerful private interests to limit the size and objectives of the federal government.

Public Policies and National Elections The spoils system, the system for selecting and supervising federal employees, was finally reformed as a result of the assassination of President Garfield. The Pendleton Civil Service Act emphasized merit and skill; it also opened new opportunities for women. Americans heatedly debated the tariff policies; popular pressure compelled Congress to take the first steps toward the regulation of business; the most divisive political issue of the era was monetary policies with inflationists wanting more money, especially silver, in circulation.

The Crisis of the 1890s Protests from Midwestern farmers over freight rates, tariffs, and the money supply resulted in popular movements of protest and reform. The Populists, a third party, funneled the discontent into politics; their emergence was but one of the many developments combining to produce a national political crises. A severe economic depression, labor unrest, and government inaction, along with the silver issue underscored the need for change. The presidential election of 1896 was an intense campaign with record voter turnout; with William McKinley's victory over William Jennings Bryan, the Republicans became established as the party of prosperity and individual progress.

REVIEW QUESTIONS

1. What social factors shaped the nature of elections in the late nine-teenth century?

2. How and why did the role of government change during this period?

3. Why did so many third parties develop during this era?

4. How might the Omaha Platform have helped farmers?

5. Why did McKinley win in 1896? How did that election differ from earlier ones?

KEY TERMS

Coxey's Army   (p. 539)
Farmers' Alliance   (p. 537)
Free silver   (p. 536)
Granger laws   (p. 527)
Greenback Party   (p. 527)

Interstate Commerce Act   (p. 534)
Mugwumps   (p. 529)
National American Woman Suffrage Association   (p. 529)
Omaha Platform   (p. 538)

Pendleton Civil Service Act   (p. 533)
Populist Party   (p. 527)
Prohibition Party   (p. 527)
Sherman Antitrust Act   (p. 534)
Sound money   (p. 535)

WHERE TO LEARN MORE

Rest Cottage, Evanston, Illinois. Frances Willard's home, from which she directed the Woman's Christian Temperance Union, is carefully preserved as a museum. The Willard Memorial Library contains more memorabilia and papers of Willard and the WCTU. **www.wctu.org/house.html**

President Benjamin Harrison's Home, Indianapolis, Indiana. President Harrison's brick Italianate mansion, completed in 1875, has been completely restored with the family's furniture and keepsakes. The former third-floor ballroom serves as a museum with exhibits of many artifacts of the Harrisons' public and private lives. **www.presidentbenjaminharrison.org/**

Fairview, Lincoln, Nebraska. A National Historic Landmark, Fairview was the home of William Jennings Bryan, who described it as "the Monticello of the West." Faithfully restored to depict the Bryan family's life in the early 1900s, it includes a museum and interpretive center. **www.bryanlgh.org/aboutus/fairviewhistory.htm**

Susan B. Anthony House National Historic Landmark, Rochester, New York. This modest house was the home of the prominent suffragist and contains Anthony's original furnishings and personal photographs. **www.susanbanthonyhouse.org/ main.html**

Rutherford B. Hayes Presidential Center, Fremont, Ohio. This complex contains President Hayes's home, office, and extensive grounds together with an excellent library and museum holding valuable collections of manuscripts, artifacts, and photographs illustrating his personal interests and political career. **www.rbhayes.org/**

James A. Garfield Home, Mentor, Ohio. Operated by the Western Reserve Historical Society as a museum, Garfield's home is the site of his successful 1880 front-porch campaign for president. **www.nps.gov/jaga/index.htm**

 For additional study resources for this chapter, go to:
www.prenhall.com/goldfield/chapter20

The women, trudging stoutly along under great difficulties, were able to complete their march only when troops of cavalry from Fort Meyers were rushed into Washington . . . No inauguration has ever produced such scenes . . .

THE JUNGLE

UPTON SINCLAIR

VOTES FOR WOMEN

The great woman suffrage parade leaves Capitol Hill and heads for the White House, March 3, 1913. Dramatic tactics and careful organizing like those that marked this parade helped secure reform in the Progressive Era. The head of a suffrage parade at Washington D.C. oil over a photograph, 1913, (Granger Collection 4E 1028.04).

21

THE PROGRESSIVE ERA
1900–1917

WHAT WAS the nature of progressivism?

WHAT ROLE did women play in Progressive Era movements?

HOW DID electoral and municipal reforms improve voting and government during the Progressive Era?

HOW WAS the executive branch strengthened under Roosevelt?

HOW DID Woodrow Wilson bring progressivism to its climax?

Five thousand women, marching in the woman suffrage pageant yesterday, practically fought their way foot by foot up Pennsylvania avenue, through a surging mass of humanity that completely defied the Washington police, swamped the marchers, and broke their procession into little companies. The women, trudging stoutly along under great difficulties, were able to complete their march only when troops of cavalry from Fort Myer were rushed into Washington to take charge of Pennsylvania avenue. No inauguration has ever produced such scenes, which in many instances amounted to little less than riots. . . .

The parade in itself, in spite of the delays, was a great success. . . . As a spectacle the pageant was entrancing. Beautiful women, posing in classic robes, passed in a bewildering array, presenting an irresistible appeal to the artistic, and completely captivating the hundred thousand spectators who struggled for a view along the entire route.

Miss Margaret Foley, bearing aloft a large "Votes for Women" flag, and Mrs. G. Farquhar, carrying an American flag, led the procession. . . . After the float reading, "We Demand an Amendment to the United States Constitution Enfranchising the Women of This Country," came a body of ushers clad in light blue capes. . . . Two large floats . . . represented the countries in which women are working for equal rights, followed by a large body of women on foot dressed in street clothes, who bore the banners and pennants of scores of suffrage associations throughout the world. . . . The Homemakers . . . were dressed in long purple robes over their street clothes. Following them came a float, "In Patriotic Service," . . . and Miss Lillian Wald, the walking leader of a large body of women who followed the float, dressed as trained nurses, with gray caps and coats.

Miss Margaret Gage and Maurice Cohen, wearing college gowns with mortar boards, represented "Education," which was followed by nearly 1,000 women of the college section. . . . A group of young girls in blue capes represented the wage-earners, followed by "A Labor Story," which depicted the crowded condition of tenements, with women and children bending over sewing machines, dirty and disheveled, in squalid quarters. . . . [Then followed] the women in the government section, all wearing light blue capes, . . . the business women, dressed in similar manner. . . . the teachers, . . . the social workers, . . . the white and pink costumed delegation of "writers," . . . club women and women clergy.

The greatest ovation was given to "General" Rosalie Jones, who led her little band of hikers from New York over rough roads and through snow and rain to march for the "cause." . . .

But there were hostile elements in the crowd through which the women marched. . . . Passing through two walls of antagonistic humanity, the marchers for the most part kept their temper. They suffered insult and closed their ears to jibes and jeers. Few faltered, although several of the older women were forced to drop out from time to time.

The pageant moved up Pennsylvania avenue with great difficulty and surrounded with some danger. Crowds surged into the streets, completely over-

IMAGE KEY

for pages 546–547

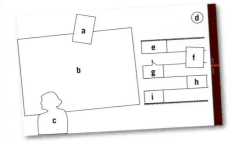

a. "The Jungle" by Upton Sinclair cover featuring a factory.

b. Photo of Women's suffrage parade in D.C., 1913.

c. Dorothy Newell has Votes for Women written on her back.

d. Bull Moose party campaign paraphernalia.

e. Flanner House Baby Clinic, about 1918. The old Flanner house Building on Colton Street was soon abandoned for better quarters.

f. Illustration "A WOMAN'S WORK IS NEVER DONE".

g. Detail of photo of Women's suffrage parade in D.C., 1913.

h. American cartoon showing President Theodore Roosevelt slaying those trusts he considered 'bad' for the public interest while restraining those whose business practices he considered 'good' for the country.

i. Woodrow Wilson (1856–1924). Oil on canvas.

whelming the police and stopping the pageant's progress. Mounted police charged into the crowds, but failed at times to drive them back, even with the free use of clubs. In more than an hour the pageant had moved only ten blocks.

Miss Inez Milholland, a New York society girl, mounted on her white horse and dressed as a herald, finally rode up beside a mounted policeman, and helped charge the crowd. Miss Milholland gesticulated and shouted at the crowd and rode her horse into it with good effect. . . .

When the surging multitude was driven back in one place it flowed back into the street at another. The pageant slowly moved along, sometimes not more than a dozen feet at a time. . . .

As a result of the unruly spirit of the biggest crowd that ever witnessed a parade on Pennsylvania avenue, or of the inactivity of the police, who seemed powerless to protect the marching suffragists, the Emergency Hospital last night was filled to overflowing. . . . While an automobile and ambulance and horse-drawn vehicle ran back and forth, with all the surgeons in the institution taking turns at riding on it, people who had fainted or been overcome by exhaustion, or crushed and trampled, were brought to the hospital.

Washington Post, March 4, 1913.

INEZ MILHOLLAND'S charge and the jumbled news accounts in the *Washington Post* convey the intensity of the woman suffrage parade on March 3, 1913. The women's difficult journey down Pennsylvania Avenue that day, illustrated critical features of life in the **Progressive Era**.

Important movements challenged traditional relationships and attitudes—here involving women's role in American life—and often met resistance. "Progressives" seeking reforms organized their supporters across lines of class, education, occupation, geography, gender, and, at times, race and ethnicity—as the variety of groups in the suffrage parade demonstrated. Rather than rely on traditional partisan politics, reformers adopted new political techniques, including lobbying and demonstrating, as nonpartisan pressure groups. Reform work begun at the local and state levels—where the suffrage movement had already met some success—inexorably moved to the national level as the federal government expanded its authority and became the focus of political interest. Finally, this suffrage demonstration revealed the diversity of the progressive movement, for the women marched, in part, against Woodrow Wilson, a fellow progressive.

Progressivism had no unifying organization, central leadership, or consensus on objectives. Instead, it represented the coalescing of different and even contradictory movements that sought changes in the nation's social, economic, and political life. But reformers did share certain convictions. They believed that to correct the disorders that industrialization and urbanization had produced required new ideas and methods. They rejected the ideology of individualism in favor of broader concepts of social responsibility, and they sought to achieve social order through organization and efficiency. Finally, most progressives believed that government itself, as the agent of public responsibility, should address social and economic problems.

The interaction among the reformers and the conflict with their opponents made the two decades before World War I a period of ferment and excitement. The progressives' achievements and failures profoundly shaped America.

Progressive Era   An era in the United States (roughly between 1900 and 1917) in which important movements challenged traditional relationships and attitudes.

WHAT WAS the nature
of progressivism?

WHERE TO LEARN MORE

★ National Museum of American
History, Smithsonian Institution,
Washington, D.C.

QUICK REVIEW

Triangle Shirtwaist Fire
◆ 1911: Fire kills 146 workers.
◆ Managers had locked the exits.
◆ The United States had the
highest rate of industrial
accidents in the world.

WHERE TO LEARN MORE

★ Lowell National Historic Park,
Lowell, Massachusetts
www.nps.gov/lowe/

THE FERMENT OF REFORM

The diversity of progressivism reflected the diverse impulses of reform. Clergy and professors provided new ideas to guide remedial action. Journalists exposed corporate excesses and government corruption and stirred public demand for reform. Business leaders sought to curtail disorder through efficiency and regulation, while industrial workers struggled to improve the horrible conditions in which they worked and lived. Women organized to protect their families and homes from new threats and even to push beyond such domestic issues. Nearly every movement for change encountered fierce opposition, while also helping America grapple with the problems of industrial society. (See the overview table "Major Progressive Organizations and Groups.")

THE CONTEXT OF REFORM: INDUSTRIAL AND URBAN TENSIONS

The origins of progressivism lay in the crises of the new urban-industrial order that emerged in the late nineteenth century. The severe depression and consequent mass suffering of the 1890s, the labor violence and industrial armies, the political challenges of Populism and an ineffective government shattered the complacency many middle-class Americans had felt about their nation and made them aware of social and economic inequities that rural and working-class families had long recognized.

By 1900, a returning prosperity had eased the threat of major social violence, but the underlying problems intensified. Big business, which had disrupted traditional economic relationships in the late nineteenth century, suddenly became bigger in a series of mergers between 1897 and 1903. Giant corporations threatened to squeeze opportunities for small firms and workers, dominate markets, and raise social tensions. They also inspired calls for public control.

Most workers still toiled nine to ten hours a day; steelworkers and textile employees usually worked twelve-hour shifts. Wages were minimal; an economist in 1905 calculated that 60 percent of all adult male breadwinners made less than a living wage. Family survival, then, often required women and children to work, often in the lowest paid, most exploited positions. Southern cotton mills employed children as young as 7; coal mines paid 12-year-old slate pickers 39 cents for a ten-hour day. Dangerous work environments and an absence of safety programs threatened not only workers' health but their lives as well. In 1911 a fire killed 146 workers, most of them young women, trapped inside the factory of the Triangle Shirtwaist Company in New York, because management had locked the exits. The fire chief found "skeletons bending over sewing machines." The United States had the highest rate of industrial accidents in the world. Half a million workers were injured and thirty thousand killed at work each year. These terrible conditions cried out for reform.

Other Americans saw additional social problems in the continuing flood of immigrants who were transforming America's cities. From 1900 to 1917, more than 14 million immigrants entered the United States, and most became urban dwellers. By 1910, immigrants and their children comprised more than 70 percent of the population of New York, Chicago, Buffalo, Milwaukee, and other cities. Most of the arrivals were so-called new immigrants from southern and eastern Europe, rather than the British, Irish, Germans, and Scandinavians who had arrived earlier. Crowding into urban slums, immigrants overwhelmed municipal sanitation, education, and fire protection services. One Russian described his new life as "all filth and sadness."

OVERVIEW

MAJOR PROGRESSIVE ORGANIZATIONS AND GROUPS

Group	Activity
Social Gospel movement	Urged churches and individuals to apply Christian ethics to social and economic problems
Muckrakers	Exposed business abuses, public corruption, and social evils through investigative journalism
Settlement House movement	Attempted through social work and public advocacy to improve living and working conditions in urban immigrant communities
National Consumers' League (1898)	Monitored businesses to ensure decent working conditions and safe consumer products
Women's Trade Union League (1903)	United workingwomen and their middle-class "allies" to promote unionization and social reform
National Child Labor Committee (1904)	Campaigned against child labor
Country Life movement	Attempted to modernize rural social and economic conditions according to urban-industrial standards
National American Woman Suffrage Association	Led the movement to give women the right to vote
Municipal reformers	Sought to change the activities and structure of urban government to promote efficiency and control
Conservationists	Favored efficient management and regulation of natural resources rather than uncontrolled development or preservation

Ethnic prejudices abounded. Woodrow Wilson, then president of Princeton University, declared in 1902: "The immigrant newcomers of recent years are men of the lowest class from the South of Italy, and men of the meaner sort out of Hungary and Poland, men out of the ranks where there was neither skill nor energy, nor any initiative or quick intelligence." Americans of the Old Stock often considered the predominantly Catholic and Jewish newcomers a threat to social stability and cultural identity and so demanded programs to reform either the urban environment or the immigrants themselves.

CHURCH AND CAMPUS

Many groups, drawing from different traditions and inspirations, responded to such economic and social issues. Reform-minded Protestant ministers created the **Social Gospel movement**, which sought to introduce religious ethics into industrial relations and appealed to churches to meet their social responsibilities. Washington Gladden, a Congregational minister in Columbus, Ohio, was shocked in 1884 by a bloody strike crushed by wealthy members of his own congregation. Gladden began a ministry to working-class neighborhoods that most churches ignored. He endorsed unions and workers' rights and proposed replacing a cruelly competitive wage system with profit sharing.

Social Gospel Movement Movement created by reform-minded Protestant ministers seeking to introduce religious ethics into industrial relations and appealing to churches to meet their social responsibilities.

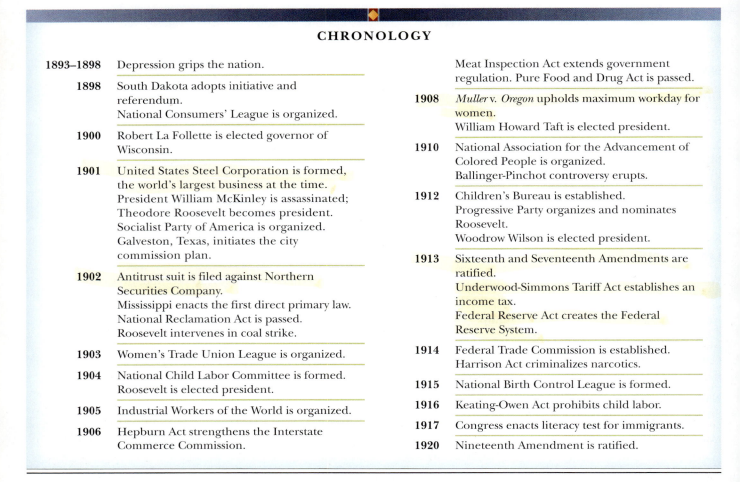

CHRONOLOGY

1893–1898	Depression grips the nation.
1898	South Dakota adopts initiative and referendum. National Consumers' League is organized.
1900	Robert La Follette is elected governor of Wisconsin.
1901	United States Steel Corporation is formed, the world's largest business at the time. President William McKinley is assassinated; Theodore Roosevelt becomes president. Socialist Party of America is organized. Galveston, Texas, initiates the city commission plan.
1902	Antitrust suit is filed against Northern Securities Company. Mississippi enacts the first direct primary law. National Reclamation Act is passed. Roosevelt intervenes in coal strike.
1903	Women's Trade Union League is organized.
1904	National Child Labor Committee is formed. Roosevelt is elected president.
1905	Industrial Workers of the World is organized.
1906	Hepburn Act strengthens the Interstate Commerce Commission. Meat Inspection Act extends government regulation. Pure Food and Drug Act is passed.
1908	*Muller* v. *Oregon* upholds maximum workday for women. William Howard Taft is elected president.
1910	National Association for the Advancement of Colored People is organized. Ballinger-Pinchot controversy erupts.
1912	Children's Bureau is established. Progressive Party organizes and nominates Roosevelt. Woodrow Wilson is elected president.
1913	Sixteenth and Seventeenth Amendments are ratified. Underwood-Simmons Tariff Act establishes an income tax. Federal Reserve Act creates the Federal Reserve System.
1914	Federal Trade Commission is established. Harrison Act criminalizes narcotics.
1915	National Birth Control League is formed.
1916	Keating-Owen Act prohibits child labor.
1917	Congress enacts literacy test for immigrants.
1920	Nineteenth Amendment is ratified.

Social Gospeler Walter Rauschenbusch, a Baptist minister, argued in his book *Christianity and the Social Crisis* (1907) that Christians should support social reform to alleviate poverty, slums, and labor exploitation. He attacked low wages for transforming workers "into lean, sallow, hopeless, stupid, and vicious young people, simply to enable some group of stockholders to earn 10 percent."

The Social Gospel movement flowered mainly among certain Protestant denominations, especially Episcopalians, Congregationalists, and Methodists. It climaxed in 1908 in the formation of the Federal Council of Churches of Christ in America. The council, representing thirty-three religious groups, adopted a program that endorsed welfare and regulatory legislation to achieve social justice. By linking reform with religion (as "applied Christianity," in the words of Washington Gladden), the Social Gospel movement gave progressivism a powerful moral drive that affected much of American life.

The Social Gospel movement provided an ethical justification for government intervention to improve the social order. Scholars in the social sciences such as Lester Ward also called for social progress through rational planning and government intervention rather than through unrestrained and unpredictable competition. Economists rejected laissez-faire principles in favor of state action to accomplish social evolution. Industrialization, declared economist Richard T. Ely, "has brought to the front a vast number of social problems whose solution is impossible without the united efforts of church, state, and science."

MUCKRAKERS

Journalists also spread reform ideas by developing a new form of investigative reporting known as **muckraking**. Samuel S. McClure sent his reporters to uncover political and corporate corruption for *McClure's Magazine*. Sensational exposés sold magazines, and soon *Cosmopolitan*, *Everybody's*, and other journals began publishing investigations of business abuses, dangerous working conditions, and the miseries of slum life.

Muckraking articles aroused indignant public demands for reform. Lincoln Steffens detailed the corrupt links between "respectable" businessmen and crooked urban politicians in a series of articles called "The Shame of the Cities." Ida Tarbell revealed John D. Rockefeller's sordid construction of Standard Oil. Muckraking novels also appeared. *The Octopus* (1901) by Frank Norris dramatized the Southern Pacific Railroad's stranglehold on California's farmers, and *The Jungle* (1906) by Upton Sinclair exposed nauseating conditions in Chicago's meatpacking industry.

THE GOSPEL OF EFFICIENCY

Many progressive leaders believed that efficiency and expertise could control or resolve the disorder of industrial society. President Theodore Roosevelt (1901–1909) praised the "gospel of efficiency." Like many other progressives, he admired corporations' success in applying management techniques to guide economic growth. Drawing from science and technology as well as from the model of the corporation, many progressives attempted to manage or direct change efficiently. They used scientific methods to collect extensive data and relied on experts for analysis and recommendations. "Scientific management" seemed the key to eliminating waste and inefficiency in government, society, and industry. Rural reformers thought that "scientific agriculture" could bring prosperity to the impoverished Southern countryside; urban reformers believed that improvements in medical science and the professionalization of physicians through uniform licensing standards could eradicate the cities' wretched public health problems.

Industrialists were drawn to the ideas of Frederick Taylor, a proponent of scientific management. Taylor proposed to increase worker efficiency through imposed work routines, speedups, and mechanization. Workers, Taylor insisted, should "do what they are told promptly and without asking questions. . . . It is absolutely necessary for every man in our organization to become one of a train of gear wheels." By assigning workers simple and repetitive tasks on machines, Taylorization made their skills expendable and enabled managers to control the production, pace of work, and hiring and firing of personnel. When labor complained, one business leader declared that unions failed "to appreciate the progressivism of the age."

Sophisticated managers of big business combinations favored government regulations that could bring about safer and more stable conditions in society and the economy. Government regulations, they reasoned, could reassure potential consumers, open markets, mandate working conditions that smaller competitors could not provide, or impose systematic procedures that competitive pressures would otherwise undercut.

LABOR'S DEMAND FOR RIGHTS

Industrial workers with different objectives also hastened the ferment of reform. Workers resisted the new rules of efficiency experts and called for improved wages and working conditions and reduced work hours. They and their middle-class

Muckraking Journalism exposing economic, social, and political evils, so named by Theodore Roosevelt for its "raking the muck" of American society.

sympathizers sought to achieve some of these goals through state intervention, demanding laws to compensate workers injured on the job, curb child labor, and regulate the employment of women. After the Triangle Shirtwaist fire, for example, urban politicians with working-class constituencies created the New York State Factory Commission and enacted dozens of laws dealing with fire hazards, machine safety, and wages and hours for women.

Workers also organized unions to improve their lot. The American Federation of Labor (AFL) claimed 4 million members by 1920, but it recruited mainly skilled workers, particularly native-born white males. New unions organized the factories and sweatshops where most immigrants and women worked. Despite strong employer resistance, the International Ladies Garment Workers Union (1900) and the Amalgamated Clothing Workers (1914) organized the garment trades, developed programs for social and economic reforms, and led their members—mostly young Jewish and Italian women—in spectacular strikes. The "Uprising of the 20,000," a 1909 strike in New York City, included months of massive rallies, determined picketing, and police repression. One observer marveled at the women strikers' "emotional endurance, fearlessness, and entire willingness to face danger and suffering."

A still more radical union tried to organize miners, lumberjacks, and Mexican and Japanese farm workers in the West, black dockworkers in the South, and immigrant factory hands in New England. Founded in 1905, the Industrial Workers of the World (IWW), whose members were known as "**Wobblies**," used sit-down strikes, sit-ins, and mass rallies, tactics adopted by other industrial unions in the 1930s and the civil rights movement in the 1960s. "Respectable people" considered the Wobblies violent revolutionaries, but most of the violence was committed against them.

EXPANDING THE WOMAN'S SPHERE

Women reformers and their organizations played a key role in progressivism. By the early twentieth century, more women than before were working outside the home—in the factories, mills, and sweatshops of the industrial economy and as clerks in stores and offices. In 1910, more than a fourth of all workers were women, increasing numbers of them married. Their importance in the work force and participation in unions and strikes challenged assumptions that woman's "natural" role was to be a submissive housewife.

Often founded for cultural purposes, women's clubs soon began adopting programs for social reform and gave their members a route to public influence. In 1914, an officer of the General Federation of Women's Clubs proudly declared that she could not find a cause for social reform that "has not received a helpful hand from the clubwomen."

Women also joined or created other organizations that pushed beyond the limits of traditional domesticity. By threatening healthy and happy homes, urban problems required that women become "social housekeepers" in the community. The National Congress of Mothers, organized in 1897, worried about crime and disease and championed kindergartens, foster-home programs, juvenile courts, and compulsory school attendance. Led by the crusading Florence Kelley, the National Consumers' League tried to protect both women wage earners and middle-class housewives by monitoring stores and factories to ensure decent working conditions and safe products. The Women's Trade Union League, or WTUL, united working women and their self-styled middle-class "allies" to unionize women workers and eliminate sweatshop conditions. Its greatest success came in the 1909 garment workers' strike when the allies—dubbed by one worker the "mink brigade"—assisted strikers with relief funds, bail money, food supplies, and public relations campaign.

Wobblies Popular name for the members of the Industrial Workers of the World (IWW).

Although most progressive women stressed women's special duties and responsibilities as social housekeepers, others began to demand women's equal rights. In 1914, for example, critics of New York's policy of dismissing women teachers who married formed a group called the Feminist Alliance and demanded "the removal of all social, political, economic and other discriminations which are based upon sex, and the award of all rights and duties in all fields on the basis of individual capacity alone."

TRANSATLANTIC INFLUENCES

A major source of America's progressive impulse lay outside its borders. European nations were grappling with many of the same problems that stemmed from industrialization and urbanization, and they provided guidance and possible solutions. As one American observer said in 1915. What "the men and women who call themselves progressive . . . propose to do is to bring the United States abreast of Germany and other European countries in the matter of remedial legislation." Progressive reformers soon learned that the political, economic, and social structures of America required modifying, adapting, or even abandoning these imported ideas, but their influence was obvious.

International influences were particularly strong in the Social Gospel movement, symbolized by William T. Stead, a British social evangelist, whose idea of a "Civic Church" (a partnership of churches and reformers) captured great attention in the United States.

Muckrakers not only exposed American problems but also looked for foreign solutions. *McClure's* sent Ray Stannard Baker to Europe in 1900 "to see why Germany is making such progress."

Institutional connections also linked progressives with European reformers. By 1912, American consumer activists, trade unionists, factory inspectors, and feminists participated in international conferences on labor legislation, child welfare, social insurance, and housing reform and returned home with new ideas and strategies. State governments organized commissions to analyze European policies and agencies for lessons that might be applicable in the United States.

SOCIALISM

The growing influence of socialist ideas also promoted the spirit of progressivism. Socialists never attracted a large following, even among workers, but their criticism of the industrial economy gained increasing attention in the early twentieth century. American socialists condemned social and economic inequities, criticized limited government, and demanded public ownership of railroads, utilities, and communications. They also campaigned for tax reforms, better housing, factory inspections, and recreational facilities for all. Muckrakers like Lincoln Steffens and Upton Sinclair were committed socialists, as were some Social Gospel ministers and labor leaders, but the most prominent socialist was Eugene Debs. In 1901, Debs helped organize the Socialist Party of America. In the next decade, the party won many local elections, especially in Wisconsin and New York, where it drew support from German and Russian immigrants, and in Oklahoma, among poor tenant farmers. Socialism was also promoted by newspapers and magazines, including the *Appeal to Reason* in Girard, Kansas, which had a circulation of 500,000 by 1906.

WHAT ROLE did immigrants and women play in Progressive-Era movements?

Striking garment workers and their supporters in the 1909 "Uprising" in New York City. Working women and their allies contributed to the growing pressure for improved working conditions.

Cornell University School of Industrial and Labor Relations.

21–3
Eugene V. Debs, "The Outlook for Socialism in the United States" (1900)

Most progressives considered socialist ideas too drastic. Nevertheless, socialists contributed to the reform ferment, by providing support for reform initiatives and by prompting progressives to push for changes to undercut increasingly attractive radical alternatives.

OPPONENTS OF REFORM

Not all Americans supported progressive reforms, and many people regarded as progressives on some issues opposed change in other areas. Social Gospeler Rauschenbusch, for instance, opposed expanding women's rights. More typically, opponents of reform held consistently traditional attitudes.

Social Gospelers themselves faced opposition. Particularly strong among evangelical denominations with rural roots, **Protestant fundamentalists** stressed personal salvation rather than social reform. "To attempt reform in the black depths of the great city," said one, "would be as useless as trying to purify the ocean by pouring into it a few gallons of spring water." The most famous evangelist was Billy Sunday, who scorned all reforms but prohibition and denounced labor unions, women's rights, and business regulation as interfering with traditional values. Declaring that the Christian mission was solely to save individual souls, he condemned the Social Gospel as "godless social service nonsense" and attacked its advocates as "infidels and atheists."

Business interests angered by exposés of corporate abuse and corruption attacked muckrakers. Major corporations like Standard Oil created public relations bureaus to improve their image and to identify business, not its critics, with the public interest. Advertising boycotts discouraged magazines from running critical stories, and credit restrictions forced some muckraking journals to suspend publication. By 1910, the heyday of muckraking was over.

Labor unions likewise encountered resistance. Led by the National Association of Manufacturers, business groups denounced unions as corrupt and radical, hired thugs to disrupt them, organized strikebreaking agencies, and used blacklists to eliminate union activists. The antiunion campaign peaked in Ludlow, Colorado, in 1914. John D. Rockefeller's Colorado Fuel and Iron Company used the state militia to shoot striking workers and their families. The courts aided employers by issuing injunctions against strikes and prohibited unions from using boycotts, one of their most effective weapons.

Progressives campaigning for government intervention and regulation also met stiff resistance. Many Americans objected to what they considered unwarranted interference in private economic matters. Their political representatives were called the "Old Guard," implying their opposition to political and economic change. The courts often supported these attitudes. In *Lochner* v. *New York* (1905), the Supreme Court overturned a maximum-hours law on the grounds that it deprived employers and employees of their "freedom of contract." Progressives constantly had to struggle with such opponents, and progressive achievements were limited by the persistence and influence of their adversaries.

QUICK REVIEW

Opponents of Reform
◆ Protestant fundamentalists.
◆ Business interests.
◆ Anti-union forces.

Protestant Fundamentalists
Religious conservatives who believe in the literal accuracy and divine inspiration of the Bible.

HOW DID the Progressives reform Society?

REFORMING SOCIETY

With their varied motives and objectives, progressives worked to transform society by improving living conditions, educational opportunities, family life, and social and industrial relations. They sought what they called "social justice," but their plans for social reform sometimes also smacked of social control—coercive efforts to impose uniform standards on a diverse population.

SETTLEMENT HOUSES AND URBAN REFORM

The spearheads for social reform were settlement houses, community centers in urban immigrant neighborhoods. Reformers created four hundred settlement houses, largely modeled after Hull House in Chicago, founded in 1889 by Jane Addams.

Most settlements were led and staffed primarily by middle-class young women. Settlement work did not immediately violate prescribed gender roles because it initially focused on the "woman's sphere": family, education, domestic skills, and cultural "uplift." Thus settlement workers organized kindergartens and nurseries; taught classes in English, cooking, and personal hygiene; held musical performances and poetry readings; and sponsored recreation.

However, settlement workers soon saw that the root problem for immigrants was widespread poverty that required more than changes in individual behavior. Unlike earlier reformers, they regarded many of the evils of poverty as products of the social environment rather than of moral weakness. Slum dwellers, Addams sadly noted, suffered from "poisonous sewage, contaminated water, infant mortality, adulterated food, smoke-laden air, juvenile crime, and unwholesome crowding." Thus settlement workers campaigned for stricter building codes to improve slums, better urban sanitation systems to enhance public health, public parks to revive the urban environment, and laws to protect women and children.

Lawrence Veiller played the leading role in the crusade for housing reform. His work at the University Settlement in New York City convinced him that "the improvement of the homes of the people was the starting point for everything." Veiller relied on settlement workers to help investigate housing conditions, prepare public exhibits depicting rampant disease in congested slums, and agitate for improvements. Based on their findings, Veiller drafted a new housing code limiting the size of tenements and requiring toilet facilities, ventilation, and fire protection. In 1901, the New York Tenement House Law became a model for other cities. To promote uniform building codes throughout the nation, the tireless Veiller founded the National Housing Association in 1910.

PROTECTIVE LEGISLATION FOR WOMEN AND CHILDREN

Settlement workers eventually concluded that only government power could achieve social justice and demanded that state and federal governments protect the weak and disadvantaged. As Veiller insisted, it was "unquestionably the duty of the state" to enforce justice in the face of "greed on the part of those who desire to secure for themselves an undue profit."

The maiming and killing of children in industrial accidents made it "inevitable," Addams said, "that efforts to secure a child labor law should be our first venture into the field of state legislation." The National Child Labor Committee, organized in 1904, led the campaign. Reformers met stiff resistance from manufacturers who used child labor, conservatives who opposed government action as an intrusion into family life, and some poor parents who needed their children's income. Child labor reformers documented the problem with extensive investigations and also benefited from the public outrage stirred by socialist John Spargo's muckraking book *The Bitter Cry of the Children* (1906). By 1914, every state but one had a minimum working age law. Effective regulation, however, required national action, for many state laws were weak or poorly enforced. (See American Views, Mother Jones and the Meaning of Child Labor in America.)

Social reformers also lobbied for laws regulating the wages, hours, and working conditions of women and succeeded in having states from New York to Oregon pass maximum-hours legislation. After the Supreme Court upheld such laws in *Muller*

21–6
Jane Addams, Twenty Years at Hull House (1910)

WHERE TO LEARN MORE
Hull House, Chicago, Illinois
www.uic.edu/jaaddams/hull/ hull_house.html

WHERE TO LEARN MORE
Lower East Side Tenement Museum, New York City, New York
www.tenement.org/

OVERVIEW

MAJOR LAWS AND CONSTITUTIONAL AMENDMENTS OF THE PROGRESSIVE ERA

Legislation	Effect
New York Tenement House Law (1901)	Established a model housing code for safety and sanitation
Newlands Act (1902)	Provided for federal irrigation projects
Hepburn Act (1906)	Strengthened authority of the Interstate Commerce Commission
Pure Food and Drug Act (1906)	Regulated the production and sale of food and drug products
Meat Inspection Act (1906)	Authorized federal inspection of meat products
Sixteenth Amendment (1913)	Authorized a federal income tax
Seventeenth Amendment (1913)	Mandated the direct popular election of senators
Underwood-Simmons Tariff Act (1913)	Lowered tariff rates and levied the first regular federal income tax
Federal Reserve Act (1913)	Established the Federal Reserve System to supervise banking and provide a national currency
Federal Trade Commission Act (1914)	Established the FTC to oversee business activities
Harrison Act (1914)	Regulated the distribution and use of narcotics
Smith-Lever Act (1914)	Institutionalized the county agent system
Keating-Owen Act (1916)	Indirectly prohibited child labor
Eighteenth Amendment (1919)	Instituted prohibition
Nineteenth Amendment (1920)	Established woman suffrage

v. *Oregon* (1908), thirty-nine states enacted new or stronger laws on women's maximum hours between 1909 and 1917. Fewer states established minimum wages for women.

Protective legislation for women posed a troubling issue for reformers. In California, for example, middle-class clubwomen favored protective legislation on grounds of women's presumed weakness. More radical progressives, as in the socialist-led Women's Trade Union League of Los Angeles, supported legislation to help secure economic independence and equality in the labor market for women, increase the economic strength of the working class, and serve as a precedent for laws improving conditions for all workers.

Progressive Era lawmakers limited protective legislation to measures reflecting the belief that women needed paternalist protection, even by excluding them from certain occupations. Laws establishing a minimum wage for women, moreover, usually set a wage level below what state commissions reported as subsistence rates. Protective legislation thus assured women not economic independence but continued dependence on husbands or fathers.

Social justice reformers forged the beginnings of the welfare state, as many states began in 1910 to provide "mothers' pensions" to indigent widows with dependent children. Twenty-one states, led by Wisconsin in 1911, enacted workers' compensation programs.

BREVARD COUNTY PARKY
  SOUTH AREA
  51 S. NIEMAN AV.
  MELB
  952-4650

424 Fourth Avenue
Indialantic, Florida 32903
(407) 984-5394

Compared to social insurance programs in Western Europe, however, these were feeble responses to the social consequences of industrialization. Proposals for health insurance and old-age pension programs went nowhere. Business groups and other conservative interests curbed the movement toward state responsibility for social welfare.

RESHAPING PUBLIC EDUCATION

Concerns about child labor overlapped with increasing attention to public schools. In 1900, for example, women's clubs in North Carolina launched a program to improve school buildings, increase teachers' salaries, and broaden the curriculum. Claiming efficiency and expertise, school administrators also pushed for changes, both to upgrade their own profession and to expand their public influence. And some intellectuals predicted that schools themselves could promote social progress and reform. Philosopher John Dewey sketched his plans for such progressive education in *The School and Society* (1899).

Between 1880 and 1920, compulsory school attendance laws, kindergartens, age-graded elementary schools, professional training for teachers, vocational education, parent-teacher associations, and school nurses became standard elements in American education. School reformers believed in both the educational soundness of these measures and their importance for countering slum environments. As Jacob Riis contended, the kindergartner would "rediscover . . . the natural feelings that the tenement had smothered."

Public education in the South lagged behind the North. After 1900, per capita expenditures for education doubled, school terms were extended, and high schools spread across the region. But the South frittered away its limited resources on a segregated educational system that shortchanged both races. South Carolina spent twelve times as much per white pupil as per black pupil. Booker T. Washington complained in 1906 that the educational reforms meant "almost nothing so far as the Negro schools are concerned." As a Northern critic observed, "To devise a school system which shall save the whites and not the blacks is a task of such delicacy that a few surviving reactionaries are willing to let both perish together."

CHALLENGING GENDER RESTRICTIONS

Most progressives held fairly conservative, moralistic views about sexuality and gender roles. Margaret Sanger, however, radically challenged conventional ideas of the social role of women. A public health nurse and an IWW organizer, she soon made the struggle for reproductive rights her personal crusade. Sanger saw in New York's immigrant neighborhoods the plight of poor women worn out from repeated pregnancies or injured or dead from self-induced knitting-needle abortions. Despite federal and state laws against contraceptives, Sanger began promoting birth control as a way to avert such tragedies. In 1914, Sanger published a magazine, *Woman Rebel,* in which she argued that "a woman's body belongs to herself alone. It does not belong to the United States of America or any other government on the face of the earth." Prohibiting contraceptives meant "enforced motherhood," Sanger declared. "Women cannot be on an equal footing with men until they have full and complete control over their reproductive function."

Women and girls in an Alabama canning factory, 1911. On the right end is Marie Colbeck, 8 years old, who shucked 6 or 7 pots of oysters a day for about 30 or 35 cents at the Alabama Canning Factory. At the left is Johnnie Schraker, 8 years old, who earned 45 cents a day after shucking oysters for 3 years.

Courtesy National Archives, photo no. 102-LH-1986

• AMERICAN VIEWS •

MOTHER JONES AND THE MEANING OF CHILD LABOR IN AMERICA

orn in Ireland in 1830, the legendary Mother Jones (Mary Harris Jones) became one of America's greatest social activists, protesting social and industrial conditions from the 1870s through the 1920s. Here she recounts an effort to end child labor, one of the most persistent progressive goals. Using the techniques of exposure and publicity characteristic of the period and employing patriotic symbols and references, Jones raised troubling questions about the concepts of social and economic opportunity that many Americans associated with national development and identity.

HOW DID Mother Jones direct public attention to child labor? How did she invoke the treasured American concept of opportunity to gain support for her goal? What did she argue was the relationship between child labor and the privileged status of other Americans? How successful was her crusade against child labor?

In the spring of 1903 I went to Kensington, Pennsylvania, where 75,000 textile workers were on strike. Of this number at least 10,000 were little children.

The workers were striking for more pay and shorter hours. Every day little children came into Union Headquarters, some with their hands off, some with the thumb missing, some with their fingers off at the knuckle. They were stooped little things, round shouldered and skinny. Many of them were not over ten years of age. . . .

We assembled a number of boys and girls one morning in Independence Park and from there we arranged to parade with banners to the court house where we would hold a meeting.

A great crowd gathered in the public square in front of the city hall. I put the little boys with their fingers off and hands crushed and maimed on a platform. I held up their mutilated hands and showed them to the crowd and made the statement that Philadelphia's mansions were built on the broken bones, the quivering hearts, and drooping heads of these children. . . .

I called upon the millionaire manufacturers to cease their moral murders, and I cried to the officials in the open windows opposite, "Some day the workers will take possession of your city hall, and when we do, no child will be sacrificed on the altar of profit."

Sanger's crusade infuriated those who regarded birth control as a threat to the family and morality. Indicted for distributing information about contraception, Sanger fled to Europe. Other women took up the cause, forming the National Birth Control League in 1915 to campaign for the repeal of laws restricting access to contraceptive information and devices.

REFORMING COUNTRY LIFE

Although most progressives focused on the city, others sought to reform rural life. They worked to improve rural health and sanitation, to replace inefficient one-room schools with modern consolidated ones under professional control, and to extend new roads and communication services into the countryside. To further these goals, President Theodore Roosevelt created the Country Life Commission in 1908.

Agricultural scientists, government officials, and many business interests also sought to promote efficient, scientific, and commercial agriculture. A key innovation was the county agent system: the U.S. Department of Agriculture and business groups placed an agent in each county to teach farmers new techniques and

The reporters quoted my statement that Philadelphia mansions were built on the broken bones and quivering hearts of children. The Philadelphia papers and the New York papers got into a squabble with each other over the question. The universities discussed it. Preachers began talking. That was what I wanted. Public attention on the subject of child labor.

The matter quieted down for a while and I concluded the people needed stirring up again. . . . I decided to go with the children to see President Roosevelt to ask him to have Congress pass a law prohibiting the exploitation of childhood. I thought that President Roosevelt might see these mill children and compare them with his own little ones who were spending the summer at the seashore at Oyster Bay. . . .

Everywhere we had meetings, showing up with living children, the horrors of child labor. . . . [In New Jersey] I called on the mayor of Princeton and asked for permission to speak opposite the campus of the University. I said I wanted to speak on higher education. The mayor gave me permission. A great crowd gathered, professors and students and the people; and I told them that the rich robbed these little children of any education of the lowest order that they might send their sons and daughters to places of higher education. . . . And I showed those professors children in our army who could scarcely read or write because they were working ten hours a day in the silk mills of Pennsylvania. . . .

[In New York] I told an immense crowd of the horrors of child labor in the mills around the anthracite region and . . . I showed them Gussie Rangnew, a little girl from whom all the childhood had gone. Her face was like an old woman's. Gussie packed stockings in a factory, eleven hours a day for a few cents a day. . . . "Fifty years ago there was a cry against slavery and men gave up their lives to stop the selling of black children on the block. Today the white child is sold for two dollars a week to the manufacturers."

. . . We marched down to Oyster Bay but the president refused to see us and he would not answer my letters. But our march had done its work. We had drawn the attention of the nation to the crime of child labor. And while the strike of the textile workers in Kensington was lost and the children driven back to work, not long afterward the Pennsylvania legislature passed a child labor law that sent thousands of children home from the mills, and kept thousands of others from entering the factory until they were fourteen years of age.

Source: The Autobiography of Mother Jones, 3rd ed. (Chicago: Kerr Publishing Company, 1977).

encourage changes in the rural social values that had spawned the Populist radicalism that most progressives decried. The Smith-Lever Act (1914) provided federal subsidies for county agents throughout the country. Its purpose, claimed Woodrow Wilson, was to produce "an efficient and contented population" in rural America.

Few farmers, however, welcomed these efforts. As one Illinois county agent said in 1915, "Farmers, as a whole, resent exceedingly those forces which are at work with missionary intent trying to uplift them." School consolidation meant the loss of community control of education; good roads would raise taxes and chiefly benefit urban business interests. Besides, most farmers believed that their problems stemmed not from rural life but from industrial society.

Even so, government agencies, agricultural colleges, and railroads and banks steadily tied farmers to urban markets. Telephones and rural free delivery of mail lessened countryside isolation but quickened the spread of city values. Improved roads and the coming of the automobile eliminated many rural villages and linked farm families directly with towns and cities. Consolidated schools wiped out the social center of rural neighborhoods and carried children out of their communities, many never to return.

SOCIAL CONTROL AND MORAL CRUSADES

The tendency toward social control evident in the movements to pass protective legislation and transform country life also marked other less attractive progressive efforts. These efforts, moreover, often meshed with the restrictive attitudes that conservative Americans held about race, religion, immigration, and morality. The result was widespread attempts to restrict certain groups and control behavior.

Many Americans wanted to limit immigration for racist reasons. Nativist agitation in California prompted the federal government to restrict Japanese immigration in 1907. Californians, including local progressives, also hoped to curtail the migration of Mexicans. A Stanford University researcher condemned Mexicans as an "undesirable class" compared to "the more progressive races."

Nationally, public debate focused on restricting the flow of new immigrants from southern and eastern Europe. Many backed their prejudice with a distorted interpretation of Darwinism, labeling the Slavic and Mediterranean peoples "inferior races." As early as 1894, nativists had organized the Immigration Restriction League, which favored a literacy test for admission, sure that it would "bear most heavily upon the Italians, Russians, Poles, Hungarians, Greeks, and Asiatics, and very lightly or not at all upon English-speaking immigrants or Germans, Scandinavians, and French." Congress enacted a literacy law in 1917.

Other nativists demanded the "Americanization" of immigrants already in the country. The Daughters of the American Revolution sought to inculcate loyalty, patriotism, and conservative values. Settlement workers and Social Gospelers also attempted to transfer their own values to the newcomers. The most prominent advocate of Americanization was a stereotypical progressive, Frances Kellor. She studied social work at the University of Chicago, worked in New York settlement houses, wrote a muckraking exposé of employment agencies that exploited women, and became director of the New York Bureau of Immigration. In 1915, she helped organize the National Americanization Committee and increasingly emphasized destroying immigrants' old-country ties and imposing an American culture.

Closely linked to progressives' worries about immigrants was their campaign for **prohibition**. Social workers saw liquor as a cause of crime, poverty, and family violence; employers blamed it for causing industrial accidents and inefficiency; Social Gospel ministers condemned the "spirit born of hell" because it impaired moral judgment and behavior. But also important was native-born Americans' fear of new immigrants. Many immigrants, in fact, viewed liquor and the neighborhood saloon as vital parts of daily life, and so prohibition became a focus of nativist hostilities, cultural conflict, and Americanization pressures.

Protestant fundamentalists also stoutly supported prohibition, working through the Anti-Saloon League, founded in 1893. Their nativism and antiurban bias surfaced in demands for prohibition to prevent the nation's cities from lapsing into "raging mania, disorder, and anarchy." With most urban Catholics and Jews opposing prohibition, the Anti-Saloon League justified imposing its reform on city populations against their will: "Our nation can only be saved by turning the pure stream of country sentiment . . . to flush out the cesspools of cities and so save civilization from pollution."

With these motivations, prohibitionists campaigned against the manufacture and sale of alcohol. Eventually, the Eighteenth Amendment made prohibition the law of the land by 1920.

Less controversial was the drive to control narcotics, then readily available, and prostitution. Fears that drug addiction was spreading, particularly among black people and immigrants, led Congress in 1914 to pass the Harrison Act, which

Prohibition A ban on the production, sale, and consumption of liquor, achieved temporarily through state laws and the Eighteenth Amendment.

prohibited the distribution and use of narcotics except for medical purposes. The progressive attack on prostitution, which was seen as symptomatic of the exploitation and disorder that affected industrial cities, resulted in state and city attacks on "red light" districts and in the federal Mann Act of 1910, which banned the interstate transport of women "for immoral purposes."

California provided other examples of progressives' interest in social control and moral reform. The state assembly, prohibited gambling, cardplaying, and prizefighting, and Los Angeles banned premarital sex and introduced artistic censorship.

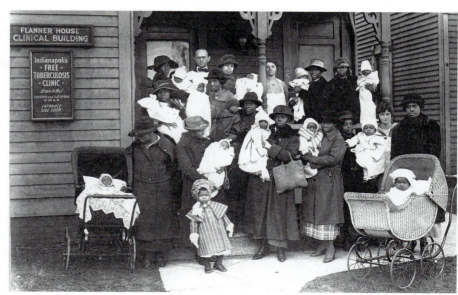

The Flanner House, a black settlement house in Indianapolis, provided the black community with many essential services, including health care. In addition to this baby clinic, pictured in 1918, it established a tuberculosis clinic at a time when the city's public hospitals refused to treat black citizens afflicted with the disease.

Indians Historical Society.

FOR WHITE PEOPLE ONLY?

Racism permeated the Progressive Era. In the South, progressivism was built on black disfranchisement and segregation. Like most white Southerners, progressives believed that racial control was necessary for social order. Governors Hoke Smith of Georgia and James Vardaman, "the White Chief," of Mississippi supported progressive reforms, but they also viciously attacked black rights. Their racist demagogy incited antiblack violence throughout the South. Antiblack race riots, like the riot produced in Atlanta by Smith's election in 1906, and lynching—defended on the floor of the U.S. Senate by a Southern progressive—were part of the system of racial control that made the era a terrible time for African Americans.

Even in the North, where relatively few black people lived, race relations deteriorated. A reporter in Pennsylvania found "this disposition to discriminate against Negroes has greatly increased within the past decade." Antiblack race riots exploded in New York in 1900 and in Springfield, Illinois—Lincoln's hometown—in 1908.

But African Americans also pursued progressive reforms. Even in the South, some black activists struggled to improve conditions. In Atlanta, for example, black women created progressive organizations and established settlement houses, kindergartens, and day-care centers. The women of the Neighborhood Union, organized in 1908, even challenged the discriminatory policies of Atlanta's board of education, demanding equal facilities and appropriations for the city's black schools. They had only limited success, but their efforts demonstrated a persisting commitment to reforming society.

In the North, African Americans more openly criticized discrimination. Ida Wells-Barnett, the crusading journalist who had fled the South for Chicago, became nationally prominent for her militant protests. She fought fiercely against racial injustices, especially school segregation, agitated for woman suffrage, and organized kindergartens and settlement houses for Chicago's black migrants.

Still more important was W.E.B. Du Bois, who campaigned tirelessly against all forms of racial discrimination. In 1905, Du Bois and other black activists met in Niagara Falls, Canada, to make plans to promote political and economic equality. In 1910, this **Niagara Movement** joined with a small group of white reformers, including Jane Addams, to organize the National Association for the Advancement of Colored People. The NAACP sought to overthrow segregation

Niagara Movement African-American group organized in 1905 to promote racial integration, civil and political rights, and equal access to economic opportunity.

and establish equal justice and educational opportunities. As its director of publicity and research, Du Bois launched the influential magazine *The Crisis* to shape public opinion. "Agitate," he counseled, "protest, reveal the truth, and refuse to be silenced." By 1918, the NAACP had 44,000 members in 165 branches.

REFORMING POLITICS AND GOVERNMENT

HOW DID electoral and municipal reforms improve voting and government during the Progressive Era?

Progressives of all kinds clamored for the reform of politics and government, but their political activism was motivated by different concerns, and they sometimes pursued competing objectives. Many wanted to change procedures and institutions to promote greater democracy and responsibility. Others hoped to improve the efficiency of government, to eliminate corruption, or to increase their own influence. All justified their objectives as necessary to adapt the political system to the nation's new needs.

WOMAN SUFFRAGE

The woman suffrage movement had begun in the mid-nineteenth century, but suffragists had been frustrated by the prevailing belief that women's "proper sphere" was the home and the family. Woman suffrage, particularly when championed as a step toward women's equality, seemed to challenge the natural order of society, and it generated much opposition among traditionalist-minded men and women.

In the early twentieth century, under a new generation of leaders like Carrie Chapman Catt, suffragists adopted activist tactics, including parades, mass meetings, and "suffrage tours" by automobile. They also organized by political districts and attracted workingwomen and labor unions. By 1917, the National American Woman Suffrage Association had over 2 million members.

But some suffrage leaders shifted arguments to gain more support. Rather than insisting on the "justice" of woman suffrage or emphasizing equal rights, they spoke of the special moral and maternal instincts women could bring to politics if allowed to vote. The suffrage movement now appeared less a radical, disruptive force than a vehicle for extending traditional female benevolence and service to society. The new image of the movement increased public support by appealing to conventional views of women. Noted one Nebraska undergraduate, women students no longer feared "antagonizing the men or losing invitations to parties by being suffragists."

Gradually, the suffrage movement began to prevail. In 1910, Washington became the first state to approve woman suffrage since the mid-1890s, followed by California in 1911 and Arizona, Kansas, and Oregon in 1912. Suffragists also mounted national action, such as the dramatic inaugural parade in March 1913 described at the beginning of this chapter. By 1919, thirty-nine states had established full or partial woman suffrage, and Congress finally approved an amendment. Ratified by the states in 1920, the **Nineteenth Amendment** marked a critical advance in political democracy.

ELECTORAL REFORM

Other electoral reforms changed the election process and the meaning of political participation. The so-called **Australian ballot** adopted by most states during the 1890s provided for secret voting and replaced the individual party tickets with an official ballot listing all candidates and distributed by public officials. The Australian ballot led to quiet, orderly elections. One Cincinnati editor, who recalled

QUICK REVIEW

Votes for Women
◆ Woman suffrage movement began in the mid-nineteenth century.
◆ Early twentieth-century leaders adopted activist tactics.
◆ Nineteenth Amendment ratified in 1920.

Nineteenth Amendment
Constitutional revision that in 1920 established women citizens' right to vote.

Australian ballot Secret voting and the use of official ballots rather than party tickets.

the "howling mobs" and chaos at the polls in previous elections, declared: "The political bummer and thug has been relegated to the background . . . while good citizenship . . . has come to the front."

Public regulation of other parts of the electoral process previously controlled by parties soon followed. Beginning with Mississippi in 1902, nearly every state provided for direct primaries to remove nominations from the boss-ridden caucus and convention system. Many states also reformed campaign practices.

The decreasing ability of parties to mobilize voters was reflected in a steady decline in voter participation, from 79 percent in 1896 to 49 percent in 1920. As parties contracted, the influence of nonpartisan organizations and pressure groups grew, promoting narrower objectives. Thus the National Association of Manufacturers (1895) and the United States Chamber of Commerce (1912) lobbied for business interests; the National Farmers Union (1902), for commercial agriculture; the American Federation of Teachers (1916), for professional educators. The organized lobbying of special-interest groups would give them greater influence over government in the future and contribute to the declining popular belief in the value of voting or participation in politics.

Disfranchisement more obviously undermined American democracy. In the South, Democrats—progressive and conservative alike—eliminated not only black voters but also many poor white voters from the electorate through poll taxes, literacy tests, and other restrictions. Republicans in the North adopted educational or literacy tests in ten states, enacted strict registration laws, and gradually abolished the right of aliens to vote. These restrictions reflected both the progressives' anti-immigrant prejudices and their obsessions with social control and with purifying politics and "improving" the electorate. Such electoral reforms reduced the political power of ethnic and working-class Americans, often stripping them of their political rights and means of influence.

MUNICIPAL REFORM

Muckrakers had exposed crooked alliances between city bosses and business leaders that resulted in wasteful or inadequate municipal services. In some cities, urban reformers attempted to break these alliances and improve conditions for those suffering most from municipal misrule. For example, in Toledo, Ohio, Samuel "Golden Rule" Jones won enough working-class votes to be elected mayor four times despite the hostility of both major parties. Serving from 1897 to 1904, Jones opened public playgrounds and kindergartens, established the eight-hour day for city workers, and improved public services. Influenced by the Social Gospel, he also provided free lodging for the homeless and gave his own salary to the poor. Other reforming mayors also fought municipal corruption, limited the political influence of corporations, and championed public ownership of utilities.

More elitist progressives attempted to change the structure of urban government. Middle-class reformers worked to replace ward elections with citywide elections which required greater resources and therefore helped swell middle-class influence at the expense of working-class wards. So did nonpartisan elections, which reformers introduced to weaken party loyalties.

Urban reformers developed two other structural innovations: the city commission and the city manager. Both attempted to institutionalize efficient, businesslike government staffed by professional administrators. By 1920, hundreds of cities had adopted one of the new plans.

Business groups often promoted these reforms. In Des Moines, for example, the president of the Commercial Club declared that "the professional politician must be ousted and in his place capable businessmen chosen to conduct the affairs of the city." Again, then, reform in municipal government often shifted political power from ethnic and working-class voters, represented however imperfectly by partisan elections, to smaller groups with greater resources.

PROGRESSIVE STATE GOVERNMENT

Progressives also reshaped state government. Some tried to democratize the legislative process, regarding the legislature—the most important branch of state government in the nineteenth century—as ineffective and even corrupt, dominated by party bosses and corporate influences. The Missouri legislature reportedly "enacted such laws as the corporations paid for, and such others as were necessary to fool the people." Populists had first raised such charges in the 1890s and proposed novel solutions adopted by many states in the early twentieth century. The **initiative** enabled reformers themselves to propose legislation directly to the electorate, bypassing an unresponsive legislature; the **referendum** permitted voters to approve or reject legislative measures.

Other reforms also expanded the popular role in state government. The **Seventeenth Amendment**, ratified in 1913, provided for the election of U.S. senators directly by popular vote instead of by state legislatures. Beginning with Oregon in 1908, ten states adopted the **recall**, enabling voters to remove unsatisfactory public officials from office.

As state legislatures and party machines were curbed, dynamic governors like Robert La Follette pushed progressive programs into law. Elected in 1900, "Fighting Bob" La Follette turned Wisconsin into "the laboratory of democracy." "His words bite like coals of fire," wrote one observer. "He never wearies and he will not allow his audience to weary." Overcoming fierce opposition from "stalwart" Republicans, La Follette established direct primaries, railroad regulation, the first state income tax, workers' compensation, and other important measures before being elected to the U.S. Senate in 1906.

La Follette also stressed efficiency and expertise. The Legislative Reference Bureau that he created was staffed by university professors to advise on public policy. He used regulatory commissions to oversee railroads, banks, and other interests. Most states followed suit, and expert commissions became an important feature of state government, gradually gaining authority at the expense of local officials.

"Experts" were presumed to be disinterested and therefore committed to the general welfare. In practice, however, regulators were subject to pressures from competing interest groups, and some commissions became captives of the very industries they were supposed to control. This irony was matched by the contradiction between the expansion of democracy through the initiative and referendum and the increasing reliance on nonelected professional experts to set and implement public policy.

THEODORE ROOSEVELT AND THE PROGRESSIVE PRESIDENCY

When a crazed anarchist assassinated William McKinley in 1901, Theodore Roosevelt entered the White House, and the progressive movement gained its most prominent leader. The son of a wealthy New York family, Roosevelt had been a New York legislator, U.S. civil service commissioner, and assistant secretary of the navy. After his exploits in the Spanish-American War, he was elected governor of New York in 1898 and vice president in 1900. His public life was matched by an active private life in which he both

---

21–12
Herbert Croly, Progressive Democracy (1914)

Initiative Procedure by which citizens can introduce a subject for legislation, usually through a petition signed by a specific number of voters.

Referendum Submission of a law, proposed or already in effect, to a direct popular vote for approval or rejection.

Seventeenth Amendment Constitutional change that in 1913 established the direct popular election of U.S. senators.

Recall The process of removing an official from office by popular vote, usually after using petitions to call for such a vote.

HOW WAS the executive branch strengthened under Roosevelt?

wrote works of history and obsessively pursued what he called the "strenuous life": boxing, wrestling, hunting, rowing, even ranching and chasing rustlers in Dakota Territory. His own son observed that Roosevelt "always wanted to be the bride at every wedding and the corpse at every funeral."

Mark Twain fretted that "Mr. Roosevelt is the Tom Sawyer of the political world of the twentieth century; always showing off; always hunting for a chance to show off; in his frenzied imagination the Great Republic is a vast Barnum circus with him for a clown and the whole world for audience." But Roosevelt's flamboyance and ambitions made him the most popular politician of the time and enabled him to dramatize the issues of progressivism and to become the first modern president.

WHERE TO LEARN MORE

Sagamore Hill, Oyster Bay, New York
www.nps.gov/sahi/

TR AND THE MODERN PRESIDENCY

Roosevelt believed that the president could do anything to meet national needs that the Constitution did not specifically prohibit. "Under this interpretation of executive power," he later recalled, "I did and caused to be done many things not previously done. . . . I did not usurp power, but I did greatly broaden the use of executive power." Indeed, the expansion of government power and its consolidation in the executive branch were among his most significant accomplishments.

Roosevelt spelled out his policy goals in more than four hundred messages to Congress, sent drafts of bills to Capitol Hill, and intervened to win passage of "his" measures. Some members of Congress resented such "executive arrogance" and "dictatorship." Roosevelt generally avoided direct challenges to the conservative Old Guard Republicans who controlled Congress, but his activities helped shift the balance of power within the national government.

Roosevelt also reorganized the executive branch. He believed in efficiency and expertise. To promote rational policymaking and public management, he staffed the expanding federal bureaucracy with able professionals. The president, complained one Republican, was "trying to concentrate all power in Washington . . . and to govern the people by commissions and bureaus."

Finally, Roosevelt exploited and skillfully handled the mass media, which made him a celebrity, "TR" or "Teddy." The publicity kept TR in the spotlight and enabled him to mold public opinion.

ROOSEVELT AND LABOR

One sign of TR's vigorous new approach to the presidency was his handling of a coal strike in 1902. Members of the United Mine Workers Union walked off their jobs, demanding higher wages, an eight-hour day, and recognition of their union. The mine owners closed the mines and waited for the union to collapse. But led by John Mitchell, the strikers held their ranks. Management's stubborn arrogance contrasted with the workers' orderly conduct and willingness to negotiate and hardened public opinion against the owners. TR's legal advisers told him that the government had no constitutional authority to intervene.

As public pressure mounted, however, Roosevelt decided to act. He invited both the owners and the union leaders to a White House conference and declared that the national interest made government action necessary. Mitchell agreed to negotiate. The owners, however, refused even to speak to the miners and demanded that Roosevelt use the army to break the union, as Cleveland had done in the Pullman strike in 1894.

Roosevelt was not a champion of labor. But furious with the owners' "arrogant stupidity" and "insulting" attitude toward the presidency, he announced that he would use the army to seize and operate the mines, not to crush the union. Questioned about the constitutionality of such an action, Roosevelt bellowed: "To hell with the Constitution when the people want coal." Reluctantly, the owners accepted the arbitration commission they had previously rejected. The commission gave the miners a 10 percent wage increase and a nine-hour day, but not union recognition, and permitted the owners to raise coal prices by 10 percent. Roosevelt described his intervention as simply giving both labor and management a "square deal." It also set important precedents for an active government role in labor disputes and a strong president acting as a steward of the public.

MANAGING NATURAL RESOURCES

Federal land policy had helped create farms and develop transportation, but it had also ceded to speculators and business interests much of the nation's forests, mineral deposits, waterpower sites, and grazing lands. A new generation believed in the **conservation** of natural resources through efficient and scientific management. Conservationists achieved early victories in the Forest Reserve Act (1891) and the Forest Management Act (1897), which authorized the federal government to withdraw timberlands from development and to regulate grazing, lumbering, and hydroelectric sites in the forests (see Map 21–1).

Roosevelt and his friend Gifford Pinchot made conservation a major focus of his presidency. Appointed in 1898 to head the new Division of Forestry (renamed the Forest Service in 1905), Pinchot brought rational management and regulation to resource development. With his advice, TR used presidential authority to triple the size of the forest reserves to 150 million acres, set aside another 80 million acres valuable for minerals and petroleum, and establish dozens of wildlife refuges. In 1908, Roosevelt held a White House conference of state and federal officials that led to the creation of the National Conservation Commission, forty-one state conservation commissions, and widespread public support for the conservation movement.

Some interests opposed conservation. Many Westerners resented having Easterners make key decisions about Western growth and saw conservation as a perpetuation of this colonial subservience. Many ranchers refused to pay federal grazing fees. Colorado arsonists set forest fires to protest the creation of forest reserves.

But Westerners were happy to take federal money for expensive irrigation projects that private capital would not undertake. They favored the 1902 National Reclamation Act, which established the **Bureau of Reclamation**. Its engineers were to construct dams, reservoirs, and irrigation canals, and the government was to sell the irrigated lands in tracts no larger than 160 acres. With massive dams and networks of irrigation canals, it reclaimed fertile valleys from the desert. Unfortunately, the bureau did not enforce the 160-acre limitation and thus helped create powerful corporate farms in the West.

CORPORATE REGULATION

Nothing symbolized Roosevelt's active presidency better than his popular reputation as a "trust buster." TR regarded the formation of large business combinations favorably, but he knew he could not ignore the public anxiety about corporate power. Business leaders and Old Guard conservatives opposed any government intervention in the large trusts, but Roosevelt knew better. "You have no conception of the revolt that would be caused if I did nothing," he said privately. TR proposed to "develop an orderly system, and such a system can only come through the gradually exercised right of efficient government control." Rather than invoking "the foolish antitrust law," he favored government regulation to prevent corporate abuses and defend the public interest. But he did sue some "bad trusts."

WHERE TO LEARN MORE

★ John Muir National Historic Site, Martinez, California
www.nps.gov/jomu/

Conservation   The efficient management and use of natural resources, such as forests, grasslands, and rivers, as opposed to preservation or controlled exploitation.

Bureau of Reclamation   Federal agency established in 1902 providing public funds for irrigation projects in arid regions.

MAP EXPLORATION
To explore an interactive version of this map, go to **http://www.prenhall.com/goldfield2/map21.1**

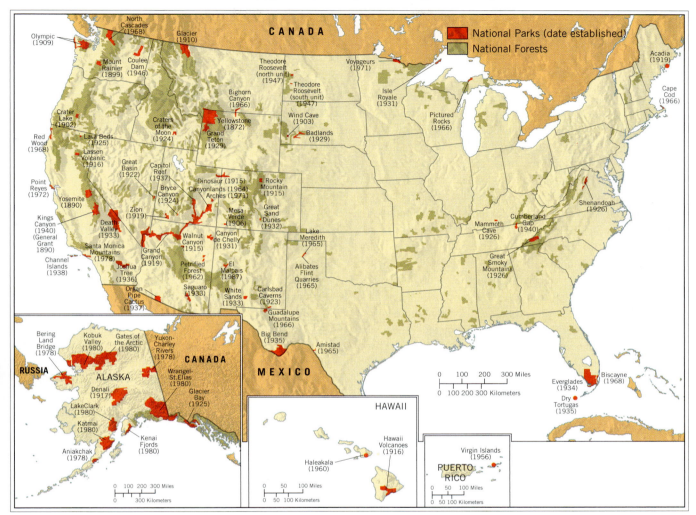

MAP 21–1

The Growth of National Forests and National Parks   Rapid exploitation of the West prompted demands to preserve its spectacular scenery and protect its remaining forests. In 1872 Yellowstone became the first National Park, and the National Forest system began in the 1890s. Conservation became increasingly important during the Progressive Era but often provoked Western hostility.

WHICH STATES have the most national forests and national parks?

In 1902, the Roosevelt administration filed its most famous antitrust suit, against the Northern Securities Company, a holding company organized by J.P. Morgan to control the railroad network of the Northwest. For TR, this suit was an assertion of government power that reassured a worried public and made corporate responsibility more likely. In 1904, the Supreme Court ordered the dissolution of the Northern Securities Company.

Elected president in his own right in 1904 over the colorless and conservative Democratic candidate Judge Alton B. Parker, Roosevelt responded to the growing popular demand for reform by pushing further toward a regulatory government.

FROM THEN TO NOW
The Environmental Movement

Many of the issues that concern environmentalists today were first raised by the conservationists and preservationists of the Progressive Era. Conservationists favored the planned and regulated management of America's natural resources for the public benefit. Led by Theodore Roosevelt, they dominated the new agencies like the Forest Service that were responsible for federal lands. In contrast, preservationists—like John Muir, who founded the Sierra Club in 1892—sought to protect wilderness from any development whatsoever. Opposing both were those who championed the uncontrolled development of public lands.

Preservationists' reasons for protecting wilderness were primarily aesthetic—to preserve natural splendors intact for future generations. By the second half of the twentieth century, however, the disturbing consequences of technological change, rapid economic development, and spiraling population growth began to raise the stakes. Air pollution from smokestack industries and automobile exhaust damaged natural vegetation and caused respiratory diseases; water pollution from sewage and chemical waste spread disease; and oil spills fouled beaches and devastated marine habitats.

Public concern over these problems gave birth to the environmental movement, which drew on the legacy of both the conservation and preservation movements but had wider interests and broader support than either. Responding to the environmental movement's quickly growing strength, Congress in the 1970s passed laws to protect endangered species, reduce pollution, limit the use of pesticides, and control hazardous waste. The Environmental Protection Agency, created in 1970, subsequently became the largest federal regulatory agency.

Again, however, as during the Progressive Era, efforts to protect the environment encountered opposition from proponents of unrestricted development, especially in the West.

In the Sagebrush Rebellion in the late 1970s and 1980s, some Westerners condemned "outside" federal regulation and tried to seize control of public lands for private exploitation. One oil company dismissed catastrophic oil spills as merely "Mother Earth letting some oil come out."

Three Republican presidents from the West—Californians Richard Nixon and Ronald Reagan and Texan George H. W. Bush, all closely tied to oil and real estate interests—sought in varying degrees to curtail environmental policies, agencies, and budgets and to promote development. This repudiation of Theodore Roosevelt's conservationism reflected the shift of the party's base to the sunbelt. As one Nixon adviser said, when a pipeline across the Alaskan wilderness was approved, "Conservation is not in the Republican ethic."

Ronald Reagan in particular was convinced that environmental protection fundamentally conflicted with economic growth. The business executives and corporate lawyers he appointed to key federal positions rescinded or weakened environmental regulations.

Congress, the courts, and the public, however, resisted efforts to weaken environmental policy. "Green" groups proliferated, demanding greater attention to environmental issues; some, like Greenpeace, undertook direct action to protect the environment, and even Western communities organized to oppose strip-mining, nuclear power plants, and toxic waste dumping.

Despite fluctuations, public opinion and mainstream politics now appear to favor greater environmental protection. Debate is sure to continue over the cost and effectiveness of specific policies. But as ever more challenging ecological problems arise—like ozone depletion and global warming—Americans are increasingly inclined to stand with Theodore Roosevelt and John Muir in looking to the federal government for effective action to meet them.

He proposed legislation "to work out methods of controlling the big corporations without paralyzing the energies of the business community."

The Hepburn Act, passed in 1906, authorized the Interstate Commerce Commission to set maximum railroad rates and extended its jurisdiction. It was a weaker law than many progressives had wanted, but it marked the first time the federal government gained the power to set rules in a private enterprise.

In the same year, Congress passed the Pure Food and Drug Act and the Meat Inspection Act. In part, this legislation reflected public demand, but many business leaders also supported government regulation of food and drugs, convinced that it would expand their markets by certifying the quality of their products and drive their smaller competitors out of business. The meat and food and drug acts did thus extend government regulation over business to protect the public health and safety, but they also served some corporate purposes.

Despite the compromises and weaknesses in the three laws, TR contended that they marked "a noteworthy advance in the policy of securing federal supervision and control over corporations." In 1907 and 1908, he pushed for an eight-hour workday, stock market regulation, and inheritance and income taxes. Republican conservatives in Congress blocked such reforms. Old Guard Republicans thought Roosevelt had extended government powers dangerously, but in fact his accomplishments had been relatively modest. As La Follette noted, Roosevelt's "cannonading filled the air with noise and smoke, which confused and obscured the line of action, but, when the battle cloud drifted by and the quiet was restored, it was always a matter of surprise that so little had really been accomplished."

TAFT AND THE INSURGENTS

TR handpicked his successor as president: a loyal lieutenant, William Howard Taft. Member of a prominent Ohio political family, Taft had been a federal judge, governor-general of the Philippines, and TR's secretary of war. Later he would serve as chief justice of the United States. But Taft's election as president in 1908, over Democrat William Jennings Bryan in his third presidential campaign, led to a Republican political disaster.

Taft did preside over a more active and successful antitrust program than Roosevelt's. He supported the Mann-Elkins Act (1910), which extended the ICC's jurisdiction to telephone and telegraph companies. Taft set aside more public forest lands and oil reserves than Roosevelt had. He also supported a constitutional amendment authorizing an income tax, which went into effect in 1913 under the **Sixteenth Amendment**. One of the most important accomplishments of the Progressive Era, the income tax would provide the means for the government to expand its activities and responsibilities.

Nevertheless, Taft soon alienated progressives and floundered into a political morass. His problems were twofold. First, Midwestern reform Republicans, led by La Follette, clashed with more conservative Republicans led by Senator Nelson Aldrich of Rhode Island. Second, Taft was politically inept. He was unable to mediate between these two groups, and the party split apart.

Reformers wanted to restrict the power of the speaker of the House, "Uncle Joe" Cannon, a reactionary who blocked reform. After seeming to promise support,

Roosevelt enjoyed this cartoon illustrating his distinction between good trusts, retrained by government regulations for public welfare, and bad trusts. On those he put his foot down.

The Granger Collection, New York

WHERE TO LEARN MORE

William Howard Taft National Historic Site, Cincinnati, Ohio

Sixteenth Amendment
Constitutional revision that in 1913 authorized a federal income tax.

Taft backed down when conservatives threatened to defeat important legislation. The insurgents in Congress never forgave what they saw as Taft's betrayal. The tariff also alienated progressives from Taft. He had campaigned in 1908 for a lower tariff to curb inflation, and Midwestern Republicans favored tariff reduction to trim the power of big business. But when they introduced tariff reform legislation, the president failed to support them. Aldrich's Senate committee added 847 amendments, many of which raised tariff rates. Taft justified his inaction as avoiding presidential interference with congressional business, but progressives concluded that Taft had sided with the Old Guard.

That perception solidified when Taft stumbled into a controversy over conservation. When Pinchot challenged secretary of the interior Richard Ballinger's role in a questionable sale of public coal lands in Alaska to a J. P. Morgan syndicate, Taft upheld Ballinger and fired Pinchot. Progressives concluded that Taft had repudiated Roosevelt's conservation policies.

In 1911, reformers formed the National Progressive League to champion La Follette for the Republican nomination in 1912. They appealed to TR for support, but Roosevelt's own position was closer to Taft's than to what he called "the La Follette type of fool radicalism." But condemning Taft as "disloyal to our past friendship . . . [and] to every canon of ordinary decency," TR began to campaign for the Republican nomination himself. In thirteen state primaries, TR won 278 delegates to only 46 for Taft. But most states did not then have primaries; that allowed Taft to dominate the Republican convention and win renomination. Roosevelt's forces formed a third party—the Progressive party—and nominated the former president. The Republican split almost guaranteed victory for the Democratic nominee, Woodrow Wilson.

WOODROW WILSON AND PROGRESSIVE REFORM

Elected president in 1912 and 1916, Woodrow Wilson mediated among differing progressive views to achieve a strong reform program, enlarge the power of the executive branch, and make the White House the center of national politics.

HOW DID Woodrow Wilson bring progressivism to its climax?

THE ELECTION OF 1912

In Congress, Southern Democrats more consistently supported reform measures than Republicans did, and Democratic leader William Jennings Bryan surpassed Roosevelt as a persistent advocate of significant political and economic reform. As the Democrats pushed progressive remedies and the Republicans quarreled during Taft's administration, Democrats achieved major victories in the state and congressional elections of 1910. To improve the party's chances in 1912, Bryan announced he would step aside. The Democratic spotlight shifted to the governor of New Jersey, Woodrow Wilson.

Born in Virginia as the son and grandson of Presbyterian ministers, Wilson combined public eloquence with a cold personality; he balanced a self-righteousness that led to stubborn inflexibility with an intense ambition that permitted the most expedient compromises. Wilson first entered public life as a conservative. In 1910, while he was president of Princeton University, New Jersey's Democratic bosses selected him for governor to head off the progressives. But once in office, Wilson championed popular reforms and immediately began to campaign as a progressive for the party's 1912 presidential nomination.

Wilson's progressivism differed from that of Roosevelt. TR emphasized a strong government that would promote economic and social order. He defended big business as inevitable and healthy provided that government control ensured that it would benefit the entire nation. Roosevelt called this program the **New Nationalism**, reflecting his belief in a powerful state and a national interest. He also supported demands for social welfare, including workers' compensation and the abolition of child labor.

Wilson was horrified by Roosevelt's vision. His **New Freedom** program rejected what he called TR's "regulated monopoly." Wilson wanted "regulated competition," with the government's role limited to breaking up monopolies through antitrust action and preventing artificial barriers like tariffs from blocking free enterprise. Wilson opposed social welfare legislation as "paternalistic."

Unable to add progressive Democrats to the Republicans who followed him into the Progressive party, TR could not win despite his personal popularity. Other reform voters embraced the Socialist candidate, Eugene V. Debs, who captured 900,000 votes—6 percent of the total. Taft played little role in the campaign. "I might as well give up as far as being a candidate," he lamented. "There are so many people in the country who don't like me."

Wilson won an easy electoral college victory, though he received only 42 percent of the popular vote. Roosevelt came in second, Taft third. The Democrats also gained control of Congress, giving Wilson the opportunity to enact his New Freedom program.

	Electoral Vote (%)	Popular Vote (%)
WOODROW WILSON (Democrat)	435 (82)	6,296,547 (42)
Theodore Roosevelt (Progressive)	88 (17)	4,118,571 (27)
William Taft (Republican)	8 (1)	3,486,720 (23)
Eugene Debs (Socialist)	–	900,672 (6)

MAP 21-2

The split within the Republican party enabled Woodrow Wilson to carry most states and became president even through he won only a minority of the popular vote

HOW IS it possible that Woodrow Wilson received 82 percent of the electoral vote but only 42 percent of the popular vote?

IMPLEMENTING THE NEW FREEDOM

Wilson built on Roosevelt's precedent to strengthen executive authority. He summoned Congress into special session in 1913 and delivered his message in person, the first president to do so since John Adams. Wilson proposed a full legislative program and worked forcefully to secure its approval. He held regular conferences with Democratic leaders and had a private telephone line installed between the Capitol and the White House to keep tabs on congressional actions. When necessary, he appealed to the public for support or doled out patronage and compromised with conservatives.

Wilson turned first to the traditional Democratic goal of reducing the high protective tariff. "The object of the tariff duties," Wilson announced, "must be effective competition." He forced through the **Underwood-Simmons Tariff Act** of 1913, the first substantial reduction in duties since before the Civil War. The act also levied the first income tax under the recently ratified Sixteenth Amendment.

Wilson next reformed the nation's banking and currency system, which was inadequate for a modernizing economy. He skillfully maneuvered a compromise measure through Congress, balancing the demands of agrarian progressives for government control with the bankers' desires for private control. The **Federal Reserve Act** of 1913 created twelve regional Federal Reserve banks that, although privately controlled, were to be supervised by the Federal Reserve Board, appointed by the president. The law also provided for a flexible national currency and improved access to credit. Serious problems remained, but the new system

New Nationalism Theodore Roosevelt's 1912 program calling for a strong national government to foster, regulate, and protect business, industry, workers, and consumers.

New Freedom Woodrow Wilson's 1912 program for limited government intervention in the economy to restore competition by curtailing the restrictive influences of trusts and protective tariffs, thereby providing opportunities for individual achievement.

Underwood-Simmons Tariff Act The 1913 reform law that lowered tariff rates and levied the first regular federal income tax.

Federal Reserve Act The 1913 law that revised banking and currency by extending limited government regulation through the creation of the Federal Reserve System.

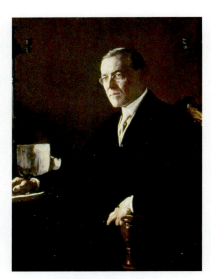

U.S. President Woodrow Wilson sits at his desk in an oil painting on canvas by Edmund Charles Tarbell.

The Granger Collection, New York

promoted the progressive goals of order and efficiency and fulfilled Wilson's New Freedom principle of introducing limited government regulation while preserving private business control.

Wilson's third objective was new legislation to break up monopolies. To this end, he initially supported the Clayton antitrust bill, which prohibited unfair trade practices and restricted holding companies. But when business leaders and other progressives strenuously objected, Wilson reversed himself. Opting for continuous federal regulation rather than for the dissolution of trusts, Wilson endorsed the creation of the **Federal Trade Commission (FTC)** to oversee business activity and prevent illegal restrictions on competition.

The Federal Trade Commission Act of 1914 embraced the New Nationalism's emphasis on positive regulation. Wilson now accepted what he had earlier denounced as a partnership between trusts and the government that the trusts would dominate. Indeed, Wilson's conservative appointments to the FTC ensured that the agency would not seriously interfere with business.

Wilson now announced that no further reforms were necessary. He refused to support woman suffrage and helped kill legislation abolishing child labor and expanding credits to farmers. Race relations provided a flagrant instance of Wilson's indifference to social justice issues. Raised in the South, he believed in segregation and backed the Southern Democrats in his cabinet when they introduced formal segregation within the government itself. Government offices, shops, restrooms, and restaurants were all segregated; employees who complained were fired.

THE EXPANSION OF REFORM

Wilson had won in 1912 only because the Republicans had split. By 1916, Roosevelt had returned to the GOP, and Wilson realized that he had to attract some of TR's former followers. Wilson therefore promoted measures he had previously condemned as paternalistic. He now also recognized that some problems could be resolved only by positive federal action. "Old political formulas," he said, "do not fit the present."

In 1916, Wilson convinced Congress to pass the Federal Farm Loan Act, which provided farmers with federally financed, long-term agricultural credits. The Warehouse Act of 1916 improved short-term agricultural credit. The Highway Act of 1916 provided funds to construct and improve rural roads.

Wilson and the Democratic Congress also reached out to labor. Wilson signed the Keating-Owen Act prohibiting the interstate shipment of products made by child labor. In 1902, Wilson had denounced Roosevelt's intervention in the coal strike, but in 1916, he broke a labor-management impasse and averted a railroad strike by helping pass the Adamson Act establishing an eight-hour day for railway workers. Wilson pushed the Kern-McGillicuddy Act, which achieved the progressive goal of a workers' compensation system for federal employees.

Wilson also promoted activist government when he nominated Louis Brandeis to the Supreme Court. Known as the "people's lawyer," Brandeis had successfully defended protective labor legislation before the conservative judiciary. Brandeis was the first Jew nominated to the court, and anti-Semitism motivated some of his opponents. Wilson overcame a vicious campaign against Brandeis and secured his confirmation.

By these actions, Wilson brought progressivism to a culmination of sorts and consolidated reformers behind him for a second term. Less than a decade earlier, Wilson the private citizen had assailed government regulation and social legislation; by 1916, he had guided an unprecedented expansion of federal power.

Federal Trade Commission
Government agency established in 1914 to provide regulatory oversight of business activity.

CONCLUSION

Progressive reformers responded to the tensions of industrial and urban development by moving to change society and government. Programs and laws to protect women, children, and injured workers testified to their compassion; the creation of new agencies and political techniques indicated their interest in order and efficiency; campaigns to end corruption, whether perceived in urban political machines, corporate influence, drunkenness, or "inferior" immigrants, illustrated their self-assured vision of the public good.

Americans had come to accept that government action could resolve social and economic problems, and the role and power of government expanded accordingly. The emergence of an activist presidency, capable of developing programs, mobilizing public opinion, directing Congress, and taking forceful action, epitomized this key development.

Progressivism had its ironies and paradoxes. It called for democratic reforms—and did achieve woman suffrage, direct legislation, and popular election of senators—but helped disfranchise black Southerners and Northern immigrants. It advocated social justice but often enforced social control. It demanded responsive government but helped create bureaucracies largely removed from popular control. It endorsed the regulation of business in the public interest but forged regulatory laws and commissions that tended to aid business. Some of these seeming contradictions reflected the persistence of traditional attitudes and the necessity to accommodate conservative opponents; others revealed the progressives' own limitations in vision, concern, or nerve.

SUMMARY

The Ferment of Reform Progressivism was a diverse movement; reformers responded to the tensions of industrialization and urbanization by developing programs to give women the right to vote, expose business abuses, end child labor, make government more efficient, manage natural resources and bring about social reform. The Social Gospel movement sought to introduce religious ethics into industrial relations; as businesses adopted Taylorization to improve workplace efficiency, workers resisted these new rules of efficiency. Opponents of reform held to traditional values and religious fundamentalism; businesses, angered by muckraking, used public relations as well as less desirable tactics to counter their critics.

Reforming Society Progressives worked to transform society by improving living conditions, educational opportunities, family life, and social and industrial relations. Settlement houses were the spearheads of social reform in urban immigrant neighborhoods; however, many reformers concluded it would take government intervention to end some of the abuses. Today's modern public school system emerged, and reformer Margaret Sanger crusaded for birth control. Nativists sought to limit immigration; the prohibition of alcohol was linked to social controls; the Eighteenth Amendment made prohibition the law of the land. The Niagara Movement sought to extend equal justice to African Americans; most Progressive reforms had not extended to them.

Reforming Politics and Government Progressives clamored for the reform of politics and the government; many wanted to change procedures and institutions to promote greater democracy; others hoped to improve the efforts of government and eliminate corruption. One of the most important achievements was woman suffrage; the Nineteenth Amendment gave women across America the right to vote. The secret ballot, initiative, referendum, recall, and direct election of senators were all introduced into the American political landscape during this period.

Theodore Roosevelt and the Progressive Presidency Progressive proponent Theodore Roosevelt entered the White House upon the assassination of President McKinley in 1901. He rejected the limited role of the Gilded Age presidents and believed it was the role of the president to meet any national needs not prohibited by the Constitution. Called the first "modern president," Roosevelt's flamboyance and ambitions made him the most popular president of the time and enabled him to take aggressive approaches toward a coal strike, conservation, "busting" trusts, and regulating business abuses. His administration marks the first time that the federal government gained the power to set rules in private enterprise.

Woodrow Wilson and Progressive Reform Progressivism was not limited to the Republican party; following Taft's administration Democrats pushed progressive remedies. President Woodrow Wilson, elected in 1912, introduced the New Freedom program; though he believed government's role should be more limited, he took steps to reduce the high protective tariff, create the Federal Reserve, break up monopolistic practices through the Federal Trade Commission, assist farmers, help workers and build highways. Wilson's "limited" view of Progressivism resulted in an unprecedented expansion of federal power.

REVIEW QUESTIONS

1. How and why did the presidency change during the Progressive Era?

2. How did the progressive concern for efficiency affect social reform efforts, public education, government, and rural life?

3. What factors, old and new, stimulated the reform movements of progressivism?

4. How did the changing role of women affect progressivism?

5. Why did the demand for woman suffrage provoke such determined support and such bitter opposition?

KEY TERMS

Australian ballot (p. 564)
Bureau of Reclamation (p. 568)
Conservation (p. 568)
Federal Reserve Act (p. 573)
Federal Trade Commission (p. 574)
Fundamentalists (p. 556)
Initiative (p. 566)
Muckraking (p. 553)

New Freedom (p. 573)
New Nationalism (p. 573)
Niagara Movement (p. 563)
Nineteenth Amendment (p. 564)
Progressive Era (p. 549)
Prohibition (p. 562)
Recall (p. 566)
Referendum (p. 566)

Seventeenth Amendment (p. 566)
Sixteenth Amendment (p. 571)
Social Gospel Movement (p. 551)
Underwood-Simmons Tariff Act (p. 573)
Wobblies (p. 554)

WHERE TO LEARN MORE

 John Muir National Historic Site, Martinez, California. The architecture and furnishings of this seventeen-room house reflect the interests of John Muir, the writer and naturalist who founded the Sierra Club and led the preservationists in the Progressive Era. **www.nps.gov/jomu/**

National Museum of American History, Smithsonian Institution, Washington, D.C. A permanent exhibition, "Parlor to Politics: Women and Reform, 1890–1925," uses design, artifacts, and recent scholarship to vividly illustrate the changing role of women in the Progressive Era. It effectively emphasizes their work in settlement houses and their growing politicization and demonstrates the importance of the work of black women's organizations.

Hull House, Chicago, Illinois. This pioneering settlement house is now a museum on the campus of the University of Illinois, Chicago. **www.uic.edu/jaddams/ hull/hull_house.html**

Lowell National Historic Park, Lowell, Massachusetts. "The Working People," a permanent exhibition, uses artifacts and photographs to chart the activities of immigrant workers at different times in the past, particularly during the Progressive Era. **www.nps.gov/lowe/**

Lower East Side Tenement Museum, New York City, New York. A six-story tenement building containing twenty-two apartments, this museum vividly illustrates the congested and unhealthy living conditions of urban immigrants from the 1870s to the early twentieth century. See **www.tenement.org/** for a virtual tour.

Sagamore Hill, Oyster Bay, New York. Theodore Roosevelt's home is now a National Historic Site and open to the public. **www.nps.gov/sahi/**

William Howard Taft National Historic Site, Cincinnati, Ohio. Taft was born in this house, the only national Taft memorial. An informative tour focuses on Taft's public and private life.

Staunton, Virginia. The birthplace and childhood home of Woodrow Wilson, restored with period furnishings, reveals many of the influences that shaped Wilson's career.

For additional study resources for this chapter, go to:
www.prenhall.com/goldfield/chapter21

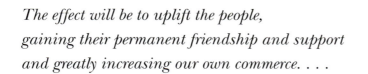

The effect will be to uplift the people, gaining their permanent friendship and support and greatly increasing our own commerce. . . .

The Spanish-American War, 1898. Uncle Sam's Latest Greatest Shortest War: cover of an American magazine, 1898, commemorating the country's swift victory in the Spanish-American War.

22

CREATING AN EMPIRE
1865–1917

WHY DID the United States build an overeas empire?

HOW DID the United States move toward expanding its influence before the 1890s?

WHAT EVENTS led to the Spanish-American War?

WHAT WAS the nature of U.S. involvement in Asia?

WHAT WAS at stake for the United States in Puerto Rico, Cuba, and Panama?

Havana, Cuba

October 1901

When the Spanish-American war was declared the United States took a step forward, and assumed a position as protector of the interests of Cuba. It became responsible for the welfare of the people, politically, mentally, and morally. The mere fact of freeing the island from Spanish rule has not ended the care which this country should give. . . . The effect will be to uplift the people, gaining their permanent friendship and support and greatly increasing our own commerce. At present there are two million people requiring clothing and food, for but a small proportion of the necessaries of life are raised on the island. It is folly to grow food crops when sugar and tobacco produce such rich revenues in comparison. The United States should supply the Cubans with their breadstuffs, even wine, fruit, and vegetables, and should clothe the people. . . . The money received for their crops will be turned over in a great measure in buying supplies from the United States. . . .

Naturally the manufacturers of the United States should have precedence in furnishing machinery, locomotives, cars, and rails, materials for buildings and bridges, and the wide diversity of other supplies required, as well as fuel for their furnaces. With the present financial and commercial uncertainty at an end the people of the island will . . . come into the American market as customers for products of many kinds.

The meeting of the Constitutional Convention on November 5th will be an event in Cuban history of the greatest importance, and much will depend upon the action and outcome of this convention as to our future control of the island. . . . I considered it unwise to interfere, and I have made it a settled policy to permit the Cubans to manage every part of their constitution-making. This has been due to my desire to prevent any possible charge of crimination being brought against the United States in the direction of their constitutional affairs. . . .

There is no distrust of the United States on the part of the Cubans, and I know of no widespread antipathy to this country, its people, or its institutions. There are, of course, a handful of malcontents, as there must be in every country. . . .

I could not well conceive how the Cubans could be otherwise than grateful to the United States for its efforts in their behalf. The reconstruction of the island has proceeded rapidly from the first, and I think the transformation is without any superior in the history of modern times. The devastation of the long war had left the island in an unparalleled condition when the United States interfered, and in the brief time since the occupation of the island by American troops the island has been completely rehabilitated—agriculturally, commercially, financially, educationally, and governmentally. This improvement has been so rapid and so apparent that no Cuban could mistake it. To doubt in the face of these facts that their liberators were not still their faithful friends would be impossible.

Major-General Leonard Wood, "The Future of Cuba," *The Independent* 54 (January 23, 1902): 193–194; and Wood, "The Cuban Convention," *The Independent* 52 (November 1, 1900): 265–266.

IMAGE KEY

for pages 578–579

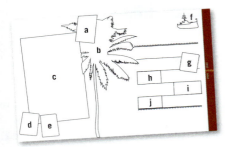

a. A colorful poster for the Panama-California Exhibition in San Diego.

b. Catalog Illustration of a Date Palm Tree ca. 1900.

c. Cover of an American magazine, 1898, commemorating the country's swift victory in the Spanish-American War.

d. Spanish American War puzzle.

e. Spanish American War game.

f. Grey And Red Battle Ship.

g. Uncle Sam rides a bicycle with globes of the western and eastern hemisphere for wheels while being watched by angry national leaders.

h. Charles Post, "Spanish Civil War."

i. Cartoon concerning the "Open Door Policy" 1899. "A Fair Field and No Favor. Uncle Sam: I'm out for commerce, not conquest."

j. Theodore Roosevelt on a steam shovel during the Panama Canal construction.

GENERAL LEONARD WOOD'S reports on Cuba, where he was military governor, captured the mixture of attitudes and motives that marked the United States's emergence as a world power. Plans for economic expansion, a belief in national mission, a sense of responsibility to help others, religious impulses and racist convictions—all combined in an uneasy mixture of self-interest and idealism that helped garner support for the new policies that the nation's leaders adopted, including American control over Cuba.

Wood himself had taken a symbolic journey in American expansionism. His earlier career had been with the troops on the American Southwestern frontier, but in 1898 he and Theodore Roosevelt formed the Rough Riders cavalry to participate in the Spanish-American War in Cuba. Upon Spain's surrender, Wood was appointed military governor of the island.

Wood's support for the war was reflected in his activities as a colonial administrator. Convinced of the superiority of American institutions, he favored their expansion. But expansion would also promote American interests. Thus while Wood brought improved sanitation, schools, and transportation to Cuba, he regarded Cubans as backward and incapable of self-government. He expected that American business interests would "naturally" benefit from his reorganization of Cuban life. Wood thus combined paternalistic or humanitarian reforms with attempts to incorporate Cuba into America's new commercial empire, fulfilling the traditional colonial role of providing raw materials and serving as a market for American products and capital.

His claim that he was not interfering with Cuba's constitutional convention was disingenuous, for he had already undertaken to limit those who could participate as voters or delegates and was devising means to restrict Cuba's autonomy. And despite his repeated insistence that the Cubans were "grateful" for the intervention of "their faithful friends," the Americans, Cubans, as well as Filipinos, Puerto Ricans, and others, rarely perceived American motives or American actions as positively as did Wood and other proponents of American expansion. Victory in the Spanish-American War had provided the United States with an empire, status as a world power, and opportunities and problems that would long shape American foreign policy.

THE ROOTS OF IMPERIALISM

The United States had a long-established tradition of expansion across the continent. Through purchase, negotiation, or conquest, the vast Louisiana Territory, Florida, Texas, New Mexico, California, and Oregon had become U.S. territory. Indeed, by the 1890s, Republican Senator Henry Cabot Lodge of Massachusetts boasted that Americans had "a record of conquest, colonization, and territorial expansion unequalled by any people in the nineteenth century." Lodge now urged the country to build an overseas empire, emulating the European model of **imperialism** based on the acquisition and exploitation of colonial possessions. Other Americans favored a less formal empire, in which U.S. interests and influence would be assured through extensive trade and investments rather than through military occupation. Still others advocated a cultural expansionism in which the nation exported its ideals and institutions.

IDEOLOGICAL ARGUMENTS

Scholars, authors, politicians, and religious leaders provided interlocking ideological arguments for the new imperialism (see the overview table "Rationales for Imperialism"). Some intellectuals, for example, invoked social Darwinism, maintaining that "the survival of the fittest" was "the law of nations as well as a law

WHY DID the United States build an overseas empire?

Imperialism The policy and practice of exploiting nations and peoples for the benefit of an imperial power either directly through military occupation and colonial rule or indirectly through economic domination of resources and markets.

OVERVIEW

RATIONALES FOR IMPERIALISM

Category	Beliefs
Racism and social Darwinism	Convictions that "Anglo-Saxons" were racially superior and should dominate other peoples, either to ensure national success, establish international stability, or benefit the "inferior" races by imposing American ideas and institutions on them.
Righteousness	The conviction that Christianity, and a supporting American culture, should be aggressively spread among the benighted peoples of other lands.
Mahanism	The conviction, following the ideas advanced by Alfred Thayer Mahan, that U.S. security required a strong navy and economic and territorial expansion.
Economics	A variety of arguments holding that American prosperity depended on acquiring access to foreign markets, raw materials, and investment opportunities.

20–3
Albert Beveridge, "The March of the Flag" (1898)

of nature." As European nations expanded into Asia and Africa in the 1880s and 1890s, seeking colonies, markets, and raw materials, these advocates argued that the United States had to adopt similar policies to ensure national success.

Related to social Darwinism was a pervasive belief in the superiority of people of English, or Anglo-Saxon, descent. To many Americans, the industrial progress, military strength, and political development of England and the United States were proof of an Anglo-Saxon superiority that carried with it a responsibility to extend the blessings of their rule to less able people. As a popular expression put it, colonialism was the "white man's burden." The political scientist John W. Burgess argued that Anglo-Saxons "must have a colonial policy" and "righteously assume sovereignty" over "incompetent" or "barbaric races" in other lands.

American missionaries also promoted expansionist sentiment. Hoping to evangelize the world, American religious groups increased the number of Protestant foreign missions sixfold from 1870 to 1900. Missionaries publicized their activities throughout the United States, generating interest in foreign developments and support for what one writer called the "imperialism of righteousness." Abroad they pursued a religious transformation that often resembled a cultural conversion, for they promoted trade, developed business interests, and encouraged Westernization through technology and education as well as religion. Sometimes, as in the Hawaiian Islands, American missionaries even promoted annexation by the United States.

The Reverend J. H. Barrows in early 1898 lectured on the "Christian conquest of Asia," suggesting that American Christianity and commerce would cross the Pacific to fulfill "the manifest destiny of the Christian Republic." Missionaries also contributed to the imperial impulse by describing their work, as Barrows did, in terms of the "conquest" of "enemy" territory. Thus while missionaries were motivated by what they considered to be idealism and often brought real benefits to other lands, especially in education and health, religious sentiments reinforced the ideology of American expansion.

STRATEGIC CONCERNS

Other expansionists were motivated by strategic concerns, shaped by what seemed to be the forces of history and geography. Alfred Thayer Mahan, a naval officer and president of the Naval War College, emphasized the importance of a strong navy for national greatness in his book *The Influence of Sea Power upon History*. Mahan also proposed that the United States build a canal across the isthmus of Panama to link its coasts, acquire naval bases in the Caribbean and the Pacific to protect the canal, and annex Hawaii and other Pacific islands. The United States must "cast aside the policy of isolation which befitted her infancy," Mahan declared, and "begin to look outward."

Mahanism found a receptive audience. Vocal advocates of Mahan's program were a group of nationalistic Republicans, predominantly from the Northeast. They included politicians like Henry Cabot Lodge and Theodore Roosevelt, journalists like Whitelaw Reid of the *New York Tribune* and Albert Shaw of the *Review of Reviews*, and diplomats and lawyers like John Hay and Elihu Root.

Such men favored imperial expansion, as Shaw wrote, "for the sake of our destiny, our dignity, our influence, and our usefulness." One British observer concluded that Mahan's influence had transformed the American spirit, serving "as oil to the flame of 'colonial expansion' everywhere leaping into life." (See American Views, "An American Views the World.")

The large navy policy popular among imperialists began in 1881, when Congress established the Naval Advisory Board. An extensive program to replace the navy's obsolete wooden ships with modern cruisers and battleships was well under way by 1890 when the first volume of Mahan's book appeared. The United States soon possessed a formidable navy, which, in turn, demanded strategic bases and coaling stations. One writer indicated the circular nature of this development by noting in 1893 that Manifest Destiny now meant "the acquisition of such territory, far and near," that would secure "to our navy facilities desirable for the operations of a great naval power."

An American missionary and her Chinese converts study the Bible in Manchuria in 1903 under a U.S. flag. American missionaries wanted to spread the Gospel albroad but inevitably spread American influence as well.

Photograph reproduced with permission of Wider Church Ministries of the United Church of Christ by permission of the Houghton Library, Harward University

ECONOMIC DESIGNS

Nearly all Americans favored economic expansion through foreign trade. Such a policy promised national prosperity: larger markets for manufacturers and farmers, greater profits for merchants and bankers, more jobs for workers. Far fewer favored the acquisition of colonies that was characteristic of European imperialism. One diplomat declared in 1890 that the nation was more interested in the "annexation of trade" than in the annexation of territory.

As early as 1844, the United States had negotiated a trade treaty with China, and ten years later, a squadron under Commodore Matthew Perry had forced the Japanese to open their ports to American products. In the late nineteenth century, the dramatic expansion of the economy caused many Americans to favor more government action to open foreign markets to American exports. Alabama Senator John Morgan had the cotton and textiles produced in the New South in mind when he warned in 1882: "Our home market is not equal to the demands of our producing and manufacturing classes and to the capital which is seeking

Mahanism The ideas advanced by Alfred Thayer Mahan, stressing U.S. naval, economic, and territorial expansion.

• AMERICAN VIEWS •

AN IMPERIALIST VIEWS THE WORLD

Theodore Roosevelt, Henry Cabot Lodge, Alfred Thayer Mahan, and other influential imperialists frequently corresponded with one another. The following excerpts are from Roosevelt's private correspondence in 1897, while he was assistant secretary of the Navy and before the Spanish-American War began.

HOW DOES Roosevelt reflect the influence of Mahan? What is Roosevelt's view of war? How does he view European states and the independence of other nations in the Western Hemisphere?

I suppose that I need not tell you that as regards Hawaii I take your views absolutely, as indeed I do on foreign policy generally. If I had my way we would annex those islands tomorrow. If that is impossible I would establish a protectorate over them. I believe we should build the Nicaraguan canal at once, and in the meantime that we should build a dozen new battleships, half of them on the Pacific Coast; and these battleships should have a large coal capacity and a consequent increased radius of action. . . . I think President Cleveland's action [in rejecting the annexation of Hawaii] was a colossal crime, and we should be guilty of aiding him after the fact if we do not reverse what he did. I earnestly hope we can make the President [McKinley] look at things our way. Last Saturday night Lodge pressed his views upon him with all his strength.

I agree with all you say as to what will be the result if we fail to take Hawaii. It will show that we either have lost, or else wholly lack, the masterful instinct which alone can make a race great. I feel so deeply about it I hardly dare express myself in full. The terrible part is to see that it is the men of education who take the lead in trying to make us prove traitors to our race.

I fully realize the importance of the Pacific coast . . . But there are big problems in the West Indies also.

Until we definitely turn Spain out of those islands (and if I had my way that would be done tomorrow), we will always be menaced by trouble there. We should acquire the Danish Islands [in the West Indies], and by turning Spain out should serve notice that no strong European power, and especially not Germany, should be allowed to gain a foothold by supplanting some weak European power. I do not fear England; Canada is a hostage for her good behavior.

I wish we had a perfectly consistent foreign policy, and that this policy was that every European power should be driven out of America, and every foot of American soil, including the nearest islands in both the Pacific and the Atlantic, should be in the hands of independent American states, and so far as possible in the possession of the United States or under its protection.

To speak with a frankness which our timid friends would call brutal, I would regard a war with Spain from two standpoints: first, the advisability on the grounds both of humanity and self-interest of interfering on behalf of the Cubans, and of taking one more step toward the complete freeing of America from European dominion; second, the benefit done our people by giving them something to think of which isn't material gain, and especially the benefit done our military forces by trying both the Navy and the Army in actual practice. I should be very sorry not to see us make the experiment of trying to land, and therefore feed and clothe, an expeditionary force [on Cuba], if only for the sake of learning from our own blunders. I should hope that the force would have some fighting to do. It would be a great lesson, and we would profit much by it.

I wish there was a chance that the [U.S. battleship] Maine was going to be used against some foreign power; by preference Germany—but I am not particular, and I'd take even Spain if nothing better offered.

Source: Reprinted by permission of the publisher from *The Letters of Theodore Roosevelt* Volume I 1868–1898, selected and edited by Elting E. Morison, Cambridge: Harvard University Press.

employment. . . . We must either enlarge the field of our traffic, or stop the business of manufacturing just where it is." More ominous, a naval officer trying to open Korea to U.S. products declared in 1878, "We must *export* these products or *deport* the people who are creating them."

Exports, particularly of manufactured goods, which grew ninefold between 1865 and 1900, did increase greatly in the late nineteenth century. Still, periodic depressions fed these fears of overproduction, and the massive unemployment and social unrest that accompanied these economic crises also provided social and political arguments for economic relief through foreign trade.

In the depression of the 1890s, this interest in foreign trade became obsessive. More systematic government efforts to promote trade seemed necessary, a conclusion strengthened by new threats to existing American markets, including higher European tariffs. Moreover, Japan and the European imperial powers began to restrict commercial opportunities in the areas of China that they controlled.

FIRST STEPS

Before the mid-1890s, the government did not pursue a policy of *isolationism* from international affairs, for the nation maintained normal diplomatic and trade ties and at times vigorously intervened in Latin America and East Asia. But in general the government deferred to the initiative of private interests, reacted haphazardly to outside events, and did little to create a professional foreign service. In a few bold if inconsistent steps, however, the United States moved toward expanding its influence.

HOW DID the United States move toward expanding its global influence before the 1890s?

SEWARD AND BLAINE

Two secretaries of state, William H. Seward, secretary under Presidents Lincoln and Andrew Johnson (1861–1869), and James G. Blaine, secretary under Presidents Garfield and Harrison (1881, 1889–1892), laid the foundation for a larger and more aggressive American role in world affairs. Seward possessed an elaborate imperial vision, based on his understanding of commercial opportunities, strategic necessities, and national destiny. Seward purchased Alaska from Russia in 1867, approved the navy's occupation of the Midway Islands in the Pacific, pushed American trade on a reluctant Japan, and repeatedly tried to acquire Caribbean naval bases (see Map 22–1). But his policy of expansion, as one observer noted, "went somewhat too far and too fast for the public," and many of his plans fizzled. Congressional opposition frustrated his efforts to obtain Haiti and the Dominican Republic and to purchase the Danish West Indies; Colombia blocked his attempt to gain construction rights for a canal across the isthmus of Panama.

Blaine was an equally vigorous advocate of expansion. He worked to extend what he called America's "commercial empire" in the Pacific. And he sought to ensure U.S. sovereignty over any canal in Panama, insisting that it be "a purely American waterway to be treated as part of our own coastline." In an effort to induce the nations of Latin America to import manufactured products from the United States rather than Europe, Blaine proposed a conference among the nations of the Western Hemisphere in 1881. The First International American Conference finally met in 1889. There Blaine called for the establishment of a customs union to reduce trade barriers. He expected this union to strengthen U.S. control of hemispheric markets. The Latin America nations, however, wary of economic subordination to the colossus of the north, rejected Blaine's plan.

WHERE TO LEARN MORE

Seward House, Auburn, New York

WHERE TO LEARN MORE

James G. Blaine House, Augusta, Maine

MAP EXPLORATION

To explore an interactive version of this map, go to **http://www.prenhall.com/goldfield2/map22.1**

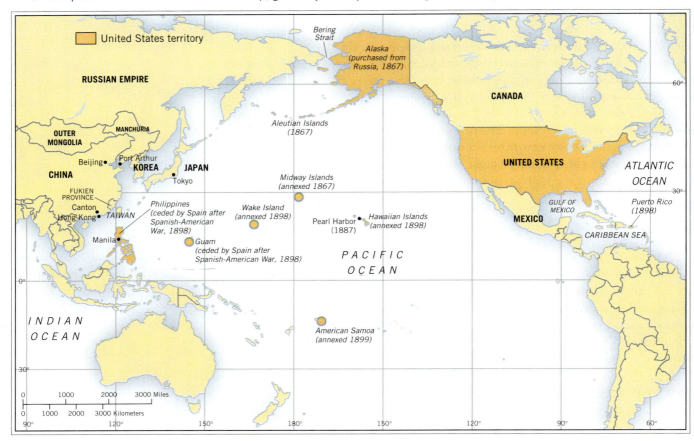

MAP 22–1

United States Expansion in the Pacific, 1867–1899   Pursuing visions of a commercial empire in the Pacific, the United States steadily expanded its territorial possessions as well as its influence there in the late nineteenth century.

WHAT DID the United States gain from its expansion in the Pacific?

HAWAII

Blaine regarded Hawaii as "indispensably" part of "the American system." As early as 1842, the United States had announced its opposition to European control of Hawaii, a key way station in the China trade where New England missionaries and whalers were active. Although the islands remained under native monarchs, American influence grew, particularly as other Americans arrived to establish sugar plantations and eventually dominate the economy.

Treaties in 1875 and 1887 integrated the islands into the American economy and gave the United States control over Pearl Harbor on the island of Oahu. In 1887, the United States rejected a proposal from Britain and France for a joint guarantee of Hawaii's independence and endorsed a new Hawaiian constitution that gave political power to wealthy white residents. The obvious next step was U.S. annexation, which Blaine endorsed in 1891.

American planters soon bid for annexation. The McKinley Tariff Act of 1890 effectively closed the U.S. market to Hawaiian sugar producers, facing them with economic ruin. At the same time, Queen Liliuokalani moved to restore native control of Hawaiian affairs. To ensure market access and protect their political authority, the American planters decided to seek annexation to the United States. In 1893, they overthrew the queen. John Stevens, the American minister, ordered U.S. Marines to help the rebels. He then declared an American protectorate over the new Hawaii government and wired Washington: "The Hawaiian pear is now fully ripe, and this is the golden hour for the United States to pluck it." A delegation from the new provisional government, containing no native Hawaiians, went to Washington to draft a treaty for annexation. President Harrison signed the pact but could not get Senate approval before the new Cleveland administration took office.

Cleveland immediately called for an investigation of the whole affair. Soon convinced that "the undoubted sentiment of the people is for the Queen, against the provisional Government, and against annexation," Cleveland apologized to the queen for the "flagrant wrong" done her by the "reprehensible conduct of the American minister and the unauthorized presence on land of a military force of the United States." But the American-dominated provisional government refused to step down, and Cleveland's rejection of annexation set off a noisy debate.

Many Republicans strongly supported annexation. One Eastern Republican manufacturer called for the annexation of Hawaii as the first step toward making the Pacific "an American ocean, dominated by American commercial enterprise for all time." On the West Coast, where California business interests had close ties with the islands, the commercial and strategic value of Hawaii seemed obvious. The *San Francisco Examiner* declared, "Hoist the Stars and Stripes. It is a case of manifest destiny." Reflecting racial imperialism, others argued that annexation would both fittingly reward the enterprising white residents of Hawaii and provide an opportunity to civilize native Hawaiians.

Democrats generally opposed annexation. They doubted, as Missouri Senator George Vest declared, whether the United States should desert its traditional principles and "venture upon the great colonial system of the European powers." The Hawaiian episode of 1893 thus foreshadowed the arguments over imperialism at the end of the century and emphasized the policy differences between Democrats and the increasingly expansionist Republicans.

CHILE AND VENEZUELA

American reactions to developments in other countries in the 1890s also reflected an increasingly assertive national policy and excitable public opinion. In 1891, American sailors on shore leave in Chile became involved in a drunken brawl that left two of them dead, seventeen injured, and dozens in jail. Encouraged by a combative navy, President Harrison threatened military retaliation against Chile, provoking an outburst of bellicose nationalism in the United States. Harrison relented only when Chile apologized and paid an indemnity.

A few years later, the United States again threatened war over a minor issue, but against a more formidable opponent. In 1895, President Cleveland intervened in a boundary dispute between Great Britain and Venezuela over British Guiana. Cleveland was motivated not only by the long-standing U.S. goal of challenging Britain for Latin American markets but also by ever more expansive notions of the **Monroe Doctrine** and the authority of the United States. Secretary of State Richard Olney sent Britain a blunt note (a "twenty-inch gun," Cleveland called it) demanding arbitration of the disputed territory and stoutly asserting American supremacy in the Western Hemisphere. Cleveland urged Congress to establish a commission to determine the boundary and enforce its decision by war if necessary. As war fever swept the United States, Britain agreed to arbitration, recognizing the limited nature of the issue that so convulsed Anglo-American relations.

WHERE TO LEARN MORE

Mission Houses,
Honolulu, Hawaii
www.missionhouses.org/

Monroe Doctrine Declaration by President James Monroe in 1823 that the Western Hemisphere was to be closed off to further European colonization and that the United States would not interfere in the internal affairs of European nations.

CHRONOLOGY

1861–1869	Seward serves as secretary of state.
1867	U.S. purchases Alaska from Russia.
1870	Annexation of the Dominican Republic is rejected.
1881	Naval Advisory Board is created.
1887	U.S. gains naval rights to Pearl Harbor.
1889	First Pan-American Conference is held.
1890	Alfred Thayer Mahan publishes *The Influence of Sea Power upon History.*
1893	Harrison signs but Cleveland rejects a treaty for the annexation of Hawaii.
1893–1897	Depression increases interest in economic expansion abroad.
1894–1895	Sino-Japanese War is fought.
1895	U.S. intervenes in Great Britain–Venezuelan boundary dispute. Cuban insurrection against Spain begins.
1896	William McKinley is elected president on an imperialist platform.
1898	Spanish-American War is fought. Hawaii is annexed. Anti-Imperialist League is organized. Treaty of Paris is signed.

1899–1902	Filipino-American War is fought.
1899	Open Door note is issued.
1901	Theodore Roosevelt becomes president.
1903	Platt Amendment restricts Cuban autonomy. Panama "revolution" is abetted by the United States.
1904	United States acquires the Panama Canal Zone. Roosevelt Corollary is announced.
1904–1905	Russo-Japanese War is fought.
1905	Treaty of Portsmouth ends the Russo-Japanese War through U.S. mediation.
1906–1909	United States occupies Cuba.
1907–1908	Gentlemen's Agreement restricts Japanese immigration.
1909	United States intervenes in Nicaragua.
1912–1933	United States occupies Nicaragua.
1914	Panama Canal opens.
1914–1917	United States intervenes in Mexico.
1915–1934	United States occupies Haiti.
1916–1924	United States occupies the Dominican Republic.
1917	Puerto Ricans are granted U.S. citizenship.
1917–1922	United States occupies Cuba.

The United States' assertion of hemispheric dominance angered Latin Americans, and their fears deepened when it decided arbitration terms with Britain without consulting Venezuela, which protested before bowing to American pressure. The further significance of the Venezuelan crisis, as Captain Mahan noted, lay in its "awakening of our countrymen to the fact that we must come out of our isolation . . . and take our share in the turmoil of the world."

THE SPANISH-AMERICAN WAR

WHAT EVENTS led to the Spanish-American War?

The forces pushing the United States toward imperialism and international power came to a head in the Spanish-American War. Cuba's quest for independence from the oppressive colonial control of Spain activated Americans' long-standing interest in the island. But few foresaw that the war that finally erupted in 1898 would dramatically change America's relationships with the rest of the world and give it a colonial empire.

THE CUBAN REVOLUTION

Cuba was the last major European colony in Latin America, with an economic potential that attracted American business interests and a strategic significance for any Central American canal. In the 1880s, Spanish control became increasingly harsh, and in 1895 the Cubans launched a revolt.

The rebellion was a classic guerrilla war in which the rebels controlled the countryside and the Spanish army the towns and cities. American economic interests were seriously affected, for both Cubans and Spaniards destroyed American property and disrupted American trade. But the brutality with which Spain attempted to suppress the revolt promoted American sympathy for the Cuban insurgents. Determined to cut the rebels off from their peasant supporters, the Spaniards herded most civilians into "reconcentration camps," where tens of thousands died of starvation and disease.

Americans' sympathy was further aroused by the sensationalist **yellow press**. To attract readers and boost advertising revenues, the popular press of the day adopted bold headlines, fevered editorials, and real or exaggerated stories of violence, sex, and corruption. A circulation war between William Randolph Hearst's *New York Journal* and Joseph Pulitzer's *New York World* helped stimulate interest in Cuban war. "Blood on the roadsides, blood on the fields, blood on the doorsteps, blood, blood, blood! The old, the young, the weak, the crippled—all are butchered without mercy," the *World* feverishly reported of Cuba. "Is there no nation wise enough, brave enough to aid this blood-smitten land?" The nation's religious press, partly because it reflected the prejudice many Protestants held against Catholic Spain, also advocated American intervention.

As the Cuban rebellion dragged on, more and more Americans advocated intervention to stop the carnage, protect U.S. investments, or uphold various principles. Expansionists like Roosevelt and Lodge clamored for intervention, but so did their opponents. Populists, for example, sympathized with a people seeking independence from colonial rule and petitioned Congress to support the crusade for Cuban freedom. In the election of 1896, both major parties endorsed Cuban independence.

GROWING TENSIONS

President William McKinley's administration soon focused on Cuba. McKinley's principal complaint was that chronic disorder in Cuba disrupted America's investments and agitated public opinion. Personally opposed to military intervention, McKinley first used diplomacy to press Spain to adopt reforms that would settle the rebellion. Following his instructions, the U.S. minister to Spain warned the Spanish government that if it did not quickly establish peace, the United States would take whatever steps it "should deem necessary to procure this result." In late 1897, Spain modified its brutal military tactics and offered limited autonomy to Cuba. But Cubans insisted on complete independence, which Spain refused to grant.

Relations between the United States and Spain deteriorated. On February 15, 1898, the U.S. battleship *Maine* blew up in Havana harbor, killing 260 men. The Spaniards were not responsible for the tragedy, which a modern naval inquiry has attributed to an internal accident. But many Americans agreed with Theodore Roosevelt, the assistant secretary of the navy, who called it "an act of dirty treachery on the part of the Spaniards" and told McKinley that only war was "compatible with our national honor."

Other pressures soon began to build on the president. Senator Lodge reported a consensus "that this situation must end. We cannot go on indefinitely with this strain, this suspense, and this uncertainty, this tottering upon the verge of war. It is killing to business." McKinley also feared that a moderate policy would endanger congressional candidates. Again Senator Lodge, although hesitant to suggest "war for political reasons," nevertheless advised McKinley, "If the war in Cuba drags on through the summer with nothing done, we shall go down in the greatest [election] defeat ever known."

QUICK REVIEW

The Press and Cuba
- Yellow press stimulated interest in Cuba.
- Newspapers emphasized violence, sex, and corruption.
- Much of America's religious press advocated American intervention.

Yellow press A deliberately sensational journalism of scandal and exposure designed to attract an urban mass audience and increase advertising revenues.

At the end of March 1898, McKinley sent Spain an ultimatum. He demanded an armistice in Cuba, an end to the reconcentration policy, and the acceptance of American arbitration, which implied Cuban independence. Desperately, Spain made concessions, abolishing reconcentration and declaring a unilateral armistice, but McKinley had already begun war preparations. He submitted a war message to Congress on April 11, asking for authority to use force against Spain "in the name of humanity, in the name of civilization, in behalf of endangered American interests." Congress declared war on Spain on April 25, 1898.

Most interventionists were not imperialists, and Congress added the **Teller Amendment** to the war resolution, disclaiming any intention of annexing Cuba and promising that Cubans would govern themselves. Congress also refused to approve either a canal bill or the annexation of Hawaii. Nevertheless, the Spanish-American War did turn the nation toward imperialism.

WAR AND EMPIRE

The decisive engagement of the war took place not in Cuba but in another Spanish colony, the Philippines, and it involved the favored tool of the expansionists, the new navy (see Map 22–2). Once war was declared, Commodore George Dewey led the U.S. Asiatic squadron into Manila Bay and destroyed the weaker Spanish fleet on May 1, 1898. The navy had long coveted Manila Bay as a strategic harbor, but other Americans, casting an eye on commercial opportunities in China, saw a greater significance in the victory. With Dewey's triumph, exulted one expansionist, "We are taking our proper rank among the nations of the world. We are after markets, the greatest markets now existing in the world." To expand this foothold in Asia, McKinley ordered troops to the Philippines, postponing the military expedition to Cuba itself.

Dewey's victory also precipitated the annexation of Hawaii, which had seemed hopeless only weeks before. Annexationists now pointed to the islands' strategic importance as steppingstones to Manila. "To maintain our flag in the Philippines, we must raise our flag in Hawaii," the *New York Sun* contended. McKinley himself privately declared, "We need Hawaii just as much and a good deal more than we did California. It is Manifest Destiny." In July, Congress approved annexation, a decision welcomed by Hawaii's white minority. Natives solemnly protested this step taken "without reference to the consent of the people of the Hawaiian Islands." Filipinos would soon face the same American imperial impulse.

Military victory also came swiftly in Cuba, once the U.S. Army finally landed in late June. Victory depended largely on Spanish ineptitude, for the American troops had to fight with antiquated weapons and wear wool uniforms in the sweltering tropics. They were issued rotting and poisoned food by a corrupt and inefficient War Department. More than five thousand Americans died of diseases and accidents brought on by such mismanagement; only 379 were killed in battle. State militias supplemented the small regular army, as did volunteer units, such as the famous Rough Riders, a cavalry unit of cowboys and eastern dandies assembled by Theodore Roosevelt.

U.S. naval power again proved decisive. In a lopsided battle on July 3, the obsolete Spanish squadron in Cuba was destroyed, isolating the Spanish army and guaranteeing its defeat. U.S. forces then seized the nearby Spanish colony of Puerto Rico without serious opposition. Humbled, Spain signed an armistice ending the war on August 12.

Americans were delighted with their military achievements, but the *Philadelphia Inquirer* cautioned, "With peace will come new responsibilities, which must be met. We have colonies to look after and develop."

WHERE TO LEARN MORE

Funston Memorial Home, Iola, Kansas
http://skyways.lib.ks.us/museums/funston/

QUICK REVIEW

Dewey's Victory
- May 1, 1898: Dewey's squadron destroys Spanish fleet in Manila Bay.
- Expansionists saw victory as an opportunity for greater U.S. presence in the region.
- McKinley followed up Dewey's victory by sending troops to the Philippines.

Teller Amendment A congressional resolution adopted in 1898 renouncing any American intention to annex Cuba.

MAP EXPLORATION

To explore an interactive version of this map, go to **http://www.prenhall.com/goldfield2/map22.2**

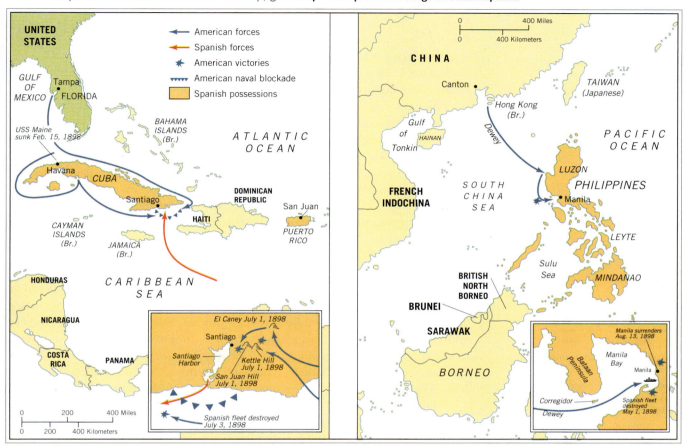

Legend:
- → American forces
- → Spanish forces
- ✶ American victories
- ⋁⋁⋁ American naval blockade
- ▮ Spanish possessions

MAP 22–2

The Spanish-American War   The United States gained quick victories in both theaters of the Spanish-American War. Its naval power proved decisive, with Commodore Dewey destroying one enemy fleet in the Philippines and a second U.S. naval force cutting off the Spanish in Cuba.

WHY DID the United States want to control the Philippines?

THE TREATY OF PARIS

The armistice required Spain to accept Cuban independence, cede Puerto Rico and Guam (a Pacific island between Hawaii and the Philippines), and allow the Americans to occupy Manila pending the final disposition of the Philippines at a formal peace conference. The acquisition of Puerto Rico and Guam indicated the expansionist nature the conflict had assumed for the United States. So did the postponement of the Philippine issue. McKinley knew that delay would permit the advocates of expansion to build public support for annexation.

But he was motivated to acquire the Philippines primarily by a determination to use the islands to strengthen America's political and commercial position in East Asia. Moreover, he believed the Filipinos poorly suited to self-rule, and he feared that Germany or Japan might seize the Philippines if the United States did not. Meeting in Paris in December, American and Spanish negotiators settled the final terms for peace. Spain agreed—despite Filipino demands for independence—to cede the Philippines to the United States.

20–5
William McKinley, "Decision on the Philippines" (1900)

The decision to acquire the Philippines sparked a dramatic debate over the ratification of the Treaty of Paris. The *United States Investor* spoke for business leaders, for example, in demanding the Philippines as "a base of operations in the East" to protect American interests in China; other economic expansionists argued that the Philippines themselves had valuable resources and were a market for American goods or warned that "our commercial rivals in the Orient" would grab the islands if the United States did not. The *Presbyterian Banner* spoke for what it termed a nearly unanimous religious press in affirming "the desirability of America's retaining the Philippines as a duty in the interest of human freedom and Christian progress."

Opponents of the treaty included such prominent figures as the civil service reformer Carl Schurz, steel baron Andrew Carnegie, social reformer Jane Addams, labor leader Samuel Gompers, and author Mark Twain. Their organizational base was the Anti-Imperialist League, which campaigned against the treaty, distributing pamphlets, petitioning Congress, and holding rallies. League members' criticisms reflected a conviction that imperialism was a repudiation of America's moral and political traditions embodied in the Declaration of Independence. The acquisition of overseas colonies, they argued, conflicted with the nation's commitment to liberty and its claim to moral superiority. They regarded as loathsome and hypocritical the transformation of a war to free Cuba into a campaign for imperial conquest and subjugation. Some African Americans derided the rhetoric of Anglo-Saxon superiority that underlay imperialism and even organized the Black Man's Burden Association to promote Philippine independence.

But other arguments were less high-minded. Many anti-imperialists objected to expansion on the racist grounds that Filipinos were inferior and unassimilable. Gompers feared that cheap Asian labor would undercut the wages and living standards of American workers. The *San Francisco Call*, representing California-Hawaiian sugar interests, also wanted no competition from the Philippines.

Finally, on February 6, 1899, the Senate narrowly ratified the treaty. Then, by a single vote, the Republicans defeated a Democratic proposal for Philippine independence once a stable government had been established; the United States would keep the islands.

William Jennings Bryan attempted to make the election of 1900 a referendum on "the paramount issue" of imperialism, promising to free the Philippines if the Democrats won. But some of the most ardent anti-imperialists were conservatives who remained loyal to McKinley because they could not tolerate Bryan's economic policies. Republicans also played on the nationalist emotions evoked by the war, especially by nominating Theodore Roosevelt for vice president. "If you choose to vote for America, if you choose to vote for the flag for which we fought," Roosevelt said, "then you will vote to sustain the administration of President McKinley." Bryan lost again, as in 1896, and under Republican leadership, the United States became an imperial nation.

IMPERIAL AMBITIONS: THE UNITED STATES AND EAST ASIA, 1899–1917

In 1899, as the United States occupied its new empire, Assistant Secretary of State John Bassett Moore observed that the nation had become "a world power. . . . Where formerly we had only commercial interests, we now have territorial and political interests as well." American policies to promote those expanded interests focused first on East Asia and Latin America, where the Spanish-American War had provided the United States with both opportunities and challenges. In Asia, the first issue concerned the fate of the Philippines, but looming beyond it were American ambitions in China, where other imperial nations had their own goals.

QUICK REVIEW

The Anti-Imperialist League
◆ Central to campaign against the Treaty of Paris (ratified 1899).
◆ League members saw treaty as a repudiation of American moral and political traditions.
◆ Many anti-imperialists objected to expansion on racist grounds.

WHAT WAS the nature of U.S. involvement in Asia?

THE FILIPINO-AMERICAN WAR

Filipino nationalists, like Cuban insurgents, were already fighting Spain for their independence before the sudden American intervention. The Filipino leader, Emilio Aguinaldo, welcomed Dewey's naval victory as the sign of a de facto alliance with the United States; he then issued a declaration of independence and proclaimed the Philippine Republic. But the Filipinos' optimism declined as American officials acted in an increasingly imperious manner toward them, first refusing to meet with the "savages," then insisting that Filipino forces withdraw from Manila or face "forcible action," and finally dismissing the claims of Aguinaldo and "his so-called government." When the Treaty of Paris provided for U.S. ownership rather than independence, Filipinos felt betrayed. Mounting tensions erupted in a battle between American and Filipino troops outside Manila on February 4, 1899, sparking a long and brutal war.

Ultimately, the United States used nearly four times as many soldiers to suppress the Filipinos as to defeat Spain in Cuba and, in a tragic irony, employed many of the same brutal methods for which it had condemned Spain. Americans often made little effort to distinguish between soldiers and noncombatants, viewing all Filipinos with racial antagonism. Before the military imposed censorship on war news, reporters confirmed U.S. atrocities; one wrote that "American troops have been relentless, have killed to exterminate men, women, and children, prisoners and captives, active insurgents and suspected people, from lads of 10 and up." A California newspaper defended such actions with remarkable candor: "Let us all be frank. WE DO NOT WANT THE FILIPINOS. WE DO WANT THE PHILIPPINES. . . . The more of them killed the better. It seems harsh. But they must yield before the superior race."

The overt racism of the war repelled African Americans. John Mitchell, a Virginia editor, condemned all the talk of "white man's burden" as deceptive rhetoric for brutal acts that could not be "defended either in moral or international law."

The Anti-Imperialist League revived, citing the war as proof of the corrosive influence of imperialism on the nation's morals and principles. Professors addressed antiwar rallies on college campuses. "Alas, what a fall," one University of Michigan professor told his audience. "Within the circuit of a single year to have declined from the moral leadership of mankind into the common brigandage of the robber nations of the world."

By 1902, however, the American military had largely suppressed the rebellion, and the United States had established a colonial government. Compared to the Americans' brutal war policies, U.S. colonial rule was relatively benign, though paternalistic. William Howard Taft, the first governor general, launched a program that brought the islands new schools and roads, a public health system, and an economy tied closely to both the United States and a small Filipino elite.

CHINA AND THE OPEN DOOR

America's determined involvement in the Philippines reflected its preoccupation with China. By the mid-1890s, other powers threatened prospects for American commercial expansion in China. Japan, after defeating China in 1895, annexed Taiwan and secured economic privileges in the mainland province of Fukien (Fujian); the major European powers then competed aggressively to claim other areas of China as their own **spheres of influence**. In Manchuria, Russia won control of Port Arthur (Lüshun) and the right to construct a railway. Germany secured a ninety-nine year lease on another Chinese port and mining and railroad privileges on the Shandong Peninsula. The British wrung special concessions in Kowloon, opposite Hong Kong, as well as a port facing the Russians in Manchuria. France gained a lease on ports and exclusive commercial privileges in southern China.

Spheres of Influence   Regions dominated and controlled by an outside power.

These developments alarmed the American business community. It was confident that given an equal opportunity, the United States would prevail in international trade because of its efficient production and marketing systems. But the creation of exclusive spheres of influence would limit the opportunity to compete. In early 1898, business leaders organized the Committee on American Interests in China to lobby Washington to promote American trade in the shrinking Chinese market. The committee persuaded the nation's chambers of commerce to petition the McKinley administration to act. And the State Department soon reported that, given overproduction for the home market, "the United States has important interests at stake in the partition of commercial facilities in regions which are likely to offer developing markets for its goods. Nowhere is this consideration of more interest than in its relation to the Chinese Empire."

In 1899, Secretary of State John Hay asked the imperial powers to maintain an **Open Door** for the commercial and financial activities of all nations within their Chinese spheres of influence. Privately, Hay had already approved a plan to seize a Chinese port for the United States if necessary to join in the partition of China, but equal opportunity for trade and investment would serve American interests far better. It would avoid the expense of military occupation, avert further domestic criticism of U.S. imperialism, and guarantee a wider sphere for American business.

The other nations replied evasively, except for Russia, which rejected the Open Door concept. In 1900, an antiforeign Chinese nationalist movement known as the Boxers laid seige to the diplomatic quarters in Beijing. The defeat of the Boxer Rebellion by a multinational military force, to which the United States contributed troops, again raised the prospect of a division of China among colonial powers. Hay sent a second Open Door note, reaffirming "the principle of equal and impartial trade" and respect for China's territorial integrity.

The Open Door became a cardinal doctrine of American foreign policy in the twentieth century. The United States promoted an informal or economic empire, as opposed to the traditional territorial colonial empire that Americans preferred to identify with European powers. Henceforth, American economic interests expected the U.S. government to oppose any developments that threatened to close other nations' economies to American penetration and to advance "private enterprise" abroad.

RIVALRY WITH JAPAN AND RUSSIA

At the turn of the twentieth century, both the Japanese and the Russians were more deeply involved in East Asia than the United States was. They expressed little support for the Open Door, which they correctly saw as favoring American interests over their own. But in pursuing their ambitions in China, the two came into conflict with each other. Japan in 1904 attacked the Russian fleet at Port Arthur and defeated the Russians in Manchuria.

In this Russo-Japanese war, American sympathies lay with Japan, for the Russians were attempting to close Manchuria to foreign trade. President Theodore Roosevelt thus welcomed the Japanese attack in the belief that "Japan is playing our game." But he soon feared that an overwhelming Japanese victory could threaten American interests as much as Russian expansionism did, so he skillfully mediated an end to the war. In the Treaty of Portsmouth in 1905, Japan won control of Russia's sphere of influence in Manchuria, half the Russian island of Sakhalin, and recognition of its domination of Korea.

This treaty marked Japan's emergence as a great power, but ironically, it worsened relations with the United States. Anti-American riots broke out in Tokyo. The Japanese people blamed Roosevelt for obstructing further Japanese gains. Tensions were then aggravated by San Francisco's decision in 1906 to segregate

---

QUICK REVIEW

Trade with China

◆ American business interests lobbied for access to China's markets.

◆ 1899: Secretary of State John Hay calls for an Open Door policy.

◆ Open Door became a central doctrine of American foreign policy.

Open Door American policy of seeking equal trade and investment opportunities in foreign nations or regions.

Asian schoolchildren to avoid affecting the "youthful impressions" of white children. Japan regarded this as a racist insult, and Roosevelt worried that "the infernal fools in California" would provoke war. Finally he got the school order rescinded in exchange for his limiting Japanese immigration. Under the **Gentlemen's Agreement**, Japan agreed not to issue passports to workers coming to the United States, and the United States promised not to prohibit Japanese immigration overtly or completely.

To calm their mutual suspicions in East Asia, the United States and Japan adopted other agreements but failed to halt the deteriorating relationship. Increasingly, Japan began to exclude American trade from its territories in East Asia and to press for further control over China. Elihu Root, Roosevelt's secretary of state, insisted that the Open Door and American access be maintained but asserted also that the United States did not want to be "a protagonist in a controversy in China with Russia and Japan or with either of them." This paradox would plague American foreign policy in Asia for decades.

Gentlemen's Agreement A diplomatic agreement in 1907 between Japan and the United States curtailing but not abolishing Japanese immigration.

IMPERIAL POWER: THE UNITED STATES AND LATIN AMERICA, 1899–1917

In Latin America, where no major powers directly challenged American objectives, the United States was more successful in exercising imperial power (see Map 22–3). In the two decades after the Spanish-American War, the United States intervened militarily in Latin America no fewer than twenty times to promote its own strategic and economic interests. Policymakers believed that these goals required restricting the influence of European nations in the region, building an isthmian canal under American control, and establishing the order thought necessary for American trade and investments to expand. Intervention at times achieved these goals, but it often ignored the wishes and interests of Latin Americans, provoked resistance and disorder, and created lasting ill will.

WHAT WAS at stake for the United States in Puerto Rico, Cuba, and Panama?

U.S. RULE IN PUERTO RICO

Well before 1898, expansionists like James G. Blaine had advocated acquiring Puerto Rico because of its strategic location in the Caribbean. During the Spanish-American War, Roosevelt urged Washington, "Do not make peace until we get" Puerto Rico. Military invasion and the Treaty of Paris soon brought the island under American rule.

In 1900, the United States established a civil government, but it was under U.S. control, and popular participation was even less than under Spain. In the so-called *Insular Cases* (1901), the Supreme Court upheld Congress's authority to establish an inferior status for Puerto Rico, as an "unincorporated territory" without promise of statehood. Disappointed Puerto Ricans pressed to end this colonial status. In 1917, the United States granted citizenship and greater political rights to Puerto Ricans, but their island remained an unincorporated territory under an American governor appointed by the president.

Economic development also disappointed most islanders, for American investors quickly gained control of the best land and pursued large-scale sugar production for the U.S. market. By 1929, the new governor—ironically, Theodore Roosevelt Jr.—found that under the domination of American capital, "poverty was wide spread and hunger, almost to the verge of starvation, common." A subsequent investigation concluded that while "the influx of capital has increased the efficiency of production and promoted general economic development," the benefits had gone largely to Americans, not ordinary Puerto Ricans, whose conditions were "deplorable." Increasingly, they left their homes to seek work in the United States.

MAP EXPLORATION

To explore an interactive version of this map, go to **http://www.prenhall.com/goldfield2/map22.3**

MAP 22–3

The United States in the Caribbean   For strategic and economic reasons, the United States repeatedly intervened in the Caribbean in the first three decades of the twentieth century. Such interventions protected the U.S. claim to dominance but often provoked great hostility among Latin Americans.

WHAT WERE the arguments for and against the repeated United States interventions in the Caribbean?

CUBA AS A U.S. PROTECTORATE

Despite the Teller Amendment, the Spanish-American War did not leave Cuba independent. McKinley opposed independence and a U.S. military government was established in the island. Only in 1900, when the Democrats made an issue of imperialism, did McKinley summon a Cuban convention to draft a constitution under the direction of the American military governor, General Leonard Wood. This constitution restricted suffrage on the basis of property and education, leaving few Cubans with the right to vote.

The United States made troop withdrawal contingent on Cuba's adding to its constitution the provisions of the **Platt Amendment**, which restricted Cuba's autonomy in diplomatic relations with other countries and in internal financial policies, required Cuba to lease naval bases to the United States, and, most important, authorized U.S. intervention to maintain order and preserve Cuban

Platt Amendment   A stipulation the United States had inserted into the Cuban constitution in 1901 restricting Cuban autonomy and authorizing U.S. intervention and naval bases.

independence. As General Wood correctly observed, "There is, of course, little or no independence left Cuba under the Platt Amendment."

Cubans quickly learned that fact when the United States prevented Cuba from extending the same trade privileges to the British that U.S. merchants enjoyed. The Open Door would not apply in the Caribbean, which was to be an American sphere of influence. To preserve that influence, the United States sent troops into Cuba three times between 1906 and 1917 (Roosevelt admitted his recurrent itch to "wipe its people off the face of the earth"). The last occupation lasted six years.

During their occupations of Cuba, the Americans modernized its financial system, built roads and public schools, and developed a public health and sanitation program that eradicated the deadly disease of yellow fever. But most Cubans thought these material benefits did not compensate for their loss of political and economic independence.

THE PANAMA CANAL

The Spanish-American War intensified the long American interest in a canal through Central America to eliminate the lengthy and dangerous ocean route around South America. Its commercial value seemed obvious, but the war emphasized its strategic importance. McKinley declared that a canal was now "demanded by the annexation of the Hawaiian Islands and the prospective expansion of our influence and commerce in the Pacific."

Theodore Roosevelt moved quickly to implement McKinley's commitment to a canal after becoming president in 1901. His canal diplomacy helped establish the assertive presidency that has characterized U.S. foreign policy in the twentieth century.

Possible canal sites included Nicaragua and Panama, then part of Colombia. A canal through Panama would require an elaborate system of locks. But the French-owned Panama Canal Company had been unsuccessfully trying to build a canal in Panama and was now eager to sell its rights to the project before they expired in 1904.

In 1902, Congress directed Roosevelt to purchase the French company's claims for $40 million and build the canal in Panama if Colombia ceded a strip of land across the isthmus on reasonable terms. Otherwise, Roosevelt was to negotiate with Nicaragua for the alternate route. In 1903, Roosevelt pressed Colombia to sell a canal zone to the United States for $10 million and an annual payment of $250,000. Colombia, however, rejected the proposal, fearing the loss of its sovereignty in Panama and hoping for more money. After all, when the Panama Canal Company's rights expired, Colombia could then legitimately collect the $40 million so generously offered the company.

Roosevelt warned "those contemptible little creatures" in Colombia that they were "imperiling their own future." Instead of using direct force Roosevelt worked with Philippe Bunau-Varilla, a French official of the Panama Canal Company, to exploit long-smoldering Panamanian discontent with Colombia. Roosevelt's purpose was to get the canal zone, Bunau-Varilla's to get the American money. Roosevelt ordered U.S. naval forces to Panama; from New York, Bunau-Varilla coordinated a revolt against Colombian authority directed by officials of the Panama Railroad, owned by Bunau-Varilla's canal company. The bloodless "revolution" succeeded when U.S. forces prevented Colombian troops from landing in Panama, although the United States was bound by treaty to maintain Colombian sovereignty. Bunau-Varilla promptly signed a treaty accepting Roosevelt's original terms for a canal zone and making Panama a U.S. protectorate. Panamanians themselves denounced the treaty for surrendering sovereignty in the zone to the United States, which took formal control of the canal zone in 1904 and completed construction of the Panama Canal in 1914.

Many Americans were appalled by what the *Chicago American* called Roosevelt's "rough-riding assault upon another republic over the shattered wreckage of international law and diplomatic usage." But others, as *Public Opinion* reported, wanted a

20–6
Theodore Roosevelt,
Third Annual Message
to Congress (1903)

"canal above all things" and were willing to overlook moral questions and approve the acquisition of the canal zone as simply "a business question." Roosevelt himself boasted, "I took the Canal Zone and let Congress debate," but his unnecessary and arrogant actions generated resentment among Latin Americans that rankled for decades.

THE ROOSEVELT COROLLARY

To protect the security of the canal, the United States increased its authority in the Caribbean. The objective was to establish conditions there that would both eliminate any pretext for European intervention and promote American control over trade and investment. "If we intend to say hands off to the powers of Europe," Roosevelt concluded, "then sooner or later we must keep order ourselves."

In his 1904 annual message to Congress, Roosevelt announced a new policy, the so-called **Roosevelt Corollary** to the Monroe Doctrine. "Chronic wrongdoing," he declared, would cause the United States to exercise "an international police power" in Latin America. The Monroe Doctrine had expressed American hostility to European intervention in Latin America; the Roosevelt Corollary attempted to justify U.S. intervention and authority in the region. Roosevelt invoked his corollary immediately, imposing American management of the debts and customs duties of the Dominican Republic in 1905. Financial insolvency was averted, popular revolution prevented, and possible European intervention forestalled.

Latin Americans vigorously resented the United States' unilateral claims to authority. By 1907, the so-called Drago Doctrine (named after Argentina's foreign minister) was incorporated into international law, prohibiting armed intervention to collect debts. Still, the United States would continue to invoke the Roosevelt Corollary to advance its interests in the hemisphere. As Secretary of State Elihu Root asserted, "The inevitable effect of our building the Canal must be to require us to police the surrounding premises." He then added, "In the nature of things, trade and control, and the obligation to keep order which go with them, must come our way."

DOLLAR DIPLOMACY

Roosevelt's successor as president, William Howard Taft, hoped to promote U.S. interests without such combative rhetoric and naked force. He described his plan as one of "substituting dollars for bullets"—using government action to encourage private American investments in Latin America to supplant European interests, promote development and stability, and gain profits for American bankers. Under this **dollar diplomacy**, American investments in the Caribbean increased dramatically during Taft's presidency from 1909 to 1913, and the State Department helped arrange for American bankers to establish financial control over Haiti and Honduras.

But Taft employed military force more frequently than Roosevelt had, with Nicaragua a major target. In 1909, Taft sent U.S. troops there to aid a revolution fomented by an American mining corporation and to seize the Nicaraguan customs houses. Under the new government, American bankers then gained control of Nicaragua's national bank, railroad, and customs service. To protect these arrangements, U.S. troops were again dispatched in 1912. To control popular opposition to the American client government, the marines remained in Nicaragua for two decades. Military power, not the social and economic improvement promised by dollar diplomacy, kept Nicaragua's minority government stable and subordinate to the United States.

Dollar diplomacy increased American power and influence in the Caribbean and tied underdeveloped countries to the United States economically and strategically, but this policy failed to improve conditions for most Latin Americans. U.S. officials remained primarily concerned with promoting American control and extracting American profits from the region, not with the well-being of its population. Not surprisingly, dollar diplomacy proved unpopular in Latin America.

Roosevelt Corollary   President Theodore Roosevelt's policy asserting U.S. authority to intervene in the affairs of Latin American nations; an expansion of the Monroe Doctrine.

Dollar diplomacy   The U.S. policy of using private investment in other nations to promote American diplomatic goals and business interests.

WILSONIAN INTERVENTIONS

Taking office in 1913, the Democrat Woodrow Wilson promised that the United States would "never again seek one additional foot of territory by conquest" but would instead work to promote "human rights, national integrity, and opportunity" in Latin America. Wilson also named as his secretary of state the Democratic symbol of anti-imperialism, William Jennings Bryan. Their generous intentions were apparent when Bryan signed a treaty with Colombia apologizing for Roosevelt's seizure of the Panama Canal Zone in 1903.

Nonetheless, Wilson believed that the United States had to expand its exports and investments abroad and that U.S. dominance of the Caribbean was strategically necessary. He also shared the racist belief that Latin Americans were inferior and needed paternalistic guidance from the United States, through military force if necessary. His self-righteousness and determination to transform other peoples' behavior led his policies to be dubbed "missionary diplomacy," but they also contained elements of Roosevelt's commitment to military force and Taft's reliance on economic power.

In 1915, Wilson ordered U.S. Marines to Haiti. The U.S. Navy selected a new Haitian president, but real authority rested with the American military, which controlled Haiti until 1934, protecting the small elite who cooperated with foreign interests and exploited their own people. As usual, American military rule improved the country's transportation, sanitation, and educational systems, but the forced-labor program that the U.S. adopted to build such public works provoked widespread resentment. In 1919, marines suppressed a revolt against American domination, killing more than three thousand Haitians.

Wilson also intervened elsewhere in the Caribbean. In 1916, when the Dominican Republic refused to cede control of its finances to U.S. bankers, Wilson ordered the marines to occupy the country. The marines ousted Dominican officials, installed a military government to rule "on behalf of the Dominican government," and ran the nation until 1924. In 1917, the United States intervened in Cuba, which remained under American control until 1922.

Wilson also involved himself in the internal affairs of Mexico. In 1913, General Victoriano Huerta seized control of the country from revolutionaries who had recently overthrown dictator Porfirio Diaz. Wilson was appalled by the violence of Huerta's power grab and was aware that opponents had organized to reestablish constitutional government.

Wilson hoped to bring the Constitutionalists to power and "to secure Mexico a better government under which all contracts and business and concessions will be safer than they have been." He authorized arms sales to their forces, led by Venustiano Carranza; pressured Britain and other nations to deprive Huerta of foreign support; and blockaded the Mexican port of Vera Cruz. In April 1914 Wilson exploited a minor incident to have the marines attack and occupy Vera Cruz. Even Carranza and the Constitutionalists denounced the American occupation as unwarranted aggression. By August, Carranza had toppled Huerta, and Wilson shifted his support to Francisco ("Pancho") Villa. But Carranza's growing popular support in Mexico and Wilson's preoccupation with World War I in Europe finally led the United States to grant de facto recognition to the Carranza government in October 1915.

Villa then began terrorizing New Mexico and Texas, hoping to provoke an American intervention that would undermine Carranza. In 1916, Wilson ordered troops under General John J. Pershing to pursue Villa into Mexico, leading Carranza to fear a permanent U.S. occupation of northern Mexico. Soon the American soldiers were fighting the Mexican army rather than Villa's bandits. On the brink of full-fledged war, Wilson finally ordered U.S. troops to withdraw in January 1917 and extended full recognition to the Carranza government. His aggressive tactics had not merely failed but had also embittered relations with Mexico.

CONCLUSION

By the time of Woodrow Wilson's presidency, the United States had been expanding its involvement in world affairs for half a century. Several themes had emerged from this activity: increasing American domination of the Caribbean, continuing interest in East Asia, the creation of an overseas empire, and the evolution of the United States into a major world power. Underlying these developments was an uneasy mixture of ideas and objectives. The American involvement in the world reflected a traditional, if often misguided, sense of national rectitude and mission. Generous humanitarian impulses vied with ugly racist prejudices as Americans sought both to help other peoples and to direct them toward U.S. concepts of religion, sanitation, capitalist development, and public institutions. American motives ranged from ensuring national security and competing with European colonial powers to the conviction that the United States had to expand its economic interests abroad. But if imperialism, both informal and at times colonial, brought Americans greater wealth and power, it also increased tensions in Asia and contributed to anti-American hostility and revolutionary ferment in Latin America. It also entangled the United States in the Great Power rivalries that would ultimately result in two world wars.

SUMMARY

The Roots of Imperialism The United States had a long tradition of expansion across the continent; now America embarked on building an overseas empire. Some Americans favored acquiring and exploiting colonies; others wanted an empire based on trade and investments; still others advocated the United States exporting its ideas and institutions. Social Darwinism, Protestant evangelism, and naval expansion were all rationales for America becoming a world power.

First Steps Despite the growing pro-imperialist arguments, America was generally passive toward foreign affairs until the end of the nineteenth century. The purchase of Alaska from Russia, the growing American commercial influence in Hawaii, and the assertion of hemispheric domination in Latin America demonstrated America's increasingly assertive national policy throughout the late 1800s.

The Spanish-American War The war originated in Cuba's quest for independence from Spain. Spain's brutality in suppressing the revolt prompted American sympathy; the sensationalist yellow press fanned the flames for war. The Spanish-American War made America an imperialist nation; the Battle of Manila Bay gave America a foothold in the Philippines; Hawaii was annexed as part of America's "Manifest Destiny"; and a short campaign in Cuba resulted in the defeat of Spanish troops there. The Treaty of Paris gave America Puerto Rico and Guam and set the stage for the acquisition of the Philippines; anti-imperialists questioned national goals and America's commitment to liberty and freedom.

Imperial Ambitions: The United States and East Asia, 1899–1917 The Filipino-American War resulted from the betrayed hope of the Filipino people for independence following the Treaty of Paris. A brutal war fought to put down rebellion resulted in America's establishing a colonial government in the Philippines. America's involvement in the Philippines reflected its interest in China; European nations and Japan claimed areas of influence in China, limiting America's options to develop trade. Involvement in China brought the United States into conflict with Japan and Russia; Japan's emergence as a great power saw growing discord between the two countries.

Imperial Power: The United States and Latin America, 1899–1917 Following the Spanish-American War, America often intervened in Latin America to promote its own strategic and economic interests; trade expanded and ill will increased. Puerto

Rico became unincorporated, Cuba, a U.S. protectorate, and land in Panama was acquired to build a canal; each was part in America's exercise of imperial power. President Theodore Roosevelt's Corollary to the Monroe Doctrine announced America's role as a policeman and debt collector; President Taft attempted dollar diplomacy; President Wilson intervened in the Caribbean, and his tactics in Mexico created lasting ill will.

REVIEW QUESTIONS

1. What were the roots of American imperialism in the late nineteenth century?
2. What factors shaped American foreign policy in the late nineteenth century?
3. Was the United States' emergence as an imperial power a break from a culmination of its earlier policies and national development?
4. What were the objectives and consequences of U.S. interventions in Latin America?

KEY TERMS

Dollar diplomacy   (p. 598)
Gentlemen's Agreement   (p. 595)
Imperialism   (p. 581)
Mahanism   (p. 583)

Monroe Doctrine   (p. 587)
Open Door   (p. 594)
Platt Amendment   (p. 596)
Roosevelt Corollary   (p. 598)

Spheres of Influence   (p. 593)
Teller Amendment   (p. 590)
Yellow press   (p. 589)

WHERE TO LEARN MORE

Mission Houses, Honolulu, Hawaii. Built between 1821 and 1841, these buildings were homes and shops of missionaries sent to Hawaii by the American Board of Commissioners for Foreign Missions. Their exhibits include furnishings and memorabilia of a group important in developing American ties with Hawaii. **www.missionhouses.org/**

Funston Memorial Home, Iola, Kansas. Operated as a museum by the Kansas State Historical Society, this is the boyhood home of General Frederick Funston, prominent in the Spanish-American War and the Filipino-American War. For a virtual tour, together with military information, political cartoons, Roosevelt correspondence, and Funston links, see **http://skyways.lib.ks.us/museums/funston/**

James G. Blaine House, Augusta, Maine. The Executive Mansion of Maine's governor since 1919, this house was formerly Blaine's home and still contains his study and furnishings from the time he served as secretary of state and U.S. senator.

Rough Riders Memorial and City Museum, Las Vegas, Nevada. Together with the nearby Castaneda Hotel, this site provides intriguing information on Roosevelt's volunteer cavalry, recruited primarily from the Southwest. **www.arco-iris.com/teddy/index.htm**

Seward House, Auburn, New York. The home of William H. Seward contains furniture and mementos from his career as secretary of state.

 For additional study resources for this chapter, go to:
www.prenhall.com/goldfield/chapter22

On the other hand, if there is little enthusiasm, the people everywhere are taking the war as a grim necessity, feeling that they have been forced into it by events beyond their control . . .

Female workers build a vehicle in an engineering shop in 1917.

The New York Times.

EXTRA
5:30 A. M.

LUSITANIA SUNK BY A SUBMARINE, PROBABLY 1,260 DEAD;
TWICE TORPEDOED OFF IRISH COAST; SINKS IN 15 MINUTES;
CAPT. TURNER SAVED, FROHMAN AND VANDERBILT MISSING;
WASHINGTON BELIEVES THAT A GRAVE CRISIS IS AT HAND

NOTICE!

23

AMERICA AND THE GREAT WAR
1914–1920

HOW WAS U.S. neutrality during World War I undermined?

WHY DID the United States join the conflict on the side of the Allies?

HOW DID the war effort threaten civil liberties?

WHAT WERE the terms of the Treaty of Versailles?

WHAT WAS the post-war backlash?

1914   1920

I have been traveling for nearly three weeks through six Middle Western States, talking about the war, with all classes of people: farmers, labor leaders, newspaper editors, college professors, business men, and state officials. I have been trying to get at the bedrock sentiment of the people regarding it, and to set it down exactly as I find it.

Almost without exception, even among those who favor the war most vigorously, the people I have talked with have commented upon the lack of popular enthusiasm for the war. The more closely these people were connected with the farmers or the workingmen, the more sweeping and positive were their statements.

The attitude of the people is wholly different from what it was at the opening of our Spanish War in 1898. There are no heroic slogans, no boastfulness, no excitement, no glamour of war. There is still a great deal of haziness about the real issues and a great deal of doubt about how far America should go beyond mere defensive measures. One of the foremost political leaders of the West, himself an ardent supporter of the war, told me that if a secret ballot were taken as to whether American armies should be sent to France, the vote would be overwhelmingly against it. It is noteworthy, also, that the newspapers are full of a-b-c explanations of the reasons why we are at war and why we should go forward with it. . . . And finally, there are nowhere as yet any evidences of the passions and the hatred which war engenders. People do not hate Germans or Austrians or Turks; nor do they love the British.

On the other hand, if there is little enthusiasm, the people everywhere are taking the war as a grim necessity, feeling that they have been forced into it by events beyond their control, and they are going forward, more or less reluctantly, with the preparations; but they are really going forward. The draft was not popular; people wished it might have been done in some other way; and in some groups of population it was hated and feared, and yet, through all this country, there has been a wonderful and complete compliance with the law. In the same way the liberty loan is not popular. There is no popular rush to subscribe, and it has required an enormous amount of organization, advertising, and pressure to sell the bonds, and yet they are being sold and will be sold. . . . And there have been no signs of any popular rush to enlist, and men have been obtained only by dint of the most vigorous advertising and pressure. It is significant also that more than half of those registered in Chicago are demanding exemption.

The only real enthusiasm that I could find was in such campaigns as that of the Red Cross, the Y.M.C.A., and here and there in work for the American Ambulance in France. The work of women everywhere for the Red Cross is remarkably organized and well supported. . . . Of the value of these activities, no matter what happens, the people are convinced.

This is as nearly a true statement of the general situation as I can make. I have met a good many men who think that this state of the popular mind, this deliberate and passionless method of doing what is regarded as a disagreeable duty, is the best possible method of getting into the great war. . . .

IMAGE KEY
for pages 602–603

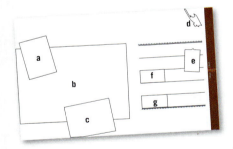

a. British Prime Minister Lloyd George, French Prime Minister George Clemenceau, and U.S. President Wilson in Versailles, Paris in 1919.

b. Women war workers working in an engineering shop, 1917.

c. The New York Times front page reports the sinking of the Lusitania in 1915.

d. British Biplane shot down

e. "Beat back the HUN:" American World War I Liberty Loan poster.

f. Women draft protesters demonstrate in front of New York's City Hall on June 16, 1917.

g. A policeman on horseback swings a truncheon at strikers on a Pittsburgh street.

> *On the other hand, I met a good many people, especially among the*
> *leaders of war organizations of various sorts, to whom the popular attitude is*
> *not only irritating but dangerous. They feel that the people are not fully*
> *awakened to the emergency, that they do not realize that the country is really*
> *at this moment at war, and that unless America meets with more enthusiasm*
> *and more speed the problems of raising money, producing food, and hurrying*
> *the training of men for armies in France the war may result in disaster.*
>
> Ray Stannard Baker, "West in Grim Business of War Without Passion," *St. Louis*
> *Post–Dispatch,* June 17, 1917.

RAY STANNARD BAKER, the famous journalist, thus described his journey across the Midwest in 1917, three years after World War I began in Europe and two months after the United States had declared war on Germany. The American people were reluctant participants, unconvinced that national interests were really involved.

But as Baker discovered, the nation's leaders were determined to whip up support for the war through "organization, advertising, and pressure." The goal would be not only to train soldiers but also to demonize Germany, mobilize the economy, and transform American social attitudes.

The Great War changed American life. Government authority increased sharply. Business, labor unions, farmers, ministers were all incorporated into the war effort. Women's organizational activities expanded dramatically; and often developed in unexpected ways. Journalists, too, put their skills to new and sometimes unfortunate uses; Baker, who had initially opposed the war, eventually went to Europe to file confidential reports for the State Department and then to control news at the Versailles Peace Conference.

Many of the changes in American life, from increased efficiency to Americanization, often reflected prewar progressivism, and the war years did promote some reforms. But the war also diverted reform energies into new channels, encouraged coercion impulses ("the passions and the hatred" which Baker found lacking in mid-1917 were soon widespread), and strengthened the conservative opposition to reform. The results were often reactionary and contributed to a postwar mood that curtailed further reform and helped defeat the peace treaty upon which so much had been gambled.

Waging Neutrality

With near unanimity, Americans supported neutrality when the Great War erupted in Europe in 1914. But American attitudes, decisions, and actions, both public and private, undercut neutrality, and the policies of governments in Berlin, London, and Washington drew the United States into the war.

HOW WAS U.S. neutrality during World War I undermined?

The Origins of Conflict

Since the 1870s, the competing imperial ambitions of the great European powers had led to economic rivalries, military expansion, diplomatic maneuvering, and international tensions. In central Europe, the expansionist Germany of Kaiser Wilhelm II allied itself with the multinational Austro-Hungarian Empire. Confronting them, Great Britain and France formed alliances with Tsarist

Russia. Observing this precarious balance of power in May 1914, an American diplomat reported anxiously, "There is too much hatred, too many jealousies." He predicted "an awful cataclysm."

On June 28, a Serbian terrorist assassinated Archduke Franz Ferdinand, the heir to the Austro-Hungarian throne. With Germany's support, Austria declared war on Serbia on July 28. Russia then mobilized its army against Austria to aid Serbia, its Slavic client state. To assist Austria, Germany declared war on Russia and then on Russia's ally France. Hoping for a quick victory, Germany struck at France through neutral Belgium; in response, Britain declared war on Germany on August 4. Soon Turkey and Bulgaria joined Germany and Austria to form the **Central Powers**. The **Allies**—Britain, France, and Russia—were joined by Italy and Japan. Britain drew on its empire for resources, using troops from India, Canada, Australia, New Zealand, and South Africa. The war had become a global conflict, waged not only in Europe but also in Africa, the Middle East, and East Asia.

Mass slaughter enveloped Europe as huge armies battled to a stalemate. The British and French faced the Germans along a line of trenches stretching across France and Belgium from the English Channel to Switzerland. The British once suffered 300,000 casualties in an offensive that gained only a few square miles before being pushed back. Machine gunners went into shock at the carnage they inflicted. In the trenches, soldiers suffered in the cold and mud, surrounded by decaying bodies and human waste, enduring lice, rats, and nightmares, and dying from disease and exhaustion. The Great War, said one German soldier, had become "the grave of nations."

AMERICAN ATTITUDES

Few Americans had expected this calamity. As one North Carolina congressman said, "This dreadful conflict of the nations came to most of us as lightning out of a clear sky." Most people believed that the United States had no vital interest in the war and would not become involved. "Our isolated position and freedom from entangling alliances," noted the *Literary Digest*, "inspire our press with the cheering assurance that we are in no peril of being drawn into the European quarrel." President Wilson issued a proclamation of neutrality and urged Americans to be "neutral in fact as well as in name . . . impartial in thought as well as in action."

However, ethnic, cultural, and economic ties bound most Americans to the British and French. Politically, too, most Americans felt a greater affinity for the democratic Western Allies. And whereas Britain and the United States had enjoyed a rapprochement since 1895, Germany had repeatedly appeared as a potential rival.

Wilson himself admired Britain's culture and government and distrusted Germany's imperial ambitions. Like other influential Americans, Wilson believed that a German victory would threaten America's economic, political, and perhaps even strategic interests. "England is fighting our fight," he said privately. Secretary of State William Jennings Bryan was genuinely neutral, but most officials favored the Allies. Early in the war, Colonel Edward House, Wilson's closest adviser on foreign affairs, wrote: "I cannot see how there can be any serious trouble between England and America, with all of us feeling as we do."

British writers, artists, and lecturers depicted the Allies as fighting for civilization against a brutal Germany that mutilated nuns and babies, shaping America's view of the conflict. Britain also cut the only German cable to the United States and censored war news to suit itself. German propaganda directed at American opinion proved ineffectual.

Sympathy for the Allies, however, did not mean that Americans favored intervention. The British ambassador complained that it was "useless" to expect any

Central Powers Germany and its World War I allies in Austria, Turkey, and Bulgaria.

Allies In World War I, Britain, France, Russia, and other belligerent nations fighting against the Central Powers but not including the United States.

"practical" advantage from the Americans' sympathy, for they had no intention of joining the conflict. Wilson was determined to pursue peace as long as his view of national interests allowed.

THE ECONOMY OF WAR

International law permitted neutral nations to sell or ship war material to all belligerents, and with the economy mired in a recession when the war began, many Americans looked to war orders to spur economic recovery. But the British navy prevented trade with the Central Powers. Only the Allies could buy American goods. Their orders for steel, explosives, uniforms, wheat, and other products, however, pulled the country out of the recession. One journalist rejoiced that "war, for Europe, is meaning devastation and death; for America a bumper crop of new millionaires and a hectic hastening of prosperity revival."

President Woodrow Wilson reads his war message to Congress, April 2, 1917. He predicted "many months of fiery trial and sacrifice ahead of us."

Library of Congress

Other Americans worried that this one-sided war trade undermined genuine neutrality. Congress even considered embargoing munitions. But few Americans supported that idea. One financial journal declared of the Allied war trade: "We need it for the profits which it yields." The German ambassador noted that American industry was "actually delivering goods only to the enemies of Germany."

A second economic issue complicated matters. To finance their war purchases, the Allies borrowed from American bankers. Initially, Secretary of State Bryan persuaded Wilson to prohibit loans to the belligerents as "inconsistent with the true spirit of neutrality." But Wilson soon ended the ban. Secretary of the Treasury William McAdoo argued that it would be "disastrous" *not* to finance the Allies' purchases, on which "our prosperity is dependent." By April 1917, American loans to the Allies exceeded $2 billion, nearly one hundred times the amount lent to Germany. These financial ties, like the war trade they underwrote, linked the United States to the Allies and convinced Germany that American neutrality was only a formality.

THE DIPLOMACY OF NEUTRALITY

This same imbalance characterized American diplomacy. Wilson acquiesced in British violations of American neutral rights while sternly refusing to yield on German actions. Wilson argued that while British violations of international law cost Americans property, markets, and time, German violations cost lives. As the *Boston Globe* noted, the British were "a gang of thieves" and the Germans "a gang of murderers. On the whole, we prefer the thieves, but only as the lesser of two evils."

When the war began, the United States asked belligerents to respect the 1909 **Declaration of London** on neutral rights. Germany agreed to do so; the British refused. Instead, Britain instituted a blockade of Germany, mined the North Sea, and forced neutral ships into British ports to search their cargoes and confiscate material deemed useful to the German war effort. Wilson branded Britain's blockade illegal and unwarranted, but by October he had conceded many of America's neutral rights to avoid conflict with Britain.

Declaration of London   Statement drafted by an international conference in 1909 to clarify international law and specify the rights of neutral nations.

CHRONOLOGY

1914	World War I begins in Europe.
	President Woodrow Wilson declares U.S. neutrality.
1915	Germany begins submarine warfare.
	Lusitania is sunk.
	Woman's Peace Party is organized.
1916	Gore-McLemore resolutions are defeated.
	Sussex Pledge is issued.
	Preparedness legislation is enacted.
	Woodrow Wilson is reelected president.
1917	Germany resumes unrestricted submarine warfare.
	The United States declares war on Germany.
	Selective Service Act establishes the military draft.
	Espionage Act is passed.
	Committee on Public Information, War Industries Board, Food Administration, and other mobilization agencies are established.
	American Expeditionary Force arrives in France.
	East St. Louis race riot erupts.
	Bolshevik Revolution occurs in Russia.

1918	Wilson announces his Fourteen Points.
	Sedition Act is passed.
	Eugene Debs is imprisoned.
	The United States intervenes militarily in Russia.
	Armistice ends World War I.
1919	Paris Peace Conference is held.
	Steel, coal, and other strikes occur.
	Red Scare breaks out.
	Prohibition amendment is adopted.
	Wilson suffers a massive stroke.
1920	Palmer Raids round up radicals.
	League of Nations is defeated in the U.S. Senate.
	Woman suffrage amendment is ratified.
	U.S. troops are withdrawn from Russia.
	Warren Harding is elected president.
1921	United States signs a separate peace treaty with Germany.

The British then prohibited food and other products that Germany had imported during peace-time, thereby interfering further with neutral shipping. One American official complained privately: "England is playing a . . . high game, violating international law every day." But when the Wilson administration finally protested, it undermined its own position by noting that "imperative necessity" might justify a violation of international law. In January 1915, Wilson yielded further by observing that "no very important questions of principle" were involved in the Anglo-American quarrels over ship seizures and that they could be resolved after the war.

This policy tied the United States to the British war effort and provoked a German response. Germany decided in February 1915 to use its submarines against Allied shipping in a war zone around the British Isles. Germany maintained that Britain's blockade and the acquiescence of neutral countries in British violations of international law made submarine warfare necessary.

Submarines could not readily follow traditional rules of naval warfare. Small and fragile, they depended on surprise attacks. They could not surface to identify themselves, as the rules mandated, without risking disaster from the deck guns of Britain's armed merchant ships, and they were too small to rescue victims of their sinkings. Yet Wilson refused to see the "imperative necessity" in German tactics that he found in British tactics, and he warned that he would hold Germany responsible for any loss of American lives or property.

In May 1915, a German submarine sank a British passenger liner, the *Lusitania*. It had been carrying arms, and the German embassy had warned Americans against traveling on the ship, but the loss of life—1,198 people, including 128 Americans—caused Americans to condemn Germany. "To speak of technicalities and the rules of war, in the face of such wholesale murder on the high seas, is a waste of time," trumpeted one magazine. Wilson saw he had to "carry out the double wish of our people, to maintain a firm front in respect of what we demand of Germany and yet do nothing that might by any possibility involve us in the war."

Wilson demanded that Germany abandon its submarine campaign. But his language was so harsh that Bryan resigned, warning that by requiring more of

Germany than of Britain, the president violated neutrality and threatened to draw the nation into war. Bryan proposed prohibiting Americans from traveling on belligerent ships. His proposal gained support in the South and West, and Senator Thomas Gore of Oklahoma and Representative Jeff McLemore of Texas introduced it in congressional resolutions in February 1916.

Wilson moved to defeat the Gore-McLemore resolutions, insisting that they impinged on presidential control of foreign policy and on America's neutral rights. In truth, the resolutions abandoned no vital national interest while offering to prevent another provocative incident. Moreover, neither law nor tradition gave Americans the right to travel safely on belligerent ships. Of the nation's "double wish," then, Wilson placed more priority on confronting what he saw as the German threat than on meeting the popular desire for peace.

In April 1916, a German submarine torpedoed the French ship *Sussex*, injuring four Americans. Wilson threatened to break diplomatic relations if Germany did not abandon unrestricted submarine warfare against all merchant vessels. This implied war. Germany promised not to sink merchant ships without warning but made its *Sussex* **Pledge** contingent on the United States' requiring Britain also to adhere to "the rules of international law universally recognized before the war." Wilson's diplomatic victory, then, was hollow. Peace for America would depend on the British adopting a course they rejected. As Wilson saw it, however, "any little German lieutenant can put us into the war at any time by some calculated outrage." Wilson's diplomacy had left the nation's future at the mercy of others.

THE BATTLE OVER PREPAREDNESS

The threat of war sparked a debate over military policy. Theodore Roosevelt and a handful of other politicians, mostly Northeastern Republicans convinced that Allied victory was in the national interest, had advocated what they called **preparedness**, a program to expand the armed forces and establish universal military training. Conservative business groups also joined the agitation, combining demands for preparedness with attacks on progressive reforms.

But most Americans opposed expensive military preparations. Leading feminists like Jane Addams, Charlotte Perkins Gilman, and Carrie Chapman Catt formed the Woman's Peace Party in 1915, and other organizations like the American League to Limit Armaments also campaigned against preparedness. William Jennings Bryan denounced the militarism of Roosevelt as a "philosophy [that] can rot a soul" and condemned preparedness as a program for turning the nation into "a vast armory with skull and cross-bones above the door."

Wilson also opposed preparedness initially, but he reversed his position when the submarine crisis with Germany intensified. In early 1916, an election year, he made a speaking tour to generate public support for expanding the armed forces. Congress soon passed the National Defense Act and the Naval Construction Act, increasing the strength of the army and authorizing a naval construction plan.

THE ELECTION OF 1916

Wilson's preparedness plans stripped the Republicans of one issue in 1916, and his renewed support of progressive reforms helped hold Bryan Democrats in line. The slogan "He Kept Us Out of War" appealed to the popular desire for peace, and the Democratic campaign became one long peace rally. Wilson disliked the peace emphasis but exploited its political appeal. He warned, "The certain prospect of the success of the Republican party is that we shall be drawn, in one form or another, into the embroilments of the European war."

Sussex **Pledge**   Germany's pledge during World War I not to sink merchant ships without warning, on the condition that Britain also observe recognized rules of international laws.

Preparedness   Military buildup in preparation for possible U.S. participation in World War I.

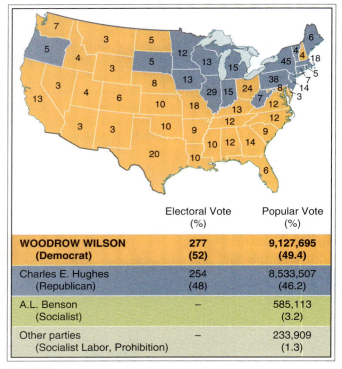

	Electoral Vote (%)	Popular Vote (%)
WOODROW WILSON (Democrat)	**277 (52)**	**9,127,695 (49.4)**
Charles E. Hughes (Republican)	254 (48)	8,533,507 (46.2)
A.L. Benson (Socialist)	–	585,113 (3.2)
Other parties (Socialist Labor, Prohibition)	–	233,909 (1.3)

MAP 23–1
The Election of 1916 Woodrow Wilson won reelection in 1916 despite a reunified Republican party by sweeping the South and West on campaign appeals to peace and progressive reform.

HOW WAS Woodrow Wilson able to win reelection in 1916 despite the reunification of the Republican party?

Self-determination The right of a people or a nation to decide on its own political allegiance or form of government without external influence.

The Republicans had hoped to regain the support of their progressive members after Roosevelt urged the Progressive party to follow him back into the GOP. But many joined the Democratic camp instead. The GOP nominated Charles Evans Hughes, a Supreme Court justice and former New York governor. The platform denounced Wilson's "shifty expedients" in foreign policy and promised "strict and honest neutrality." Unfortunately for Hughes, Roosevelt's attacks on Wilson for not pursuing a war policy persuaded many voters that the GOP was a war party. "If Hughes is defeated," wrote one observer, "he has Roosevelt to thank for it."

The election was the closest in decades (see Map 23–1). When California narrowly went for Wilson, it decided the contest. The desire for peace, all observers concluded, had determined the election.

DESCENT INTO WAR

Still, Wilson knew that war loomed, and he made a last effort to avert it. In January 1917, he sketched out the terms of what he called a "peace without victory." Anything else, he warned, would only lead to another war. The new world order should be based on national equality and **self-determination**, arms reductions, freedom of the seas, and an international organization to ensure peace. It was a distinctly American vision.

But both the Allies and the Central Powers had sacrificed too much to settle for anything short of outright victory. Germany wanted to annex territory in eastern Europe, Belgium, and France and to take over Belgian and French colonies in Africa; Austria sought Balkan territory. The Allies wanted to destroy German military and commercial power, weaken the Austro-Hungarian empire, take Germany's colonies in Africa, and supplant Turkish influence in the Middle East. One British leader denounced Wilson as "the quintessence of a prig" for suggesting that after three years of "this terrible effort," the two sides should accept American principles rather than their own national objectives.

Germany now moved to win the war by cutting the Allies off from U.S. supplies. On January 31, Germany unleashed its submarines in a broad war zone.

Wilson was now virtually committed to a war many Americans opposed. He broke diplomatic relations with Germany and asked Congress to arm American merchant vessels. When the Senate refused, Wilson invoked an antipiracy law of 1819 and armed the ships anyway. Although no American ships had yet been sunk, he also ordered the naval gun crews to shoot submarines on sight. Wilson's own secretary of the navy warned that these actions violated international law and were a step toward war. Huge rallies across America demanded peace.

Yet several developments soon shifted public opinion. On March 1, Wilson released an intercepted message from the German foreign minister, Arthur Zimmermann, to the German minister in Mexico. It proposed that in the event of war between the United States and Germany, Mexico should ally itself with Germany; in exchange, Mexico would recover its "lost territory in Texas, New Mexico, and Arizona." The Zimmermann note produced a wave of hostility toward Germany and increased support for intervention in the war, especially in the Southwest, which had opposed involvement. A revolution in Russia overthrew the tsarist regime and established a provisional government. Russia was now "a fit partner" for the United States, said Wilson. When submarines sank four American freighters in mid-March, anti-German feeling broadened.

On April 2, 1917, Wilson delivered his war message, declaring that neutrality was no longer possible, given Germany's submarine "warfare against mankind." To build support for joining a war that most people had long regarded with revulsion and as alien to American interests, Wilson set forth the nation's war goals as simple and noble. The United States would not fight for conquest or domination but for "the ultimate peace of the world and for the liberation of its peoples. . . . The world must be made safe for democracy."

After vigorous debate, the Senate passed the war resolution 82 to 6 and the House 373 to 50. On April 6, 1917, the United States officially entered the Great War, what Representative Claude Kitchin of North Carolina predicted would be "one vast drama of horrors and blood, one boundless stage upon which will play all the evil spirits of earth and hell."

WHERE TO LEARN MORE

National Infantry Museum,
Fort Benning, Georgia
www.benningmwr.com/index.cfm

WAGING WAR IN AMERICA

Mobilizing for military intervention was a massive undertaking. "It is not an army that we must shape and train for war," announced President Wilson; "it is a Nation." The government reorganized the economy to emphasize centralized management, developed policies to control public opinion and suppress dissent, and transformed the role of government itself. Mobilization often built on progressives' moralism and sense of mission. In other respects, however, the war experience withered the spirits of reformers. In many different ways, people on the home front—like soldiers in Europe—would participate in the Great War; all would find their lives changed.

WHY DID the United States join the conflict on the side of the Allies?

MANAGING THE WAR ECONOMY

Federal and state governments developed a complex structure of agencies and controls for every sector of the economy (see the overview table "Major Government Wartime Agencies"). Supervised by the Council of National Defense, these agencies shifted resources to war-related enterprise, increased production of goods and services, and improved transportation and distribution.

The most important agency was the **War Industries Board (WIB)**. Led by financier Bernard Baruch, the WIB exercised unprecedented powers over industry by setting prices, allocating scarce materials, and standardizing products and procedures to boost efficiency. Yet Baruch was not an industrial dictator; he aimed at business-government integration. The WIB promoted major business interests, helped suspend antitrust laws, and guaranteed huge corporate profits. So many business leaders became involved in the WIB that there was a popular outcry against business infiltration of the government, and one corporate executive admitted, "We are all making more money out of this war than the average human being ought to." Some progressives began to see the dangers, and business leaders the advantages, of government economic intervention.

Under William McAdoo, the Railroad Administration operated the nation's railroads as a unified system to move supplies and troops efficiently. Centralized management eliminated competition, permitted improvements in equipment, and brought great profits to the owners but higher prices to the general public.

Equally effective and far more popular was the Food Administration, headed by Herbert Hoover. Hoover persuaded millions of Americans to accept meatless and

War Industries Board (WIB) The federal agency that reorganized industry for maximum efficiency and productivity during World War I.

OVERVIEW

MAJOR GOVERNMENT WARTIME AGENCIES

Agency	Purpose
War Industries Board	Reorganized industry to maximize wartime production
Railroad Administration	Modernized and operated the nation's railroads
Food Administration	Increased agricultural production, supervised food distribution and farm labor
National War Labor Board	Resolved labor-management disputes, improved labor conditions, and recognized union rights as means to promote production and efficiency
Committee on Public Information	Managed propaganda to build public support for the war effort

QUICK REVIEW

National War Labor Board

◆ Federal and state governments created agencies to oversee the war-time economy.

◆ The National War Labor Board guaranteed the rights of unions to organize and bargain collectively.

◆ Labor unions sharply increased their membership under this protection.

wheatless days so that the Food Administration could feed military and foreign consumers. Half a million women went door to door to secure food conservation pledges from housewives. City residents planted victory gardens in parks and vacant lots.

Hoover also worked closely with agricultural processors and distributors. Farmers profited from the war, too. To encourage production, he established high prices for farm commodities, and agricultural income rose 30 percent. The Food Administration organized the Woman's Land Army to recruit women to work in the fields, providing sufficient farm labor despite the military draft. Most states formed units of the Boys' Working Reserve for agricultural labor. Agribusinesses in the Southwest persuaded the federal government to permit them to import Mexicans to work under government supervision and be housed in special camps.

In exchange for labor's cooperation, the National War Labor Board guaranteed the rights of unions to organize and bargain collectively. With such support, labor unions sharply increased their membership. The labor board also encouraged improved working conditions, higher wages, and shorter hours. These improvements limited labor disputes during the war, and Secretary of War Newton Baker praised labor as "more willing to keep in step than capital." But when unions like the Industrial Workers of the World did not keep in step, the government suppressed them.

These and other government regulatory agencies reinforced many long-standing trends in the American economy, from the consolidation of business to the commercialization of agriculture and the organization of labor. They also set a precedent for governmental activism that would prove valuable during the crises of the 1930s and 1940s.

WOMEN AND MINORITIES, NEW OPPORTUNITIES, OLD INEQUALITIES

The reorganization of the economy also had significant social consequences, especially for women and African Americans. In response to labor shortages, women took jobs previously closed to them. Besides farm work, they built airplanes, produced guns and ammunition, manufactured tents and cartridge belts, and worked in a wide variety of other heavy and light industries. "One of the lessons from the war," said one manufacturer, "has been to show that women can do exacting work."

Harriot Stanton Blatch, a suffragist active in the Food Administration, estimated that a million women had replaced men in industry, where "their drudgery is for the first time paid for."

Many working women simply shifted to other jobs where their existing skills earned better wages and benefits. The reshuffling of jobs among white women opened new vacancies for black women in domestic, clerical, and industrial employment. As black women replaced white women in the garment and textile industries, social reformers spoke of "a new day for the colored woman worker." But racial as well as gender segregation continued to mark employment, and wartime improvements were temporary.

The war helped middle-class women reformers achieve two long-sought objectives: woman suffrage and prohibition. Emphasizing the national cooperation needed to wage the war, one magazine noted that "arbitrarily to draw the line at voting, at a time when every man and woman must share in this effort, becomes an absurd anomaly." Even Woodrow Wilson finally endorsed the reform, terming it "vital to the winning of the war." Congress approved the suffrage amendment, which was ratified in 1920. Convinced that abstaining from alcohol would save grain and make workers and soldiers more efficient, Congress also passed the prohibition amendment, which was ratified in 1919.

The demand for industrial labor caused a huge migration of black people from the rural South, where they had had little opportunity, few rights, and no hope. Half a million African Americans moved north during the war, doubling and tripling the black population of Chicago, Detroit, and other industrial cities.

Unfortunately, fearful and resentful white people started race riots in Northern cities. In East St. Louis, Illinois, where thousands of black Southerners sought defense work, a white mob in July 1917 murdered at least thirty-nine black people. The *Literary Digest* noted, "Race-riots in East St. Louis afford a lurid background to our efforts to carry justice and idealism to Europe." And Wilson was told privately that the riot was "worse than anything the Germans did in Belgium."

FINANCING THE WAR

To finance the war, the government borrowed money and raised taxes. Business interests favored the first course, but Southern and Western progressives argued that taxation was more efficient and equitable and would minimize war profiteering. California Senator Hiram Johnson noted, "Our endeavours to impose heavy war profit taxes . . . have brought into sharp relief the skin-deep dollar patriotism of some of those who have been loudest in declamations on war and in their demands for blood." Nevertheless, the tax laws of 1917 and 1918 established a graduated tax structure with increased taxes on large incomes, corporate profits, and wealthy estates.

The government raised two-thirds of the war costs by borrowing. Most of the loans came from banks and wealthy investors, but the government also campaigned to sell **Liberty Bonds** to the general public. Celebrities went to schools, churches, and rallies to persuade Americans to buy bonds as their patriotic duty. "Every person who refuses to subscribe," Secretary of the Treasury McAdoo told a California audience, "is a friend of Germany."

CONQUERING MINDS

The government also tried to promote a war spirit among the American people by establishing propaganda agencies and enacting legislation to control social attitudes and behavior. This program drew from the restrictive side of progressivism

QUICK REVIEW

Women and the War
◆ The war opened jobs in industry for women.
◆ New job opportunities appeared for black women.
◆ Middle-class women reformers achieved two objectives: woman suffrage and prohibition.

Liberty Bonds Interest-bearing certificates sold by the U.S. government to finance the American World War I effort.

Female workers stack bricks from wheel barrows at a brickyard under the supervision of a man in a suit.

National Archives and Records Administration

but also reflected the interests of more conservative forces. The Wilson administration adopted this program of social mobilization because many Americans opposed the war, including German Americans with ethnic ties to the Central Powers, Irish Catholics and Russian Jews who condemned the Allies for persecution and repression, Scandinavian immigrants averse to military service, pacifists, radicals who denounced the war as capitalist and imperialist, and many others.

To rally Americans behind the war effort, Wilson established the **Committee on Public Information (CPI)** under George Creel. Despite its title, the CPI sought to manipulate, not inform, public opinion. Creel described his goal as winning "the fight for the *minds* of men, for the 'conquest of their convictions.'" The CPI flooded the country with press releases, advertisements, cartoons, and canned editorials. It made newsreels and war movies to capture public attention. It hired artists to draw posters, professors to write pamphlets in twenty-three languages, and poets to compose war poems for children.

Other government agencies launched similar campaigns. The Woman's Committee of the Council of National Defense established the Department of Educational Propaganda and Patriotic Education. This agency worked to win over women who opposed the war.

Government propaganda had three themes: national unity, the loathsome character of the enemy, and the war as a grand crusade for liberty and democracy. Germans were depicted as brutal, even subhuman, rapists and murderers. The campaign suggested that any dissent was unpatriotic, if not treasonous, and dangerous to national survival. This emphasis on unreasoning conformity helped prompt hysterical attacks on German Americans, radicals, and pacifists.

SUPPRESSING DISSENT

The government also suppressed dissent, now officially branded disloyalty. For reasons of their own, private interests helped shape a reactionary repression that tarnished the nation's professed idealistic war goals.

Congress rushed to stifle antiwar sentiment. The **Espionage Act** provided heavy fines and up to twenty years in prison for obstructing the war effort, a vague phrase but one "omnipotently comprehensive," warned one Idaho senator who opposed the law. "No man can foresee what it might be in its consequences." In fact, the Espionage Act became a weapon to crush dissent and criticism. In 1918, Congress passed the still more sweeping **Sedition Act**. Based on state laws in the West designed to suppress labor radicals, the Sedition Act provided severe penalties for speaking or writing against the draft, bond sales, or war production or for criticizing government personnel or policies. Senator Hiram Johnson lamented: "It is war. But, good God, . . . when did it become war upon the American people?"

Postmaster General Albert Burleson banned antiwar or radical newspapers and magazines from the mail, suppressing literature so indiscriminately that one observer said he "didn't know socialism from rheumatism." The reactionary

Committee on Public Information (CPI) Government agency during World War I that sought to shape public opinion in support of the war effort through newspapers, pamphlets, speeches, films, and other media.

Espionage Act Law whose vague prohibition against obstructing the nation's war effort was used to crush dissent and criticism during World War I.

Sedition Act Broad law restricting criticism of America's involvement in World War I or its government, flag, military, taxes, or officials.

attorney general, Thomas Gregory, made little distinction between traitors and pacifists, war critics, and radicals. Eugene Debs was sentenced to ten years in prison for a "treasonous" speech in which he declared it "extremely dangerous to exercise the right of free speech in a country fighting to make democracy safe in the world." By war's end, a third of the Socialist party's national leadership was in prison, leaving the party in shambles.

Gregory also enlisted the help of private vigilantes, including several hundred thousand members of the reactionary American Protective League, which sought to purge radicals and reformers from the nation's economic and political life. They wiretapped telephones, intercepted private mail, burglarized union offices, broke up German-language newspapers, harassed immigrants, and staged mass raids, seizing thousands of people they claimed were not doing enough for the war effort.

State and local authorities established 184,000 investigating and enforcement agencies known as councils of defense or public safety committees. They encouraged Americans to spy on one another, required people to buy Liberty Bonds, and prohibited teaching German in schools or using the language in religious services and telephone conversations. When Oklahoma abolished German in its schools, a newspaper crowed: "German Deader than Latin Now." (See American Views, Mobilizing America for Liberty.") In Tulsa, a member of the county council of defense shot and killed someone for making allegedly pro-German remarks. The council declared its approval, and community leaders applauded the killer's patriotism.

"Beat Back the Hun," a poster to induce Americans to buy Liberty Bonds, demonizes the enemy in a raw, emotional appeal. Liberty bond drives raised the immense sum of $23 billion.

The Granger Collection, New York

Members of the business community exploited the hysteria to promote their own interests at the expense of farmers, workers, and reformers. As one Wisconsin farmer complained, businessmen "now under the guise of patriotism are trying to ram down the farmers' throats things they hardly dared before." On the Great Plains from Texas to North Dakota, the business target was the Nonpartisan League, a radical farm group demanding state control or ownership of banks, grain elevators, and flour mills. Although the League supported the war, oversubscribed bond drives, and had George Creel affirm its loyalty, conservatives depicted it as seditious to block its advocacy of political and economic reforms. Minnesota's public safety commission proposed a "firing squad working overtime" to deal with League members. Public officials and self-styled patriots broke up the League's meetings and whipped and jailed its leaders.

In the West, business interests targeted labor organizations, especially the Industrial Workers of the World. In Arizona, for example, the Phelps-Dodge Company armed and paid a vigilante mob to seize twelve hundred striking miners, many of them Wobblies and one-third of them Mexican Americans, and herd them into the desert without food or water. Federal investigators found that the company and its thugs had been inspired not by "considerations of patriotism" but by "ordinary strike-breaking motives." Corporate management was merely "raising the false cry of 'disloyalty' " to suppress workers' complaints.

Nonetheless, the government itself used the army to break loggers' support for the IWW in the Pacific Northwest, and it raided IWW halls across the country in September 1917. The conviction of nearly two hundred Wobblies on charges

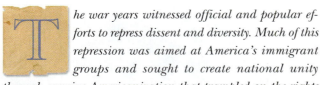

MOBILIZING AMERICA FOR LIBERTY

he war years witnessed official and popular efforts to repress dissent and diversity. Much of this repression was aimed at America's immigrant groups and sought to create national unity through coercive Americanization that trampled on the rights and values that the nation claimed to be defending. The following is an official proclamation of Governor W.L. Harding of Iowa, issued May 23, 1918.

WHAT IS the rationale for the governor's proclamation? What do you think of his interpretation of the constitutional guarantees of individual rights? What other "inconvenience or sacrifice" might the proclamation impose on minorities? How might the proclamation incite vigilantism?

The official language of the United States and the State of Iowa is the English language. Freedom of speech is guaranteed by federal and State Constitutions, but this is not a guaranty of the right to use a language other than the language of this country—the English language. Both federal and State Constitutions also provide that "no laws shall be made respecting an establishment of religion or prohibiting the free exercise thereof." Each person is guaranteed freedom to worship God according to the dictates of his own conscience, but this guaranty does not protect him in the use of a foreign language when he can as well express his thought in English, nor entitle the person who cannot speak or understand the English language to employ a foreign language, when to do so tends in time of national peril, to create discord among neighbors and citizens, or to disturb the peace and quiet of the community.

Every person should appreciate and observe his duty to refrain from all acts or conversation which may excite suspicion or produce strife among the people, but in his relation to the public should so demean himself that every word and act will manifest his loyalty to his country and his solemn purpose to aid in achieving victory for our army and navy and the permanent peace of the world . . . .

The great aim and object of all should be unity of purpose and a solidarity of all the people under the flag for victory. This much we owe to ourselves, to posterity, to our country, and to the world.

Therefore, the following rules should obtain in Iowa during the war:

First. English should and must be the only medium of instruction in public, private, denominational, or other similar schools.

Second. Conversation in public places, on trains, and over the telephone should be in the English language.

Third. All public addresses should be in the English language.

Fourth. Let those who cannot speak or understand the English language conduct their religious worship in their homes.

This course carried out in the spirit of patriotism, though inconvenient to some, will not interfere with their guaranteed constitutional rights and will result in peace and tranquility at home and greatly strengthen the country in battle. The blessings of the United States are so great that any inconvenience or sacrifice should willingly be made for their perpetuity.

Therefore, by virtue of authority in me vested, I, W.L. Harding, Governor of the State of Iowa, commend the spirit of tolerance and urge that henceforth the within outlined rules be adhered to by all, that petty differences be avoided and forgotten, and that, united as one people with one purpose and one language, we fight shoulder to shoulder for the good of mankind.

Source: B.F. Shambaugh, ed., *Iowa and War* (Iowa City; State Historical Society of Iowa, 1919).

22–2
Boy Scouts of America
from, "Boy Scouts Support
the War Effort" (1917)

of sedition in three mass trials in Illinois, California, and Kansas crippled the nation's largest industrial union.

The government was primarily responsible for the war hysteria. It encouraged suspicion and conflict by its own inflammatory propaganda, repressive laws, and violation of basic civil rights, by supporting extremists who used the war for their own purposes, and by not opposing mob violence against German Americans.

WAGING WAR AND PEACE ABROAD

While mobilizing the home front, the Wilson administration undertook an impressive military effort to help the Allies defeat the Central Powers. Wilson also struggled to secure international acceptance for his plans for a just and permanent peace.

THE WAR TO END ALL WARS

When the United States entered the war, the Allied military position was dire. The losses from three years of trench warfare had sapped military strength and civilian morale. French soldiers mutinied after 120,000 casualties in five days; the German submarine campaign was devastating the British. On the eastern front, the Russian army collapsed, and the Russian government gradually disintegrated.

What the Allies needed, said French Marshal Joseph Joffre in April 1917, was simple: "We want men, men, men." In May, Congress passed the **Selective Service Act of 1917**, establishing conscription. More than 24 million men eventually registered for the draft, and nearly 3 million entered the army when their numbers were drawn in a national lottery. Almost two million more men volunteered, as did more than ten thousand women who served in the navy. Nearly one-fifth of America's soldiers were foreign-born (Europeans spoke of the "American Foreign Legion"); 367,000 were black people.

Civilians were transformed into soldiers in hastily organized training camps operated according to progressive principles. Prohibition prevailed in the camps; the poorly educated and largely working-class recruits were taught personal hygiene; worries about sin and inefficiency produced campaigns against venereal disease; and immigrants were taught English and American history. Some units were ethnically segregated: At Camp Gordon, Georgia, Italians and Slavs had separate units with their own officers. Racial segregation was more rigid. The navy assigned black sailors to menial positions, and the army used black soldiers primarily as gravediggers and laborers. But one black combat division was created, and four black regiments fought under French command. France decorated three of these units with its highest citations for valor.

The first American troops landed in France in June 1917. This American Expeditionary Force (AEF) was commanded by General John J. Pershing. Full-scale American intervention did not begin until the late spring of 1918 (see Map 23–2). The influx of American troops in June and July tipped the balance toward Allied victory. By July 18, the German chancellor later acknowledged, "even the most optimistic among us knew that all was lost."

In July, Wilson also agreed to commit fifteen thousand American troops to intervene in Russia. Russia's provisional government had collapsed when the **Bolsheviks**, or Communists, had seized power in November 1917. Under V.I. Lenin, the Bolsheviks had then signed an armistice with Germany in early 1918, which freed German troops for the summer offensive in France. The Allies' interventions were designed to reopen the eastern front and help overthrow the Bolshevik government. Lenin's call for the destruction of capitalism and imperialism alarmed the Allied leaders. One Wilson adviser urged the "eradication" of the Russian government. Soon American and British troops were fighting Russians in an effort to influence Russia's internal affairs. U.S. forces remained in Russia until 1920, but these military interventions failed.

On the western front, the Allies launched their own advance. In late September an American army over 1 million strong attacked German trenches in the Argonne Forest. Some soldiers had been drafted only in July and had spent

HOW DID the war effort threaten civil liberties?

WHERE TO LEARN MORE

W

Fort George G. Meade Museum, Fort Meade, Maryland

22–5
Eugene Kennedy, A "Doughboy" Describes the Fighting Front (1918)

WHERE TO LEARN MORE

W

General John J. Pershing Boyhood Home, Laclede, Missouri
www.mostateparks.com/ pershingsite.htm

Selective Service Act of 1917   The law establishing the military draft for World War I.

Bolshevik   Member of the Communist movement in Russia that established the Soviet government after the 1917 Russian Revolution.

MAP EXPLORATION

To explore an interactive version of this map, go to **http://www.prenhall.com/goldfield2/map23.2**

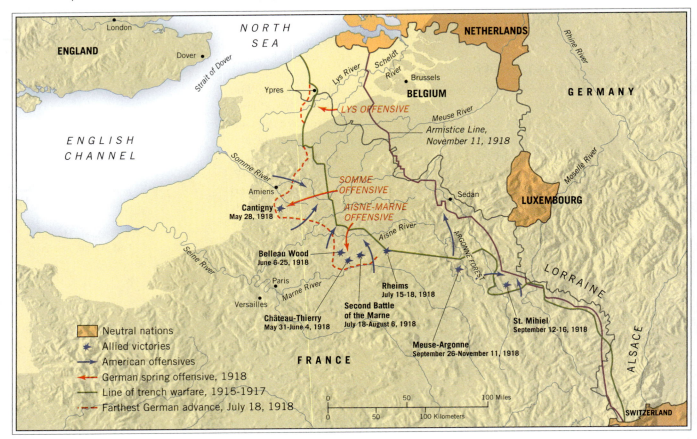

MAP 23–2
The Western Front, 1918 After three years of trench warfare, the arrival of large numbers of American troops in 1918 enabled the Allies to launch an offensive that drove back the Germans and forced an armistice.

AT THE time of the armistice, how far back had the Germans been forced to retreat from their farthest advance?

WHERE TO LEARN MORE

★ Sgt. Alvin C. York Homeplace and State Historic Site, Pall Mall, Tennessee
www.alvinyork.org

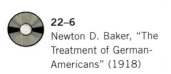

22–6
Newton D. Baker, "The Treatment of German-Americans" (1918)

more time traveling than training. One officer worried, "With their unfamiliarity with weapons, a gun was about as much use as a broom in their hands." Nevertheless, the Americans advanced steadily, despite attacks with poison gas and heavy artillery. Lieutenant Maury Maverick (later a Texas congressman) described the shelling: "We were simply in a big black spot with streaks of screaming red and yellow, with roaring giants in the sky tearing and whirling and roaring." An exploding shell terrified him: "There is a great swishing scream, a smash-bang, and it seems to tear everything loose from you. The intensity of it simply enters your heart and brain, and tears every nerve to pieces."

The battle for the Argonne raged for weeks. One German general reported that his exhausted soldiers faced Americans who "were fresh, eager for fighting, and brave." But he found their sheer numbers most impressive. Despite severe casualties, the AEF helped the British and French defeat the enemy. Soon thereafter, Germany asked for peace. On November 11, 1918, an armistice ended the Great War. More than 115,000 Americans were among the 8 million soldiers and 7 million civilians dead.

THE FOURTEEN POINTS

The armistice was only a step toward final peace. President Wilson had already enunciated American war objectives on January 8, 1918, in a speech outlining what became known as the Fourteen Points. In his 1917 war message, Wilson had advocated a more democratic world system, and this new speech spelled out how to achieve it. But Wilson also had a political purpose. The Bolsheviks had published the secret treaties the Allies had signed dividing up the economic and territorial spoils of war. Lenin called for an immediate peace based on the liberation of all colonies, self-determination for all peoples, and the rejection of annexations and punitive indemnities. Wilson's Fourteen Points reassured the American and Allied peoples that they were fighting for more than imperialist gains and offered an alternative to what he called Lenin's "crude formula" for peace.

Eight of Wilson's points proposed creating new nations, shifting old borders, or assuring self-determination for peoples previously subject to the Austrian, German, or Russian empires. The point about Russia called on all nations to evacuate Russian territory and permit Russia "an unhampered and unembarrassed opportunity for the independent determination of her own political development" under "institutions of her own choosing." Another five points invoked principles to guide international relations: freedom of the seas, open diplomacy instead of secret treaties, reduction of armaments, free trade, and the fair settlement of colonial claims. Wilson's fourteenth and most important point proposed a league of nations to carry out these ideals and ensure international stability.

Wilson and the German government had these principles in mind when negotiating the armistice. The Allies, however, had never explicitly accepted the Fourteen Points. While Wilson favored a settlement that would promote international stability and economic expansion, he recognized that the Allies sought "to get everything out of Germany that they can."

Convinced of the righteousness of his cause, Wilson decided to attend the peace conference in Paris himself. But Wilson weakened his position before he even set sail. First, he urged voters to support Democratic candidates in the November 1918 elections to indicate approval of his peace plans. But the electorate, responding primarily to domestic problems like inflation, gave the Republicans control of both houses of Congress. This meant that a treaty would have to be approved by Senate Republicans angry that Wilson had tried to use war and peace for partisan purposes. Second, Wilson refused to consult with Senate Republicans on plans for the peace conference and failed to name important Republicans to the Paris delegation. It would be Wilson's treaty, but Republicans would feel no responsibility to approve it.

THE PARIS PEACE CONFERENCE

The peace conference opened on January 18, 1919. Meeting at the Palace of Versailles, the delegations were dominated by the principal Allied leaders themselves: Wilson of the United States, David Lloyd George of Britain, Georges Clemenceau of France, and Vittorio Orlando of Italy. The Central Powers and Bolshevik Russia were excluded. Clemenceau remarked, "God gave us the Ten Commandments and we broke them. Mr. Wilson has given us the Fourteen Points. We shall see."

Wilson himself had broken two of the Fourteen Points before the conference began. He had acquiesced in Britain's rejection of freedom of the seas, and he had sent U.S. troops to intervene in Russia in violation of its right to self-determination.

WHERE TO LEARN MORE

Wisconsin Veterans Museum,
Madison, Wisconsin

For months, the conference debated Wilson's other goals and the Allies' demands for compensation and security. Lloyd George later commented, with reference to the self-righteous Wilson and the assertive Clemenceau, "I think I did as well as might be expected, seated as I was between Jesus Christ and Napoleon Bonaparte." Under protest, Germany signed the **Treaty of Versailles** on June 28, 1919. Its terms were far more severe than Wilson had proposed or Germany had anticipated. Germany had to accept sole responsibility for starting the war; to pay huge reparations to the Allies; to give up land to France, Poland, Belgium, and Denmark; to cede its colonies; to limit its army and navy; and to promise not to manufacture or purchase armaments.

Wilson gained some acceptance of self-determination. As the German, Austro-Hungarian, Turkish, and Russian empires had collapsed at the end of the war, nationalist groups had proclaimed their independence. On one hand, the peace settlement formally recognized these new nation-states in Eastern Europe. On the other hand, France, Italy, Romania, and Japan all annexed territory regardless of the wishes of the inhabitants. Germans were placed under Polish control in Silesia and Czech control in Bohemia. Austrians were not allowed to merge with Germany. And the conference sanctioned colonialism by establishing a trusteeship system that enabled France, Britain, and Japan to take over German colonies and Turkish territory.

Moreover, the Allied leaders endorsed the changes in eastern Europe in part because the new states there were anti-Communist. Western leaders soon called these countries the *cordon sanitaire*, a barrier against Bolshevism. Indeed, the Allies at Versailles were preoccupied with Bolshevik Russia, which one of Wilson's aides called the "black cloud of the east, threatening to overwhelm and swallow up the world." The Allies hoped to isolate and weaken Bolshevik Russia. This hostility to Russia, like the punitive terms for Germany and the concessions to imperial interests, boded ill for a stable and just postwar order.

But Wilson hoped that the final section of the Versailles treaty would resolve the flaws of the agreement by establishing his great international organization to preserve peace: the **League of Nations**. The Covenant, or constitution, of the League was built into the treaty. Its crucial feature, Article Ten, bound the member nations to guarantee each other's independence, which was Wilson's concept of collective security. Sailing home, he mused: "Well, it is finished, and, as no one is satisfied, it makes me hope we have made a just peace; but it is all on the lap of the gods."

Treaty of Versailles The treaty ending World War I and creating the League of Nations.

League of Nations International organization created by the Versailles Treaty after World War I to ensure world stability.

WHAT WERE the terms of the Treaty of Versailles?

WAGING PEACE AT HOME

Wilson was determined to defeat opposition to the peace treaty. But many Americans were engaged in their own struggles with the new conditions of a nation suddenly at peace but riven by economic, social, and political conflict shaped by the war experience. Wilson's battle for the League of Nations would fail tragically. The other conflicts would rage until the election of 1920 restored a normalcy of sorts.

BATTLE OVER THE LEAGUE

Most Americans favored the Versailles treaty. A survey of fourteen hundred newspapers found fewer than two hundred opposed. Thirty-three governors and thirty-two state legislatures approved of the League of Nations. But when Wilson called for the Senate to accept "the moral leadership . . . and confidence of the world" by ratifying the treaty, he met resistance. Republican opponents of the treaty raised serious questions. Nearly all Democrats favored the treaty, but they were a minority; some Republicans had to be converted for the treaty to be approved.

Progressive Republican senators, such as Robert La Follette and Hiram Johnson, led one group of opponents. Called the **Irreconcilables**, they opposed participation in the League of Nations, which they saw as designed to perpetuate the power of imperialist countries. Article Ten, they feared, would require the United States to help suppress rebellions in Ireland against British rule or to enforce disputed European borders. Most of the Irreconcilables gave priority to restoring civil liberties and progressive reform at home.

A larger group of opponents, the **Reservationists**, were led by Senator Henry Cabot Lodge, the chair of the Senate Foreign Relations Committee. They regarded Article Ten as eroding congressional authority to declare war. They also fretted that the League might interfere with domestic questions, such as immigration laws. Lodge held public hearings on the treaty to rouse and focus opposition. German Americans resented the war guilt clause; Italian and Polish Americans complained that the treaty did not satisfy the territorial ambitions of Italy and Poland; Irish Americans condemned the treaty's failure to give self-determination to Ireland. Many progressives also criticized the treaty's compromises on self-determination, reparations, and colonies.

When Lodge proposed reservations or amendments to the treaty, Wilson opened "a direct frontal attack" on his opponents. If they wanted war, he declared, he would "give them a belly full." In early September 1919, Wilson set out across the country to win popular support for the League. In three weeks, he traveled 8,000 miles and delivered thirty-seven speeches. He collapsed in Pueblo, Colorado. Confused and in tears, Wilson mumbled, "I seem to have gone to pieces." Taken back to Washington, Wilson on October 2 suffered a massive stroke that paralyzed his left side and left him psychologically unstable and temporarily blind. Wilson's physician and his wife, Edith Galt Wilson, kept the nature of his illness secret from the public, Congress, and even the vice president and cabinet. The administration was immobilized.

By February 1920, Wilson had partially recovered, but he remained suspicious and quarrelsome. He still refused to compromise to win Senate approval of the treaty. On March 19, 1920, the Senate killed the treaty.

ECONOMIC READJUSTMENT AND SOCIAL CONFLICT

The League was not the only casualty of the struggle to conclude the war. Grave problems shook the United States in 1919 and early 1920. An influenza epidemic had erupted in Europe in 1918 among the massed armies. It now hit the United States, killing perhaps 700,000 Americans, far more than had died in combat.

Meanwhile, the Wilson administration had no plans for an orderly reconversion of the wartime economy. The secretary of the Council of National Defense later reported, "the mobilization that had taken many months was succeeded by an instantaneous demobilization." The government canceled war contracts and dissolved the regulatory agencies. Noting that "the war spirit of cooperation and sacrifice" had disappeared with the Armistice, Bernard Baruch decided to "turn industry absolutely free" and abolished the War Industries Board as of January 1, 1919. Other agencies followed in such haste that turmoil engulfed the economy.

The army discharged 600,000 soldiers still in training camps; the navy brought AEF soldiers home from France. With no planning or assistance, troops were hustled

Irreconcilables   Group of U.S. senators adamantly opposed to ratification of the Treaty of Versailles after World War I.

Reservationists   Group of U.S. senators favoring approval of the Treaty of Versailles, after amending it to incorporate their reservations.

A policeman on horseback swings a truncheon at strikers on a Pittsburgh street.

Corbis/Bettman

back into civilian life. There they competed for scarce jobs with workers recently discharged from the war industries.

As unemployment mounted, the removal of wartime price controls brought runaway inflation. The cost of food, clothing, and other necessities more than doubled over prewar rates. The return of the soldiers caused a serious housing shortage, and rents skyrocketed. Farmers also suffered from economic readjustments. Net farm income declined by 65 percent between 1919 and 1921. Farmers who had borrowed money for machinery and land to expand production for the war effort were left impoverished and embittered.

Women also lost their wartime economic advances. Returning soldiers took away their jobs. Male trade unionists insisted that women go back to being housewives. One New York union maintained that "the same patriotism which induced women to enter industry during the war should induce them to vacate their positions after the war." At times, male workers struck to force employers to fire women. "During the war they called us heroines," one woman complained, "but they throw us on the scrapheap now." By 1920, women constituted a smaller proportion of the work force than they had in 1910.

The postwar adjustments also left African Americans disappointed. During the war, they had agreed with W. E. B. Du Bois to "forget our special grievances and close our ranks shoulder to shoulder with our own white fellow citizens." They had contributed to the fighting and home fronts. Now, housing shortages and job competition interacted with racism in 1919 to produce race riots in twenty-six towns and cities, resulting in at least 120 deaths. In Chicago, thirty-eight people were killed and more than five hundred injured in a five-day riot that began when white thugs stoned to death a black youth swimming too near "their" beach. White rioters then fired a machine gun from a truck hurtling through black neighborhoods. But black residents fought back, no longer willing, the *Chicago Defender* reported, "to move along the line of least resistance as did their sires." Racial conflict was part of a postwar battle between Americans hoping to preserve the new social relations fostered by the war effort and those wanting to restore prewar patterns of power and control.

Even more pervasive discontents roiled as America adjusted to the postwar world. More than 4 million angry workers launched a wave of 3,600 strikes in 1919. They were reacting not only to the soaring cost of living, which undermined the value of their wages, but also to employers' efforts to reassert their authority and destroy the legitimacy labor had won by its participation in the war effort. The abolition of government controls on industry enabled employers not only to raise prices but also to rescind their recognition of unions and reimpose objectionable working conditions. In response, strikers demanded higher wages, better conditions, and recognition of unions and the right of collective bargaining.

The greatest strike involved the American Federation of Labor's attempt to organize steelworkers, who endured dangerous conditions and twelve-hour shifts. When the steel companies refused to recognize the union or even discuss issues, 365,000 workers went out on strike in September 1919. Strikers in Pennsylvania pointed out that they had worked "cheerfully, without strikes or trouble of any kind" during the war to "make the world safe for democracy" and that they now sought "industrial democracy." Employers hired thugs to beat the strikers, used strikebreakers to take their jobs, and exploited ethnic and racial divisions among them. Management also portrayed the strikers as disruptive radicals influenced by Bolshevism. After four months, the strike failed.

Employers used the same tactic to defeat striking coal miners. Coal operators claimed that Russian Bolsheviks financed the strike to destroy the American economy. Attorney General Mitchell Palmer secured an injunction against the strike under the authority of wartime legislation. Since the government no longer controlled coal prices or enforced protective labor rules, miners complained bitterly that the war had ended for corporations but not for workers.

Two municipal strikes in 1919 also alarmed the public when their opponents depicted them as revolutionary attacks on the social order. In Seattle in February, the Central Labor Council called a general strike to support 35,000 shipyard workers striking for higher wages and shorter hours. When 60,000 more workers from 110 local unions also walked out, the city ground to a halt. Seattle's mayor, business leaders, and newspapers attacked the strikers as Bolsheviks and anarchists. Threatened with military intervention, the labor council called off the strike. In Boston, the police commissioner fired police officers for trying to organize a union to improve their inadequate pay. In response, the police went on strike. As in Seattle, Boston newspapers, politicians, and business leaders attributed the strike to Bolshevism. Governor Calvin Coolidge mobilized the National Guard and gained nationwide acclaim when he stated, "There is no right to strike against the public safety by anybody, anywhere, anytime." The police were all fired; many of their replacements were war veterans.

RED SCARE

The strikes contributed to an anti-Bolshevik hysteria that swept the country in 1919. This **Red Scare** reflected fears that the Bolshevik revolution in Russia might spread to the United States. Steeped in the antiradical propaganda of the war years, many Americans were appalled by Russian Bolshevism, described by the *Saturday Evening Post* as a "compound of slaughter, confiscation, anarchy, and universal disorder." Their alarm grew in 1919 when Russia established the Third International to foster revolution abroad, and a few American socialists formed the American Communist Party. But the Red Scare also reflected the willingness of antiunion employers, ambitious politicians, sensational journalists, zealous veterans, and racists to exploit the panic to advance their own purposes.

The Red Scare reached panic levels by mid-1919. Bombs mailed anonymously to several prominent people on May Day seemed proof enough that a Bolshevik conspiracy threatened America. The Justice Department, Congress, and patriotic organizations like the American Legion joined with business groups to suppress radicalism, real and imagined. The government continued to enforce the repressive laws against Wobblies, socialists, and other dissenters. Indeed, Wilson and Attorney General Palmer called for more stringent laws. State governments harassed and arrested hundreds.

Palmer created a new agency, headed by J. Edgar Hoover, to suppress radicals and impose conformity. Its war on radicalism became the chief focus of the

QUICK REVIEW

Labor Unrest
- Efforts to roll back war-time gains upset workers.
- 4 million workers launched 3,600 strikes in 1919.
- The largest strike involved efforts to organize steelworkers.

Red Scare Post-World War I public hysteria over Bolshevik influence in the United States directed against labor activism, radical dissenters, and some ethnic groups.

Justice Department. Hoover collected files on labor leaders and other "radical agitators" from Senator La Follette to Jane Addams, issued misleading reports on Communist influence in labor strikes and race riots, and contacted all major newspapers "to acquaint people like you with the real menace of evil-thinking, which is the foundation of the Red Movement." Indeed, the Justice Department itself promoted the Red Scare hysteria, which Palmer hoped would lead to his presidential nomination and Hoover hoped would enhance his own power and that of his bureau.

In November 1919, Palmer and Hoover began raiding groups suspected of subversion. A month later, they deported 249 alien radicals, including the anarchist Emma Goldman, to Russia. Rabid patriots endorsed such actions. One minister favored deporting radicals "in ships of stone with sails of lead, with the wrath of God for a breeze and with hell for their first port." In January 1920, Palmer and Hoover rounded up more than four thousand suspected radicals in thirty-three cities. Without warrants, they broke into union halls, club rooms, and private homes, assaulting and arresting everyone in sight. People were jailed without access to lawyers; some were beaten into signing false confessions. In Lynn, Massachusetts, thirty-nine people meeting to organize a bakery were arrested for holding a revolutionary caucus. The *Washington Post* clamored, "There is no time to waste on hairsplitting over infringement of liberty."

Other Americans began to recoil from the excesses and illegal acts. Assistant Secretary of Labor Louis Post stopped further deportations by demonstrating that most of the arrested were "working men of good character, who are not anarchists or revolutionists, nor politically or otherwise dangerous in any sense." When Palmer's predictions of a violent attempt to overthrow the government on May 1, 1920, came to naught, most Americans agreed with the *Rocky Mountain News*: "We can never get to work if we keep jumping sideways in fear of the bewhiskered Bolshevik." Even one conservative Republican concluded that "too much has been said about Bolshevism in America." But if the Red Scare faded in mid-1920, the hostility to immigrants, organized labor, and dissent it reflected endured.

THE ELECTION OF 1920

The Democratic coalition that Wilson had cobbled together on the issues of progressivism and peace came apart after the war. Workers resented the administration's hostility to the postwar strikes. Ethnic groups brutalized by the Americanization of the war years blamed Wilson for the war or condemned his peace settlement. Farmers grumbled about wartime price controls and postwar falling prices. Wartime taxes and the social and economic turmoil of 1919–1920 alienated the middle class. In the words of Kansas journalist William Allen White, Americans were "tired of issues, sick at heart of ideals, and weary of being noble." They yearned for what Republican presidential candidate Warren Harding of Ohio called "normalcy."

The Republican ticket in 1920 symbolized the reassurance of simpler times. Harding was a genial, Old Guard conservative. His running mate, Calvin Coolidge, governor of Massachusetts, owed his nomination to his handling of the Boston police strike.

Wilson called the election of 1920 "a great and solemn referendum" on the League of Nations, but the League was not a decisive issue in the campaign.

Harding defeated Democratic nominee James Cox, former governor of Ohio, in a landslide. "The Democrats are inconceivably unpopular," wrote Walter Lippmann, a prominent journalist. Harding received 16 million popular votes to Cox's 9 million. Running for president from his prison cell, Socialist Eugene Debs polled nearly a million votes. Not even his closest backers considered Harding qualified for the White House, but as Lippmann said, the nation's "public spirit was exhausted" after the war years. The election of 1920 was "the final twitch" of America's "war mind."

CONCLUSION

The Great War disrupted the United States and much of the rest of the world. The initial American policy of neutrality yielded to sentimental and substantive links with the Allies and the pressure of German submarine warfare. Despite popular opposition. America joined the conflict when its leaders concluded that national interests demanded it. Using both military and diplomatic power, Woodrow Wilson sought to secure a more stable and prosperous world order, with an expanded role for the United States. But the Treaty of Versailles only partly fulfilled his hopes, and the Senate refused to ratify the treaty and its League of Nations. The postwar world order would be unstable and dangerous.

Participation in the war, moreover, had changed the American government, economy, and society. Some of these changes, including the centralization of the economy and an expansion of the regulatory role of the federal government, were already under way; some offered opportunities to implement progressive principles or reforms. Woman suffrage and prohibition gained decisive support because of the war spirit. But other consequences of the war betrayed both progressive impulses and the democratic principles the war was allegedly fought to promote. The suppression of civil liberties, manipulation of human emotions, repression of radicals and minorities, and exploitation of national crises by narrow interests helped disillusion the public. The repercussions of the Great War would linger for years, at home and abroad.

WHAT WAS the postwar backlash?

SUMMARY

Waging Neutrality Few Americans were prepared for the Great War that erupted in Europe in 1914; fewer still envisioned the United States becoming involved in the war. The Central Powers and the Allies were involved in mass slaughter and stalemate in Europe; America had no vital interest in the war, but it did not stay strictly neutral. The economy of America became closely tied with Britain and the Allies, the President sympathized with the Allied cause, and German submarine warfare tied the United States to the British war effort. The desire for peace determined the results of the 1916 election; in 1917 America entered the war as Germany decided to resume unrestricted submarine warfare and the contents of the Zimmermann Note, linking Germany to Mexico's recovering the Southwest, were exposed.

Waging War in America In addition to mobilizing for military invention, the government reorganized the economy to emphasize centralized management and developed policies to control public opinion and suppress dissent. In response to labor shortages women and minorities entered the work force, obtaining jobs which had previously been closed to them; individual citizens planted victory gardens and bought Liberty Bonds to help the war effort. Government propaganda to rally Americans painted the enemy as subhuman; dissent was viewed as unpatriotic; Americans were encouraged to spy on one another; basic civil rights were violated.

Waging War and Peace Abroad The American involvement in the Great War turned the tide and ensured Allied victory. Having stopped the German advance on the Western Front, the Allies, with fresh American troops, began a counteroffensive that ended the war with an armistice on November 11, 1918. President Wilson envisioned the postwar world based on the Fourteen Points and attended the Paris Peace Conference convinced of the righteousness of his peace plans. The Allied leaders were more interested in revenge and retribution than righteousness. The Treaty of Versailles imposed harsh restrictions on Germany; the specter of Bolshevism hung over the peace conference; fear of communism impacted decisions made by the delegates.

Waging Peace at Home While most Americans favored the Versailles treaty, the senators who had to vote on the treaty were largely opposed to it. The Irreconcilables opposed participation in the League of Nations, and the Reservationists feared the power of the League and the erosion of Congressional authority. The Treaty of Versailles was never approved by the United States. The vote in the Senate was not the only war casualty: An influenza epidemic, the reconversion to a peacetime economy, housing shortages, unemployment, labor unrest, and the Red Scare wearied Americans. By 1920, Americans wanted a return to "normalcy" and elected Warren Harding as president in a landslide victory.

REVIEW QUESTIONS

1. What were the major arguments for and against U.S. entry into the Great War?

2. How and why did the United States shape public opinion in World War I?

3. How did groups exploit the war crisis and the government's propaganda and repression?

4. What were the arguments for and against American ratification of the Treaty of Versailles?

KEY TERMS

Allies (p. 606)
Bolshevik (p. 617)
Central Powers (p. 606)
Committee on Public Information (CPI) (p. 614)
Declaration of London (p. 607)
Espionage Act (p. 614)

Irreconcilables (p. 621)
League of Nations (p. 620)
Liberty Bonds (p. 613)
Preparedness (p. 609)
Red Scare (p. 623)
Reservationists (p. 621)
Sedition Act (p. 614)

Selective Service Act of 1917 (p. 617)
Self-determination (p. 610)
Sussex **Pledge** (p. 609)
Treaty of Versailles (p. 620)
War Industries Board (WIB) (p. 611)

WHERE TO LEARN MORE

 National Infantry Museum, Fort Benning, Georgia. This sprawling collection of weapons, uniforms, and equipment includes exhibits on World War I. **www.benningmwr. com/index.cfm**

Fort George G. Meade Museum, Fort Meade, Maryland. This museum contains unparalleled exhibits depicting U.S. military life during World War I, including artifacts, photographs, and French and American tanks designed for trench warfare.

General John J. Pershing Boyhood Home, Laclede, Missouri. Maintained by the Missouri State Park Board, Pershing's restored nineteenth-century home exhibits some of his personal belongings and papers. **www.mostateparks.com/pershingsite.htm**

Sgt. Alvin C. York Homeplace and State Historic Site, Pall Mall, Tennessee. The home of America's greatest military hero of World War I contains fascinating artifacts, including York's letters written in the trenches. **www.alvincyork.org**

Wisconsin Veterans Museum, Madison, Wisconsin. The most stunning museum of its size in the United States, this large building combines impressive collections of artifacts ranging from uniforms to tanks, with substantive exhibits and video programs based on remarkable historical research. It both documents and explains the participation of Wisconsin soldiers in the nation's wars, including the Spanish-American War and World War I.

For additional study resources for this chapter, go to: **www.prenhall.com/goldfield/chapter23**

Happy times were here again.

Toward a Modern America: The 1920's. "More than a car. FORD.
A National Institution" poster, 1923.

24

TOWARD A MODERN AMERICA
THE 1920s

WHY WERE the 1920s referred to as the "Roaring Twenties?"

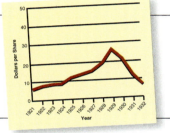

HOW DID big business shape the economy of the 1920s?

WHAT WAS the Great Migration, and how did it affect social life in the 1920s?

HOW DID new systems of distributing, marketing, and communication create culture?

WHAT CONFLICTS divided social groups in the 1920s?

WHAT WERE the reasons for U.S. involvement overseas in the 1920s?

Happy times were here again. American industry, adopting Henry Ford's policy of mass production and low prices, was making it possible for everybody to have his share of everything. The newspapers, the statesmen, the economists, all agreed that American ingenuity had solved the age-old problem of poverty. There could never be another depression. . . .

The war had done something to Henry, it had taught him a new way to deal with his fellow men. . . . He became more abrupt in his manner, more harsh in his speech. "Gratitude?" he would say. "There's no gratitude in business. Men work for money." . . . From now on he was a business man, and held a tight rein on everything. This industry was his, he had made it himself, and what he wanted of the men he hired was that they should do exactly as he told them. . . .

Every worker had to be strained to the uttermost limit, every one had to be giving the last ounce of energy he had in his carcass. . . . They were tired when they started in the morning, and when they quit they were grey and staggering with fatigue, they were empty shells out of which the last drop of juice had been squeezed. . . .

Henry Ford was now getting close to his two million cars a year goal. . . . From the moment the ore was taken out of the ship at the River Rouge plant [in Detroit], through all the processes turning it into steel and shaping it into automobile parts with a hundred-ton press, and putting five thousand parts together into a car which rolled off the assembly line under its own power—all those processes were completed in less than a day and a half!

Some forty-five thousand different machines were now used in the making of Ford cars, in sixty establishments scattered over the United States. . . . Henry Ford was remaking the roads of America, and in the end he would remake the roads of the world—and line them all with filling stations and hot-dog stands of the American pattern.

Upton Sinclair, *The Flivver King: A Story of Ford–America.* (Chicago: Charles H. Kerr Publishing Company, 1999).

IMAGE KEY

for pages 628–629

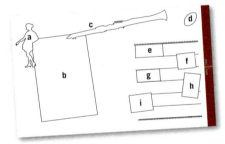

a. Silent film star Gertrude Olmstead wears a ruffled flapper dress with a striped hat in 1925.

b. Toward A Modern America: The 1920's More than a car. FORD. A National Institution "poster", 1923.

c. A clarinet.

d. An old football.

e. Men are shown piecing together automobiles on an assembly line in the Rouge Plant of the Ford Motor Company.

f. The price of stocks through the 1920s and early 30s.

g. A Black family from the south arrives in Chicago, ca. 1910.

h. Campbell's Tomato Soup ad.

i. Women dressed in the white robes and hoods of the Ku Klux Klan in 1924.

UPTON SINCLAIR'S 1906 novel *The Jungle* graphically depicted the wretched conditions endured by Chicago's immigrant meatpacking workers. In *The Flivver King*, Sinclair portrayed the rise of the automobile industry and the revolutionizing vision of Henry Ford—the entrepreneur who symbolized modern America to the world.

"Machinery," proclaimed Henry Ford, "is the new Messiah." Ford had introduced the moving assembly line at his automobile factory on the eve of World War I, and, by 1925, it was turning out a Model T car every ten seconds. Mass production was becoming a reality; in fact, the term originated in Henry Ford's 1926 description of the system of flow production techniques popularly called "Fordism." The system symbolized the nation's booming economy: In the 1920s, Europeans used the word Fordize as a synonym for Americanize. Ford coupled machines and technology with managerial innovations. He established the "five-dollar day," twice the prevailing wage in Detroit's auto industry, and slashed the workweek from forty-eight to forty

CHRONOLOGY

1915	Ku Klux Klan is founded anew.
1919	Volstead Act is passed.
1920	Urban population exceeds rural population for the first time. Warren Harding is elected president. Prohibition takes effect. First commercial radio show is broadcast. Sinclair Lewis publishes *Main Street*.
1921	Sheppard-Towner Maternity and Infancy Act is passed. Washington Naval Conference limits naval armaments.
1922	Fordney-McCumber Act raises tariff rates. Sinclair Lewis publishes *Babbitt*.

	Country Club Plaza in Kansas City opens.
1923	Harding dies; Calvin Coolidge becomes president.
1924	National Origins Act sharply curtails immigration. Coolidge is elected president.
1925	Scopes trial is held in Dayton, Tennessee. F. Scott Fitzgerald publishes *The Great Gatsby*
1927	Charles A. Lindbergh flies solo across the Atlantic.
1928	Kellogg-Briand Pact is signed. Herbert Hoover is elected president.
1929	Ernest Hemingway publishes *A Farewell to Arms*.

hours. These changes, Ford argued, would reduce the costs of labor turnover and boost consumer purchasing power, leading to further profits from mass production.

The assembly line, however, alienated workers, and even Ford himself conceded that the repetitive operations of the assembly line were "so monotonous that it scarcely seems possible that any man would care to continue long at the same job." Ford first tried to adapt his mostly immigrant workers to these conditions through an Americanization program. His "Education Department" taught classes in English, sobriety, obedience, and industrial efficiency to the unskilled laborers entering the factory. After the course, they participated in a symbolic pageant: They climbed into a huge "melting pot," fifteen feet across and seven feet deep. After Ford managers stirred the pot with ten-foot ladles, the workers emerged wearing new clothes and waving American flags—new Americans made for the factory system.

When the labor market became more favorable to management in the early 1920s, Ford relied on discipline to control workers. To maximize profits and increase efficiency, he prohibited talking, whistling, sitting, or smoking on the job. Ford also banned unions and used spies to guard against their formation.

But Ford remained conflicted about the changes he saw and had helped facilitate. Cars and cigarettes were among the most intensively advertised goods in the 1920s, and for some they signaled rebellion and freedom. Women in short skirts and the rise of the Jazz Age—all contributed to what Ford saw as the evils of the "new America." Embracing nativism and protestantism, Ford, an ardent anti-Semite, blamed Jewish Americans for radicalism and labor organization and singled out the "International Jew" for allegedly controlling the financial community.

Henry Ford—and Fordism itself—thus reflected the complexity of the 1920s. Economic growth and technological innovation were paired with social conflict as traditions were destroyed, values displaced, and new people incorporated into a society increasingly industrialized, urbanized, and dominated by big business. Industrial production and national wealth soared, buoyed by new techniques and markets for consumer goods. Business values pervaded society and dominated government, which promoted business interests.

But not all Americans prospered. Many workers were unemployed, and the wages of still more were stagnant or falling. Farmers endured grim conditions and worse prospects. Social change brought pleasure to some and deep concern to others. City factories like the Ford Works attracted workers from the countryside, increasing urbanization; rapid suburbanization opened other horizons. Leisure activities flourished, and new mass media promoted modern ideas and stylish products. Workers would have to achieve personal satisfaction through consumption—and not production. But such experiences often proved unsettling, and some Americans sought reassurance by imposing their cultural or religious values on everyone around them. The tumultuous decade thus had many unresolved issues, much like the complex personality of Henry Ford himself. And Ford so dominated the age that when college students were asked to rank the greatest people of all time, Ford came in third—behind Christ and Napoleon.

The Economy that Roared

Following a severe postwar depression in 1920 and 1921, the American economy boomed through the remainder of the decade. Gross domestic product soared nearly 40 percent; output per worker-hour, or productivity, rose 72 percent in manufacturing; average per capita income increased by a third. Although the prosperity was not evenly distributed and some sectors of the economy were deeply troubled, most Americans welcomed the industrial expansion and business principles of the "New Era." (See American views, "The Cult of Business.")

WHY WERE the 1920s
referred to as the "roaring twenties"?

Boom Industries

Many factors spurred the economic expansion of the 1920s. The huge wartime and postwar profits provided investment capital that enabled business to mechanize. Mass production spread quickly in American industry; machine-made standardized parts and the moving assembly line increased efficiency and production. Businesses steadily adopted the scientific management principles of Frederick W. Taylor. These highly touted systems, though often involving little more than an assembly-line "speed-up," also boosted efficiency. In factories, electric motors cut costs and improved manufacturing; in homes, electricity spurred demand for new products. Henry Ford was right: Mass production and consumption went hand in hand. Although not one in ten farm families had access to electric power, most other families did by 1929, and many bought electric sewing machines, vacuum cleaners, washing machines, and other labor-saving appliances.

The automobile industry drove the economy. Sales rose from about 1.9 million vehicles in 1920 to nearly 5 million by 1929. The automobile industry also employed one of every fourteen manufacturing workers and stimulated other industries from steel to rubber and glass. It created a huge new market for the petroleum industry and fostered oil drilling in Oklahoma, Texas, and Louisiana. It also encouraged the construction industry, a mainstay of the 1920s economy.

New industries also sprang up. The aviation industry grew rapidly, with government support. The U.S. Post Office subsidized commercial air service by providing air mail contracts to private carriers. Congress then authorized commercial passenger service over the mail routes, with regular traffic opening in 1927 between Boston and New York. By 1930, more than one hundred airlines criss-crossed America.

The Great War had stimulated the chemicals industry. The government confiscated chemical patents from German firms and transferred them to U.S. companies like Du Pont. With this advantage, Du Pont in the 1920s became a

WHERE TO LEARN MORE

Henry Ford Museum
and Greenfield Village,
Dearborn, Michigan
www.hfmgv.org

• AMERICAN VIEWS •

THE CULT OF BUSINESS

uring the 1920s, publicists and politicians joined manufacturers and merchants in proclaiming that business promoted not only material but also social and even spiritual well-being. In The Man Nobody Knows *(1924), advertising executive Bruce Barton portrayed Jesus Christ as the founder of modern business. The following excerpt from an article by Edward E. Purinton, a popular lecturer on business values and efficiency, makes even more extensive claims for business.*

HOW ACCURATE are Purinton's claims of great opportunity in the corporate world of the 1920s? Of occupational mobility in the factory economy? What does this view of business imply about the role of government? How might Protestant fundamentalists have viewed the cult of business?

Among the nations of the earth today America stands for one idea: Business. National opprobrium? National opportunity. For in this fact lies, potentially, the salvation of the world.

Through business, properly conceived, managed, and conducted, the human race is finally to be redeemed. How and why a man works foretells what he will do, think, have, give, and be. And real salvation is in doing, thinking, having, giving, and being—not in sermonizing and theorizing. . . .

What is the finest game? Business. The soundest science? Business. The truest art? Business. The fullest education? Business. The fairest opportunity? Business. The cleanest philanthropy? Business. The sanest religion? Business.

You may not agree. That is because you judge business by the crude, mean, stupid, false imitation of business that happens to be located near you.

The finest game is business. The rewards are for everybody, and all can win. There are no favorites—Providence always crowns the career of the man who is worthy. And in this game there is no "luck"—you have the fun of taking chances but the sobriety of guaranteeing certainties. The speed and size of your winnings are for you alone to determine. . . .

The soundest science is business. All investigation is reduced to action, and by action proved or disproved. The idealistic motive animates the materialistic method. . . . Capital is furnished for the researches of "pure science"; yet pure science is not regarded pure until practical. Competent scientists are suitably rewarded—as they are not in the scientific schools. . . .

The fullest education is business. A proper blend of study, work and life is essential to advancement. The whole man is educated. Human nature itself is the open book that all business men study; and the mastery of a page of this educates you more than the memorizing of a dusty tome from a library shelf. In the school of business, moreover, you teach yourself and learn most from your own mistakes. What you learn here you live out, the only real test.

The fairest opportunity is business. You can find more, better, quicker chances to get ahead in a large business house than anywhere else on earth. . . . Recognition of better work, of keener and quicker thought, of deeper and finer feeling, is gladly offered by the men higher up, with early promotion the rule for the man who justifies it. There is, and can be, no such thing as buried talent in a modern business organization. . . .

The sanest religion is business. Any relationship that forces a man to follow the Golden Rule rightfully belongs amid the ceremonials of the church. A great business enterprise includes and presupposes this relationship. I have seen more Christianity to the square inch as a regular part of the office equipment of famous corporation presidents than may ordinarily be found on Sunday in a verbalized but not vitalized church congregation. . . . You can fool your preacher with a sickly sprout or a wormy semblance of character, but you can't fool your employer. I would make every business house a consultation bureau for the guidance of the church whose members were employees of the house. . . .

The future work of the businessman is to teach the teacher, preach to the preacher, admonish the parent, advise the doctor, justify the lawyer, superintend the statesman, fructify the farmer, stabilize the banker, harness the dreamer, and reform the reformer.

Source: Edward E. Purinton, "Big Ideas from Big Business," *Independent,* April 16, 1921. National Weekly Corp., New York.

chemical empire producing plastics, finishes, dyes, and organic chemicals, which it developed into enamels, rayon, and cellophane.

The new radio and motion picture industries also flourished. Commercial broadcasting began in 1920. By 1927, there were 732 stations, and Congress created what became the Federal Communications Commission (FCC) to prevent wave band interference. Corporations dominated the new industry. Westinghouse, RCA, and General Electric began opening strings of stations in the early 1920s.

The motion picture industry became one of the nation's five largest businesses. Twenty thousand movie theaters sold 100 million tickets a week. Hollywood studios were huge factories, producing films on an assembly-line basis. While Americans watched Charlie Chaplin showcase his comedic genius in films like *The Gold Rush* (1925), corporations like Paramount were integrating production with distribution and exhibition to maximize control and profit and eliminate independent producers and theaters.

CORPORATE CONSOLIDATION

A wave of corporate mergers swept over the 1920s economy. Great corporations swallowed up thousands of small firms. Particularly significant was the spread of oligopoly—the control of an entire industry by a few giant firms. Three companies—Ford, General Motors, and Chrysler—produced 83 percent of the nation's cars. In the electric light and power industry, nearly four thousand local utility companies were merged into a dozen holding companies. By 1929, the nation's two hundred largest corporations controlled nearly half of all nonbanking corporate wealth.

Oligopolies also dominated finance and marketing. By 1929, a mere 1 percent of the nation's banks controlled half of its banking resources. In marketing, national chain stores like A&P and Woolworth's displaced local retailers.

The corporate consolidation of the 1920s provoked little public opposition. Americans mostly accepted that size brought efficiency and productivity.

OPEN SHOPS AND WELFARE CAPITALISM

Business also attacked labor. In 1921, the National Association of Manufacturers organized an **open shop** campaign to break union shop contracts, which required all employees to be union members. Denouncing collective bargaining as un-American, businesses described the open shop, in which union membership was not required and usually prohibited, as the "American plan." They forced workers to sign so-called **yellow dog contracts** that bound them to reject unions to keep their jobs. Business also used boycotts to force employers into a uniform antiunion front. Bethlehem Steel, for example, refused to sell steel to companies employing union labor. Where unions existed, corporations tried to crush them, using spies or hiring strikebreakers.

Some companies advocated a paternalistic system called **welfare capitalism** as an alternative to unions. Eastman Kodak, General Motors, U.S. Steel, and other firms provided medical services, insurance pensions and vacations for their workers to persuade workers to rely on the corporation. Welfare capitalism, however, covered scarcely 5 percent of the work force and often benefited only skilled workers who were already tied to the company through seniority. Moreover, it was directed primarily at men.

Corporations in the 1920s also promoted company unions, management-sponsored substitutes for labor unions. Company unions were usually forbidden to handle wage and hour issues. Their function was to implement company policies and undermine real unionism.

Open shop Factory or business employing workers whether or not they are union members; in practice, such a business usually refuses to hire union members and follows antiunion policies.

Yellow-dog contracts Employment agreements binding workers not to join a union.

Welfare capitalism A paternalistic system of labor relations emphasizing management responsibility for employee well-being.

Partly because of these pressures, membership in labor unions fell from 5.1 million in 1920 to 3.6 million in 1929. But unions also contributed to their own decline. Conservative union leaders neglected ethnic and black workers in mass production industries. Nor did they try to organize women, nearly one-fourth of all workers by 1930. The growing numbers of white-collar workers regarded themselves as middleclass and beyond the scope of union action.

With increasing mechanization and weak labor unions, workers suffered from job insecurity and stagnant wages. Real wages (purchasing power) did improve, but most of the improvement came before 1923 and reflected falling prices more than rising wages. After 1923, American wages stabilized. The failure to raise wages when productivity was increasing threatened the nation's long-term prosperity. In short, rising national income largely reflected salaries and dividends, not wages.

Overall, the gap between rich and poor widened during the decade. By 1929, 71 percent of American families earned less than what the U.S. Bureau of Labor Statistics regarded as necessary for a decent living standard. The maldistribution of income meant that eventually Americans would be unable to purchase the products they made.

The expansion of consumer credit, rare before the 1920s, offered temporary relief by permitting consumers to buy goods over time. General Motors introduced consumer credit on a national basis to create a mass market for expensive automobiles. By 1927, two-thirds of automobiles were purchased on the installment plan. However, installment loans simply added interest charges to the price of products.

22–9
Warren G. Harding, Campaign Speech at Boston (1920)

SICK INDUSTRIES

Several "sick" industries dragged on the economy. Coal mining, textile and garment manufacturing, and railroads suffered from excess capacity (too many mines, factories and lines), shrinking demand, low returns, and management-labor conflicts. Unemployment in the coal industry approached 30 percent; by 1928, a reporter found "thousands of women and children literally starving to death" in Appalachia and the remaining miners held in "industrial slavery." The textile industry coped with overcapacity and declining demand by shifting operations from New England to the cheap-labor South, employing girls and young women for fifty-six-hour weeks at 18 cents an hour. Nevertheless, textile companies remained barely profitable.

American agriculture never recovered from the 1921 depression. Agricultural surpluses and shrinking demand forced down prices. After the war, foreign markets dried up, and demand for cotton slackened. Moreover, farmers' wartime expansion left them heavily mortgaged. Many small farmers lost their land and became tenants or farm hands. By the end of the 1920s, the average per capita income for people on the nation's farms was only one-fourth that of Americans off the farm.

THE BUSINESS OF GOVERNMENT

The Republican surge in national politics also shaped the economy. In the 1920 election, the Republican slogan was "Less government in business, more business in government." Under such direction, the federal government advanced business interests at the expense of other objectives.

REPUBLICAN ASCENDANCY

Republicans in 1920 had retained control of Congress and put Warren Harding in the White House. Harding was neither capable nor bright, but he had a genial touch that contrasted favorably with Wilson. He pardoned Eugene Debs, whom

HOW DID the big business shape the economy of the 1920s?

WHERE TO LEARN MORE

★ Warren G. Harding House,
Marion, Ohio
www.ohiohistory.org/places/harding

WHERE TO LEARN MORE

★ George Norris Home,
McCook, Nebraska
**www.nebraskahistory.org/sites/
norris/index.htm**

QUICK REVIEW

The Teapot Dome Scandal

◆ Corruption and scandals plagued the Harding administration.

◆ Albert Hall, the secretary of the interior, leased petroleum reserves in exchange for cash and cattle.

◆ As a result of his part in the Teapot Dome scandal, Fall went to prison.

Wilson had refused to release from prison, and he spoke out against racial violence. He also helped shape the modern presidency by supporting the Budget and Accounting Act of 1921, which gave the president authority over the budget and created the Budget Bureau and the General Accounting Office. Two of his cabinet appointees, Secretary of Commerce Herbert Hoover and Secretary of the Treasury Andrew Mellon, shaped economic policy throughout the 1920s.

Hoover made the Commerce Department the government's most dynamic office. He cemented its ties with the leading sectors of the economy, expanded its collection and distribution of industrial information, pushed to exploit foreign resources and markets, and encouraged innovation. Hoover's goal was to expand prosperity by making business efficient, responsive, and profitable. Andrew Mellon had a narrower goal. A wealthy banker and industrialist, he pressed Congress to reduce taxes on businesses and the rich. Despite the opposition of progressives, Mellon lowered maximum tax rates and eliminated wartime excess-profits taxes in 1921.

The Harding administration promoted business interests in other ways, too. The tariff of 1922 raised import rates to protect industry from foreign competition. Attorney General Harry Daugherty aided the business campaign for the open shop. And the Republicans also curtailed government regulation. By appointing advocates of big business to the Federal Trade Commission, the Federal Reserve Board, and other regulatory agencies established earlier by the progressives, Harding made government the collaborator rather than the regulator of business. Progressive Republican Senator George Norris of Nebraska angrily asked, "If trusts, combinations, and big business are to run the government, why not permit them to do it directly rather than through this expensive machinery which was originally honestly established for the protection of the people of the country against monopoly?"

Finally, Harding reshaped the Supreme Court into a still more aggressive champion of business. He named the conservative William Howard Taft as chief justice and matched him with three other pro-business justices. The Court struck down much of the government economic regulation adopted during the Progressive Era, invalidated restraints on child labor and a minimum wage law for women, and approved restrictions on labor unions.

GOVERNMENT CORRUPTION

The green light that Harding Republicans extended to private interests led to corruption and scandals. Harding appointed friends and cronies who saw public service as an opportunity for graft. The head of the Veterans Bureau went to prison for cheating disabled veterans of $200 million. Albert Fall, the secretary of the interior, leased the petroleum reserves set aside by progressive conservationists to oil companies in exchange for cash, bonds, and cattle for his New Mexico ranch. Exposed for his role in the Teapot Dome scandal, named after a Wyoming oil reserve, Fall became the first cabinet officer in history to go to jail. Attorney General Daugherty escaped a similar fate by destroying records and invoking the Fifth Amendment.

Harding was appalled as the scandals began to unfold. He died shortly thereafter, probably of a heart attack.

COOLIDGE PROSPERITY

On August 3, 1923, Vice President Calvin Coolidge was sworn in as president by his father while visiting his birthplace in rural Vermont, thereby reaffirming his association with traditional values. This image reassured Americans troubled by the Harding scandals.

Coolidge supported business with ideological conviction and cultivated a deliberate inactivity calculated to lower expectations of government. He endorsed Secretary of the Treasury Mellon's ongoing efforts to reverse the progressive tax policies of the Wilson years and backed Secretary of Commerce Hoover's efforts on behalf of the business community (although he privately sneered at Hoover as the "Wonder Boy"). Coolidge continued, like Harding, to install business supporters in the regulatory agencies. To chair the Federal Trade Commission he appointed an attorney who had condemned the agency as "an instrument of oppression and disturbance and injury instead of help to business." The *Wall Street Journal* crowed, "Never before, here or anywhere else, has a government been so completely fused with business."

"Coolidge prosperity" determined the 1924 election. The Democrats, took 103 ballots to nominate the colorless, conservative Wall Street lawyer John W. Davis. A more interesting opponent for Coolidge was Robert La Follette, nominated by discontented farm and labor organizations that formed a new Progressive party. La Follette campaigned against "the power of private monopoly over the political and economic life of the American people." The Republicans, backed by immense contributions from business, denounced La Follette as an agent of Bolshevism. The choice, Republicans insisted, was "Coolidge or Chaos." Thus instructed, Americans chose Coolidge, though barely half the electorate bothered to vote.

THE FATE OF REFORM

The fate of women's groups illustrated the difficulties reformers faced in the 1920s. At first, the adoption of woman suffrage prompted politicians to champion women's reform issues. In 1920, both major parties endorsed many of the goals of the new **League of Women Voters**. Within a year, many states had granted women the right to serve on juries, several enacted equal pay laws, and Wisconsin adopted an equal rights law. Congress passed the **Sheppard-Towner Maternity and Infancy Act**, the first federal social welfare law, in 1921. It provided federal funds for infant and maternity care, precisely the type of protective legislation that the suffragists had described as women's special interest.

But thereafter women reformers gained little. As it became clear that women did not vote as a bloc but according to their varying social and economic backgrounds, Congress lost interest in "women's issues." In 1929, Congress killed the Sheppard-Towner Act. Nor could reformers gain ratification of a child labor amendment after the Supreme Court invalidated laws regulating child labor. Conservatives attacked women reformers as "Bolsheviks."

Disagreements among women reformers and shifting interests also limited their success. The National Woman's Party campaigned for an Equal Rights Amendment, but other reformers feared that such an amendment would nullify the progressive laws that protected working women. Reform organizations lost their energy, and many younger women rejected the public concerns of progressive feminists for what the president of the Women's Trade Union League called "cheap hopes and cheaper materialism."

CITIES AND SUBURBS

The 1920 census reported that, for the first time, more Americans lived in urban than in rural areas. The trend toward urbanization accelerated in the 1920s as millions of Americans fled the depressed countryside for the booming cities. This massive population movement interacted with technological innovations to reshape cities, build suburbs, and transform urban life (see Map 24–1).

WHERE TO LEARN MORE

Calvin Coolidge Homestead, Plymouth, Vermont
www.calvin-coolidge.org/ pages/homestead

League of Women Voters   League formed in 1920 advocating for women's rights, among them the right for women to serve on juries and equal pay laws.

Sheppard-Towner Maternity and Infancy Act   The first federal social welfare law, passed in 1921, providing federal funds for infant and maternity care.

WHAT WAS the Great Migration, and how did it affect social life in the 1920s?

MAP EXPLORATION
To explore this map, go to **http://www.prenhall.com/goldfield2/map24.1**

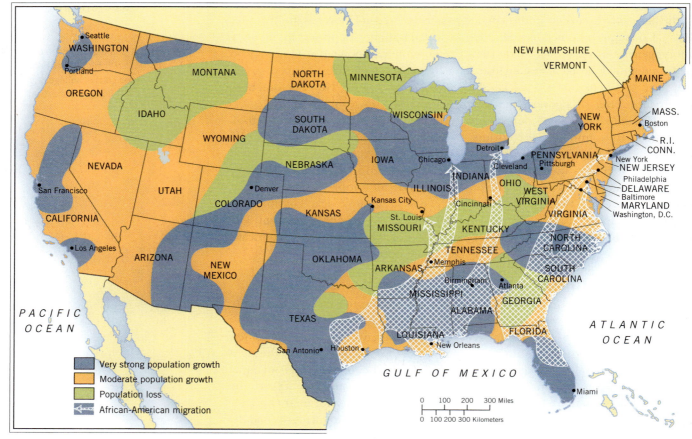

MAP 24–1

Population Shifts, 1920–1930 Rural Americans fled to the cities during the 1920s, escaping a declining agricultural economy to search for new opportunities. African Americans in particular left the rural South for Eastern and Midwestern cities, but the urban population also jumped in the West and in the South itself.

WHY DID certain states and areas gain population during this period, and why did others see population decreases?

EXPANDING CITIES

Urbanization affected all regions of the country. The older industrial cities of the Northeast and Upper Midwest attracted migrants from the rural South and distressed Appalachia. Rural Southerners also poured into Atlanta, Birmingham, Memphis, and Houston. Little more than jungle before 1914, Miami became the fastest-growing city in the United States during the 1920s—"the Magic City." In the West, Denver, Portland, and Seattle (each a regional economic hub) and several California cities grew rapidly. By 1930 Los Angeles was the nation's fifth-largest city, with over 1.2 million people.

The population surge transformed the urban landscape. As land values soared, developers built skyscrapers. By the end of the decade, American cities had nearly four hundred skyscrapers taller than twenty stories. The tallest, New York's 102-story Empire State Building, symbolized the urban boom.

THE GREAT BLACK MIGRATION

A significant feature of the rural-to-urban movement was the **Great Migration** of African Americans from the South in search of job opportunities. Prosperity created jobs, and with the decline in European immigration, black workers filled the positions previously given to new immigrants. Though generally the lowest paid and least secure jobs, they were better than sharecropping in the rural South. Black men worked as unskilled or semiskilled laborers; black women became domestics in white homes. More than a million and a half African Americans moved to Northern cities in the 1920s.

Black ghettos developed in most Northern cities more because of prejudice than the wishes of the migrants. With thousands of newcomers limited to certain neighborhoods by racist restrictions, housing shortages developed. High rents and low wages forced black families to share inferior and unsanitary housing that threatened their health and safety. In Pittsburgh, only 20 percent of black houses had bathtubs and only 50 percent had indoor toilets.

However, the Great Migration also increased African Americans' racial consciousness and power. In 1928 black Chicagoans elected the first black man to Congress since the turn of the century. Mutual aid societies and fraternal orders proliferated. Churches were particularly influential.

Another organization also sought to appeal to poor black ghetto dwellers. The Universal Negro Improvement Association (UNIA), organized by Marcus Garvey, a Jamaican immigrant to New York, rejected the NAACP's goal of integration. A black nationalist espousing racial pride, Garvey exhorted African Americans to migrate to Africa to build a "free, redeemed, and mighty nation." UNIA organized many enterprises, including groceries, restaurants, laundries, a printing plant, and the Black Star Steamship Line. UNIA attracted half a million members, the first black mass movement in American history. When Garvey was convicted of mail fraud and deported, however, the movement collapsed.

Racial pride also found expression in the **Harlem Renaissance**, an outpouring of literature, painting, sculpture, and music. Inspired by African-American culture and black urban life, writers and artists created works of power and poignancy. The poetry of Langston Hughes reflected the rhythm and mood of jazz and the blues.

BARRIOS

Hispanic migrants also entered the nation's cities in the 1920s, creating their own communities, or *barrios*. Fifty thousand Puerto Ricans settled in New York, mostly in East ("Spanish") Harlem, where they found low-paying jobs. Far more migrants arrived from Mexico, usually settling in Western and Southwestern cities. The *barrios*, with their own businesses, churches, and cultural organizations, created a sense of permanency.

These communities enabled the newcomers to preserve their cultural values and build social institutions like *mutualistas* (mutual aid societies) that helped them get credit, housing, and health care. But the *barrios* also reflected the hostility that Hispanics encountered in American cities, for racism often restricted them to such districts. The number of Mexicans in Los Angeles tripled during the 1920s to nearly 100,000, but segregation confined them to East Los Angeles. Other areas of the city boasted of being "restricted to the white race."

Some Hispanics fought discrimination. *La Orden de Hijos de America* (The Order of the Sons of America), organized in San Antonio in 1921, campaigned against inequities in schools and the jury system. In 1929, it helped launch the larger League of United Latin American Citizens (LULAC), which would help advance civil rights for all Americans.

WHERE TO LEARN MORE

Smithsonian Institution, Washington, D.C.

23–1
F. J. Grimke, "Address of Welcome to the Men Who Have Returned from the Battlefront" (1919)

Great Migration The mass movement of African Americans from the rural South to the urban North, spurred especially by new job opportunities during World War I and the 1920s.

Harlem Renaissance A new African-American cultural awareness that flourished in literature, art, and music in the 1920s.

THE ROAD TO SUBURBIA

As fast as the cities mushroomed in the 1920s, the suburbs grew twice as fast. Automobiles created the modern suburb for it enabled people to live in formerly remote areas. A single-family house surrounded by a lawn became the social ideal, a pastoral escape from the overcrowded and dangerous city. Many suburbs excluded African Americans, Hispanics, Jews, and working-class people.

Suburbanization and the automobile brought other changes. In 1922, J.C. Nichols opened the Country Club Plaza, the first suburban shopping center, in Kansas City; it provided free, off-street parking. Department stores and other large retailers began leaving the urban cores for the suburbs, where both parking and more affluent customers were waiting. Drive-in restaurants began with Royce Hailey's Pig Stand in Dallas in 1921. Later in the decade, the first fast-food franchise chain, White Tower, appeared, with its standardized menu and building. To serve the automobile, governments spent more on road construction and maintenance. By 1930, road construction was the largest single item in the national budget.

MASS CULTURE IN THE JAZZ AGE

The White Tower chain symbolized a new society and culture. Urbanization and the automobile joined with new systems of distributing, marketing, and communications to mold a mass culture of standardized experiences and interests. Not all Americans participated equally in the new culture, however, and some attacked it.

ADVERTISING THE CONSUMER SOCIETY

Advertising and its focus on increasing consumption shaped the new society. Advertisers exhorted consumers via newspapers, billboards, streetcar signs, junk mail, radio, movies, and even skywriting. They sought to create a single market where everyone, regardless of region and ethnicity, consumed brand-name products. Advertisers attempted to stimulate new wants by ridiculing previous models or tastes as obsolete, acclaiming the convenience of a new brand, or linking the latest fashion with status or sex appeal.

The home became a focus of consumerism. Middle- and upper-class women purchased mass-produced household appliances, such as electric irons, toasters, vacuum cleaners, washing machines, and refrigerators. Working-class women bought packaged food, ready-made clothing, and other consumer goods to lighten their workload. Advertisers attempted to redefine the housewife's role as primarily that of a consumer, purchasing goods for her family.

A shifting labor market also promoted mass consumption. The increasing number of white-collar workers had more time and money for leisure and consumption. Women clerical workers, the fastest growing occupational group, found in the purchase of clothes and cosmetics a sign of social status and an antidote to workplace monotony.

Under the stimulus of advertising, consumption increasingly displaced the traditional virtues of thrift, prudence, and avoidance of debt. Installment buying became common. By 1928, 85 percent of furniture, 80 percent of radios, and 75 percent of washing machines were bought on credit. But with personal debt rising more than twice as fast as incomes, even aggressive advertising and credit could not indefinitely prolong the illusion of a healthy economy.

LEISURE AND ENTERTAINMENT

During the 1920s, Americans also spent more on recreation and leisure, important features of the new mass society. Millions of people packed into movie theaters whose ornate style symbolized their social importance. Movies helped set national trends in dress, language, and behavior. Studios made films to attract the largest audiences and fit prevailing stereotypes. Cecil B. De Mille titillated audiences while reinforcing conventional standards with religious epics, like *The Ten Commandments* (1923) or *The King of Kings* (1927).

Radio also helped mold national popular culture. The first radio network, the National Broadcasting Company (NBC), was formed in 1926. Soon it was charging $10,000 to broadcast commercials to a national market. Networks provided standardized entertainment, personalities, and news to Americans across the nation. Radio incorporated listeners into a national society. Rural residents welcomed the "talking furniture" for giving them access to the speeches, sermons, and business information available to city-dwellers.

The phonograph allowed families to listen to music of their choice in their own homes. Record companies promoted dance crazes, such as the Charleston, and developed regional markets for country, or "hillbilly," music in the South and West as well as a "race market" for blues and jazz among the growing urban population, black and white. The popularity of the trumpet player Louis Armstrong and other jazz greats gave the decade its nickname, the **Jazz Age**.

Jazz derived from African-American musical traditions. The Great Migration spread it from New Orleans and Kansas City to cities throughout the nation. Its improvisational and rhythmic characteristics differed sharply from older and more formal music and were often condemned by people who feared that jazz would undermine conventional restraints on behavior. But conductor Leopold Stokowski defended jazz as, "an expression of the times, of the breathless, energetic, superactive times in which we are living; it is useless to fight against it."

Professional sports also flourished and became more commercialized. Millions of Americans, attracted by the popularity of such celebrities as Babe Ruth of the New York Yankees, crowded into baseball parks to follow major league teams. Ruth treated himself as a commercial commodity, hiring an agent, endorsing Cadillacs and alligator shoes, and defending a salary in 1932 that dwarfed that of President Hoover by declaring, "I had a better year than he did."

Another celebrity who captured popular fascination was the aviator Charles Lindbergh, who flew alone across the Atlantic in 1927. In the *Spirit of St. Louis*, a tiny airplane built on a shoestring budget, Lindbergh fought bad weather and fatigue for thirty-four hours before landing to a hero's welcome in Paris. Named its first "Man of the Year" by *Time*, one of the new mass-circulation magazines, Lindbergh won adulation and awards from Americans who still valued the image of individualism.

THE NEW MORALITY

The promotion of consumption and immediate gratification weakened traditional self-restraint and fed a desire for personal fulfillment. The failure of wartime sacrifices to achieve promised glories deepened Americans' growing disenchantment

The soup for men who eat to win!

MEN with the success-habit eat wisely and well, both. They enjoy Campbell's Tomato Soup regularly and they get from it a sparkle and zest, which tell in the day's work. All of the rich, tonic goodness. All of the famous tomato healthfulness. 12 cents a can.

Advertisements for brand-name products, like this 1929 ad for Campbell's tomato soup, often tried to link simple consumption with larger issues of personal success and achievement.

By permission of Campbell Soup Company

Jazz Age   The 1920s, so called for the popular music of the day as a symbol of the many changes taking place in the mass culture.

with traditional values. The social dislocations of the war years and growing urbanization accelerated moral and social change. Sexual pleasure became an increasingly open objective, as the growing availability of birth control information enabled women to enjoy sex with less fear of pregnancy; and movie stars like Clara Bow, known as "the It Girl," and Rudolph Valentino flaunted sexuality to mass audiences. Traditionalists worried as divorce rates, cigarette consumption, and hemlines went up while respect for parents, elders, and clergy went down.

Young people seemed to embody the new morality. Rejecting conventional standards, they embraced the era's frenzied dances, bootleg liquor, smoking, more revealing clothing, and sexual experimentation. They welcomed the freedom from parental control that the automobile afforded. The "flapper"—a frivolous young woman with short hair and a skimpy skirt who danced, smoked, and drank in oblivious self-absorption—was a major obsession.

But the new morality was neither as new nor as widespread as its advocates and critics believed. Signs of change had appeared before the war in new clothing fashions, social values, and public amusements among working-class and ethnic groups. But most Americans still adhered to traditional beliefs and values. Moreover, the new morality offered only a limited freedom. Women remained subject to traditional double standards, with marriage and divorce laws, property rights, and employment opportunities biased against them.

THE SEARCHING TWENTIES

Many writers rejected what they considered the materialism, conformity, and provincialism of the emerging mass culture. Their criticism made the postwar decade one of the most creative periods in American literature. The brutality and hypocrisy of the war stimulated their disillusionment and alienation. What Gertrude Stein called the **Lost Generation** considered, in the words of F. Scott Fitzgerald, "all Gods dead, all wars fought, all faiths in man shaken." Ernest Hemingway, wounded as a Red Cross volunteer during the war, rejected idealism in his novel *A Farewell to Arms* (1929), declaring that he no longer saw any meaning in "the words *sacred, glorious*, and *sacrifice.*"

Novelists also turned their attention to American society. In *The Great Gatsby* (1925), Fitzgerald traced the self-deceptions of the wealthy. Sinclair Lewis ridiculed middle-class society and its narrow business culture in *Babbitt* (1922), whose title character provided a new word for the smug and shallow.

WHERE TO LEARN MORE

F. Scott and Zelda Fitzgerald Museum, Montgomery, Alabama **www.alabamatravel.org/central/ szfm.html**

WHAT CONFLICTS

divided social groups in the 1920s?

CULTURE WARS

Despite the blossoming of mass culture and society in the 1920s, conflicts divided social groups. Some of these struggles involved reactions against the new currents in American life, including technological and scientific innovations, urban growth, and materialism. But movements to restrict immigration, enforce prohibition, prohibit the teaching of evolution, and even sustain the Ku Klux Klan did not have simple origins, motives, or consequences. The forces underlying the culture wars of the 1920s would surface repeatedly in the future (see the Overview table "Issues in the Culture Wars of the 1920s" on p. 644).

NATIVISM AND IMMIGRATION RESTRICTION

For years, many Americans, from racists to reformers, had campaigned to restrict immigration. In 1917, Congress required immigrants to pass a literacy test. But renewed immigration after the war revived the anti-immigration movement, and the propaganda of the war and Red Scare years generated public support for more restriction. Depicting immigrants as radicals, racial inferiors, religious subversives, or criminals, nativists clamored for congressional action.

The Emergency Quota Act of 1921 reduced immigration by about two-thirds and established quotas for nationalities on the basis of their numbers in the United States in 1910. Coolidge himself urged that America "be kept American," meaning white, Anglo-Saxon, and Protestant. Congress adopted this racist rationale in the **National Origins Act of 1924**, which proclaimed its objective to be the maintenance of the "racial preponderance" of "the basic strain of our population." This law restricted immigration quotas to 2 percent of the foreign-born population of each nationality as recorded in the 1890 census, which was taken before the mass immigration from southern and eastern Europe. Another provision excluded Japanese immigrants.

Other actions targeted Japanese residents in America. California, Oregon, Washington, Arizona, and other Western states prohibited them from owning or leasing land. In 1922, the Supreme Court ruled that, as nonwhites, they could never become naturalized citizens. Dispirited by the prejudice of the decade, Japanese residents hoped for fulfillment through their children, the **Nisei**, who were American citizens by birth.

Ironically, as a U.S. territory, the Philippines was not subject to the National Origins Act, and Filipino immigration increased ninefold during the 1920s. Similarly, because the law did not apply to immigrants from the Western Hemisphere, Mexican immigration also grew. Nativists lobbied to exclude Mexicans, but agribusiness interests in the Southwest blocked any restrictions on low-cost migrant labor.

THE KU KLUX KLAN

Nativism was also reflected in the popularity of the revived Ku Klux Klan, the goal of which, according to its leader, was to protect "the interest of those whose forefathers established the nation." Although founded in Georgia in 1915 and modeled on its Reconstruction predecessor, the new Klan was a national, not a Southern, movement and claimed several million members by the mid-1920s. Admitting only native-born white Protestants, the Klan embodied the fears of a traditional culture threatened by social change. Ironically, its rapid spread owed much to modern business and promotional techniques as hundreds of professional recruiters raked in hefty commissions selling Klan memberships to those hoping to defend their way of life.

In part the Klan was a fraternal order, providing entertainment, assistance, and community for its members. Its picnics, parades, charity drives, and other social and family-oriented activities—perhaps a half million women joined the Women of the Ku Klux Klan—sharply distinguished the organization from both the small, secretive Klan of the nineteenth century and the still smaller, extremist Klan of the later twentieth century.

But the Klan also exploited racial, ethnic, and religious prejudices, attacking African Americans in the South, Mexicans in Texas, Japanese in California, and Catholics and Jews everywhere. A twisted religious impulse ran through much of the Klan's organization and activities. It hired itinerant Protestant ministers to spread its message, erected altars and flaming crosses at its meetings, and sang Klan lyrics to the tunes of well-known hymns. The Klan also resorted to violence. In 1921, for example, a Methodist minister who belonged to the Klan murdered a Catholic priest on his own doorstep, and other Klansmen burned down Catholic churches.

National Origins Act of 1924   Law sharply restricting immigration on the basis of immigrants' national origins and discriminating against southern and eastern Europeans and Asians.

Nisei   U.S. citizens born of immigrant Japanese parents.

OVERVIEW

ISSUES IN THE CULTURE WARS OF THE 1920S

Issue	Proponent view	Opponent view
The new morality	Promotes greater personal freedom and opportunities for fulfillment	Promotes moral collapse
Evolutionism	A scientific advance linked to notions of progress	A threat to religious belief
Jazz	Modern and vital	Unsettling, irregular, vulgar, and primitive
Immigration	A source of national strength from ethnic and racial diversity	A threat to the status and authority of old-stock white Protestants
Great Migration	A chance for African Americans to find new economic opportunities and gain autonomy and pride	A threat to traditional white privilege, control, and status
Prohibition	Promotes social and family stability and reduces crime	Restricts personal liberty and increases crime
Fundamentalism	An admirable adherence to traditional religious faith and biblical injunctions	A superstitious creed given to intolerant interference in social and political affairs
Ku Klux Klan	An organization promoting community responsibility, patriotism, and traditional social, moral, and religious values	A group of religious and racial bigots given to violent vigilantism and fostering moral and public corruption
Mass culture	Increases popular participation in national culture; provides entertainment and relaxation	Promotes conformity, materialism, mediocrity, and spectacle
Consumerism	Promotes material progress and higher living standards	Promotes waste, sterility, and self-indulgence

The Klan also ventured into politics, with some success, but it eventually encountered resistance. In the North, Catholic workers disrupted Klan parades. In the South, too, Klan excesses provoked a backlash. After the Klan in Dallas flogged sixty-eight people in a "whipping meadow" along the Trinity River in 1922, respect turned to outrage. Newspapers demanded that the Klan disband, and district attorneys began to prosecute Klan thugs. Elsewhere the Klan was stung by revelations of criminal behavior and corruption. By 1930, the Klan had nearly collapsed.

PROHIBITION AND CRIME

Like the Klan, prohibition both reflected and provoked social tensions in the 1920s. In 1920 the Eighteenth Amendment, prohibited the manufacture, sale, or transportation of alcoholic beverages. Congress then passed the **Volstead Act**, which defined the forbidden liquors and established the Prohibition Bureau to enforce the law. But many social groups, especially among urban ethnic communities, opposed

Volstead Act The 1920 law defining the liquor forbidden under the Eighteenth Amendment and giving enforcement responsibilities to the Prohibition Bureau of the Department of the Treasury.

prohibition, and the government could not enforce the law where public opinion did not endorse it.

Evasion was easy. By permitting alcohol for medicinal, sacramental, and industrial purposes, the Volstead Act enabled doctors, priests, and druggists to satisfy their friends' needs. City dwellers made "bathtub gin," and rural people distilled "moonshine." Bootleggers often operated openly.

The huge profits encouraged organized crime—which had previously concentrated on gambling and prostitution—to develop elaborate liquor distribution networks. Crime "families" used violence to enforce contracts, suppress competition, and attack rivals. In Chicago, Al Capone's army of nearly a thousand gangsters killed hundreds.

Gradually, even many "drys"—people who had initially favored prohibition—dropped their support, horrified by the boost it gave organized crime and worried about a general disrespect for law that it promoted. In 1933, thirty-six states ratified an amendment repealing what Herbert Hoover had called a "noble experiment."

Indiana Klanswomen pose in their regalia in 1924. The Klan combined appeals to traditional family and religious values with violent attacks upon those who were not white, native-born Protestants.

Getty Image Inc./Image Bank

OLD-TIME RELIGION AND THE SCOPES TRIAL

Religion provided another fulcrum for traditionalists attempting to stem cultural change. Protestant fundamentalism, which emphasized the infallibility of the Bible, including the Genesis story of Adam and Eve, emerged at the turn of the century as a conservative reaction to religious modernism and the social changes brought by the mass immigration of Catholics and Jews; the growing influence of science and technology; and the secularization of public education. But the fundamentalist crusade to reshape America became formidable only in the 1920s.

Fundamentalist groups, colleges, and publications sprang up throughout the nation, especially in the South. The anti-Catholic sentiment exploited by the Klan was but one consequence of fundamentalism's insistence on strict biblical Christianity. A second was the assault on Darwin's theory of evolution which contradicted literal interpretations of biblical Creation. Fundamentalist legislators tried to prevent teaching evolution in public schools in at least twenty states. In 1925, Tennessee forbade teaching any idea contrary to the biblical account of human origins.

Social or political conservatism, however, was not an inherent part of old-time religion. The most prominent antievolution politician, William Jennings Bryan, feared that Darwinism promoted political and economic conservatism. The survival of the fittest, he complained, elevated force and brutality, ignored spiritual values and democracy, and discouraged altruism and reform. How could a person fight for social justice "unless he believes in the triumph of right?"

The controversy over evolution came to a head when the **American Civil Liberties Union (ACLU)** responded to Tennessee's violation of the constitutional separation of church and state by offering to defend any teacher who tested the anti-evolution law. John Scopes, a high school biology teacher in Dayton, Tennessee, did so and was arrested. Scopes's trial riveted national attention after Bryan agreed to assist the prosecution and Clarence Darrow, a famous Chicago lawyer and prominent atheist, volunteered to defend Scopes.

Millions of Americans tuned their radios to hear the first trial ever broadcast. Though the local jury took only eight minutes to convict Scopes, fundamentalists suffered public ridicule from reporters like H. L. Mencken, who sneered at the "hillbillies" and "yokels" of Dayton. But fundamentalism retained religious influence and would again challenge science and modernism in American life.

WHERE TO LEARN MORE

Rhea County Courthouse and Museum, Dayton, Tennessee

23–2
The Sahara of the Bozart (1920)

FROM THEN TO NOW
The Culture Wars

Cultural conflict raged through American society in the 1920s as people reacted to great social changes, including new roles for women, increasing ethnic and racial diversity, rapid urbanization, and the "new morality." Nativists demanded immigration restriction; the Ku Klux Klan played on fears of racial, ethnic, and religious minorities; prohibitionists grappled with the minions of Demon Rum; and Protestant fundamentalists campaigned to prohibit the teaching of evolution in public schools.

Such conflicts are rooted in the moral systems that give people identity and purpose. As a result, the challenges of the Great Depression and World War II dampened but did not extinguish them. Beginning in the 1960s, fueled as before by challenges to traditional values and beliefs—African American demands for civil rights, opposition to the Vietnam War, the women's rights movement and women's growing presence in the workplace, a new wave of immigration (dominated this time by Asians and Latin Americans), the gay rights movement—cultural conflict flared again and continues to burn.

In the 1920s nativists succeeded in curtailing immigration with the passage of the National Origins Act of 1924. In 1994, the people of California approved Proposition 187, which barred undocumented aliens from public schools and social services. Again, as in the 1920s, fundamentalists are mounting an attack against the teaching of evolution in public schools, sometimes seeking to persuade local school boards to give equal time to the pseudoscience of creationism. And today rap and rock-and-roll provoke the same kind of worried condemnation that jazz provoked in the 1920s.

The central battleground of today's culture wars, however, is women's rights, and especially abortion rights. Ever since the Supreme Court ruled in *Roe v. Wade* in 1973 that women had a right to an abortion, opponents, primarily religious conservatives, have sought to curtail or abolish that right in the name of "family values." Antiabortion protests became increasingly violent in the 1980s and 1990s. Demonstrators have harassed women trying to enter abortion clinics, clinics have been bombed, and several abortion providers have been murdered. Although the Supreme Court has upheld *Roe* v. *Wade* and laws restraining demonstrations at abortion clinics, it has also upheld state laws imposing limits on abortion rights. Abortions have become harder to obtain in many parts of the country.

Gay rights is another new battleground in the culture wars. Religious conservatives, again in the name of "family values," have sought to counter efforts to extend civil rights protections to gays and lesbians. In 1992, for example, Colorado approved a measure (overturned by the Supreme Court in 1996) that prohibited local governments from passing ordinances protecting gays and lesbians from discrimination.

The hostility to the Catholic Church and Catholic immigrants that had long been characteristic of American nativism has been largely absent from the current culture wars. On the contrary, conservative Catholics have joined forces with evangelical Protestants on many fronts, particularly on abortion and gay rights.

According to one popular analysis, the antagonists in today's culture wars are, on one side, those who find authority in transcendent universal sources like those that religious traditions lay claim to, and, on the other, those who find authority in society and human reason. From this perspective, perhaps the most prominent recent engagement in the culture wars was the impeachment of President Clinton. Republican leader Tom DeLay of Texas, for example, declared in 1999 that the impeachment debate was "about relativism versus absolute truth." Polls, however, showed that most Americans were more tolerant and flexible, willing to separate the president's public performance from his personal morality. With the failure to convict Clinton, one Republican lamented. "We probably have lost the culture war." But given the deeply rooted convictions that motivate it, cultural conflict is likely to remain a persistent undercurrent in American life.

The packed courtroom for the Scopes Trial in 1925 illustrates the intense interest that Americans have persistently taken in conflicts stemming from differing cultural values and ethical visions.

Getty Images Inc.

A New Era in the World?

Abroad, as at home, Americans in the 1920s sought peace and economic order. Rejection of the Treaty of Versailles and the League of Nations did not foreshadow isolationism. Indeed, in the 1920s, the United States became more deeply involved in international matters than ever before in peacetime.

WHAT WERE the reasons for U.S. involvement overseas in the 1920s?

WAR DEBTS AND ECONOMIC EXPANSION

The United States was the world's dominant economic power in the 1920s, changed by the Great War from a debtor to a creditor nation. The loans that the United States had made to its allies during the war troubled the nation's relations with Europe throughout the decade. American insistence on repayment angered Europeans, who saw the money as a U.S. contribution to the joint war effort against Germany. Moreover, high American tariffs blocked Europeans from exporting goods to the United States and earning dollars to repay their debts. Eventually, the United States readjusted the terms for repayment, and American bankers extended large loans to Germany, which used the money to pay reparations to Britain and France, whose governments then used the same money to repay the United States. This unstable system depended on a constant flow of money from the United States.

America's global economic role expanded in other ways as well. By 1929, the United States was the world's largest exporter, responsible for one-sixth of all exports. American investment abroad more than doubled between 1919 and 1930. To expand their markets and avoid foreign tariffs, many U.S. companies became **multinational corporations**, establishing branches or subsidiaries abroad. Ford built assembly plants in England, Japan, Turkey, and Canada. American oil companies invested in foreign oil fields, especially in Latin America. The United Fruit Company developed such huge operations in Central America that it often dominated national economies.

The government worked to open doors for American businesses in foreign countries. Secretary of Commerce Hoover's Bureau of Foreign Commerce opened fifty offices around the world to boost American business. Secretary of State Charles Evans Hughes negotiated access to Iraqi oil fields for U.S. oil companies. The government also exempted bankers and manufacturers from antitrust laws to exploit foreign markets.

REJECTING WAR

Although government officials cooperated with business leaders to promote American strategic and economic interests, they had little desire to use force in the process. Popular reaction against the Great War, strengthened by a strong peace movement, constrained policymakers. Indeed, the State Department sought to restrict the buildup of armaments among nations.

At the invitation of President Harding, delegations from nine nations met at the Washington Naval Conference in 1921 to draft a treaty to reduce battleship tonnage and suspend the building of new ships for a decade. The terms virtually froze the existing balance of naval power, with the first rank assigned to Britain and the United States, followed by Japan and then France and Italy. The U.S. Senate ratified the treaty with only one dissenting vote. The United States made a more dramatic gesture in 1928 when it helped draft the **Kellogg-Briand Pact**. Signed by sixty-four nations, the treaty renounced aggression and outlawed war. Without provisions for enforcement, however, it was little more than symbolic.

QUICK REVIEW

America's Economic Power

- U.S. was the world's dominant economic power in the 1920s.
- U.S. war-time loans to European countries were a trouble spot throughout the decade.
- To expand their markets and avoid tariffs, many U.S. companies became multinational corporations.

Multinational corporations   Firms with direct investments, branches, factories, and offices in a number of countries.

MANAGING THE HEMISPHERE

The United States continued to dominate Latin America to promote its own interests through investments, control of the Panama Canal, invocation of the Monroe Doctrine, and military intervention.

In response to American public opinion, the peace movement, and Latin American nationalism, the United States did retreat from the extreme gunboat diplomacy of the Progressive Era, withdrawing troops from the Dominican Republic and Nicaragua. But Haiti remained under U.S. occupation throughout the decade, American troops stayed in Cuba and Panama, and the United States directed the financial policies of other Latin American countries. Moreover, it sent the marines into Honduras in 1924 and back to Nicaragua in 1926. Such interventions provoked further Latin American hostility. "We are hated and despised," said one American businessman in Nicaragua. "This feeling has been created by employing American marines to hunt down and kill Nicaraguans in their own country."

The anger of Latin Americans prompted the State Department to draft the Clark Memorandum. This document, not published until 1930, receded from the Roosevelt Corollary and helped prepare the way for the so-called Good Neighbor Policy toward Latin America. Still, the United States continued to dominate the hemisphere.

HERBERT HOOVER AND THE FINAL TRIUMPH OF THE NEW ERA

As the national economy steamed ahead in 1928, the Republicans chose as their presidential candidate Herbert Hoover, a man who symbolized the policies of prosperity and the New Era. Hoover was not a politician—he had never been elected to office—but a successful administrator who championed rational and efficient economic development. Hoover's stiff managerial image was softened by his humanitarian record and his roots in rural Iowa.

The Democrats, in contrast, chose a candidate who evoked the cultural conflicts of the 1920s. Alfred E. Smith, four-term governor of New York, was a Catholic, an opponent of prohibition, and a Tammany politician tied to the immigrant constituency of New York City. His nomination plunged the nation into cultural strife. Rural fundamentalism, anti-Catholicism, prohibition, and nativism were crucial factors in the campaign. The fundamentalist assault was unrelenting. A Baptist minister in Oklahoma City warned his congregation: "If you vote for Al Smith, you're voting against Christ and you'll all be damned."

But Hoover was in fact the more progressive candidate. Sympathetic to labor, sensitive to women's issues, hostile to racial segregation, and favorable to the League of Nations, Hoover had always distanced himself from what he called "the reactionary group in the Republican party." By contrast, despite supporting state welfare legislation to benefit his urban working-class constituents, Smith was essentially conservative and opposed an active government. Moreover, he was as parochial as his most rural adversaries and never attempted to reach out to them. With the nation still enjoying the economic prosperity so closely associated with Hoover and the Republicans, the Democrats were routed.

But 1928 would be the Republicans' final triumph for a long time. The prosperity of the 1920s was ending, and the country faced a future dark with poverty.

WHERE TO LEARN MORE

★ Herbert Hoover National Historic Site, West Branch, Iowa

American President Herbert Hoover in a color engraving.
The Granger Collection, New York

CONCLUSION

The New Era of the 1920s changed America. Technological and managerial innovations produced giant leaps in productivity, new patterns of labor, a growing concentration of corporate power, and high profits. Government policies from protective tariffs and regressive taxation to a relaxation of regulatory laws reinforced the triumphs of a business elite over traditional cautions and concerns.

The decade's economic developments stimulated social change, drawing millions of Americans from the countryside to the cities, creating an urban nation, and fostering a new ethic of materialism, consumerism, and leisure and a new mass culture based on the automobile, radio, the movies, and advertising. This social transformation swept up many Americans but left others unsettled by the erosion of traditional practices and values. The concerns of traditionalists found expression in campaigns for prohibition and against immigration, the revival of the Ku Klux Klan, and the rise of religious fundamentalism. Intellectuals denounced the materialism and conformity they saw in the new social order and fashioned new artistic and literary trends.

But the impact of the decade's trends was uneven. Mechanization increased the productivity of some workers but cost others their jobs; people poured into the cities while others left for the suburbs; prohibition, produced conflict, crime, and corruption; government policies advanced some economic interests but injured others. Even the notion of a "mass" culture obscured the degree to which millions of Americans were left out of the New Era. With no disposable income and little access to electricity, rural Americans scarcely participated in the joys of consumerism; racial and ethnic minorities were often isolated in ghettos and barrios; and many workers faced declining opportunities. Although living standards rose for many Americans and the rich expanded their share of national wealth, much of the population fell below the established poverty level. The unequal distribution of wealth and income made the economy vulnerable to a disastrous collapse.

SUMMARY

The Economy that Roared Following a postwar depression in 1920 and 1921, the American economy boomed through the rest of the decade. Mechanization of production, investment, new industries such as broadcasting and motion pictures and the automobile industry drove the economy. Oligopoly eliminated competition; Americans accepted the idea that size brought efficiency and productivity. While many businesses boomed, "sick" industries such as textiles, coal mining, agriculture and railroads dragged the economy down. Not all Americans shared in the economic boom; the gap between rich and poor widened.

The Business of Government The Republican surge in national politics also shaped the economy; a business government went hand in hand with a business country. Government regulation was curtailed, business supporters were installed in regulatory agencies, and the Supreme Court became a champion of business. While the Progressive party had little impact on politics, progressivism was not dead but had lost much of its energy and focus.

Cities and Suburbs By 1920 more Americans lived in urban than rural areas: the massive population movement interacted with technological innovations to reshape cities, build automobile-accessible suburbs, and transform urban life. The South was the most rapidly urbanizing region; however, African Americans left the South for job opportunities in Midwestern and Northern cities; increased racial pride found expression in the Harlem Renaissance. Puerto Ricans and Mexicans moved into U.S. cities creating their own communities. Suburbs grew more rapidly than cities as middle-class enclaves created by automobiles.

Mass Culture in the Jazz Age Fast food chains symbolized a new society and culture; advertising and its focus on increasing consumption shaped the new society. Brand-name goods, mass consumption, and buying on credit became hallmarks of the new American economy. People also spent more on recreation and leisure; radio, the phonograph, and the movies competed with college football, professional baseball, and boxing during the Jazz Age. The social dislocations and America's growing disenchantment with traditional values fueled the new morality among the young; writers of the Lost Generation criticized the new era.

Culture Wars Despite the new mass culture of the 1920's, conflicts divided social groups. Some of these struggles involved reactions against the new currents in American life, including technical and scientific innovation, urban growth, and materialism. Nativism, racism, religion, dislike of modernism and the expanding role of science, and the desire to return to and strengthen traditional rural values were all underlying issues in the culture wars.

A New Era in the World? The United States was changed by the Great War into a creditor nation. The loans made to the Allies troubled America's relations with Europe as America insisted on repayment; however, high tariffs blocked Europe exporting goods and earning money to repay those debts. America's global economic role expanded and companies became multinational corporations; Europe and Latin America resented this economic invasion. Reaction to the Great War resulted in America, along, with sixty-four other nations, outlawing war in 1928.

Herbert Hoover and the Triumph of the New Era Herbert Hoover's election as president in 1928 seemed the "final triumph over poverty"; in 1929, the Great Depression would begin.

REVIEW QUESTIONS

1. How did the automobile industry affect the nation's economy and society in the 1920s?

2. What factors characterized the "boom industries" of the 1920s? What factors characterized the "sick industries"?

3. What role did politics play in the public life of the 1920s?

4. How did the World War I experience shape the 1920s?

5. What was the U.S. level of involvement in world affairs in the 1920s?

KEY TERMS

Great Migration   (p. 639)

Harlem Renaissance   (p. 639)

Jazz Age   (p. 641)

League of Women Voters   (p. 637)

Multinational corporations   (p. 647)

National Origins Act of 1924   (p. 643)

Nisei   (p. 643)

Open shop   (p. 634)

Sheppard-Towner Maternity and
Infancy Act   (p. 637)

Volstead Act   (p. 644)

Welfare capitalism   (p. 634)

Yellow-dog contracts
(p. 634)

WHERE TO LEARN MORE

F. Scott and Zelda Fitzgerald Museum, Montgomery, Alabama. The novelist and his wife lived a short while in this house in her hometown. **www.alabamatravel.org/central/szfm.html**

Smithsonian Institution, Washington, D.C. "From Farm to Factory," a permanent exhibition at the National Museum of American History, splendidly portrays the human side of the Great Migration.

Herbert Hoover National Historic Site, West Branch, Iowa. Visitors may tour Hoover's birth-place cottage, presidential library, and museum.

Henry Ford Museum and Greenfield Village, Dearborn, Michigan. Among many fascinating exhibits, "The Automobile in American Life" particularly and superbly demonstrates the importance of the automobile in American social history. **www.hfmgv.org**

George Norris Home, McCook, Nebraska. This museum, operated by the Nebraska State Historical Society, is dedicated to a leading progressive Republican of the 1920s. **www.nebraskahistory.org/sites/norris/index.htm**

Warren G. Harding House, Marion, Ohio. Harding's home from 1891 to 1921 is now a museum with period furnishings. **www.ohiohistory.org/places/harding**

Rhea County Courthouse and Museum, Dayton, Tennessee. The site of the Scopes Trial, the courtroom appears as it did in 1925; the museum contains memorabilia related to the trial.

Calvin Coolidge Homestead, Plymouth, Vermont. Operated by the Vermont Division of Historic Sites, the homestead preserves the exact interiors and furnishings from when Coolidge took the presidential oath of office there in 1923. **www.calvin-coolidge.org/pages/homestead** and **www.dhca.state.vt.us./HistoricSites/sites.htm**

 For additional study resources for this chapter, go to:
www.prenhall.com/goldfield/chapter24

Advertising and the Modern Woman

DURING the 1920s, for the first time in American history, consumer demand was the chief impetus to economic growth. As a direct consequence, the 1920s witnessed the emergence of advertising as a major industry. Most of the ads from this period promoted benefits that had little to do with product. Why? The simplest explanation is that the ad agency and the manufacturer believed that youth and feminine beauty would sell. By the late twenties, advertisements for all sorts of products touted the "modern young woman" as the arbiter of taste and beauty. In so doing, the advertisers signaled a deep shift in American culture. Which specific feminine characteristics are promoted in the advertisements shown here?

The image of a young, attractive woman in this Lucky Strike ad from the 1920s is much more prominent than the product she is promoting. How does the ad make the connection between cigarettes and feminine beauty? What is the underying message of the command to "reach for a Lucky—instead of a sweet?"

ADS-TOBACCO

"Reach for a Lucky – instead of a sweet"

LUCKY STRIKE
"IT'S TOASTED"
CIGARETTES

"A flavor that completely satisfies"

Billie Burke
Popular American Actress

"It's toasted"
No Throat Irritation-No Cough.

© 1929, The American Tobacco Co., Manufacturers

The Creoles of Louisiana are of the
purest French and Spanish blood and their
charm is the charm of courtly France and
of patrician Spain.
A distinguishing mark of their aristocratic ancestry is their wonderful hair, thick,
dark, lustrous and beautiful.

The Wonder of Creole Hair

CREOLE charm has been as much admired in aristocratic European circles
as in America. Empress Josephine, wife of Napoleon, was a Creole.
Queen Hortense of Holland and Prince Eugene, Viceroy of Italy, were Creoles. The glorious Creole hair has always
been especially admired. The hair is a special pride and care of the Creoles and for generations La Creole Hair Dressing has
been favorite among them. It preserves the youthful color and beauty of the hair even through advanced years.

La Creole Ends Gray Hair

La Creole not alone prevents gray hair. La Creole treatment will bring back
to its youthful color and beauty, hair that has become gray, gray-streaked, or
faded. La Creole contains no dyes. It promotes the youthfully vigorous
healthy condition of hair and scalp which nature intended. Its effect on
the hair is gradual but certain. Two to five weeks treatment is required to
bring back any shade—lightest brown to deepest black—whatever the natural
color was. After that an occasional application will preserve the vigorous
healthy color permanently.

Good taste and good breeding approve the use of La Creole and there is
no reason for making any secret of its use, though it can never be detected.
La Creole must not be confused with dyes—it can not give a dyed look
and there is nothing to stain the scalp or to wash or rub off. It makes the
hair soft, wavy, lustrous and beautiful. Eliminates dandruff.
Absolutely guaranteed to bring back the hair's color or money refunded.
Send coupon for booklet "La
Creole—Hair Beautiful." Shows
style of hair dressing best suited
to each type of face.

At Drug Stores and Toilet Counters, Price $1.00
If your Dealer can't supply you, send his name and address.
We will see that you are supplied.

VAN VLEET-MANSFIELD LABORATORIES
132 Tenth Street, Memphis, Tenn.

Van Vleet-Mansfield Laboratories
132 Tenth St., Memphis, Tenn.
Please send booklet "La Creole—Hair
Beautiful," teaching the hair dress most
becoming to each individual.

Name ....
Address ....
City .... State ....

▲
Virtually all ads during this period, except those aimed explicitly at
African Americans, avoided any ethnic or racial references. "La Creole"
ads are exceptions. The product name itself referred to a specific Community of people in Louisiana, descendants of French settlers. But the
term was also used to refer to individuals of mixed racial background.
How does the "La Creole" ad deal with this? What does that suggest for
how you might interpret the other ads?

This ad for a line of hair products created and
manufactured by Madame C.J. Walker, one of the
first African-American millionaires. The ad promises
"fascinating beauty" to users of its product.
▼

*You, too,
may be a
fascinating beauty*

PERHAPS YOU ENVY the girl with irresistible
beauty, whose skin is flawless and velvety,
whose hair has a beautiful silky sheen, the girl
who receives glances of undoubted admiration.

You need not envy her. Create new beauty
for yourself by using Madam C. J. Walker's
famous beauty preparations.

When Madam Walker and her associates
started to develop her beauty preparations,
which are now used all over the world, they
perfected their toiletries step by step.

Each preparation was beyond the point of
experiment before it was followed by another.
Each preparation's wide use and high merit
were always proved. Today they are unsurpassed.

Try these products and you won't have reason
to envy another girl her lovely hair and her
charming complexion.

You can obtain any of these marvelous preparations at your nearest
druggist or from a Madam C. J. Walker agent (there's one near
you) or write the company direct at Indianapolis.

**Madam
C.J. WALKER'S
Beauty Preparations**

THESE ARE BUT FOUR OF EIGHTEEN MADAM C. J. WALKER BEAUTY PREPARATIONS—AS FINE AS MONEY CAN BUY

I remembered seeing the people passing on their way to California . . . It hurt me to see the people in their rickety old cars, their clothes in tatters, escaping from the drought and the dust bowls.

NRA
MEMBER
U.S.

WE DO OUR PART

CIVILIAN CONSERVATION CORPS
U S
Co. 272

Work Pays America!
PROSPERITY

WORKS PROGRESS ADMINISTRATION

Hands in their pockets, hungry men stand numbly in one of New York City's breadlines. Said one observer: "The wretched men, many without overcoats or decent shoes, usually began to line up soon after six o'clock— in good weather or bad, rain or snow."

25

THE GREAT DEPRESSION
AND THE NEW DEAL
1929–1939

WHAT TRIGGERED
the Great Depression?

WHY DID Herbert Hoover's actions
to resolve the Great Depression fail?

WHAT WERE
the main achievements
of the early New Deal?

YEARS OF DUST

RESETTLEMENT ADMINISTRATION
Rescues Victims
Restores Land to Proper Use

WHICH ECONOMIC
and social reforms made up
the "Second New Deal?"

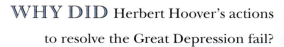

WHAT IMPACT did New Deal
programs have on women and minorities?

WHY WERE late New Deal reforms unsuccessful?

My mother had two small babies on her hands. When I became sickly, Grandmother Josefa took me home with her, and I never returned to my parents. . . . My grandmother's house was located on the 'American' side of town, but there was nothing they could do about it because she was there before anybody else. . . . My grandmother worked very hard; I grew up in the Depression.

When it was time for me to go to school I was assigned to [the] Mexican side of town. We were segregated; [the] Anglo children were sent to Roosevelt and the Mexican children who lived closer to Roosevelt [still] had to go down to Harding. I'll admit, there was a lot of discrimination in those years.

During the Depression my grandmother sewed piecework for the WPA. My dad helped out when he could [and] Uncle Ernesto also worked. He used to dig graves.

The Depression years were very, very hard. I remember seeing the people passing on their way to California. . . . It hurt me to see the people in their rickety old cars, their clothes in tatters, escaping from the drought and the dust bowls.

—*Oral Testimony,*

Carlotta Silvas Martin
Star Route One
Albertville, Ala.

January 1, 1936

On April 27 [1933], according to the New York Times, *Paul Schneider, aged forty-four, a sick and crippled Chicago school teacher, shot himself to death. His widow, left with three children, stated that he had not been paid for eight months. . . . Less than a month after Paul Schneider's discouragement drove him to suicide, the militant action of Chicago teachers—patient no more . . . resulted in the payment of $12,000,000 due them for the last months of 1932. Their pay for the five months of 1933 is still owed them. Five hundred of them are reported to be in asylums and sanitariums as a result of the strain. . . .*

These are the conditions facing teachers fortunate enough to be employed. What of the unemployed? . . . "We are always hungry," wrote [one unemployed teacher]. "We owe six months' rent. . . . We live every hour in fear of eviction. . . . My sister, a typist, and I . . . have been out of work for two years. . . . We feel discouraged . . . and embittered. We are drifting, with no help from anyone."

—*Eunice Langdon,*

The Nation,
August 16, 1933

IMAGE KEY
for pages 654–655

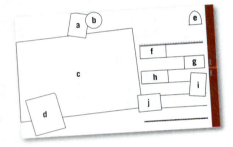

a. The National Recovery Agency seal with an eagle holding a cog in one talon and lightning bolts in the other over the slogan "We Do Our Part."
b. The Civilian Conservation Corps Emblem.
c. Hungry men stand in a bread line in New York City.
d. A Works Progress Administration poster, depicting a farmer and a miner shaking hands.
e. An old fashioned radio in a wooden cabinet.
f. Anxious citizens crowd along Wall Street sidewalks while automobiles edge down the street on Black Tuesday October 29, 1929.
g. Mexican farm Workers, pecan shell homes that rent for 50 cents a week in San Antonio, TX.
h. Gov. Franklin D. Roosevelt shakes hands with a poor mine worker during campaign trip.
i. Ben Shahn, "Years of Dust," 1936. Poster for the Resettlement Administration.
j. Isaac Soyer, "Employment Agency." Oil on canvas, 34 1/2" × 45".

I am sitting in the city free employment bureau. It's the women's section. We have been sitting here now for hours. We sit here every day, waiting for a job. There are no jobs. . . .

. . . [W]e don't talk much. . . . There is a kind of humiliation. . . . We look away from each other. We look at the floor.

—Meridel LeSeur,

"Women on the Breadlines,"
1932

Dear Mrs. Roosevelt,

I am now 15 years old and in the 10th grade. I have always been smart but I never had a chance as all of us is so poor. I hope to complete my education, but I will have to quit school I guess if there is no clothes can be bought. (Don't think that we are on the relief.) Mother has been a faithful servant for us to keep us togather. I don't see how she has made it.

Mrs. Roosevelt, don't think I am just begging, but that is all you can call it I guess. . . . Do you have any old clothes you have throwed back. You don't realize how honored I would feel to be wearing your clothes.

—Your friend,

M.I.

"Carlotta Silvas Martin: A Mexican American Childhood during the Depression" and "Meridel LeSeur: The Despair of Unemployed Women," both from Susan Ware, *Modern American Women: A Documentary History* (New York: McGraw-Hill Higher Education, 2002), pp. 162–165, 145–146, respectively; Letter to Eleanor Roosevelt, January 1, 1936, **http://www.newdeal.feri.org/eleanor/mi0136.htm**; Eunice Langdon, "The Teacher Faces the Depression," *The Nation* 137 (August 16, 1933): 182–187.

CARLOTTA SILVAS MARTINE, Eunice Langdon, and Meridel Le Seur convey some of the trauma of the Great Depression, but no one voice can capture its devastating effects. The American economy collapsed, leaving millions of people jobless, homeless, or in fear of foreclosure, eviction, and even starvation. Men, women, and children saw their families and dreams shattered and felt the humiliation of standing in bread lines or begging for clothes or food scraps. The winter of 1932–1933 was particularly cruel. Unemployment soared. Hunger was so widespread in Kentucky and West Virginia that one relief committee limited its handouts to those who were at least 10 percent below their normal weight for their height. In Chicago, half the people were without jobs. In the drought-stricken Great Plains families left their farms and took to the road to escape the darkened skies of the "Dust Bowl".

The election of Franklin D. Roosevelt, however, lifted spirits and hopes throughout the nation. Jobless Americans enthusiastically responded to his

New Deal, taking jobs with such programs as the Works Progress Administration (WPA). They also wrote to FDR and Eleanor Roosevelt, asking for advice and assistance and thanking the President and the First Lady for their compassionate support and leadership. Throughout all such letters ran the common theme: the belief among poor and unemployed Americans that for the first time there were people in the White House who cared about them.

The economic collapse hit hardest those industries dominated by male workers, leaving mothers and wives with new roles as the family breadwinners, sometimes straining family relationships and men's sense of purpose and respect.

Race and ethnicity further complicated the problems of both joblessness and relief. Southern states routinely denied African Americans relief assistance as did Southwestern states for Hispanic Americans. Despite some progress in assisting African Americans, the New Deal failed to overcome traditional attitudes and practices that targeted women and minorities and reinforced local prejudice and segregation.

Hard times, then, both united and divided the American people, and although the federal activism of the 1930s achieved neither full recovery nor systematic reform, it restored confidence to many Americans and transformed the nation's responsibilities for the welfare of its citizens. By the end of the decade, President Roosevelt was no longer worried that the economy—indeed society itself—teetered on the edge of catastrophe; his gaze now fixed abroad where even more ominous developments, he believed, threatened the nation's future and security.

New Deal The economic and political policies of the Roosevelt administration in the 1930s.

Hard Times in Hooverville

The prosperity of the 1920s ended in a stock market crash that revealed the flaws honeycombing the economy. As the nation slid into a catastrophic depression, factories closed, employment and incomes tumbled, and millions lost their homes, hopes, and dignity. Some protested and took direct action; others looked to the government for relief.

WHAT TRIGGERED the Great Depression?

Crash!

The buoyant prosperity of the New Era collapsed in October of 1929 when the stock market crashed. After peaking in September, the market suffered several sharp checks, and on October 29, "Black Tuesday," panicked investors dumped their stocks at any price. The slide continued for months, and then years. It hit bottom in July 1932. By then, the stock of U.S. Steel had plunged from 262 to 22, Montgomery Ward from 138 to 4.

The Wall Street crash marked the beginning of the **Great Depression**, but it did not cause it. The depression stemmed from weaknesses in the New Era economy. Most damaging was the unequal distribution of wealth and income. By 1929, the richest 0.1 percent of American families had as much total income as the bottom 42 percent (see Figure 25.1). With more than half the nation's people living at or below the subsistence level, there was not enough purchasing power to maintain the economy.

A second factor was that oligopolies dominated American industries. Their power led to "administered prices," prices kept artificially high and rigid rather than determined by supply and demand. By not responding to purchasing power, this

Great Depression The nation's worst economic crisis, extending through the 1930s, producing unprecedented bank failures, unemployment, and industrial and agricultural collapse.

system not only helped bring on economic collapse but also dimmed prospects for recovery.

Weaknesses in specific industries had further unbalanced the economy. Agriculture suffered from overproduction, declining prices, and heavy debt; so did the coal and textile industries. Poorly managed and regulated, banks had contributed to the instability of prosperity; they now threatened to spread the panic and depression.

International economic difficulties also contributed to the depression. Shut out from U.S. markets by high tariffs, Europeans had depended on American investments to manage their debts and reparation payments from the Great War. The stock market crash dried up the flow of American dollars to Europe, causing financial panics and industrial collapse and making the Great Depression global. In turn, European nations curtailed their imports of American goods and defaulted on their debts, further debilitating the U.S. economy. American exports fell by 70 percent from 1929 to 1932. As foreign markets shrank, so did hopes for economic recovery.

Government policies also bore some responsibility for the crash and depression. Failure to enforce antitrust laws had encouraged oligopolies and high prices; failure to regulate banking or the stock market had permitted financial recklessness. Reducing tax rates on the wealthy had also encouraged speculation and contributed to the maldistribution of income. Opposition to labor unions and collective bargaining helped keep workers' wages and purchasing power low. The absence of an effective agricultural policy and the high tariffs that inhibited foreign trade and reduced markets for agricultural products hurt farmers in the same way. In short, the same government policies that shaped the booming 1920s economy also pointed to economic disaster.

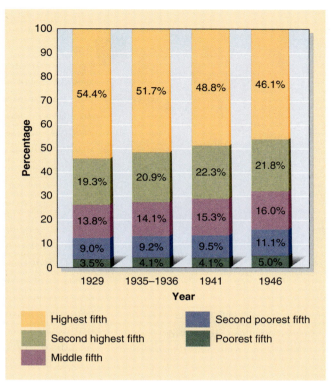

FIGURE 25.1

Distribution of Income in the United States, 1929–1946

An unequal distribution of income contributed to the Great Depression by limiting purchasing power. Only slight changes occurred until after World War II, but other factors gradually stabilized the national economy.

Source: U.S. Bureau of the Census

THE DEPRESSION SPREADS

By early 1930, factories had shut down or cut back, and industrial production plummeted; by 1932, it was scarcely 50 percent of its 1929 level. Steel mills operated at 12 percent of capacity, auto factories at 20 percent. Unemployment skyrocketed, as an average of 100,000 workers a week were fired in the first three years after the crash. By 1932, one-fourth of the labor force was out of work. Personal income dropped by more than half between 1929 and 1932; by 1933, industrial workers had average weekly wages of only $16.73. Moreover, the depression began to feed on itself in a vicious circle: Shrinking wages and employment cut into purchasing power, causing business to slash production again and lay off workers, thereby further reducing purchasing power.

The depression particularly battered farmers. Commodity prices fell by 55 percent between 1929 and 1932, stifling farm income. Unable to pay their mortgages, many farm families lost their homes and fields. "We have no security left," cried one South Dakota farm woman. "Foreclosures and evictions at the point of sheriff's guns are increasing daily."

Urban families were also evicted when they could not pay their rent. Some moved in with relatives; others lived in **Hoovervilles**—the name reflects the bitterness directed at the president—shacks where people shivered, suffered,

Hoovervilles Shantytowns, sarcastically named after President Hoover, in which unemployed and homeless people lived in makeshift shacks, tents, and boxes.

and starved. Oklahoma City's vast Hooverville covered 100 square miles; one witness described its hapless residents as squatting in "old, rusted-out car bodies," orange crates, and holes in the ground.

Soup kitchens became standard features of the urban landscape, but charities and local communities could not meet the massive needs, and neither state nor federal governments had welfare or unemployment compensation programs. To survive, people planted gardens in vacant lots and back alleys and tore apart empty houses or tapped gas lines for fuel. In immigrant neighborhoods, social workers found a "primitive communism" in which people shared food, clothing, and fuel.

"WOMEN'S JOBS" AND "MEN'S JOBS"

Gender segregation had concentrated women in low-paid service, sales, and clerical jobs that shrank less than the heavy industries where men predominated. But traditional attitudes also reinforced opposition to female employment itself, especially that of married women. As one Chicago civic organization complained, "They are holding jobs that rightfully belong to the God-intended providers of the household." The city council of Akron, Ohio, resolved that public agencies and private employers should stop employing wives. Three-fourths of the nation's school systems refused to hire married women as teachers, and two-thirds dismissed female teachers who married. Many private employers, especially banks and insurance companies, also fired married women.

Few men sought positions in the fields associated with women, so firing women simply aggravated the suffering of families already reeling from the depression. Despite hostility, the proportion of married women in the work force increased in the 1930s as women took jobs to help their families survive.

FAMILIES IN THE DEPRESSION

"I have watched fear grip the people in our neighborhood around Hull House," wrote Jane Addams as the depression deepened in 1931 and family survival itself seemed threatened. Divorce declined because it was expensive, but desertion increased, and marriages were postponed. Birthrates fell. Husbands and fathers, the traditional breadwinners, were often humiliated and despondent when laid off from work. One social worker observed in 1931: "Like searing irons, the degradation, the sheer terror and panic which loss of job brings, the deprivation and the bitterness have eaten into men's souls."

The number of female-headed households increased. Not only did some women become wage earners, but to make ends meet, many women sewed their own clothing and raised and canned vegetables. Some also took on extra work at home. In San Antonio, one in every ten families had boarders, and in Alabama, housewives took in laundry at 10 cents a week.

Some parents sacrificed their own well-being to protect their children. One witness described "the uncontrolled trembling of parents who have starved themselves for weeks so that their children might not go hungry." In New York City, 139 people, most of them children, died of starvation and malnutrition in 1933. Many teenagers who left home so that younger children would have more to eat suffered from starvation, exposure, illness, and accidents. The California Unemployment Commission concluded that the depression had left the American family "morally shattered. There is no security, no foothold, no future."

QUICK REVIEW

Gendered Attitudes About Work
- Women were concentrated in low-paid service, sales, and clerical jobs.
- Traditional attitudes reinforced opposition to female employment.
- Few men sought work in fields associated with women.

"LAST HIRED, FIRST FIRED"

With fewer resources and opportunities, racial minorities were less able than other groups to absorb the economic pain. African Americans, reported a sociologist at Howard University in 1932, were "the last to be hired and the first to be fired." Black unemployment rates were more than twice the rate for white people. Jobless white workers now sought the menial jobs traditionally reserved for black workers, such as street cleaning and domestic service. Religious and charitable organizations often refused to care for black people. Local and state governments set higher requirements for black people than for white people to receive relief and provided them with less aid. The Urban League reported, "at no time in the history of the Negro since slavery has his economic and social outlook seemed so discouraging." African Americans were "hanging on by the barest thread."

Hispanic Americans also suffered. As mostly unskilled workers, they faced increasing competition for decreasing jobs paying declining wages. They were displaced even in the California agricultural labor force, which they had dominated. Other jobs were lost when Arizona, California, and Texas barred Mexicans from public works and highway construction jobs. Vigilantes threatened employers who hired Mexicans rather than white Americans. Economic woes and racism drove nearly half a million Mexican immigrants and their American-born children from the United States in the 1930s. Local authorities in the Southwest encouraged the federal government to deport Mexicans and offered free transportation to Mexico.

PROTEST

Bewildered and discouraged, most Americans responded to the depression with resignation. But others engaged in protests, ranging from small desperate gestures like stealing food and coal to more dramatic deeds. In Louisiana, women seized a train to call attention to the needs of their families; in New Jersey, in the "bloodless battle of Pleasantville," one hundred women held the city council hostage to demand assistance.

Communists organized the jobless into "unemployment councils" that staged hunger marches, demonstrated for relief, and blocked evictions. Mothers facing eviction in Chicago told their children: "Run quick and find the Reds." Socialists built similar organizations, including Baltimore's People's Unemployment League. However, local authorities often suppressed their protests. In 1932, police fired on the Detroit Unemployment Council as it marched to demand food and jobs, killing four marchers and wounding many more.

Rural protests also broke out. In the Midwest, the Farmers' Holiday Association stopped the shipment of produce to urban markets, hoping to drive up prices. A guerrilla war broke out as farmers blocked roads and halted freight trains, dumped milk in ditches, and fought bloody battles with deputy sheriffs. In Iowa, farmers beat sheriffs and mortgage agents and nearly lynched a lawyer conducting foreclosure proceedings.

HERBERT HOOVER AND THE DEPRESSION

The Great Depression challenged the optimism, policies, and philosophy of Herbert Hoover. The president took unprecedented steps to resolve the crisis but shrank back from the interventionist policies activists urged. His failures, personal as well as political and economic, led to his repudiation and opened the way to a new deal.

Many Mexican farm Workers lived in pecan shell homes that rented for 50 cents a week; this one in San Antonio, TX.

National Archives and Records Administration

WHERE TO LEARN MORE

Herbert Hoover National Historic Site, West Branch, Iowa
www.nps.gov/heho

WHY DID Herbert Hoover's actions to resolve the Great Depression Fail?

CHRONOLOGY

1929   Stock market crashes.

1932   Farmers' Holiday Association organizes rural protests in the Midwest.
Reconstruction Finance Corporation is created to assist financial institutions.
Bonus Army is routed in Washington, D.C.
Franklin D. Roosevelt is elected president.

1933   Emergency Banking Act is passed.
Agricultural Adjustment Administration (AAA) is created to regulate farm production.
National Recovery Administration (NRA) is created to promote industrial cooperation and recovery.
Federal Emergency Relief Act provides federal assistance to the unemployed.
Civilian Conservation Corps (CCC) is established to provide work relief in conservation projects.
Public Works Administration (PWA) is created to provide work relief on large public construction projects.
Civil Works Administration (CWA) provides emergency winter relief jobs.
Tennessee Valley Authority (TVA) is created to coordinate regional development.

1934   Securities and Exchange Commission (SEC) is established.
Indian Reorganization Act reforms Indian policy.
Huey Long organizes the Share-Our-Wealth Society.
Democrats win midterm elections.

1935   Supreme Court declares NRA unconstitutional.
National Labor Relations Act (Wagner Act) guarantees workers' rights to organize and bargain collectively.
Social Security Act establishes a federal social insurance system.
Banking Act strengthens the Federal Reserve.
Revenue Act establishes a more progressive tax system.
Resettlement Administration is created to aid dispossessed farmers.
Rural Electrification Administration (REA) is created to help provide electric power to rural areas.
Soil Conservation Service is established.
Emergency Relief Appropriation Act authorizes public relief projects for the unemployed.
Works Progress Administration (WPA) is created.
Huey Long is assassinated.

1936   Supreme Court declares AAA unconstitutional.
Roosevelt is reelected president.
Sit-down strikes begin.

1937   Chicago police kill workers in Memorial Day Massacre.
FDR tries but fails to expand the Supreme Court.
Farm Security Administration (FSA) is created to lend money to small farmers to buy and rehabilitate farms.
National Housing Act is passed to promote public housing projects.
"Roosevelt Recession" begins.

1938   Congress of Industrial Organizations (CIO) is founded.
Fair Labor Standards Act establishes minimum wage and maximum hours rules for labor.
Roosevelt fails to "purge" the Democratic party.
Republicans make gains in midterm elections.

THE LIMITS OF VOLUNTARISM

Hoover fought economic depression more vigorously than any previous president, but he believed that voluntary, private action was preferable to federal intervention. In promoting voluntarism, Hoover first secured business leaders' pledges to maintain employment and wage levels. But most corporations soon repudiated these pledges, slashed wages, and laid off workers. Hoover complained, "You know, the only trouble with capitalism is capitalists; they're too damn greedy." Still, he rejected government action.

Hoover created the President's Organization for Unemployment Relief to help raise private funds for voluntary relief agencies. Charities and local authorities, he believed, should help the unemployed; direct federal relief would expand government power and undermine the recipients' character. He vetoed congressional attempts to aid the unemployed. "The American way of relieving distress," said Hoover, was through "the voluntary agencies of self help in the community."

But private programs to aid the unemployed scarcely existed. Private charitable groups like the Salvation Army, church associations, and ethnic societies quickly exhausted their resources. Nor could local governments cope. New York City provided relief payments of $2.39 a week for an entire family, and other cities much less. By 1932, more than one hundred cities made no relief appropriations at all, and the commissioner of charity in Salt Lake City reported that people were sliding toward starvation. Only eight state governments provided even token assistance.

Hoover blundered not in first relying on charities and local governments for relief but in refusing to admit that they were inadequate. As the depression worsened, Hoover adopted more activist policies. He persuaded Congress to cut taxes to boost consumers' buying power, and he increased the public works budget. The Reconstruction Finance Corporation (RFC), established in January 1932, lent federal funds to banks, insurance companies, and railroads so that their recovery could "trickle down" to ordinary Americans.

But these programs satisfied few Americans who saw Hoover as indifferent to their suffering and a reactionary protector of privileged business interests. (See American Views, "An Ohio Mayor on Unemployment and Relief.")

Bonus Marchers battling police in Washington, D.C., in 1932. Police and military assaults on these homeless veterans infuriated Americans and prompted Democratic Presidential nominee Franklin D. Roosevelt to declare, "Well, this will elect me."

National Archives and Records Administration

REPUDIATING HOOVER: THE 1932 ELECTION

Hoover's treatment of the **Bonus Army** symbolized his unpopularity and set the stage for the 1932 election. In 1932, unemployed veterans of World War I gathered in Washington, demanding payment of service bonuses not due until 1945. Hoover refused to meet with them, and Congress rejected their plan. But ten thousand veterans erected a shantytown at the edge of Washington and camped in vacant public buildings. General Douglas MacArthur disobeyed Hoover's cautious orders and on July 28 led cavalry, infantry, and tanks against the ragged Bonus Marchers. The troops cleared the buildings and assaulted the shantytown, dispersing the veterans and their families and setting their camp on fire.

"What a pitiful spectacle is that of the great American Government, mightiest in the world, chasing unarmed men, women, and children with army tanks," commented the *Washington News*. The administration tried to brand the Bonus Marchers as Communists and criminals, but official investigations refuted such claims. The incident confirmed Hoover's public image as harsh and insensitive.

In the summer of 1932, with no prospects for victory, Republicans renominated Hoover. Confident Democrats selected Governor Franklin D. Roosevelt of New York, who pledged "a new deal for the American people." Born into a wealthy family in 1882, FDR had been educated at Harvard, trained in the law, and schooled in politics, as a state legislator, assistant secretary of the navy, and the Democratic vice presidential nominee in 1920. In 1921, Roosevelt contracted polio, which paralyzed him from the waist down, leaving him dependent on braces or crutches. His continued involvement in politics owed much to his wife, Eleanor. A social reformer, she became a Democratic activist, organizing women's groups and campaigning across New York. In a remarkable political comeback, FDR was elected governor in 1928 and reelected in 1930.

The 1932 Democratic platform differed little from that of the Republicans, and Roosevelt spoke in vague or general terms. He knew that the election would

25–1
Herbert Hoover, Speech at New York City (1932)

QUICK REVIEW

The 1932 Election
♦ Republicans renominated Hoover.
♦ The Democratic platform differed little from the Republican platform.
♦ Franklin D. Roosevelt's victory was a repudiation of Hoover.

Bonus Army   Unemployed veterans of World War I gathering in Washington in 1932 demanding payment of service bonuses not due until 1945.

◆ AMERICAN VIEWS ◆

AN OHIO MAYOR ON UNEMPLOYMENT AND RELIEF

Joesph Heffernan was the mayor of Youngstown, Ohio, when the nation sank into the Great Depression. Like other industrial cities, Youngstown soon confronted widespread unemployment and distress. In this document, written in 1932, Heffernan describes the obstacles he faced in responding to the suffering.

WHAT WOULD Heffernan think of President Hoover's belief that private charities and local authorities would provide unemployment relief? What did Heffernan see as obstacles to a public response to the depression? What did he fear would be the consequences of the failure to devise a rational and humane system of relief?

[In 1930] I asked for a bond issue of $1,000,000 for unemployment relief. Many leading business men went out of their way to show their disapproval. One of them . . . said to me: "You make a bad mistake in talking about the unemployed. Don't emphasize hard times and everything will be all right." An influential newspaper chastised me for "borrowing trouble"; the depression would be

over, the editor maintained, before relief would be needed. . . . The gravity of the situation was so deliberately misrepresented by the entire business community that when the bond issue finally came to a ballot, in November 1930, it was voted down.

Thus we passed into the early days of 1931–fourteen months after the first collapse—with no relief in sight except that which was provided by the orthodox charities. Not a single move had been made looking toward action by a united community.

Strange as it may seem, there was no way in which the city government could embark upon a program of its own. We had no funds available for emergency relief, and without specific authorization from the people we could not issue bonds. . . .

As time went on, business conditions showed no improvement. Every night hundreds of homeless men crowded into the municipal incinerator, where they found warmth even though they had to sleep on heaps of garbage. In January 1931, I obtained the cooperation of the City Council to convert an abandoned police station into a "flop

---

be a repudiation of Hoover more than an endorsement of himself. Indeed, FDR carried every state south and west of Pennsylvania.

In the months before his inauguration, the depression worsened, with rising unemployment, plunging farm prices, and spreading misery. When teachers in Chicago, unpaid for months, fainted in their classrooms from hunger, it symbolized the imminent collapse of the nation itself. The final blow came in February 1933 when desperate Americans rushed to withdraw their funds from the tottering bank system. State governments shut the banks to prevent their failure. Hoover concluded, "We are at the end of our string."

LAUNCHING THE NEW DEAL

WHAT WERE the main achievements of the early New Deal?

In the midst of national anxiety, Franklin D. Roosevelt pushed forward an unprecedented program to resolve the crises of a collapsing financial system, crippling unemployment, and agricultural and industrial breakdown and to promote reform. The early New Deal achieved successes and attracted support, but it also had limitations and generated criticism that suggested the need for still greater innovations.

house." The first night it was filled, and it has remained filled ever since. I made a point of paying frequent visits to this establishment so that I could see for myself what kind of men these down-and-outers were, and I heartily wish that those folk who have made themselves comfortable by ignoring and denying the suffering of their less fortunate neighbors could see some of the sights I saw. There were old men gnarled by heavy labor, young mechanics tasting the first bitterness of defeat, clerks and white-collar workers learning the equality of misery, derelicts who fared no worse in bad times than in good, Negroes who only a short time before had come from Southern cotton fields, now glad to find any shelter from the cold, immigrants who had been lured to Van Dyke's "land of youth and freedom"— each one a personal tragedy, and all together an overwhelming catastrophe for the nation. . . .

This descent from respectability, frequent enough in the best of times, has been hastened immeasurably by two years of business paralysis, and the people who have been affected in this manner must be numbered in millions. This is what we have accomplished with our bread lines and soup kitchens. I know, because I have seen thousands of these defeated, discouraged, hopeless men and women, cringing and fawning as they come to ask for public aid. It

is a spectacle of national degeneration. That is the fundamental tragedy for America. If every mill and factory in the land should begin to hum with prosperity to-morrow morning, the destructive effect of our haphazard relief measures would not work itself out of the nation's blood until the sons of our sons had expiated the sins of our neglect.

Even now there are signs of rebellion against a system so out of joint that it can only offer charity to honest men who want to work. Sometimes it takes the form of social agitation, but again it may show itself in a revolt that is absolute and final. Such an instance was reported in a Youngstown newspaper on the day I wrote these lines:—

Father Of Ten Drowns Self

. . . Out of work two years, Charles Wayne, aged 57, father of ten children, stood on the Spring Common bridge this morning. . . . He took off his coat, folded it carefully, and jumped into the swirling Mahoning River. Wayne was born in Youngstown and was employed by the Republic Iron and Steel Company for twenty-seven years as a hot mill worker. "We were about to lose our home," sobbed Mrs. Wayne. "And the gas and electric companies had threatened to shut off the service."

Source: Joseph L. Heffernan, "The Hungry City: A Mayor's Experience with Unemployment," *Atlantic Monthly*, May 1932, pp. 538–540, 546 5.

ACTION NOW!

On March 4, 1933, Franklin Delano Roosevelt became president and immediately reassured the American people. He insisted that "the only thing we have to fear is fear itself—nameless, unreasoning, unjustified terror, which paralyzes needed efforts to convert retreat into advance." And he promised "action, and action now!" In the first three months of his administration, the famous Hundred Days of the New Deal, the Democratic Congress passed many important laws (see the Overview table "Major Laws of the Hundred Days" on p. 666).

Roosevelt's program reflected a mix of ideas, some from FDR himself, some from a diverse group of advisers, including academic experts dubbed the "brain trust," politicians, and social workers. It also incorporated principles from the progressive movement, precedents from the Great War mobilization, and even plans from the Hoover administration. FDR had set its tone in his campaign when he declared, "The country needs, and, unless I mistake its temper, the country demands bold, persistent experimentation. . . . Above all, try something."

On March 5, FDR proclaimed a national bank holiday, closing all remaining banks. Congress then passed his Emergency Banking Act, a conservative measure that extended government assistance to sound banks and reorganized the weak ones.

WHERE TO LEARN MORE

Center for the New Deal Studies, Roosevelt University, Chicago, Illinois

OVERVIEW

MAJOR LAWS OF THE HUNDRED DAYS

Law	Objective
Emergency Banking Act	Stabilized the private banking system
Agricultural Adjustment Act	Established a farm recovery program based on production controls and price supports
Emergency Farm Mortgage Act	Provided for the refinancing of farm mortgages
National Industrial Recovery Act	Established a national recovery program and authorized a public works program
Federal Emergency Relief Act	Established a national system of relief
Home Owners Loan Act	Protected homeowners from mortgage foreclosure by refinancing home loans
Glass-Steagall Act	Separated commercial and investment banking and guaranteed bank deposits
Tennessee Valley Authority Act	Established the TVA and provided for the planned development of the Tennessee River Valley
Civilian Conservation Corps Act	Established the CCC to provide work relief on reforestation and conservation projects
Farm Credit Act	Expanded agricultural credits and established the Farm Credit Administration
Securities Act	Required full disclosure from stock exchanges
Wagner-Peyser Act	Created a U.S. Employment Service and encouraged states to create local public employment offices

Fireside chats Speeches broadcast nationally over the radio in which President Franklin D. Roosevelt explained complex issues and programs in plain language, as though his listeners were gathered around the fireside with him.

Federal Deposit Insurance Corporation (FDIC) Government agency that guarantees bank deposits, thereby protecting both depositors and banks.

Securities and Exchange Commission (SEC) Federal agency with authority to regulate trading practices in stocks and bonds.

Prompt government action, coupled with a reassuring **fireside chat** over the radio by the president, restored popular confidence in the banks. When they reopened on March 13, deposits exceeded withdrawals. "Capitalism," said Raymond Moley of the brain trust, "was saved in eight days." In June, Congress created the **Federal Deposit Insurance Corporation (FDIC)** to guarantee bank deposits up to $2,500.

The financial industry was also reformed. The Glass-Steagall Act separated investment and commercial banking to curtail risky speculation. The Securities Act reformed the sale of stocks to prevent the insider abuses that had characterized Wall Street, and in 1934, the **Securities and Exchange Commission (SEC)** was created to regulate the stock market. Two other financial measures in 1933 created the Home Owners Loan Corporation and the Farm Credit Administration, which enabled millions to refinance their mortgages.

CREATING JOBS

Roosevelt also provided relief for the unemployed. The Federal Emergency Relief Administration (FERA) furnished funds to state and local agencies. Directed by Harry Hopkins, FERA spent over $3 billion before it ended in 1935, and by then Hopkins and FDR had developed new programs that provided work relief to preserve both the skills and the morale of recipients. The Civil Works Administration (CWA) hired laborers to build roads, teachers to staff rural schools, and singers to give public performances. The Public Works Administration (PWA) provided work relief and stimulated the economy by building schools, hospitals, courthouses, airports, dams, and bridges. One of FDR's personal ideas, the Civilian Conservation Corps (CCC) employed 2.5 million young men to work on reforestation and flood control projects, build roads and bridges in national forests and parks, restore Civil War battlefields, and fight forest fires.

HELPING SOME FARMERS

In May 1933, Congress established the Agricultural Adjustment Administration (AAA) to combat the depression in agriculture caused by crop surpluses and low prices. The AAA subsidized farmers who agreed to restrict production. The objective was to boost farm prices to parity, a level that would restore farmers' purchasing power to its 1914 level. In the summer of 1933, the AAA paid southern farmers to plow up 10 million acres of cotton and midwestern farmers to bury 9 million pounds of pork. Restricting production in hard times caused public outrage.

But agricultural conditions improved. Farm prices rose from 52 percent of parity in 1932 to 88 percent in 1935, and gross farm income rose by 50 percent. Not until 1941, however, would income exceed the level of 1929, a poor year for farmers. Moreover, some of the decreased production and increased prices stemmed from devastating droughts and dust storms on the Great Plains. The AAA itself harmed poor farmers while aiding larger commercial growers. As southern planters restricted their acreage, they dismissed tenants and sharecroppers, and with AAA payments, they bought new farm machinery, reducing their need for farm labor. Thus while big producers moved toward prosperity, many small farmers were forced into a pool of rural labor for which there was decreasing need or into the cities, where there were no jobs.

The Supreme Court declared the AAA unconstitutional in 1936, but new laws established the farm subsidy program for decades to come. Increasing mechanization and scientific agriculture kept production high and farmers dependent on government intervention.

THE FLIGHT OF THE BLUE EAGLE

The New Deal attempted to revive American industry with the National Industrial Recovery Act (NIRA), which created the National Recovery Administration (NRA). The NRA sought to halt the slide in prices, wages, and employment by suspending antitrust laws and authorizing industrial and trade associations to draft codes setting production quotas, price policies, wages and working conditions, and other business practices. The codes promoted the interests of business generally and big business in particular, but Section 7a of the NIRA guaranteed workers the rights to organize unions and bargain collectively.

Hugh Johnson became director of the NRA and persuaded business leaders to cooperate in drafting codes and the public to patronize participating companies, indicated by the NRA Blue Eagle insignia. Corporate leaders, however, used the NRA to advance their own goals and discriminate against small producers, consumers, and labor. Employers also violated Section 7a, even using violence to smother unions. The NRA did little to enforce Section 7a, and Johnson—strongly probusiness—denounced all strikes. Workers felt betrayed.

Roosevelt tried to reorganize the NRA, but it remained controversial until the Supreme Court declared it unconstitutional in 1935.

CRITICS RIGHT AND LEFT

Though the early New Deal had not ended the depression, its efforts to grapple with problems, its successes in reducing suffering and fear, and Roosevelt's own skills carried the Democratic party to victory in the 1934 elections. But New Deal policies also provoked criticism.

WHERE TO LEARN MORE

Civilian Conservation Corps Interpretive Center, Whidbey Island, Washington

QUICK REVIEW

The National Recovery Administration (NRA)

♦ Sought to halt the slide in prices, wages, and employment.

♦ Tended to help business, often at the expense of labor.

♦ Declared unconstitutional in 1935.

WHERE TO LEARN MORE

★ Labor Museum and Learning
Center of Michigan,
Flint, Michigan

QUICK REVIEW

Critique of the New Deal

◆ Conservative critics of the
expansion of government gained
little support.

◆ Many on the left saw the early
New Deal as a "Raw Deal."

◆ Popular pressure mounted for
more aggressive policies.

Conservatives complained that the expansion of government activity and its regulatory role weakened the autonomy of American business. They also condemned the efforts to aid nonbusiness groups as socialistic, particularly the "excessive" spending on unemployment relief and the "instigation" of labor organizing. By 1934, as *Time* magazine reported, "Private fulminations and public carpings against the New Deal have become almost a routine of the business day." These critics attracted little popular support, however.

More realistic criticism came from the left. In 1932, FDR had campaigned for "the forgotten man at the bottom of the economic pyramid," and some radicals argued that the early New Deal had forgotten the forgotten man. In Arkansas and Tennessee, socialists in 1934 helped organize sharecroppers into the Southern Tenant Farmers Union protesting the "Raw Deal" they had received from the AAA. A broader labor militancy in 1934 also pressed Roosevelt. Workers acted as much against the failure of the NRA to enforce Section 7a as against recalcitrant corporations. The number of workers participating in strikes leaped from 325,000 in 1932 (about the annual average since 1925) to 1.5 million in 1934. From dockworkers in Seattle and copper miners in Butte to streetcar drivers in Milwaukee and shoemakers in Boston, workers demanded their rights.

Employers moved to crush the strikes, often using complaisant police and private strikebreakers. In Minneapolis, police shot sixty-seven teamsters, almost all in the back as they fled an ambush arranged by employers; in Toledo, company police and National Guardsmen attacked autoworkers with tear gas, bayonets, and rifle fire. At times, the workers held their ground. But against such powerful opponents, they needed help to achieve their rights.

Popular discontent was also mobilized by four prominent individuals demanding government action to assist groups neglected by the New Deal. Representative William Lemke of North Dakota, an agrarian radical leader of the Nonpartisan League, objected to the New Deal's limited response to farmers crushed by the depression. The AAA's strategy of simply restricting production, he thundered, was an "insane policy in the midst of hunger, misery, want, and rags." He sought government financial aid for farmers and policies favoring inflation, a traditional rural demand.

Francis Townsend, a California physician, called for a government pension to all Americans over the age of 60, provided they retire from work and spend their entire pension. This promised to extend relief to the many destitute elderly, open jobs for the unemployed, and stimulate economic recovery. Over five thousand Townsend Clubs lobbied for government action to help the elderly poor.

Father Charles Coughlin, a Catholic priest in the Detroit suburb of Royal Oak, threatened to mobilize another large constituency against the limitations of the early New Deal. Thirty million Americans listened eagerly to his weekly radio broadcasts mixing religion with anti-Semitism and demands for social justice and financial reform. After concluding that FDR's policies favored "the virile viciousness of business and finance," Coughlin organized the National Union for Social Justice to lobby for his goals. With support among lower-middle-class, heavily Catholic, urban ethnic groups, Coughlin posed a real challenge to Roosevelt's Democratic party.

Senator Huey P. Long of Louisiana wanted more comprehensive social welfare policies, but he also wanted to be president. In 1934, he organized the Share-Our-Wealth Society. His plan to end poverty and unemployment called for confiscatory taxes on the rich to provide every family with a decent income, health coverage, education, and old-age pensions. Within months, Long's organization claimed more than 27,000 clubs and 7 million members.

These dissident movements raised complex issues and simple fears. They built on concerns about the New Deal, with programs often ill-defined or impractical. Nevertheless, their popularity warned Roosevelt that government action was needed to satisfy reform demands and assure his reelection in 1936.

CONSOLIDATING THE NEW DEAL

In 1935, Roosevelt undertook economic and social reforms that some observers have called the Second New Deal. The new measures shifted the relative weights accorded to the constant objectives of recovery, relief, and reform. This new phase reflected the persisting depression, growing political pressures, and the progressive inclinations of key New Dealers, including FDR himself.

LIFTING UP AND WEEDING OUT

"In spite of our efforts and in spite of our talk," Roosevelt told the new Congress in 1935, "we have not weeded out the overprivileged and we have not effectively lifted up the underprivileged." To do so, he developed "must" legislation, to which his allies in Congress added. One of the new laws protected labor's rights to organize and bargain collectively. Drafted by Senator Robert Wagner of New York to replace Section 7a, the Wagner National Labor Relations Act, dubbed "Labor's Magna Carta," guaranteed workers' rights to organize unions and forbade employers to adopt unfair labor practices, such as firing union activists or forming company unions. The law also set up the National Labor Relations Board (NLRB) to enforce these provisions, protect workers from coercion, and supervise union elections.

Of greater long-range importance was the Social Security Act. It provided unemployment compensation, old-age pensions, and aid for dependent mothers and children and the blind. The conservative nature of the law appeared in its stingy benefit payments, its lack of health insurance, and its exclusion of more than a fourth of all workers, including many in desperate need of protection, such as farm laborers and domestic servants. Moreover, unlike in other nations, the old-age pensions were financed through a regressive payroll tax on both employees and employers rather than through general tax revenues. Thus the new system was more like a compulsory insurance program. Despite its weaknesses, however, the Social Security Act was one of the most important laws in American history. It provided, Roosevelt pointed out, "at least some measure of protection to the average citizen and to his family against the loss of a job and against poverty-ridden old age."

Among other reform measures, the Banking Act of 1935 increased the authority of the Federal Reserve Board over the nation's currency and credit system and decreased the power of the private bankers whose irresponsible behavior had contributed to the depression and the appeal of Father Coughlin. The Revenue Act of 1935 provided for graduated income taxes and increased estate and corporate taxes. Opponents called it the Soak the Rich Tax, but with its many loopholes, it was scarcely that. Nevertheless, it set a precedent for progressive taxation and attracted popular support.

The Second New Deal also responded belatedly to the environmental catastrophe that had turned much of the Great Plains into a "Dust Bowl" (see Map 25–1). Since World War I, farmers had stripped marginal land of its native grasses to plant wheat. When drought and high winds hit the plains in 1932, crops failed, and nothing held the soil. Dust storms blew away millions of tons of topsoil, despoiling the land and darkening the sky 1,000 miles away. Families abandoned their farms in droves.

WHICH ECONOMIC

and social reforms made up the "Second New Deal"?

25–2
Share the Wealth

QUICK REVIEW

The Social Security Act

◆ Provided unemployment compensation, old-age pensions, and aid for dependent mothers and children and the blind.

◆ The law excluded more than a fourth of all workers and did not include health insurance.

◆ Funded by a regressive payroll tax.

A sullen mother stares vacantly between her two children in a migrant labor camp in Nipomo, California in 1936. This photograph, commissioned by the FSA, came to symbolize the Great Depression for many people.

Courtesy of the Library of Congress

MAP EXPLORATION
To explore an interactive version of this map, go to
http://www.prenhall.com/goldfield2/map25.1

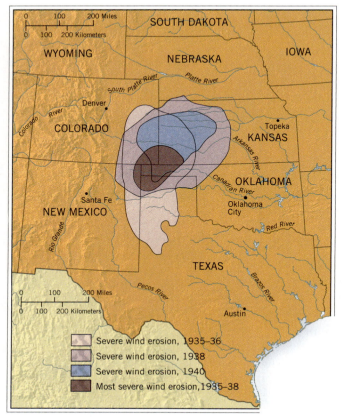

Severe wind erosion, 1935–36
Severe wind erosion, 1938
Severe wind erosion, 1940
Most severe wind erosion, 1935–38

MAP 25–1
The Dust Bowl Years of overcultivation, drought, and high winds created the Dust Bowl, which most severely affected the southern Great Plains. Federal relief and conservation programs provided assistance, but many residents fled the area, often migrating to California.

WHY WAS this drought particularly damaging to people in this region?

In 1935, Roosevelt established the Resettlement Administration to focus on land reform and help poor farmers. Under Rexford Tugwell, this agency initiated soil erosion projects and attempted to resettle impoverished farmers on better land, but the problem exceeded its resources. Congress moved to save the land, if not its people, by creating the Soil Conservation Service in 1935.

EXPANDING RELIEF

Relief remained critical in the Second New Deal. With millions still unemployed, Roosevelt pushed through Congress in 1935 the Emergency Relief Appropriation Act, authorizing $5 billion—at the time the largest single appropriation in history—for emergency public employment. Roosevelt created the Works Progress Administration (WPA) under Hopkins, who set up work relief programs to assist the unemployed and boost the economy. Before its end in 1943, the WPA gave jobs to 9 million people (more than a fifth of the labor force) and spent nearly $12 billion. Three-fourths of its expenditures went on construction projects that could employ manual labor: the WPA built 125,000 schools, post offices, and hospitals; 8,000 parks; nearly 100,000 bridges; and enough roads and sewer systems to circle the earth thirty times. From New York City's La Guardia Airport to Atlanta's sewer system to irrigation ditches in the Far West, the WPA laid much of the nation's basic infrastructure on which it still relies.

The WPA also developed work projects for unemployed writers, artists, musicians, and actors. "Why not?" said FDR. "They are human beings. They have to live." These WPA programs allowed people to use their talents while surviving the depression, increased popular access to cultural performances, and established a precedent for federal support of the arts.

The National Youth Administration (NYA), another WPA agency, gave part-time jobs to students, enabling 2 million high school and college students to stay in school, learn skills, and do productive work. Law student Richard M. Nixon earned 35 cents an hour doing research in the library. Lyndon Johnson, a Texas NYA official, believed that "if the Roosevelt administration had never done another thing, it would have been justified by the work of this great institution for salvaging youth."

THE ROOSEVELT COALITION AND THE ELECTION OF 1936

The 1936 election gave Americans an opportunity to judge FDR and the New Deal. Conservatives alarmed at the expansion of government, businesspeople angered by regulation and labor legislation, and well-to-do Americans furious with tax reform decried the New Deal. But they were a minority. Even the presidential candidate they supported, Republican Governor Alf Landon of Kansas, endorsed much of the New Deal, criticizing merely the inefficiency and cost of some of its programs. The reforms of 1935 had undercut the arguments of critics on the left, and the assassination of Huey Long in the same year had removed their ablest

FROM THEN TO NOW
Social Security

No politician will "ever scrap my social security program." So predicted FDR when he signed the Social Security Act in 1935. He based his confidence on the provisions in the act that linked benefits to payroll deductions. Because workers contributed to the program, they would feel a "right to collect their pensions and unemployment benefits." But Roosevelt could not have imagined just how successful the Social Security program would become. Expanded over the years since the 1930s, it now assists 44 million Americans, including the elderly, the disabled, and the survivors of contributors to the program. Certain poverty would confront half the nation's elderly without their monthly checks.

But the successful expansion of the program has also called its future into question. By 2030, the number of eligible recipients will double, but the number of employees paying Social Security taxes will increase by only 17 percent. Annual funding deficits of more than $100 billion loom ahead.

Still, as FDR predicted, no political leader dares to propose "scrapping" Social Security. Rather, proposals to solve this problem reflect conflicting views about the expansion of the federal government—and especially its efforts to promote social welfare—that began with the New Deal. No longer does the public overwhelmingly endorse federal responsibility for solving social problems as it did during the economic crisis of the 1930s. On the contrary, an increasingly intense backlash against "big government" emerged in the 1960s, ultimately finding its champion in the 1980s in Republican President Ronald Reagan, who declared, "Government is not the solution to our problems; government is the problem." Reagan's administration sought to reduce the size of government and curtail its regulatory oversight of American business. This "Reagan Revolution" appealed to those who never supported government responsibility for social welfare and to those who had lost trust in the government's ability to fulfill that role. By the 1990s, even Democratic President Bill Clinton declared an end to the era of "big government."

Support has grown for private initiatives to replace government programs, and now critics are pressing to "privatize" the Social Security system itself. They have proposed such sweeping changes as limiting benefits to contributors only and requiring contributors to invest their Social Security accounts themselves, including in the stock market. The predicted payoff would be larger earnings.

Opponents of these critics argue for reforming, not overturning, the current Social Security system. Privatization, they argue, would undermine Social Security's fundamental principle: to guarantee retirees a dependable income base. Investing retirement savings in the stock market subjects them to market volatility, which might benefit some people but could leave others with serious losses just when they were ready to retire. Privatization would also eliminate the special assistance that Social Security provides to large families, couples with one partner who has had no or limited earnings, and low-income earners.

Rather than scrap the current system, reformers propose other changes. They suggest taxing all workers for Social Security, many, especially in state and local governments, are now outside the system. Extending the age of eligibility to receive benefits, justified by the increasing life expectancy of Americans, would also bolster the Social Security funds. Another proposal would abandon the current investment strategy but have a quasi-private government entity manage the system's portfolio. Such changes would enable Social Security to continue meeting the needs of all citizens.

The current argument over Social Security echoes the disputes of the 1930s about the role and function of our government and reflects continuing differences over the degree to which the government should attempt to make American society more equitable. Finding a solution to funding Social Security in the new century will require addressing the issue of America's core values.

FDR signs the Social Security Act in 1935, establishing a program that would grow in size and importance in subsequent decades. To the left in a dark suit is Senator Robert F. Wagner; behind FDR is Secretary of Labor Frances Perkins. All three were influential in shaping an activist federal government that some Americans would later decry as unnecessary.

AP/Wide World Photos

WHERE TO LEARN MORE

★ Franklin D. Roosevelt Home and
Presidential Library,
Hyde Park, New York
www.fdrlibrary.marist.edu

WHAT IMPACT did
New Deal programs have on
women and minorities?

Congress of Industrial Organizations
An alliance of industrial unions
that spurred the 1930s organizational drive among the mass-production
industries.

politician. They formed the Union party and nominated William Lemke for the presidency, but they were no longer a threat.

The programs and politicians of the New Deal had created an invincible coalition behind Roosevelt. The New Deal's agricultural programs reinforced the traditional Democratic allegiance of white Southerners while attracting many Western farmers. Labor legislation clinched the active support of the nation's workers. Middle-class voters, whose homes had been saved and whose hopes had been raised, also joined the Roosevelt coalition.

So did urban ethnic groups, who had benefited from welfare programs and received unprecedented recognition. FDR named the first Italian American to the federal judiciary, for example, and appointed five times as many Catholics and Jews to government positions as the three Republican presidents had during the 1920s. African Americans voted overwhelmingly Democratic for the first time. Women, too, were an important part of the Roosevelt coalition. As one campaigner said to a roaring crowd in 1936, "Many women in this country when they vote for Franklin D. Roosevelt will also be thinking with a choke in the throat of Eleanor Roosevelt!"

This political realignment produced a landslide. Roosevelt polled 61 per-cent of the popular vote and the largest electoral vote margin ever recorded, 523 to 8. Landon even lost Kansas, his own state, and Lemke received fewer than 900,000 votes. Democrats also won huge majorities in Congress.

THE NEW DEAL AND AMERICAN LIFE

T he landslide of 1936 reflected the impact the New Deal had on Ameri-cans. Government programs changed daily life, and ordinary people often helped shape the new policies.

LABOR ON THE MARCH

The labor revival in the 1930s reflected both workers' determination and gov-ernment support. Workers wanted not merely to improve their wages and bene-fits but also to gain union recognition and union contracts to limit arbitrary managerial authority and achieve some control over the workplace. The Wagner Act sparked a wave of labor activism. But if the government ultimately protected union rights, the unions themselves had to form locals, recruit members, and demonstrate influence in the workplace.

At first, the American Federation of Labor (AFL), with its reliance on craft-based unions and its reluctance to organize immigrant, black, and women work-ers, was unprepared for the rush of industrial workers seeking unionization. More progressive labor leaders formed the Committee for Industrial Organization (CIO) within the AFL. They campaigned to unionize workers in the steel, auto, and rub-ber industries, all notoriously hostile to unions. AFL leaders insisted that the CIO disband and then in 1937 expelled its unions. The militants reorganized as the sep-arate **Congress of Industrial Organizations**.

The split roused the AFL to increase its own organizing activities, but it was primarily the new CIO that put labor on the march. It inspired workers previously neglected. The CIO's interracial union campaign in the Birmingham steel mills, said one organizer, was "like a second coming of Christ" for black workers, who wel-comed the union as a chance for social recognition as well as economic opportunity. The CIO also employed new and aggressive tactics, particularly the sit-down strike, in which workers, rather than picketing outside the factory, simply sat inside the plant, thereby blocking both production and the use of strikebreakers. Upton Sinclair said, "For seventy-five years big business has been sitting down on the American people, and now I am delighted to see the process reversed."

Sit-down strikes paralyzed General Motors in 1937 after it refused to recognize the United Auto Workers. GM tried to force the strikers out of its Flint, Michigan, plants by turning off the heat, using police and tear gas, and threatening strikers' families. The strikers held out, and after six weeks GM signed a contract with the UAW. Chrysler soon followed suit. Ford refused to recognize the union until 1941, often violently disrupting organizing efforts.

Steel companies also used violence against unionization. In the Memorial Day Massacre in Chicago in 1937, police guarding a plant of the Republic Steel Company fired on strikers and their families, killing ten people as they tried to flee. Scores more were wounded and beaten. A Senate investigation found that Republic and other companies "dominate their employees, deny them their constitutional rights, promote disorder and disharmony, and even set at naught the powers of the government itself." Federal court orders finally forced the companies to bargain collectively.

New Deal labor legislation, government investigations and court orders, and the federal refusal to use force against strikes helped the labor movement secure basic rights for American workers. Union membership leaped from under 3 million in 1932 to 9 million by 1939, and workers won higher wages, better working conditions, and more economic democracy.

WOMEN AND THE NEW DEAL

As federal programs proliferated in 1933, a Baltimore women's group urged the administration to "come out for a square and new deal for women." Although women did gain increased attention and influence, government and society remained largely bound by traditional values.

New Deal relief programs had a mixed impact on workingwomen. Formal government policy required "equal consideration" for women and men, but local officials so flouted this requirement that Eleanor Roosevelt urged Harry Hopkins to "impress on state administrators that the women's programs are as important as the men's. They are so apt to forget us!" Women on relief were restricted to "women's work"— more than half worked on sewing projects, regardless of their skills—and were paid scarcely half what men received. And although women constituted nearly a fourth of the labor force, they obtained only 19 percent of the jobs created by the WPA, 12 percent by the FERA, and 7 percent by the CWA. The CCC excluded women altogether. Still, relief agencies provided crucial assistance to women in the depression.

Other New Deal programs also had mixed benefits for women. Many NRA codes mandated lower wage scales for women than for men, which officials justified as reflecting "long-established customs." But by raising minimum wages, the NRA brought relatively greater improvements to women, who were concentrated in the lowest-paid occupations, than to male workers. The Social Security Act did not cover domestic servants, waitresses, and women who worked in the home but did help mothers with dependent children.

Women also gained political influence under the New Deal. Molly Dewson, the director of the Women's Division of the Democratic party, exercised considerable political power and helped shape the party's campaigns. Around Dewson revolved a network of women, linked by friendships and experiences in the National Consumers' League, Women's Trade Union League, and other progressive reform organizations. Appointed to positions in the Roosevelt administration, they helped develop and implement New Deal social legislation. Secretary of Labor Frances Perkins was the first

25–3
Mrs. Henry Weddington, Letter to President Roosevelt (1938)

WHERE TO LEARN MORE

★ Eleanor Roosevelt National
Historic Site,
Hyde Park, New York
www.nps.gov/elro

woman cabinet member and a key member of the network; other women were in the Treasury Department, the Children's Bureau, and relief and cultural programs.

Eleanor Roosevelt roared across the social and political landscape of the 1930s, pushing for women's rights, demanding reforms, traveling across the country, writing newspaper columns and speaking over the radio, developing plans to help unemployed miners and abolish slums. FDR rebuffed her critics with a jaunty, "Well, that is my wife; I can't do anything about her." Indeed, Eleanor Roosevelt had become a symbol of the growing importance of women in public life.

MINORITIES AND THE NEW DEAL

Although Roosevelt deplored racial abuses, he never pushed for civil rights legislation, fearing to antagonize the influential Southern Democrats in Congress whose support he needed. For similar reasons, many New Deal programs discriminated against African Americans. The CCC segregated black workers; NRA codes so often specified lower wages and benefits for black workers relative to white workers or even excluded black workers from jobs that the black press claimed NRA stood for "Negro Run Around" or "Negroes Ruined Again."

However, African Americans did benefit from the New Deal's welfare and economic programs. W. E. B. Du Bois asserted that "large numbers of colored people in the United States would have starved to death if it had not been for the Roosevelt policies." And key New Dealers campaigned against racial discrimination. Eleanor Roosevelt, prodded FDR to appoint black officials, wrote articles supporting racial equality, and flouted segregationist laws. Attacked by white racists, she was popular in the black community. As black votes in Northern cities became important, more pragmatic New Dealers also began to pay more attention to black needs.

African Americans themselves pressed for reforms, and FDR took more interest in their economic and social problems. He prohibited discrimination in the WPA in 1935, and the NYA adopted enlightened racial policies. Roosevelt also appointed black people to important positions, including the first black federal judge. Many of these officials began meeting regularly at the home of Mary McLeod Bethune of the National Council of Negro Women. Dubbed the Black Cabinet, they worked with civil rights organizations, fought discrimination in government, influenced patronage, and stimulated black interest in politics.

WHERE TO LEARN MORE

★ Bethune Museum and Archives
National Historic Site,
Washington, D.C.

Under the New Deal, black illiteracy dropped because of federal education projects, and the number of black college students and graduates more than doubled, in part because the NYA provided student aid to black colleges. New Deal relief and public health programs reduced black infant mortality rates and raised life expectancy rates. Conditions for black people continued to lag behind those for white people, and discrimination persisted, but the black switch to the Roosevelt coalition reflected the New Deal's benefits.

Native Americans also benefited from the New Deal. The CCC particularly appealed to their interests and skills. More than eighty thousand Indians received training in agriculture, forestry, and animal husbandry, along with basic academic subjects. CCC projects, together with those undertaken by the PWA and the WPA, built schools, hospitals, roads, and irrigation systems on reservations.

New Deal officials also refocused government Indian policy, which had undermined tribal authority and promoted assimilation by reducing Indian landholding and attacking Indian culture. Appointed commissioner of Indian affairs in 1933, John Collier prohibited interference with Indian religious or cultural life, directed the Bureau of Indian Affairs to employ more Indians, and prevented Indian schools from suppressing native languages and traditions. The Indian Reorganization Act of 1934, often called the Indians' New Deal, guaranteed

religious freedom, reestablished tribal self-government, and halted the sale of tribal lands. It also provided funds to expand Indian landholdings, support Indian students, and establish tribal businesses.

Hispanic Americans received less assistance from the New Deal. Its relief programs
aided many Hispanics in California and the Southwest but ignored those who were not
citizens. And by excluding agricultural workers, neither the Social Security Act nor the
Wagner Act gave Mexican Americans much protection or hope. Farm workers remained largely unorganized, exploited, and at the mercy of agribusinesses.

THE NEW DEAL: NORTH, SOUTH, EAST, AND WEST

"We are going to make a country," President Roosevelt declared, "in which no one
is left out." And with that statement along with his belief that the federal government
must take the lead in building a new "economic constitutional order," FDR ensured
that his New Deal programs and policies fanned out throughout the nation, bolstering the stock market and banking in New York, constructing public housing for
poor immigrant families and African Americans in most major cities, and building
schools, roads, and bridges in all regions of the United States. Ironically, the New
Deal also offered special benefits to the South, traditionally averse to government
activism, and to the West, which considered itself the land of rugged individualism.

The New Deal's agricultural program boosted farm prices and income more
in the South than any other region. By controlling cotton production, it also promoted diversification; its subsidies financed mechanization. The resulting modernization helped replace an archaic sharecropping system with an emergent
agribusiness. The rural poor were displaced, but the South's agricultural economy advanced.

The New Deal also improved Southern cities. FERA and WPA built urban
sewer systems, airports, bridges, roads, and harbor facilities. Whereas Northern cities
had already constructed such facilities themselves—and were still paying off their
debts—the federal government largely paid for such modernization in the South,
giving its cities an economic advantage.

Federal grants were supposed to be awarded to states in proportion to their
own expenditures, but Southern politicians refused to contribute their share of the
costs. Nationally, the federal proportion of FERA expenditures was 62 percent; in
the South, it was usually 90 percent and never lower than 73 percent.

Federal money enabled Southern communities to balance their own budgets,
preach fiscal orthodoxy, and maintain traditional claims of limited government.
Even Southerners acknowledged the hypocrisy of the region's invocation of state's
rights. "We recognize state boundaries when called on to give," noted the *Houston
Press*, "but forget them when Uncle Sam is doing the giving."

The federal government had a particularly powerful impact on the South with
the **Tennessee Valley Authority (TVA)**, launched in 1933 (see Map 25–2). Coordinating activities across seven states, the TVA built dams to control floods and generate hydroelectric power, produced fertilizer, fostered agricultural and forestry development,
encouraged conservation, improved navigation, and modernized school and health
systems. Its major drawback was environmental damage that only became apparent later.
Over a vast area of the South, it provided electricity for the first time.

The New Deal further expanded access to electricity by establishing the Rural
Electrification Administration (REA) in 1935. Private companies had refused to
extend power lines into the countryside because it was not profitable, consigning
90 percent of the nation's farms to drudgery and darkness. The REA revolutionized farm life by sponsoring rural nonprofit electric cooperatives. By 1950, 78 percent of American farms had electricity.

American educator and activist Mary
McLeod Bethune.
Courtesy of the Library of Congress

Tennessee Valley Authority (TVA)
Federal regional planning agency established to promote conservation,
produce electric power, and encourage economic development in seven
southern states.

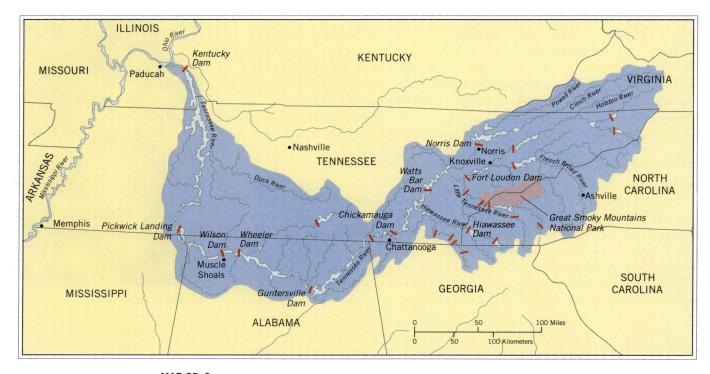

MAP 25–2

The Tennessee Valley Authority   By building dams and hydroelectric power plants, the TVA controlled flooding and soil erosion and generated electricity that did much to modernize a large region of the Upper South.

WHAT ECONOMIC and social impact did the Tennessee Valley Authority have on the Upper South?

The New Deal also changed the West. Westerners received the most federal money per capita in welfare, relief projects, and loans. Western farmers and cattle raisers were saved by federal payments, and even refugees from the Dust Bowl depended on relief assistance and medical care in federal camps.

The Bureau of Reclamation, established in 1902, built huge dams to control the Western river systems, promote large-scale development, prevent flooding, produce cheap hydroelectric power, and create reservoirs and canal systems to bring water to farms and cities. By furnishing capital and expertise, the government subsidized and stimulated western economic development, particularly the growth of agribusiness.

Westerners welcomed such assistance but rarely shared the federal goals of rational resource management. Instead, they often wanted to continue to exploit the land and resented federal supervision as colonial control. In practice, however, the government worked in partnership with the West's agribusinesses and timber and petroleum industries.

THE NEW DEAL AND PUBLIC ACTIVISM

Despite Hoover's fear that government responsibility would discourage local initiative, New Deal programs, in fact, often encouraged or empowered groups to shape public policy and social and economic behavior. Moreover, because the administration worried about centralization, some federal agencies fostered what New Dealers called "grass-roots democracy." The AAA set up committees totaling more than 100,000 people to implement agricultural policy and held referendums on crop controls; local advisory committees guided the various federal arts projects; federal management of the West's public grasslands mandated cooperation with associations of livestock raisers.

At times, federal programs allowed previously unrepresented groups to contest traditionally dominant interests. Often seeing greater opportunities for participation and influence in federal programs than in city and state governments, community groups even campaigned to expand federal authority. In short, depression conditions and New Deal programs actually increased citizen involvement in public affairs.

EBBING OF THE NEW DEAL

A fter his victory in 1936, Roosevelt committed himself to further reforms. "The test of our progress," he declared in his second inaugural address, "is not whether we add more to the abundance of those who have much; it is whether we provide enough for those who have too little." But determined opponents, continuing economic problems, and the president's own misjudgments blocked his reforms and deadlocked the New Deal.

WHY WERE late New Deal reforms unsuccessful?

CHALLENGING THE COURT

During Roosevelt's first term, the Supreme Court had declared unconstitutional several important measures. FDR complained that the justices held "horse-and-buggy" ideas about government that prevented the president and Congress from responding to changes. He decided to restructure the federal judiciary and, in early 1937, proposed legislation authorizing a new judge for each one serving past the age of 70. Additional judges, he said, would increase judicial efficiency, but his real goal was to appoint new judges more sympathetic to the New Deal.

His court plan led to a divisive struggle. The proposal was perfectly legal, but Republicans and conservative Democrats attacked the plan as a scheme to "pack" the Court and subvert the separation of powers among the three branches of government. Even many liberals expressed reservations. The Court itself undercut support for FDR's proposal by upholding the Social Security and Wagner Acts. Congress rejected Roosevelt's plan.

Roosevelt's challenge to the Court hurt the New Deal. It worried the public, split the Democratic party, and revived conservatives. Opponents promptly attacked other New Deal policies, from support for unions to progressive taxation. Henceforth, a conservative coalition of Republicans and Southern Democrats in Congress blocked FDR's reforms.

MORE HARD TIMES

A sharp recession beginning in August 1937 added to Roosevelt's problems. As the economy improved in 1936, Roosevelt decided to cut federal expenditures and balance the budget, but private investment and employment remained stagnant, and the economy plunged. A record decline in industrial production canceled the gains of the previous two years, and unemployment leaped from 7 million to 11 million. Republicans delighted in attacking the "Roosevelt recession," although it stemmed from retrenchment policies they themselves advocated.

In 1938, Roosevelt reluctantly increased spending, based on the principles of British economist John Maynard Keynes. As Marriner Eccles of the Federal Reserve Board explained, the federal government had to serve as the "compensatory agent" in the economy: It should use deficit spending to increase demand and production when private investment declined and raise taxes to pay its debt and cool the economy when business activity became excessive. New appropriations for the PWA and other government programs revived the faltering economy, but only the vast expenditures for World War II would bring full recovery.

POLITICAL STALEMATE

The recession interrupted the momentum of the New Deal and strengthened its opponents. In late 1937, their leaders in Congress issued a "conservative manifesto" decrying New Deal fiscal, labor, and regulatory policies. Holding seniority in a Congress malapportioned in their favor, they blocked most of Roosevelt's reforms. None of his "must" legislation passed a special session of Congress in December. In 1938, Congress rejected tax reforms and reduced corporate taxes. The few measures that passed were heavily amended. The Fair Labor Standards Act established maximum hours and minimum wages for workers but authorized so many exemptions that one New Dealer asked "whether anyone is subject to this bill."

To protect the New Deal, Roosevelt turned again to the public, with whom he remained immensely popular. In the 1938 Democratic primaries, he campaigned against the New Deal's conservative opponents. But FDR could not transfer his personal popularity to the political newcomers he supported. What his foes attacked as a "purge" failed. Roosevelt lost further political leverage when the Republicans gained seventy-five seats in the House and seven in the Senate and thirteen governorships.

The Democrats retained majorities in both houses of Congress, but the Republican revival and the survival of the conservative Southern Democrats guaranteed that the New Deal had gone as far as it ever would. With Roosevelt in the White House and his opponents controlling Congress, the New Deal ended in political stalemate.

GOOD NEIGHBORS AND HOSTILE FORCES

Even before FDR's conservative opposition derailed the New Deal, the President felt the impact of congressional limitations in foreign policy. Isolationists in Congress counseled against any U.S. involvement in world affairs. Republican Senator Gerald Nye established a committee in 1934 to investigate the origins of U.S. involvement in what many Americans termed the European War. The Nye Committee exposed the greed of big business and intimated that President Woodrow Wilson had gone to war to save profits for capitalists—and not democracy for the world. Jobless and homeless Americans reacted with anger to the committee's findings and public sentiment against fighting another "foreign" war hardened. Roosevelt himself believed that the gravity of the nation's economic depression warranted a primary focus on domestic recovery, and in the early years of his presidency, he took few international initiatives.

Those actions he did take related directly to salvaging America's desperate economy. In 1933, key business leaders informed FDR that they would welcome the opportunity to expand trade to the Soviet Union, and the President extended formal recognition of the Soviet Union in November 1933.

Enhancing trade opportunities also figured prominently in Roosevelt's policies in the Western hemisphere where he extended the Good Neighbor policy begun by President Herbert Hoover who had removed all U.S. troops from Latin America. Still, the Great Depression strained U.S.-Latin American relations, sending economic shock waves throughout Central and South America and helping propel to power ruthless dictators who ruled with U.S. support. In Cuba FDR supported a coup, which resulted in the coming to power of the infamous dictator Fulgencio Batista, whose domination lasted until it was overthrown by Fidel Castro in 1959.

FDR also worked to encourage trade by reducing tariffs. Between 1929 and 1933, the volume of trade worldwide had fallen by 40 percent and American exports had plummeted by 60 percent. Secretary of State Cordell Hull finalized trade agreements with Latin American nations that sharply increased U.S. exports to its southern neighbors. Good neighbors were also good trading partners.

NEUTRALITY AND FASCISM

During his first term as president, Roosevelt generally avoided involvement in Europe's problems, but the aggressive actions of Adolf Hitler in Germany ultimately led Roosevelt to try to educate the American public, still resentful of U.S. participation in World War I, about the fascist danger that was spreading in Europe. Hitler came to power in 1933, shortly before FDR entered the White House, and he pledged to restore German pride and nationalism in the aftermath of the Versailles Treaty. As the leader of the National Socialist Workers Party—the Nazis—Hitler established a **fascist government**—a one-party dictatorship—closely aligned with corporate interests, committed to a "biological world evolution," and determined to establish a new empire, the Third Reich. He vowed to destroy Bolshevik radicalism and purify the German "race" by eliminating those he deemed undesirable, especially Jewis, whom Hitler blamed for most, if not all, Germany's ills.

Others aided the spread of fascism. Benito Mussolini, who had assumed power in Italy in 1922, attacked Ethiopia in 1935. The following year, a conservative military officer, Francisco Franco, led an uprising in Spain, and with the assistance of Italy and Germany, overthrew the Spanish Republic to create an authoritarian government. Meanwhile, Hitler remilitarized the Rhineland in 1936 and in 1938 he annexed Austria.

But the aggressive actions of Germany and Italy failed to eclipse American fears of being led into another European war. Congress passed four Neutrality Acts designed to continue America's trade with its world partners but prohibit the president from taking sides in the mounting European crisis. The first act, passed in 1935, prohibited Americans from traveling to a war zone, banned loans to belligerent nations, and instituted an embargo on armaments to belligerents. In 1937 Congress added a "cash-and-carry" provision that required belligerent nations to pay for American goods in advance of their shipment. President Roosevelt reluctantly signed the bill into law but continued to work to heighten public awareness of the dangers of Nazism.

In 1938, Hitler demanded the Sudetenland from Czechoslovakia. The French and British, following a policy of appeasement, met in Munich in September 1938, with Hitler and Mussolini and abandoned the Czechs, yielding the Sudetenland to Hitler in exchange for a weak promise of no more annexations.

In America, too, the sentiment was for peace at all costs, and Hitler did not regard the United States as a threat to his expansionist plan: He held FDR in low esteem and denounced America as a racially mixed nation of intellectual inferiors. "Transport a German to Kiev," Hitler declared, "and he remains a perfect German. But transplant him to Miami, and you make a degenerate out of him—in other words, an American." Isolationism also combined with anti-Semitism and with division among America's Jewish leadership to insure that the United States would not become a haven for Jews suffering under Nazi brutality. News of Nazi atrocities against Jews, particularly the violent pogrom, known as *Kristallnacht* (the Night of the Broken Glass) in November 1938, shocked the American Press. Although the United States recalled its ambassador from Berlin to protest the pogrom, the United States failed to alter its restrictive immigration quota system, the 1924 National Origins Act, to provide refuge for German Jews. Unchallenged,

Fascist government   A government subscribing to a philosophy of dictatorship that merges the interests of the state, armed forces, and big business.

On November 9, 1938 Nazi Germany launched an assault on Jews, destroying their businessess and burning their synagogues. This street scene in Berlin shows the shattered windows of Jewish businesses. Nazi leader Joseph Goebbels recorded the event, known as Kristallnacht, in his diary: "Yesterday: Berlin. There, all proceded fantastically. One fire after another. It is good that way. . . . 100 dead. But no German property damaged."

UPI/Corbis–Bettmann

Hitler pressed on with his campaign of terror, herding Jews, Slavs, homosexuals, and handicapped citizens into concentration camps.

As Europe edged closer to war, the relationship between the United States and Japan, periodically tense, became more strained. Japan resented U.S. economic interests in East Asia and was offended by American immigration policy which excluded Japanese immigrants. The United States regarded Japan's desires for empire as threatening but also needed Japan as a trading partner, especially in the economically depressed 1930s. Consequently in September 1931, when Japan seized Manchuria and then went to war with China, the United States merely condemned the actions, and although President Roosevelt denounced "the epidemic of world lawlessness", in 1937 and called for a "quarantine" of aggressors, he refused to risk war with Japan.

EDGING TOWARD INVOLVEMENT

After the Munich agreement, President Roosevelt moved away from domestic reform toward preparedness for war, fearful that conflict in Europe was unavoidable and determined to revise the neutrality laws. In his State of the Union address in January 1939, FDR explained that "our neutrality laws" might "actually give aid to an aggressor and deny it to the victim." By the fall of that year, he had won support for eliminating the prohibition of arms and adding armaments to the list of cash-and-carry items—a revision that would enable the United States to provide important assistance to Britain and France in the winter of 1939–1940. Hitler's defiance of the Munich agreement and his seizure of all of Czechoslovakia in March 1939 anticipated his next move toward Poland later that summer and also convinced the British and the French that war was imminent.

CONCLUSION

The Great Depression and the New Deal mark a major divide in American history. The depression cast doubt on the traditional practices, policies, and attitudes that underlay not only the nation's economy but its social and political institutions and relationships as well. The New Deal failed to restore prosperity, but it did bring partial economic recovery. Moreover, its economic policies, from banking and securities regulation to unemployment compensation, farm price supports, and minimum wages, created barriers against another depression. The gradual adoption of compensatory spending policies also expanded the government's role in the economy. Responding to the failures of both private organizations and state and local governments, the federal government also assumed the obligation to provide social welfare. "Better the occasional faults of a Government that lives in a spirit of charity," Roosevelt warned, "than the constant omission of a Government frozen in the ice of its own indifference."

The New Deal brought political changes, too. The role of the presidency expanded; the federal government, rather than state or local governments, became the focus of public interest and expectations; and the Roosevelt coalition made the Democrats the dominant national party for years to come. Political constraints limited some New Deal efforts, particularly to curtail racial discrimination or protect the rural and urban poor, but the New Deal did change American life. By 1939, as international relations deteriorated, FDR was already considering a shift, as he later said, from Dr. New Deal to Dr. Win-the-War.

SUMMARY

Hard Times in Hooverville The prosperity of the 1920s ended in a stock market crash that revealed the flaws in the economy. As the nation slid into a catastrophic depression, factories closed, employment and incomes tumbled, and millions lost their homes, hopes, and dignity. Some protested and took direct action; others looked to the government for relief. The stock market crash of 1929 marked the beginning of the Great Depression but did not cause it. Contributing factors were the uneven distribution of wealth and income; industries dominated by oligarchies; overproduction in agriculture and other industries; declining prices; government policies; and European debts.

Herbert Hoover and the Depression President Hoover took unprecedented steps to resolve the growing economic crises, but he believed that voluntary private relief was preferable to federal intervention. The scope of the depression overwhelmed anything that private individuals and agencies could manage; Hoover blundered by refusing to admit a more activist approach was needed. The Reconstruction Finance Corporation lent funds that could "trickle down" to the public. The treatment of the Bonus Army symbolized Hoover's unpopularity and set the stage for the election of Franklin D. Roosevelt.

Launching the New Deal In the midst of national anxiety, Franklin D. Roosevelt pushed forward an unprecedented program to resolve the crises of a collapsing financial system, crippling unemployment, and agricultural and industrial breakdown and to promote reform. After initially addressing the banking crises, the New Deal went on to establish relief agencies and promote economic recovery. The New Deal achieved successes and attracted support but it also had limitations and generated criticism that suggested the need for still greater innovations.

Consolidating the New Deal In 1935 Roosevelt undertook additional economic and social reforms. Labor's right to organize and bargain collectively was addressed, the path-breaking Social Security Act was passed, and the Works Progress Administration was created. The administration also responded to the environmental crises that had turned the Great Plains into a dustbowl and driven the "Okies" to California. The 1936 election gave Americans an opportunity to judge the New Deal and Roosevelt. Political realignment resulted: Former Republican constituents voted Democratic and produced a landslide victory for the president.

The New Deal and American Life The election of 1936 revealed the impact the New Deal had on Americans. Industrial workers mobilized to secure their rights; women and minorities gained increased, if still limited, opportunities to participate in American society; and Southerners and Westerners benefited from government programs like the TVA that they turned to their own advantage. Government programs changed daily life, and ordinary people often helped shape the new policies.

Ebbing of the New Deal After his 1936 election, Roosevelt committed himself to further reforms, but his misjudgment blocked some efforts and deadlocked others. Regarding the Supreme Court as an adversary, Roosevelt attempted to restructure the federal judiciary; his attempt to "pack" the court hurt the New Deal. A 1937 recession caused by the New Deal's lack of aggressiveness caused the administration to adopt Keynesian economic theories and have the government use deficient spending to increase demand and production.

Good Neighbors and Hostile Forces While isolationists in Congress counseled against involvement in foreign affairs, fascism was spreading in Europe and Asia. In his first term Roosevelt followed a policy of neutrality; after the Munich crises, Hitler's intentions toward the world and Germany's Jewish citizens had become more defined and threatening. America's relationship with Japan continued to deteriorate; by 1939, the "epidemic of world lawlessness" was edging the United States toward involvement.

REVIEW QUESTIONS

1. Why did President Hoover's emphasis on voluntarism fail to resolve the Great Depression?

2. What were the relief programs of the New Deal, and what did they achieve?

3. What were the criticisms of the early New Deal?

4. What were the major issues between management and labor in the 1930s?

5. How did the role of the federal government change in the 1930s?

KEY TERMS

Bonus Army   (p. 663)
Congress of Industrial Organizations (p. 672)
Fascist government   (p. 679)
Federal Deposit Insurance Corporation (FDIC)   (p. 665)

Fireside chats   (p. 665)
Great Depression   (p. 658)
Hoovervilles   (p. 659)
New Deal   (p. 658)

Securities and Exchange Commission (SEC)   (p. 665)
Tennessee Valley Authority (TVA) (p. 675)

WHERE TO LEARN MORE

Center for New Deal Studies, Roosevelt University, Chicago, Illinois. The center contains political memorabilia, photographs, papers, and taped interviews dealing with Franklin D. Roosevelt and the New Deal; it also sponsors an annual lecture series about the Roosevelt legacy.

Herbert Hoover National Historic Site, West Branch, Iowa. This 186-acre site contains the birthplace cottage and grave of Herbert Hoover as well as his presidential library and museum, which contains a reconstruction of Hoover's White House office. **www.nps.gov/heho**; **www.hoover.archives.gov**

Labor Museum and Learning Center of Michigan, Flint, Michigan. Exhibits trace the history of the labor movement, including the dramatic "Sit-Down Strike" of 1936–1937.

Franklin D. Roosevelt Home and Presidential Library, Hyde Park, New York. The Roosevelt home, furnished with family heirlooms, and the spacious grounds, where FDR is buried, personalize the president and provide insights into his career. The nearby library has displays and exhibitions about Roosevelt's presidency, and the Eleanor Roosevelt Wing is dedicated to the career of ER. **www.fdrlibrary.marist.edu**

Eleanor Roosevelt National Historic Site, Hyde Park, New York. These two cottages, where Eleanor Roosevelt worked and, after 1945, lived, contain her furniture and memorabilia. Visitors can also watch a film biography of ER and tour the grounds of this retreat where she entertained personal friends and world leaders. **www.nps.gov/elro**

Civilian Conservation Corps Interpretive Center, Whidbey Island, Washington. This stone and wood structure, built as a CCC project, now houses exhibits and artifacts illustrating the history of the CCC.

Bethune Museum and Archives National Historic Site, Washington, D.C. This four-story townhouse was the home of Mary McLeod Bethune, a friend of Eleanor Roosevelt and the director of the New Deal's Division of Negro Affairs, and the headquarters of the National Council of Negro Women, which Bethune founded in 1935. Exhibits feature the contributions of black activist women and activities of the civil rights movement.

 For additional study resources for this chapter, go to:
www.prenhall.com/goldfield/chapter25

The event was not spectacular, no fuses burned, no lights flashed. But to us it meant that release of atomic energy on a large scale would be only a matter of time.

GROW VITAMINS AT YOUR KITCHEN DOOR
Enter VICTORY GARDEN CONTEST
REGISTER 404 S. 8th ST. MAY 1-15
CONSUMER INTEREST DIVISION. MINNEAPOLIS DEFENSE COUNCIL. A WAR CHEST AGENCY

On June 6, 1944, American, British, and Canadian forces seized a beachhead in German-occupied France. The landings began the final phase of World War II in Europe, which ended eleven months later with German surrender to the U.S., Britain, the Soviet Union, and their allies.

26

WORLD WAR II
1939–1945

WHY WERE most Americans reluctant to get involved in World War II?

WHY DID the United States need a strategy for a two-front war?

HOW WAS the United States transformed socially and economically by the war?

HOW DID the Allies win the war?

December, 1942

The scene [under the stadium] at The University of Chicago would have been confusing to an outsider, if he could have eluded the security guards and gained admittance. He would have seen only what appeared to be a crude pile of black bricks and wooden timbers. . . .

Finally, the day came when we were ready to run the experiment. We gathered on a balcony about 10 feet above the floor of the large room in which the structure had been erected. Beneath us was a young scientist, George Weil, whose duty it was to handle the last control rod that was holding the reaction in check. . . .

Finally, it was time to remove the control rods. Slowly, Weil started to withdraw the main control rod. On the balcony, we watched the indicators which measured the neutron count and told us how rapidly the disintegration of the uranium atoms under their neutron bombardment was proceeding.

At 11:35 A.M., the counters were clicking rapidly. Then, with a loud clap, the automatic control rods slammed home. The safety point had been set too low.

It seemed a good time to eat lunch. During lunch everyone was thinking about the experiment but nobody talked much about it.

At 2:30, Weil pulled out the control rod in a series of measured adjustments. Shortly after, the intensity shown by the indicators began to rise at a slow but ever-increasing rate. At this moment we knew that the self-sustaining [nuclear] reaction was under way.

The event was not spectacular, no fuses burned, no lights flashed. But to us it meant that release of atomic energy on a large scale would be only a matter of time.

Enrico Fermi, in *The First Reactor* (Washington: U.S. Department of Energy, 1982), accessed at **http://hep.uchicago.edu/cp**; Laura Fermi, *Atoms in the Family* (Chicago: University of Chicago Press, 1954); Laura Fermi, "The Fermis' Path to Los Alamos," in Lawrence Badash, Joseph O. Hirschfelder, and Herbert P. Broida, eds. *Reminiscences of Los Alamos, 1943–45* (Boston and Dordrecht: D. Reidel Publishing Co.).

IMAGE KEY

for pages 684–685

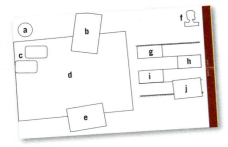

a. A cloth patch with a yellow star of David that all Jews had to wear under the Nazi regime.

b. Victory Garden Poster.

c. All POWs had to carry identification (ID) tags with them at all times. These two came from the Oflag XVIIA and Stelag VI/A camps in Germany.

d. American soldiers landing on the coast of France at Normandy on 6 June 1944 (D-Day).

e. Unusually addressed letters to Winston Churchill.

f. The explosion of an atomic bomb.

g. Mpa of central Europe.

h. Pearl Harbor Attack, 7 December 1941. Motor launch rescues a man from the water, alongside the burning USS West Virginia (BB-48); USS Tennessee (BB-43) is inboard.

i. Wartime marriages, Chicago, IL, August 20, 1943.

j. D-Day invasion.

ENRICO FERMI was describing the first controlled nuclear chain reaction—the critical experiment from which atomic weapons and atomic power would soon develop. Fermi himself had emigrated to the United States to escape the growing repression of Fascist Italy in 1938. When the United States entered World War II, Fermi, other atomic scientists, and their families moved to Los Alamos, a science city that the government built in northern New Mexico, where isolation was supposed to ensure secrecy and help the United States win the race with Nazi Germany to develop atomic weapons.

The Fermis were not the only family to give Los Alamos a multinational flavor. Niels Bohr had fled Denmark to escape Nazi invasion. Edward Teller was a Hungarian who had studied in Germany. Hans Bethe had left Germany, and Stanislaus Ulam was the only member of his family to survive the Nazi conquest of Poland. Absent were scientists from the Soviet Union, which was bearing the worst of the fighting against Germany but was excluded from the secret of the atomic bomb.

The men and women racing to perfect the atomic bomb knew that victory was far from certain. Allied defeat in a few key battles could have resulted in stand-off or Axis victory. Not until 1944 did American economic power allow the United States and its allies to feel confident of victory. A new weapon might end the war more quickly or make the difference between victory and defeat.

The war's domestic impacts were as profound as its international consequences. The war highlighted racial inequalities, gave women new opportunities, and fostered growth in the South and West. By devastating the nation's commercial rivals, compelling workers to retrain and factories to modernize, World War II left the United States dominant in the world economy. It also increased the size and scope of the federal government and built an alliance among the armed forces, big business, and science that helped shape postwar America.

THE DILEMMAS OF NEUTRALITY

Opinion polls in the fall of 1941 showed that most voters still hoped to avoid war. President Roosevelt's challenge was to lead the United States toward rearmament and support for Great Britain and China without alarming a reluctant public.

THE ROOTS OF WAR

The roots of World War II can be found in the aftereffects of World War I. The peace settlement after that war created a set of small new nations in Eastern Europe that were vulnerable to aggression from large neighbors such as Germany and the Soviet Union. Italy and Japan thought that the Treaty of Versailles failed to recognize their stature as world powers. Many Germans were convinced that Germany had been betrayed rather than defeated in 1918. In the 1930s, economic crisis and political instability fueled the rise of right-wing dictatorships that offered territorial expansion by military conquest as the way to redress old rivalries, dominate trade, and gain access to raw materials.

Japanese nationalists believed that Japan should expel the French, British, Dutch, and Americans from Asia and create a **Greater East Asia Co-Prosperity Sphere**, in which Japan gave the orders and other Asian peoples complied. When war with China erupted in 1937, Japan took many of the key cities and killed tens of thousands of civilians in the "rape of Nanking" but failed to dislodge the government of Jiang Jieshi (Chi-ang Kai-shek) and settled into a war of attrition.

Italian aggression led to the conquest of Ethiopia in 1935 and intervention in Spain in support of General Francisco Franco's right-wing rebels.

In Germany, Adolf Hitler made himself the German Führer, or absolute leader in 1934. Proclaiming the start of a thousand-year Reich (empire), he combined the historic German interest in eastward expansion with a long tradition of German racial superiority. The Slavs of eastern Europe were to be pushed aside to provide more territory for a growing German population, and the Jews, who were prominent in German business and professional life, were to be driven from the country. In 1935, the "Nuremberg laws" denied civil rights to Jews and the campaign against them intensified. The Nazi government began expropriating Jewish property and excluded Jews from most employment.

Germany and Italy formed the Rome-Berlin Axis in October 1936 and the Tripartite Pact with Japan in 1940, leading to the term **Axis Powers** to describe the aggressor nations. Political dissidents in all three nations were suppressed in the but Hitler's Germany was the most repressive. The Nazi concentration camp was a device for political terrorism. Hitler decreed that opponents should disappear

WHY WERE most Americans reluctant to get involved in World War II?

Greater East Asia Co-Prosperity Sphere Japanese nationalists believed that Japan should expel the French, British, Dutch, and Americans from Asia and create this sphere in which Japan would give the orders and other Asian peoples would comply.

Axis Powers The opponents of the United States and its allies in World War II.

The raspy-voiced Adolf Hitler had a remarkable ability to stir the German people. He and his inner circle made skillful use of propaganda, exploiting German resentment over the country's defeat in World War I and, with carefully staged mass rallies, such as this event in 1938, inspiring an emotional conviction of national greatness.

Bildarchiv Preubisher Kulterbesitz, Berlin

26–2
Charles Lindbergh, Radio Address (1941)

Blitzkrieg German war tactic in World War II ("lightning war") involving the concentration of air and armored firepower to punch and exploit holes in opposing defensive lines.

into "night and fog." The concentration camps would evolve into forced labor camps and then into hellish extermination camps.

HITLER'S WAR IN EUROPE

Germany invaded Poland on September 1, 1939. Western journalists covering the three-week conquest of Poland coined the term **Blitzkrieg**, or "lightning war," to describe the German tactics. Armored divisions with tanks and motorized infantry punched quick holes in defensive positions and raced forward 30 or 40 miles per day.

Striking from a central position against scattered enemies, Hitler chose the targets and timing of each new front: east to smash Poland in September 1939; north to capture Denmark and Norway in April and May 1940; west to defeat the Netherlands, Belgium, and France in May and June 1940; south into the Balkans, enlisting Hungary, Romania, and Bulgaria as allies and conquering Yugoslavia and Greece in April and May 1941. He also launched the Battle of Britain in the second half of 1940, sending bombers in an unsuccessful effort to pound Britain into submission.

In June 1941, having failed to knock Britain out of the war, Hitler invaded the Soviet Union (officially the Union of Soviet Socialist Republics, or USSR). The attack caught the Red Army off guard, because the Nazis and Soviets had signed a nonagression pact in 1939, and the USSR had helped dismember Poland. Nevertheless, from June until December 1941, more than 3 million Germans, Italians, and Romanians pushed eastward, encircling and capturing entire Soviet armies. Before desperate Soviet counterattacks and a bitter winter stopped the German tanks, the Axis powers had reached the outskirts of Moscow, and they expected to finish the job in the spring.

TRYING TO KEEP OUT

"We Must Keep Out!" shouted the September 7, 1939, *Chicago Daily News*. Most Americans wanted to avoid foreign quarrels. People who opposed intervention in the European conflict considered themselves realists. Drawing their lessons from 1914–1918, they assumed that the same situation applied in 1939. For more than two years after the invasion of Poland, strong isolationist sentiment shaped public debate and limited President Roosevelt's ability to help Britain and its allies.

Much of the emotional appeal of neutrality came from disillusionment with the American crusade in World War I, which had failed to make the world safe for democracy. Many opponents of intervention wanted the United States to protect its traditional spheres of interest in Latin America and the Pacific. Like George Washington, whose Farewell Address they quoted, they wanted to avoid becoming entangled in the perpetual quarrels of the European nations.

Noninterventionists spanned the political spectrum from left-leaning labor unions to such ultraconservative business tycoons as Henry Ford, from radicals who wanted the European nations to fight themselves into exhaustion to admirers of Hitler and Mussolini. Any move to intervene in Europe had to take these different views into account, meaning that Roosevelt had to move the United States slowly and carefully to the side of Britain.

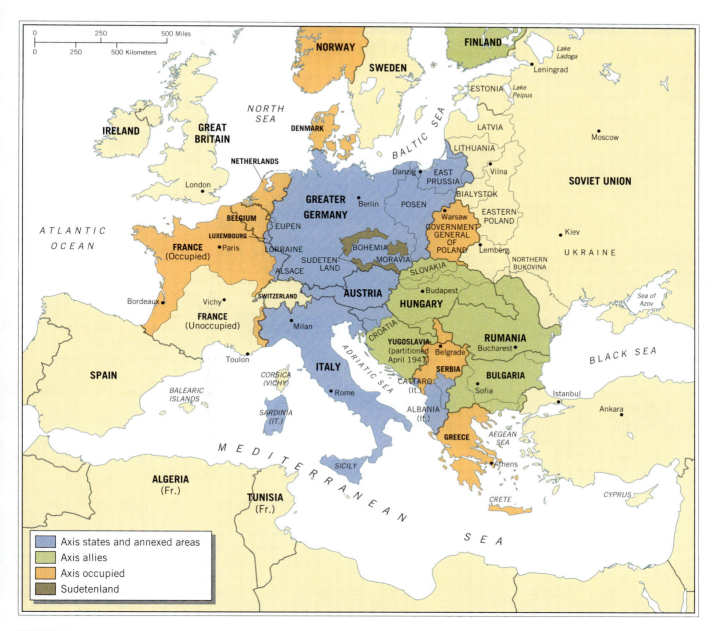

MAP 26–1

Axis Europe, 1941, on the Eve of Hitler's Invasion of the Soviet Union   After almost two years of war, the Axis powers controlled most of Europe, from the Atlantic Ocean to the Soviet border through annexation, military conquest, and alliances. Failure to force Britain to make peace caused Hitler to look eastward in 1941 to attempt the conquest of the Soviet Union.

HOW WAS Germany's central location in Europe both a strength and a weakness?

CHRONOLOGY

1931	Japan invades Manchuria.
1933	Hitler takes power in Germany.
1935	Congress passes first of three Neutrality acts. Italy invades Ethiopia.
1936	Germany and Italy form the Rome Berlin Axis. Civil war erupts in Spain.
1937	Japan invades China.
1938	Germany absorbs Austria. Munich agreement between Germany, Britain and France.
1939	Germany and the Soviet Union sign a nonagression pact. Germany absorbs Czechoslovakia. Germany invades Poland; Great Britain and France declare war on Germany.
1940	Germany conquers Denmark, Norway, Belgium, the Netherlands, and France. Japan, Germany, and Italy sign the Tripartite Pact. Germany bombs England in the Battle of Britain. The United States begins to draft men into the armed forces. Franklin Roosevelt wins an unprecedented third term.
1941	The United States begins a lend-lease program to make military equipment available to Great Britain and later the USSR. The Fair Employment Practices Committee is established. Germany invades the Soviet Union. Roosevelt and Churchill issue the Atlantic Charter. Japan attacks U.S. military bases in Hawaii.
1942	American forces in the Philippines surrender to Japan. President Roosevelt authorizes the removal and internment of Japanese Americans living in four western states. Naval battles in the Coral Sea and off the island of Midway blunt Japanese expansion. U.S. forces land in North Africa. Soviet forces encircle a German army at Stalingrad. The first sustained and controlled nuclear chain reaction takes place at the University of Chicago.
1943	U.S. and British forces invade Italy, which makes terms with the Allies. Race conflict erupts in riots in Detroit, New York, and Los Angeles. The landing of Marines on Tarawa initiates the island-hopping strategy. U.S. war production peaks. Roosevelt, Churchill, and Stalin confer at Tehran.
1944	Allied forces land in Normandy. The U.S. Navy destroys Japanese sea power in the battles of the Philippine Sea and Leyte Gulf. The Battle of the Bulge is the last tactical setback for the Allies.
1945	Roosevelt, Stalin, and Churchill meet at Yalta to plan the postwar world. The United States takes the Pacific islands of Iwo Jima and Okinawa. Franklin Roosevelt dies; Harry S Truman becomes president. Germany surrenders to the United States, Great Britain, and the USSR. The United Nations is organized at an international meeting in San Francisco. Potsdam Conference. Japan surrenders after the detonation of atomic bombs over Hiroshima and Nagasaki.

EDGING TOWARD INTERVENTION

Because 85 percent of the American people agreed that the nation should fight only if directly attacked, Roosevelt had to chip away at neutrality. In October 1939, lawmakers reluctantly passed the Neutrality Act of 1939 allowing arms sales to belligerent nations on a "cash and carry" basis. In control of the Atlantic, France and Britain were the only expected customers.

Isolationism helps explain why the United States accepted only a few thousand Jewish refugees. Anti-Semitism at the State Department also contributed to tight enforcement of immigration quotas, and polls showed that the public supported restricted immigration.

The collapse of France in June 1940 scared Americans into rearming. In the summer of 1940, Congress voted to expand the army to 2 million men, build 19,000 new war planes, and add 150 ships to the navy. September brought the nation's first peacetime draft.

26–2
Franklin Delano Roosevelt,
Annual Message to Congress
(1941)

In the same month, the United States concluded a "destroyer deal" with Britain, trading fifty old destroyers for the use of bases on British territories in the Caribbean, Bermuda, and Newfoundland.

In the presidential election of 1940, the big campaign issue was therefore whether FDR's unprecedented try for a third term represented arrogance or legitimate concern for continuity in a time of peril. The voters gave Roosevelt 55 percent of their votes to defeat his Republican opponent, Wendell Wilkie. The president pledged that no Americans would fight in a foreign war, but if the United States were attacked, he said privately, the war would no longer be "foreign."

THE BRINK OF WAR

In January 1941, Roosevelt proposed the "lend-lease" program, which allowed Britain to "borrow" military equipment for the duration of the war. Roosevelt compared the program to lending a garden hose to a neighbor whose house had caught fire. Senator Robert Taft of Ohio countered that it was more like lending chewing gum—you wouldn't want it back after it was used. Behind the scheme was Britain's inability to go on paying for American goods.

The Committee to Defend America by Aiding the Allies argued the administration's position. In opposition, the America First Committee claimed that lend-lease would allow the president to declare anything a "defense article." Congress finally passed the measure in March 1941, giving Great Britain an unlimited line of credit.

FDR soon began an undeclared war in the North Atlantic. Roosevelt instructed the navy to report sightings of German submarines to the British. In September, the U.S. destroyer *Greer* clashed with a German submarine. Roosevelt proclaimed a "shoot on sight" policy for German subs and told the navy to escort British convoys to within 400 miles of Britain. In reply, German submarines torpedoed and damaged the destroyer *Kearny* on October 17 and sank the destroyer *Reuben James* with the loss of more than 100 lives on October 30. The United States was approaching outright naval war with Germany.

The **Atlantic Charter** of August 1941 provided a political umbrella for American involvement. Meeting off Newfoundland, Roosevelt and British prime minister Winston Churchill agreed that the first priority was to defeat Germany; Japan was secondary. Echoing Woodrow Wilson, Roosevelt also insisted on a commitment to oppose territorial change by conquest, to support self-government and promote freedom of the seas.

Some historians think that Roosevelt's goal in the North Atlantic was to support Britain short of war. Others believe that he accepted the inevitability of war but hesitated to outpace public opinion. In this second interpretation, FDR wanted to eliminate Hitler without going to war if possible, with war if necessary. "I am waiting to be pushed into the situation," he told his secretary of the treasury.

That final shove came in the Pacific rather than the Atlantic. In 1940, as part of its rearmament program, the United States decided to build a "two-ocean navy." This decision antagonized Japan. Japan had achieved roughly 70 percent of U.S. naval strength by late 1941. However, America's buildup promised to reduce that ratio to only 30 percent by 1944. Furthermore, the United States was gradually restricting Japan's vital imports of steel, iron ore, and aluminum. In July 1941, after Japan occupied French Indochina, Roosevelt froze Japanese assets in the United States, blocked petroleum shipments, and began to build up U.S. forces in the Philippines. Both militarily and economically, it looked in Tokyo as if 1942 was Japan's last chance for victory.

Japanese war planners never seriously considered an actual invasion of the United States or expected a decisive victory. They hoped that attacks on American Pacific bases would shock the United States into letting Japan have its way in Asia or at least win time to create impenetrable defenses in the central Pacific.

QUICK REVIEW

Undeclared War
- March 1941: Lend-lease program approved by Congress.
- FDR ordered navy to offer support to Britain.
- August 1941: Atlantic Charter lays out British and American war aims.

Atlantic Charter   Statement of common principles and war aims developed by President Franklin Roosevelt and British Prime Minister Winston Churchill at a meeting in August 1941.

December 7, 1941

It now seems that Roosevelt wanted to restrain the Japanese with bluff and intimidation so that the United States could focus on Germany. FDR also recognized the possibility of a two-front war—at least a 20 percent chance, he told military advisers in January 1941. Because the United States cracked Japanese codes, it knew by November that Japanese military action was imminent but expected the blow to come in Southeast Asia.

Instead, the Japanese fleet sailed a 4,000-mile loop through the empty North Pacific, avoiding merchant shipping and American patrols. Before dawn on December 7, six Japanese aircraft carriers launched 351 planes in two unopposed bombing strikes on Pearl Harbor, Hawaii.

Americans counted their losses: eight battleships, eleven other warships, and nearly all military aircraft damaged or destroyed; and 2,403 people killed. Fortunately, dockyards, drydocks, and oil storage tanks remained intact because the Japanese admiral had refused to order a third attack. And the American carriers, at sea on patrol, were unharmed.

Speaking to Congress the following day, Roosevelt proclaimed December 7, 1941, "a date which will live in infamy." He asked for—and got—a declaration of war against the Japanese. Hitler and Mussolini declared war on the United States on December 11.

Holding the Line

WHY DID the United States need a strategy for a two-front war?

In 1940, Admiral Isoroku Yamamoto, the chief of Japan's Combined Fleet, weighed the chances of victory against the United States and Great Britain: "If I am told to fight regardless of the consequences, I shall run wild for the first six months or a year, but I have utterly no confidence for the second or third year." The admiral was right. As it turned out, Japan's conquests reached their limit after six months, but early 1942, it was far from clear that that would be so. In Europe, Allied fortunes went from bad to worse in the first half of 1942. Decisive turning points did not come until November 1942, a year after the United States had entered the war.

Stopping Germany

In December 1941, the United States plunged into a truly global war that was being fought on six distinct fronts. In North Africa, the British battled Italian and German armies that were trying to seize the Suez Canal. On the **Eastern Front**, Soviet armies held defensive positions. In the North Atlantic, merchant ships dodged German submarines. In China, Japan controlled the most productive provinces but could not crush Chinese resistance, which was supported by supplies airlifted from British India. In Southeast Asia, Japanese troops attacked the Philippines, the Dutch East Indies, New Guinea, Malaya, and Burma. In the central Pacific, the Japanese fleet faced the U.S. Navy.

Despite the popular desire for revenge against Japan, the United States decided to defeat Germany first, as Germany was far stronger than Japan. Defeat of Japan would not assure the defeat of Germany, especially if it crushed the Soviet Union or starved Britain into submission. In contrast, a strategy that helped the Soviets and British survive and then destroyed German military power would doom Japan.

The strategy recognized that the Eastern Front held the key to Allied hopes. In 1941, Germany had seized control of 45 percent of the Soviet population, 47 percent of its grain production, and more than 60 percent of its coal, steel, and

Eastern Front The area of military operations in World War II located east of Germany in eastern Europe and the Soviet Union.

aluminum industries. Hitler next sought to destroy Soviet capacity to wage war. He targeted southern Russia, an area rich in grain and oil. The German thrust was also designed to eliminate the British from the Middle East.

The German offensive opened with stunning success. Every day's advance, however, stretched supply lines. Tanks ran out of fuel and spare parts. The horses that pulled German supply wagons died for lack of food.

Disaster came at Stalingrad (present-day Volgograd), an industrial center on the western bank of the Volga River. In September and October, 1942, German, Italian, and Romanian soldiers fought their way house by house into the city.

The Red Army delivered a counterstroke on November 18 that cut off 330,000 Axis soldiers. Airlifts kept the Germans fighting for two more months, but they surrendered in February 1943.

THE SURVIVAL OF BRITAIN

In 1940 and 1941, from bases in France, German submarines (greatly improved since World War I) intercepted shipments of oil from Nigeria, beef from Argentina, minerals from Brazil, and weapons from the United States. Through the end of 1941, German "tonnage warfare" sank merchant vessels faster than they could be replaced.

The **Battle of the Atlantic** forced the British to reduce their reliance on the Atlantic supply lines. Between 1939 and 1944, planning and rationing cut Britain's need for imports in half. The British also organized protected convoys. Grouping the merchant ships into convoys with armed escorts "hardened" the targets and made them more difficult to find in the wide ocean. Roosevelt's destroyer deal of 1940 and U.S. naval escorts in the western Atlantic in 1941 thus contributed directly to Britain's survival.

Nevertheless, German submarines (known as U-boats from *Unterseeboot*) operated as far as the Caribbean and the Carolinas in 1942. In June, U-boats sank 144 ships; drowned sailors washed up on Carolina beaches. Only the extension of the convoy system to American waters forced the subs back toward Britain. Meanwhile, Allied aircraft began to track submarines with radar, spot them with searchlights as they maneuvered on the surface, and attack them with depth charges. New sonar systems allowed escort ships to measure submarines' speed and depth. By the spring of 1943, American shipyards were also launching ships faster than the Germans could sink them.

British ground fighting in 1942 centered in North Africa. By October 1942, Field Marshal Erwin Rommel's German and Italian forces were within striking distance of the Suez Canal. At **El Alamein** between October 23 and November 5, 1942, however, General Bernard Montgomery, with twice Rommel's manpower and tanks, forced the enemy to retreat and lifted the danger to the Middle East.

RETREAT AND STABILIZATION IN THE PACIFIC

Striking the Philippines a few hours after Hawaii, the Japanese gained another tactical surprise (see Map 26–2), destroying most American air power on the ground and isolating U.S. forces. Between February 27 and March 1, Japan brushed aside a combined American, British, Dutch, and Australian fleet in the Battle of the Java Sea, and a numerically inferior Japanese force had seized Singapore.

In the spring Japan pushed the British out of Burma and overwhelmed Filipino and U.S. defensive positions on the Bataan peninsula. On May 6, the last American bastion, the island fortress of Corregidor in Manila Bay, surrendered.

The first check to Japanese expansion came on May 7–8, 1942, in the Battle of the Coral Sea, where U.S. aircraft carriers halted a Japanese advance toward

Battle of the Atlantic The long struggle between German submarines and the British and U.S. navies in the North Atlantic from 1940 to 1943.

MAP EXPLORATION

To explore an interactive version of this map, go to **http://www.prenhall.com/goldfield2/map26.2**

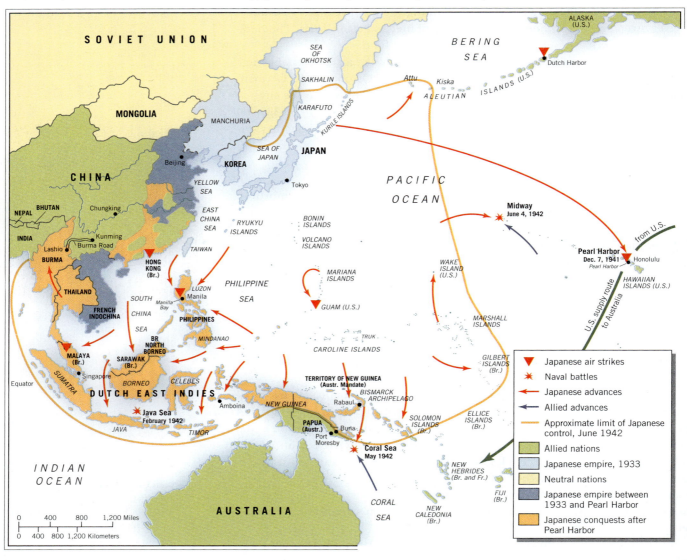

MAP 26–2

World War II in the Pacific, from Pearl Harbor to Midway   The first six months after the Japanese attack on Pearl Harbor brought a string of Japanese victories and conquests in the Pacific, the islands southeast of Asia, and the British colonies of Malaya and Burma. Japan's advance was halted by a standoff battle in the Coral Sea, a decisive U.S. naval victory at Midway, and the length and vulnerability of Japanese supply lines to its most distant conquests.

HOW WAS Japan able to mount a series of victories in the Pacific after their attack on Pearl Harbor?

Australia. In June, the Japanese struck at the island of Midway, 1,500 miles northwest of Honolulu. Their goal was to destroy American carrier forces. Having cracked Japanese radio codes, U.S. forces were aware of the plan for a diversionary invasion of the Aleutian Islands. On the morning of June 4, U.S. Navy dive bombers found the Japanese fleet and sank or crippled three aircraft carriers in five minutes; another Japanese carrier sank later in the day. The Battle of Midway ended Japanese efforts to expand in the Pacific.

MOBILIZING FOR VICTORY

News of the Japanese attack on Pearl Harbor shattered a bright Sunday afternoon. Elliott Johnson was eating in a Chinese restaurant in Portland, Oregon, when the proprietor burst from the kitchen with a portable radio; the line was two blocks long by the time he got to the marine recruiting office.

War changed the lives of most Americans. Millions of men and women served in the armed forces and millions more worked in defense factories. The number of civilian employees of the federal government quadrupled to 3.8 million. Meanwhile, youngsters saved tin foil, collected scrap metal, and followed the freedom-fighting stories of Wonder Woman in the comics. The war effort gave Americans a common purpose that softened the divisions of region, class, and national origin while calling attention to continuing inequalities of race.

ORGANIZING THE ECONOMY

The need to fight a global war brought a huge expansion of the federal government. The War Manpower Commission allocated workers among vital industries and the military. The War Production Board invested $17 billion for new factories and managed $181 billion in war-supply contracts, favoring big corporations with experience in large-scale production.

The Office of Price Administration (OPA) fought inflation with price controls and rationing that began with tires, sugar, and coffee and eventually included meat, butter, gasoline, and shoes. Consumers used ration cards and ration stamps to obtain scarce products. By slowing price increases, the OPA helped to convince Americans to buy the war bonds that financed half the war spending. Americans also felt the bite of the first payroll deductions for income taxes as the government secured revenues and soaked up some of the high wages that would have pushed inflation. By 1945 the federal budget was $98 billion, eleven times as large as in 1939, and the national debt had increased more than sixfold.

Industry had reluctantly begun to convert from consumer goods to defense production in 1940 and 1941. Although corporations hated to give up the market for toasters and automobiles just as Americans had more money, the last passenger car for the duration of the war rolled off the assembly line in February 1942. Existing factories retooled to make war equipment, and huge new facilities turned out thousands of planes and ships. The United States applied mass production technology to aircraft production at a time when Japan was still building warplanes one at a time and Germany in small batches.

Most defense contracts went to such established industrial states as Michigan, New York, and Ohio, but in the South and West, the war marked the takeoff of what Americans would later call the Sunbelt. Albuquerque, New Mexico more than doubled in population during the 1940s. War-boom cities, such as San Diego (up 92 percent in population in the 1940s) and Mobile (up 68 percent), bustled with activity and hummed with tension. Factories operated three shifts, movies ran around the clock, and workers filled the streets after midnight.

The hordes of war workers found housing scarce. Workers in Seattle's shipyards and Boeing plants scrounged for living space in offices, tents, chicken coops, and rooming houses where "hot beds" rented in shifts. The situation was similar in small towns.

The results of war production were staggering—an estimated 40 percent of the world's military production was coming from the United States by 1944. The productivity of U.S. workers increased 30 percent between 1939 and 1945. Surging

A wartime shopper uses ration coupons to purchase groceries.
©Bettmann/Corbis

farm income pulled agriculture out of its long slump. The rich certainly got richer, but overall per capita income doubled, and the poorest quarter of Americans made up some of the ground lost during the Great Depression.

THE ENLISTMENT OF SCIENCE

"There wasn't a physicist able to breathe who wasn't doing war work," remembered Professor Philip Morrison. At the center of the scientific enterprise was Vannevar Bush, former dean at the Massachusetts Institute of Technology. As head of the newly established Office of Scientific Research and Development, Bush guided spending on research and development that dwarfed previous scientific work and set the pattern of massive federal support for science that continued after the war.

The biggest scientific effort was the drive to produce an atomic bomb. As early as 1939, Albert Einstein had written FDR about the possibility of such a weapon and the danger of falling behind the Germans. In late 1941, Roosevelt established what became known as the **Manhattan Project**. On December 2, 1942, scientists manipulated graphite rods inserted in a stack of uranium ingots until they were certain they could trigger and control a self-sustaining nuclear reaction.

The Manhattan Project moved from theory to practice in 1943. Physicist J. Robert Oppenheimer directed the young scientists at Los Alamos in designing a nuclear fission bomb. Engineers in other new science cities tried two approaches to producing the fissionable material. Richland, Washington, burgeoned into a sprawling metropolis that supported the creation of plutonium at the Hanford Engineer Works. Oak Ridge, Tennessee, near Knoxville, was built around gaseous diffusion plants.

Plutonium from Hanford fueled the first bomb tested at the Trinity site, 100 miles from Alamogordo, New Mexico, on July 16, 1945. The explosion astonished even the physicists; Oppenheimer quoted from Hindu scriptures as he tried to comprehend the results: "Now I am become death, destroyer of worlds."

MEN AND WOMEN IN THE MILITARY

By 1945, 8.3 million men and women were on active duty in the army and army air forces and 3.4 million in the navy and Marine Corps, totals exceeded only by the Soviet Union. In total, some 350,000 women and more than 16 million men served in the armed forces; 292,000 died in battle, 100,000 survived prisoner-of-war camps, and 671,000 returned wounded.

Twenty-five thousand American Indians served in the armed forces, most in racially integrated units. Because the Navajo were one of the few tribes that had not been studied by German anthropologists, their language was unknown to the Axis armies. More than three hundred Navajo were "code-talkers" who served in radio combat-communication teams in the Pacific theater.

Approximately 1 million African Americans also served in the armed forces during World War II. As it had since the Civil War, the army organized black soldiers in segregated units and often assigned them to the more menial jobs, excluding them from combat until manpower shortages forced changes in policy.

Black soldiers encountered discrimination on and off the base. Towns adjacent to army posts were sometimes off limits to blacks. At some Southern bases, German prisoners of war watched movies from the first rows along with white GIs while African-American soldiers watched from the back. Military courts were quick to judge and harsh to punish when black GIs were the accused. Despite the obstacles, all-black units, such as the 761st Tank Battalion and the 99th Pursuit Squadron, earned distinguished records. More broadly, the war experience helped

WHERE TO LEARN MORE

Los Alamos County Historical Museum and Bradbury Science Museum, Los Alamos, New Mexico

25–5
A. Philip Randolph, "Why Should We March?" (1942)

Manhattan Project The effort, using the code name Manhattan Engineer District, to develop an atomic bomb under the management of the U.S. Army Corps of Engineers during World War II.

to invigorate postwar efforts to achieve equal rights, as had also been true after World War I.

The nation had a different—but also mixed—reaction to the women who joined the armed forces. The armed services tried not to change established gender roles. Many of the women in uniform hammered at typewriters, worked switchboards, inventoried supplies. Others, however, worked close to combat zones as photographers, code analysts, and nurses.

The greatest departure from expected roles was the work of the 1,074 members of the Women's Airforce Service Pilots (WASPS), a civilian auxiliary of the U.S. Army Air Forces. From 1942 to 1944, they ferried military aircraft across the United States, towed targets for antiaircraft practices, and tested new planes. Nevertheless, WASPS were not allowed to carry male passengers, and the unit was dissolved when the supply of male pilots caught up with the demand.

THE HOME FRONT

The war inexorably penetrated everyday life. Residents in war-production cities had to cope with throngs of new workers, many of whom were unattached males—young men waiting for their draft call and older men without their families. Military and defense officials worried about sexually transmitted diseases and pressured cities to shut down their vice districts.

Americans put their lives on fast forward. Couples who had postponed marriage because of the depression could afford to marry as the economy picked up. Altogether, the war years brought 1.2 million "extra" marriages, compared to the rate for the period 1920–1939.

The war's impact on families was gradual. The draft started with single men, then called up married men without children, and finally tapped fathers in 1943. Left at home were millions of "service wives," whose compensation from the government was $50 per month.

The war had mixed effects on children. "Latchkey children" of working mothers often had to fend for themselves, but middle-class kids whose mothers stayed home could treat the war as an interminable scout project, with salvage drives and campaigns to sell war bonds. Between the end of the school day and suppertime, children listened as Captain Midnight, Jack Armstrong, and Hop Harrigan ("America's ace of the airways") fought the Nazis and Japanese on the radio.

The federal government tried to keep civilians of all ages committed to the war. It encouraged scrap drives and backyard victory gardens. The government also managed news about the fighting. Censors screened soldiers' letters. Early in the war, they blocked publication of most photographs of war casualties, although magazines such as *Life* were full of haunting images. Censors also authorized photographs of enemy atrocities to motivate the public.

Government officials had a harder time controlling Hollywood. The Office of War Information wanted propaganda in feature films, but not so heavy-handed that it drove viewers from theaters. War films revealed the nation's racial attitudes, often drawing distinctions between "good" and "bad" Germans but uniformly portraying Japanese as subhuman and repulsive. The most successful films dramatized the courage of the Allies. *Mrs. Miniver* (1942) showed the British transcending class differences in their battle with the Nazis. *So Proudly We Hail* (1943) celebrated the heroism of navy nurses in the Pacific theater.

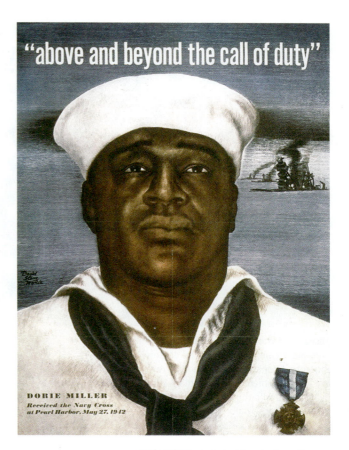

"above and beyond the call of duty"

DORIE MILLER
Received the Navy Cross
at Pearl Harbor, May 27, 1942

Dorie Miller, a mess attendant on the battleship West Virginia, received the Navy Cross for "extraordinary courage" during the Japanese attack on Pearl Harbor. Miller helped to pull the Arizona's captain to safety and then manned a machine gun and shot down several Japanese planes. The War Department used Miller on recruiting posters such as this one but neglected to point out that it continued to restrict black recruits mostly to kitchen and other service jobs.

Courtesy of the Library of Congress

Members of Women Fliers of America
examine an aircraft engine. The organization had been asked by the U.S. Army to identify women with more than 200 flying hours who might ferry planes, freeing military aviators for other duties.

Getty Image Inc./Hutton Archive Photos

QUICK REVIEW

Rosie the Riveter
- Demand for labor drew women into the workplace.
- Companies opened positions for women in nontraditional jobs.
- Government funded daycare programs to help women enter the workforce.

NEW WORKERS

As draft calls took men off the assembly line, women changed the composition of the industrial work force. The war gave them new job opportunities that were embodied in the image of Rosie the Riveter. The acute shortage of welders and other skilled workers, opened thousands of journeyman positions to women, work that was far more lucrative than waiting tables or sewing in a clothing factory. Aircraft companies, which compounded labor shortages by stubborn "whites only" hiring, developed new power tools and production techniques to accommodate the smaller average size of women workers, increasing efficiency for everyone along the production line.

By July 1944, fully 19 million women held paid jobs, up 6 million in four years. Women's share of government jobs increased from 19 to 38 percent and their share of manufacturing jobs from 22 to 33 percent. Some women worked out of patriotism. Many others, however, needed to support their families and already had years of experience in the work force. As one of the workers recalled of herself and a friend, "We both had to work, we both had children, so we became welders, and if I might say so, damn good ones."

Americans did not know how to respond to the growing numbers of working women. Many worried that their employment would undermine families. The federal government assisted female entry into the labor force by funding day-care programs that served 600,000 children. Employment recruitment posters showed strong, handsome women with rolled-up sleeves and wrenches in hand, but men and women assumed that women would want to return to the home after victory; they were to work when the nation needed them and quit when the need was past.

Mexican-American workers made special contributions to the war effort. As defense factories and the military absorbed workers, western farms and railroads faced an acute shortage of workers. In 1942, the United States and Mexico negotiated the *bracero* program, under which the Mexican government recruited workers to come to the United States on six-to-twelve month contracts. Although *bracero* workers still faced discrimination, the U.S. government tried to improve working conditions because it wanted to keep public opinion in Latin America favorable to the Allied cause.

The war was a powerful force for the assimilation of Native Americans. Forty thousand moved to off-reservation jobs; they were a key labor force for military supply depots throughout the West. The average cash income of Indian households tripled during the war. Many stayed in cities at its end. The experience of the war accelerated the fight for full civil rights. Congress had made Indians citizens in 1924, but several states continued to deny them the vote. Activists organized the National Congress of American Indians in 1944 and began the efforts that led the U.S. Supreme Court in 1948 to require states to grant voting rights.

African Americans, too, found economic advancement through war jobs. Early in the mobilization, labor leader A. Philip Randolph of the Brotherhood of Sleeping Car Porters worked with Walter White of the NAACP to plan a "Negro March on Washington" to protest racial discrimination by the federal government.

To head off a major embarrassment, Roosevelt issued Executive Order 8802 in June 1941, barring racial discrimination in defense contracts and creating the **Fair Employment Practices Committee (FEPC)**; the order coined a phrase that reverberated powerfully through the coming decades: "No discrimination on grounds of race, color, creed, or national origin."

But white resistance to black coworkers remained strong. In Mobile, New Orleans, and Jacksonville, agreements between shipyards and segregated unions blocked skilled black workers from high-wage jobs. Attempts to overturn discrimination could lead to violence. When the Alabama Dry Dock Company integrated its work force in May 1943, white workers rioted. Nevertheless, African-American membership in labor unions doubled, and wartime prosperity raised the average black income from 41 percent of the white average in 1939 to 61 percent by 1950.

In 1942, the federal government removed Japanese Americans from parts of four western states and interned them in isolated camps scattered through the West.

AP/Wide World Photos

CLASHING CULTURES

As men and women migrated in search of work, they also crossed or collided with traditional boundaries of race and region. African-American migration out of the South accelerated in the early 1940s. Many of the migrants headed for well-established black neighborhoods in Northern cities. Others created new African-American neighborhoods in Western cities. White Southerners and black Northerners with different ideas of racial etiquette found themselves side by side in West Coast shipyards. In the Midwest, black migrants from the South and white migrants from Appalachia competed for the same high-wage jobs and scarce apartments.

Tensions between black and white residents exploded in at least fifty cities in 1943 alone. In June 1943, an argument over the use of Detroit's Belle Isle Park set off three days of violence: Twenty-five black people and nine white people died in the most serious racial riot of the war.

Tensions were simultaneously rising between Mexican Americans and Anglos. As the Mexican community in Los Angeles swelled to an estimated 400,000, newspapers published anti-Mexican articles. On June 6, 1943, off-duty sailors and soldiers attacked Latinos on downtown streets and invaded Mexican-American neighborhoods. The attacks dragged on for a week of sporadic violence against black people and Filipinos as well as Latinos.

INTERNMENT OF JAPANESE AMERICANS

On February 19, 1942, President Roosevelt issued Executive Order 9066, which authorized the secretary of war to define restricted areas and remove civilian residents who were threats to national security. The primary targets were 112,000 Japanese Americans in California and parts of Washington, Oregon, and Arizona. Japanese immigrants and their children in the Western states had experienced forty years of hostility and racial prejudice. The outbreak of war triggered anti-Japanese hysteria

Fair Employment Practices Committee (FEPC) Federal agency established in 1941 to curb racial discrimination in war production jobs and government employment.

• AMERICAN VIEWS •

THE INTERNMENT OF JAPANESE AMERICANS IN 1942

In the spring of 1942, the U.S. army ordered that Japanese Americans in four western states be relocated to internment camps distant from the Pacific Coast. Monica Itoe Stone describes the experience of her Seattle family as they were transferred to temporary quarters before they were moved again to Idaho.

HOW DO the expectations of *issei* (immigrants who had been born in Japan) differ from those of *nisei* (their American-born children, including the author of this memoir)? Why did the U.S. army wait five months after Pearl Harbor before beginning the internment? Does the management of the assembly and internment suggest anything about stereotypes of Japanese Americans?

General DeWitt kept reminding us that E day, evacuation day, was drawing near. "E day will be announced in the very near future. If you have not wound up your affairs by now, it will soon be too late."

. . . On the twenty-first of April, a Tuesday, the general gave us the shattering news. "All the Seattle Japanese will be moved to Puyallup by May 1. Everyone must be registered Saturday and Sunday between 8 A.M. and 5 P.M."

Up to that moment, we had hoped against hope that something or someone would intervene for us. Now there was no time for moaning. A thousand and one details must be attended to in this one week of grace. Those seven days sputtered out like matches struck in the wind, as we rushed wildly about. Mother distributed sheets, pillowcases and blankets, which we stuffed into seabags. Into the two suitcases, we packed heavy winter overcoats, plenty of sweaters, woolen slacks and skirts, flannel pajamas and scarves. Personal toilet articles, one tin plate, tin cup and silverware completed our luggage. The one seabag and two suitcases apiece were going to be the backbone of our future home, and we planned it carefully.

Henry went to the Control Station to register the family. He came home with twenty tags, all numbered "10710," tags to be attached to each piece of baggage, and one to hang from our coat lapels. From then on, we were known as Family #10710.

[On the day set for relocation] we climbed into the truck. . . . As we coasted down Beacon Hill bridge for the last time, we fell silent, and stared out at the delicately flushed, morning sky of Puget Sound. We drove through bustling Chinatown, and in a few minutes arrived on the corner of Eighth and Lane. This area was ordinarily lonely and deserted but now it was gradually filling up with silent, labeled Japanese. . . .

Finally at ten o'clock, a vanguard of Greyhound busses purred in and parked themselves neatly along

and gave officials an excuse to take action against both enemy aliens (immigrants who retained Japanese citizenship) and their American-born children. As the U.S. general commanding on the West Coast put it, "A Jap is a Jap. It makes no difference whether he is an American citizen or not."

At the end of April 1942, Japanese in the coastal states were given a week to organize their affairs and report to assembly centers, where they were housed before being moved to ten internment camps in isolated locations in the western interior (see American Views, "Internment of Japanese Americans: Life in Camp Harmony"). Here, they were housed in tar-paper barracks, hemmed in by barbed wire fences, and guarded by military police. The victims reacted to the hardship and stress in different ways. Several thousand second-generation Japanese Americans renounced their citizenship in disgust. But many others demonstrated their loyalty by cooperating with the authorities, finding sponsors who would help them move to the curb. The crowd stirred and murmured. The bus doors opened and from each, a soldier with rifle in hand stepped out and stood stiffly at attention by the door. The murmuring died. It was the first time I had seen a rifle at such close range and I felt uncomfortable. . . .

Newspaper photographers with flash-bulb cameras pushed busily through the crowd. One of them rushed up to our bus, and asked a young couple and their little boy to step out and stand by the door for a shot. They were reluctant, but the photographers were persistent and at length they got out of the bus and posed, grinning widely to cover their embarrassment. We saw the picture in the newspaper shortly after and the caption underneath it read, "japs good-natured about evacuation."

Our bus quickly filled to capacity. . . . The door closed with a low hiss. We were now the Wartime Civil Control Administration's babies.

About noon we crept into a small town. . . . and we noticed at the left of us an entire block filled with neat rows of low shacks, resembling chicken houses. Someone commented on it with awe, "Just look at those chicken houses. They sure go in for poultry in a big way here." Slowly the bus made a left turn, drove through a wire-fenced gate, and to our dismay, we were inside the over-sized chicken farm. . . .

The apartments resembled elongated, low stables about two blocks long. Our home was one room, about 18 by 20 feet, the size of a living room. There was one small window in the wall opposite the one door. It was bare except for a small, tinny wood-burning stove crouching in the center. The flooring consisted of two by fours laid directly on the earth, and dandelions were already pushing their way up through the cracks. . . .

I stared at our little window, unable to sleep. I was glad Mother had put up a makeshift curtain on the window for I noticed a powerful beam of light sweeping across it every few seconds. The lights came from high towers placed around the camp where guards with Tommy guns kept a twenty-four hour vigil. I remembered the wire fence encircling us, and a knot of anger tightened in my breast. What was I doing behind a fence like a criminal? If there were accusations to be made, why hadn't I been given a fair trial? Maybe I wasn't considered an American anymore. My citizenship wasn't real, after all. Then what was I? I was certainly not a citizen of Japan as my parents were. On second thought, even Father and Mother. . . . had little tie with their mother country. In their twenty-five years in America, they had worked and paid their taxes to their adopted government as any other citizen.

Of one thing I was sure. The wire fence was real. I no longer had the right to walk out of it. It was because I had Japanese ancestors. It was also because some people had little faith in the ideas and ideals of democracy.

Source: Monica Itoi Sone, *Nisei Daughter* (Seattle: University of Washington Press, 1979).

other parts of the country, or joining the 442nd Regimental Combat Team, the most decorated American unit in the European war.

Although the U.S. Supreme Court sanctioned the removals in *Korematsu* v. *United States* (1944), the nation officially recognized its liability with the Japanese Claims Act of 1948, for many internees had lost property that they had been powerless to protect. The nation acknowledged its broader moral responsibility in 1988, when Congress approved redress payments to each of the sixty thousand surviving evacuees.

By contrast Hawaii treated Japanese Americans much differently. Hawaii's long history as a multiethnic society made residents and officials disinclined to look for a racial scapegoat. Less than 1 percent of Hawaii's Japanese American population of 160,000 was interned. The treatment of mainland Japanese Americans also contrasted with the situation of German Americans and Italian Americans. Only tiny fractions of their total populations were interned or had their movements restricted.

THE END OF THE NEW DEAL

Roosevelt's New Deal had run out of steam in 1938. The war had reinvigorated his political fortunes by focusing national energies on foreign policy, over which presidents have the greatest power. After the 1942 election left Congress in the hands of Republicans, conservative lawmakers ignored proposals that war emergency housing be used to improve the nation's permanent housing stock, abolished the National Resources Planning Board, curtailed rural electrification, and crippled the Farm Security Administration.

For the presidential election of 1944, the Republicans nominated Governor Thomas Dewey of New York, who had made his reputation as a crime-fighting district attorney. The Democrats renominated Roosevelt for a fourth term. Missouri Senator Harry S Truman, a tough investigator of American military preparedness, replaced liberal New Dealer Henry Wallace as Roosevelt's running mate, which appeased Southern Democrats.

Roosevelt supporters argued that the nation could not afford to switch leaders in the middle of a war, but Dewey's vigor and relative youth (he was twenty years younger than FDR) pointed up the president's failing health and energy. Voters gave Roosevelt 432 electoral votes to 99, but the narrowing gap in the popular vote—54 percent for Roosevelt and 46 percent for Dewey—made the Republicans eager for 1948.

WAR AND PEACE

HOW DID the Allies win the war?

In January 1943, the U.S. War Department completed the world's largest office building, the Pentagon. The building housed 23,000 workers along 17.5 miles of corridors. The gray walls of the Pentagon symbolized an American government that was outgrowing its prewar roots.

GATHERING ALLIED STRENGTH

American and British landings in North Africa in 1942 and Italy in 1943 satisfied the British desire to secure Western influence in the Mediterranean and Middle East, but they pleased neither American policymakers nor the Soviet Union. U.S. leaders wanted to justify massive mobilization with a war-winning campaign and to strike across Europe to occupy the heart of Germany. Stalin needed a full-scale invasion of western Europe to divert German forces from the Eastern Front.

In fact, 1943 was the year in which the Allies gained the edge in quality of equipment, capacity for war production, and military sophistication. The United States poured men and equipment into Britain. The Soviets recruited, rearmed, and upgraded new armies, despite enormous losses in 1941 and 1942 and rebuilt munitions factories beyond German reach. As Soviet soldiers reconquered western Russia and the Ukraine, they marched in 13 million pairs of American-made boots and traveled in 51,000 jeeps and 375,000 Dodge trucks made available from U.S. lend-lease assistance.

Meeting in Casablanca in January 1943, Roosevelt and Churchill demanded the "unconditional surrender" of Italy, Germany, and Japan; the phrase meant no deals that kept the enemy governments or leaders in power. Ten months later, the Allied leaders huddled again. Roosevelt and Churchill met with China's Jiang in Cairo and then flew on to meet Stalin in Tehran. At Tehran, the United States and Britain promised to invade France within six months. "We leave here," said the three leaders, "friends in fact, in spirit, in purpose."

The superficial harmony barely survived the end of the war. Stalin and his generals scoffed at the small scale of early U.S. efforts. Roosevelt's ideal of self-determination for all peoples seemed naive to Churchill, who wanted the major powers to carve out realistic spheres of influence in Europe. It was irrelevant to Stalin, who wanted control of eastern Europe.

TURNING THE TIDE IN EUROPE

The United States had entered the ground war in Europe with Operation TORCH. Against little opposition, British and American troops under General Dwight Eisenhower landed in French Morocco and Algeria on November 8, 1942 (see Map 26–3). The puppet French government in place there, which had collaborated with the Nazis, now switched sides, giving the Allies footholds in North Africa.

German tanks in February 1943 counterattacked U.S. divisions at Kasserine Pass in the Atlas Mountains of Tunisia. Learning quickly from this tactical defeat, Allied troops forced the Axis in Africa to surrender in May. Eisenhower had already demonstrated his ability to handle the politics of military leadership, skills he perfected commanding a multinational army for the next two and a half years.

The central Mediterranean remained the focus of U.S. and British action for the next year. The British proposed strikes in southern Europe. U.S. Army Chief of Staff George Marshall and President Roosevelt agreed first to the action in North Africa and then to invade Italy in 1943. In July and August, Allied forces led by Montgomery and Patton overran Sicily. As Sicily fell, the Italian king and army forced Mussolini from power and began to negotiate peace with Britain and America (but not the Soviet Union). In September, the Allies announced an armistice with Italy, and Eisenhower's troops landed south of Naples. Germany responded by occupying the rest of Italy.

As American military planners had feared, the Italian campaign soaked up Allied resources. Week after week, the experience of GIs on the line was the same: "You wake up in the mud and your cigarettes are all wet and you have an ache in your joints and a rattle in your chest." Despite months of bitter fighting, the Allies controlled only two-thirds of Italy when the war there ended on May 1, 1945.

On the Eastern Front, the climactic battle of the German-Soviet war had erupted on July 5, 1943. The Germans sent three thousand tanks against the Kursk Salient. Soviet generals had prepared a defense in depth with three thousand tanks of their own. When the attack finally stalled, it marked the last great German offensive until December 1944.

OPERATION OVERLORD

On **D-Day**–June 6, 1944–the western Allies landed on the coast of Normandy in northwestern France. Six divisions went ashore from hundreds of attack transports carrying four thousand landing craft. Dozens of warships and twelve thousand aircraft provided support. One British and two American airborne divisions dropped behind German positions. When the sun set on the "longest day," the Allies had a tenuous toehold in France.

The Allies secured their beachheads and landed 500,000 men and 100,000 vehicles within two weeks. However, the German defenders kept the Allies along a narrow coastal strip. **Operation OVERLORD**, the code name for the entire campaign across northern France, met renewed success in late July and August. U.S. troops finally broke through German lines around the town of St.-Lô and then drew a ring around the Germans that slowly closed on the town of Falaise. The Germans lost a quarter of a million troops. The German command chose to regroup closer to Germany rather than fight in France. The Allies liberated Paris on August 25.

QUICK REVIEW

The Beginning of the End
♦ Allies gained footholds in North Africa.
♦ Allies took control of much of Italy.
♦ German's last offensive in Russia turned back.

D-Day   June 6, 1944, the day of the first paratroop drops and amphibious landings on the coast of Normandy, France, in the first stage of Operation OVERLORD during World War II.

Operation OVERLORD   U.S. and British invasion of France in June 1944 during World War II.

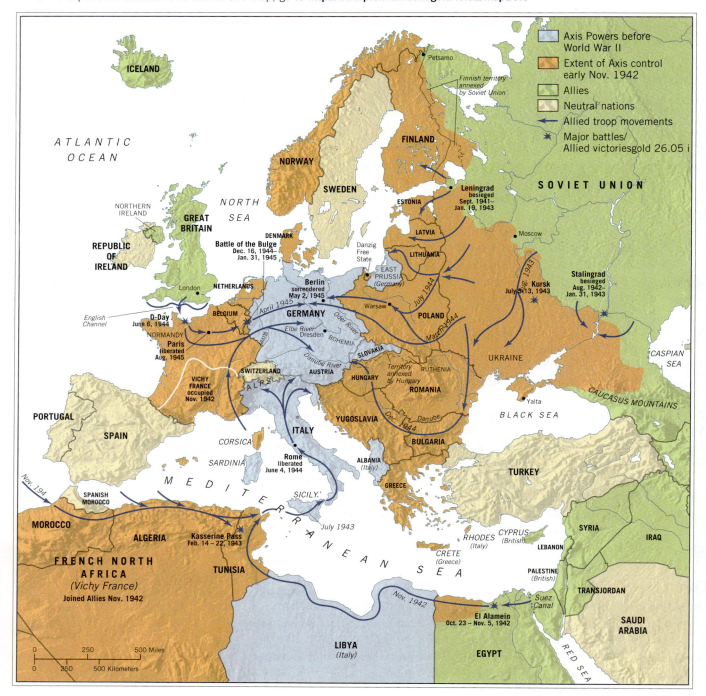

MAP 26–3

World War II in Europe, 1942–1945   Nazi Germany had to defend its conquests on three fronts. Around the Mediterranean, American and British forces pushed the Germans out of Africa and Southern Italy, while guerrillas in Yugoslavia pinned down many German troops. On the eastern front, Soviet armies advanced hundreds of miles to drive the German army out of the Soviet Union and eastern Europe. In June 1944, U.S. and British landings opened the western front in northern France for a decisive strike at the heart of Germany.

WHAT WERE the turning points in the war in Europe?

On the Eastern Front, by the end of 1944, the Red Army had entered the Balkans and reached central Poland. With the end in sight, the Soviets had suffered nearly 20 million casualties and sustained the heaviest burden in turning back Nazi tyranny.

VICTORY AND TRAGEDY IN EUROPE

In the last months of 1944, massive air strikes finally reduced German war production. The new American P-51 escort fighter helped B-17 bombers overfly Germany in relative safety after mid-1944. Thousand-bomber raids on railroads and oil facilities began to cripple the German economy. The raids also forced Germany to devote 2.5 million workers to air defense and damage repair. Politics rather than military need governed the final great action of the European air war. British and U.S. bombers in February 1945 staged a terror raid on the nonindustrial city of Dresden, packed with refugees, filled with great art, and undefended by the Germans; a firestorm fueled by incendiary bombs and rubble from blasted buildings killed tens of thousands of civilians without military justification.

Hitler struck a last blow on December 16, 1944. Stripping the Eastern Front of armored units, he launched twenty-five divisions against thinly held U.S. positions in the Ardennes Forest of Belgium. He hoped to split U.S. and British forces by capturing the Belgian port of Antwerp. Taking advantage of snow and fog that grounded Allied aircraft, the Germans drove a 50-mile bulge into U.S. lines. But the German thrust literally ran out of gas beyond the town of Bastogne. The Battle of the Bulge never seriously threatened the outcome of the war.

The Nazi empire collapsed in the spring of 1945. American and British divisions crossed the Rhine in March and enveloped Germany's industrial core. The Soviets drove through eastern Germany toward Berlin. On April 25, American and Red Army troops met on the Elbe River. Hitler committed suicide on April 30 in his concrete bunker deep under devastated Berlin, which surrendered to the Soviets on May 2. The Nazi state formally capitulated on May 8.

The defeat of Germany revealed appalling evidence of the evil at the heart of the Nazi ideology of racial superiority. The "final solution" to what Hitler thought of as the "Jewish problem" went far beyond slave labor. The elite SS, Hitler's personal army within the Nazi party, in 1942 set out to eliminate all of Europe's Jews. The evidence of genocide—systematic racial murder—is irrefutable. At Auschwitz and Treblinka, the SS organized the extermination of up to 6 million Jews and 1 million Poles, Gypsies, and others who failed to fit the Nazi vision of the German master race. Prisoners arrived by forced marches and cattle trains. Those who were not worked or starved to death were herded into gas chambers and then incinerated in huge crematoriums. Soviet troops could scarcely believe what they saw as they overran the death camps and freed the few survivors of what we now call the **Holocaust**.

THE PACIFIC WAR

Washington divided responsibilities in the Pacific theater. General Douglas MacArthur operated in the islands that stretched between Australia and the Philippines. Admiral Chester Nimitz commanded in the central Pacific. The Allies planned to isolate Japan from its southern conquests. The British moved from India to retake Burma. The Americans advanced along the islands of the southern Pacific to retake the Philippines. With Japan's army still tied down in China, the Americans then planned to bomb Japan into submission.

The Pacific campaigns of 1944, often called **island hopping**, were the American naval version of the *Blitzkrieg*. Planes from American carriers controlled the air, allowing the navy and land forces to isolate and capture the most strategically located Japanese-held islands while bypassing the rest (see Map 26–4).

WHERE TO LEARN MORE

Air Force Museum,
Dayton, Ohio

WHERE TO LEARN MORE

United States Holocaust Memorial
Museum, Washington, D.C.
http://www.ushmm.urlorg

WHERE TO LEARN MORE

Museum of the Pacific War,
Fredericksburg, Texas

Holocaust   The systematic murder of millions of European Jews and others deemed undesirable by Nazi Germany.

Island hopping   The Pacific campaigns of 1944 that were the American naval versions of the *Blitzkrieg*.

MAP 26–4

World War II in the Pacific, 1942–1945 The Allied strategy against Japan was to cut off Japan's southern conquests by retaking the central Pacific islands, the Philippines, and Burma and then to strike at the Japanese home islands. Submarine warfare and massive air attacks from November 1944 to August 1945 crippled Japan's capacity to wage war. The detonation of atomic bombs over Hiroshima and Nagasaki then forced surrender on August 15, 1945.

WHY WAS Japan unable to maintain its conquests in the Pacific?

Racial hatred animated both sides in the Pacific war and fueled a "war without mercy." Americans often characterized Japanese soldiers as vermin. In turn, the Japanese viewed Americans as racial mongrels and called them demons.

MacArthur used a version of the bypass strategy in the Solomon Islands and New Guinea, leapfrogging over Japanese strong points. The invasion of the Philippines repeated the approach by landing on Leyte, in the middle of the island chain. The Philippine campaign also destroyed the offensive capacity of the Japanese fleet. In the Battle of Leyte Gulf, the U.S. military sank four Japanese battleships, four carriers, and ten cruisers. The Japanese home islands were left with no defensive screen against an expected invasion.

During 1943 and 1944, submarines choked off food, oil, and raw materials bound for Japan and island bases. By 1945, imports to Japan were one-eighth of the 1940 level. Heavy bombing of Japan began in early 1944. A fire-bomb raid on Tokyo on the night of March 9, 1945, killed 124,000 people and left 1 million homeless. Overall, conventional bombing destroyed 42 percent of Japan's industrial capacity. By the time the United States captured the islands of Iwo Jima and Okinawa in fierce fighting (April–June 1945) and neared the Japanese home islands, Japan's position was hopeless.

SEARCHING FOR PEACE

At the beginning of 1945, the Allies sensed victory. Conferring from February 4 to 11 in the Ukrainian town of Yalta, Roosevelt, Stalin, and Churchill debated plans for the postwar world. The most important American goal was to enlist the USSR in finishing off the Pacific war. Americans hoped that a Soviet attack on Manchuria would tie down enough Japanese troops to reduce U.S. casualties in invading Japan. Stalin repeated his intent to declare war on Japan within three months of victory in Europe, in return for a free hand in Manchuria.

The most that Roosevelt could coax from Stalin were vague pledges to allow participation of non-Communists in coalition governments in eastern Europe. Stalin also agreed to join a new international organization, the United Nations.

Conservative critics later charged that the Western powers "gave away" eastern Europe at the **Yalta Conference**. In fact, the Soviet Union gained little that it did not already control. In East Asia as well, the Soviets could seize the territories that the agreements granted them.

On April 12, two months after Yalta, Roosevelt died of a cerebral hemorrhage. Harry Truman, the new president, was a shrewd politician, but his experience was limited; Roosevelt had not even told him about the Manhattan Project. Deeply distrustful of the Soviets, Truman first ventured into personal international diplomacy in July 1945 at a British-Soviet-American conference at Potsdam, near Berlin. Most of the sessions debated the future of Germany. The leaders endorsed the expulsion of ethnic Germans from eastern Europe and moved the borders of Poland 100 miles west into historically German territory. Truman also made it clear that the United States expected to dominate the occupation of Japan. Its goal was to democratize the Japanese political system and reintroduce Japan into the international community—a policy that succeeded. The **Potsdam Declaration** on July 26 summarized U.S. policy and gave Japan an opening for surrender. However, the declaration failed to guarantee that Emperor Hirohito would not be tried as a war criminal. The Japanese response was so cautious that Americans read it as rejection.

Secretary of State James Byrnes now urged Truman to use the new atomic bomb, tested just weeks earlier. Japan's ferocious defense of Okinawa and suicide missions by thousands of *kamikaze* pilots had confirmed American fears that the Japanese would fight to the death. In contrast, the bomb offered a quick end to the conflict, and it might intimidate Stalin (see the overview table "The Decision to Use the Atomic Bomb"). In short, a decision not to use atomic weapons was never a serious alternative.

In early August, the United States dropped two of three available nuclear bombs on Japan. On August 6 at Hiroshima the first bomb killed at least eighty thousand people and poisoned thousands more with radiation. A second bomb three days later at Nagasaki took another forty thousand lives. Japan ceased hostilities on August 14 and surrendered formally on September 2. The world has wondered ever since if the United States might have defeated Japan without resorting to atomic bombs, but recent research shows that the bombs were the shock that allowed the Emperor and peace advocates to overcome military leaders who wanted to fight to the death.

QUICK REVIEW

Preparations for Victory
- February 1945: Allies debate plans for postwar world at Yalta.
- Soviets solidified their hold on Eastern Europe.
- July 26, 1945: Potsdam Declaration fails to produce a definitive response from Japan.

Yalta Conference   Meeting of U.S. President Franklin Roosevelt, British Prime Minister Winston Churchill, and Soviet Premier Joseph Stalin held in February 1945 to plan the final stages of World War II and postwar arrangements.

Potsdam Declaration   Statement issued by the United States during a meeting of U.S. President Harry Truman, British Prime Minister Winston Churchill, and Soviet Premier Joseph Stalin in which the United States declared its intention to democratize the Japanese political system and reintroduce Japan into the international community.

OVERVIEW

THE DECISION TO USE THE ATOMIC BOMB

Americans have long argued whether the use of atomic bombs on the Japanese cities of Hiroshima and Nagasaki was necessary to end the war. Several factors probably influenced President Truman's decision to use the new weapon:

Military necessity	Truman later argued that the use of atomic bombs was necessary to avoid an invasion of Japan that would have cost hundreds of thousand of lives. Military planners expected Japanese soldiers to put up the same kind of suicidal resistance in defense of the home islands as they had to American landings at the Philippines, Iwo Jima, and Okinawa. More recently, historians have argued that the Japanese military was near collapse and that an invasion would have met far less resistance than feared.
Atomic diplomacy	Some historians believe that Truman used atomic weapons to overawe the Soviet Union and induce it to move cautiously in expanding its influence in Europe and East Asia. Truman and his advisers were certainly aware of how the bomb might influence the Soviet leadership.
Domestic politics	President Roosevelt and his chief military advisers had spent billions on the secret atomic bomb project without the knowledge of Congress or the American public. The managers of the Manhattan Project may have believed that only proof of its military value would quiet critics and justify the huge cost.
Momentum of war	The United States and Britain had already adopted wholesale destruction of German and Japanese cities as a military tactic. Use of the atomic bomb looked like a variation on fire bombing, not the start of a new era of potential mass destruction. In this context, some historians argue, President Truman's choice was natural and expected.

CONCLUSION

World War II made and unmade families. It gave millions of women new responsibilities and then sent them back to the kitchen. It put money in pockets that had been emptied by the Great Depression and turned struggling business owners into tycoons.

Most of the 16 million men and women in uniform served in support jobs that keep the war machine going.

World War II adventure movies in which Americans always win leave the impression that triumph was necessary and inevitable. In fact, victory was the hard-fought result of public leadership and military effort. Under other leadership, for example, the United States might have stood aside until it was too late to reverse the Axis conquest of Europe and East Asia.

The war unified the nation in new ways while confirming old divisions. People of all backgrounds shared a common cause.

But nothing broke the barriers that separated white and black Americans. Unequal treatment in a war for democracy outraged black soldiers, who returned to fight for civil rights. The uprooting of Japanese Americans was another reminder of racial prejudice.

FROM THEN TO NOW
Nuclear Weapons

On May 11 and 12, 1998, India tested five nuclear weapons in its western desert. Two weeks later, Pakistan tested its own nuclear weapons. Neighbors and bitter rivals, the two became the sixth and seventh nations to publicly acknowledge the possession of a nuclear arsenal. Now the tensions between them, which had long fueled border clashes and twice erupted in open warfare, had become another factor in the delicate calculus of nuclear terror that has confronted the world since Hiroshima.

It has been a central goal of U.S. policy since 1945 to limit the number of nations with atomic weapons and place ceilings on the size of nuclear arsenals. The goal became more urgent when the Soviet Union deployed its own nuclear weapons after 1949, establishing the "balance of terror" that haunted the decades-long Cold War between the United States and the Soviet Union.

Two key steps toward reducing the nuclear threat were the Limited Test Ban Treaty of 1963—in which the United States, Britain, and the USSR outlawed atmospheric nuclear testing (see Chapter 30)—and the Nuclear Non-Proliferation Treaty, which was signed in 1968 and extended indefinitely in 1995. One hundred eighty nations have agreed not to acquire nuclear weapons, and five acknowledged nuclear powers—the United States, Russia, Britain, France, China—have agreed to eventual elimination of their own weapons.

The power of international opinion was clearly not enough to convince India and Pakistan to abandon their nuclear weapons programs, but it has been effective elsewhere in the 1990s. One justification of the Gulf War in 1991 (see Chapter 33) was to prevent Iraq from developing nuclear arms, and Iraqi interference with United Nations inspection teams triggered bombing raids on Iraq in 1998–1999. The United States also orchestrated pressure on North Korea to cancel a suspected nuclear weapons program and admit international inspectors.

The 1990s saw advances in efforts to reduce the huge nuclear stockpiles of the United States and Russia. The first Strategic Arms Limitation Treaty (START I) went into effect in 1994. The United States and Russia agreed to retain a maximum of eight thousand warheads each. START II, if implemented, would cut the total to three thousand each. The breakup of the Soviet Union and the economic challenges that have confronted its constituent republics have created fears about the diversion of warheads into the hands of terrorists. The United States, however, has helped to pay for dismantling of Russian warheads and their removal from Ukraine and Kazakhstan, both formerly parts of the Soviet Union.

The frightening proliferation and growth of nuclear arsenals that began with the Manhattan Project and continued into the 1980s may be ending. The 1990s, on the contrary, may have marked the beginning of a new era of shrinking nuclear capacity, despite reversals like those in India and Pakistan. South Africa, for example, announced in 1993 that it had destroyed six warheads that it had manufactured secretly. And planned reductions in the largest nuclear arsenals offer hope that the trend will continue in the new century.

The lessons of World War II influenced the thinking of presidents from Eisenhower in the 1950s to George H. W. Bush in the 1990s. Even though the United States ended 1945 with the world's mightiest navy, biggest air force, and only atomic bomb, the instability that had followed World War I made Western leaders nervous about the shape of world politics.

One result in the postwar era was conflict between the United States and the Soviet Union, which became the Cold War. At home, international tensions fed pressure for social and political conformity. Fifteen years of economic depression and sacrifice made the postwar generation sensitive to perceived threats to steady jobs and stable families. For the next generation, the unresolved business of World War II would haunt American life.

SUMMARY

The Dilemmas of Neutrality In the late 1930s President Roosevelt's challenge was to lead the United States toward rearmament and support nations at war with fascism without alarming the public. The roots of World War II were to be found in the after-effects of the first World War; as Germany marched from victory to victory from 1939 to 1941, strong isolationist sentiment in America shaped public debate and limited attempts to help Britain and the Soviet Union. The swift collapse of France and radio broadcasts describing the bombing of London frightened Americans; the Lend Lease Act, an undeclared naval war, and the Atlantic Charter drew America closer to war. The final shove came in the Pacific with the attack on Pearl Harbor; in December 1941 America entered World War II.

Holding the Line Despite the popular desire to defeat Japan, the Allies planned to defeat Germany first. The Soviet Union held the Eastern front in the Battle of Stalingrad; the British fought back in the Battle of the Atlantic; German troops in North Africa were forced to retreat; Japanese expansion came to a halt at the Battle of the Coral Sea and Battle of Midway. By the end of 1942 the tide was turning; in mid-1943 the Allies could begin to plan for victory with confidence.

Mobilizing for Victory The need to fight a global war brought a huge expansion of the federal government; price controls and rationing fought inflation, industry mobilized for defense production, and the Manhattan Project ushered in the age of atomic energy. The war penetrated every facet of everyday life; women and minorities changed the composition of the industrial work force. The government saw Japanese Americans as threats and interned them in camps throughout the West. The war required more than a thirtyfold expansion of the U.S. military; soldiers came from across the American spectrum. While women in the military received unequal treatment, African Americans fared worse.

War and Peace Plans for ending the war were drawn up at Casablanca and Tehran; Italy was invaded in 1943; Operation Overlord opened the second front in Europe; in 1944 Germany was being battered from the east and west. As Allied troops entered Germany and discovered the death camps, the extent of what is now called the Holocaust became clear. Through the island hopping campaign in the Pacific, American forces neared the Japanese home islands; in 1945 President Truman chose to use the atomic bomb to end the war with Japan. The postwar world would prove to be a challenge; the Yalta and Potsdam conferences divided Europe into spheres that would last for almost fifty years.

REVIEW QUESTIONS

1. What arguments did Americans make against involvement in the war in Europe? Why did President Roosevelt and many others believe it necessary to block German and Japanese expansion?

2. How did mobilization for World War II alter life in the United States? What opportunities did it open for women?

3. What factors were decisive in the defeat of Germany?

4. What was the U.S. strategy against Japan, and how well did it work?

5. What role did advanced science and technology play in World War II? How did the scientific lead of the United States affect the war's outcome?

KEY TERMS

Allies (p. 687)
Atlantic Charter (p. 691)
Axis Powers (p. 687)
Battle of the Atlantic (p. 693)
Blitzkrieg (p. 688)
D-Day (p. 703)

Eastern Front (p. 692)
Fair Employment Practices Committee (p. 699)
Greater East Asia Co-Prosperity Sphere (p. 687)
Holocaust (p. 705)

Island hopping (p. 705)
Manhattan Project (p. 696)
Operation OVERLORD (p. 703)
Postdam Declaration (p. 707)
Yalta Conference (p. 707)

WHERE TO LEARN MORE

 Air Force Museum, Dayton, Ohio. Visitors can walk among World War II fighter planes and bombers, including the B-29 that dropped the atomic bomb in Nagasaki, and learn about the role of aviation in the war.

Museum of the Pacific War, Fredericksburg, Texas. In the birthplace of Admiral Chester Nimitz, this new museum is an excellent introduction to the war with Japan.

Los Alamos County Historical Museum and Bradbury Science Museum, Los Alamos, New Mexico. The museum traces the origins of atomic energy for military and civilian uses. Nearby is the Los Alamos County Historical Museum, which gives the feel of everyday life in the atomic town.

United States Holocaust Memorial Museum, Washington, D.C. The Holocaust Museum gives visitors a deeply moving depiction of the deadly impacts of Nazi ideas in the 1930s and 1940s. The museum's website at **http://www.ushmm.urlorg** also explores virtually every facet of the Holocaust experience for Jews during World War II.

For additional study resources for this chapter, go to:
www.prenhall.com/goldfield/chapter26

To my mind we are in a situation no less dangerous than the one we were facing in 1939, and it is of the greatest importance that we realize it. We must realize . . . that democracy will not be saved by ideals alone.

As international tensions rose with the onset of the Cold War, Americans wondered how to prepare for a possible nuclear war. Many families stocked extra food and water and bought a battery-powered radio, but few actually installed backyard bomb shelters like the one being tested by this family in a Long Island suburb not far from Levittown.

27

FALLOUT SHELTER

THE COLD WAR AT HOME AND ABROAD

1946–1952

WHAT WAS the catalyst for the economic boom that began in 1947?

HOW WAS Harry Truman able to win the 1948 presidential election?

WHAT WERE the origins of the Cold War?

WHAT WERE the major conflicts of the early Cold War?

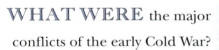

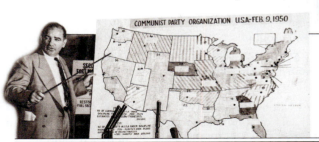

WHAT WAS the "Second Red Scare?"

1952

1946

My eyes popped when I got to town hall because the lobby and the stairs leading up to the hearing room were loaded with people. The upstairs hallway was jammed and the room was packed. People were standing along the walls. I remember there were a lot of children, toddlers—some in strollers—and many babies held by men and women. We expected there would be quite a turnout. But the extent of the crowd was a big surprise to me. . . . The meeting itself was rather brief. There were some speeches. No screaming and yelling the way people do at town meetings today. Everyone was quiet, anxious. I remember one guy in uniform, holding a baby, made a strong statement. These people were desperate. It was very moving. When the decision was announced, the crowd broke into applause.

Levittown was the last place on the planet I thought I would be living. But, as it turned out, we moved there because the house was such a good buy. . . . We loved living there. I came into work and told [Newsday managing editor Alan] Hathway that I would be eating crow for the rest of my days.

Bernadette Rischer Wheeler, in "Levittown at Fifty: Long Island Voices," at **www.lihistory.com/specsec/hsvoices.htm**; originally published in *Newsday*.

IMAGE KEY
for pages 712–713

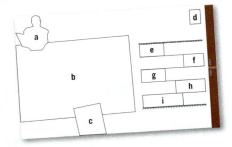

a. A man sitting reading "The Mirror" with a headline about Lucille Ball.

b. "The Cold War At Home and Abroad 1946-52." Photo of mother and father with 3 children in fallout shelter.

c. The North Atlantic Treaty Organization treaty with signature and seal.

d. "Fallout shelter" sign.

e. Unidentified model displaying a kitchen interior, photo 1950's.

f. American President Harry Truman shakes hands with supporters from a train car during a rally in the 1948 presidential campaign.

g. Civilians atop bombed out ruins of buildings watching American C-54 cargo plane fly overhead during Allied airlift to bring food & supplies to beseiged citizens of Soviet controlled Berlin.

h. Soldiers in Korea.

i. Senator Joseph McCarthy points to Oregon on an organizational map implying Communist Party organization in the United States.

Cold War The political and economic confrontation between the Soviet Union and the United States that dominated world affairs from 1946 to 1989.

BERNADETTE WHEELER was a reporter for *Newsday*, the daily newspaper for the Long Island suburbs of New York, who covered the birth of the new community of Levittown. She remembers the meeting on May 21, 1947, when the local governing board approved construction of the new subdivision. The size of the crowd indicates the severity of the housing shortage after World War II and the intense desire of Americans to return to normal life. After years of hardship, they defined American ideals in terms of economic opportunity and the chance to enjoy national prosperity. Over the next decade, the residents who moved to Levittown and thousands of other new subdivisions would start the baby boom and rekindle the economy with their purchases of automobiles, appliances, and televisions.

This yearning to enjoy the promise of American life after years of sacrifice helps to explain why Americans reacted so fiercely to new challenges and threats. They watched as congressional conservatives and President Truman fought over the fate of New Deal programs. More worrisome was the confrontation with the Soviet Union that was soon being called the **Cold War**. Triggered by the Soviet Union's imposition of communist regimes throughout eastern Europe, the Cold War grew into a global contest between the United States and the Soviets. By the time real war broke out in Korea in 1950, many Americans were venting their frustration by blaming international setbacks on internal subversion and by trying to root out suspected "reds."

The Cold War would shape the United States and the world for a generation. Massive rearmament allowed U.S. presidents to act as international policemen in the name of democratic values—a vast change from earlier American goals to remain disengaged from the problems of other nations. Defense spending also reshaped American industry and helped stimulate twenty-five years of economic growth. The Cold War narrowed the range of political discussion, making many of the left-wing ideas of the 1930s taboo by the 1950s. It also made racial segregation and limits on immigration into international embarrassments and thus nudged the nation to live up to its ideals.

LAUNCHING THE GREAT BOOM

When World War II ended, Americans feared that demobilization would bring a rerun of the inflation and unemployment that had followed World War I. In the first eighteen months of peace, rising prices, labor-management strife, and shortages of everything from meat to automobiles confirmed their anxiety. In 1947 and 1948, however, an economic expansion began that lasted for a quarter century. That prosperity would finance a military buildup and an activist foreign policy.

RECONVERSION CHAOS

Japan's sudden surrender took U.S. officials by surprise. They had planned on taking two years to phase out military spending and reintroduce veterans to the domestic economy. Now their plans were obsolete. The Pentagon, already scaling back defense spending, canceled $15 billion in war contracts in the first forty-eight hours after the victory over Japan. Public pressure demanded that the military release the nation's 12 million servicemen and servicewomen as rapidly as possible. GIs in Europe and the South Pacific waited impatiently for their discharge determined by length of time in uniform, service overseas, combat decorations, and number of children.

Veterans came home to shortages of both food in the grocery stores and consumer goods in the department stores. Automobiles were especially scarce; the number of vehicles registered in the United States had declined by 4 million during the war. For the privilege of spending a few hundred dollars on a junker, consumers sometimes had to pay used-car dealers for so-called accessories like $150 batteries and $100 lap robes.

Inflation squeezed factory workers, who had accepted wage controls during the war effort. Since 1941, prices had risen twice as fast as base wages. In the fall of 1945, more and more workers went on strike to redress the balance. By January 1946, some 1.3 million auto, steel, electrical, and packinghouse workers were off the job. Strikes in these basic industries shut other factories down for lack of supplies. Presidential committees finally crafted settlements that allowed steel and auto workers to make up ground lost during the war, but they also allowed corporations to pass on higher costs to consumers. One Republican senator complained of "unionists who fatten themselves at the expense of the rest of us." Bill Nation, who inspected window moldings at a GM plant in Detroit, wondered who the senator was talking about. The strike gave him an hourly raise of 18 cents, pushing his weekly income to $59. After paying for food, housing, and utilities, that left $13.44 for Bill, his wife, and their five children to spend on clothes, comic books, and doctor bills.

ECONOMIC POLICY

The **Employment Act of 1946** and the **Taft-Hartley Act** of 1947 represented contradictory liberal and conservative approaches to the peacetime economy.

The Employment Act was an effort by congressional liberals to ward off economic crisis by fine-tuning government taxation and spending. It started as a proposal to ensure everyone's "right to a useful and remunerative job." Watered down in the face of business opposition, it still defined economic growth and high employment as national goals. It also established the **Council of Economic Advisers** to assist the president.

In fact, more than 2 million women provided some slack by leaving the labor force outright, so that unemployment rates were far lower than economists had predicted. Federal agencies hastened their departure by publishing pamphlets

QUICK REVIEW

Post-war Economic Problems
- Military spending and military service came to an abrupt halt.
- Veterans came home to shortages in food and consumer goods.
- Inflation contributed to labor unrest.

Taft-Hartley Act   Federal legislation of 1947 that substantially limited the tools available to labor unions in labor-management disputes.

Council of Economic Advisers   Board of three professional economists established in 1946 to advise the president on economic policy.

American actors Dana Andrews and Virginia Mayo portray Fred and Marie Derry in the 1946 movie *The Best Years of Our Life*, a film about WWII soldiers returning from war and adjusting to their post-war lives.

RKO Radio Pictures/Hulton Archive

QUICK REVIEW

The Taft-Hartly Act (1947)

◆ Effort to reverse gains made by labor in the 1930s.
◆ Public anger over strikes made passage of the act possible.
◆ Many middle-class Americans believed labor had gone too far.

---

asking *men* the pointed question, "Do you want your wife to work after the war?" In addition, consumer spending from a savings pool of $140 billion in bank accounts and war bonds created a huge demand for workers to fill. Total employment rose rather than fell with the end of the war.

From the other end of the political spectrum, the Taft-Hartley Act climaxed a ten-year effort by conservatives to reverse the gains made by organized labor in the 1930s. The act passed in 1947 because of anger about continuing strikes. For many Americans, the chief culprit was John L. Lewis, head of the United Mine Workers. The burly, bushy-browed, and combative Lewis was instantly recognizable—loved by his workers and hated by nearly everyone else. In April 1946, a forty-day coal strike cut into industrial production. The coal settlement was only days old when the nation faced an even more crippling walkout by railroad workers. Many middle-class Americans were convinced that organized labor needed to be curbed.

In November 1946, Republicans capitalized on the problems of reconversion chaos, labor unrest, and dissatisfaction with Truman. Their election slogan was simple: "Had enough?" The GOP won control of Congress for the first time since the election of 1928.

Adopted by the now firmly conservative Congress, the Taft-Hartley Act was a serious counterattack by big business on the power of large unions. It barred the closed shop (the requirement that all workers hired in a particular company or plant be union members) and blocked secondary boycotts (strikes against suppliers or customers of a targeted business). The federal government could postpone a strike by imposing a "cooling-off period," which gave companies time to stockpile their output. Officers of national unions had to swear they were not Communists or Communist sympathizers, even though corporate executives had no similar obligation. The bill passed over Truman's veto.

THE GI BILL

Another landmark law for the postwar era passed Congress without controversy. Popularly known as the **GI Bill of Rights**, the Servicemen's Readjustment Act of 1944 was designed to ease veterans back into the civilian mainstream. Rather than pay cash bonuses to veterans, as after previous wars, Congress tied benefits to specific public goals. The GI Bill guaranteed loans for buying a house or farm or starting a business. The program encouraged veterans to attend college with money for tuition and books plus monthly stipends.

The GI Bill made college degrees accessible to men with working-class backgrounds. In the peak year of 1947, veterans made up half of all college students. "We're all trying to get where we would have been if there hadn't been a war," one vet attending Indiana University told *Time* magazine. Veterans helped convert the college degree—once available primarily to the socially privileged—into a basic business and professional credential.

An unfortunate side effect of the GI tide was to crowd women out of classrooms, although sixty thousand servicewomen did take advantage of educational benefits. Women's share of bachelor's degrees dropped from 40 percent in 1940 to 25 percent in 1950. The most common female presence on many campuses was working wives trying to make up the gap between Veterans Administration (VA) checks and the expenses of new families.

ASSEMBLY-LINE NEIGHBORHOODS

Americans faced a housing shortage after the war. In 1947, fully 3 million married couples were unable to set up their own household. Most doubled up with relatives while they waited for the construction industry to respond. Hunger for housing

---

GI Bill of Rights Legislation in June 1944 that eased the return of veterans into American society by providing educational and employment benefits.

was fierce. Eager buyers lined up for hours and paid admission fees to tour model homes or to put their names in drawings for the opportunity to buy.

The solution started with the federal government and its VA mortgage program. By guaranteeing repayment, the VA allowed veterans to get home purchase loans from private lenders without a down payment. Eyeing the mass market created by the federal programs, William Levitt, a New York builder who had developed defense housing projects, built two thousand rental houses for veterans on suburban Long Island in 1947. His basic house had 800 square feet of living space in two bedrooms, living room, kitchen, bath, and unfinished attic waiting for the weekend handyman. It gave new families a place to start. There were six thousand **Levittown** houses by the end of 1948 and more than seventeen thousand by 1951.

Other successful builders bought hundreds of acres of land, put in utilities for the entire tract, purchased materials by the carload, and kept specialized workers busy on scores of identical houses. Floor plans were square, simple, and easy for semiskilled workers to construct. For the first time, kitchens across America were designed for preassembled cabinets and appliances in standard sizes. "On-site fabrication" was mass production without an assembly line. Work crews at the Los Angeles suburb of Lakewood started a hundred houses a day as they moved down one side of the street and back up the other.

From 1946 through 1950, the federal government backed $20 billion in VA and New Deal era Federal Housing Administration (FHA) loans, approximately 40 percent of all home mortgage debt. Housing starts neared 2 million in the peak year of 1950. By the end of the 1940s, 55 percent of American households owned their homes. The suburban population grew much faster than the population of central cities, and the population outside the growing reach of metropolitan areas actually declined.

Unfortunately, the suburban solution to housing shortages also had costs. Vast new housing tracts tended to isolate women and children and did little to help African Americans. Discrimination excluded black workers and their families from new housing. Federal housing agencies and private industry worsened the problem by **redlining** older neighborhoods, which involved withholding home purchase loans and insurance coverage from inner-city areas.

Public and private actions kept black people in deteriorating inner-city ghettos. When severe flooding in 1948 drove thousands of African Americans from wartime temporary housing in Portland, Oregon, for example, their only choice was to crowd into the city's small black neighborhood. Chicago landlords squeezed an estimated 27,000 black migrants per year into run-down buildings, subdividing larger apartments into one-room "kitchenette" units with sinks and hot plates but no private bathrooms. Families that tried to find new homes in white neighborhoods on the edge of black ghettos often met violence—rocks through windows, fire bombs, milling mobs of angry white people.

STEPS TOWARD CIVIL RIGHTS

A new generation of black leaders began working to reduce the gap between America's ideal of equality and its performance. At the same time, a wave of lynchings and racist violence surged across the South after the war; special targets were black veterans who tried to register to vote. However, many white people felt uneasy about the contradiction between a crusade for freedom abroad and racial discrimination at home.

Caught between pressure from black leaders and the fear of alienating Southern Democrats, President Truman in 1946 appointed the Committee on Civil Rights, whose report developed an agenda for racial justice that would take two

QUICK REVIEW

Housing Shortages
- Americans faced housing shortages after the war.
- The VA mortgage program allowed veterans to purchase homes without a down payment.
- Builders responded with mass-produced housing.

Levittown Suburban Long Island community of postwar rental houses built by William Levitt for veterans of World War II.

Redlining The withholding of home purchase loans and insurance coverage from inner-city older neighborhoods by federal housing agencies and private industry.

CHRONOLOGY

1944	Servicemen's Readjustment Act (GI Bill) is passed.
1945	United Nations is established.
1946	Employment Act creates Council of Economic Advisers. George Kennan sends his "long telegram." Winston Churchill delivers his "iron curtain" speech.
1947	Truman Doctrine is announced. Truman establishes a federal employee loyalty program. Kennan explains containment policy in an anonymous article in *Foreign Affairs*. Marshall Plan begins providing economic aid to Europe. HUAC holds hearings in Hollywood. Taft-Hartley Act rolls back gains of organized labor. National Security Act creates the National Security Council and the Central Intelligence Agency.
1948	Communists stage coup in Czechoslovakia. Berlin airlift overcomes Soviet blockade. Truman orders desegregation of the armed forces. Selective Service is reestablished. Truman wins reelection.
1949	North Atlantic Treaty Organization is formed. Communist Chinese defeat Nationalists. Soviet Union tests an atomic bomb. Department of Defense is established.
1950	Senator McCarthy begins his Red hunt. Alger Hiss is convicted of perjury. NSC-68 is drafted and accepted as U.S. policy. Korean War begins.
1951	Senate Internal Security Subcommittee begins hearings. Truman relieves MacArthur of his command. Julius and Ethel Rosenberg are convicted of conspiring to commit espionage. Truce talks begin in Korea.
1952	United States tests the hydrogen bomb. Eisenhower is elected president.

decades to put into effect. The Justice Department began to support antisegregation lawsuits filed by the NAACP.

The president also ordered "equality of treatment and opportunity" in the armed services in July 1948. The army in particular dragged its feet, hoping to limit black soldiers to 10 percent of enlistees. Manpower needs and the fighting record of integrated units in Korea from 1950 to 1953 persuaded the reluctant generals. Over the next generation, African Americans would find the military an important avenue for career opportunities.

More Americans were interested in the lowering of racial barriers in professional team sports. Individual black champions already included heavy-weight boxer Joe Louis and sprinter Jesse Owens. Jack Roosevelt (Jackie) Robinson, a proud and gifted African-American athlete, opened the 1947 baseball season as a member of the Brooklyn Dodgers. Robinson was the first African American to play for the modern major leagues. In the segregated society of the 1940s, Robinson also found himself a powerful symbol of racial change.

CONSUMER BOOM AND BABY BOOM

Americans celebrated the end of the war with weddings; the marriage rate in 1946 surpassed even its wartime high. By 1950, the median age at which women married would be just over 20 years—lower than at any previous time in the twentieth century. The United States ended the 1940s with 7 million more married couples than at the decade's start.

New marriages jump-started the "baby boom," as did already married couples who decided to catch up after postponing childbearing during the war. In the early 1940s, an average of 2.9 million children per year were born in the United States; in 1946–1950, the average was 3.6 million. Those 3.5 million "extra" babies needed diapers, swing sets, lunch boxes, bicycles, and school rooms. Fast-growing families also needed to stock up on household goods. Out of an average household income of roughly $4,000 in 1946 and 1947, a family of four had $300 to $400 a year for the furnishings and appliances that manufacturers were beginning to produce in growing volume. William Levitt tried to humorously capture the American satisfaction with the fruits of free enterprise when he said in 1948 that "no man who owns his house and lot can be a Communist; he has too much to do."

TRUMAN, REPUBLICANS, AND THE FAIR DEAL

From new radios to new homes to new jobs, the economic gains of the postwar years propelled Americans toward the political center. After fifteen years of economic crisis and world war, they wanted to enjoy prosperity. They wanted to keep the gains of the New Deal—but without risking new experiments.

Recognizing this attitude, Harry Truman and his political advisers tried to define policies acceptable to moderate Republicans as well as Democrats. This meant creating a bipartisan coalition to block Soviet influence in western Europe and defending the core of the New Deal's social and economic agenda at home.

This political package is known as the strategy of the "vital center," after the title of a 1949 book by Arthur Schlesinger Jr. The book linked anti-Communism in foreign policy with efforts to enact inclusive social and economic policies—to extend freedom abroad and at home at the same time. The vital center reflected the political reality of the Cold War years, when Democrats had to prove that they were tough on Communism before they could enact domestic reforms.

TRUMAN'S OPPOSITION

In his campaign for a full term as president in 1948, Truman faced not only the Republicans but also new fringe parties on the far right and far left that allowed him to position himself in the moderate center. The blunt, no-nonsense Missourian entered the campaign an underdog; he soon looked like the country's best option for steering a steady course.

Truman's formal opponents represented the American Progressive party (an amalgam of left-leaning political groups), the **Dixiecrats** (officially the States' Rights Democrats), and the Republicans. The president also ran against the Republican-controlled "donothing 80th Congress," which he used as a punching bag at every opportunity.

Progressive candidate Henry Wallace cast himself as the prophet for "the century of the common man." His background as a plant geneticist and farm journalist prepared him to deal with domestic policy but not world affairs. After Truman fired him from the cabinet in 1946 for advocating a conciliatory stance toward the Soviets, Wallace went to Europe to praise the USSR and denounced U.S. foreign policy. On his return, most liberal Democrats ran the other way when Wallace organized the Progressive party, leaving the Communist party to supply many of his campaign workers.

Wallace argued that the United States was forcing the Cold War on the Soviet Union and undermining American ideals by diverting attention from poverty and racism at home. He wanted to repeal the draft and destroy atomic weapons. His arguments had merit, for the United States was becoming a militarized society, but Wallace was the wrong person to change American minds. With his shy

HOW WAS Harry Truman able to win the 1948 presidential election?

WHERE TO LEARN MORE

Harry S Truman National Historical Site, Library, and Museum, Independence, Missouri
www.nps.gov/hstr/

Dixiecrats   States' Rights Democrats.

personality, disheveled appearance, and fanaticism about health food, he struck most voters as a kook rather than a statesman.

At the other political extreme were the Southerners who walked out when the 1948 Democratic National Convention called for full civil rights for African Americans. Mayor Hubert Humphrey of Minneapolis challenged the Democratic party "to get out of the shadow of states' rights and walk forthrightly into the bright sunshine of human rights."

When the angry Southerners met to nominate their own candidate, however, the South's important politicians stayed away. Major Southern newspapers called the revolt futile and narrow-minded.

Tom Dewey, Truman's strongest opponent, had been an effective governor of New York and represented the moderate Eastern establishment within the Republican party. Fortunately for Truman, Dewey lacked the common touch. Smooth on the outside, he alienated people who should have been his closest supporters. He was an arrogant campaigner, refusing to interrupt his morning schedule to talk to voters. He acted like a snob and dressed like the groom on a wedding cake.

Dewey was also saddled with the results of the 80th Congress (1947–1948). Truman used confrontation with Congress to rally voters who had supported the New Deal. Vote for me, Truman argued, to protect the New Deal, or vote Republican to bring back the days of Herbert Hoover. After his nomination in July 1948, Truman called Congress back into session and dared Republicans to enact all the measures for which *their* party claimed to stand. Congress did nothing, and Truman had more proof that the Republicans were all talk and no show.

WHISTLE-STOPPING ACROSS AMERICA

In the 1948 presidential campaign, a major candidate crisscrossed the nation by rail for the last time and made hundreds of speeches from the rear platforms of trains. For the first time, national television broadcast the two party conventions. The Republican campaign issued a printed T-shirt that read "Dew-It With Dewey"— the earliest advertising T-shirt in the collections of the Smithsonian Institution.

Truman was a widely read and intelligent man who cultivated the image of a backslapper. "I'll mow 'em down . . . and I'll give 'em hell," he told his vice presidential running mate, Senator Alben Barkley of Kentucky. Crowds across the country greeted him with "Give 'em hell, Harry!" He covered 31,700 miles in his campaign train and gave ten speeches a day.

On the advice of political strategist Clark Clifford, Truman tied Dewey to inflation, housing shortages, and fears about the future of Social Security. In industrial cities, he hammered at the Taft-Hartley Act. In the West, he pointed out that Democratic administrations had built dams and helped turn natural resources into jobs. He called the Republicans the party of privilege and arrogance. The Democrats, he said, offered opportunity for farmers, factory workers, and small business owners.

Truman got a huge boost from Dewey's unwillingness to fight. Going into the fall with a huge lead in the public opinion polls, Dewey sought to avoid mistakes. He failed to counter Truman's attacks and packed his speeches with platitudes: "Our streams abound with fish." "You know that your future is still ahead of you." "Peace is a blessing that we all share." The results astounded the pollsters, who had stopped sampling opinion in mid-October—just as a swing to Truman gathered strength. Wallace and Thurmond each took just under 1.2 million votes. Dewey received nearly 22 million popular votes and 189 electoral votes, but Truman won more than 24 million popular votes and 303 electoral votes (see Map 27–1).

American President Harry Truman shakes hands with supporters from a train car during a rally in the 1948 presidential campaign.

AP/Wide World Photos

TRUMAN'S FAIR DEAL

Truman hoped to build on the gains of the New Deal. In his State of the Union address in January 1949, he called for a **Fair Deal** for all Americans. He promised to extend the New Deal and ensure "greater economic opportunity for the mass of the people."

In the Housing Act of 1949, the federal government reaffirmed its concern about families who had been priced out of the private market. Passed with the backing of conservative Senator Robert Taft—"Mr. Republican" to his admirers—the act provided money for local housing agencies to buy, level, and resell land for housing. The intent was to level slums and replace them with affordable modern apartments. The program never worked as intended because of scanty appropriations and poor design of the replacement housing, but it established the goal of decent housing for all Americans.

In 1950, Congress revitalized the weak Social Security program. Benefits went up by an average of 80 percent, and 10.5 million additional people received old-age and survivors' insurance. Most of the new coverage went to rural and small-town people.

Congress rejected other Fair Deal proposals that would remain on the national agenda for decades. A plan to alter the farm subsidy system to favor small farmers rather than agribusiness went nowhere. A Senate filibuster killed a permanent Fair Employment Practices Commission to fight racial discrimination in hiring. The medical establishment blocked a proposal for national health insurance as "socialistic." The overall message from Truman's second term was clear: Americans liked what the New Deal had given them but were hesitant about new initiatives.

CONFRONTING THE SOVIET UNION

In 1945, the United States and the Soviet Union were allies, victorious against Germany and planning the defeat of Japan. By 1947, they were engaged in a diplomatic and economic confrontation and soon came close to war over the city of Berlin.

Over the next forty years, the United States and the USSR contested for economic, political, and military influence around the globe in a Cold War. The heart of Soviet policy was control of eastern Europe as a buffer zone against Germany. The centerpiece of American policy was to link the United States, western Europe, and Japan into an alliance of overwhelming economic power. Both sides spent vast sums on conventional military forces and atomic weapons that held the world in a balance of terror. They also competed for political advantage in Asia and Africa as newly independent nations replaced European colonial empires.

Americans and Soviets frequently interpreted each other's actions in the most threatening terms, turning miscalculations and misunderstandings into crises. At home, a U.S. public that had suffered through nearly two decades of economic depression and war reacted to international problems with frustration and anger.

MAP EXPLORATION

To explore an interactive version of this map, go to
http://www.prenhall.com/goldfield2/map27.1

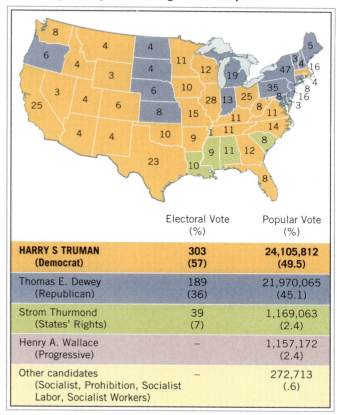

	Electoral Vote (%)	Popular Vote (%)
HARRY S TRUMAN (Democrat)	**303** **(57)**	**24,105,812** **(49.5)**
Thomas E. Dewey (Republican)	189 (36)	21,970,065 (45.1)
Strom Thurmond (States' Rights)	39 (7)	1,169,063 (2.4)
Henry A. Wallace (Progressive)	–	1,157,172 (2.4)
Other candidates (Socialist, Prohibition, Socialist Labor, Socialist Workers)	–	272,713 (.6)

MAP 27–1

The Election of 1948   Harry Truman won a narrow victory in the presidential election of 1948 by holding many of the traditionally Democratic states of the South and West and winning key industrial states in the Midwest. His success depended on the coalition of rural and urban interests that Franklin Roosevelt had pulled together in the 1930s.

WHY DO you think industrial states in the Midwest supported Harry S Truman in the 1948 presidential election?

WHAT WERE the origins of the Cold War?

THE END OF THE GRAND ALLIANCE

The Yalta Conference of February 1945 had recognized military realities by marking out rough spheres of influence. The Soviet defeat of Germany on the Eastern Front had made the USSR the only military power in eastern Europe. The American and British attacks through Italy and France had made the Western allies dominant in western Europe and the Mediterranean. The Soviets, Americans, British, and French shared control of defeated Germany, each with its own occupation zone of the country and its own sector of Berlin. The Western allies had the better of the bargain. Defeated Italy and Japan, whose reconstruction was firmly in Western hands, had far greater economic potential than Soviet-controlled Bulgaria, Romania, or Hungary.

The victorious powers argued bitterly about Germany and eastern Europe. For Poland, Truman and his advisers claimed that Yalta had assumed open elections on the American model. The Soviet Union saw Poland as the historic invasion route from the west; it claimed that Yalta had ensured that any Polish government would be friendly to Soviet interests and acted to guarantee that this would be so.

The United States tried to involve the USSR and eastern Europe in new international organizations, such as the United Nations (U.N.). The Washington-based **International Monetary Fund (IMF)** and the **World Bank** were designed to revive international trade. The IMF stabilized national currencies against the short-term pressures of international trade. The World Bank drew on the resources of member nations to make economic development loans to governments for such projects as new dams or agricultural modernization. These organizations ensured that a reviving world economy would revolve around the industrial and technological power of the United States.

In 1946, the United States also presented a plan in the United Nations to control atomic energy. Bernard Baruch suggested that an international agency should oversee all uranium production and research on atomic explosives, but this plan was unacceptable to the Soviets, who did not want to open their atomic energy program to outside control or inspection. On-site inspection would remain a problem in arms control negotiations for the next half-century.

American leaders were also becoming convinced of Soviet aggressiveness. In February 1946, George Kennan, a senior American diplomat in Moscow, sent a "long telegram" to the State Department. He depicted a USSR driven by expansionist Communist ideology. The Soviets, he argued, would constantly probe for weaknesses in the capitalist world. The best response was firm resistance to protect the western heartlands.

Lacking the strength to shape Europe on its own, Great Britain repeatedly nudged the United States into blocking Soviet influence. Speaking at Westminster College in Missouri in March 1946, Winston Churchill warned that the USSR had dropped an "iron curtain" across the middle of Europe and urged a firm Western response.

Truman's foreign policy advisers shared the belief in an aggressive Soviet Union. Administration leaders did not fear an immediate Soviet military threat to the United States itself, for they knew that World War II had exhausted the USSR, but they also knew that the Soviets were strong enough to brush aside the U.S. occupation forces in Germany. Added to military apprehension were worries about political and economic competition. Communist parties in war-ravaged Europe and Japan were exploiting discontent. In Asia and Africa, the allegiance of nationalists who were fighting for independence from France, Great Britain, and the Netherlands remained in doubt. America's leaders worried that much of the Eastern Hemisphere might fall under Soviet control and turn its back on North America.

WHERE TO LEARN MORE

United Nations Headquarters, New York, New York
www.un.org

27–1
George F. Kennan,
"Long Telegram" (1946)

International Monetary Fund
International organization established in 1945 to assist nations in maintaining stable currencies.

World Bank   Designed to revive postwar international trade, it drew on the resources of member nations to make economic development loans to governments for such projects as new dams or agricultural modernization.

Truman and the "wise men" who made up his foreign policy circle ignored examples of Soviet caution and conciliation. The Soviets withdrew troops from Manchuria in northern China and acquiesced in America's control of defeated Japan. They allowed a neutral but democratic government in Finland and technically free elections in Hungary and Czechoslovakia (although it was clear that Communists would do well there). They demobilized much of their huge army and reduced their forces in eastern Europe while expecting a falling out between capitalist Britain and the United States.

However, the Soviet regime also did more than enough to justify American fears. The USSR pressured Turkey to give it partial control of the exit from the Black Sea. It retained troops in northern Iran until warned out by the United States. The Soviets were ruthless in support of Communist control in Bulgaria, Romania, and Poland. U.S. policymakers read these Soviet actions as a rerun of Nazi aggression and determined not to let a new totalitarian threat undermine Western power.

THE TRUMAN DOCTRINE AND THE MARSHALL PLAN

Early in 1947, Truman and his advisers decided on decisive action. The British could no longer afford to back the Greek government that was fighting Communist rebels, and U.S. officials feared that a Communist takeover in Greece would threaten the stability of Italy, France, and the Middle East. On March 12, he told Congress that the United States faced a "fateful hour." Taking the advice of Senator Arthur Vandenberg to "scare the hell out of the country," he said that only the appropriation of $400 million to fight Communism in Greece and Turkey could secure the free world. Congress agreed, and the United States became the dominant power in the eastern Mediterranean.

In a sweeping declaration that became known as the **Truman Doctrine**, the president pledged that "It must be the policy of the United States to support free peoples who are resisting attempted subjugation by armed minorities or by outside pressures. . . . I believe that our help should be primarily through economic and financial aid, which is essential to economic stability and orderly political processes."

Meanwhile, Europe was sliding toward chaos. Germany was close to famine after the bitter winter of 1946–1947. Western European nations were bankrupt and unable to import raw materials for their factories. Overstressed medical systems could no longer control diseases such as tuberculosis. Communist parties had gained in Italy, France, and Germany.

Secretary of State George C. Marshall announced the European Recovery Plan on June 5, 1947. What the press quickly dubbed the **Marshall Plan** committed the United States to help rebuild Europe. The United States invited Soviet and eastern European participation, but the Soviets refused, instead organizing their eastern European satellites in their own association for Mutual Economic Assistance, or Comecon, in 1949. In western Europe, the aid from the Marshall Plan totaled $13.5 billion over four years. It met many of Europe's economic needs and quieted class conflict. Because Europeans spent much of the aid on U.S. goods and machinery and because economic recovery promised markets for U.S. products, business and labor both supported it. In effect, the Marshall Plan created an "empire by invitation" in which Americans and Europeans jointly planned European recovery.

U.S. policy in Japan followed the pattern set in Europe. As supreme commander of the Allied Powers, General Douglas MacArthur acted as Japan's postwar dictator. He tried to change the values of the old war-prone Japan through social reform, democratization, and demilitarization. At the end of 1947, however,

Truman Doctrine President Harry Truman's statement in 1947 that the United States should assist other nations that were facing external pressure or internal revolution.

Marshall Plan Secretary of State George C. Marshall's European Recovery Plan of June 5, 1947, committing the United States to help in the rebuilding of post-World War II Europe.

Berlin in 1948 was still a devastated city of gutted buildings and heaps of rubble. When the Soviet Union shut off ground access to Berlin's British, French, and American occupation zones, the city also became a symbol of the West's Cold War resolve. Allied aircraft lifted in food, fuel, and other essentials for West Berliners for nearly a year until the Soviets ended the blockade.

Getty Images/Time Life Pictures

Berlin blockade   Three-hundred-day Soviet blockade of land access to United States, British, and French occupation zones in Berlin, 1948–1949.

Central Intelligence Agency (CIA)   Agency established in 1947 that coordinates the gathering and evaluation of military and economic information on other nations.

National Security Council   The formal policymaking body for national defense and foreign relations, created in 1947 and consisting of the president, the secretary of defense, the secretary of state, and others appointed by the president.

North Atlantic Treaty Organization (NATO)   Organization of ten European countries, Canada, and the United States whom together formed a mutual defense pact in April, 1949.

policymakers were fearful of economic collapse and political chaos, just as in Europe. The "reverse course" in occupation policy aimed to make Japan an economic magnet for other nations in East Asia, pulling them toward the American orbit and away from the Soviet Union. MacArthur reluctantly accepted the new policy of "economic crank-up" by preserving Japan's corporate giants and encouraging American investment. At American insistence, the new Japan accepted American bases and created its own "self-defense force" (with no capacity for overseas aggression).

George Kennan summed up the new American policies in the magazine *Foreign Affairs* in July 1947. Writing anonymously as "X," Kennan warned that the emerging Cold War would be a long conflict with no quick fixes.

SOVIET REACTIONS

The bold American moves in the first half of 1947 put the USSR on the defensive. East of the iron curtain, Hungarian Communists expelled non-Communists from a coalition government. Bulgarian Communists shot opposition leaders. Romania, Bulgaria, and Hungary signed defense pacts with the Soviet Union.

In early 1948, the Soviets targeted Czechoslovakia. For three years, a neutral coalition government there based on the model of Finland had balanced trade with the West with a foreign policy friendly to the USSR. In February 1948, while Russian forces assembled on the Czech borders, local communists pushed aside Czechoslovakia's democratic leadership and turned the nation into a dictatorship and Soviet satellite within a week.

The climax of the Soviet reaction came on June 24, 1948, when Soviet troops blockaded surface traffic into Berlin, cutting off the U.S., British, and French sectors. The immediate Soviet aim was to block Western plans to merge their three occupation zones into an independent federal republic (West Germany). Rather than abandon 2.5 million Berliners or shoot their way through, the Western nations responded to the **Berlin blockade** by airlifting supplies to the city. Planes landed every two minutes at Berlin's Tempelhof Airport. Stalin decided not to intercept the flights. After eleven months, the Soviets abandoned the blockade, making the Berlin airlift a triumph of American resolve.

AMERICAN REARMAMENT

The coup in Czechoslovakia and the Berlin blockade shocked American leaders and backfired on the Soviets. Congress responded in 1948 by reinstating the military draft and increasing defense spending by 30 percent.

The United States had already begun to modernize and centralize its national security apparatus. The National Security Act of July 1947 created the **Central Intelligence Agency (CIA)** and the **National Security Council (NSC)**. The CIA handled intelligence gathering and covert operations. The NSC assembled top diplomatic and military advisers in one committee. In 1949, legislation also created the Department of Defense to oversee the army, navy, and air force (independent from the army since 1947).

In April 1949, ten European nations, the United States, and Canada signed the North Atlantic Treaty as a mutual defense pact. American commitments to the **North Atlantic Treaty Organization (NATO)** included military aid and the deployment of U.S. troops in western Europe. As Republican Senator Robert Taft warned in the ratification debate, NATO was the sort of "entangling alliance" that the United States had avoided for 160 years. It was also the insurance policy that western Europeans required if they were to accept the dangers as well as the benefits of a revived Germany, which was economically and militarily necessary for a strong Europe.

Two years later, the United States signed similar but less comprehensive agreements in the western Pacific: the ANZUS Pact with Australia and New Zealand and a new treaty with the Philippines. The alliances reassured Pacific allies who were nervously watching the United States negotiate a unilateral peace treaty with Japan (ignoring the Soviet Union). Taken together, peacetime rearmament and mutual defense pacts amounted to a revolution in American foreign policy.

COLD WAR AND HOT WAR

The first phase of the Cold War reached a crisis in the autumn of 1949. The two previous years had seen an uneasy equilibrium in which American success in southern and western Europe and the standoff over Berlin (the blockade ended in May 1949) balanced the consolidation of Soviet power in eastern Europe. Now, suddenly, two key events seemed to tilt the world balance against the United States and its allies. In September, Truman announced that the Soviet Union had tested its own atomic bomb. A month later, the Chinese Communists under Mao Zedong (Mao Tse-tung) took power in China. The following summer, civil war in Korea sucked the United States into a fierce war with communist North Korea and China. The United States government accelerated a forty-year arms race with the Soviet Union.

WHAT WERE the major conflicts of the early Cold War?

THE NUCLEAR SHADOW

Experts in Washington had known that the Soviets were working on an A-bomb, but the news shocked the average citizen. In 1946, advocates of civilian control had won a small victory when Congress gave control of atomic energy to the new Atomic Energy Commission (AEC). The AEC tried to balance research on atomic power with continued testing of new weapons. Now Truman told the AEC to double the output of fissionable uranium and plutonium for "conventional" nuclear weapons.

A more momentous decision soon followed. Truman decided in January 1950 to authorize work on the "super" bomb—the thermonuclear fusion weapon that would become the hydrogen bomb (H-bomb). As would be true in future nuclear defense debates, the underlying question was how much capacity for nuclear destruction was enough. (See American Views, "Deciding on a Nuclear Arms Race.")

Nuclear weapons proliferated in the early 1950s. The United States exploded the first hydrogen bomb in the South Pacific in November 1952. Releasing one hundred times the energy of the Hiroshima bomb, the detonation tore a mile-long chasm in the ocean floor. Great Britain became the third nuclear power in the same year. The Soviet Union tested its own hydrogen bomb only nine months after the U.S. test.

Under the guidance of the Federal Civil Defense Administration, Americans learned that they should always keep a battery-powered radio and tune to 640 or 1240 on the AM dial for emergency information when they heard air raid sirens. Schoolchildren learned to hide under their desks if they saw the blinding flash of a nuclear detonation.

Soldiers were exposed to posttest radiation with minimal protection. Nuclear tests in the South Pacific dusted fishing boats with radioactivity and forced islanders to abandon contaminated homes. Radioactive fallout from Nevada testing

QUICK REVIEW

Nuclear Weapons
- Truman ordered in the Atomic Energy Commission to double the production of materials for nuclear weapons.
- The U.S. began work on the hydrogen bomb.
- The U.S. tested the first hydrogen bomb in 1952.

• AMERICAN VIEWS •

DECIDING ON A NUCLEAR ARMS RACE

I n 1950, the United States began work on a hydrogen (thermonuclear) bomb. The decision locked the United States and the Soviet Union into a nuclear arms race that lasted another forty years. In the first document reprinted here, an excerpt from a letter to President Truman written on November 25, 1949, Lewis Strauss, chairman of the Atomic Energy Commission, urged work on the H-bomb. In the second, scientist Edward Teller agreed. A refugee from Nazi-dominated Europe who had worked at Los Alamos, Teller remained an advocate of massive defense spending through the 1980s.

HOW DID memories of World War II affect this Cold War decision? How did U.S. policymakers evaluate the intentions of the Soviet Union?

Lewis Strauss,
November 1949:

Dear Mr. President:

As you know, the thermonuclear (super) bomb was suggested by scientists working at Los Alamos during the war. . . . I believe that the United States must be as completely armed as any possible enemy. From this, it follows that I believe it unwise to renounce, unilaterally, any weapon which an enemy can reasonably be expected to possess. I recommend that the President direct the Atomic Energy Commission to proceed with the development of the thermonuclear bomb, at highest priority. . . . Obviously the current atomic bomb as

well as the proposed thermonuclear weapon are horrible to contemplate. All war is horrible. Until, however, some means is found of eliminating war, I cannot agree with those of my colleagues who feel that an announcement should be made by the President to the effect that the development of the thermonuclear weapon will not be undertaken by the United States at this time. This is because I do not think the statement will be credited in the Kremlin . . . and because primarily until disarmament is universal, our arsenal must be not less well equipped than with the most potent weapons that our technology can devise.

Edward Teller,
March 1950:

President Truman has announced that we are going to make a hydrogen bomb. . . . The scientist is not responsible for the law of nature. It is his job to find out how these laws operate. . . . However, it is not the scientist's job to determine whether a hydrogen bomb should be constructed, whether it should be used, or how it should be used. This responsibility rests with the American people and their chosen representatives. Personally, as a citizen, I do not know in what other way President Truman could have acted. . . . To my mind we are in a situation no less dangerous than the one we were facing in 1939, and it is of the greatest importance that we realize it. We must realize. . . . that democracy will not be saved by ideals alone.

Source: Lewis L. Strauss, *Men and Decisions* (1962).

contaminated large sections of the West and increased cancer rates among "downwinders" in Utah. Weapons production and atomic experiments contaminated vast tracts in Nevada, Washington, and Colorado and left huge environmental costs for later generations.

THE COLD WAR IN ASIA

Communist victory in China's civil war was as predictable as the Soviet nuclear bomb but no less controversial. American military and diplomatic missions in the late 1940s pointed out that the collapse of Jiang Jieshi's Nationalist regime was nearly inevitable, given its corruption and narrow support. But advocates for Jiang, mostly conservative Republicans from the Midwest and West, were certain that

Truman's administration had done too little. "China asked for a sword," complained one senator, "and we gave her a dull paring knife." Critics looked for scapegoats. Foreign service officers who had honestly analyzed the weakness of the Nationalists were accused of Communist sympathies and hounded from their jobs. The results were damage to the State Department and tragedy for those unfairly branded as traitors.

NSC-68 AND AGGRESSIVE CONTAINMENT

The turmoil of 1949 led to a comprehensive statement of American strategic goals. In April 1950, the State Department prepared a sweeping report known as **National Security Council Paper 68 (NSC-68).** The document described a world divided between the forces of "slavery" and "freedom" and assumed that the Soviet Union was actively and broadly aggressive, motivated by greed for territory and a "fanatic faith" in Communism. To defend civilization itself, said the experts, the United States should use as much force as needed to resist Communist expansion anywhere and everywhere.

Truman and his advisors in 1947 and 1948 had hoped to contain the Soviets by diplomacy and by integrating the economies of Europe and Japan with that of the United States. Now that the Soviets had the atomic bomb, NSC-68 argued that the United States needed to press friendly nations to rearm and to make its former enemies into military allies. It also argued the need for the nation to acquire expensive conventional forces to defend Europe. NSC-68 thus advocated nearly open-ended increases in the defense budget (which in fact tripled between 1950 and 1954).

Although it was not a public document, NSC-68's portrait of implacable Communist expansion would have made sense to most Americans; it certainly did to Harry Truman. The outbreak of war in Korea at the end of June 1950 seemed to confirm that Communism was a military threat. The thinking behind the report led the United States to approach the Cold War as a military competition and to view political changes in Africa and Asia as parts of a Soviet plan.

WAR IN KOREA, 1950–1953

The success of Mao and the Chinese Communists forced the Truman administration to define national interests in East Asia and the western Pacific. The most important U.S. interest was Japan, still an industrial power despite its devastating defeat. The United States had shaped a more democratic Japan that would be a strong and friendly trading partner. Protected by American armed forces, Japan would be part of a crescent of offshore strong points that included Alaska, the Philippines, Australia, and New Zealand.

Two questions remained unresolved at the start of 1950 (and were still troublesome at the turn of the century). One was the future of Taiwan and the remnants of Jiang's regime. The other question was Korea, whose own civil war would soon bring the world to the brink of World War III.

The Korean peninsula is the closest point on the Asian mainland to Japan. With three powerful neighbors—China, Russia, and Japan—Korea had always had to fight for its independence. As World War II ended, Soviet troops had moved down the peninsula from the north and American forces had landed in the south, creating a situation similar to that in Germany. The 38th parallel, which Russians and Americans set as the dividing line between their zones of occupation, became a de facto border. The United States in 1948 recognized an independent South Korea, with its capital at Seoul, under a conservative government led by Syngman Rhee. Rhee's support came from large landowners and a police force trained by

27–3
National Security Council Memorandum Number 68 (1950)

National Security Council Paper 68 (NSC-68)   Policy statement that committed the United States to a military approach to the Cold War.

MAP EXPLORATION

To explore an interactive version of this map, go to
http://www.prenhall.com/goldfield2/map27.2

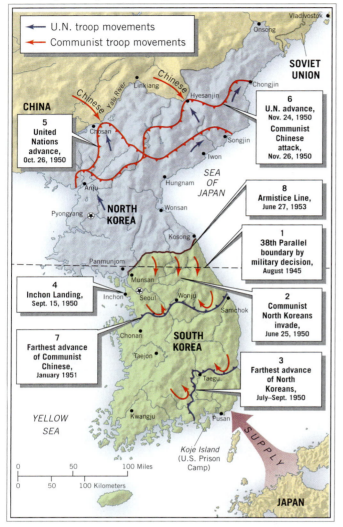

MAP 27–2

The Korean War   After rapid reversals of fortune in 1950 and early
1951, the war in Korea settled into stalemate. Most Americans agreed
with the need to contain Communist expansion but found it deeply
frustrating to fight for limited objectives rather than total victory.

WAS A stalemate the inevitable end to the Korean War?
Why or why not?

Korean War   Pacific war started on
June 25, 1950, when North Korea,
helped by Soviet equipment and Chinese training, attacked South Korea.

the Japanese between 1910 and 1945. The Soviets recognized a separate North Korea, whose leader, Kim Il Sung, advocated radical social and political change. Both leaders
hoped to unify all Koreans under their own rule, and each
crushed political dissent and tried to undermine the other
with economic pressure and commando raids.

United States military planners assumed that U.S. air
power in Japan could neutralize unfriendly forces on the Korean peninsula. But Korea remained politically important as
the only point of direct confrontation with the Soviet Union
in Asia.

On June 25, 1950, North Korea, helped by Soviet equipment and Chinese training, attacked South Korea, starting
the **Korean War**, which lasted until 1953 (see Map 27–2).
Truman and Secretary of State Dean Acheson believed that
Moscow lay behind the invasion. They worried that the attack
was a ploy to suck America's limited military resources into
Asia before a bigger war came in Europe or the Middle East.
The war was really an intensification of an ongoing civil war
that Stalin was willing to exploit. Kim originated the inva-
sion plan and spent a year persuading Stalin to agree to it.
Stalin hoped that the conquest of South Korea would force
Japan to sign a favorable treaty with the USSR.

As the South Korean army collapsed, Truman committed American ground troops from Japan on June 30. The
United States also had the diplomatic good fortune of securing an endorsement from the United Nations. Because the
USSR was boycotting the UN, the Korean conflict remained
officially a United Nations action, although U.S. Generals
Douglas MacArthur, Matthew Ridgway, and Mark Clark ran
the show as the successive heads of the U.N. command.

THE POLITICS OF WAR

The first U.S. combat troops were outnumbered, outgunned,
and poorly trained. They could not stop the North Koreans.
By early August, the Americans clung to a narrow toehold
around the port of Pusan on the tip of the Korean peninsula. As reinforcements arrived from the United States, however, MacArthur transformed the war with a daring amphibious
counterattack at Inchon, 150 miles behind North Korean
lines. The North Korean army was already overextended and
exhausted. It collapsed and fled north.

MacArthur and Washington officials disregarded warn-
ings by China that it would enter the war if the United States tried to reunite Korea
by force. U.S. and South Korean troops rolled north, drawing closer and closer to
the boundary between North Korea and China.

Chinese forces attacked MacArthur's command in late October but then
disappeared. MacArthur dismissed the attacks as a token gesture. But on November 26, the Chinese struck the overextended American columns. They had massed
300,000 troops without detection by American aviation. Their assault drove the U.N.
forces into a two-month retreat that again abandoned Seoul.

In March 1951, with the U.N. forces again pushing north, Truman prepared to offer a cease-fire that would have preserved the separate nations of South and North Korea. MacArthur tried to preempt the president by demanding that China admit defeat or suffer the consequences. He then published a direct attack on the administration's policy of limiting the Asian war to ensure the security of Europe.

To protect civilian control of the armed forces, he was forced to relieve MacArthur of his commands on April 11, 1951. The general returned to parades and a hero's welcome when he addressed a joint session of Congress. He quoted a line from an old barracks song: "Old soldiers never die; they just fade away." But Truman remained in charge of the war.

In Korea itself, U.S. and South Korean forces stabilized a strong defensive line that cut diagonally across the 38th parallel. For two years, U.N. and Communist armies faced boredom that alternated with fierce inch-by-inch battles for territory with names like Heartbreak Ridge and Pork Chop Hill. In the air, the arrival of new F-86 Saberjets in 1952 allowed American pilots to clear the skies of Chinese aviators in Russian-made MIG 15s.

After 1950, the Chinese were careful to keep their war planes north of the ground combat zone, the Russians had stayed out of the war, and the United States was willing to accept a divided Korea.

Truce negotiations stalled over the political decision to turn free choice for Chinese POWs into a symbol of resistance to Communism. Nearly half of the 140,000 U.S. casualties came after the truce talks started. The war was a decisive factor behind the Republican victory in the November 1952 elections and dragged on until June 1953, when an armistice returned the peninsula roughly to its pre-war political division.

The blindly ambitious attack into North Korea was one of the great failures of intelligence and strategic leadership in American military history. Nearly everyone in Washington shared the blame for letting the excitement of battlefield victories obscure limited war aims. Civilian leaders couldn't resist the desire to roll back Communism. Truman hoped for a striking victory before the 1950 congressional elections. The Joint Chiefs of Staff failed to question a general with MacArthur's heroic reputation. MacArthur himself allowed ambition and wishful thinking to jeopardize his army.

The war in Korea was a preview of Vietnam fifteen years later. American leaders found themselves propping up an undemocratic regime to defend democracy. Both North Koreans and South Koreans engaged in savage political reprisals as the battlefront shifted back and forth. American emphasis on the massive application of firepower led U.S. forces to demolish entire villages to kill single snipers. General Curtis Le May estimated that Air Force bombings killed a million Koreans.

The Korean War helped to legitimize the United Nations. In Washington, it confirmed the ideas behind NSC-68, with its call for the United States to lead an anti-Communist alliance. Two days after the North Korean invasion, President Truman ordered the Seventh Fleet to protect the Nationalist Chinese on Taiwan, a decision that guaranteed twenty years of hostility between the United States and the People's Republic of China. In the same month, the United States began to aid France's struggle to retain control over its colony of Indochina, which included Laos, Cambodia, and Vietnam.

In Europe, the United States pushed to rearm West Germany as part of a militarized NATO and sent troops to Europe as a permanent defense force. It increased military aid to European governments and secured a unified command for the national forces allocated for NATO. The unified command made West German rearmament acceptable to France and the smaller nations of western Europe.

WHERE TO LEARN MORE

General Douglas MacArthur Memorial, Norfolk, Virginia

WHAT WAS the "Second Red Scare"?

THE SECOND RED SCARE

The Korean War reinforced the second Red Scare, an assault on civil liberties that stretched from the mid-1940s to the mid-1950s and dwarfed the Red Scare of 1919–1920. Legitimate concerns about espionage mixed with suspicions that Communist sympathizers in high places were helping Stalin and Mao (see the overview table "The Second Red Scare").

Efforts to root out suspected subversives operated on three tracks. National and state governments established loyalty programs to identify and fire suspect employees. The courts punished members of suspect organizations. Congressional and state legislative investigations followed the whims of committee chairs. Anti-Communist crusaders often relied on dubious evidence and eagerly believed the worst. They also threatened basic civil liberties.

THE COMMUNIST PARTY AND THE LOYALTY PROGRAM

The Communist party in the United States was actually in rapid decline after World War II. Many intellectuals had left the party over the Nazi-Soviet Pact in 1939. And the postwar years brought a series of failures. In 1946, Walter Reuther defeated a Communist for the presidency of the huge United Auto Workers union, and other large CIO unions froze Communists out of leadership positions.

Nevertheless, Republicans used red-baiting as a campaign technique in 1944 and 1946, setting the stage for a national loyalty program. Republicans in 1944 tried to frighten voters about "commydemocrats" by linking FDR, CIO labor unions, and Communism. Democrats slung their own mud by trying to convince voters that Hitler preferred the Republicans. Two years later, Republican campaigners told the public that the basic choice was "between Communism and Republicanism." The argument helped dozens of Republicans, including a young navy veteran named Richard Nixon, win congressional seats.

President Truman responded to the Republican landslide with a loyalty program for federal employees, initiated in March 1947 with Executive Order 9835. Order 9835 authorized the attorney general to prepare a list of "totalitarian, Fascist, Communist, or subversive" organizations and made membership or even "sympathetic association" with such groups grounds for dismissal. The loyalty program applied to approximately 8 million Americans working for the federal government or defense contractors; similar state laws affected another 5 million.

Many accusations were just malicious gossip, but allegations stayed in a worker's file even if refuted. Many New Dealers and people associated with presumably liberal East Coast institutions were targets. An Interior Department official boasted that he had been especially effective in squeezing out graduates of Harvard and Columbia.

Federal employees worked under a cloud of fear. Loyalty boards asked about religion, racial equality, and a taste for foreign films; they also tried to identify homosexuals, who were thought to be targets for blackmail by foreign agents. The loyalty program resulted in 1,210 firings and 6,000 resignations under Truman and comparable numbers during Dwight Eisenhower's first term from 1953 to 1956.

NAMING NAMES TO CONGRESS

The congressional hunt for subversives had its roots in 1938 when Congressman Martin Dies, a Texas Democrat, created the Special Committee on Un-American Activities. Originally intended to ferret out pro-Fascists, the Dies Committee evolved into the permanent **House Committee on Un-American Activities (HUAC)** in 1945. It investigated "un-American propaganda" that attacked constitutional government.

House Committee on Un-American Activities (HUAC)   Originally intended to ferret out pro-Fascists, it later investigated "un-American propaganda" that attacked constitutional government.

OVERVIEW

THE SECOND RED SCARE

Type of Anti-Communist Effort	Key Tools	Results
Employee loyalty programs	U.S. attorney general's list of subversive organizations	Thousands of federal and state workers fired, careers damaged
Congressional investigations	HUAC McCarren Committee Army-McCarthy hearings	Employee blacklists, harassment of writers and intellectuals
Criminal prosecutions	Trials for espionage and conspiracy to advocate violent overthrow of the U.S. government	Convictions of Communist party leaders (1949), Rosenbergs (1951)

One of HUAC's juiciest targets was Hollywood. In 1946, Americans bought an average of 90 million tickets every *week*. But Hollywood's reputation for loose morals, high living, foreign-born directors, Jewish producers, and left-leaning writers aroused the suspicions of many congressmen. HUAC sought to make sure that no un-American messages were being peddled through America's most popular entertainment.

When the hearings opened in October 1947, studio executives assured HUAC of their anti-Communism. So did popular actors Gary Cooper and Ronald Reagan. In contrast, eight screenwriters and two directors—the Hollywood Ten—refused to discuss their past political associations, citing the free speech protections of the First Amendment to the Constitution. HUAC countered with citations for contempt of Congress. The First Amendment defense failed when it reached the Supreme Court, and the ten went to jail in 1950.

HUAC changed the politics of Hollywood. Before 1947, it had been fashionable to lean toward the left. After the hearings, it was imperative to tilt the other way. The government refused to let British-born Charlie Chaplin reenter the United States in 1952 because of his left-wing views. Other actors, writers, and directors found themselves on the Hollywood blacklist, banned from jobs where they might insert Communist propaganda into American movies.

At the start of 1951, the new Senate Internal Security Subcommittee joined the sometimes bumbling HUAC. The McCarran Committee, named for the Nevada senator who chaired it, targeted diplomats, labor union leaders, professors, and schoolteachers. The real point of the investigations was not to force personal confessions from witnesses but to badger them into identifying friends and associates who might have been involved in suspect activities.

The only sure way to avoid "naming names" was to respond to every question by citing the Fifth Amendment to the Constitution, which protects Americans from testifying against themselves. Many Americans wrongly assumed that citing the amendment was a sure sign of guilt, not a matter of principle, and talked about "Fifth Amendment Communists."

State legislatures imitated Congress by searching for "Reducators" among college faculty in such states as Oklahoma, Washington, and California. College presidents frequently fired faculty who took the Fifth Amendment. The experience of an economics professor fired from the University of Kansas City after testimony before the McCarran Committee was typical. He found it hard to keep any job once his name had been in the papers. A local dairy fired him because it thought its customers might be uneasy having a radical handle their milk bottles.

27–2
Ronald Reagan, Testimony Before the House Un-American Activities Committee (1947)

SUBVERSION TRIALS

In 1948, the Justice Department indicted the leaders of the American Communist party under the Alien Registration Act of 1940. Eleven men and women were convicted in 1949 of conspiring to advocate the violent overthrow of the United States government through their speech and publications. Some of the testimony came from Herbert Philbrick, an advertising manager and FBI informer who had posed as a party member. Philbrick parlayed his appearance into a bestseller titled *I Led Three Lives* and then into a popular television series on which the FBI foiled Communist spies every Friday night.

Then, in 1948, former Communist Whittaker Chambers named Alger Hiss as a Communist with whom he had associated in the 1930s. Hiss, who had held important posts in the State Department, sued Chambers for slander. As proof, Chambers gave Congressman Richard Nixon microfilms that he had hidden inside a pumpkin on his Maryland farm. Tests seemed to show that the "pumpkin papers" were State Department documents that had been copied on a typewriter that Hiss had once owned. The Justice Department indicted Hiss for perjury—lying under oath. A first perjury trial ended in deadlock, but a second jury convicted Hiss in January 1950.

The essence of the Hiss case has been a matter of faith, not facts. Even his enemies agreed that any documents he might have stolen were of limited importance. His smugness as a member of the East Coast establishment enraged them. To his opponents, Hiss stood for every wrong turn that the nation had taken since 1932. Many supporters believed that he had been framed. Both sides claimed support from Soviet records that became public in the 1990s.

In 1950, the British arrested nuclear physicist Klaus Fuchs, who confessed to passing atomic secrets to the Soviets when he worked at Los Alamos in 1944 and 1945. The "Fuchs spy ring" soon implicated Julius and Ethel Rosenberg, New York radicals of strong beliefs but limited sophistication. Convicted in 1951 of the vague charge of conspiring to commit espionage, they were sent to the electric chair in 1953 after refusing to buy a reprieve by naming other spies.

As in the case of Alger Hiss, the government had a plausible but not airtight case against the Rosenbergs. There is no doubt that Julius Rosenberg was a convinced Communist, and he was likely a minor figure in an atomic spy net, but it is likely that Ethel Rosenberg was charged with crimes to pressure her husband into confessing.

SENATOR MCCARTHY ON STAGE

The best-remembered participant in the second Red Scare was Senator Joseph McCarthy of Wisconsin. He burst into national prominence on February 9, 1950. In a rambling speech in Wheeling, West Virginia, he supposedly stated: "I have here in my hand a list of 205 that were known to the Secretary of State as being members of the Communist party and who, nevertheless, are still working and shaping the policy of the State Department." McCarthy's rise to fame climaxed with an incoherent six-hour speech to the Senate. He tried to document the charges by mixing previously exposed spies with people who no longer worked for the government or who never had worked for it. Over the next several years, his speeches were full of multiple untruths. He threw out so many accusations that the facts could never catch up.

Senators treated McCarthy as a crude outsider in their exclusive club, but voters in 1950 turned against his most prominent opponents. In 1951, McCarthy even called George Marshall, now serving as secretary of defense, an agent of Communism. The idea was ludicrous. Marshall was one of the most upright Americans of his generation, the architect of victory in World War II and a key contributor to the stabilization of Europe. Nevertheless, McCarthy was so popular that the Republicans featured him at their 1952 convention. That fall, the Re-

Senator Joseph McCarthy points to Oregon on an organizational map implying Communist Party organization in the United States.

UPI/Corbis/Bettmann

publicans' presidential candidate, Dwight Eisenhower, appeared on the same campaign platform with McCarthy and conspicuously failed to defend George Marshall—who was chiefly responsible for Eisenhower's fast-track career.

McCarthy's personal crudeness made him a media star but eventually undermined him. Given control of the Senate Committee on Government Operations in 1953, one of his investigations targeted the U.S. Army's promotion of an army dentist with a supposedly subversive background. Two months of televised hearings revealed the emptiness of the charges. The cameras also put McCarthy's style on trial. "Have you no decency?" asked the army's lawyer Joseph Welch at one point.

The end came quickly. McCarthy's "favorable" rating in the polls plummeted. The comic strip *Pogo* began to feature a foolishly menacing figure with McCarthy's face named Simple J. Malarkey. The U.S. Senate finally voted 67 to 22 in December 1954 to condemn McCarthy for conduct "unbecoming a Member of the Senate." When he died from alchoholism in 1957, he was repudiated by the Senate and ignored by the media.

UNDERSTANDING MCCARTHYISM

The antisubversive campaign now called **McCarthyism**, however, died a slower death. Legislation, such as the Internal Security Act (1950) and the Immigration and Nationality Act (1952), remained as tools of political repression. HUAC continued to mount investigations as late as the 1960s.

Fear of Communist subversion reached deep into American society. In the early 1950s, Cincinnati's National League baseball team tried out a new name. Harking back to its origins as the Red Stockings, the team was now the "Redlegs," not the "Reds," to avoid associations with Communism. Cities and states required loyalty oaths from their employees; Ohio even required oaths from recipients of unemployment compensation.

In retrospect, at least four factors made Americans afraid of Communist subversion. One was a legitimate but exaggerated concern about atomic spies. A second was an undercurrent of anti-Semitism and nativism, for many labor organizers and Communist party members (like the Rosenbergs) had Jewish and eastern European backgrounds. Third was Southern and Western resentment of the nation's Ivy League elite. Most general, finally, was that it was basically reassuring if Soviet and Chinese Communist successes were the result of American traitors rather than Communist strengths.

Partisan politics mobilized the fears and resentments into a political force. From 1946 through 1952, the conservative wing of the Republican party used the Red Scare to attack New Dealers and liberal Democrats. The Republican elite used McCarthy until they won control of the presidency and Congress in 1952 and then abandoned him.

McCarthyism Anti-Communist attitudes and actions associated with Senator Joe McCarthy in the early 1950s, including smear tactics and innuendo.

CONCLUSION

The Cold War stayed cool because each side achieved its essential goals. The Soviet Union controlled eastern Europe, while the United States built increasingly strong ties with the NATO nations and Japan. Though the result was a stalemate that would last through the 1980s, it nevertheless absorbed huge shares of Soviet and American resources and conditioned the thinking of an entire generation.

The shift from prewar isolationism to postwar internationalism was one of the most important changes in the nation's history. To many of its advocates, internationalism represented a commitment to spread political democracy to other nations. As the 1950s and 1960s would show, the results often contradicted the ideal when the United States forcibly imposed its will on other peoples. However, the new internationalism highlighted and helped change domestic racial attitudes.

The Truman years brought increasing stability. The economic chaos of 1946 faded quickly. By identifying liberalism at home with anti-Communism abroad, Truman's efforts to define a vital center helped protect the New Deal. If the Republicans had won in 1948, they might have dismantled the New Deal. By 1952, both presidential candidates affirmed the consensus that placed economic opportunity at the center of the national agenda. The suburban housing boom seemed to turn the dream of prosperity into reality for millions of families.

The United States emerged from the Truman years remarkably prosperous. It was also more secure from international threats than many nervous Americans appreciated. The years from 1946 to 1952 set the themes for a generation that believed that the United States could do whatever it set its mind to. As the world moved slowly toward greater stability in the 1950s, Americans were ready for a decade of confidence.

SUMMARY

Launching the Great Boom Americans feared demobilization would bring inflation and unemployment, but the immediate postwar years ushered in an economic expansion that would last a quarter century; the resulting prosperity would finance a military buildup and activist foreign policy. Veterans benefited from VA mortgages and the GI Bill of Rights; the need for family housing fueled a boom and suburbs expanded; the housing boom was a product of the consumer and baby booms. The first steps toward civil rights for African Americans were taken; the crusade for freedom abroad had contrasted with the racial discrimination faced at home.

Truman, Republicans, and the Fair Deal The economic gains of the postwar years propelled Americans toward the political center; after depression and war they wanted prosperity. In his campaign for a full term as president in 1948, Truman faced third-party candidates in addition to Republican Thomas Dewey. Truman appealed to average Americans and his victory astounded the pollsters. The Fair Deal showed that Americans liked what the New Deal had given them but were hesitant about major new initiatives.

Confronting the Soviet Union By 1947 the former allies were involved in a conflict that came to be known as the Cold War. Both sides assumed the other's ill will, spent vast amounts on military forces and atomic weapons, and competed for political advantage around the globe. As the "iron curtain" divided Europe, the Marshall Plan committed the United States to aid European recovery. The announcement of the Truman Doctrine brought Soviet reactions climaxing in the Berlin blockade; the formation of the CIA, NSC, and signing mutual defense pacts such as NATO amounted to a revolution in American foreign policy.

Cold War and Hot War The news that the Soviet Union and China had developed nuclear bombs helped begin the "arms race" and the fear of nuclear war multiplied the apprehensions of the Cold War. America's strategic goals were outlined in NSC-68: America would use force to counter communist aggression: The first use of this policy was in Korea. North Korea, helped by Soviet equipment and Chinese training, attacked South Korea. The Korean War, which lasted until 1953, had global consequences and was a preview of another war to come.

The Second Red Scare The Korean War reinforced the second Red Scare, an assault on civil liberties that dwarfed the Red Scare of 1919–1920. The Cold War fanned fears of Communist subversion on American soil. Legitimate concerns about espionage mixed with suspicions that Communist sympathizers in high places were helping China and the Soviet Union. Loyalty programs and the Congressional hunt for subversives such as that by Senator Joseph McCarthy showed how deep the fear of Communists was in the country.

REVIEW QUESTIONS

1. What were the key differences between Harry Truman and congressional Republicans about the legacy of the New Deal?

2. How did the postwar years expand opportunity for veterans and members of the working class? How did they limit opportunities for women?

3. What foreign policy priorities did the United States set after 1945?

4. How did the Cold War change character in 1949 and 1950?

KEY TERMS

Berlin blockade   (p. 724)
Central Intelligence Agency   (p. 724)
Cold War   (p. 714)
Council of Economic Advisers
(p. 715)
Dixiecrats   (p. 719)
GI Bill of Rights   (p. 716)
House Committee on Un-American
Activities (HUAC)   (p. 730)

International Monetary Fund
(p. 722)
Korean War   (p. 728)
Levittown   (p. 717)
Marshall Plan   (p. 723)
McCarthyism   (p. 733)
National Security Council   (p. 724)
National Security Council Paper 68
(NSC-68)   (p. 727)

North Atlantic Treaty Organization
(NATO)   (p. 724)
Redlining   (p. 717)
Taft-Hartley Act   (p. 715)
Truman Doctrine   (p. 723)
World Bank   (p. 722)

WHERE TO LEARN MORE

Harry S Truman National Historical Site, Library, and Museum, Independence, Missouri. The museum has exhibits on Truman's political career and U.S. history during his administration. Also in Independence is the Harry S Truman Courtroom and Office, with exhibits on his early career. **www.nps.gov/hstr/**

General Douglas MacArthur Memorial, Norfolk, Virginia. The MacArthur Memorial in downtown Norfolk commemorates the career of a key figure in shaping the postwar world.

United Nations Headquarters, New York, New York. A tour of the United Nations complex in New York is a reminder of the new organizations for international cooperation that emerged from World War II. **www.un.org**

 For additional study resources for this chapter, go to:
www.prenhall.com/goldfield/chapter27

We were trapped. And I thought, Okay,
so I'm going to die here, in school . . .
Even the adults, the school officials, were panicked,
feeling like there was no protection . . .
[A] gentleman, who I believed to be the police chief,
said . . . "I'll get them out." And we were taken
to the basement of this place.

MISSILE EQUIPMENT
MARIEL PORT FACILITY
4 NOVEMBER 1962

4 MISSILE TRANSPORTERS

OXIDIZER TRAI

OXIDIZER TRAILERS

WE INSIST!
MAX ROACH'S - FREEDOM NOW SUITE

8002

CANDID

FEATURING ABBEY LINCOLN
COLEMAN HAWKINS, OLATUNJI

Elvis Presley swivels onto his toes
while singing into a microphone
on stage with his band.

28

THE CONFIDENT YEARS
1953–1964

HOW DID the "Decade of Affluence" alter social and religious life in America?

WHAT IMPACT did Dwight Eisenhower's foreign policy have on U.S. relations with the Soviet Union?

WHAT WAS John F. Kennedy's approach to dealing with the Soviet Union?

WHAT WAS the significance of *Brown* v. *Board of Education of Topeka?*

HOW DID Lyndon B. Johnson continue the domestic agenda inherited from the Kennedy administration?

1953 | 1964

The first day I was able to enter Central High School [in Little Rock, Arkansas, September 23, 1957], what I felt inside was terrible, wrenching, awful fear. On the car radio I could hear that there was a mob. I knew what a mob meant and I know that the sounds that came from the crowd were very angry. So we entered the side of the building, very, very fast. Even as we entered there were people running after us, people tripping other people. . . . There has never been in my life any stark terror or any fear akin to that.

I'd only been in the school a couple of hours and by that time it was apparent that the mob was just overrunning the school. Policemen were throwing down their badges and the mob was getting past the wooden sawhorses because the police would no longer fight their own in order to protect us. So we were all called into the principal's office, and there was great fear that we would not get out of this building. We were trapped. And I thought, Okay, so I'm going to die here, in school. . . . Even the adults, the school officials, were panicked, feeling like there was no protection. . . . [A] gentleman, who I believed to be the police chief, said . . . "I'll get them out." And we were taken to the basement of this place. And we were put into two cars, grayish blue Fords. And the man instructed the drivers, he said, "Once you start driving, do not stop." And he told us to put our heads down. "This guy revved up his engine and he came up out of the bowels of this building, and as he came up, I could just see hands reaching across this car, I could hear the yelling, I could see guns, and he was told not to stop. "If you hit somebody, you keep rolling,' cause the kids are dead." And he did just that, and he didn't hit anybody, but he certainly was forceful and aggressive in the way he exited this driveway, because people tried to stop him and he didn't stop. He dropped me off at home. And I remember saying, "Thank you for the ride," and I should've said, "Thank you for my life."

Melba Patillo Beals in Henry Hampton and Steve Frayer, eds., *Voices of Freedom: An Oral History of the Civil Rights Movement from the 1950s through the 1980s* (New York: Bantam, 1990).

IMAGE KEY

for pages 736–737

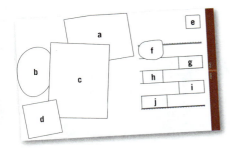

a. Russian nuclear missiles photographed at Mariel Port facility in Cuba, with illustrative tags describing various equipment.

b. A drawing of the Sputnik satellite appears on a playing card from a card game about the space race.

c. Elvis Presley swivels onto his toes while singing into a microphone on stage with his band.

d. The album cover of "We Insist!" by Max Roach depicts African American men at a lunch counter during a sit-in.

e. 1960 Presidential candidates Richard Milhous Nixon and John F. Kennedy during a televised debate.

f. Suburban family standing in front of their 1948 Levittown house in 1950.

g. Children huddle below their desks in an elementary school classroom during an air raid drill.

h. President Kennedy's TV address on the Cuban Missile Crisis.

i. Elizabeth Eckford is heckled by a white student while integrating Central High School in Little Rock, Arkansas in 1957. Many other white students surround the girl.

j. LBJ takes the oath of office on the ride back to Washington, D.C. from Dallas, after the assassination of JFK.

MELBA PATTILLO was one of the nine African-American students who entered previously all-white Central High in 1957. Her enrollment in the high school, where she managed to last through a year of harassment, was a symbolic step in the journey toward greater racial equality in American society. School integration in Little Rock implemented the U.S. Supreme Court decision in the case of *Brown* v. *Board of Education* in 1954, which declared that racially segregated schools violated the mandate that all citizens receive equal protection of the law. The violence with which some white residents of Little Rock responded, and the courage of the students, was a key episode in the civil rights revolution that spanned roughly a decade from the *Brown* decision to the Voting Rights Act of 1965.

The struggle for full civil rights for all Americans was rooted in national ideals, but it was also shaped by the continuing tensions of the Cold War. President Dwight Eisenhower acted against his own inclinations and sent federal troops to keep the

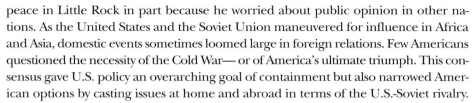

peace in Little Rock in part because he worried about public opinion in other nations. As the United States and the Soviet Union maneuvered for influence in Africa and Asia, domestic events sometimes loomed large in foreign relations. Few Americans questioned the necessity of the Cold War— or of America's ultimate triumph. This consensus gave U.S. policy an overarching goal of containment but also narrowed American options by casting issues at home and abroad in terms of the U.S.-Soviet rivalry.

Melba Pattillo's life after Little Rock also reflects the increasing economic opportunities available to most Americans. She eventually graduated from San Francisco State University, earned a master's degree from Columbia University, and become a television reporter and writer. San Francisco State, which was rapidly expanding, was itself part of the great expansion of higher education that helped millions of Americans move into middle-class jobs and neighborhoods. The prosperous years from 1953 to 1964 spread the economic promise of the 1940s across American society. Young couples could afford large families and new houses. Labor unions grew conservative because cooperation with big business offered immediate gains for their members.

Despite challenges at home and abroad, Americans were confident during the decade after the Korean War. They expected corporations to use scientific research to craft new products and medical researchers to conquer diseases. When the USSR challenged U.S. preeminence and launched the first artificial space satellite in 1957, Americans redoubled efforts to regain what they considered their rightful world leadership in science and technology.

A DECADE OF AFFLUENCE

Americans in the 1950s believed in the basic strength of the United States. Examples of self-assurance were everywhere. Television's *General Electric Theater* was third in the ratings in 1956–1957. Every week, its host, Ronald Reagan, a popular Hollywood lead from the late 1930s, stated, "At General Electric, progress is our most important product." Large, technologically sophisticated corporations were introducing new marvels: Orlon sweaters and Saran Wrap, long-playing records and Polaroid cameras.

Social and intellectual conformity assured a united front. National leaders argued that strong families were bulwarks against Communism and that church-going inoculated people against subversive ideas. Under the lingering cloud of McCarthyism, the range of political ideas that influenced government policy was narrower than in the 1930s and 1940s. Nevertheless, disaffected critics began to voice the discontents that exploded in the 1960s and 1970s.

WHAT'S GOOD FOR GENERAL MOTORS

Dwight Eisenhower presided over the prosperity of the 1950s. Both Democrats and Republicans had courted him as a presidential candidate in 1948. Four years later, he picked the Republicans and easily defeated Democrat Adlai Stevenson, the moderately liberal governor of Illinois.

Publicists tried a variety of labels for Eisenhower's domestic views: "progressive moderation," "New Republicanism," "dynamic conservatism." Satisfied with postwar America, Eisenhower accepted much of the New Deal but saw little need for further reform. In a 1959 poll, liberals considered him a fellow liberal and conservatives thought him a conservative.

Eisenhower's first secretary of defense, "Engine Charlie" Wilson, had headed General Motors. At his Senate confirmation hearing, he proclaimed, "For years,

HOW DID the "Decade of Affluence" alter social and religious life in America?

I thought what was good for the country was good for General Motors and vice versa." Wilson's statement captured a central theme of the 1950s.

The economy in the 1950s gave Americans much to like. Between 1950 and 1964, output grew by a solid 3.2 percent per year. Automobile production, on which dozens of other industries depended, neared 8 million vehicles per year in the mid-1950s; less than 1 percent of new car sales were imports.

In the 1950s American workers' productivity, or output per worker, increased steadily. Average wages rose faster than consumer prices in nine of eleven years between 1953 and 1964. The steel and auto industries gave their workers a middle-class way of life. In turn, labor leaders lost interest in radical changes in American society. In 1955, the older and politically more conservative American Federation of Labor absorbed the younger Congress of Industrial Organizations. The new AFL-CIO positioned itself as a partner in prosperity and foe of Communism at home and abroad.

Industrial cities offered members of minority groups factory jobs at wages that could support a family. African Americans worked through the Urban League, the National Association of Colored Women, and other race-oriented groups to secure fair employment laws and jobs with large corporations. Many Puerto Rican migrants to New York found steady work in the Brooklyn Navy Yard. Mexican-American families in San Antonio benefited from maintenance jobs at the city's military bases.

However, there were never enough family-wage jobs for all of the African-American and Latino workers who continued to move to Northern and Western cities. Many Mexican Americans were still migrant farm laborers and workers in nonunionized sweatshops. Minority workers were usually the first to suffer from the erosion of industrial jobs that began in the 1960s.

To cut costs and accelerate Native American assimilation, Congress pushed the policy of termination between 1954 and 1962. The government sold tribal land and assets, distributed the proceeds among tribal members, and terminated its treaty relationship with the tribe. Termination cut thousands of Indians adrift from the security of tribal organizations. The Bureau of Indian Affairs also encouraged Indians to move to large cities, but jobs were often unavailable.

RESHAPING URBAN AMERICA

If Eisenhower's administration opted for the status quo on many issues, it nevertheless reshaped American cities around an agenda of economic development. In 1954, Congress transformed the public housing program into urban renewal. Cities used federal funds to replace low-rent businesses and run-down housing on the fringes of their downtowns with new hospitals, civic centers, sports arenas, office towers, and luxury apartments.

Los Angeles demolished the seedy Victorian mansions of Bunker Hill, just northwest of downtown, for a music center and bank towers. A mile to the north was Chavez Ravine, whose Mexican-American population lived in substandard housing but maintained a lively community. When conservative opposition blocked plans for public housing, the residents were evicted, and Dodger Stadium was built. Here as elsewhere, urban showplaces rose at the expense of minority groups.

The Eisenhower administration also revolutionized American transportation. The **Federal Highway Act of 1956** created a national system of Interstate and Defense Highways. The legislation wrapped a program to build 41,000 miles of freeways in the language of the Cold War. The roads would be wide and strong enough for trucks hauling military hardware; they were also supposed to make it easy to evacuate cities in case of a Soviet attack.

Federal Highway Act of 1956
Measure that provided federal funding to build a nationwide system of interstate and defense highways.

Interstates halved the time of city-to-city travel. They were good for General Motors, the steel industry, and the concrete industry, requiring the construction equivalent of sixty Panama Canals. The highways promoted long-distance trucking at the expense of railroads. As with urban renewal, the bulldozers most often plowed through African-American or Latino neighborhoods.

The beltways or perimeter highways that began to ring most large cities made it easier and more profitable to develop new subdivisions and factory sites than to reinvest in city centers. Federal grants for sewers and other basic facilities further cut suburban costs. Continuing the pattern of the late 1940s, suburban growth added a million new single-family houses per year.

COMFORT ON CREDIT

The 1930s had taught Americans to avoid debt. The 1950s taught them to buy on credit. Families financed their new houses with 90 percent FHA mortgages and 100 percent VA mortgages. They filled the rooms by signing installment contracts at furniture and appliance stores and charging the drapes and carpeting on department store credit cards. The value of consumer debt, excluding home mortgages, tripled from 1952 to 1964.

New forms of marketing facilitated credit-based consumerism. The first large-scale suburban shopping center was Northgate in Seattle, which assembled all the pieces of the full-grown mall. By the end of the decade, developers were building malls with 1 million square feet of shopping floor. At the start of the 1970s, the universal credit card (Visa, MasterCard) made shopping even easier.

Where cities of the early twentieth century had been built around the public transportation of streetcars and subways, the 1950s depended on private automobiles. Interstate highways sucked retail business from small-town main streets to interchanges on the edge of town. Nationally franchised motels and fast-food restaurants sprang up along suburban shopping strips, pioneered by Holiday Inn (1952) and McDonald's (nationally franchised in 1955).

More extreme than the mall were entirely new environments for high-intensity consumption and entertainment that appeared in the Southwest, such as Las Vegas with its hotel-casinos. Opening in Orange County, California, in 1955, Disneyland was safe and artificial— a never-ending state fair without the smells and dust.

THE NEW FIFTIES FAMILY

Family life in the Eisenhower years departed from historic patterns. Prosperity allowed children to finish school and young adults to marry right after high school. Young women faced strong social pressure to pursue husbands rather than careers. The proportion of single adults reached its twentieth-century low in 1960. At all social levels, young people married quickly and had an average of three children spaced closely together. Family activities replaced the street corner for kids and the neighborhood tavern for men. Strong families, said experts, defended against Communism by teaching American values.

Television was made to order for the family-centered fifties. By 1960, fully 87 percent of households had sets. Popular entertainment was now enjoyed in the privacy of the home, rather than in a crowd. Situation comedies were the most popular programs. Successful shows depicted families who had northern European names and lived in single-family houses with friendly neighbors representing the 1950s ideal of American success.

Television sets were major pieces of living room furniture in the 1950s. This 1951 Motorola ad from Woman's Home Companion emphasizes television as a source of family togetherness, a popular theme in the 1950s.

Gaslight Advertising Archives, Inc. NY

 28–1
Ladies Home Journal, "Young Mother" (1956)

Television programming helped limit women's roles by power of example. Women in the fifties had a smaller share of new college degrees and professional jobs. Despite millions of new electric appliances, the time spent on housework *increased.* Magazines proclaimed that proper families maintained distinct roles for dad and mom, who was urged to find fulfillment in a well-scrubbed house and children.

But in reality the number of employed women reached new highs. By 1960, nearly 35 percent of all women held jobs, including 7.5 million mothers with children under 17.

INVENTING TEENAGERS

Teenagers in the 1950s joined adults as consumers of movies, clothes, and automobiles. Advertisers tapped and expanded the growing youth market by promoting a distinct "youth culture," an idea that became omnipresent in the 1960s and 1970s. While psychologists pontificated on the special problems of adolescence, many cities matched their high schools to the social status of their students: college-prep curricula for middle-class neighborhoods, vocational and technical schools for future factory workers, and separate schools or tracks for African Americans and Latinos.

All teenagers shared rock-and-roll, a new music of the mid-1950s that adapted the rhythm-and-blues of urban blacks for a white mass market. Rock music drew vitality from poor white Southerners (Buddy Holly, Elvis Presley), Hispanics (Richie Valens), and, in the 1960s, the British working class (the Beatles). Record producers played up the association between rock music and youthful rebellion.

TURNING TO RELIGION

Leaders from Dwight Eisenhower to FBI Director J. Edgar Hoover advocated churchgoing as an antidote for Communism. Regular church attendance grew from 48 percent of the population in 1940 to 63 percent in 1960. Congress created new connections between religion and government when it added "under God" to the Pledge of Allegiance in 1954 and required currency to bear the phrase "In God We Trust" in 1955.

Radio and television preachers added a new dimension to religious life. Bishop Fulton J. Sheen brought vigorous anti-Communism and Catholic doctrine to millions of TV viewers who would never have entered a Catholic church. Norman Vincent Peale blended popular psychology with Protestantism. His book *The Power of Positive Thinking* (1952) told readers to "stop worrying and start living" and sold millions of copies.

Another strand in the religious revival was revitalized evangelical and fundamentalist churches. During the 1950s, the theologically and socially conservative Southern Baptists became the largest Protestant denomination. Evangelist Billy Graham continued the grand American tradition of the mass revival meeting. Graham was a pioneer in the resurgence of evangelical Christianity that stressed an individual approach to belief and social issues. "Before we can solve the economic, philosophical, and political problems in the world," he said, "pride, greed, lust, and sin are going to have to be erased."

African-American churches were community institutions as well as religious organizations. Black congregations in Northern cities swelled in the postwar years and often supported extensive social service programs. In Southern cities, churches were centers for community pride and training grounds for the emerging civil rights movement.

Boundaries between many Protestant denominations blurred as church leaders emphasized national unity. Supreme Court decisions sowed the seeds for later

CHRONOLOGY

1953	CIA-backed coup returns the Shah to power in Iran. USSR detonates hydrogen bomb.
1954	Vietnamese defeat the French. Geneva conference divides Vietnam. United States and allies form SEATO. Supreme Court decides *Brown* v. *Board of Education of Topeka* CIA overthrows the government of Guatemala. China provokes a crisis over Quemoy and Matsu.
1955	Salk polio vaccine is announced. Black riders boycott Montgomery, Alabama, bus system. USSR forms the Warsaw Pact. AFL and CIO merge.
1956	Interstate Highway Act is passed. Soviets repress Hungarian revolt. Israel, France, and Britain invade Egypt.
1957	U.S. Army maintains law and order in Little Rock. Soviet Union launches *Sputnik.*
1958	United States and USSR voluntarily suspend nuclear tests.
1959	Fidel Castro takes power in Cuba. Nikita Khrushchev visits the United States.
1960	U-2 shot down over Russia. Sit-in movement begins in Greensboro, North Carolina.
1961	Bay of Pigs invasion fails. Kennedy establishes the Peace Corps. Vienna summit fails. Freedom rides are held in the Deep South. Berlin crisis leads to construction of the Berlin Wall.
1962	John Glenn orbits the earth. Cuban missile crisis brings the world to the brink. Michael Harrington publishes *The Other America.*
1963	Civil rights demonstrations rend Birmingham. Civil rights activists march in Washington. Betty Friedan publishes *The Feminine Mystique.* Limited Test Ban Treaty is signed. Ngo Dinh Diem is assassinated in South Vietnam. President Kennedy is assassinated.
1964	Civil Rights Act is passed. Freedom Summer is organized in Mississippi. Office of Economic Opportunity is created. Gulf of Tonkin Resolution is passed. Wilderness Act launches the modern environmental movement.
1965	Medical Care Act establishes Medicare and Medicaid. Elementary and Secondary Education Act extends direct federal aid to local schools. Selma-Montgomery march climaxes era of nonviolent civil rights demonstrations. Voting Rights Act suspends literacy tests.

political activism among evangelical Christians. In *Engel* v. *Vitale* (1962), the Court said that public schools could not require children to start the school day with group prayer. *Abington Township* v. *Schempp* (1963) prohibited devotional Bible reading in the schools. Such decisions alarmed many evangelicals.

THE GOSPEL OF PROSPERITY

Writers and intellectuals often marveled at the prosperity of Eisenhower's America. William H. Whyte Jr. searched American corporations for the changing character of the United States in *The Organization Man* (1956). Historian David Potter brilliantly analyzed Americans in *People of Plenty* (1954), contending that their national character had been shaped by the abundance of natural resources. In *The Affluent Society* (1958), economist John Kenneth Galbraith predicted that the challenge of the future would be to ensure the fair distribution of national wealth.

Officially, the American message was that abundance was a natural by-product of a free society. In fact, it was easy to present prosperity as a goal in itself, as Vice President Richard Nixon did when he represented the United States at a technology exposition in Moscow in 1959. The American exhibit included a complete six-room ranch house. In its "miracle kitchen," Nixon engaged Soviet Communist party chairman Nikita Khrushchev in a carefully planned "kitchen debate." The vice president claimed that the "most important thing" for Americans was "the right to choose": "We have so many different manufacturers and many different kinds of washing machines so that the housewives have a choice."

THE UNDERSIDE OF AFFLUENCE

The most basic criticism of the ideology of prosperity was the simplest— that affluence concealed vast inequalities. Michael Harrington wrote *The Other America* (1962) to remind Americans about the "underdeveloped nation" of 40 to 50 million poor people who had missed the last two decades of prosperity.

C. Wright Mills found dangers in the way that the Cold War distorted American society at the top. *The Power Elite* (1956) described an interlocking alliance of big government, big business, and the military. The losers in a permanent war economy, said Mills, were economic and political democracy.

Other critics targeted the alienating effects of consumerism and the conformity of homogeneous suburbs. Sociologist David Riesman saw suburbia as the home of "other-directed" individuals who lacked inner convictions.

There was far greater substance to increasing dissatisfaction among women. In 1963, Betty Friedan's book *The Feminine Mystique* followed numerous articles in *McCall's*, *Redbook*, and the *Ladies' Home Journal* about the unhappiness of college-educated women who were expected to find total satisfaction in kids and cooking. What Friedan called "the problem that has no name" was a sense of personal emptiness. "I got up one morning," remembered Geraldine Bean, "and I got my kids off to school. I went in to comb my hair and wash my face, and I stood in front of the bathroom mirror crying . . . because at eight-thirty in the morning I had my children off to school. I had my housework done. There was absolutely nothing for me to do the rest of the day." She went on to earn a Ph.D. and win election to the board of regents of the University of Colorado.

QUICK REVIEW

Critique of the Ideology of Prosperity

◆ Some critics argued that affluence concealed inequality.

◆ Others were concerned about the alienating effects of consumerism.

◆ Many women became dissatisfied with their assigned role in society.

WHAT IMPACT did

Dwight Eisenhower's foreign policy have on U.S. relations with the Soviet Union?

FACING OFF WITH THE SOVIET UNION

Americans got a reassuring new face in the White House in 1953, but not new policies toward the world. The United States pushed ahead in an arms race with the Soviet Union, stood guard on the borders of China and the Soviet empire, and judged political changes in Latin America, Africa, and Asia for their effect on the global balance of power.

WHY WE LIKED IKE

In the late twentieth century, few leaders were able to master both domestic policy and foreign affairs. Some presidents, such as Lyndon Johnson, were more adept at social problems than diplomacy. In contrast, Richard Nixon and George H.W. Bush were more interested in the world outside the United States.

Dwight Eisenhower was one of these "foreign policy presidents." He had helped hold together the alliance that defeated Nazi Germany and built NATO into an effective force in 1951–1952. He then sought the Republican nomination, he said, to ensure that the United States kept its international commitments. He sealed his victory in 1952 by emphasizing foreign policy expertise, telling a Detroit campaign audience that "to bring the Korean war to an early and honorable end . . . requires a personal trip to Korea. I shall make that trip . . . I shall go to Korea."

Many of the Eisenhower administration's accomplishments were things that didn't happen. Eisenhower refused to dismantle the social programs of the New Deal. He exerted American political and military power around the globe but avoided war.

It helped Eisenhower's political agenda if Americans thought of him as a smiling grandfather. The "Ike" who gave rambling, incoherent answers at White House press conferences was controlling information and keeping the opposition guessing. When his press secretary advised him to duck questions at one press conference, Ike replied, "Don't worry, I'll just confuse them." He was easily re-elected in 1956.

A BALANCE OF TERROR

The backdrop for U.S. foreign policy was the growing capacity for mutual nuclear annihilation. The old balance of power had become a balance of terror.

The Eisenhower administration's doctrine of massive retaliation took advantage of superior American technology while economizing on military spending. Eisenhower compared uncontrolled military spending to crucifying humankind on a "cross of iron." "Every gun that is fired," he warned, "every warship launched, every rocket fired signifies . . . a theft from those who hunger and are not fed, those who are cold and not clothed." The administration concentrated military spending where the nation already had the greatest advantage—on atomic weapons, instead of attempting to match the land armies of the Soviet Union and China. In response to any serious attack, the United States would direct maximum force against the homeland of the aggressor. The National Security Council in 1953 made reliance on "massive retaliatory damage" by nuclear weapons official policy.

The doctrine grew even more fearful as the Soviet Union developed its own hydrogen bombs. The chairman of the Atomic Energy Commission terrified the American people by mentioning casually that the Soviets could now obliterate New York City. Signs for air raid shelters posted on downtown buildings, air raid drills in schools, and appearance of radioactivity in milk supplies in the form of the isotope strontium 90 carried by fallout made the atomic threat very immediate.

The USSR added to worries about atomic war by launching the world's first artificial satellite. On the first Sunday of October 1957, Americans discovered that *Sputnik*— Russian for "satellite"— was orbiting the earth. The Soviets soon lifted a dog into orbit while U.S. rockets fizzled on the pad. Soviet propagandists claimed that their technological "first" showed the superiority of Communism, and Americans wondered if the United States had lost its edge. The new **National Aeronautics and Space Administration (NASA)** took over the satellite program in 1958.

The crisis was more apparent than real. The combination of Soviet rocketry and nuclear capacity created alarm about a missile gap. The USSR was said to be building hundreds of intercontinental ballistic missiles (ICBMs) to overwhelm American air defenses designed to intercept piloted bombers. Although there was no such gap, Eisenhower was unwilling to reveal secret information that might have allayed public anxiety.

CONTAINMENT IN ACTION

Someone who heard only the campaign speeches in 1952 might have expected sharp foreign policy changes under Eisenhower, but there was more continuity than change. John Foster Dulles, Eisenhower's secretary of state, had attacked the Democrats as defeatists and appeasers. He demanded that the United States liberate eastern Europe from Soviet control and encourage Jiang Jieshi to attack Communist China. In 1956, Dulles proudly claimed that tough-minded diplomacy had repeatedly brought the United States to the verge of war: "We walked to the brink and looked it in the face. We took strong action."

In fact, Eisenhower viewed the Cold War in the same terms as Truman. Caution replaced campaign rhetoric about "rolling back" Communism. Around the periphery of the Communist nations, from eastern Asia to the Middle East to Europe, the United States accepted the existing sphere of Communist influence but attempted to block its growth, a policy most Americans accepted.

WHERE TO LEARN MORE **W**

Kansas Cosmosphere, Hutchinson, Kansas
www.cosmo.org

WHERE TO LEARN MORE **W**

National Air and Space Museum, Washington, D.C.
www.nasm.edu

National Aeronautics and Space Administration (NASA) Federal agency created in 1958 to manage American space flights and exploration.

The American worldview assumed both the right and the need to intervene in the affairs of other nations, especially in Latin America, Asia, and Africa. Policymakers saw these nations as markets for U.S. products and sources of vital raw materials. When political disturbances arose in these states, the United States blamed Soviet meddling to justify U.S. intervention. If Communism could not be rolled back in eastern Europe, the CIA could still undermine anti-American governments in the third world. The Soviets themselves took advantage of local revolutions even when they did not instigate them.

Twice during Eisenhower's first term, the CIA subverted democratically elected governments that seemed to threaten U.S. interests. In Iran, which had nationalized British and U.S. oil companies in an effort to break the hold of western corporations, the CIA in 1953 backed a coup that toppled the government and helped the young Shah, or monarch, gain control. The Shah then cooperated with the United States until his overthrow in 1979. In Guatemala, the leftist government was upsetting the United Fruit Company. When the Guatemalans accepted weapons from the Communist bloc in 1954, the CIA imposed a regime friendly to U.S. business (see Map 28–1).

For most Americans in 1953, democracy in Iran was far less important than ending the war in Korea and stabilizing relations with China. Eisenhower declined to escalate the Korean War by blockading China and sending more U.S. ground forces. Instead he shifted atomic bombs to Okinawa, only 400 miles from China. The nuclear threat, along with the continued cost of the war on both sides, brought the Chinese to a truce that left Korea divided into two nations.

In Vietnam, on China's southern border, France was fighting to maintain its colonial rule against rebels who combined Communist ideology with fervor for national independence under the leadership of Ho Chi Minh. The United States picked up three-quarters of the costs, but the French military position collapsed in 1954. The French had had enough, and Eisenhower was unwilling to join another Asian war. A Geneva peace conference in 1954 "temporarily" divided Vietnam into a Communist north and a non-Communist south and scheduled elections for a single Vietnamese government.

The United States then replaced France as the supporter of pro-Western Vietnamese in the south. Washington's client was Ngo Dinh Diem, an anti-Communist from South Vietnam's Roman Catholic elite. U.S. officials encouraged Diem to put off the elections and backed his efforts to construct an authoritarian South Vietnam. Ho meanwhile consolidated the northern half as a Communist state that claimed to be the legitimate government for all Vietnam. The United States further reinforced containment in Asia by creating the **Southeast Asia Treaty Organization (SEATO)** in 1954.

Halfway around the world, there was a new crisis when three American friends—France, Britain, and Israel— ganged up on Egypt, each for its own reasons. On October 29, 1956, Israel attacked Egypt. A week later, British and French forces attempted to seize the canal. The United States forced a quick cease-fire, partly to maintain its standing with oil-producing Arab nations. The war left Britain and France dependent on American oil that Eisenhower would not provide until they left Egypt.

In Europe, Eisenhower accepted the status quo because conflicts there could result in nuclear war. In 1956, challenges to Communist rule arose in East Germany, Poland, and Hungary and threatened to break up the Soviet empire. The Soviets replaced liberal Communists in East Germany and Poland with hard-liners. In Hungary, however, open warfare broke out. Hungarian freedom fighters in Budapest used rocks and fire bombs against Soviet tanks while pleading in vain for Western aid. NATO would not risk war with the USSR. Tens of thousands of Hungarians died and 200,000 fled when the Soviets crushed the resistance.

Southeast Asia Treaty Organization (SEATO) Mutual defense alliance signed in 1954 by the United States, Britain, France, Thailand, Pakistan, the Philippines, Australia, and New Zealand.

MAP EXPLORATION

To explore an interactive version of this map, go to **http://www.prenhall.com/goldfield2/map28.1**

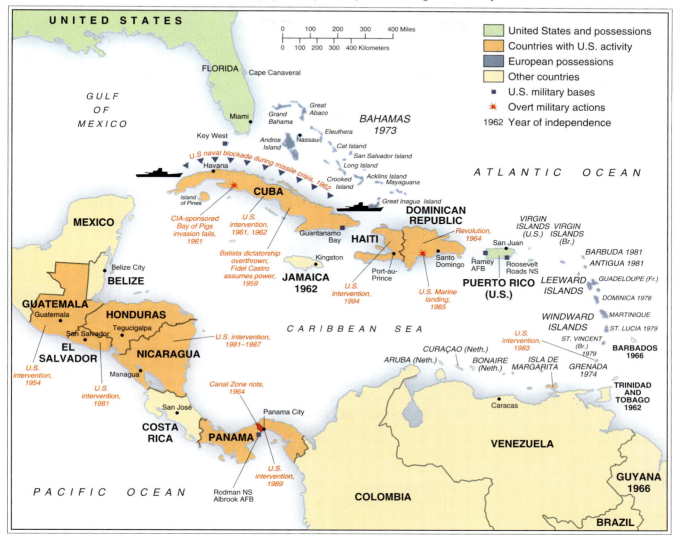

MAP 28–1

U.S. Intervention around the Caribbean since 1954   The United States has long kept a careful eye on the politics of neighboring nations to its south. In the second half of the twentieth century, the United States has frequently used military assistance or force to influence or intervene in Caribbean and Central American nations. The most common purpose has been to counter or undermine left-leaning governments; some interventions, as in Haiti, have been intended to stabilize democratic regimes.

WHAT WAS the effect of U.S. involvement in the Caribbean?

GLOBAL STANDOFF

As documents from both sides of the Cold War become available, historians have realized what dangerously different meanings the two sides gave to confrontations between 1953 and 1964.

A good example was the U-2 affair of 1960, which derailed progress toward nuclear disarmament. Both countries voluntarily suspended nuclear tests in 1958 and prepared for a June 1960 summit meeting in Paris, where Eisenhower intended to negotiate a test ban treaty.

But on May 1, 1960, Soviet air defenses shot down an American U-2 spy plane over the heart of Russia and captured the pilot, Francis Gary Powers. Designed to soar above the range of Soviet antiaircraft missiles, U-2s had assured American officials that there was no missile gap.

When Moscow trumpeted the news of the downing, Eisenhower took personal responsibility in hopes that Khrushchev would accept the U-2 as an unpleasant reality of international espionage. Unfortunately, the planes meant something very different to the Soviets, touching their festering sense of inferiority. They had stopped protesting the flights in 1957 because complaints were demeaning. The Americans thought that silence signaled acceptance. When Eisenhower refused to apologize in Paris, Khrushchev stalked out. Disarmament was set back for years.

The most important aspect of Eisenhower's foreign policy was continuity. The administration pursued containment as defined under Truman. The Cold War consensus, however, prevented the United States from seeing the nations of the developing world on their own terms. By viewing every independence movement and social revolution as part of the competition with Communism, American leaders created unnecessary problems.

JOHN F. KENNEDY AND THE COLD WAR

John Kennedy was a man of contradictions. A Democrat, he presided over policies whose direction was set under Eisenhower. Despite stirring rhetoric about leading the nation toward a **New Frontier** of scientific and social progress, he recorded his greatest failures and successes in the continuing Cold War. (See American Views, "Two Presidents Assess the Implication of the Cold War.")

THE KENNEDY MYSTIQUE

Kennedy won the presidency over Richard Nixon in a cliffhanging 1960 election that was more about personality and style than substance (see Map 28–2). Both candidates were determined not to yield another inch to Communism. The charming and eloquent Kennedy narrowly skirted scandal in his personal life. Well publicized as a war hero from World War II, he tempered ruthless ambition with respect for public service. His forthright campaigning allayed voter concern about his Roman Catholicism. Nixon had wider experience and was a shrewd tactician, but he was also self-righteous and awkward.

Television was crucial to the outcome. The campaign featured the first televised presidential debates. In the first session, Nixon actually gave better replies, but his nervousness and a bad makeup job turned off millions of viewers who admired Kennedy's energy. Nixon never overcame the setback. Kennedy's televised inauguration was the perfect setting for his impassioned plea for national unity: "My fellow Americans," he challenged, "ask not what your country can do for you— ask what you can do for your country."

Kennedy brought dash to the White House. His beautiful and refined wife, Jackie, outshined previous first ladies. Kennedy's staff and large family played touch football, not golf. No president had shown such verve since Teddy Roosevelt. People began to talk about Kennedy's "charisma," his ability to lead by sheer force of personality.

KENNEDY'S MISTAKES

Talking tough to satisfy more militant countrymen, Kennedy and Khrushchev pushed each other into corners, continuing the problems of mutual misunderstanding. When Khrushchev promised in January 1961 to support "wars of national liberation,"

New Frontier John F. Kennedy's domestic and foreign policy initiatives, designed to reinvigorate a sense of national purpose and energy.

he was really fending off Chinese criticism. But Kennedy over-reacted in his first State of the Union address by asking for more military spending.

Three months later, Kennedy fed Soviet fears of American aggressiveness by sponsoring an invasion of Cuba. At the start of 1959, Fidel Castro replaced another Cuban dictator, Fulgencio Batista.

When fourteen hundred anti-Castro Cubans landed at Cuba's **Bay of Pigs** on April 17, 1961, they were following a plan from the Eisenhower administration. The CIA had trained and armed the invaders and convinced Kennedy that the landing would trigger spontaneous uprisings. But when Kennedy refused to commit American armed forces to support them, Cuban forces captured the attackers.

Kennedy followed the Bay of Pigs debacle with a hasty and ill-prepared summit meeting with Khrushchev in Vienna in June that left the Soviets with the impression that the president was weak. To exploit Kennedy's perceived vulnerability, the USSR renewed tension over Berlin, deep within East Germany. The divided city served as an escape route from Communism for hundreds of thousands of East Germans. Khrushchev now threatened to transfer the Soviet sector in Berlin to East Germany, which had no treaty obligations to France, Britain, or the United States. If the West had to deal directly with East Germany for access to Berlin, it would have to recognize a permanently divided Germany. Kennedy sounded the alarm; he doubled draft calls, called up reservists, and warned families to build fallout shelters. Boise, Idaho, families paid $100 for a share in a community shelter with its own power plant and hospital.

Rather than confront the United States directly, however, the Soviets and East Germans on August 13, 1961, built the **Berlin Wall** around the western sectors of Berlin while leaving the access route to West Germany open. In private, Kennedy accepted the wall as a clever way to stabilize a dangerous situation: "A wall," he said, "is a hell of a lot better than a war."

GETTING INTO VIETNAM

American involvement in Vietnam dated from the mid-1950s when the United States replaced France, the former colonial power there, as the supporter of the anti-Communist Vietnamese who had established a government in the southern part of Vietnam. North Vietnam was ruled by Communists under the leadership of Ho Chi Minh who had defeated the French in 1954.

An international conference that negotiated the French withdrawal had called for elections for a single Vietnamese government. The Eisenhower administration, however, encouraged its client in the south, Ngo Dinh Diem from the country's Catholic elite, to put off elections and to establish an independent South Vietnam. Meanwhile, Ho's Communist state in the north claimed to be the legitimate government for all Vietnam.

Kennedy saw U.S. support for Diem as an opportunity to reassert America's commitment to containment. Although Diem's forces controlled the cities with the help of a Vietnamese elite that had also supported the French, Communist insurgents,

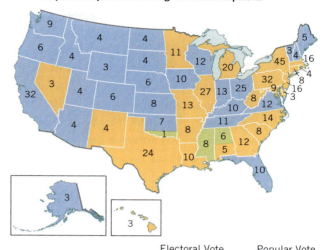

MAP EXPLORATION

To explore an interactive version of this map, go to
http://www.prenhall.com/goldfield2/map28.2

	Electoral Vote (%)	Popular Vote (%)
JOHN F. KENNEDY (Democrat)	**303 (56)**	**34,226,731 (49.9)**
Richard M. Nixon (Republican)	219 (41)	34,108,157 (49.7)
Other	15 (3)	197,029 (.4)

Note: Fifteen electors voted for Harry Byrd, although he had not been an active candidate. Minor party candidates took a tiny percentage of the popular vote.

MAP 28–2
The Election of 1960   The presidential election of 1960 was one of the closest in American history. John Kennedy's victory depended on his appeal in Northern industrial states with large Roman Catholic populations and his ability to hold much of the traditionally Democratic South. Texas, the home state of his vice presidential running mate Lyndon Johnson, was vital to the success of the ticket.

WHY DID most Western states not support Kennedy?

Bay of Pigs   Site in Cuba of an unsuccessful landing by fourteen hundred anti-Castro Cuban refugees in April 1961.

Berlin Wall   Wall erected by East Germany in 1961 that isolated West Berlin from the surrounding areas in Communist-controlled East Berlin and East Germany.

• AMERICAN VIEWS •

TWO PRESIDENTS ASSESS THE IMPLICATIONS OF THE COLD WAR

In speeches two days apart in January 1961, outgoing President Dwight Eisenhower and incoming President John Kennedy offered contrasting interpretations of America's Cold War crusade. Eisenhower spoke with concern about the effects of defense spending on American society. Kennedy promised an unlimited commitment of resources to achieve national goals.

WHY DID Kennedy define the American mission to the world so broadly? Why did Eisenhower warn about the dangers of pursuing that mission? Do the selections show basic agreement or disagreement about the goals of national policy?

Dwight D.Eisenhower
Farewell Address,
January 18, 1961

Our military organization today bears little relation to that known by any of my predecessors in peacetime. . . . This conjunction of an immense military establishment and a large arms industry is new in the American experience. The total influence— economic, political, even spiritual—is felt in every city, every State house, every office of the federal government. We recognize the imperative need for this development. Yet we must not fail to comprehend its grave implications. . . .

In the councils of government, we must guard against the acquisition of unwarranted influence, whether sought or unsought, by the military-industrial complex. The potential for the disastrous rise of misplaced power exists and will persist.

We must never let the weight of this combination endanger our liberties or democratic processes. We should take nothing for granted. Only an alert and knowledgeable citizenry can compel the proper meshing of the huge industrial and military machinery of defense with our peaceful methods and goals.

John F. Kennedy
Inaugural Address,
January 20, 1961

Let the word go forth from this time and place, to friend and foe alike, that the torch has been passed to a new generation of Americans—born in this century, tempered by war, disciplined by a hard and bitter peace, proud of our ancient heritage—and unwilling to witness or permit the slow undoing of those human rights to which this nation has always been committed, and to which we are committed today at home and around the world.
Let every nation know, whether it wishes us well or ill, that we shall pay any price, bear any burden, meet any hardship, support any friends, oppose any foe to assure the survival and the success of liberty.

known as the **Viet Cong**, were gaining strength in the countryside. The United States sent Diem more weapons and increasing numbers of civilian and military advisors.

U.S. aid did not work. Despite overoptimistic reports and sixteen thousand American troops, Diem's government was losing the loyalty—"the hearts and minds"—of many South Vietnamese. North Vietnam's support for the Viet Cong offset the effect of U.S. assistance. Diem further weakened his position by crushing opposition from Vietnamese Buddhists. In frustration, Kennedy's administration tacitly approved a coup that killed Diem and his brother on November 1, 1963 and replaced them with an ineffectual military junta.

MISSILE CRISIS: A LINE DRAWN IN THE WAVES

On October 15, 1962 reconnaissance photos revealed Soviets at work on launching sites in Cuba from which Soviet-operated nuclear missiles could hit the United States. Top officials spent five exhausting and desperate days sorting through options. Doing nothing meant political disaster. Full-scale invasion of Cuba was

Viet Cong Communist rebels in South Vietnam who fought the pro-American government established in South Vietnam in 1954.

infeasible on short notice, and "surgical" air strikes were technically impossible. Secretary of Defense Robert McNamara suggested demanding removal of the missiles and declaring a naval "quarantine" against the arrival of further offensive weapons. A blockade would buy time for diplomacy.

Kennedy imposed the blockade in a terrifying speech on Monday, October 22. He emphasized the "deceptive" deployment of the Soviet missiles and raised the specter of nuclear war. Americans would have been even more afraid had they known that some of the missiles were operational and that Soviets in Cuba were authorized to use them in self-defense. On Friday, Khrushchev offered to withdraw the missiles in return for an American pledge not to invade Cuba. On Saturday, a second communication raised a new complaint about American missiles on the territory of NATO allies. The letter was the result of pressure by Kremlin hard-liners and Khrushchev's own wavering. Kennedy decided to accept the first letter and ignore the second. The United States pledged not to invade Cuba and secretly promised to remove obsolete Jupiter missiles from Turkey.

Why did Khrushchev risk the Cuban gamble? One reason was to protect Castro as a symbol of Soviet commitment to anti-Western regimes in the developing world. Kennedy had tried to preempt Castroism in 1961 by launching the **Alliance for Progress**, an economic development program for Latin America that tied aid to social reform. However, the United States had also orchestrated the Bay of Pigs invasion and funded a CIA campaign to sabotage Cuba and assassinate its leaders. Castro and Khrushchev had reason to fear the worst.

Khrushchev also hoped to redress the strategic balance. Intermediate-range rockets gave the USSR a nuclear club over western Europe, but in October 1962, the USSR had fewer than fifty ICBMs to aim at the United States and China. The United States was creating a defensive triad of a thousand land-based Minuteman missiles, five hundred long-range bombers, and six hundred Polaris missiles on nuclear submarines targeted on the USSR. The strategic imbalance had sustained NATO during the Berlin confrontation, but forty launchers in Cuba with two warheads each would have doubled the Soviet capacity to strike at the United States.

Soviet missiles in Cuba thus flouted the Monroe Doctrine and posed a real military threat. In the end, both sides were cautious. Khrushchev backed down rather than fight. Kennedy fended off hawkish advisers who wanted to destroy Castro. The world had trembled, but neither nation wanted war over "the missiles of October." In the long run, the crisis accelerated the global arms race. Never again, Soviet leaders vowed, would they submit to American nuclear superiority.

SCIENCE AND FOREIGN AFFAIRS

The two superpowers competed through science as well as diplomacy. A Russian, Yuri Gagarin, was the first human to orbit the earth, on April 12, 1961. American John Glenn did not match Gagarin's feat until February 1962. Kennedy committed the United States to placing an American astronaut on the moon by 1970.

The Soviet Union and the United States were also fencing about nuclear weapons testing. After the three-year moratorium, tests resumed in 1961–1962. Both nations worked on multiple targetable warheads, antiballistic missiles, and other innovations that might destabilize the balance of terror.

After the missile crisis showed his toughness, however, Kennedy had enough political maneuvering room to respond to pressure from liberal Democrats and groups like Women Strike for Peace and the Committee for a Sane Nuclear Policy by giving priority to disarmament. In July 1963, the United States, Britain, and the USSR signed the **Limited Test Ban Treaty**, which outlawed nuclear testing in the atmosphere, in outer space, and under water, and invited other nations to join in. A more comprehensive

The Kennedy family in Hyannis Port in August of 1962.

Cecil Soughton, White House/John Fitzgerald Kennedy Library, Boston

QUICK REVIEW

The Cuban Missile Crisis
- October 15, 1962: U.S. acquires evidence of construction of missile launching sites in Cuba.
- In response, Kennedy imposed a blockade.
- The Soviets removed the launchers in exchange for removal of U.S. missiles from Turkey and a U.S. promise not to invade Cuba.

 28–2
John F. Kennedy, Cuban Missile Address (1962)

Alliance for Progress   Program of economic aid to Latin America during the Kennedy administration.

Limited Test Ban Treaty   Treaty, signed by the United States, Britain, and the Soviet Union, outlawing nuclear testing in the atmosphere, in outer space, and under water.

treaty was impossible because the Soviet Union refused on-site inspections. France and China, the other nuclear powers, refused to sign, and the treaty did not halt weapons development, but it was the most positive achievement of Kennedy's foreign policy and a step toward later disarmament treaties.

RIGHTEOUSNESS LIKE A MIGHTY STREAM: THE STRUGGLE FOR CIVIL RIGHTS

WHAT WAS the significance of *Brown* v. *Board of Education of Topeka?*

Linda Brown of Topeka, Kansas, was a third-grader whose parents were fed up with sending her past an all-white public school to attend an all-black school a mile away. The Browns volunteered to help the NAACP challenge Topeka's school segregation by trying to enroll Linda in their neighborhood school, beginning a legal challenge that reached the Supreme Court. Three years later, on May 17, 1954, in ***Brown*** **v.** ***Board of Education of Topeka***, the justices reversed the 1896 case of *Plessy* v. *Ferguson* by ruling that sending black children to "separate but equal" schools denied them equal treatment under the Constitution.

GETTING TO THE SUPREME COURT

The *Brown* decision climaxed a twenty-five-year campaign to reenlist the federal courts on the side of equal rights. The work began in the 1930s when Charles Hamilton Houston, dean of Howard University's law school, trained a corps of civil rights lawyers. Working on behalf of the NAACP, he hoped to erode *Plessy* by suits focused on interstate travel and professional graduate schools (the least defensible segregated institutions because states seldom provided alternatives). In 1938, Houston's student Thurgood Marshall, a future Supreme Court justice, took over the NAACP job.

The *Brown* case combined lawsuits from Delaware, Virginia, South Carolina, the District of Columbia, and Kansas. In each instance, students and families braved community pressure to demand equal access to a basic public service. Viewing public education as central for the equal opportunity that lay at the heart of American values, the Court weighed the *consequences* of segregated school systems and concluded that separate meant unequal.

Brown also built on efforts by Mexican Americans in the Southwest to assert their rights of citizenship. In 1946, the federal courts had prohibited segregation of Mexican-American children in California schools. Eight years later, the Supreme Court forbade Texas from excluding Mexican Americans from juries.

DELIBERATE SPEED

Racial segregation by law was largely a Southern problem, the legacy of Jim Crow laws from early in the century. At first, Americans elsewhere thought of racial injustice as a regional issue.

Southern responses to *Brown* emphasized regional differences. Few Southern communities desegregated schools voluntarily. Their reluctance was bolstered in 1955 when the Supreme Court allowed segregated states to carry out the 1954 decision "with all deliberate speed" rather than immediately. The following year, 101 Southern congressmen and senators issued the **Southern Manifesto**, which asserted that the Court decision was unconstitutional. President Eisenhower privately deplored the desegregation decision, which violated his sense of states' rights and upset Republican attempts to gain southern votes.

The first crisis came in Little Rock, Arkansas, in September 1957. The city school board admitted nine African Americans to Central High, only to be upstaged by Governor Orval Faubus. Claiming to fear violence, he surrounded Central with

Brown v. *Board of Education of Topeka* Supreme Court decision in 1954 that declared that "separate but equal" schools for children of different races violated the Constitution.

Southern Manifesto   A document signed by 101 members of Congress from Southern states in 1956 that argued that the Supreme Court's decision in *Brown* v. *Board of Education of Topeka* itself contradicted the Constitution.

the National Guard and turned the new students away. Meanwhile, segregationists stirred up white fears. Under intense national pressure, Faubus withdrew the Guard, and a howling crowd surrounded the school. When the black students entered anyway, the mob threatened to storm the building. The police had to sneak them out after two hours. Fuming at the governor's defiance of federal authority, which bordered on insurrection, Eisenhower reluctantly nationalized the National Guard and sent in the 101st Airborne Division to keep order. Eight of the students endured a year of harassment in the hallways of Central.

The breakthrough in school integration did not come until the end of the 1960s, when the courts rejected further delays and federal authorities threatened to cut off education funds. As late as 1968, only 6 percent of African-American children in the South attended integrated schools. By 1973, the figure was 90 percent.

PUBLIC ACCOMMODATIONS

Most Southern states separated the races in bus terminals and movie theaters. They required black riders to take rear seats on buses. They labeled separate restrooms and drinking fountains for "colored" users. Hotels denied rooms to black people, and restaurants refused them service.

The struggle to end segregated facilities started in Montgomery, Alabama. On December 1, 1955, Rosa Parks, a seamstress who worked at a downtown department store, refused to give up her bus seat to a white passenger and was arrested. Parks acted spontaneously, but she was part of a network of civil rights activists who wanted to challenge segregated buses and was the secretary of the Montgomery NAACP. As news of her action spread, the Women's Political Council, a group of college-trained black women, initiated a mass boycott of the privately owned bus company. Martin Luther King Jr., a twenty-six-year-old pastor, galvanized a mass meeting with a speech that quoted the biblical prophet Amos: "We are determined here in Montgomery to work and fight until justice runs down like water, and righteousness like a mighty stream."

A car pool substituted for the buses despite police harassment. As the boycott survived months of pressure, the national media began to pay attention. After nearly a year, the Supreme Court agreed that the bus segregation law was unconstitutional.

Victory in Montgomery depended on the steadfastness of African-American involvement. Participants cut across the class lines that had divided black Southerners. Success also revealed the discrepancy between white attitudes in the Deep South and national opinion. For white Southerners, segregation was a local concern best defined as a legal or constitutional matter. For other Americans, it was increasingly an issue of the South's deviation from national moral norms.

The Montgomery boycott won a local victory and made King famous. King formed the **Southern Christian Leadership Conference (SCLC)**, but four African-American college students in Greensboro, North Carolina, started the next phase of the struggle. On February 1, 1960, they sat down at the segregated lunch counter in Woolworth's, waiting through the day without being served. Their patient courage brought more demonstrators; within two days, eighty-five students packed the store. Nonviolent sit-ins spread throughout the South.

In a comparatively sophisticated border city like Nashville, Tennessee, sit-ins integrated lunch counters. Elsewhere they precipitated white violence and mass arrests. Like soldiers on a battlefield, nervous participants in sit-ins and demonstrations drew strength from one another. "If you don't have courage," said one young woman in Albany, Georgia, "you can borrow it." SCLC leader Ella Baker helped the students form a new organization, the **Student Nonviolent Coordinating Committee (SNCC)**.

WHERE TO LEARN MORE

National Afro-American Museum and Cultural Center, Wilberforce, Ohio www.ohiohistory.org/places/afroam/

Southern Christian Leadership Conference (SCLC) Black civil rights organization founded in 1957 by Martin Luther King Jr., and other clergy.

Student Nonviolent Coordinating Committee (SNCC) Black civil rights organization founded in 1960 and drawing heavily on younger activists and college students.

The year 1961 brought "freedom rides" to test the segregation of interstate bus terminals. The idea came from James Farmer of the **Congress of Racial Equality (CORE)**. Two buses carrying black and white passengers met only minor problems in Virginia, the Carolinas, and Georgia, but Alabamians burned one of the buses and attacked the riders in Birmingham, where they beat demonstrators senseless and clubbed a Justice Department observer. The governor and police refused to protect the freedom riders. The riders traveled into Mississippi under National Guard protection but were arrested at the Jackson bus terminal. Freedom rides continued through the summer.

MARCH ON WASHINGTON, 1963

John Kennedy was a tepid supporter of the civil rights movement and entered office with no civil rights agenda. He appointed segregationist judges to mollify Southern congressmen and would have preferred that black protestors stop disturbing the fragile Democratic party coalition.

In the face of slow federal response, the SCLC concentrated for 1963 on rigidly segregated Birmingham. April began with sit-ins and marches that aimed to integrate lunch counters, restrooms, and stores and secure open hiring for some clerical jobs. Birmingham's commissioner of public safety, Bull Connor, used fire hoses to blast demonstrators against buildings and roll children down the streets. When demonstrators fought back, his men chased them with dogs. Continued marches brought the arrest of hundreds of children. King's own "Letter from Birmingham City Jail" stated the case for protest: "We have not made a single gain in civil rights without determined legal and nonviolent pressure. . . . Freedom is never voluntarily given by the oppressor; it must be demanded by the oppressed."

The events in Alabama had forced President Kennedy to board the freedom train with an eloquent June 11 speech and to send a civil rights bill to Congress. "Are we to say . . . that this is the land of the free, except for Negroes, that we have no second-class citizens, except Negroes . . . ? Now the time has come for the nation to fulfill its promise."

On August 28, 1963, a quarter of a million black and white people marched to the Lincoln Memorial. The day gave Martin Luther King Jr. a national pulpit. His call for progress toward Christian and American goals had immense appeal. Television cut away from afternoon programs for his "I Have a Dream" speech. The March on Washington demonstrated the mass appeal of civil rights and its identification with national values.

"LET US CONTINUE"

The optimism of the March on Washington shattered with the assassination of John Kennedy in November 1963. In 1964 and 1965, however, President Lyndon Johnson pushed through Kennedy's legislative agenda and much more.

DALLAS, 1963

In November 1963, President Kennedy visited Texas to patch up feuds among Texas Democrats. On November 22, the president's motorcade took him near the Texas School Book Depository building in Dallas, where Lee Harvey Oswald had stationed himself at a window on the sixth floor. When Kennedy's open car swung into the sights of his rifle, Oswald fired three shots that wounded Texas Governor John Connally and killed the president. As doctors vainly treated the president in a hospital emergency room, Dallas police arrested Oswald. Vice President Lyndon Johnson took the oath of office as president on Air Force One while the blood-spattered Jacqueline Kennedy looked

28–3
John Lewis, Address at the March on Washington (1963)

Congress of Racial Equality (CORE)
Civil rights group formed in 1942 and committed to nonviolent civil disobedience.

HOW DID Lyndon Johnson continue the domestic agenda inherited from the Kennedy administration?

on. Two days later, as Oswald was being led to a courtroom, Texas nightclub owner Jack Ruby killed Oswald with a handgun, in full view of TV cameras.

Lee Oswald was a twenty-four-year old misfit. He had served in the Marines and worked maintaining U-2 spy planes before defecting to the Soviet Union. He returned to the United States after three years with a fervent commitment to Fidel Castro's Cuban revolution. He visited the Soviet and Cuban embassies in Mexico City in September trying to drum up a job, but neither country thought him worth hiring.

Some Americans believe there is more to the story. Why? One possibility is that Oswald seems too insignificant to be responsible on his own for the murder of a charismatic president. The sketchy job done by the Warren Commission, appointed to investigate the assassination, calmed fears in the short run but left loose ends that have fueled conspiracy theories.

All of the theories remain unproved. Logic holds that the simplest explanation for cutting through a mass of information is usually the best. Oswald was a social misfit with a grievance against American society. Ruby was an impulsive man who told his brother on his deathbed that he thought he was doing the country a favor.

WAR ON POVERTY

Five days after the assassination, Lyndon Johnson claimed Kennedy's progressive aura for his new administration. "Let us continue," he told the nation, promising to implement Kennedy's policies. Lyndon Johnson was a professional politician who had reached the top through Texas politics and congressional infighting. Johnson's presence on the ticket in 1960 had helped elect Kennedy by attracting Southern voters, but he lacked Kennedy's polish and easy relations with the Eastern elite. He had entered public life with the New Deal in the 1930s and believed in its principles. Johnson, not Kennedy, was the true heir of Franklin Roosevelt.

Johnson inherited a domestic agenda that the Kennedy administration had defined but not enacted. Initiatives in education, medical insurance, tax reform, and urban affairs had stalled or been gutted by conservatives in Congress.

When Michael Harrington's study *The Other America* became an unexpected bestseller, Kennedy had taken notice. As poverty captured public attention, Kennedy's economic advisers devised a community action program that emphasized education and job training, a national service corps, and a youth conservation corps.

Johnson made Kennedy's antipoverty package his own. Adopting Cold War rhetoric, he declared "unconditional war on poverty." The core of Johnson's program was the **Office of Economic Opportunity (OEO)**. Established under the direction of Kennedy's brother-in-law R. Sargent Shriver in 1964, the OEO operated the Job Corps for school dropouts, the Neighborhood Youth Corps for unemployed teenagers, the Head Start program to prepare poor children for school, and VISTA (Volunteers in Service to America), a domestic Peace Corps. OEO's biggest effort went to Community Action Agencies. By 1968, more than five hundred such agencies provided health and educational services. Despite flaws, the **War on Poverty** improved life for millions of Americans.

CIVIL RIGHTS, 1964–1965

In Johnson's view, segregation not only deprived African Americans of access to opportunity but also distracted Southern white people from their own poverty and underdevelopment.

One solution was the **Civil Rights Act of 1964**, which Kennedy had introduced but Johnson got enacted. The law prohibited segregation in public accommodations, such as hotels, restaurants, gas stations, theaters, and parks, and outlawed employment discrimination on federally assisted projects. It also created

WHERE TO LEARN MORE

Sixth Floor Museum, Dallas, Texas
www.jfk.org

WHERE TO LEARN MORE

National Civil Rights Museum,
Memphis, Tennessee
http://www.civilrightsmuseum.org

Office of Economic Opportunity (OEO) Federal agency that coordinated many programs of the War on Poverty between 1964 and 1975.

War on Poverty Set of programs introduced by Lyndon Johnson between 1963 and 1966 designed to break the cycle of poverty by providing funds for job training, community development, nutrition, and supplementary education.

Civil Rights Act of 1964 Federal legislation that outlawed discrimination in public accommodations and employment on the basis of race, skin color, sex, religion, or national origin.

the Equal Employment Opportunity Commission (EEOC) and included gender in a list of categories protected against discrimination, a provision whose consequences were scarcely suspected in 1964.

Even as Congress was debating the 1964 law, **Freedom Summer** moved political power to the top of the civil rights agenda. Organized by SNCC, the Mississippi Summer Freedom Project was a voter registration drive that sent white and black volunteers to the small towns and back roads of Mississippi. The target was a Southern political system that used rigged literacy tests and intimidation to keep black people from voting. In Mississippi in 1964, only 7 percent of eligible black people were registered voters. Freedom Summer gained sixteen hundred new voters and taught two thousand children in SNCC-run Freedom Schools at the cost of beatings, bombings, church arson, and the murder of three project workers.

Another outgrowth of the SNCC effort was the Mississippi Freedom Democratic Party (MFDP), a biracial coalition that bypassed Mississippi's all-white Democratic party, followed state party rules, and sent its own delegates to the 1964 Democratic convention. To preserve party harmony, President Johnson refused to expel the "regular" Mississippi Democrats and offered instead to seat two MFDP delegates and enforce party rules for 1968. The MFDP walked out. Fannie Lou Hamer, a MFDP delegate, remembered, "We learned the hard way that even though we had all the law and all the righteousness on our side— that white man is not going to give up his power to us. We have to build our own power."

Lyndon Johnson and Martin Luther King Jr. agreed on the need for federal voting legislation when King visited the president in December 1964 after winning the Nobel Peace Prize. For King, power at the ballot box would help black Southerners take control of their own communities. For Johnson, voting reform would fulfill the promise of American democracy. It would also benefit the Democratic party by replacing with black voters the white Southerners who were drifting toward anti-integration Republicans.

The target for King and the SCLC was Dallas County, Alabama, where only 2 percent of eligible black voters were registered, compared with 70 percent of white voters. Peaceful demonstrations started in January 1965. By early February, jails in the county seat of Selma held 2,600 black people whose offense was marching to the courthouse to demand the vote. The campaign climaxed with a march from Selma to the state capital of Montgomery. SNCC leader John Lewis remembered, "I don't know what we expected. I think maybe we thought we'd be arrested and jailed, or maybe they wouldn't do anything to us. I had a little knapsack on my shoulder with an apple, a toothbrush, toothpaste, and two books in it: a history of America and a book by [Christian theologian] Thomas Merton."

On Sunday, March 7, five hundred marchers crossed the bridge over the Alabama River to meet a sea of state troopers. The troopers gave them two minutes to disperse and then attacked on foot and horseback "as if they were mowing a big field." The attack drove the demonstrators back in bloody confusion while television cameras rolled.

As violence continued, Johnson addressed a joint session of Congress to demand a voting rights law: "Our mission is at once the oldest and the most basic of this country: to right wrong, to do justice, to serve man." He ended with the refrain of the civil rights movement: "We shall overcome."

Johnson signed the **Voting Rights Act** on August 6, 1965. The law outlawed literacy tests and provided for federal voting registrars in states where registration or turnout in 1964 was less than 50 percent of eligible population. It applied initially in seven southern states. Black registration in these states jumped from 27 percent to 55 percent within the first year. In 1975, Congress extended coverage to Hispanic voters in the Southwest. By the end of 1992, Virginia had elected a black governor, and nearly

Freedom Summer Voter registration effort in rural Mississippi organized by black and white civil rights workers in 1964.

Voting Rights Act Legislation in 1965 that overturned a variety of practices by which states systematically denied voter registration to minorities.

every southern state had sent black representatives to Congress. Less obvious but just as revolutionary were the thousands of African Americans and Latinos who won local offices and the new moderation of white leaders who had to satisfy black voters.

WAR, PEACE, AND THE LANDSLIDE OF 1964

Johnson had maintained Kennedy's commitment to South Vietnam. On the advice of Kennedy hold-overs like Defense Secretary Robert McNamara, he stepped up commando raids and naval shelling of North Vietnam. On August 2, North Vietnamese torpedo boats attacked the U.S. destroyer *Maddox* in the Gulf of Tonkin while it was eavesdropping on North Vietnamese military signals. Two days later, the *Maddox* and the *C. Turner Joy* reported another torpedo attack (probably false sonar readings). Johnson ordered a bombing raid and asked Congress to authorize "all necessary measures" to protect American forces and stop further aggression. Congress passed the **Gulf of Tonkin Resolution** with only two nay votes.

Johnson's Republican opponent, Senator Barry Goldwater of Arizona, a former Air Force pilot, wanted aggressive confrontation with Communism. Campaign literature declared that "extremism in the defense of liberty is no vice," raising visions of vigilantes and mobs. Goldwater's campaign made Johnson look moderate. Johnson pledged not "to send American boys nine or ten thousand miles from home to do what Asian boys ought to be doing for themselves" while Goldwater proposed an all-out war.

Johnson's 61 percent of the popular vote was the greatest margin ever recorded in a presidential election. Democrats racked up two-to-one majorities in Congress. For the first time in decades, liberal Democrats could enact their domestic program without begging votes from conservative Southerners or Republicans, and Johnson could achieve his goal of a **Great Society** based on freedom and opportunity for all.

The result in 1965 was a series of measures that Johnson rushed through Congress before his political standing began to erode and Vietnam distracted national attention. The National Endowment for the Humanities, National Endowment for the Arts, and highway beautification were part of the Great Society for the middle class. The Wilderness Act (1964), an early success of the modern environmental movement, preserved 9.1 million acres from all development.

More central to Johnson's vision were efforts to increase opportunity for all. As he told a July 1965 news conference, "When I was young, poverty was so common that we didn't know it had a name. An education was something that you had to fight for. . . . It is now my opportunity to help every child get an education, to have every family get a decent home, and to help bring healing to the sick and dignity to the old." The Elementary and Secondary Education Act was the first general federal aid program for public schools, allocating $1.3 billion for textbooks and special education. The Higher Education Act funded low-interest student loans and university research facilities. The Medical Care Act created federally funded health insurance for the elderly (**Medicare**) and helped states offer medical care to the poor (**Medicaid**). The Appalachian Regional Development Act funded economic development in the depressed mountain counties of twelve states from Georgia to New York and proved a long-run success.

The United States came closer to winning the war on poverty than the war in Vietnam. New or expanded social insurance and income support programs, such as Medicare, Medicaid, Social Security, and food stamps, cut the proportion of poor people from 22 percent of the American population in 1960 to 13 percent in 1970. Infant mortality dropped by a third because of improved nutrition and better access to health care for mothers and children. Taken together, the political results of the 1964 landslide moved the United States far toward Lyndon Johnson's vision of an end to poverty and racial injustice.

WHERE TO LEARN MORE

Birmingham Civil Rights Institute Museum, Birmingham, Alabama
www.bcri.bham.al.us

WHERE TO LEARN MORE

Martin Luther King, Jr., National Historical Site, Atlanta, Georgia
http://www.nps.gov/malu/

Gulf of Tonkin Resolution   Request to Congress from President Lyndon Johnson in response to North Vietnamese torpedo boat attacks in which he sought authorization for "all necessary measures" to protect American forces and stop further aggression.

Great Society   Theme of Lyndon Johnson's administration, focusing on poverty, education, and civil rights.

Medicare   Basic medical insurance for the elderly, financed through the federal government; program created in 1965.

Medicaid   Supplementary medical insurance for the poor, financed through the federal government; program created in 1965.

CONCLUSION

From 1953 to 1964, consistent goals guided American foreign policy including vigilant anti-Communism and the confidence to intervene in trouble spots around the globe. At home, the Supreme Court's *Brown* decision introduced a decade-long civil rights revolution. However, many patterns of personal behavior and social relations remained unchanged. Women faced similar expectations from the early fifties to the early sixties. Churches showed more continuity than change.

In retrospect, it is remarkable how widely and deeply the Cold War shaped U.S. society. Fundamental social institutions, such as marriage and religion, got extra credit for their contributions to anti-Communism. The nation's long tradition of home-grown radicalism was virtually silent in the face of the Cold War consensus. Even economically meritorious programs like more money for science and better roads went down more easily if linked to national defense.

SUMMARY

A Decade of Affluence President Eisenhower presided over the prosperity of the 1950s. He claimed the "political middle" and accepted much of the New Deal but saw little need for further reform. Under Eisenhower, workers had more disposable income and credit-based consumerism expanded; suburbs and the "car culture" grew. Families were seen as part of the anti-Communist crusade. The "youth culture" emerged, but religious affiliation, the belief in prosperity, and social conformity characterized the era. Vast inequalities were concealed; many had missed out on "affluent America" and many women were unhappy in their "perfect" world.

Facing Off with the Soviet Union The actions of the United States and Soviet Union created a bipolar world: Each was a magnetic pole with countries aligning themselves or attempting to remain neutral. The Soviet launching of the *Sputnik* satellite concerned Americans who thought they were technologically superior; America's worldview of the right and need to intervene in areas that were possible Communist takeover targets resulted in an expansion of containment. "Brinksmanship" characterized this period in the Cold War.

John F. Kennedy and the Cold War John F. Kennedy won over Richard Nixon in a close election in 1960; television was a critical element. Kennedy's administration dealt with the Bay of Pigs invasion, a new Berlin crisis and the building of the Berlin Wall, growing American involvement in Vietnam, and the Cuban Missile crisis. Kennedy supported science as well as diplomacy; he committed the United States to placing an American astronaut on the moon and signed the Limited Test Ban Treaty which was a step toward later disarmament treaties.

Righteousness Like a Mighty Stream: The Struggle for Civil Rights The Supreme Court's *Brown* decision made the growing effort to secure equal legal treatment for African Americans a challenge to American society. The first phase of the civil rights struggle built from the Supreme Court's decision in 1954 to a vast gathering at the Lincoln Memorial in 1963. In between African Americans chipped away at racial segregation of schools, universities, and public facilities with boycotts, sit-ins, and lawsuits, forcing segregationists to choose between integration and violent defiance.

"Let Us Continue" After President Kennedy's assassination, Lyndon Johnson inherited a domestic agenda that was based on the knowledge that poverty was a widespread American problem. Johnson's passionate commitment to economic betterment accompanied a commitment to civil rights. War on Poverty and Great Society measures were passed before Johnson's enlargement of the Vietnam War eroded his political standing; the United States moved closer to addressing the effects of poverty and racial injustice than ever before.

REVIEW QUESTIONS

1. What were the sources of prosperity in the 1950s and 1960s? How did prosperity shape cities, family life, and religion?
2. What did American leaders think was at stake in Vietnam, Berlin, and Cuba?
3. Who initiated and led the African-American struggle for civil rights?
4. In what new directions did Lyndon Johnson take the United States?
5. Why was school integration the focus of such strong conflict?

KEY TERMS

Alliance for Progress   (p. 751)
Bay of Pigs   (p. 749)
Berlin Wall   (p. 749)
Brown v. *Board of Education of Topeka* (p. 752)
Civil Rights Act of 1964   (p. 755)
Congress of Racial Equality (CORE) (p. 754)
Federal Highway Act of 1956 (p. 740)
Freedom Summer   (p. 756)

Great Society   (p. 757)
Gulf of Tonkin Resolution   (p. 757)
Limited Test Ban Treaty   (p. 751)
Medicaid   (p. 757)
Medicare   (p. 757)
National Aeronautics and Space Administration (NASA)   (p. 745)
New Frontier   (p. 748)
Office of Economic Opportunity (OEO)   (p. 755)

Southeast Asia Treaty Organization (SEATO)   (p. 746)
Southern Christian Leadership Conference (SCLC)   (p. 753)
Southern Manifesto   (p. 752)
Student Nonviolent Coordinating Committee (SNCC)   (p. 753)
Viet Cong   (p. 750)
Voting Rights Act   (p. 756)
War on Poverty   (p. 755)

WHERE TO LEARN MORE

- **National Air and Space Museum, Washington, D.C.** Part of the Smithsonian Institution's complex of museums in Washington, the Air and Space Museum is the richest source for artifacts and discussion of the American space program. **www.nasm.edu**

- **Kansas Cosmosphere, Hutchinson, Kansas.** A rich collection of artifacts and equipment from the U.S. space program. **www.cosmo.org**

- **Sixth Floor Museum, Dallas, Texas.** Occupying the sixth floor of the former Texas School Book Depository building, exhibits examine the life, death, and legacy of John F. Kennedy. **www.jfk.org**

- **Birmingham Civil Rights Institute Museum, Birmingham, Alabama.** This museum and archive deal with the background of Southern racial segregation, civil rights activism, and the 1963 demonstrations in Birmingham. **www.bcri.bham.al.us**

- **Martin Luther King, Jr., National Historical Site, Atlanta, Georgia.** The birthplace and grave of Reverend King are the nucleus of a park set in the historic black neighborhood of Auburn. **http://www.nps.gov/malu/**

- **National Civil Rights Museum, Memphis, Tennessee.** Located in the Lorraine Motel, where Martin Luther King, Jr., was killed, the museum traces the participants, background, and effects of key events in the civil rights movement. **http://www.civilrightsmuseum.org**

- **National Afro-American Museum and Cultural Center, Wilberforce, Ohio.** The exhibit "From Victory to Freedom: Afro-American Life in the Fifties" looks at home, family, music, and religion. **www.ohiohistory.org/places/afroam/**

- **John F. Kennedy Library and Museum, Boston, Massachusetts.** Exhibits offer a sympathetic view of Kennedy's life and achievements. **www.cs.umb.edu/jfklibrary/**

 For additional study resources for this chapter, go to:
www.prenhall.com/goldfield/chapter28

We opened the hatch and Neil, with me as navigator, began backing out the tiny opening. It seemed like a small eternity before I heard Neil say, "That's one small step for man . . . one giant leap for mankind."

The shootings at Kent State University in May 1970 reflected the deep divisions in American society created by the Vietnam War, including those between antiwar college students and young people serving in the armed forces.

FARMWORKERS SAY

BOYCOTT ICEBERG LETTUCE

29

SHAKEN TO THE ROOTS
1965–1980

HOW DID the national consensus of the 1950s and early 1960s unravel?

WHAT CHALLENGES did American cities face in the late 1960s and 1970s?

WHY DID America's view of the war in Vietnam change in 1968?

WHAT WAS the legacy of Richard Nixon's presidency?

HOW WAS Jimmy Carter's idealism a frustration to his success as president?

1980

1965

Contact light! O.K., engine stop. . . . Houston, Tranquility Base here. The Eagle has landed! . . .

We opened the hatch and Neil, with me as navigator, began backing out of the tiny opening [in the Lunar Module Eagle]. It seemed like a small eternity before I heard Neil say, "That's one small step for man. . . . one giant leap for mankind." In less than fifteen minutes I was backing awkwardly out of the hatch and onto the surface to join Neil, who, in the tradition of all tourists, had his camera ready to photograph my arrival.

I took off jogging to test my maneuverability. The exercise gave me an odd sensation and looked even more odd when I later saw the films of it. With bulky suits on, we seemed to be moving in slow motion. . . . At one point, I re-marked that the surface was "Beautiful, beautiful. Magnificent desolation." I was struck by the contrast between the starkness of the shadows and the desert-like barrenness of the rest of the surface. It ranged from dusty gray to light tan and was unchanging except for one startling sight: our LM sitting there with its black, silver and bright yellow-orange thermal coating shining brightly in the otherwise colorless landscape.

During a pause in experiments, Neil suggested we proceed with the flag. . . . To our dismay the staff of the pole wouldn't go far enough into the lunar surface. . . . I dreaded the possibility of the American flag collapsing into the lunar dust in front of the television camera.

Edgar Cortright, ed., *Apollo Expeditions to the Moon* (Washington: NASA SP 350, 1975).

IMAGE KEY
for pages 760–761

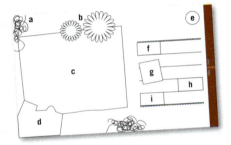

a. Damaged cassette tape evocative of the Watergate scandal.
b. Daisies represent the "Flower Power" mindset.
c. A weeping young woman kneels beside the body of a protester during the 1970 riots at Kent State University in Ohio.
d. Caeser Chávez.
e. Anti war peace button.
f. Crowds gather to hear Martin Luther King, Jr. speak.
g. Vietnamese refugees.
h. President Nixon announces he will resign effective noon Friday in this Thursday, August 8, 1974 file photo shown during a broadcast from the Oval Room of the White House.
i. Egyptian president Anwar el-Sadat, US President Jimmy Carter, and Israeli Prime Minister Menachem Begin share a three-way handshake after signing an Arab-Israeli peace treaty on March 26, 1979. The three leaders agreed on the terms of the treaty at Camp David in September 1978.

BUZZ ALDRIN AND NEIL ARMSTRONG, on July 20, 1969, complet-ed the longest journey that any person had yet taken. Landing the Apollo 11 lunar module on the moon climaxed a five-day trip across the quarter million miles sep-arating the earth from the moon. Six and a half hours after the landing, Arm-strong and Aldrin were the first humans to walk on the moon's surface.

The Apollo 11 expedition combined science and Cold War politics. The American flag waving on the lunar surface was a symbol of victory in one phase of the space race between the United States and Soviet Union. NASA had been working since 1961 to meet John F. Kennedy's goal of a manned trip to the moon before the end of the decade. After Apollo II, American astronauts made five more trips to the moon between 1969 and 1972, which helped to restore the na-tion's standing as the world's scientific and technological leader.

Despite Apollo's success, however, the United States was increasingly shak-en in the later 1960s and 1970s. The failure to win an easy victory in Vietnam erod-ed the nation's confidence and fueled bitter divisions. Most Americans had agreed about the goals of the Cold War, the benefits of economic growth, and the value of equal opportunity. Stalemate in Southeast Asia, political changes in third world countries, and an oil supply crisis in the 1970s challenged U.S. influence in the world. Frustrated with slow progress toward racial equality, many minority Amer-icans advocated separation rather than integration, helping to plunge the nation's cities into crisis, while other Americans began to draw back from some of the ob-jectives of racial integration.

Political scandals, summarized in three syllables as "Watergate," undercut faith in government. Fifteen years of turmoil forced a grudging recognition of limits to American military power, economic capacity, governmental prerogatives, and even the ideal of a single American dream.

THE END OF CONSENSUS

Pleiku is a town in Vietnam 240 miles north of Saigon (now Ho Chi Minh City). In 1965, Pleiku was the site of a South Vietnamese army headquarters and American military base. At 2 A.M. on February 7, Viet Cong attacked the U.S. base, killing eight Americans and wounding a hundred. The national security adviser, McGeorge Bundy, in Saigon on a fact-finding visit; Ambassador Maxwell Taylor; and General William Westmoreland, the commander of U.S. forces South Vietnam recommended a retaliatory air strike against North Vietnam. President Johnson concurred, and navy bombers roared off aircraft carriers. A month later, Johnson ordered a full-scale air offensive.

The attack at Pleiku triggered plans that were waiting to be put into effect since the Gulf of Tonkin resolution the previous summer. The official reason for the bombing was to pressure North Vietnam to negotiate an end to the war. As the South Vietnamese government lost control of the countryside, air strikes on North Vietnam looked like an easy way to redress the balance. In the back of President Johnson's mind were the need to prove his toughness and the mistaken assumption that China was aggressively backing North Vietnam.

The air strikes pushed the United States over the line from propping up the South Vietnamese government to leading the war effort. A president who desperately wanted a way out of Southeast Asia kept adding American forces. The war in Vietnam would distract the United States from the goals of the Great Society, drive Johnson from office, set back progress toward global stability, and divide the American people.

DEEPER INTO VIETNAM

Advisers persuaded Lyndon Johnson that controlled military escalation—a middle course between withdrawal and all-out war—could secure Vietnam (see Map 29–1). They failed to understand the extent of popular opposition to the official government in Saigon and the willingness of North Vietnam to sacrifice to achieve national unity.

The air war required ground troops to protect bases in South Vietnam. Marines landed on March 8. More bombs, a pause, an offer of massive U.S. aid—nothing brought North Vietnam to the negotiating table. Johnson dribbled in new forces and expanded their mission from base security to combat. On July 28, he finally gave General William Westmoreland, the commander of U.S. forces in Vietnam, doubled draft calls and an increase in U.S. combat troops from 75,000 to 275,000 by 1966.

Secretary of Defense Robert McNamara was clear about the change: "We have relied on South Vietnam to carry the brunt. Now we would be responsible for a satisfactory military outcome." American forces in South Vietnam reached their maximum of 543,000 in August 1969. In all, more than 2 million Americans served in Vietnam.

The U.S. strategy on the ground was **search and destroy**. As conceived by Westmoreland, it used sophisticated surveillance and heavily armed patrols to locate enemy detachments, which could then be destroyed by air strikes, artillery, and reinforcements carried in by helicopter.

HOW DID the national consensus of the 1950s and early 1960s unravel?

WHERE TO LEARN MORE

Vietnam Veterans Memorial, Washington, D.C.
www.nps.gov/vive/

search and destroy U.S. military tactic in South Vietnam, using small detachments to locate enemy units and then massive air, artillery, and ground forces to destroy them.

MAP 29–1

The War in Vietnam   The United States attacked North Vietnam with air strikes but confined large-scale ground operations to South Vietnam and Cambodia. In South Vietnam, U.S. forces faced both North Vietnamese army units and Viet Cong rebels, all of whom received supplies by way of the so-called Ho Chi Minh Trail, named for the leader of North Vietnam. The coordinated attacks on cities and towns throughout South Vietnam during the Tet Offensive in 1968 surprised the United States.

WHAT WERE the shortcomings of American military strategy in Vietnam?

CHRONOLOGY

1962 Rachel Carson publishers *Silent Spring*
Port Huron Statement launches Students for a Democratic Society.

1965 Congress approves Wilderness Act.
Malcolm X is assassinated. Residents of Watts neighborhood in Los Angeles riot.

1967 African Americans riot in Detroit and Newark.

1968 Viet Cong launches Tet Offensive.
James Earl Ray kills Martin Luther King Jr.
Lyndon Johnson declines to run for reelection.
SDS disrupts Columbia University.
Sirhan Sirhan kills Robert Kennedy.
Peace talks start between the United States and North Vietnam.
Police riot against antiwar protesters during the Democratic National Convention in Chicago.
Richard Nixon is elected president.

1969 Neil Armstrong and Buzz Aldrin walk on the moon.

1970 United States invades Cambodia.

National Guard units kill students at Kent State and Jackson State Universities.

Earth Day is celebrated.

Environmental Protection Agency is created.

1971 *New York Times* publishes the secret "Pentagon Papers."
President Nixon freezes wages and prices.
"Plumbers" unit is established in the White House.

1972 Nixon visits China.
United States and Soviet Union adopt SALT I.

Operatives for Nixon's reelection campaign break into Democratic headquarters in the Watergate complex in Washington, D.C.

1973 Paris accords end direct U.S. involvement in South Vietnamese war.
United States moves to all-volunteer armed forces.
Watergate burglars are convicted.
Senate Watergate hearings reveal the existence of taped White House conversations.
Spiro Agnew resigns as vice president, is replaced by Gerald Ford.
Arab states impose an oil embargo after the third Arab-Israeli War.

1974 Nixon resigns as president, is succeeded by Gerald Ford.

1975 Communists triumph in South Vietnam.
United States, USSR, and European nations sign the Helsinki Accords.

1976 Jimmy Carter defeats Gerald Ford for the presidency.

1978 Carter brings the leaders of Egypt and Israel to Camp David for peace talks.

1979 SALT II agreement is signed but not ratified.
OPEC raises oil prices.
Three Mile Island nuclear plant comes close to disaster.
Iranian militants take U.S. embassy hostages.

1980 Iranian hostage rescue fails.
Soviet troops enter Afghanistan.
Ronald Reagan defeats Jimmy Carter for the presidency.

However, most opponents were South Vietnamese guerrillas forcing the United States to make repeated sweeps through farms and villages. The enemy were difficult for Americans to recognize among farmers and workers, making South Vietnamese society itself the target. Massive American firepower killed thousands of Vietnamese and made millions refugees.

Pilots dropped tons of bombs on the "Ho Chi Minh Trail," a network of supply routes from North Vietnam to South Vietnam through the mountains of neighboring Laos. Despite the bombing, thousands of workers converted rough paths into roads that were repaired as soon as they were damaged. Air assault on North Vietnam itself remained "diplomatic," intended to force North Vietnam to stop intervening in the South Vietnamese civil war. Since Ho Chi Minh considered North and South to be one country, the American goal was unacceptable. Attacking North Vietnam's poorly developed economy, the United States soon ran out of targets.

VOICES OF DISSENT

At home, protest against the war quickly mounted. In the 1950s, McCarthyism had intimidated dissenters on the left. Now antiwar activists and college students challenged the "Cold Warriors."

"Realists," such as Senator William Fulbright, the chairman of the Senate Foreign Relations Committee, argued that the war was a dangerous distraction from the country's vital interests in regions such as Europe, and a waste of American lives and resources. More radical critics saw the roots of the war in basic flaws in the American character and system. Some called it an example of economic imperialism that revealed the power of multinational corporations to control American foreign policy. A generation later, some of the same criticisms would reappear in arguments against the North American Free Trade Agreement (NAFTA) and the World Trade Organization.

In 1966 and 1967, antiwar activity accelerated into direct confrontation. Protesters blocked munitions trains. Peace organizations sent representatives to North Vietnam to explore possible solutions. Religious groups condemned the war.

Much of the anger was directed against the military draft administration, the **Selective Service System**. Draft deferral criteria favored the middle class and helped make Vietnam a working-class conflict. Full-time college enrollment was grounds for a deferment; so was the right diagnosis from the right doctor. As a result, enlistees and draftees tended to be small-town or innercity working-class youths. They were also young. In World War II, the average GI had been in his mid-twenties. The typical soldier in Vietnam was 19 or 20. Women who served as military nurses tended to come from the same background. The resentment the draft created eroded the alliance between working-class Americans and the Democratic party.

Military service also deepened the racial gap. In 1965 African Americans made up 11 percent of the nation's population but were 24 percent of the soldiers killed in Vietnam. This disparity forced the Defense Department to revise its combat assignments. Martin Luther King Jr. joined the protest in 1967. King called the war a moral disaster and a new form of colonialism whose costs weighed most heavily on the poor.

As protests mounted, draft resistance provided a direct avenue to attack the war. Young men burned their draft cards, fled to Canada, or applied for conscientious objector status on moral or religious grounds. A few were jailed for refusing to cooperate in any way with the Selective Service System. And a handful of activists invaded draft-board offices and tried to destroy files. By 1969, over half the men drafted in California were refusing to show up, and thousands were prosecuted for draft evasion.

The popular media portrayed the conflicting visions of the war. While antiwar songs climbed the charts, an aging John Wayne portrayed a heroic American soldier saving South Vietnam in the movie *The Green Berets*, and country singer Merle Travis spoke for many small-town Americans who supported the war in "Okie from Muskogee" (where they didn't burn draft cards).

NEW LEFT AND COMMUNITY ACTIVISM

The antiwar movement was part of a growing grass-roots activism that took much of its tone from the university-based **Students for a Democratic Society (SDS)**. The group was important for its ideas, not its size. Its Port Huron Statement, adopted in 1962, called for grass-roots action and "participatory democracy." SDS tried to harness youthful disillusionment about consumerism, racism, and imperialism. It thought of itself as a "New Left" that was free from the doctrinal squabbles that hampered the old left of the 1930s and 1940s.

Many of the original SDS leaders were also participants in the civil-rights movement. The same was true of Mario Savio, founder of the **Free Speech Movement (FSM)** at the University of California at Berkeley in 1964. Savio hoped to build a

Selective Service System   Federal agency that coordinated military conscription before and during the Vietnam War.

Students for a Democratic Society (SDS)   The leading student organization of the New Left of the early and mid-1960s.

Free Speech Movement (FSM) Student movement at the University of California, Berkeley, formed in 1964 to protest limitations on political activities on campus.

multi-issue "community of protest" around the idea of "a free university in a free society." FSM protests climaxed with a December sit-in that led to 773 arrests and stirred protest on other campuses.

What SDS wanted to do with its grass-roots organizing resembled the federal community-action programs associated with the war on poverty. The **Model Cities Program** (1966) invited residents of poor neighborhoods to write their own plans for using federal funds to improve local housing, education, health services, and job opportunities. Model Cities assemblies challenged the racial bias in programs like urban renewal and helped train community leaders.

The lessons of grass-roots reform strengthened democracy from the bottom up. Activists staffed food cooperatives, free clinics, women's health groups, and drug counseling centers. Community-based organization was a key element in self-help efforts by African Americans, Asian Americans, and Latinos. Neighborhood associations and community-development corporations that provided affordable housing and jobs extended the "backyard revolution" into the 1980s and beyond. Social conservatives, such as antiabortionists, used the same techniques on behalf of their own agendas.

THE FEMINIST CRITIQUE

A revived feminism was another result of the ferment of the 1960s. Important steps in this revival included the Presidential Commission on the Status of Women in 1961; the addition of gender as one of the categories protected by the Civil Rights Act of 1964 (see Chapter 28); and creation of the National Organization for Women (NOW) in 1966.

Mainstream feminism targeted unequal opportunity in the job market. College-educated baby boomers encountered "glass ceilings" and job discrimination, in which companies hired less qualified men who "needed the job" rather than more qualified women who supposedly did not. Throughout the mid-1960s and 1970s, activists battled to open job categories to women, who proved that they could indeed use tools or pick stocks on Wall Street. They also battled for equal pay for everyone with equal qualifications and responsibilities.

Changes in sexual behavior paralleled efforts to equalize treatment in the workplace. More reliable methods of contraception, especially birth-control pills introduced in the early 1960s, gave women greater control over childbearing. A new sexual revolution eroded the double standard that expected chastity of women but tolerated promiscuity among men. One consequence was a singles culture that accepted sexual activity between unmarried men and women.

Women's liberation took off as a social and political movement in 1970 and 1971 as influential books probed the roots of inequality between men's and women's opportunities. Women shared their stories and ideas in small "consciousness-raising" sessions. Within a few years, millions of women had recognized events and patterns in their lives as discrimination based on gender. The feminist movement, and specific policy measures related to it, put equal rights

Antiwar protests were simultaneously symbolic and disruptive. Some activists dumped jars of animal blood over draft-board records. Others tried to block munitions trains. In October 1967, a hundred thousand people marched on the Pentagon and surrounded it with the light of burning draft cards. Some in front stuck flowers in the rifle barrels of the soldiers ringing the building; others kicked and spat. The troops and police cleared the grounds with tear gas and clubs.

Corbis–Bettman

29–4
National Organization for Women, Statement of Purpose (1966)

Model Cities Program Effort to target federal funds to upgrade public services and economic opportunity in specifically defined urban neighborhoods between 1966 and 1974.

A hippie gestures the peace sign while standing in a meadow.

Getty Images, Inc.–Taxi

Counterculture   Various alternatives to mainstream values and behaviors that became popular in the 1960s, including experimentation with psychedelic drugs, communal living, a return to the land, Asian religions, and experimental art.

and the fight against sexism (a word no one knew before 1965) on the national agenda and changed how Americans thought about the relationships between men and women. Feminists highlighted rape as a crime of violence and called attention to the burdens the legal system placed on rape victims. In the 1980s and 1990s, they also challenged sexual harassment in the workplace, gradually refining the boundaries between acceptable and unacceptable behavior.

YOUTH CULTURE AND COUNTERCULTURE

Millions of young people in the second half of the 1960s expressed their alienation from American society by sampling drugs or chasing the rainbow of a youth culture. Some just smoked marijuana, grew long hair, and listened to psychedelic rock. Others plunged into ways of life that scorned their middle-class backgrounds. The middle aged and middle class ignored the differences and dubbed the rebellious young "hippies." A high point of the youth culture was the 1969 Woodstock rock festival in New York State, a weekend of "sex, drugs, and rock-and-roll" for 400,000 young people.

But within the youth culture was a smaller and more intense **counterculture** that added Eastern religion, social radicalism, and evangelistic belief in the drug LSD. The Harvard professor Timothy Leary and the writer Aldous Huxley claimed that hallucinogenic or psychedelic drugs, such as mescaline and LSD, would swing open the "doors of perception." Rock lyrics began to reflect the drug culture, and young people talked about Leary's advice to "tune in, turn on, and drop out." The mecca of the dropouts was San Francisco's Haight-Ashbury district, but hippie neighborhoods sprang up around university campuses across the country.

The cultural rebels of the late 1950s and early 1960s had been trying to combine personal freedom with new social arrangements. Many hippies were more interested in drugs than with politics or poetry. Serious exploration of societal alternatives was left for the minority who devoted themselves to the political work of the New Left, communal living, women's liberation, and other movements.

SOUNDS OF CHANGE

The youth culture was shaped by films and philosophers, by pot and poets, but above all by music. Many changes in American society are mirrored in the abrupt shift from the complacent rock-and-roll of the early 1960s to the more provocative albums of mid-decade: Bob Dylan's *Highway 61 Revisited* (1965), the Beatles *Rubber Soul* (1965) and *Sergeant Pepper's Lonely Hearts Club Band* (1967), the Jefferson Airplane's *Surrealistic Pillow* (1967). Musicians were increasingly self-conscious of themselves as artists and social critics.

At the start of the decade, the African-American roots of rock-and-roll were unmistakable, but there was no social agenda. Elvis Presley and the Everly Brothers kept the messages personal. Music that criticized American society initially found a much smaller audience through the folk-music revival. Folk singers, such as Pete Seeger and Joan Baez, drew on black music, white country music, and old labor-organizing songs to keep alive dissenting voices.

Then, in an artistic revolution, the doors opened to a new kind of rock music. The Beatles' immense popularity opened the way for such hard-edged British bands as the Rolling Stones and The Who to introduce social criticism and class consciousness into rock lyrics. San Francisco's new psychedelic-rock scene included performers such as the Jefferson Airplane, the Grateful Dead, Buffalo Springfield and Janis Joplin.

Bob Dylan transformed the music scene. His music was musically exciting and socially critical in a way that expressed much of the discontent of American young people. Dylan paved the way for later singers like Bruce Springsteen and Kurt Cobain.

The transformation of rock in the mid-1960s invited far more explicit treatment of sex and illegal drugs than was previously accepted in pop music. Jim Morrison and The Doors, Lou Reed and the Velvet Underground, and Jimi Hendrix exploded onto the scene in 1967. Their driving rhythms and sexually aggressive stage personalities blended the tensions of big cities with influences from white rock and roll and black rhythm and blues. By 1972, both Morrison and Hendrix were dead of hard living and drug abuse. Meanwhile, *Rolling Stone* magazine had published its first issue in November 1967, giving the new sounds a forum for serious analysis.

COMMUNES AND CULTS

Thousands of Americans in the late 1960s and 1970s formed "intentional communities" or "communes." Their members usually tried to combine individual freedom and spontaneity with cooperative living. Rural communes usually located on marginal land too poor to support commercial farming; members pored over *The Whole Earth Catalog* (1968) to figure out how to live on the land. Members of urban communes occupied large old houses and tried to pursue experiments in socialism, environmentalism, or feminism.

Communes were artificial families, financed by inheritances, food stamps, and handicraft sales, and they suffered from the same inequality between men and women that was fueling the feminist revolt. Like natural families, they were emotional hothouses; most collapsed because their members had incompatible goals.

Far more organized were exotic religious communities. Following an American tradition, they have offered tightly knit group membership and absolute answers to basic questions of human life. One of the most successful has been the Holy Spirit Association for the Unification of World Christianity (Unification Church), which Sun Myung Moon brought from Korea to the United States in 1973. Converts ("Moonies") have never numbered more than a few tens of thousands, but Moon amassed a huge fortune and dabbled in conservative politics.

Americans usually hear about cults only if they clash with authorities or end in disaster. Most tragic was the case of Jim Jones, who founded the People's Temple in California on a program of social justice but became dictatorial and abusive. He moved nearly a thousand followers to Guyana in South America and violently resisted efforts to penetrate his walls of secrecy. An investigation of abuses within the colony led to the murder of Congressman Leo Ryan and mass suicide by nine hundred of Jones's followers, who drank cyanide-laced punch on November 18, 1978.

At the Newport (Rhode Island) Jazz Festival in 1963, Joan Baez and Bob Dylan performed as folksingers who worked in the tradition of protest songs. Two years later in Newport, Dylan shocked the popular music world by replacing his acoustic instrument with an amplified guitar and backup and jump-starting a fruitful blending of folk, country, and rock music into radical new sounds.

AP/Wide World Photos

CITIES UNDER STRESS

In the confident years after World War II, big cities had an upbeat image. The typical movie with a New York setting opened with a shot of the towering Manhattan skyline and plunged into the bustling business or theater districts. By the 1970s, however, slums and squalid back streets dominated popular imagery.

The message in films and and on television was that cities had become places of random and frequent violence.

WHAT CHALLENGES
did American cities face in the late 1960s and 1970s?

DIAGNOSING AN URBAN CRISIS

Central cities had a special burden in caring for the domestic poor. Baltimore had 27 percent of the Maryland population in 1970 but 66 percent of the state's welfare recipients. Boston had 14 percent of the Massachusetts population but 32 percent of the welfare clients. Impoverished, and often fragmented, families needed schools to serve as social-work agencies as well as educational institutions. Poor people with no other access to health care treated city hospital emergency rooms as the family doctor.

Many urban problems were associated with the "second ghettos" created by the migration of 2.5 million African Americans from Southern farms to Northern and Western cities in the 1950s and 1960s. At the start of World War II, black Americans had been much more rural than white Americans. By 1970, they were more urban. One-third of all African Americans lived in the twelve largest cities, crowding into ghetto neighborhoods.

Postwar black migrants found systems of race relations that limited their access to decent housing, to the best schools, and to many unionized jobs. Many black families also had to face industrial layoffs and plant closures in the 1970s and 1980s. Already unneeded in the South because of the mechanization of agriculture, the migrants found themselves equally unwanted in the industrial North, caught in decaying neighborhoods and victimized by crime.

Because ghettos grew block by block, middle-class black families had to pioneer as intruders into white neighborhoods and then see ghetto problems crowd in behind them. Their children faced the seductions of the street, which became increasingly violent with the spread of handguns and illegal drugs.

Central cities faced additional financial problems unrelated to poverty and race. Much of their infrastructure was 50 to 100 years old by the 1960s and 1970s, and it was wearing out. This decay of urban utility and transportation systems was a by-product of market forces and public policy. Private developers often borrowed money saved through Northeastern bank accounts, insurance policies, and pension funds to finance new construction in the suburbs. The defense budget pumped tax dollars from the old industrial cities into the South and West.

High local taxes in older cities was one result, for the American system of local government demands that cities and the poor help themselves. By the early 1970s, the average resident of a central city paid roughly twice the state and local taxes per $1,000 of income as the average suburbanite. As Mayor Moon Laundreau of New Orleans commented, "We've taxed everything that moves and everything that stands still; and if anything moves again, we tax that, too."

RACIAL RIOTING

African Americans and Hispanics who rioted in city streets in the mid-1960s were fed up with lack of job opportunities, and with substandard housing and crime in their neighborhoods. Prominent black writers, such as James Baldwin in *The Fire Next Time* (1963), had warned of mounting anger. Suddenly the fires were real. Before they subsided, the riots scarred most big cities and killed two hundred people, most of them African Americans.

The explosion of the Watts neighborhood in Los Angeles fixed the danger of racial unrest in the public mind. Trouble started on August 11, 1965, when a white highway-patrol officer arrested a young African American for drunken driving. Loud complaints drew a crowd, and the arrival of Los Angeles police turned the bystanders into an angry mob that attacked passing cars. Rioting, looting, and arson spread through Watts until the National Guard occupied the neighborhood on August 14 and 15.

28–2
Stokely Carmichael and Charles Hamilton, from Black Power (1968)

QUICK REVIEW

Urban Problems

◆ Minorities and the poor were concentrated in urban centers.

◆ Postwar black migrants to the north found themselves with limited access to better houses, schools, and jobs.

◆ Cities faced decaying infrastructure and high taxes.

The outburst frightened white Americans. In most previous race riots, whites had used violence to keep blacks "in their place." In Watts, blacks were the instigators. The primary targets were the police and ghetto businesses that had reputations for exploiting their customers. The National Advisory Commission on Civil Disorders concluded in 1968 that most property damage was the "result of deliberate attacks on white-owned businesses characterized in the Negro community as unfair or disrespectful." In short, the riots were protests about the problems of ghetto life.

After Watts, Americans expected "long hot summers" and got them. Scores of cities suffered riots in 1966, including one by Puerto Ricans in Chicago that protested the same problems blacks faced. In 1967, the worst violence was in Newark, New Jersey, and in Detroit, where forty-three deaths and blocks of blazing buildings stunned television viewers.

Few politicians wanted to admit that African Americans and Hispanics had serious grievances. Their impulse was to blame riffraff and outside agitators—"lawbreakers and mad dogs," to quote California Governor Ronald Reagan. This theory was wrong. Almost all participants were younger neighborhood residents who were representative of the African-American population. Their violence came from the frustration of rising expectations. Despite the political gains of the civil rights movement, unemployment remained high, and the police treated all black people as potential criminals. The urban riots were political actions to force the problems of African Americans onto the national agenda.

MINORITY SEPARATISM

Minority separatism tapped the same anger. The phrase **"Black Power"** challenged the central goal of the civil rights movement, which sought full participation in American life. The term came from frustrated SNCC leader Stokely Carmichael in 1966: "We've been saying freedom for six years—and we ain't got nothing. What we're going to start saying now is 'Black Power'!"

Black power translated many ways—control of one's own community through the voting machine, celebration of the African-American heritage, creation of a parallel society that shunned white institutions. At the personal level, it was a synonym for black pride.

Black Power also meant increased interest in the **Nation of Islam**, or Black Muslims, who combined a version of Islam with radical separatism. It was strongest in Northern cities, where it offered an alternative to the life of the ghetto streets.

In the early 1960s, Malcolm X emerged as a leading Black Muslim. Growing up as Malcolm Little, he was a streetwise criminal until he converted to the Nation of Islam in prison. After his release, Malcolm preached that blacks should stop letting whites set the terms by which they judged their appearance, communities, and accomplishments. He emphasized the African cultural heritage and economic self-help and proclaimed himself an extremist for black rights. Rivals within the movement assassinated him in February 1965, but his ideas lived on in *The Autobiography of Malcolm X.*

The **Black Panthers** pursued similar goals. Bobby Seale and Huey Newton saw African-American ghettos as internal colonies in need of self-determination. They created the Panthers in 1966 and recruited Eldridge Cleaver as the group's chief publicist.

The Panthers shadowed police patrols to prevent mistreatment of African Americans and carried weapons into the California State Legislature in May 1967 to protest gun control. They also promoted community-based self-help efforts, and ran political candidates. Unlike the rioters in Watts, the Panthers

Black Power Philosophy emerging after 1965 that real economic and political gains for African Americans could come only through self-help, self-determination, and organizing for direct political influence.

Nation of Islam Religious movement among black Americans that emphasizes self-sufficiency, self-help, and separation from white society.

Black Panthers Political and social movement among black Americans, founded in Oakland, California, in 1966 and emphasizing black economic and political power.

Some members of the Black Panther party raised funds to pay for the legal fees of those arrested and charged with various offenses, such as Bobby Seale and Ericka Huggins. The Panthers advocated a radical economic, social, and educational agenda that made the group the target of a determined campaign of suppression by the police and the FBI.

Magnum Photos Inc.

had a political program, if not the ability to carry it through. The movement was shaken when Newton was convicted of manslaughter for killing a police officer, Cleaver fled to Algeria, and a police raid killed Chicago Panther leader Fred Hampton.

Latinos in the Southwest developed a their own "Brown Power" movement in the late 1960s, but the best-known Hispanic activism combined social protest with the crusading spirit of earlier labor union organizing campaigns. César Chávez organized the multiracial United Farm Workers (UFW) among Mexican-American agricultural workers in California in 1965. UFW demands included better wages and safer working conditions. Because farm workers were not covered by the National Labor Relations Act of 1935, the issue was whether farm owners would recognize the union as a bargaining agent and sign a contract. Chávez supplemented work stoppages with national boycotts against table grapes, lettuce, and brands of wine, making *la huelga* ("the strike") into *la causa* for urban liberals. Although the UFW had only limited success, Chávez's toughness and self-sacrifice gave both Chicanos and the country a new hero.

Latino political activism had strong appeal for young people. Many rejected assimilation and began to talk about *la raza* ("the people"), whose language and heritage descended from centuries of Mexican history. "Chicano" itself was a slang term with insulting overtones that was now adopted as a badge of pride and cultural identity.

Native Americans also fought both for equal access to American society and to preserve cultural traditions through tribal institutions. Some Native American used media-oriented protest, such as seizing the abandoned Alcatraz Island (1969–1971) to assist "Red Power." Indians in Minneapolis created the **American Indian Movement (AIM)** in 1968 to increase economic opportunity, stop police mistreatment and to assert their distinctiveness within American society.

Black Power, Brown Power, and Red Power were all efforts by minorities to define themselves through their own heritage, not simply by looking in the mirror of white society. They thus questioned the American assumption that everyone wanted to be part of the same homogeneous society.

SUBURBAN INDEPENDENCE: THE OUTER CITY

The 1970 census found more people living in the suburban counties of metropolitan areas (37 percent) than in central cities (31 percent) or in small towns and rural areas (31 percent). By the late 1960s, these suburbs were becoming "outer cities," whose inhabitants had little need for the old central city and felt no personal connection to, or responsibility for, old city neighborhoods. For them, suburban malls and shopping strips were the new American Main Street and suburban communities the new Middle America.

Suburbs captured most new jobs, leaving the urban poor with fewer opportunities for employment. In the fifteen largest metropolitan areas, the number of central city jobs fell by 800,000 in the 1960s, while the number of suburban jobs rose by 3.2 million. The shift from rail to air for business travel accentuated suburban job growth. Sales representatives and executives could arrive at airports

American Indian Movement (AIM)
Group of Native-American political activists who used confrontations with the federal government to publicize their case for Indian rights.

on the edge of town, and transact business without ever going downtown. Around many cities, suburban retailing, employment, and services fused into so-called "edge cities." Suburban rings also gained a growing share of public facilities including colleges and major league sports franchises.

Suburban political power grew along with economic clout. In 1962, the Supreme Court in the case of *Baker v. Carr* overturned laws that treated counties or other political subdivisions as the units to be represented in state legislatures. The Court said that legislative seats should be apportioned on the basis of population. This principle of "one person, one vote" broke the stranglehold of rural counties on state governments, but the big beneficiaries were fast-growing suburbs. By 1975, suburbanites held the largest block of seats in the House of Representatives—131 suburban districts, 130 rural, 102 central city, and 72 mixed.

School integration controversies in the 1970s reinforced a tendency for suburbanites to separate themselves from city problems. In *Swann v. Charlotte-Mecklenburg Board of Education* (1971), the U.S. Supreme Court held that crosstown busing was an acceptable solution to the *de facto* segregation that resulted from residential patterns within a single school district. When school officials around the country failed to achieve racial balance, federal judges ordered their own busing plans. Some white people resented the practice and for many Americans, the image of busing for racial integration was fixed in 1975, when white citizens in Boston resisted busing black students to largely white high schools. The goal of equal opportunity clashed with equally strong values of neighborhood, community, and ethnic solidarity.

Because the Supreme Court also ruled that busing programs normally stopped at school-district boundaries, suburbs with independent districts escaped school integration. One result was to make busing self-defeating, for it caused white families to move out of the integrating school district or place their children in private academies. Busing also caused suburbanites to defend their political independence fiercely. In Denver, for example, a by-product of court-ordered busing included incorporation or expansion of several large suburbs and a state constitutional amendment that blocked further expansion of the city boundaries (and thus of the Denver school district).

Baker v. Carr U.S. Supreme Court decision in 1962 that allowed federal courts to review the appointment of state legislative districts and established the principle that such districts should have roughly equal populations ("one person, one vote").

Swann v. Charlotte-Mecklenburg Board of Education U.S. Supreme Court decision in 1971 that upheld cross-city busing to achieve the racial integration of public schools.

THE YEAR OF THE GUN, 1968

In 1968, mainstream Americans turned against the war in Vietnam, student protest and youth counter-culture turned ugly, and political consensus shattered.

WHY DID America's view of the war in Vietnam change in 1968?

THE TET OFFENSIVE

The longer the Vietnam War continued and the less interest that China or the Soviet Union showed in it, the less valid the conflict seemed to the American people. It looked more and more like a war for pride, not national security.

At the end of 1967, U.S. officials were overconfidently predicting victory. They also fell for a North Vietnamese feint by committing U.S. forces to the defense of Khe Sanh, a strongpoint near the North-South border. The defense was a tactical success for the United States but thinned its forces elsewhere in South Vietnam. Then, at the beginning of Tet, the Vietnamese New Year on January 30, 1968, the Viet Cong attacked cities across South Vietnam. In the capital, Saigon, they even hit the U.S. embassy. U.S. and South Vietnamese troops repulsed the attacks, but the offensive was a psychological blow that convinced the American public that the war was quicksand.

Images from Vietnam went direct to the evening television news; it was a "living room war." A handful of images stayed in people's memories—a Buddhist monk burning himself to death in protest; a child with flesh peeled off by napalm; a South Vietnamese official executing a captive on the streets of Saigon.

In the wake of the Tet crisis, General Westmoreland's request for 200,000 more troops forced a political and military reevaluation. Clark Clifford, the new secretary of defense, as well as twenty "wise men"—the big names of the Cold War—told the president that the war was unwinnable. The best option was disengagement.

LBJ's Exit

Minnesota's liberal Senator Eugene McCarthy had decided to challenge Johnson in the presidential primaries. Because he controlled the party organizations in two-thirds of the states, Johnson ignored the first primary in New Hampshire. Enthusiastic college students staffed McCarthy's campaign. McCarthy won a startling 42 percent of the popular vote and twenty of twenty-four delegates in the March 16 election. The vote proved that the political middle ground would no longer hold.

By showing Johnson's vulnerability, New Hampshire also drew Robert Kennedy into the race. Younger brother of the former president, Kennedy inspired both fervent loyalty and strong distaste. In the 1950s, he had worked for Senator Joe McCarthy and had been a reluctant supporter of civil rights during his brother's administration. More than other mainstream politicians of the 1960s, however, he touched the hearts of Hispanic and African-American voters as well as the white working class.

Facing political challenges and an unraveling war, on March 31, 1968, Johnson announced a halt to most bombing of North Vietnam, opening the door for negotiations. He then astounded the country by withdrawing from the presidential race. As he told an aide, the war made him feel like a hitchhiker in a hailstorm: "I can't run, I can't hide, and I can't make it stop." Hoping to save his domestic program, he served out his term with few friends and little credit for his accomplishments.

Red Spring

In the months that followed the Tet crisis, grass-roots rebellion shook the Soviet grip on eastern Europe. University students in Poland protested the stifling of political discussion. Alexander Dubèek, the new leader of the Czech Communist party, brought together students and the middle class around reforms that caused people to talk about "Prague Spring"—a blossoming of democracy inside the iron curtain. In August, the Soviets sent in their tanks to crush the reforms and bring Czechoslovakia back into line.

Students protested across Europe. In Paris, student demonstrations against the Vietnam War turned into attacks on the university system and the French government. Students fought police in the Paris streets in the first days of May. Radical industrial workers called a general strike. The government nearly toppled.

At Columbia University in New York, African-American students and its SDS chapter had several grievances. One was the university's cooperation with the Pentagon-funded Institute for Defense Analysis. Another was its plan to build a gymnasium on park land that might better serve the residents of Harlem. Some students

---

WHERE TO LEARN MORE

Lyndon B. Johnson National Historic Park, Johnson City, Texas
www.nps.gov/lypo/

QUICK REVIEW

Student Protests in the Spring of 1968

- University students and members of the middle-class in Poland and Czechoslovakia sought reforms.
- Students across Europe protested the war in Vietnam.
- Students at Columbia University occupied five buildings.

wanted changes in university policy, others a confrontation that would recruit new radicals. They occupied five university buildings, including the library and the president's office, for a week in April until police evicted them. The "battle of Morningside Heights" (the location of Columbia) gave Americans a glimpse of the gap that divided radicalized students from national institutions.

VIOLENCE AND POLITICS

On April 4, 1968, ex-convict James Earl Ray shot and killed Martin Luther King Jr. as he stood on the balcony of a Memphis motel. King's death triggered a climactic round of violence in black ghettos. Fires devastated the West Side of Chicago and downtown Washington, D.C. The army guarded the steps of the Capitol, ready to protect Congress from its fellow citizens.

The shock of King's death was still fresh when another political assassination stunned the nation. On June 5, Robert Kennedy won California's primary election. He was still behind Vice President Hubert Humphrey in the delegate count but coming on strong. As Kennedy walked out of the ballroom at his headquarters in the Ambassador Hotel in Los Angeles, a Jordanian immigrant named Sirhan Sirhan put a bullet in his brain.

Kennedy's death ensured the Democratic nomination for Humphrey, a liberal who had loyally supported Johnson's war policy. After his nomination, Humphrey faced Republican Richard Nixon and Independent George Wallace. Nixon positioned himself as the candidate of the political middle and claimed he had a secret plan for winning the war. Wallace appealed to white Southerners and working-class Northerners who feared black militancy and hated "the ivory-tower folks with pointed heads."

Both got great help from the Democratic Convention, held in Chicago on August 26–29. While Democrats feuded among themselves, Chicago Mayor Richard Daley and his police department monitored antiwar protesters. Leaders of the National Mobilization Committee to End the War in Vietnam were experienced peace activists—people who had long fought against nuclear weapons in the 1950s and the Vietnam War. They wanted to embarrass the Johnson-Humphrey administration by marching to the convention hall on nomination night. Mixed in were the **Yippies**. The term supposedly stood for Youth International Party. The Yippies planned to attract young people to Chicago with a promise of street theater, media events, and confrontation that would puncture the pretensions of the power structure.

On August 28, the same night that Democratic delegates were nominating Humphrey, protesters and Yippies had congregated in Grant Park, across Michigan Avenue from downtown hotels. Undisciplined police waded into the crowds with clubs and tear gas. Young people fought back with rocks and bottles. Television caught the hours of violence that ended when the National Guard separated police from demonstrators. On the convention floor, Senator Abraham Ribicoff of Connecticut decried "Gestapo tactics" on the streets of Chicago. Mayor Daley shouted back obscenities. For Humphrey, the convention was a catastrophe, alienating liberal Democrats.

Election day gave Wallace 13.5 percent of the popular vote, Humphrey 42.7 percent of the popular vote and 191 electoral votes, and Nixon 43.4 percent of the popular vote and 301 electoral votes. The national media saw Wallace in terms of bigotry and backlash against civil rights. But many of Wallace's northern backers were unhappy with both parties.

Dr. Martin Luther King, Jr.
Corbis/Bettmann

QUICK REVIEW

The 1968 Democratic Convention

◆ August 26–29: Democrats meet to nominate Hubert Humphrey.

◆ Antiwar protesters march on the convention hall.

◆ Undisciplined police helped precipitate violence between the police and the protesters.

NIXON AND WATERGATE

WHAT WAS the legacy of
Richard Nixon's presidency?

The new president was an unlikely politician. After losing a 1962 race for governor of California, he announced that he was quitting politics and that the press would no longer have Dick Nixon "to kick around." In 1968, he skillfully sold a "new Nixon" to the media. Seven years later, the press was his undoing as it uncovered the Watergate scandal.

GETTING OUT OF VIETNAM, 1969–1973

Nixon had no secret plan to end the war. Protests culminated in 1969 with the Vietnam Moratorium on October 15, when 2 million protesters joined rallies across the country. Disaffection also mounted in Vietnam. Nurses found their idealism strained as they treated young men maimed in thousands of nasty skirmishes in the jungles and mountains. Racial tensions sapped morale on the front lines. Troops lost discipline, took drugs, and hunkered down waiting for their tours of duty to end. Soldiers "fragged" (killed) their own gung-ho or racist officers, and the high command had to adapt its code of justice to keep an army on the job.

Nixon and Vice President Spiro Agnew responded by trying to isolate the antiwar opposition, but Nixon also reduced the role of U.S. ground forces. He claimed that his policies represented "the great silent majority of my fellow Americans." Agnew blamed bad morale on journalists and intellectuals—on "nattering nabobs of negativism" and "an effete corps of impudent snobs."

The New Left had already split into factions. About a hundred angry SDS members declared themselves the Weather Underground in 1969, taking their name from a Bob Dylan lyric. They tried to disrupt Chicago and Washington with window-smashing "days of rage." Three Weatherpeople blew themselves up with a homemade bomb in New York in 1970. Others bombed a University of Wisconsin building and killed a student.

Nixon's secretary of defense, Melvin Laird, responded to the antiwar sentiment with "Vietnamization," withdrawing U.S. troops as fast as possible without undermining the South Vietnamese government. In July 1969, the president announced the "**Nixon Doctrine**." The policy substituted weapons and money for men. Americans rearmed and expanded the South Vietnamese army and surreptitiously bombed Communist bases in neutral Cambodia.

The secret war against Cambodia culminated on April 30, 1970 with an invasion. Americans who had hoped that the war was fading away were outraged. Students shut down hundreds of colleges. At Kent State University in Ohio, the National Guard was called in to maintain order. On May 4, one unit fired on a group of nonthreatening students and killed four of them. At Jackson State University in Mississippi, two students were also killed when troops fired on their dormitory.

The Cambodian "incursion" extended the military stalemate in Vietnam to United States policy. In December 1970, Congress repealed the Gulf of Tonkin Resolution and prohibited use of U.S. ground troops outside South Vietnam. Cambodia, however, was already devastated. The U.S. invasion had opened the way for the bloodthirsty Khmer Rouge, who killed millions of Cambodians in the name of working-class revolution. Only ninety thousand U.S. ground troops were still in Vietnam by early 1972. A final air offensive in December smashed much of Hanoi into rubble and helped force four and a half years of peace talks to a conclusion.

The cease-fire began on January 27, 1973. The United States promised not to increase its military aid to South Vietnam. Immediately after coming to terms with North Vietnam, Nixon suspended the draft in favor of an all-volunteer military.

QUICK REVIEW

The Nixon Doctrine
- Nixon responded to antiwar protesters by reducing the role of U.S. ground forces in Vietnam.
- "Vietnamization": The withdrawal of U.S. troops as fast as possible without undermining the South Vietnamese government.
- The Nixon Doctrine substituted weapons and money for troops.

Nixon Doctrine   President Nixon's new American policy (1969) toward Asia in which the United States would honor treaty commitments but would gradually disengage and expect Asian nations to handle military defense on their own.

The shootings at Kent State University in May 1970 reflected the deep divisions in American society created by the Vietnam War, including those between antiwar college students and those serving in the armed forces.

© John Paul Filo/Hutton/Archive

NIXON AND THE WIDER WORLD

To his credit, Richard Nixon took American foreign policy in new directions even while he was struggling to escape from Vietnam and Cambodia. He hoped to distract the American people from frustration in Southeast Asia with more important accomplishments elsewhere.

Nixon's first foreign policy success was a gift from Kennedy and Johnson. NASA had been working since 1961 to meet Kennedy's goal of a manned trip to the moon before the end of the decade. On July 20, 1969 the lunar lander *Eagle* detached from the command module circling the moon and landed on the level plain known as the Sea of Tranquillity. Six hours later, Armstrong was the first human to walk on the moon.

For Nixon and Henry Kissinger, his national security adviser (and later secretary of state), foreign policy was about the balance of world economic and military power and securing the most advantageous agreements, alliances, and military positions. In particular, they hoped to trade improved relations with China and the USSR for help in settling the Vietnam War.

China was increasingly isolated within the Communist world. In 1969, it almost went to war with the USSR. Nixon was eager to take advantage of Chinese-Soviet tension. In April 1971 secret talks led to an easing of the American trade

WHERE TO LEARN MORE

Richard Nixon Library and Birthplace, Yorba Linda, California
www.nixonfoundation.org/index.shtml

WHERE TO LEARN MORE

★ Titan Missile Museum,
Green Valley, Arizona
www.pimaair.org/titan_0.1.htm

embargo begun in 1950 and a tour of China by a U.S. table tennis team. Kissinger then arranged for Nixon's startling visit to Mao Zedong in Beijing in February 1972.

Playing the "China card" helped improve relations with the Soviet Union. The Soviets needed increased trade with the United States and a counterweight to China, the United States was looking for help in getting out of Vietnam, and both countries wanted to limit nuclear armaments. Protracted negotiations led to arms agreements known as **SALT**—the **Strategic Arms Limitation Treaty**—that Nixon signed in Moscow in May 1972. The agreements blocked creation of extensive antiballistic missiles (ABM) systems but failed to limit bombers, cruise missiles, or multiple independently targeted warheads on single missiles.

Diplomats used the French word *détente*, meaning easing of tension, to describe the new U.S. relations with China and the Soviet Union. It facilitated travel between the United States and China. It allowed U.S. farmers to sell wheat to the Soviets. More broadly, détente implied that the United States and China recognized mutual interests in Asia and that the United States acknowledged the Soviet Union as an equal in world affairs.

COURTING MIDDLE AMERICA

Nixon designed domestic policy to help him win reelection. His goal was to solidify his "Middle American" support; the strategy targeted the suburbs and the South. The Nixon White House preferred not to deal with troubled big cities. Spokesmen announced that the "urban crisis" was over and then dismantled the urban initiatives of Johnson's Great Society. Instead, Nixon tilted federal assistance to the suburbs. The centerpiece of his **New Federalism** was General Revenue Sharing (1972). By 1980, it had transferred more than $18 billion from the federal treasury to the states and more than $36 billion to local governments. Revenue sharing grants supplemented the general funds of every full-service government, whether a city of 2 million or a suburban town of five hundred.

Nixon pursued the southern strategy through Supreme Court nominations of Southerners Clement Haynsworth of Florida and G. Harrold Carswell of Alabama. Although the Senate rejected both as unqualified, the nominations nonetheless gave Nixon a reputation as a champion of the white South. He hoped to move cautiously in enforcing school desegregation, but a task force led by Secretary of Labor George Shultz crafted an approach that allowed substantial desegregation.

OIL, OPEC, AND STAGFLATION

More troublesome was inflation, one of Lyndon Johnson's unpleasant legacies. One of the causes was LBJ's decision to fight in Vietnam without tax increases until 1968. An income tax cut in 1969, supported by both parties, made the situation worse. Inflation eroded the value of savings and pensions. It also made U.S. goods too expensive for foreign buyers and generated a trade deficit.

After the 1972 election, inflation came roaring back. The main cause was sharp increases in the cost of energy. Angry at American support for Israel in the Arab-Israeli War of October 1973, Arab nations imposed an embargo on oil exports that lasted from October 1973 to March 1974. Gasoline and heating oil became scarce and expensive. The shortages eased when the embargo ended, but the **Organization of Petroleum Exporting Countries (OPEC)** had challenged the ability of the industrial nations to dictate world economic policy.

Americans switched off unused lights, turned down thermostats, and put on sweaters. Congress required states to enforce a highway speed limit of 55 miles

SALT (Strategic Arms Limitation Treaty)   Treaty signed in 1972 by the United States and the Soviet Union to slow the nuclear arms race.

détente   (French for "easing of tension") Used to describe the new U.S. relations with China and the Soviet Union in 1972.

New Federalism   President Richard Nixon's policy to shift responsibilities of government programs from the federal level to the states.

Organization of Petroleum Exporting Countries (OPEC)   Cartel of oil-producing nations in Asia, Africa, and Latin America that gained substantial power over the world economy in the mid-to late-1970s by controlling the production and price of oil.

per hour to get federal highway funds and enacted the first fuel economy standards for automobiles. More efficient imports captured a third of the U.S. car market by 1980.

After thirty years at the top, the United States could no longer dominate the world economy by itself. Germany and Japan now had economies as modern as that of the United States. In 1971, stagflation was the new term to describe the painful combination of inflation, high unemployment, and flat economic growth that matched no one's economic theory but everyone's daily experience.

AMERICANS AS ENVIRONMENTALISTS

In the turbulent 1970s, resource conservation grew into a multifaceted environmental movement. Environmentalism dealt with serious problems. It was broad enough for both scientific experts and activists, for both Republican Richard Nixon and Democrat Jimmy Carter.

After the booming 1950s, Americans had started to pay attention to the damage that advanced technologies and industrial production did to natural systems. Rachel Carson's *Silent Spring* in 1962 described the side effects of DDT and other pesticides on animal life. In her imagined future, spring was silent because all the birds had died of pesticide poisoning. Meanwhile, an offshore oil well polluted the beaches of Santa Barbara, California, in 1969. Fire danced across the Cuyahoga River in Cleveland when industrial discharges ignited.

On April 22, children in ten thousand schools and 20 million other people took part in Earth Day, an occasion first conceived by Wisconsin Senator Gaylord Nelson. Earth Day gained a grass-roots following in towns and cities across the country.

The mainstream media discovered the ravaged planet; so did a politically savvy president. Nixon had already signed the National Environmental Policy Act on January 1, 1970, and later in the year created the **Environmental Protection Agency (EPA)** to enforce environmental laws. The rest of the Nixon years brought legislation on clean air, clear water, pesticides, hazardous chemicals, and endangered species that made environmental management and protection part of governmental routine.

Americans began to realize that low-income and minority communities had more than their share of environmental problems. Residents near the Love Canal in Buffalo, New York, discovered in 1978 that an entire neighborhood was built on land contaminated by decades of chemical dumping. Activists sought to understand the health effects and force compensation, paving the way for the **Superfund** cleanup legislation. (See American View, "Grassroots Community action.") African Americans often lived downstream and downwind of heavily polluting industries. Landfills and waste disposal sites were frequently located near minority neighborhoods. Efforts to fight environmental racism became important in many minority communities.

FROM DIRTY TRICKS TO WATERGATE

Subordinates learned during his first administration that Richard Nixon would condone dishonest actions—"dirty tricks"—if they stood to improve his political position. In 1972 and 1973, dirty tricks grew from a scandal into a constitutional crisis when Nixon abused the power of his office to cover up wrongdoing and hinder criminal investigations.

The chain of events that undermined Nixon's presidency started with the **Pentagon Papers**. In his last year as secretary of defense, Robert McNamara had

Environmental Protection Agency (EPA)   Federal agency created in 1970 to oversee environmental monitoring and cleanup programs.

Pentagon Papers   Classified Defense Department documents on the history of the United States' involvement in Vietnam, prepared in 1968 and leaked to the press in 1971.

• AMERICAN VIEWS •

GRASSROOTS COMMUNITY ACTION

I n the 1950s, a major chemical company closed a waste dump in Niagara Falls, New York. The site, known as Love Canal, was soon surrounded by a park, school, and hundreds of modest homes. Residents put up with noxious odors and seepage of chemical wastes until 1978, when they learned that the State Health Department was concerned about the health effects on small children and pregnant women. Over the next two years, residents battled state and federal bureaucracies and reluctant politicians for accurate information about the risks they faced and then for financial assistance to move from the area (often their homes represented their only savings). In October, 1980, President Carter signed a bill to move all families permanently from the Love Canal area.

One of the leaders of the grassroots movement was housewife Lois Gibbs. The following excerpts from her story show her increasing sophistication as a community activist, starting by ringing doorbells in 1978 and ending with national television exposure in 1980. Although the Love Canal case itself was unusual, community based organizations in all parts of the country learned the tactics of effective action in the 1960s and 1970s.

WHAT PUBLIC programs in the 1960s and 1970s gave citizens experience in grassroots action? How might the Internet change the tactics of community organizing?

Knocking on Doors

I decided to go door-to-door with a petition. It seemed like a good idea to start near the school, to talk to the mothers nearest it. I had already heard that a lot of the residents near the school had been upset about the chemicals for the past couple of years. I thought they might help me. I had never done anything like this. . . . I was afraid a lot of doors would be slammed in my face, that people would think I was some crazy fanatic. But I decided to do it anyway. . . . and knocked on my first door. There was no answer. I just stood there, not knowing what to do. It was an usually warm June day and I was perspiring. I thought: What am I doing here? I must be crazy. People are going to think I am. Go home, you fool! And that's just what I did.

It was one of those times when I had to sit down and face myself. I was afraid of making a fool of myself, I had scared myself, and I had gone home. When I got there, I sat at the kitchen table with my petition in my hand, thinking. Wait. What if people do slam doors in your face? People may think you're crazy. But what's more important—what people think or your child's health? Either you're going to do something or

---

commissioned a report on America's road to Vietnam. The documents showed that the country's leaders had planned to expand the war even while they claimed to be looking for a way out. In June 1971, one of the contributors to the report, Daniel Ellsberg, leaked it to the *New York Times*. Its publication infuriated Nixon.

In response, the White House compiled a list of journalists and politicians who opposed Nixon. As White House staffer John Dean put it, the president's men could then "use the available federal machinery [Internal Revenue Service, FBI] to screw our political enemies." Former CIA employees E. Howard Hunt and G. Gordon Liddy became the chief "plumbers," as the group was known because its job was to prevent leaks of information. The plumbers cooked up schemes to embarrass political opponents and ransacked the office of Ellsberg's psychiatrist.

Early in 1972, Hunt went to work for CREEP—the Committee to Re-Elect the President—while Liddy took another position on the presidential staff. CREEP had already raised millions from corporations and was hatching plans to undermine Democrats with rumors and pranks. Then, on June 17, 1972, five inept burglars hired with CREEP funds were caught breaking into the Democratic National Committee office in Washington's **Watergate** apartment building. Nixon initiated

Watergate   A complex scandal involving attempts to cover up illegal actions taken by administration officials and leading to the resignation of President Richard Nixon in 1974.

you're going to have to admit you're a coward and not do it. . . .

The next day, I went out on my own street to talk to people, I knew. It was a little easier to be brave with them. If I could convince people I knew—friends— maybe it would be less difficult to convince others. . . . I went to the back door, as I always did when I visited a neighbor. Each house took about twenty or twenty-five minutes. . . .

Phil Donahue and Political Action

The *Phil Donahue Show* called. They wanted us to appear on their June 18 show. The reaction in the office was different this time, compared to the show in October 1978. In October, everyone was excited. "Phil Donahue—wow!" Now, residents reacted differently. "Donahue. That's great press. Now we'll get the politicians to move!" . . . Now our people looked at the show as a tool to use in pushing the government to relocate us permanently. By this time we understood how politicians react to public pressure, how to play the political game. We eagerly agreed to go, and found forty other residents to go with us. . . .

[After arriving in Chicago] We then planned how we would handle the *Phil Donahue Show*. . . . We had to get the real issues across. Each resident was assigned an issue. One told of the chromosome tests. Another was to concentrate on her multiple miscarriages. Another was to ask for telegrams from across the country to the White House in support of permanent relocation. I coached them to get their point in, no matter the question asked. For example, if Donahue asked what you thought of the mayor, and your assignment was to discuss miscarriages, you should answer: "I don't like the mayor because I have had three miscarriages and other health problems, and he won't help us." Or; "My family is sick, and the mayor won't help us. That's why we need people to send telegrams to the White House for permanent relocation." . . . The residents were great! Each and every one followed through with our plan.

In July, I went on a speaking tour of California arranged by Jane Fonda and Tom Hayden. I visited many sites with problems similar to ours. I was able to give advice, based on our experiences. I told the leaders of each community that it wasn't hopeless that they could win. "Stick with it. We are!"

Source: Lois Marie Gibbs, as told to Murray Levine, *Love Canal: My Story* (Albany: State University of New York Press, 1982), pp. 12–13, 161–64.

a coverup. On June 23, he ordered his assistant H. R. Haldeman to warn the FBI off the case with the excuse that national security was involved. Nixon compounded this obstruction of justice by arranging a $400,000 bribe to keep the burglars quiet. The coverup worked in the short run.

Nixon's opponent in the 1972 election was South Dakota Senator George Mc-Govern, an impassioned opponent of the Vietnam War. McGovern was honest, intelligent, and well to the left on issues like the defense budget and legalization of marijuana. He did not appeal to the white Southerners and blue-collar Northerners. An assassination attempt that took George Wallace out of national politics also helped Nixon win in a landslide.

The coverup began to come apart with the trial of the Watergate burglars in January 1973. Federal Judge John Sirica used the threat of heavy sentences to pressure one burglar into a statement that implied that higher-ups had been involved. Meanwhile, the *Washington Post* was linking Nixon's people to dirty tricks and illegal campaign contributions. The White House scrambled to find a defensible story. Nixon now began to coach people on what they should tell investigators, claimed his staff had lied to him, and tried to set up John Dean to take the fall.

In the late spring and early summer, attention shifted to the televised hearings of the Senate's Select Committee on Presidential Campaign Activities. Its chair was Sam Ervin of North Carolina. A parade of White House and party officials described their own pieces in the affair, often accusing each other and revealing the plumbers and the enemies list. The real questions, it became obvious, were what the president knew and when he knew it. It seemed to be John Dean's word against Richard Nixon's.

A bombshell turned the scandal into a constitutional crisis. A mid-level staffer told the committee that Nixon made tape recordings of his White House conversations. Both the Senate and the Watergate special prosecutor, Archibald Cox, subpoenaed the tapes. Nixon refused to give them up. In late October, after he failed to cut a satisfactory deal, he fired his attorney general and the special prosecutor. Many Americans thought that these actions proved that Nixon had something to hide. In April 1974, he finally issued *edited* transcripts of the tapes, with foul language deleted and key passages missing. Finally, on July 24, 1974, the U.S. Supreme Court ruled unanimously that Nixon had to deliver sixty-four tapes to the new special prosecutor.

In Congress, Republicans joined Democrats in voting three articles of impeachment: for hindering the criminal investigation of the Watergate breakin, for abusing the power of the presidency by using federal agencies to deprive citizens of their rights, and for ignoring the committee's subpoena for the tapes. Before the full House could vote on the articles of impeachment, Nixon delivered the tapes containing direct evidence that he had participated in the coverup on June 23, 1972, and had been lying ever since. On August 8 he announced his resignation, effective the next day.

Watergate was two separate but related stories. On one level, it was about individuals, Nixon and his cronies who wanted to win so badly they repeatedly broke the law. Nixon paid for his overreaching ambition with the end of his political career; more than twenty others paid with jail terms.

On another level, the crisis was a lesson about the Constitution. The separation of powers allowed Congress and the courts to rein in a president who had spun out of control.

THE FORD FOOTNOTE

Gerald Ford was the first president who had been elected neither president nor vice president. Ford was Nixon's appointee to replace Spiro Agnew, who resigned and pleaded no contest to charges of bribery and income tax evasion in 1973. On September 8, Ford pardoned Richard Nixon for "any and all crimes" committed while president. Since Nixon had not yet been indicted, the pardon saved him from future prosecution. He also offered clemency to thousands of draft resisters.

Détente continued. American diplomats joined the Soviet Union and thirty other European nations in the capital of Finland to sign the **Helsinki Accords**, which called for increased commerce between the Eastern and Western blocs and human rights guarantees. They also legitimized the national boundaries that had been set in eastern Europe in 1945.

At home the economy slid into recession; unemployment climbed above 10 percent; inflation diminished the value of savings and wages.

Ford was the Republican presidential candidate in the 1976 election. His Democratic opponent was a political enigma. James Earl Carter Jr. had been a navy officer, a farmer, and governor of Georgia. Carter and other new style Southern politicians left race-baiting behind to talk like modern New Dealers. He appealed to Democrats as someone who could reassemble LBJ's political coalition and return the South to the Democratic party. In his successful campaign, Carter presented himself as an alternative to party hacks and Washington insiders.

Helsinki Accords Agreement in 1975 among NATO and Warsaw Pact members that recognized European national boundaries as set after World War II and included guarantees of human rights.

JIMMY CARTER: IDEALISM AND FRUSTRATION IN THE WHITE HOUSE

As an outsider in Washington's political establishment, Carter had one great advantage: freedom from the narrow mind-set of experts who talk only to each other. However, he lacked both the knowledge of key political players and the experience to resolve legislative gridlock.

HOW WAS Jimmy Carter's idealism a frustration to his success as president?

CARTER, ENERGY, AND THE ECONOMY

Carter was refreshingly low-key. After his inauguration, he walked from the Capitol to the White House as Jefferson had. He signed official documents "Jimmy." He tended to tell the public what he thought rather than what pollsters said the people wanted to hear.

Carter's approach to politics reflected his training as an engineer. He was analytical, logical, and given to breaking a problem into its component parts. He filled his cabinet with experts rather than political operators. He didn't seem to understand the basic rules of Washington politics. For example, he and his cabinet officers developed policies and made appointments without consulting key congressional committee chairs.

The biggest domestic problem remained the economy, which slid into another recession in 1978. Another jump in petroleum prices helped make 1979 and 1980 the worst years for inflation in the postwar era. Carter himself was a fiscal conservative whose impulse was to cut federal spending. This worsened unemployment and alienated liberal Democrats, who wanted to revive the Great Society.

CLOSED FACTORIES AND FAILING FARMS

Ford and Carter both faced massive problems of economic transition that undercut their efforts to devise effective government programs.

Industrial decay stalked such "gritty cities" as Allentown, Pennsylvania; Trenton, New Jersey; and Gary, Indiana. Communities whose workers had made products in high volume for mass markets found that technological revolutions made them obsolete. Critics renamed the old manufacturing region of the Northeast and Midwest the Rustbelt in honor of its abandoned factories.

Plant closures were only one facet of business efforts to increase productivity by substituting machinery for employees. Between 1947 and 1977, American steelmakers doubled output while cutting their work force from 600,000 to 400,000. Lumber companies used economic recession in the early 1980s to automate mills and rehired only a fraction of their workers when the economy picked up. High interest rates in the early 1980s, the result of a ballooning federal deficit (see Chapter 30), attracted foreign investors and strengthened the dollar.

Carter simultaneously proposed a comprehensive energy policy. He asked Americans to make energy conservation the moral equivalent of war—to accept individual sacrifices for the common good. Congress created the Department of Energy but refused to raise taxes on oil and natural gas to reduce consumption. However, the Energy Policy and Conservation Act (1978) did encourage alternative energy sources to replace foreign petroleum. Big oil companies poured billions of dollars into western Colorado to squeeze a petroleum substitute from shale. Solar energy research prospered. Breezy western hillsides sprouted "wind farms" to wring electricity out of the air.

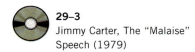

29–3
Jimmy Carter, The "Malaise" Speech (1979)

However, antinuclear activism blocked one obvious alternative to fossil fuels. In the late 1970s, activists staged sit-ins at the construction sites of nuclear plants. A near-meltdown at the Three Mile Island nuclear plant in Pennsylvania in March 1979 stalemated efforts to expand nuclear power capacity.

When the OPEC price hikes undermined the inflation-fighting effort in the summer of 1979, Carter proposed new steps to solve the energy crisis. A cabinet reshuffle a few days later was supposed to show that he was firmly in charge, but instead conveyed the message that he was erratic. By 1979, opinion leaders had decided that Carter was not capable of leading the nation and then interpreted every action as confirming that belief.

BUILDING A COOPERATIVE WORLD

Despite troubles on the home front, Carter's first two years brought foreign policy success that reflected a new vision of a multilateral world. He appointed Andrew Young—a fellow Georgian with long experience in the civil rights movement—as ambassador to the United Nations, where he worked effectively to build bridges to third-world nations.

Carter's moral convictions were responsible for a new concern with human rights around the globe. He criticized the Soviet Union for preventing free speech and denying its citizens the right to emigrate, angering Soviet leaders, who didn't expect the human rights clauses of the Helsinki Accords to be taken seriously. Carter also withheld economic aid from South Africa, Guatemala, Chile, and Nicaragua, which had long records of human rights abuses. In Nicaragua, the change in policy helped left-wing Sandinista rebels topple the Somoza dictatorship.

The triumph of the new foreign policy was the **Camp David Agreement** between Egypt and Israel. Carter risked his reputation and credibility in September 1978 to bring Egyptian President Anwar el-Sadat and Israeli Prime Minister Menachem Begin together at Camp David, the presidential retreat. A formal treaty signed in Washington on March 26, 1979 normalized relations between Israel and its most powerful neighbor and led to Israeli withdrawal from the Sinai Peninsula.

NEW CRISES ABROAD

The Soviets ignored the human rights provisions of the Helsinki Accords. Soviet advisers or Cuban troops intervened in African civil wars. At home, Cold Warriors who had never accepted détente found it easier to attack Carter than Nixon.

Carter inherited negotiations for SALT II—a strategic arms limitation treaty that would have reduced both the American and Soviet nuclear arsenals—from the Ford administration. SALT II met stiff resistance in the Senate. Opponents claimed it would create a "window of vulnerability" in the 1980s that would invite the Soviets to launch a nuclear first strike. Carter tried to counter criticism by stepping up defense spending, starting a buildup that would accelerate under Ronald Reagan.

Hopes for SALT II vanished on January 3, 1980, when Soviet troops entered Afghanistan. Muslim tribespeople unhappy with modernization had attacked Afghanistan's pro-Communist government, which invited Soviet intervention. The situation resembled the American involvement in South Vietnam. In the end, it took the Soviets a decade to find a way out.

The final blow to Carter's foreign policy came in Iran. Since 1953, the United States had strongly backed Iran's monarch, the Shah. The Shah modernized

Camp David Agreement Agreement to reduce points of conflict between Israel and Egypt, hammered out in 1977 with the help of U.S. President Jimmy Carter.

Iran's economy but jailed political opponents. U.S. aid and oil revenues helped him build a vast army, but the Iranian middle class despised his authoritarianism, and Muslim fundamentalists opposed modernization. Revolution toppled the Shah at the start of 1979.

The upheaval installed a nominally democratic government, but the Ayatollah Ruhollah Khomeini, a Muslim cleric who hated the United States, exercised real power. Throughout 1979, Iran grew increasingly anti-American. After the United States allowed the exiled Shah to seek medical treatment in New York, a mob stormed the U.S. embassy in Tehran on November 4, 1979, and took more than sixty Americans hostage. They demanded that Carter surrender the Shah.

Television brought pictures of blindfolded hostages and anti-American mobs burning effigies of Uncle Sam and wrapping American flags around garbage. The administration tried economic pressure and diplomacy, but Khomeini had no desire for accommodation. When Iran announced in April 1980 that the hostages would remain in the hands of the militants rather than be transferred to the government, Carter ordered an airborne rescue. The attempt misfired when three of eight helicopters malfunctioned and one crashed in the Iranian desert. The fiasco added to the national embarrassment. The United States and Iran finally reached agreement on the eve of the 1980 election. The hostages gained their freedom after 444 days at the moment Ronald Reagan took office as the new president.

The hostage crisis consumed Jimmy Carter the way that Vietnam had consumed Lyndon Johnson. It gripped the public and stalemated other issues. For weeks, Carter's tragedy was that "his" Iranian crisis was the fruit of policies hatched by the Eisenhower administration and pursued by every president since then, all of whom overlooked the Shah's despotic government because of his firm anti-Communism.

After thirty years in which the United States had viewed the entire world as a Cold War battlefield, Carter was willing to accept the developing world on its own terms. His human rights efforts showed that evangelical religious convictions could be tied to progressive aims. Iranian rage at past policies of the sort Carter hoped to change destroyed his ability to direct a new course.

CONCLUSION

A period of remarkable prosperity ended in 1974. Long lines at gas stations suggested that prosperity was fragile. Cities and regions began to feel the costs of obsolete industries. Environmental damage caused many Americans to reconsider the goal of economic expansion.

American withdrawal from Vietnam in 1973 and the collapse of the South Vietnamese government in 1975 were defeats; the United States ended up with little to show for a long and painful war. SALT I stabilized the arms race, but it also recognized that the Soviet Union was an equal. The American nuclear arsenal might help deter a third world war, but it could not prevent the seizure of hostages in Iran.

The nation finished the 1970s more egalitarian than it had been in the early 1960s but also more divided. More citizens had the opportunity to advance economically and to seek political power, but there were deepening fissures between social liberals and cultural conservatives, old and new views about roles for women, rich and poor, white and black people.

SUMMARY

The End of Consensus The failure to win an easy victory in Vietnam eroded the nation's confidence and fueled bitter division about the nation's goals. Operation Rolling Thunder in the air and search and destroy missions on the ground were not "wining" the war; protest against the war at home quickly followed America's decision to use combat forces. The tone of the debate over Vietnam turned nastier, much of the anger directed at the draft. The antiwar movement reflected a growing grass-roots activism on college campuses, among women, and the Woodstock generation counterculture.

Cities Under Stress Exploding metropolitan areas needed money for streets, schools, and sewers. Many urban problems were associated with the creation of "second ghettos" due to immigration in the 1950s and 1960s. A series of riots scarred most big cities during the 1960s; the riots were protests about the problems of ghetto life but were often blamed on "outsiders." Minority separatism tapped into the same anger that caused the riots. The Black Power movement, Hispanic activism in the Southwest, and the American Indian Movement all questioned the American assumption that everyone wanted to be a part of the same homogeneous society, a society increasingly becoming "suburbanized."

The Year of the Gun, 1968 1968 was a watershed year that forced American society to rethink the role of government. Mainstream Americans began questioning the war in Vietnam after the Tet Offensive; President Johnson was advised that the war was unwinnable on acceptable terms. Facing political challenges, Johnson announced a halt to the bombing of North Vietnam and his withdrawal from the presidential race. The assassinations of Martin Luther King Jr. and Robert Kennedy and the riots at the Democratic National Convention captured America's attention. Richard Nixon captured the presidency in 1968 with a secret plan to end the war and an appeal to middle America.

Nixon and Watergate President Nixon had no plan to end the Vietnam War and antiwar sentiment grew; while the Nixon Doctrine and "Vietnamization" made it appear the United States was withdrawing from Southeast Asia, the bombing of Cambodia intensified. The 1973 ceasefire confirmed American withdrawal from Vietnam; in 1975 South Vietnam collapsed. To his credit, Nixon took American foreign policy in new directions, improving relations with the Soviet Union and China, and the administration passed numerous laws relating to environmental issues. Nixon abused the power of his office in the Watergate scandal and resigned before he could be impeached; Gerald Ford, who had been appointed vice president, succeeded him.

Jimmy Carter: Idealism and Frustration in the White House Washington outsider Jimmy Carter's major domestic challenge was the economy. A recession, an energy crisis, the deindustrization of America, and the transformation of the family farm to agribusiness challenged the president upon his election. Carter's moral convictions brought attention to human rights issues abroad. The signing of the Camp David Agreement between Egypt and Israel was a high point; hopes for reducing nuclear arsenals ended when the Soviet Union invaded Afghanistan. The Iranian hostage crisis consumed the Carter administration and helped contribute to Ronald Reagan's 1980 victory.

REVIEW QUESTIONS

1. Why did the United States fail in Vietnam? What factors limited President Johnson's freedom of action there?

2. How did racial relations change between 1965 and 1970?

3. Why was 1968 a pivotal year for American politics and society?

4. What were the implications of détente? How and why did U.S. influence over the rest of the world change during the 1970s?

5. How did the backgrounds of Presidents Johnson, Nixon, and Carter shape their successes and failures as national leaders?

6. Why was the "space race" important for the United States?

KEY TERMS

American Indian Movement (AIM) (p. 772)
Baker v. Carr (p. 773)
Black Panthers (p. 771)
Black Power (p. 771)
Camp David Agreement (p. 784)
Counterculture (p. 768)
Détente (p. 778)
Environmental Protection Agency (p. 779)

Free Speech Movement (FSM) (p. 776)
Helsinki Accords (p. 782)
Model Cities Program (p. 767)
Nation of Islam (p. 771)
New Federalism (p. 778)
Nixon Doctrine (p. 776)
Organization of Petroleum Exporting Countries (OPEC) (p. 778)

Pentagon Papers (p. 779)
SALT (Strategic Arms Limitation Treaty) (p. 778)
Search and destroy (p. 763)
Selective Service System (p. 766)
Students for a Democratic Society (SDS) (p. 766)
Swann v. Charlotte-Mecklenburg Board of Education (p. 773)
Watergate (p. 780)

WHERE TO LEARN MORE

 Lyndon B. Johnson National Historical Park, Johnson City, Texas. Johnson's ranch, southwest of Austin, gives visitors a feeling for the open landscape in which Johnson spent his early years. **www.nps.gov/lypo/**

Vietnam Veterans Memorial, Washington, D.C. A simple wall engraved with the names of the nation's Vietnam War dead is testimony to one of the nation's most divisive wars. **www.nps.gov/vive/**

Richard Nixon Library and Birthplace, Yorba Linda, California. Exhibits trace Nixon's political career and related world events with a sympathetic interpretation. **www.nixonfoundation.org/index.shtml**

Titan Missile Museum, Green Valley, Arizona. The Green Valley complex near Tucson held eighteen Titan missiles. They were deactivated after SALT I, and the complex is now open to visitors. **www.pimaair.org/titan_01.htm**

For additional study resources for this chapter, go to:
www.prenhall.com/goldfield/chapter29

Iconic Images of the Vietnam Era

PRESIDENTS HAVE their picture taken shaking hands with visitors countless times. Usually they are of interest only to the visitors. What do you think made the photograph of President Nixon with Elvis Presley of interest to so many? During the late 1960s and early 1970s violence at home and overseas was distressingly commonplace. What do you think made the photographs of Mary Vecchio and Kim Phuk so memorable?

Television famously brought the Vietnam War "into the living room." Nonetheless some of the most memorable images of the era were photographs. What is it about particular images that turn them into iconic representations of a moment of history? Pictured here are three such photographs. The first shows Richard Nixon and Elvis Presley in the Oval Office. Fifteen years earlier, Presley had scandalized the "older generation" with his uninhibited gyrations. Nixon, then and later, always campaigned for "family values." Next is a photograph of a student reacting to the killing of a classmate on May 4, 1970 at Kent State University in Ohio. The preceeding week Nixon had ordered U.S. troops into Cambodia to destroy North Vietnamese supply routes and command centers. Campuses across the country erupted and in Ohio, the governor called in the National Guard to quell the demonstrations at Kent State. Guard soldiers fired on the students, killing the young man shown this photograph. The third photograph shows the impact on an American napalm attack upon the children of a South Vietnamese village.

◀ **This is the single most requested item in the National Archives which contain, among other national treasures, originals of the Declaration of Independence, the Constitution, and the Bill of Rights.** President Nixon and Elvis Presley met at the singer's request. He had volunteered to work in the administration's anti-drug crusade. The president, looking for a way to reach out to young people, readily agreed. He appointed Presley a "deputy" in the anti-drug war. Presley was, at the time, addicted to a variety of uppers, downers, and other medications.

◄ **Mary Vecchio reacting to the death of fellow student Jeff Miller.** John Filo, a Kent State student and photographer for the yearbook, won a Pulitzer Prize for the picture. It appeared on the cover of *Newsweek* magazine with the caption "Nixon's Home Front."

© John Paul Filo/Getty Images - Hulton Archive

This Pulitzer Prize-winning photograph of 9-year-old Kim Phuc, center, running after an aerial napalm attack on her village in 1972 was taken by Associated Press photographer Nick Ut (Cong Ut). Kim suffered burns over 65% of her body. She survived and is now a peace activist. ►

AP/Wide World Photos

"All the men are gone in our family," Mom was actually saying for the Khmer Rouge spies to hear. "They are only girls. Don't kill them. We are the only members left of the family " . . . We were lying to them about our identity. It was a horrible game.

Washington, D.C.: President and Mrs. Ronald Reagan dance early January 21, 1981 at the Smithsonian Museum of American History, the last stop on a tour of inaugural balls. Mrs. Reagan wore a one-shoulder white satin sheath gown by James Galanos to the fetes.

30

THE REAGAN REVOLUTION
AND A CHANGING WORLD
1981–1992

WHAT ECONOMIC
and social changes occurred
during the Reagan administration?

WHAT foreign policy measures
did Ronald Reagan employ
in dealing with the Soviet Union
and the Middle East?

HOW DID America's
population change in the 1980s?

WHAT WERE the culture wars?

1992

1981

The Khmer Rouge marched into the city [Phnom Penh, the capital of Cambodia], dressed in black. . . . Young Khmer Rouge [Marxist revolutionary] soldiers, eight or ten years old, were dragging their rifles, which were taller than them. . . . The whole city, more than two million people was forced out of their homes into the streets. My family walked until we reached Mao Tse-Tung Boulevard, the main boulevard in Phnom Penh. All the population of the city was gathered there. The Khmer Rouge were telling everyone to leave the city.

Although my two middle children were safe in France, my oldest and youngest daughters were close beside me. Parika was only seven. Mealy, who was nineteen, carried her infant son. I kept my children huddled together. As soon as a parent let go, a child would be lost in the huge crowd. . . . And the Khmer Rouge kept ordering everybody, "You must go forward." They shot their guns in the air. Even during the middle of the night the procession was endless. The Khmer Rouge kept shooting and we kept moving forward. . . .

Recently I saw the movie Doctor Zhivago, *about the Russian Revolution. If you compare that to what happened in Phnon Penh, the movie is only on a very small scale. Even* Killing Fields *only gives you part of the idea of what happened in Cambodia. The reality was much more incredible. . . .*

Each night, when we came back to the village from working in the fields, Mom would say, "Children, let's all go to sleep." She would quietly warn me that the wood had eyes and ears. She'd say, "It's nine o'clock now. Go to sleep. . . . There is nothing else to do but work. All the men are gone in our family." Mom was actually saying for the Khmer Rouge spies to hear, "They are only girls. Don't kill them. We are the only members left of the family." . . . We were lying to them about our identity. It was a horrible game.

If you hid your identity, that meant you wanted your past forgotten. We had changed from people who were intellectual, who used to think independently. . . . You became humiliated, allowed to live only as a slave. . . . We were accepted into the United States thanks to my husband's military service. . . . My daughters and I flew to the United States on July 4, 1979. . . . As we landed, I thought, "This is real freedom." . . .

I've found that America is a country where people have come from all over the world. You do your job, you get paid like anybody else, and you're accepted. But Cambodians I know in France, like my sister, feel differently. People are not accepted if they are not French. But in America you're part of the melting pot. . . . In 1983, I came to Los Angeles for my daughter Monie's wedding. I decided to stay. . . . Long Beach has the largest concentration of Cambodians in the country. I called the community center in Long Beach. They said they had no job openings. So I decided to get involved in running a store. . . . Donut shops are very American. . . .

All that refugees have is our work, our dreams. Do I still hurt from what happened in the past? When I opened my mouth to tell you my story, I don't know where my tears came from. . . . My daughters don't like to talk

IMAGE KEY
for pages 790–791

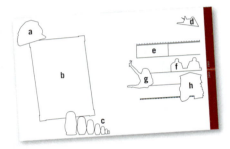

a. A piece of the fallen Berlin Wall.

b. President Ronald Reagan and First Lady Nancy Reagan dance at his first inaugural at the Smithsonian on January 21, 1981.

c. Nesting dolls of Communist or Russian leaders Boris Yeltsin, Mikhail Gorbechev, Leonid Brezhnev, Nikita Khruschev, Joseph Stalin, Vladimir Lenin, and Czar Nicholas II.

d. The black flying wing design of the stealth bomber resembles a bat.

e. Traders on the floor of the new York Stock Exchange work frantically as panic selling swept Wall Street, Monday, October 19, 1987. The Dow Jones Industrial average plunged more than 500 points for the biggest one-day loss in history.

f. Mikhail Gorbachev and Reagan sign INF treaty at the White House.

g. Hispanic female student raises her hand in class.

h. Abortion rights advocate Inga Coulter stands next to pro life protester Elizabeth McGee during clashing demonstrations outside the Supreme Court building.

about the past in Cambodia. They want to forget and think about their fu-
ture. They ask me why I would talk about the past with anybody. I said, "The
past cannot be erased from my memory."

Celia Noup in Al Santoli, *New Americans: An Oral History* (New York, 1988).

CELIA NOUP taught school for twenty years in Cambodia, which borders on South Vietnam. In 1975, after a long civil war, the Communist Khmer Rouge insurgents took over Cambodia's capital, Phnom Penh, and forced its inhabitants into the countryside to work in the fields. Four years later, Noup managed to make her way to a refugee camp in neighboring Thailand and then to the United States. Here she joined hundreds of thousands of other refugees who arrived in the later 1970s and 1980s from war-devastated nations such as Cambodia, Vietnam, Laos, Ethiopia, and Afghanistan. Within a decade, she was working from 5:00 A.M. to 7:00 P.M. in her own donut shop near Los Angeles airport and worrying about helping her children buy houses.

Celia Noup's life shows some of the ways that new waves of immigration from Asia, Latin America, and Africa have changed the United States over the last generation. Immigrants fueled economic growth in the 1980s and 1990s with their labor and their drive to succeed in business. They revitalized older neighborhoods in cities from coast to coast and changed the ethnic mix of major cities. And they created new racial tensions that found their way into national political debates about immigration and into open conflict in places such as Miami and Los Angeles.

Noup's story is also a reminder of the drawn-out consequences of the U.S. involvement in Vietnam and the long shadow of the Cold War. The Cambodian civil war was fueled by the Vietnamese war and the American invasion of Cambodia in 1969. American refugee policy was humanitarian, but also political, opening the door to people fleeing Communist regimes but holding it shut against refugees from right-wing dictatorships. In Washington, foreign policy decisions in the 1980s started with the desire of a new administration to reaffirm American toughness after failures in Vietnam and ended with the astonishing evaporation of the Cold War.

By the end of Ronald Reagan's presidency (1981– 89), new rules governed domestic affairs as well as international relations. Since World War II, politics had followed a well-thumbed script. Lessons about full employment and social services that were accepted in 1948 still applied in 1968 or 1972. In the 1980s, however, Americans decided to reverse the growth of federal government responsibilities that had marked both Republican and Democratic administrations since the 1930s. By the 1990s, the center of U.S. politics had shifted substantially to the right, and even a "liberal" Democrat like Bill Clinton would sound like an Eisenhower Republican. The backdrop to the political changes was massive readjustments in the American economy that began in the 1970s with the decline of heavy industry and then continued to shift employment from factory jobs to service jobs in the 1980s. The ideology of unregulated markets celebrated economic success and made "yuppies" or young urban professionals the center of media attention. But behind the lifestyle stories was a troubling reality: a widening gap between the rich and poor. The result by 1992 was a nation that was much more secure in the world than it had been in 1980, but also more divided against itself.

REAGAN'S DOMESTIC REVOLUTION

WHAT ECONOMIC and social changes occurred during the Reagan administration?

WHERE TO LEARN MORE

Ronald Reagan Boyhood Home, Dixon, Illinois

Political change began in 1980, when Ronald Reagan and running mate George H. W. Bush rode American discontent to a decisive victory in the presidential election (see Map 30–1). Building on a conservative critique of American policies and developing issues that Jimmy Carter had placed on the national agenda, Reagan presided over revolutionary changes in American government and policies. He was a "Teflon president" who managed to take credit for successes but avoid blame for problems, and he rolled to a landslide reelection in 1984 and set the stage for George H. W. Bush's victory in 1988. The consequences of his two terms included an altered role for government, powerful but selective economic growth, and a shift of domestic politics away from bread-and-butter issues toward moral or lifestyle concerns.

An unresolved question is whether Ronald Reagan planned an economic revolution, or simply presided over changes initiated by others. Most memoirs by White House insiders and books by journalists suggest the latter. But even if Reagan was acting out a role that was scripted by others, he was a hit at the polling place. Americans voted *against* Jimmy Carter in 1980, but they enthusiastically voted *for* Reagan in 1984.

REAGAN'S MAJORITY

Ronald Reagan reinvented himself several times on the way to the White House. A product of small-town Illinois, he succeeded in Hollywood in the late 1930s as a romantic lead actor while adopting the liberal politics common at the time. After World War II, he moved to the political right as a spokesman for big business. In two terms as governor of California, he spoke for a state and then a nation that were drifting toward more conservative values and expectations.

Reagan tapped into nostalgia for a simpler America. Although he was 69 when elected, his Hollywood background made it easy for him to use popular films to make his points. He once threatened to veto legislation by challenging Congress with Clint Eastwood's "Make my day." Many blockbuster movies reinforced two of Reagan's messages. One was the importance of direct confrontation with bad guys. The second was the incompetence of government bureaucracies, whose elitist mistakes could only be set right by tough individuals, like the movie heroes Dirty Harry and Rambo.

Some of Reagan's most articulate support came from anti-Communist stalwarts who feared that the United States was losing influence in the world. Despite Jimmy Carter's tough actions in 1979 and 1980 and increased defense spending, such conservatives had not trusted him to do enough. The inability to free the hostages in Iran grated. The Panama Canal and SALT II treaties seemed to give away American power. Soviet military buildup, charged the critics, was creating a "window of vulnerability."

Other Reagan voters directed their anger at government bureaucracies. Christian conservatives worried that social activists were using the federal courts to alter traditional values. Wealthy entrepreneurs from the fast-growing South and West believed that Nixon-era federal offices such as the Environ-

	Electoral Vote (%)	Popular Vote (%)
RONALD REAGAN (Republican)	**489 (91)**	**43,201,220 (50.9)**
Jimmy Carter (Democrat)	49 (9)	34,913,332 (41.2)
John B. Anderson (Independent)	–	5,581,379 (6.6)
Other candidates (Libertarian)	–	921,299 (1.1)

MAP 30–1
The Election of 1980   Ronald Reagan won in a landslide in 1980. Independent candidate John Anderson took more votes from Jimmy Carter than from Reagan, but Reagan's personal magnetism was a powerful political force. His victory confirmed the shift of the South to the Republican Party.

WHAT DID Reagan's victory tell about voters' desire for change in 1980?

CHRONOLOGY

1973	Roe v. Wade: Supreme Court struck down state laws banning abortion in the first trimester of pregnancy.
1980	Ronald Reagan is elected president.
1981	Economic Recovery and Tax Act, reducing personal income tax rates, is passed. Reagan breaks strike by air traffic controllers. AIDS is recognized as a new disease
1982	Nuclear freeze movement peaks. United States begins to finance Contra rebels against the Sandinista government in Nicaragua. Equal Rights Amendment fails to achieve ratification.
1983	241 Marines are killed by a terrorist bomb in Beirut, Lebanon. Strategic Defense Initiative introduced. U.S. invades Grenada.
1984	Reagan wins reelection.
1985	Mikhail Gorbachev initiates economic and political reforms in the Soviet Union.
1986	Tax Reform Act is adopted.
1987	Congress holds hearings on the Iran-Contra scandal. Reagan and Gorbachev sign the Intermediate Nuclear Force treaty.
1988	George Bush is elected president.
1989	Communist regimes in eastern Europe collapse; Germans tear down Berlin Wall. Financial crisis forces federal bailout of many savings and loans. United States invades Panama to capture General Manuel Noriega.
1990	Iraq invades Kuwait; and United States sends forces to the Persian Gulf. West Germany and East Germany reunite. Americans with Disabilities Act is adopted.
1991	Persian Gulf War: Operation Desert Storm drives the Iraqis from Kuwait. Soviet Union dissolves into independent nations. Strategic Arms Reduction Treaty (START) is signed.
1992	Acquittal of officers accused of beating Rodney King triggers Los Angeles riots.

mental Protection Agency and the Occupational Safety and Health Administration, were choking their businesses in red tape.

The key to Reagan's reforms, however, was disaffected blue-collar and middle-class voters who deserted the Democrats. Reagan's campaign hammered on the question; "Are you better off than you were four years ago?" Many white blue-collar voters were alienated by affirmative action and busing for school integration. They also worried about inflation and blamed their difficulties on runaway government spending.

Reagan also made the Republicans seem exciting. In the mid 1980s young people in their twenties and early thirties saw the Republicans as the party of energy and new ideas, leaving the Democrats to the middle-aged and elderly.

In the election of 1984, Democrats sealed their fate by nominating Walter Mondale, who had been vice president under Carter. Mondale was earnest, honest, and dull. Reagan ran on the theme, "It's Morning in America," with the message that a new age of pride and prosperity had begun. He won reelection with 98 percent of the electoral votes. His election confirmed that the American public found conservative ideas increasingly attractive.

30–1
Ronald Reagan, First Inaugural Address (1981)

THE NEW CONSERVATISM

Reagan's approach to public policy drew on conservative intellectuals who offered a critique of the New Deal-New Frontier approach to American government. Some of the leading figures were journalists and academics who feared that the antiwar movement had undermined the anti-Communist stance and that social changes were corrupting mainstream values. *Commentary* and The Public Interest magazines became platforms for these neoconservative arguments.

Edward Banfield's radical ideas about the failures of the Great Society set the tone of the neoconservative analysis. In *The Unheavenly City* (1968), he argued that

Ronald Reagan and his wife Nancy celebrate Reagan's inauguration as president.

Corbis–Bettman

QUICK REVIEW

The Conservative Critique

◆ Free markets work better than government programs.

◆ Government intervention does more harm than good.

◆ Government assistance saps the initiative of the poor.

30–2
Ronald Reagan, Speech to the House of Commons (1982)

Economic Recovery and Tax Act of 1981 (ERTA) A major revision of the federal income tax system.

Deregulation Reduction or removal of government regulations and encouragement of direct competition in many important industries and economic sectors.

---

liberal programs failed because inequality is based on human character and rooted in the basic structure of society; government action can solve only the problems that require better engineering, such as pollution control, better highways, or the delivery of explosives to military targets. Government's job was to preserve public order, not to right wrongs or encourage unrealistic expectations.

Other conservative writers elaborated Banfield's ideas. Charles Murray's 1984 book, *Losing Ground*, argued that welfare assistance encouraged dependency and discouraged individual efforts at self-improvement. The editorial page of the *Wall Street Journal* became a national forum for outspoken versions of neoconservatism.

The common themes of the conservative critique were simple: Free markets work better than government programs; government intervention does more harm than good; government assistance may be acceptable for property owners, but it saps the initiative of the poor. In 1964, three-quarters of Americans had trusted Washington "to do what is right." By 1980, three-quarters were convinced that the federal government wasted tax money. The neoconservatives offered the details to support Reagan's own summary: "Government is not the solution to our problems; government is the problem." The cumulative effect of the neoconservative arguments was to trash the word "liberal" and convince many Americans that labor unions and minorities were "special interests" but that oil tycoons, defense contractors, and other members of Reagan's coalition were not.

The conservative cause found support in new "think tanks" and political lobbying organizations, such as the Manhattan Institute, the Heritage Foundation, and the American Enterprise Institute, where conservative analysts could develop policy proposals and opinion pieces for newspapers. The cumulative effect shifted political discussion in a conservative direction between 1975 and 1990.

Conservatives promoted their ideology with new political tactics. Targeted mailings raised funds and mobilized voters. Radio talk shows spread the conservative message.

REAGANOMICS: DEFICITS AND DEREGULATION

The heart of the 1980s revolution was the **Economic Recovery and Tax Act of 1981 (ERTA)**, which reduced personal income tax rates by 25 percent over three years. The explicit goal was to stimulate business activity by lowering taxes overall and slashing rates for the rich. Cutting the government's total income by $747 billion over five years, ERTA meant less money for federal programs and more money in the hands of consumers and investors to stimulate economic growth.

Reagan's first budget director, David Stockman, later revealed a second goal. Because defense spending and Social Security were politically untouchable, Congress would find it impossible to create and fund new programs without cutting old ones. The first year's tax reductions were accompanied by cuts of $40 billion in federal aid to mass transit, school lunches, and similar programs. If Americans still wanted social programs, they could enact them at the local or state level.

The second part of the economic agenda was to free eager capitalists from government regulations to increase business initiative, innovation, and efficiency. The **deregulation** revolution built on a head start from the 1970s. A federal antitrust case had split the unified Bell System of AT&T and its subsidiaries into seven regional telephone companies and opened long-distance service to competition.

Congress also deregulated air travel in 1978. The result has been cheaper and more frequent air service for major hubs and poorer and more expensive service for small cities. The transformation of telecommunications similarly meant more choices for sophisticated consumers but higher prices for basic phone service.

Corporate America used the Reagan administration to attack environmental legislation as "strangulation by regulation." Vice President George Bush headed the White House Task Force on Regulatory Relief, which delayed or blocked regulations on hazardous wastes, automobile emissions, and exposure of workers to chemicals on the job.

Most attention, however, went to the instantly controversial appointment of Colorado lawyer James Watt as Secretary of the Interior. He was sympathetic to a Western movement known as the **Sagebrush Rebellion**, which wanted the vast federal land holdings in the West transferred to the states for more rapid economic use. He blamed air pollution on natural emissions from trees and compared environmentalists to both Nazis and Bolsheviks. Federal resource agencies sold trees to timber companies at a loss to the Treasury, expanded offshore oil drilling, and expedited exploration for minerals.

The early 1980s also transformed American financial markets. Individual Retirement Accounts (IRAs), a creation of the 1981 tax act, made millions of households into new investors. Dollars poured from savings accounts into higher-paying money market funds. Savings and loans had traditionally been conservative financial institutions that funneled individual savings into safe home mortgages. Under new rules, they began to compete for deposits by offering high interest rates and reinvested the money in much riskier commercial real estate. By 1990, the result would be a financial crisis in which bad loans destroyed hundreds of S&Ls, especially in the Southwest.

Corporate raiders snapped up "cash cows," profitable and cash-rich companies that could be milked of profits and assets. Dealmakers brought together often mismatched companies into huge conglomerates. They raised money with "junk bonds," high-interest, high-risk securities that could be paid off only in favorable conditions. The merger mania channeled capital into paper transactions rather than investments in new equipment and products. Another effect was to damage the economies of small and middle-sized communities by transferring control of local companies to outside managers.

CRISIS FOR ORGANIZED LABOR

The flip side of the economic boom was another round in the Republican offensive against labor unions. Reagan set the tone when he fired more than eleven thousand members of the Professional Air Traffic Controllers Organization for violating a no-strike clause in their hiring agreements. He claimed to be enforcing the letter of the law, but the message to organized labor was clear. Over the next eight years, the National Labor Relations Board and other federal agencies also weakened the power of collective bargaining.

As union membership declined and unions struggled to cope with the changing economy, corporations demanded wage rollbacks and concessions on working conditions as trade-offs for continued employment. Workers faced the threat that employers might move a factory overseas or sell out to a new owner, who could close a plant, and reopen without a union contract.

Another cause for shrinking union membership was the decline of blue-collar jobs, from 36 percent of the American work force in 1960 to roughly 25 percent at the end of the 1990s. Although unions made up part of the loss from manufacturing by recruiting government workers, such as police officers, teachers,

Sagebrush Rebellion   Political movement in the Western states in the early 1980s that called for easing of regulations on the economic issue of federal lands and the transfer of some or all of those lands to state ownership.

and bus drivers, many white-collar jobs in the private sector were in small firms and offices that were difficult to organize.

The corporate merger mania of the 1980s added to unions' woes. Takeover specialists loaded old companies with new debt, triggering efforts to cut labor costs, sell off plants, or raid pension funds for cash to pay the interest. Manufacturing employment in the 1980s declined by nearly 2 million jobs, with the expansion of high-tech manufacturing concealing much higher losses in traditional industries. In sum, while corporate merger specialists steered their BMWs along the fast lane to success, displaced mill hands drove battered pickups along potholed roads to nowhere.

AN ACQUISITIVE SOCIETY

The national media in the early 1980s discovered "yuppies," or young urban professionals, who were both a marketing category and a symbol of social change. These upwardly mobile professionals supposedly defined themselves by elitist consumerism and flocked to such upscale retailers as Neiman-Marcus and Bloomingdale's.

Far richer than yuppies were wheeler-dealers who made themselves into media stars of finance capitalism. *Forbes* magazine began to publish an annual list of the nation's 400 richest people. Before he admitted to violating the law against profiting from insider information, the corporate-merger expert Ivan Boesky had told a business-school audience; "Greed is all right. . . . You shouldn't feel guilty," epitomizing an era of big business takeovers driven by paper profits rather than underlying economic fundamentals. The superficial glamour of this era of acquisitiveness and corporate greed had its underside of loneliness and despair. Young novelists in the 1980s like Bret Easton Ellis and Jay McInerny explored the emptiness of life among the privileged. Tom Wolfe's bestselling novel *The Bonfire of the Vanities* (1987), depicted a New York where the art dealers and stockbrokers of glitzy Manhattan meet the poor of the devastated South Bronx only through an automobile accident to their mutual incomprehension and ruin.

New movements in popular music reacted to the acquisitive 1980s. Punk rock lashed out at the emptiness of 1970s disco sounds and the commercialization of youth culture. Grunge bands expressed alienation from consumerism. Hip-Hop originated among African Americans and Latinos in New York, soon adding the angry and often violent lyrics of rap. Rap during the 1980s was about personal power and sex, but it also dealt with social inequities and deprivation and tapped some of the same anger and frustration that had motivated black power advocates in the 1960s. It crossed into the mainstream culture with the help of MTV, which had begun broadcasting in 1981, but its hard-edged "attitude" undercut any sense of complacency about an inclusive American society.

POVERTY AMID PROSPERITY

Federal tax and budget changes had different effects on the rich and poor. (see Figure 30.1) The 1981 tax cuts came with sharp increases in the Social Security tax, which hit lower-income workers the hardest. The tax changes meant that the average annual income of households in the bottom 20 percent declined and that many actually paid higher taxes, while those in the top fifth increased their share of after-tax income at the expense of everyone else.

Cities and their residents absorbed approximately two-thirds of the cuts in the 1981–1982 federal budget. Provisions for accelerated depreciation (tax write-offs) of factories and equipment in the 1981 tax act encouraged the abandonment of center-city factories in favor of new facilities in the suburbs. One result was a growing jobs-housing mismatch. There were often plenty of jobs in the suburbs, but the poorer people who most needed the jobs were marooned in city slums and dependent on public transit that seldom served suburban employers.

Federal tax and spending policies in the 1980s decreased the security of middle-class families. As the economy continued to struggle through dein-dustrialization, average wage rates fell in the 1980s when measured in real purchasing. The squeeze put pressure on traditional family patterns and pushed into the workforce women who might

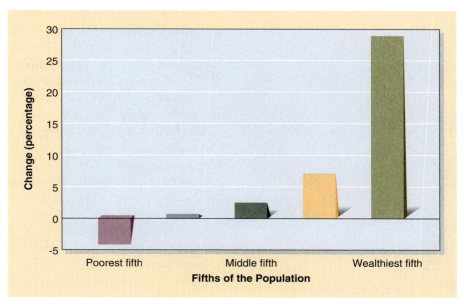

otherwise have stayed home. Even with two incomes, many families found it hard to buy a house because of skyrocketing prices in urban markets and sky-high interest rates. The national home ownership rate actually fell for the first time in almost fifty years, from 66 to 64 percent of American households. Many Americans no longer expected to surpass their parents' standard of living.

Corporate downsizing and white-collar jobs.   Corporate "downsizing" meant that lower-paying office jobs fell under the same pressures as factory jobs. Companies increasingly computerized and automated their operations and replaced full-time employees with "temps" who shifted from job to job and were not eligible for company benefits. Takeovers sometimes eliminated even more white-collar jobs. A targeted company could lose its entire management and support staff. The expectation for a college graduate who joined a large corporation of a "job for life" (often true in the 1950s and 1960s) became dubious.

The chill of corporate "downsizing" hit white-collar families most heavily toward the end of the 1980s. Big business consolidations delivered improved profits by squeezing the ranks of middle managers as well as assembly-line workers. With fewer workers to supervise and with new technologies to collect and distribute information, companies could complete their cost cutting by trimming administrators. Takeovers sometimes meant the elimination of the entire management and support staff of target companies. In the 1950s, a college graduate could sign on with a large corporation like IBM or General Motors, advance through the ranks, and expect to retire from the same company. Now the expectation of a "job for life" looked dubious; AT&T, for one example, eliminated 76,000 jobs— one-fifth of its total— between 1985 and 1989. Those white-collar workers whose jobs survived clung to them more firmly than ever. The combined result was to clog the ladder of economic opportunity for college graduates, making the cab-driving Ph.D. and the *barrista* with the B.A. popular clichés.

Increase in the poverty rate.   At the lower end of the economic ladder, the proportion of Americans living in poverty increased. After declining steadily from 1960 to a low of 11 percent in 1973, the poverty rate climbed back to the 13 to 15 percent range. Although the economy in the 1980s created lots of new jobs, half of them paid less than poverty-level wages. Conservative critics began to talk about an underclass of Americans permanently outside the mainstream economy because

FIGURE 30.1
Changes in Real Family Income, 1980–1990
In the 1980s, the poor got poorer, the middle class made slight gains, and the most affluent 20 percent of the American people did very well. Tax changes that helped well-off households were one factor. Another factor was the erosion of "family-wage jobs" in manufacturing.

of poor education, drug abuse, or sheer laziness. In fact, most of the nation's millions of poor people lived in households with employed adults. In 1992, fully 18 percent of all full-time jobs did not pay enough to lift a family of four out of poverty.

Most women, even those working full time, did not earn as much as men. In the 1960s and 1970s, the average working woman earned just 60 percent of the earnings of the average man. Only part of the wage gap could be explained by measurable factors, such as education or experience. The gap narrowed in the 1980s, with women's earnings rising to 74 percent of men's by 1996 but falling back to 72 percent in 2000.

Despite a narrowing of the income gap between working men and women (which was the result of both a decline in men's earnings and the success of better-educated younger women), women constituted nearly two-thirds of poor adults at the end of the 1980s. While only 6 percent of married-couple households were below the poverty level, 32 percent of households headed by a woman without a husband present were poor. The feminization of poverty and American reliance on private support for child rearing also meant that children had a higher chance of living in poverty than adults and that poor American children were worse off than their peers in other advanced nations.

Falling below even the working poor were growing numbers of homeless Americans. In the 1980s, a new approach to the treatment of the mentally ill reduced the population of mental hospitals from 540,000 in 1960 to only 140,000 in 1980. Deinstitutionalized patients were supposed to receive community-based treatment, but many ended up on the streets and in overnight shelters. New forms of self-destructive drug abuse, such as crack addiction, joined alcoholism. A boom in downtown real estate destroyed old skid-row districts with their bars, missions, and dollar-a-night hotels.

These factors tripled the number of permanently homeless people during the early and middle 1980s, from 200,000 to somewhere between 500,000 to 700,000. For every person in a shelter on a given night, two people were sleeping on sidewalks, in parks, in cars, and in abandoned buildings.

CONSOLIDATING THE REVOLUTION: GEORGE H.W. BUSH

In 1988 George H.W. Bush, Reagan's vice president for eight years, won the presidential election with 56 percent of the popular vote and 40 out of 50 states. As someone who had survived twenty years of bureaucratic infighting, his watchword was prudence. Using a comparison from baseball, Bush described himself as the sort of guy who would play the averages and "bunt 'em over" rather than go for the big inning.

Michael Dukakis, the Democratic nominee in 1988, was a dry, by-the-numbers manager who offered the American people "competence." The Bush campaign director, Lee Atwater, looked for "hot-button" issues and found that Dukakis as governor of Massachusetts had delayed cleanup of Massachusetts Bay, favored gun control, and had vetoed a bill requiring schoolchildren to recite the Pledge of Allegiance (arguing correctly that it would be overturned in the courts). Even more damaging, Massachusetts officials had allowed a murderer named Willie Horton a weekend furlough from prison, during which he had committed a brutal rape. Pro-Bush advertisements tapped into real worries among the voters—fear of crime, racial tension (Horton was black), worry about eroding social values. George Bush,

WHERE TO LEARN MORE

The Causes of Homelessness in America
http://www.stanford.edu/class/e297c/poverty_prejudice/soc_sec/hcauses.htm

despite his background in prep schools and country clubs, came out looking tough as nails, while the Democrats looked inept.

The ads locked Bush into a rhetorical war on crime and drugs. Americans had good cause to be worried about public safety, but most were generally unaware that the likelihood of becoming the target of a violent crime had leveled off and would continue to fall in the 1990s or that crime was far worse in minority communities than elsewhere.

The Bush administration stepped up the fight against illegal drugs. By 1990, 50 percent of federal prison inmates were in jail for drug offenses.

Bush believed that Americans wanted government to leave them alone. The major legislation from his administration was a transportation bill that shifted federal priorities from highway building toward mass transit and the **Americans with Disabilities Act** (1990) to prevent discrimination against people with physical handicaps. In the areas of crime and health care, however, Bush's lack of leadership left continuing problems.

The same attitude produced weak economic policies. The massive budget deficits of the 1980s combined with growing trade deficits swelled the national debt and turned the United States from an international creditor to a debtor nation. Despite pledging "no new taxes" in his campaign, Bush backed into a tax increase in 1990. Voters found it hard to forget the president's waffling and attempts to downplay the importance of this decision.

The "Rodney King riot" of April 1992 in Los Angeles was a reminder of the nation's inattention to the problems of race and poverty. Rodney King was a black motorist who had been savagely beaten by police officers while being arrested after a car chase on March 3, 1991. A nearby resident captured the beating on

An affluent family pedals by a group of homeless people in Santa Barbara, California. In the 1980s a combination of rising housing prices and the closure of most mental hospitals pushed increasing numbers of Americans onto the streets. Estimates of the number of homeless Americans in the late 1980s ranged from 300,000 to 3 million, depending on the definition of homelessness and the political goals of the estimator.

P. F. Bentley, Time Magazine © TimePix

Americans with Disabilities Act
Legislation in 1992 that banned discrimination against physically handicapped persons in employment, transportation, and public accommodations.

videotape from his apartment. Within two days, the tape was on national television. It confirmed the worst black fears about police behavior. Early the next year, the four officers stood trial for unjustified use of force before a suburban jury. The unexpected verdict of not guilty on April 29 stirred deep anger that escalated into four days of rioting that left fifty-eight people dead, mostly African Americans and Latinos.

The disorder was far more complex than the Watts outbreak of 1965. Central American and Mexican immigrants accounted for about one-third of the 12,000 arrests. As in 1965, some targets were white passers-by and symbols of white authority. But angry black people also targeted hundreds of Korean-owned and Vietnamese-owned shops as symbols of economic discrimination.

THE SECOND (SHORT) COLD WAR

Ronald Reagan considered the Soviet Union not a coequal nation with legitimate world interests but an "evil empire," like something from the *Star Wars* movies. After the era of détente, global tensions had started to mount in the late 1970s. They were soon higher than they had been since the 1960s.

CONFRONTING THE USSR

Who renewed the Cold War after Nixon's diplomacy of détente and Carter's early efforts at negotiation? The Soviets had pursued military expansion in the 1970s, and in 1980 were supporting Marxist regimes in civil wars in Angola, Ethiopia, Nicaragua, and especially Afghanistan. Given the aging Soviet leadership and the economic weaknesses revealed in the late 1980s, however, it makes more sense to see the Soviets as muddling along rather than executing a well-planned global strategy.

The new Reagan administration reemphasized central Europe as the focus of superpower rivalry. To counter improved Soviet armaments, the United States began to place cruise missiles and midrange Pershing II missiles in Europe in 1983. NATO governments approved the action, but it frightened millions of their citizens.

The controversy over the new missile systems was part of new thinking about nuclear weaponry. Multiple warheads on U.S. missiles already allowed Washington to target 25,000 separate places in the Soviet Union. National Security Directive D-13 (1981) stated that a nuclear war might be winnable, despite its enormous costs. All Americans needed for survival, said one administration official, were "enough shovels" to dig fallout shelters.

The nuclear freeze campaign caught the imagination of many Americans in 1981 and 1982. Drawing on the experience of the antiwar movement, it sought to halt the manufacture and deployment of new atomic weapons by the great powers. The movement gained urgency when a group of distinguished scientists argued that the smoke and dust thrown up by an atomic war would devastate the ecology of the entire globe by triggering "nuclear winter." Nearly a million people turned out for a nuclear freeze rally in New York in 1982.

In response, Reagan announced the **Strategic Defense Initiative (SDI)** or "Star Wars" program in March 1983. SDI would deploy new defenses that could intercept and destroy ballistic missiles as they rose from the ground and arced through space. Ideas included superlasers, killer satellites, and clouds of projectiles to rip missiles to shreds before they neared their targets. Few scientists thought that SDI could work. Nevertheless, President Reagan found SDI appealing, for it offered a way around the balance of terror.

WHAT FOREIGN policy measures did Reagan employ in dealing with the Soviet Union and the Middle East?

QUICK REVIEW

The New Arms Race
- The Reagan administration reemphasized central Europe as the focus of superpower rivalry.
- Pershing 11 missiles were placed in Europe in 1983.
- A National Security Directive stated that the U.S. might be able to win a nuclear war.

Strategic Defense Initiative (SDI)
President Reagan's program, announced in 1983, to defend the United States against nuclear missile attack with untested weapons systems and sophisticated technologies.

RISKY BUSINESS: FOREIGN POLICY ADVENTURES

Reagan kept the United States out of a major war and backed off in the face of serious trouble. Foreign interventions were designed to achieve symbolic victories rather than the global balance of power. The exception was the Caribbean and Central America.

Lebanon was the model for Reagan's small-scale military interventions. Israel invaded Lebanon in 1982 to clear Palestinian guerrillas from its borders. The Israeli army found itself bogged down in civil war. Reagan sent U.S. Marines to preserve the semblance of a Lebanese state and provide a face-saving exit for Israel. But the Marines were on an ill-defined "presence mission" that angered Arabs. In October 1983, a car bomb killed 241 Marines. The remainder were soon gone, confirming the Syrian observation that Americans were "short of breath" when it came to Middle East politics.

The administration had already found an easier target. Only days after the disaster in Beirut, U.S. troops invaded the small independent Caribbean island of Grenada. A left-leaning government had invited Cuban help in building an airfield, which the U.S. feared would turn into a Cuban military base. Two thousand American troops overcame Cuban soldiers who were thinly disguised as construction workers, "rescued" American medical students, and put a more sympathetic and locally popular government in power.

The Caribbean was also the focus of a secret foreign policy operated by the CIA and then by National Security Council staff. The target was Nicaragua, the Central American country where leftist Sandinista rebels had overthrown the Somoza dictatorship in 1979. Reagan and his people were determined to prevent Nicaragua from becoming "another Cuba," especially when Sandinistas helped left-wing insurgents in neighboring El Salvador. The CIA organized perhaps ten thousand "Contras" from remnants of Somoza's national guard. From bases in Honduras, they harassed the Sandinistas with sabotage and raids. Reagan called the Contras "freedom fighters."

Constitutional trouble started when an unsympathetic Congress blocked U.S. funding for the Contras. Under the direction of CIA director William Casey, Lieutenant Colonel Oliver North flouted the law by organizing aid from private donors while serving on the staff of the National Security Council.

Even shadier were arms-for-hostages negotiations with Iran. The United States in 1985 joined Israel in selling five hundred antitank missiles to Iran. The deal followed stern public pronouncements that the United States would never negotiate with terrorists, and it violated this nation's official trade embargo against Iran. Iran helped in securing the release of several Americans held hostage in Lebanon by pro-Iranian radicals, but other hostages were soon taken. Colonel North funneled proceeds from the arms sales to the Contras, in a double evasion of the law.

Like Watergate, the Iran-Contra affair was a two-sided scandal. First was the blatant misjudgment of operating a secret and bumbling foreign policy that depended on international arms dealers and ousted Nicaraguan military officers. Second was a concerted effort to cover up the actions. North shredded relevant documents and lied to Congress. In his final report in 1994, Special Prosecutor Lawrence Walsh found that President Reagan and Vice President Bush participated in efforts to withhold information and mislead Congress.

American policy in Asia was a refreshing contrast with Central America and the Middle East. In the Philippines, American diplomats helped push corrupt President Ferdinand Marcos out and opened the way for a popular uprising to put Corazon Aquino in office. Secretary of State George Shultz made sure that the

United States supported popular democracy while reassuring the Philippine military. In South Korea, the United States similarly helped ease out an unpopular dictator by firmly supporting democratic elections that brought in a more popular but still pro-U.S. government.

EMBRACING PERESTROIKA

Thaw in the Cold War started in Moscow. Mikhail Gorbachev became general secretary of the Communist party in 1985. Gorbachev was the picture of vigor compared to his three sick or elderly predecessors, Leonid Brezhnev, Yuri Andropov, and Constantin Chernenko. He was a master of public relations who charmed western Europe's leaders and public. Gorbachev startled Soviet citizens by urging *glasnost*, or political openness and free discussion of issues. He followed by setting the goal of *perestroika*, or restructuring of the painfully bureaucratic Soviet economy.

Gorbachev also decided that he needed to reduce the crushing burden of Soviet defense spending if the USSR was to have any chance of modernizing. During Reagan's second term, the Soviets offered one concession after another in a relentless drive for arms control.

Reagan cast off decades of belief in the dangers of Soviet Communism and took Gorbachev seriously. He was willing to abandon many of his most fervent supporters. He frightened his own staff when he met Gorbachev in Iceland in the summer of 1986 and accepted the principle of deep cuts in strategic forces. Reagan explained that when he railed against the "evil empire," he had been talking about Brezhnev and the bad old days; Gorbachev and *glasnost* were different.

In the end, Reagan negotiated the **Intermediate Nuclear Force (INF)** agreement over the strong objections of the CIA and the Defense Department but with the support of Secretary of State Shultz. Previous treaties had only slowed the growth of nuclear weapons. The new pact matched Soviet SS-20s with American cruise missiles as an entire class of weapons that would be destroyed, with on-site inspections for verification.

CRISIS AND DEMOCRACY IN EASTERN EUROPE

As a believer in personal diplomacy, George Bush based much of his foreign policy on his changing attitudes toward Mikhail Gorbachev. He started lukewarm, talking tough to please the Republican right wing. Before 1989 was over, however, the president had decided that Gorbachev was OK. For the next two years, the United States pushed reform in Europe while being careful not to damage Gorbachev's position at home.

The people of eastern Europe overcame both American and Soviet caution. Gorbachev had urged his eastern European allies to emulate *perestroika*. Poland and Hungary were the first satellite nations to eject their Communist leadership in favor of democracy in mid-1989. When East Germans began to flee westward through Hungary, the East German regime bowed to mounting pressure and opened the Berlin Wall on November 9. By the end of 1989, there were new governments in Czechoslovakia, Romania, Bulgaria, and East Germany. These largely peaceful revolutions destroyed the military and economic agreements that had harnessed the satellites to the Soviet economy. The USSR swallowed hard, accepted the loss of its satellites, and slowly withdrew its army from eastern Europe.

Events in eastern Europe left German reunification as a point of possible conflict. West German Chancellor Helmut Kohl removed one obstacle when he reassured Poland and Russia that Germany would seek no changes in the boundaries drawn after World War II. By July 1990, the United States and USSR had agreed that a reunited Germany would belong to NATO. The decision satisfied France and Britain

---

WHERE TO LEARN MORE

The Intermediate Nuclear Force Agreement (INF)
http://www.state.gov/www/global/arms/treaties/infl.html

Glasnost Russian for "openness" applied to Mikhail Gorbachev's encouragement of new ideas and easing of political repression in the Soviet Union.

Perestroika Russian for "restructuring," applied to Mikhail Gorbachev's efforts to make the Soviet economic and political systems more modern, flexible, and innovative.

Intermediate Nuclear Force Agreement (INF) Disarmament agreement between the United States and the Soviet Union under which an entire class of missiles would be removed and destroyed and on-site inspections would be permitted.

that a stronger Germany would still be under the influence of the Western allies. In October, the two Germanies completed their political unification, although it would be years before their mismatched economies functioned as one.

Throughout these events, the Bush administration proceeded cautiously. Bush tried not to push the Soviet Union too hard and infuriate Russian hard-liners. "I don't want to do something that would inadvertently set back the progress," he said.

The final act in the transformation of the USSR began with an attempted coup against Mikhail Gorbachev in August, 1991 of old-line Communist bureaucrats. But they turned out to be bumblers and drunks who hadn't secured military support and even failed to take over radio and television stations. Boris Yeltsin, president of the Russian Republic, organized the resistance. Within three days, the plotters themselves were under arrest.

Before the month was out, the Soviet parliament banned the Communist party. By December, Gorbachev had resigned, and all of the fifteen component republics of the Soviet Union had declared their independence. The superpower Union of Soviet Socialist Republics ceased to exist. Russia remained the largest and strongest of the new states followed by Ukraine and Kazakhstan.

Analysts agree that the relentless pressure of American defense spending helped bankrupt and undermine the USSR. It is an open question whether this same American defense spending also weakened the United States' economy and its ability to compete in the world marketplace. Some scholars see the demise of the Soviet empire as ultimate justification for forty years of Cold War. Dissenters argue the opposite— that the collapse of European Communism shows that American leaders had magnified its threat.

A more definitive answer may lie in what scholars learn about Soviet Cold War policy when they explore the Russian archives.

THE FIRST PERSIAN GULF WAR

On August 2, 1990, President Saddam Hussein of Iraq seized the neighboring country of Kuwait. The conquest gave Iraq control of 20 percent of the world's oil production and reserves. Bush demanded unconditional withdrawal, enlisted European and Arab allies in an anti-Iraq coalition, and persuaded Saudi Arabia to accept substantial U.S. forces for its protection against Iraqi invasion. Within weeks, the Saudis were host to tens of thousands of U.S. soldiers and hundreds of aircraft.

Iraq was a dictatorship that had just emerged from an eight-year war with Iran. Saddam Hussein had depended on help from the United States and Arab nations in this war, but Iraq was now economically exhausted. Kuwait itself was a small, rich nation whose ruling dynasty enjoyed huge oil royalties. The U.S. State Department had signaled earlier in 1990 that it might support some concessions by Kuwait to Iraq. Saddam Hussein read the signal as an open invitation to do what he wanted.

The Iraqis gave Bush a golden opportunity to assert America's world influence. The importance of Middle Eastern oil helped enlist France and Britain as military allies and secure billions of dollars from Germany and Japan. A short-term oil glut also meant that the industrial nations could boycott Iraqi production. The collapse of Soviet power and Gorbachev's interest in cooperating with the United States meant that the Soviets would not interfere with U.S. plans.

President Bush and his advisers offered a series of justifications for American actions. First and most basic were the desire to punish armed aggression and the need to protect Iraq's other neighbors, although there was scant evidence of Iraqi preparations against Saudi Arabia. Sanctions and diplomatic pressure might also have brought withdrawal from most or all of Kuwait. However, additional

WHERE TO LEARN MORE

A Concrete Curtain: The Life and Death of the Berlin Wall
http://www.wall-berlin.org/ gb/berlin.htm

QUICK REVIEW

The Fall of Gorbachev and the Soviet Union

- ◆ August 1991: old-line communists attempt a coup against Gorbachev.
- ◆ Boris Yeltsin organized the successful resistance to the plotters.
- ◆ Gorbachev resigned and all fifteen Soviet republics declared their independence.

30–3
George Bush, Address to the Nation Announcing Allied Military Action in the Persian Gulf (1991)

First Persian Gulf War   War (1991) between Iraq and a U.S.-led coalition that followed Iraq's invasion of Kuwait and resulted in the expulsion of Iraqi forces from that country.

WHERE TO LEARN MORE

★ The Gulf War
http://www.pbs.org/wgbh/pages/
frontline/gulf/

American objectives— to destroy Iraq's capacity to create atomic weapons and to topple Saddam's regime— would require direct military action.

The Persian Gulf itself offered an equally golden opportunity to the American and allied armed forces. The United States could try out the tactics of armored maneuver and close land-air cooperation that the Pentagon had devised to protect Germany against Soviet invasion.

In October, Bush decided to increase the number of American troops in Saudi Arabia to 580,000. The United States also secured a series of increasingly tough United Nations resolutions that culminated in November 1990 with Security Council Resolution 678, authorizing "all necessary means" to liberate Kuwait. The president convinced Congress to agree to military action under the umbrella of the U.N.

War began one day after the U.N.'s January 15 deadline for Iraqi withdrawal from Kuwait. **Operation Desert Storm** opened with massive air attacks on command centers, transportation facilities, and Iraqi forward positions. The air war also seriously hurt Iraqi civilians by disrupting utilities and food supplies.

Americans watched CNN's live transmission of Baghdad under bombardment in fascination. The forty-day rain of bombs was the prelude to a ground attack. On February 24, 1991, U.S. and allied forces swept into Iraq and advanced directly to liberate Kuwait. A cease-fire came one hundred hours after the start of the ground war. Allied forces suffered only 240 deaths in action, compared to perhaps 100,000 for the Iraqis. Militarily, overwhelming the Iraqis turned out to be easy.

The United States hoped to replace Saddam Hussein without disrupting Iraqi society. Instead, the hundred-hour war incited armed rebellions against Saddam by Shi'ite Muslims in southern Iraq and by Kurds in the north. Since Bush and his advisers were unwilling to get embroiled in a civil war, they stood by while Saddam crushed the uprisings. Saddam Hussein became a hero to many in the Islamic world simply by remaining in power. But Bush had accomplished exactly what he wanted— the restoration of the status quo.

In 2003, however, his son, President George W. Bush, was to launch the second Gulf War with the explicit purpose of toppling Saddam's regime (see Chapter 31).

Operation Desert Storm Code name for the successful offensive against Iraq by the United States and its allies in the Persian Gulf War (1991).

Growth In The Sunbelt

HOW DID America's
population change in the 1980s?

The rise in the military and defense spending from the late 1970s through the early 1990s and the Persian Gulf War, were two of the most powerful sources of growth in the **Sunbelt**, the Southern and Western regions of the United States. Americans had discovered this "new" region in the 1970s. Kevin Phillips's book *The Emerging Republican Majority* (1969) first popularized the term "Sunbelt." Phillips pointed out that people and economic activity had been flowing southward and westward since World War II, shifting the balance of power away from the Northeast.

The Sunbelt was a region of conservative voting habits where Republicans solidified their status as a majority party, a process continuing to the present. In the 1990s, the region's economic power was reflected in a conservative tone in both the Republican and Democratic parties and in the prominence of Southern political leaders. (see Map 30–2).

The rise of the Sunbelt, which is anchored by Florida, Texas, and California, reflected the leading economic trends of the 1970s and 1980s, including military spending, immigration from Asia and Latin America, and recreation and retirement spending. Corporations liked the business climate of the South, which had weak labor laws, low taxes, and lower costs of living and doing business.

Sunbelt The states of the American South and Southwest.

MAP EXPLORATION

To explore an interactive version of this map, go to **http://www.prenhall.com/goldfield2/map30.2**

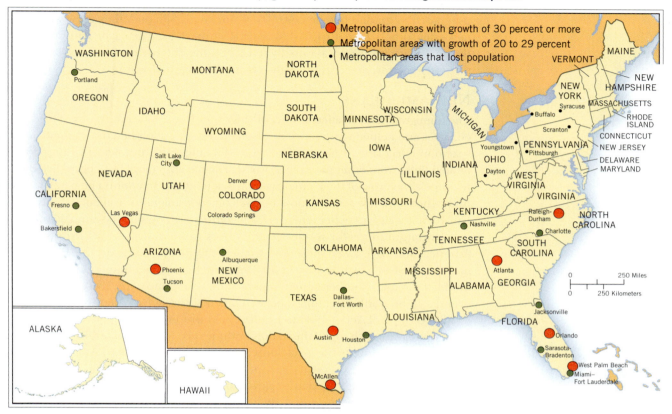

MAP 30–2

Fast-Growing and Shrinking Metropolitan Areas, 1900–2000   In the 1990s, boom cities were found in the Southeast, Southwest, and on the West Coast. In contrast, all of the large metropolitan areas that lost population were in Ohio, New York, or Pennsylvania, the area hardest hit by the decline of jobs in established manufacturing industries.

WHAT ECONOMIC forces contributed to the growth of some cities and the decline of others?

THE DEFENSE BOOM

The Vietnam buildup and reinvestment in the military during the Carter (1977–1981) and Reagan (1981–1989) administrations fueled the growth of the Sunbelt. Over the forty years from the Korean conflict to the first Persian Gulf War, the United States made itself the mightiest military power ever known. Military bases and defense contractors remolded the economic landscape, as mild winters and clear skies for training and operations helped the South and West attract more than 75 percent of military payrolls.

Big cities and small depended on defense spending. Southern California thrived on more than 500,000 jobs in the aircraft industry. Visitors to Colorado Springs could drive past sprawling Fort Carson and visit the new Air Force Academy, opened in 1958. Sunk deep from view was the North American Air Defense command post beneath Cheyenne Mountain. Malmstrom Air Force Base transformed Great Falls, Montana, from a manufacturing and transportation center into a coordinating center for Minuteman missiles targeted at Moscow and Beijing.

Defense spending underwrote the expansion of American science and technology. Nearly one-third of all engineers worked on military projects. Large universities, such as MIT, Michigan, CalTech, and Stanford, were leading defense contractors. The modern electronics business started in New York, Boston and the San Francisco Bay Area with research and development for military uses, such as guided-missile controls. California's Silicon Valley grew with military sales long before it turned to consumer markets. The space component of the aerospace industry was equally reliant on the defense economy. NASA's centers were scattered across the South from Florida to Houston.

NEW AMERICANS

The **Immigration and Nationality Act of 1965**, transformed the ethnic mix of the United States and helped to stimulate the Sunbelt boom. It abolished the national quota system in effect since 1924 that had favored immigrants from western Europe and limited those from other parts of the world. The old law's racial bias contradicted the self-proclaimed role of the United States as a defender of freedom. The new law gave preference to family reunification and welcomed immigrants from all nations. The United States also accepted refugees from communism outside the annual limits.

Immigration reform opened the doors to Mediterranean Europe, Latin America, and Asia. Legal migration to the United States surged from 1.1 million in 1960–1964 to nearly 4 million for 1990–1994. Nonlegal immigrants may have doubled the total number of newcomers in the 1970s and early 1980s. Meanwhile, over 2 million nonlegal immigrants had taken advantage of the Immigration Reform and Control Act of 1986 to legalize their presence in the United States.

Immigration changed the nation's ethnic mix. Members of officially defined ethnic and racial minorities accounted for 30 percent in 2000. Asians and Hispanics were the fastest growing group. (See Table 30.1)

The largest single group of new Americans came from Mexico. Mexican Americans are the largest minority group in many Southwestern and Western states. They were also transforming neighborhoods in Chicago and other midwestern cities and changing everything from politics to the Catholic church.

The East Coast has meanwhile welcomed migrants from the West Indies and Central America. Many Puerto Ricans, who hold U.S. citizenship, came to Philadelphia and New York in the 1950s and 1960s. Other countries sending large numbers of immigrants include Haiti, the Dominican Republic, Guatemala, Honduras, Nicaragua, El Salvador, and Jamaica. Cuban refugees from Castro's regime concentrated in Miami and in major cities such as Chicago and New York.

Another great immigration has occurred eastward across the Pacific. Chinese, Filipinos, Koreans, Samoans, and other Asians and Pacific Islanders constituted only 6 percent of newcomers to the United States in 1965, but nearly half of all arrivals in 1990. The numbers of ethnic Chinese in the United States jumped from a quarter of a million in 1965 to 1,645,000 in 1990.

The most publicized Asian immigrants were refugees from Indochina after Communist victories in 1975. Many settled on the West Coast. The San Francisco Bay area, for example, had more than a dozen Vietnamese-language newspapers, magazines, and cable television programs.

Recent immigrants have found both economic possibilities and problems. On the negative side, immigration has added to the numbers of nonunion workers. But immigrants also added to the pool of talent and ambition in the expanding economy of the mid-1980s and 1990s. The 130,000 Vietnamese immigrants of 1975 now have an average adjusted income above the national average. Asians and Pacific islanders by 2000 constituted 22 percent of students in California's public universities. Many newcomers have opened groceries, restaurants, and other businesses. Juan Fernandez found it easier to set up a successful car repair

Immigration and Nationality Act of 1965 Federal legislation that replaced the national quota system for immigration with new limits for each hemisphere.

TABLE 30.1
Major Racial and Ethnic Minorities in the United States

1960 Population (in millions)	Percentage of total	2000 Population (in millions)	Percentage of total
American Indians	0.5	0.3	2.5 0.9
Asians and Pacific Islanders	1.1	0.6	10.6 3.7
African Americans	18.9	10.5	34.7 12.3
Hispanics	Not available		35.3 12.5

shop in Gary, Indiana, than in Guadalajara, Mexico, because his fellow immigrants prefer a Spanish-speaking mechanic. Asian-born business owners have filled retail vacuums in central city neighborhoods abandoned by chain stores.

OLD GATEWAYS AND NEW

The new immigration had its most striking effects in coastal and border cities. New York again became a great mixing bowl of the American population. By 1990, some 28 percent of the population of New York City was foreign-born, compared to 42 percent at the height of European immigration in 1910. ZIP code 11373 in North Queens was reportedly the most diverse neighborhood in the world.

Southern and Western cities became gateways for immigrants from Latin America and Asia. Los Angeles emerged as "the new Ellis Island." As *Time* magazine put it in 1983, the arrival of more than 2 million immigrants altered "the collective beat and bop of L.A." In 1960, a mere 1 percent of the Los Angeles County population was Asian and 11 percent was Hispanic. By 2000, the figures for a population of 9.5 million were 12 percent Asian and 45 percent Hispanic. The sprawling neighborhoods of East Los Angeles make up the second-largest Mexican city in the world. One hundred languages are spoken among students entering Los Angeles schools.

New York and Los Angeles are world cities as well as immigrant destinations. Like London and Tokyo, they are capitals of world trade and finance, with international banks and headquarters of multinational corporations. The deregulation of international finance and the explosive spread of instant electronic communication in the 1980s confirmed their importance as global decision centers.

Similar factors turned Miami into the economic capital of the Caribbean. Half a million Cuban businessmen, white-collar workers, and their families moved to the United States between 1959 and 1980 to escape Castro's government. Most of the newcomers stayed in South Florida. Their success in business made Miami and helped to attract two million Latin American tourists and shoppers during the 1980s. Miami also has hundreds of offices for corporations engaged in U.S.-Latin American trade.

Cross-border communities in the Southwest, such as El Paso, Texas and Juarez, Mexico, or San Diego, California and Tijuana, Mexico, are "Siamese twins joined at the cash register." Employees with work permits commute from Mexico to the United States. American popular culture flows southward. Bargain hunters and tourists pass in both directions.

Both nations have promoted the cross-border economy. The Mexican government in the mid-1960s began to encourage a "platform economy" by allowing companies on the Mexican side of the border to import components and inputs duty-free as long as 80 percent of the items were reexported and 90 percent of the workers were Mexicans. The intent is to encourage American corporations to locate assembly plants south of the border. Such *maquila* industries can employ lower-wage workers and avoid strict antipollution laws (leading to serious threats to public health on both sides of the border). From the Gulf of Mexico to the Pacific Ocean, eighteen hundred *maquiladora* plants employed half a million workers. North of the border, U.S. factories supplied components under laws that meshed with the Mexican regulations.

THE GRAYING OF AMERICA

Retirees were another factor contributing to the growth of the Sunbelt. Between 1965 and 2000, the number of Americans aged 65 and over jumped from 18.2 million to 35 million, or 12.4 percent of the population. For the first time, most Americans could expect to survive into old age. The "young old" are people in their sixties and seventies who remain sharp, vigorous, and financially secure because of better private pensions, Social Security, and Medicare. The "old old" are the 9 million people in their eighties and nineties who often require daily assistance, although data show that improved medical services have made such Americans healthier and more self-sufficient than they were ten or twenty years ago.

Older Americans have become a powerful voice in public affairs. They tend to vote against local taxes but fight efforts to slow the growth of Social Security, even though growing numbers of the elderly are being supported by a relatively smaller proportion of working men and women. By the 1990s, observers noted increasing resentment among younger Americans, who fear that public policy is biased against the needs of men and women in their productive years. In turn, the elderly fiercely defend the programs of the 1960s and 1970s that have kept many of them from poverty. Protecting Medicare and Social Security was one of the Democrats' best campaign issues in 1996 and 2000, after Republicans suggested cuts in spending growth.

Retired Americans changed the social geography of the United States. Much growth in the South and Southwest has been financed by money earned in the Northeast and Midwest and transferred by retirees. Florida in the 1980s absorbed nearly 1 million new residents aged sixty or older. California, Arizona, Texas, the Carolinas, and the Ozark Mountains of Missouri and Arkansas have all attracted retirees, many of them in age-segregated communities such as Sun City near Phoenix.

VALUES IN COLLISION

In 1988, two very different religious leaders sought a presidential nomination. Pat Robertson's campaign for the Republican nomination tapped deep discontent with the changes in American society since the 1960s. A television evangelist, Robertson used the mailing list from his 700 Club program to mobilize conservative Christians and pushed the Republican Party further to the right on family and social issues. Jesse Jackson, a civil-rights leader and minister from Chicago, mounted a grassroots campaign with the opposite goal of moving the Democratic Party to the left on social and economic policy. Drawing on his experience in the black civil-rights movement, he assembled a "Rainbow Coalition" that included labor unionists, feminists, and others whom Robertson's followers feared. Both Jackson and Robertson used their powerful personalities and religious convictions to inspire support from local churches and churchgoers.

In diagnosing social ills, Robertson pointed to the problems of individual indulgence, while Jackson pointed to racism and economic inequality. Their sharp divergence expressed differences in basic values that divided Americans in the 1980s and beyond. In substantial measure, the conflicts were rooted in the social and cultural changes of the 1960s and 1970s that had altered traditional institutions, especially the 1950s ideal of a "Ward and June Cleaver" family. Changes in roles and expectations among women and new openness about gay and lesbian sexuality were particularly powerful in dividing American churches and politics.

In Swann v. Charlotte-Mecklenburg Board of Education (1971), the U.S. Supreme Court held that crosstown busing was an acceptable solution to de facto segregation that resulted from residential patterns within a single school district. When school officials failed to achieve racial balance, federal judges ordered their own busing plans. For many Americans, the image of busing for racial integration was fixed in 1975 when white people in Boston reacted with violence against black students who were bused to largely white high schools in the South Boston and Charlestown neighborhoods. The goal of equal opportunity clashed with equally strong values of neighborhood, community, and ethnic solidarity.

Busing was self-defeating, for it caused white families to move out of the integrating school district or to place their children in private academies, as happened frequently in the South. Busing also caused suburbanites to defend their political independence fiercely.

Zoning was another powerful tool of suburban self-defense. Restrictive building codes, requirements for large lots, and expensive subdivision fees could price all but the rich out of the local housing market. Many suburbs refused to zone land for apartments. As one Connecticut suburbanite put it, for a moderate-income family to hope to move into one of the state's most exclusive suburbs was "like going into Tiffany and demanding a ring for $12.50. Tiffany doesn't have any rings for $12.50. Well, Greenwich is like Tiffany."

However, as continued decentralization pushed the suburban share of the U.S. population toward 50 percent in the 1990s, most suburban rings displayed the full range of American society with the same economic, traffic, and pollution problems as the central cities.

NEW MEANINGS FOR AMERICAN FAMILIES

The political and social changes of the 1960s altered the patterns and meaning of family life. Americans began to rethink ideas about families and to emphasize personal identities in addition to traditional family roles. Women redefined themselves as individuals and workers as well as wives and mothers. Gays and lesbians asserted that their sexual orientations were not aberrations from "normal" family patterns but were valid in their own right. As average life spans lengthened, older Americans found personal satisfaction and political influence as members of their own communities and interest groups.

If one result of changing family patterns was new political groupings and new policies, another was deep confusion. In 1992, Vice 'President Dan Quayle earned headlines, and some derision, by criticizing the television comedy *Murphy Brown* for a positive and unrealistic portrayal of its lead character as a single mother. In the same year, however, 98 percent of Americans agreed that the label "family" applied to a married couple living with their children and 81 percent also applied "family" to the *Murphy Brown* scenario of an unwed mother living with her child. More than a quarter were even comfortable using "family" for two lesbian women or two gay men living together and raising children.

THE FEMINIST CRITIQUE

The growing dissatisfaction of many women with the domestic role expected of them in the 1950s helped set the stage for a revived feminism. Important steps in this revival included the Presidential Commission on the Status of Women in 1961;

WHAT WERE the culture wars?

the addition of gender as one of the categories protected by the Civil Rights Act of 1964; and creation of the National Organization for Women (NOW) in 1966.

Throughout the 1970s, activists battled to open one job category after another to women who proved that they could indeed use tools, run computers, or pick stocks on Wall Street. They also battled for equal pay for everyone with equal qualifications and responsibilities.

Changes in sexual behavior paralleled efforts to equalize treatment in the workplace. More reliable methods of contraception, especially birth control pills introduced in the early 1960s, gave women greater control over child-bearing. In some ways a replay of ideas from the 1920s, a new sexual revolution eroded the double standard that expected chastity of women but tolerated promiscuity among men. One consequence was a singles culture that accepted sexual activity between unmarried men and women.

Feminist radicals caught the attention of the national media with a demonstration against the 1968 Miss America pageant. Protesters crowned a sheep as Miss America and set out barrels for women who wanted to make a statement by tossing their bras and makeup in the trash.

Women's liberation took off as a social and political movement in 1970 and 1971. Within a few years, millions of women had recognized events and patterns in their lives as discrimination based on gender.

WOMEN'S RIGHTS AND PUBLIC POLICY

Congress wrote key goals of the feminist movement into law in the early 1970s. Title IX of the Educational Amendments (1972) to the Civil Rights Act prohibited discrimination by sex in any educational program receiving federal aid. In the same year, Congress sent the Equal Rights Amendment (ERA) to the states for ratification. The amendment read, "Equal rights under the law shall not be denied or abridged by the United States or by any state on account of sex." More than twenty states ratified quickly in the first few months and another dozen after increasingly tough battles in state legislatures. The ERA then stalled, three states short, when the time limit for ratification expired in 1982.

In January 1973, the U.S. Supreme Court expanded the debate about women's rights with the case of **_Roe_ v. _Wade_**. Voting 7 to 2, the Court struck down state laws forbidding abortion in the first three months of pregnancy and set guidelines for abortion during the remaining months. Drawing on the earlier decision of _Griswold v. Connecticut_, which dealt with access to information about birth control, the justices held that the Fourteenth Amendment includes a right to privacy that blocks states from interfering with a woman's right to terminate pregnancy.

The feminist movement and specific policy measures related to it put equal rights and the fight against sexism (a word no one knew before 1965) on the national agenda and gradually changed how Americans thought about the relationships between men and women. Feminists focused attention on rape as a crime of violence, calling attention to the burdens the legal system placed on rape victims. In the 1980s and 1990s, they also challenged sexual harassment in the workplace, gradually refining the boundaries between acceptable and unacceptable behavior.

These changes came in the context of increasingly sharp conflict over the feminist agenda. Both the ERA and _Roe_ stirred impassioned support and equally passionate opposition. Opponents of the ERA worried about unisex restrooms (not a problem on commercial airliners) and women in the military (not a problem in the Persian Gulf War). Also fueling the debate was a deep split between the mainstream feminist view of women as fully equal individuals and the contrary belief that women had a special role as anchors of families, an updating of the nineteenth-century idea of separate spheres.

Roe v. _Wade_ U.S. Supreme Court decision (1973) that disallowed state laws prohibiting abortion during the first three months (trimester) of pregnancy and established guidelines for abortion in the second and third trimesters.

The most sweeping change in the lives of American women did not come from federal legislation or court cases but from the growing likelihood that a married woman would work outside the home. In 1960, some 32 percent of married women were in the labor force; forty years later, 69 percent were working or looking for work (along with 69 percent of single women). Federal and state governments slowly responded to the changing demands of work and family with new policies such as a federal child care tax credit.

One reason for more working women was inflation in the 1970s and declining wages in the 1980s, both of which eroded the ability of families to live comfortably on one income. Between 1979 and 1986, fully 80 percent of married households saw the husband's income fall in constant dollars. The result, headlined the *Wall Street Journal* in 1994: "More Women Take Low-Wage Jobs Just So Their Families Can Get By." One young woman juggled community college courses and full-time work as an insurance company clerk, earning more than her husband brought home as a heavy equipment operator. Another worked at the drive-up window of a shopping center bank and cleaned offices on Saturdays to help pay the mortgage on a house purchased before her husband's employer imposed pay cuts.

A second reason for the increase in working women from 29 million in 1970 to 66 million in 2000 was increasing need for "women's jobs" like data entry clerks, reservation agents, and nurses. Indeed, the American economy still divides job categories by sex. Despite some movement toward gender-neutral hiring in the 1970s job types were more segregated by sex than by race in the early 1990s.

COMING OUT

New militancy among gay men and lesbians drew on several of the social changes of the late 1960s and 1970s. Willingness to acknowledge nonstandard sexual behavior was part of a change in public values. Tactics of political pressure came from the antiwar and civil rights movements. The timing, with a series of key events from 1969 to 1974, coincided with that of women's liberation.

Gay activism spread from the biggest cities to smaller communities, from the coasts to Middle America. New York police had long harassed gay bars and their customers. When police raided Manhattan's Stonewall Inn in June 1969, patrons fought back in a weekend of disorder. The **"Stonewall Rebellion"** was a catalyst for homosexuals to assert themselves as a political force. San Francisco also became a center of gay life. By the late 1970s, the city had more than three hundred business and social gathering places identified as gay and lesbian.

With New Yorkers and San Franciscans as examples, more and more gay men and lesbians "came out," or went public about their sexual orientation. They published newspapers, organized churches, and lobbied politicians for protection of basic civil rights such as equal access to employment, housing, and public accommodations. They staged "gay pride" days and marches. In 1974, the American Psychiatric Association eliminated homosexuality from its official list of mental disorders.

Life in gay communities took an abrupt turn in the 1980s when a new worldwide epidemic began to affect the United States. Scientists first identified a new disease pattern, **acquired immune deficiency syndrome (AIDS)**, in 1981. The name described the symptoms resulting from the human immunodeficiency virus (HIV), which destroys the body's ability to resist disease. HIV is transferred through blood and semen. In the 1980s, the most frequent American victims were gay men and intravenous drug users.

A decade later, it was clear that HIV/AIDS was a national and even global problem. By the end of 1998, AIDS had been responsible for 411,000 deaths in the United States, transmission to heterosexual women was increasing, and HIV infection had spread to every American community.

AIDS quilt, Washington, D.C., October, 1992

Lisa Quinones/Black Star

Stonewall Rebellion   On June 27, 1969, patrons fought back when police raided the gay Stonewall Inn in New York.

Acquired Immune Deficiency Syndrome (AIDS)   A complex of deadly pathologies resulting from infection with the human immunodeficiency virus (HIV).

FROM THEN TO NOW
Women and Work in American Offices

At the end of the twentieth century, women filled the majority of America's office-based jobs. More women than men worked as office managers, receptionists, library administrators, bank tellers, travel agents, administrative assistants, insurance agents, bookkeepers, and other desk-and-computer occupations.

In 1997, women made up 46 percent of the American labor force. Seven out of ten of these women worked in professional, managerial, technical, administrative support, and sales positions. They ranged from corporate CEOs and college professors to clerks in state motor vehicle offices and the voices that take your orders and reservations when you dial 800.

This employment pattern, which most Americans now take for granted, is the product of 140 years of gradual change that began with, and was triggered by, the Civil War. Before the Civil War, American women found employment as domestic servants, sometimes as mill operatives, and increasingly as schoolteachers, but not as office workers. Clerks were men— sometimes settled into lower-status white-collar careers and sometimes learning a business from the inside before rising into management. Their jobs consisted of copying letters and documents by hand, tracing orders and correspondence, and keeping financial records.

The Civil War, however, sharply increased the flow of government paperwork while diverting young men into military service. The U.S. Treasury Department in Washington responded in 1862 by hiring women to sort and package federal bonds and currency. Treasury officials fretted about the moral implications of mixing men and women in offices but overcame these concerns when they found that women were both cheap and reliable workers. By 1870, several hundred women worked in Washington's federal offices, enough for a character in a novel about the Hayes administration (1877–1881) to comment that he could learn from a glance to "single out the young woman who supported her family upon her salary and the young woman who bought her ribbons with it; the widow who fed half-a-dozen children."

As the national economy grew in the late nineteenth century, it generated ever-increasing flows of information. New technologies such as telephones and typewriters routinized clerical work. These trends increased the need for desk workers, a need largely filled by middle-class women, whose literacy was often guaranteed by the high school diplomas that went disproportionately to women in the later nineteenth century. As women workers filled new downtown skyscrapers, the central districts of large cities lost some of their rough edges and grew more respectable as centers of shopping and entertainment.

By 1900, the division of labor that would characterize the first half of the twentieth century was in place. Women comprised 76 percent of the nation's stenographers and typists and 29 percent of its cashiers, bookkeepers, and accountants. For the most part, however, they occupied the lower echelons of the office hierarchy. It was men who determined what was to be said; women who transcribed, transmitted, recorded, and filed their messages. Only in recent decades have women begun successfully to challenge that established order.

By the 1990s, Americans were accustomed to open discussion of gay sexuality, if not always accepting of its reality. Television stars and other entertainers could "come out" and retain their popularity. So could politicians in selected districts. On the issue of gays in the military, however, Congress and the Pentagon were more cautious, accepting a policy that made engaging in homosexual acts, though not sexual orientation itself, grounds for discharge.

Churches in Change

Americans take their search for spiritual grounding much more seriously than do citizens of other industrial nations. Roughly half of privately organized social activity (such as charity work) is church related. In the mid-1970s, 56 percent of Americans said that religion was "very important" to them, compared to only 27 percent of Europeans.

However, mainline Protestant denominations that traditionally defined the center of American belief struggled after 1970. The United Methodist Church, the Presbyterian Church U.S.A., the United Church of Christ, and the Episcopal Church battled internally over the morality of U.S. foreign policy, the role of women in the ministry, and the reception of gay and lesbian members. While they were strengthened by the ecumenical impulse, which united denominational branches that had been divided by ethnicity or regionalism, they gradually lost their predominant position among American churches, perhaps because ecumenism diluted the certainty of their message.

By contrast, evangelical Protestant churches have benefited from the direct appeal of their message and from strong roots in the booming Sunbelt. Members of evangelical churches (25 percent of white Americans) now outnumber the members of mainline Protestant churches (20 percent). Major evangelical denominations include Baptists, the Church of the Nazarene, and the Assemblies of God. Fundamentalists, defined by a belief in the literal truth of the Bible, are a subset of evangelicals. So are 8 to 10 million Pentecostals and charismatics, who accept "gifts of the spirit," such as healing by faith and speaking in tongues.

Outsiders know evangelical Christianity through "televangelists." Spending on religious television programming rose from $50 to $600 million by 1980. By the 1970s, it reached 20 percent of American households. (See American Views, "The Religious Imperative in Politics.")

Behind the glitz and hype of the television pulpit, evangelical churches emphasized religion as an individual experience focused on personal salvation. They also offered communities of faith to stabilize fragmented lives in a changing society.

Another important change in national religious life has been the continuing "Americanization" of the Roman Catholic church following the Second Vatican Council in 1965, in which church leaders sought to respond to postwar industrial society. In the United States, Roman Catholicism moved toward the center of American life, while Asian and Latino immigrants brought new vigor to many parishes and many inner-city churches have been centers for social action. Yet, modernization also sparked a conservative backlash in the church and Catholics disagree about whether priests should be allowed to marry and other adaptations to American culture.

CULTURE WARS

In the 1950s and 1960s, Americans argued most often over foreign policy, racial justice, and the economy. Since the 1980s, they have also quarreled over beliefs and values, especially as the patterns of family life have become more varied. In these quarrels, religious belief has heavily influenced politics as individuals and groups try to shape America around their particular, and often conflicting, ideas of the godly society. Americans who are undogmatic in religion are often liberal in politics as well, while religious and political conservatism also tend to go together.

The division on social issues is related to theological differences within Protestantism. The "conservative" emphasis on personal salvation and the literal truth of the Bible also expresses itself in a desire to restore "traditional" social patterns. Conservatives worry that social disorder occurs when people follow personal impulses and pleasures. In contrast, the "liberal" or "modern" emphasis on the universality of the Christian message restates the Social Gospel with its call to build the Kingdom of God through social justice and may recognize divergent pathways toward truth. Liberals worry that greed in the unregulated marketplace creates disorder and injustice.

The cultural conflict also transcends the historic three-way division of Americans among Protestants, Catholics, and Jews. Catholic reformers, liberal Protestants, and Reform Jews may agree on issues of cultural values. The same may be true of conservative Catholics, fundamentalist Protestants, and Orthodox Jews.

• AMERICAN VIEWS •

THE RELIGIOUS IMPERATIVE IN POLITICS

The strong religious faith of many Americans can drive them to different stands on political issues. The letter below written by Jerry Falwell in 1987 to potential supporters of the Moral Majority, reflects the politically conservative outlook of many evangelical Christians. Falwell is pastor of the Thomas Road Baptist Church in Lynchburg, Virginia. He founded the Moral Majority, a conservative religious lobbying and educational organization, in 1979 and served as its president until 1987. The second document, from an open letter issued by the Southside United Presbyterian Church in Tucson in 1982, expresses the conviction of other believers that God may sometimes require civil disobedience to oppose oppressive government actions. The letter explains the church's reasons for violating immigration law to offer sanctuary to refugees from repressive Central American regimes supported by the United States.

HOW DO Falwell and the Southside Presbyterian Church define the problems that demand a religious response? Are there any points of agreement? How does each statement balance the claims of God and government?

From the Reverend Jerry Falwell: I believe that the overwhelming majority of Americans are sick and tired of the way that amoral liberals are trying to corrupt our nation from its commitment to freedom, democracy, traditional morality, and the free enterprise system.

And I believe that the majority of Americans agree on the basic moral values which this nation was founded upon over 200 years ago.

Today we face four burning crises as we continue in this Decade of Destiny the 1980s loss of our freedom by giving in to the Communists; the destruction of the family unit; the deterioration of the free enterprise system; and the crumbling of basic moral principles which has resulted in the legalizing of abortion, widespread pornography, and a drug problem of epidemic proportions.

That is why I went to Washington, D.C., in June of 1979, and started a new organization The Moral Majority.

Right now you may be wondering: "But I thought Jerry Falwell was the preacher on the Old-Time Gospel Hour television program?"

You are right. For over twenty-four years I have been calling the nation back to God from the pulpit on radio and television.

But in recent months I have been led to do more than just preach. I have been compelled to take action.

I have made the commitment to go right into the halls of Congress and fight for laws that will save America. . . .

I will still be preaching every Sunday on the Old-Time Gospel Hour and I still must be a husband and father to my precious family in Lynchburg, Virginia.

But as God gives me the strength, I must do more. I must go into the halls of Congress and fight for laws that will protect the grand old flag . . . for the sake of our children and grandchildren.

From Southside United Presbyterian Church.

We are writing to inform you that Southside Presbyterian Church will publicly violate the Immigration and Nationality Act, Section 274 (A). . . .

We take this action because we believe the current policy and practice of the United States Government with regard to Central American refugees is illegal and immoral. We believe our government is in violation of the 1980 Refugee Act and international law by continuing to arrest, detain, and forcibly return refugees to the terror, persecution, and murder in El Salvador and Guatemala.

We believe that justice and mercy require the people of conscience actively assert our God-given right to aid anyone fleeing from persecution and murder. . . .

We beg of you, in the name of God, to do justice and love mercy in the administration of your office. We ask that "extended voluntary departure" be granted to refugees from Central America and that current deportation proceedings against these victims be stopped.

Until such time, we will not cease to extend the sanctuary of the church. . . . Obedience to God requires this of us all.

Sources: Gary E. McCuen, ed., *The Religious Right* (G. E. McCuen Publishers, 1989); Ann Crittenden, *Sanctuary* (Weidenfeld and Nicolson, 1988).

Conservatives have initiated the culture wars, trying to stabilize what they fear is an American society spinning out of control because of sexual indulgence. In fact, the evidence on the sexual revolution is mixed. Growing numbers of teenagers reported being sexually active in the 1970s, but the rate of increase tapered off in the 1980s. The divorce rate began to drop after 1980. Births to teenagers dropped after 1990, and the number of two-parent families increased. Most adults remain monogamous, according to data from 1994.

There was, however, an astonishing eagerness to talk about sex in the 1990s and this set the stage for religiously rooted battles over two sets of issues. One cluster revolves around so-called family values, questioning the morality of access to abortion, the acceptability of homosexuality, and the roles and rights of women. A second set of concerns has focused on the supposed role of public schools in undermining morality through sex education, unrestricted reading matter, nonbiblical science, and the absence of prayer. Opinion polls show clear differences among religious denominations on issues such as censorship of library books, acceptability of racially segregated neighborhoods, freedom of choice in terminating pregnancy, and homosexuality, and efforts to restrict legal access to abortion mobilized thousands of "right to life" advocates in the late 1980s and early 1990s.

A culturally conservative issue with great popular appeal in the early 1990s was an effort to prevent states and localities from protecting homosexuals against discrimination. Under the slogan "No special rights," antigay measures passed in Cincinnati, Colorado, and Oregon in 1993 and 1994, only to have the Supreme Court overturn the Colorado law in *Romer* v. *Evans* (1996). Public support for lesbian and gay civil rights varies with different issues (strong support for equal employment opportunity, much less for granting marriage rights to same-sex couples) and whether the issues are framed in terms of specified rights for gays or in terms of the right of everyone, including gays, to be free from government interference with personal decisions, such as living arrangements and sexual choices.

In December 1993, the U.S. Supreme Court heard arguments on whether states could require protesters to remain a certain distance from abortion clinics. These anti-abortion and pro-abortion protesters revealed the deep divisions over this and other issues in the culture wars.

AP/Wide World Photos

CONCLUSION

Americans entered the 1980s searching for stability. The 1970s had brought unexpected and uncomfortable change. America's global postwar dominance seemed to recede even as traditional values appeared under siege in the U.S. itself. Ronald Reagan's presidential campaign played to these insecurities by promising to revitalize the older ways of life and restore the United States to its former influence.

Taken as a whole, it is fair to call the years from 1981 through 1992 the era of the Reagan revolution. The astonishing collapse of the Soviet Union ended forty years of Cold War. The fifty-year expansion of federal government programs to deal with economic and social inequities was reversed. Prosperity alternated with recessions that shifted the balance between regions. Economic inequality increased after narrowing for a generation at the same time that more and more leaders proclaimed that unregulated markets could best meet social needs. Middle-class Latinos and African Americans made substantial gains while many other minority Americans sank deeper into poverty.

Every revolution has its precursors. Intellectuals had been clarifying the justifications for Reagan administration actions since the 1960s. The Reagan-Bush years

extended changes that had begun in the 1970s, particularly the conservative economic policies and military buildup of the troubled Carter administration. In retrospect, the growing weakness of the USSR should also have been apparent in the same decade, had not the United States been blinded by its fear of communist power. Intervention in the Persian Gulf amplified American policies that had been in place since the CIA intervened in Iran in 1953. The outbreak of violence in Los Angeles after the Rodney King verdict showed that race relations were as tense as they had been in the 1960s.

In 1992, the United States was the undisputed world power. Its economy was poised for a surge of growth. It was the leader in scientific research and the development of new technologies. Its military capacities far surpassed those of any rival and seemed to offer a free hand in shaping the world— capacities that would be tested and utilized in the new century.

SUMMARY

Reagan's Domestic Revolution Political change began in 1980, when Ronald Reagan and his running mate George H.W. Bush, rode American discontent to a decisive victory in the presidential election. Building on a neoconservative critique of American public policies and issues from the Carter administration, Reagan presided over revolutionary changes in American government and policies. The consequences of his two terms included an altered role for government, powerful but selected economic growth, and a shift of domestic policy toward lifestyle concerns. Reaganomics and a new prosperity contrasted with corporate "downsizing" and an increase in the poverty rate.

The Second (Short) Cold War Reagan regarded the Soviet Union as an "evil empire." By the end of 1991 the Soviet Union was gone, Communist regimes had ended in Eastern Europe, and the Berlin Wall had come down. The Cold War had finally ended with the help of the relentless pressure of American spending on defense helping bankrupt the Soviet Union. Reagan's foreign policy was marked by the invasion of Granada, the overthrowing of a Panamanian strong man, assistance to Nicaraguan Contras, and the revelation of the Iran-Contra affair. In 1991, President George H.W. Bush intervened in the Persian Gulf in response to Iraq's invasion of Kuwait; the war fascinated millions who watched it live on television; America won the war but not the peace.

Growth in the Sunbelt The emergence of the Sunbelt as a center of population and source of conservative voting strength, the immigration "boom," the demographic and ethnic changes in American cities, and the graying of America are all characteristics of America since 1981. Much of the Sunbelt growth has come from retired Americans and new job seekers. Older Americans have now become a powerful voice in public affairs. Immigration has significantly changed the American ethnic mix; while the largest single group of immigrants is Hispanic, immigrants from Asia, Russia, Eastern Europe, and the Middle East are reflected in the 10.4 percent of the population that is foreign-born.

Values in Collision In the 1950s and 1960s Americans argued most often about foreign policy, racial injustice, and the economy. Since that time, they have also quarreled over beliefs and values, especially as patterns in family life have become more varied. In substantial measure these conflicts were rooted in the social and cultural changes of the 1960s and 1970s that had altered traditional institutions. Changes in roles and expectations among women and new openness about gay and lesbian sexuality were particularly powerful in dividing American churches and politics. Abortion rights and the conservative backlash, the increase of women in the work force, and the new "culture wars" were part of modern America.

REVIEW QUESTIONS

1. Was there a Reagan revolution in American politics? Did Reagan's presidency change the economic environment for workers and business corporations?

2. How did American ideas about the proper role of government change during the 1980s?

3. What caused the breakup of the Soviet Union and the end of the Cold War?

4. How did immigration from other nations affect different regions in America?

5. What changes in family roles and sexual behavior became divisive political issues?

KEY TERMS

Acquired immune deficiency syndrome (AIDS)   (p. 813)
Americans with Disabilities Act (p. 801)
Deregulation   (p. 796)
Economic Recovery and Tax Act of 1981 (ERTA)   (p. 796)

Glasnost   (p. 804)
Immigration and Nationality Act of 1965   (p. 808)
Intermediate Nuclear Force Agreement   (p. 804)
Operation Desert Storm   (p. 806)
First Persian Gulf War   (p. 805)

Perestroika   (p. 804)
Roe v. *Wade*   (p. 812)
Sagebrush Rebellion   (p. 797)
Stonewall Rebellion   (p. 813)
Strategic Defense Initiative (SDI) (p. 802)
Sunbelt   (p. 806)

WHERE TO LEARN MORE

🛡 **Ronald Reagan Boyhood Home, Dixon, Illinois.** The home where Reagan lived from 1920 to 1923 tells relatively little about Reagan himself but a great deal about the small-town context that shaped his ideas.

🛡 **The Causes of Homelessness in America.** Social and political policies since the 1980s that have contributed to the gap between rich and poor and the rise of homelessness. http://www.stanford.edu/class/e297c/poverty_prejudice/soc_sec/bcauses.htm

🛡 **The Intermediate Nuclear Force Agreement (INF).** The full text document of the INF agreement between the United States and the Soviet Union, the first true nuclear disarmament treaty. http://www.state.gov/www/global/arms/treaties/infl.html

🛡 **The Gulf War.** Read about the Persian Gulf War commanders, see testimony of American combat soldiers, and learn about the events leading up to the invasion. http://www.pbs.org/wgbh/pages/frontline/gulf/

🛡 **A Concrete Curtain: The Life and Death of the Berlin Wall.** Traces the wall from creation in the 1960s to its destruction after the collapse of communist East Germany. Http:www.wall-berlin.org/gb/berlin.htm

 For additional study resources for this chapter, go to:
   www.prenhall.com/goldfield/chapter30

. . . the looks on the faces of the people
coming out of the city that day will haunt me forever . . .
everyone was the same color . . . dust white . . .
women crying . . . men crying . . . we must never forget
the men and women that died that day . . .

Black smoke billows through lower Manhattan during the collapse of the World Trade Center.

31

COMPLACENCY AND CRISIS
1993–2003

HOW DID Bill Clinton dominate the politics of the "center?"

WHAT IMPACT did information technologies have on the economy in the 1990s?

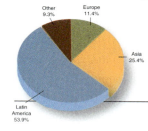

Other 9.3%
Europe 11.4%
Asia 25.4%
Latin America 53.9%

HOW DID the make-up of the American population change in the 1990s?

WHAT WERE the policies of George W. Bush during his first two years in office?

HOW DID 9/11 affect American views on security and affairs?

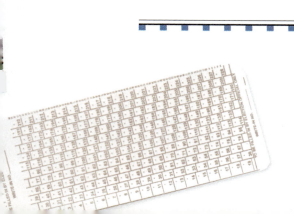

IMAGE KEY

for pages 820–821

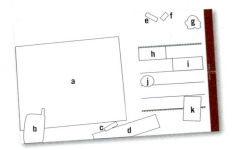

a. Black smoke billowing through lower Manhattan during the collapse of the World Trade Center.

b. A cell phone like those used by many in the stricken World Trade Center Towers to call for help or give their families their last goodbyes.

c. Computer chips have come to symbolize the boom of the 1990s.

d. A paper voting card like those used in Florida in the contentious 2000 presidential election.

e, f. Computer chips.

g. A gas mask used as protection from a chemical or biological attack.

h. Bill Clinton campaigning in 1992; shown surrounded by a crowd.

i. S.V. Marshall High School students join other Mississippi teens in building more than 125 new high-speed multimedia computers during a Computer Blitz Build at Jackson State University e-Center.

j. A pie chart showing the population shifts of the 1990s.

k. A soldier stops to watch the sunset during military exercises in Kuwait, November 18, 2002.

I'm a firefighter for the FDNY [Fire Department New York]. I had gotten off the night before. . . . My friend woke me up early that morning to borrow my car to take his sick cat to the vet. . . . I was up so I went to my local bagel store for my coffee and paper. . . . when I heard a lady scream a plane had hit the Trade Center. . . . I thought since it was a beautiful day that perhaps a Cessna with the pilot having a heart attack had accidentally done this. . . . I ran home to put the TV on. . . . as soon as I saw what damage was done I knew this wasn't any Cessna. . . . my god people were jumping . . . phone rang it was a fellow from my station and he hadn't turned his TV on yet. . . . I screamed to him to turn his #*#* TV on. . . .

When the second plane hit. . . . I said goodbye and told him I was going in. . . . I jumped in my car and was off to the races. . . . the highway was closed. . . . but open for us. . . . I had the gas pedal to the floor as I headed toward the city looking out my window I see both towers burning. . . . when I hear a rumble and see the south tower #2 fall. . . . I have to get my gear so I pull off the highway going down the on ramp. . . . arriving at the firehouse everyone's in shock and we know we gotta get there now to help. . . . as we're getting ready to leave the 2nd tower fell. . . . we commandeer a bus and we're off. . . .

We arrived at a staging area and then finally got the ok to go in. . . . who's in charge? . . . Shoes, papers, and dust are everywhere. . . . we wait til [building] 7 collapses. . . . chief gets us into the site by going thru the financial center and bam there we are. . . . pieces of the outside wall sticking out of the highway. . . . cars on fire . . . buses gutted. . . . I saw numerous acts of courage that day both civilian and uniformed. . . . the looks on the faces of the people coming out of the city that day will haunt me forever . . . everyone was the same color. . . . dust white. . . . women crying. . . . men crying. . . . we must never forget the men and women that died that day. . . . their sacrifice will live on for generations to come. . . .

Source: John McNamara Story #400, The September 11 Digital Archive, 13 April, 2002, **http://911digitalarchive.org/stories/details/400**

JOHN MCNAMARA was one of the many off-duty New York City fire fighters who rushed to the World Trade Center after the terrorist attack on September 11, 2001. Hijacking four commercial jetliners, the terrorists crashed one plane into the Pentagon and one into each of the twin towers of the World Trade Center, 110-story buildings that housed 50,000 workers at the peak of the workday. Millions of Americans watched in horror as television showed first one tower and then the other burned and disintegrated. September 11 was an occasion for terror and courage. Passengers on the fourth plane fought the hijackers and made sure that it crashed in a Pennsylvania field rather than hit a fourth target. Altogether, 479 police officers, fire fighters, and other emergency workers died in the collapse of the towers. Thousands of volunteers rushed to help. The total confirmed death toll was 2,795 in New York, 184 at the Pentagon, and 40 in Pennsylvania.

The attacks, masterminded by the Al-Qaeda network of Muslim extremists, ended a decade of prosperity at home and complacency about the place of the United States in the world. In their aftermath, as Americans became aware of millions of Muslim neighbors and tried to balance civil liberties against national security, they realized how diverse the nation had become. For most of the 1990s, prosperity allowed politics to focus on social issues, such as health care and education, as well as on bitterly partisan but often superficial battles over personalities and presidential behavior. However, the terrorists attacked buildings that were symbols of the nation's economic and military power. The aftermath of the attacks deepened a business recession that had followed a decade of growth spurred by new technologies. The vulnerability of the targets also undermined Americans' sense of security and isolation from world problems, underscored the global reach of terrorism, and made understanding its sources more necessary than ever.

THE POLITICS OF THE CENTER

I n Bill Clinton's race for president in 1992, the "war room" was the decision center where Clinton and his staff planned tactics and countered Republican attacks. On the wall was a sign with a simple message: "It's the economy, stupid." It was a reminder that victory lay in emphasizing everyday problems that George H.W. Bush had neglected.

The message also revealed an insight into the character of the United States in the 1990s. What mattered most were down-to-earth issues, not the distant problems of foreign policy.

POLITICAL GENERATIONS

Every fifteen to twenty years, a new group of voters and leaders comes to power, driven by the desire to fix the mess that the previous generation left behind. The leaders who dominated the 1980s believed that the answer was to turn the nation's social and economic problems over to the market while asserting America's influence and power around the world.

In the mid-1990s the members of "Generation X" came of voting age with deep worries about the foreclosing of opportunities. They worried that previous administrations had neglected social problems and let the competitive position of the United States deteriorate.

Young and successful but not widely known as governor of Arkansas, Democrat Bill Clinton's campaign for the 1992 nomination overcame minimal name recognition and his use of a student deferment to avoid military service in Vietnam. Clinton made sure that the Democrats fielded a full baby boomer (and Southern) ticket by choosing the equally youthful Tennessean Albert Gore Jr. as his running mate.

Bush won renomination by beating back archconservative Patrick Buchanan. The party platform conformed to the beliefs of the Christian right. At the Republican National convention in Houston, Pat Buchanan called for a crusade against unbelievers. His startling speech was a reminder of how religious belief was reshaping American politics.

The wild card was Texas billionaire Ross Perot, whose independent campaign started with an appearance on a television talk show. Perot also tried to claim the political center, appealing to the middle of the middle-class—to small business owners, middle managers, and professionals who had approved of Reagan's antigovernment rhetoric but distrusted his corporate cronies. But, Perot's behavior became increasingly erratic.

HOW DID Bill Clinton dominate the politics of the center?

QUICK REVIEW

Candidates for President in 1992

◆ Republican George H.W. Bush: Ronald Reagan's vice president.

◆ Democrat Bill Clinton: little known governor of Arkansas.

◆ Independent Ross Perot: Texas billionaire and political maverick.

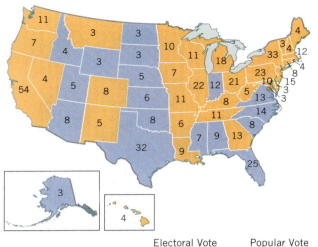

	Electoral Vote (%)	Popular Vote (%)
BILL CLINTON (Democrat)	**370** **(69)**	**43,728,275** **(43.2)**
George Bush (Republican)	168 (31)	38,167,416 (37.7)
H. Ross Perot (United We Stand, America)	–	19,237,247 (19.0)

MAP 31–1

The Election of 1992   Bill Clinton defeated George H.W. Bush in 1992 by reviving the Democratic Party in the industrial Northeast and enlisting new Democratic voters in the western states, where he appealed both to Hispanic immigrants and to people associated with fast-growing high-tech industries. He won reelection in 1996 with the same pattern of support. However, the coalition was an unstable combination of "Old Democrats," associated with older industries and labor unions, and "New Democrats," favoring economic change, free trade, and globalization.

WHAT FACTOR'S led to George H.W. Bush's downfall in the election of 1992?

Bosnia   A nation in southeast Europe that split off from Yugoslavia and became the site of bitter civil and religious war, requiring NATO and U.S. intervention in the 1990s.

Kosovo   Province of Yugoslavia where the United States and NATO intervened militarily in 1999 to protect ethnic Albanians from expulsion.

Bush campaigned as a foreign policy expert, but he ignored anxieties about the nation's direction at home. In fact, voters in November ranked the economy first as an issue, the deficit second, health care third, and foreign policy eighth. Clinton hammered away at economic concerns and the need for change from the Reagan-Bush years. He presented himself as a new, pragmatic, and livelier Democrat.

Election day gave the Clinton-Gore ticket 43 percent of the popular vote, Bush 38 percent, and Perot 19 percent. Millions who voted for Perot were casting a protest vote for "none of the above" and against "politics as usual" rather than hoping for an actual Perot victory. Clinton ran best among voters over 65, who remembered FDR and Harry Truman, and voters under 30.

POLICING THE WORLD

Clinton inherited an expectation that the United States could keep the world on an even keel. U.S. diplomats helped broker an Israel-PLO accord that gave Palestinians self-government in Gaza and the West Bank, only to watch extremists on both sides undermine the accords and plunge Israel into a near-civil war by 2002. The United States in 1994 used diplomatic pressure to persuade North Korea to promise to suspend building nuclear weapons. The world also benefited from a gradual reduction of nuclear arsenals and from a 1996 treaty to ban the testing of nuclear weapons.

Given the national distaste for overseas entanglements, Clinton used military power with caution. He inherited a U.S. military presence in Somalia (in northeastern Africa) but withdrew American forces when their humanitarian mission of guarding food relief to starving Somalis was overshadowed by the need to take sides in a civil war. In Haiti he restored an elected president.

Clinton also reluctantly committed the United States to a multinational effort to end bloody civil war in ethnically and religiously divided **Bosnia** in 1995.

The American military revisited the same part of Europe in 1999, when the United States and Britain led NATO's intervention in **Kosovo**. The majority of people in this Yugoslav province were ethnic Albanians who chafed under the control of the Serb-controlled Yugoslav government. When a Kosovar independence movement began a rebellion, the Yugoslavs responded with brutal repression. To protect the Kosovars, NATO began a bombing campaign that targeted Yugoslav military bases and forces in Kosovo. In June, Yugoslavia agreed to withdraw its troops and make way for a multinational NATO peacekeeping force, marking a measured success for U.S. policy.

To satisfy Russia, the peacekeeping force that entered Kosovo in June was technically a U.S. operation, but it was a reinvented NATO that negotiated with Yugoslavia.

The new NATO is a product of the new Europe of the 1990s. A key step was expansion into the former Soviet sphere in eastern Europe. In 1999, NATO formally admitted Poland, Hungary, and the Czech Republic. Three years later, NATO agreed to give Russia a formal role in its discussions further eroding the barriers of the Cold War.

CLINTON'S NEOLIBERALISM

Domestic policy attracted Clinton's greatest interest, and his first term can be divided into two parts. In 1993–1994, he worked with a slim Democratic majority in Congress to modernize the American economy, taking advantage of an economic upturn that lasted for most of the decade. In 1995 and 1996, however he faced solid Republican majorities, the result of a Republican sweep in the November 1994 elections.

The heart of Clinton's agenda was efforts to make the United States economy more equitable domestically and more competitive internationally; these goals marked Clinton as a **neoliberal** who envisioned a partnership between a leaner government and a dynamic private sector. Steps to "reinvent" government cut federal employment below Reagan administration levels. A new tax bill increased taxes on the top 1.2 percent of households. The Earned Income Tax Credit, a Nixon-era program that helped lift working Americans out of poverty, was expanded. In early 1993, Clinton pushed through the Family and Medical Leave Act, which provided up to twelve weeks of unpaid leave for workers with newborns or family emergencies and had been vetoed twice by George H.W. Bush.

Clinton's biggest setback was the failure of comprehensive health-care legislation. The goals seemed simple at first: containment of health-care costs and extension of basic medical insurance to all Americans under age 65. In the abstract, voters agreed that something needed to be done. So did individuals like the twenty-five-year-old photographer's assistant who found herself facing cancer surgery without savings or health insurance: "I work full-time, and because it's a very small business, we don't get any benefits. . . . It just devastated everybody financially. And that shouldn't happen. That's the American dream that's lost."

Unfortunately the plan that emerged from the White House ran to 1,342 pages of complex regulations, with something for everyone to dislike. Senior citizens worried about limits on Medicare spending. Insurance companies did not want more regulations. Businesses did not want the costs of insuring their workers. Taxpayers did not want to pay for wider medical insurance coverage through higher taxes or rationing of medical services. The reform effort went nowhere.

If Reagan avoided blame for mistakes, Clinton in his first two years in office seemed to avoid credit for successes despite his legislative accomplishments. Both the president and his wife attracted bitter hatred from the far right, of a sort previously reserved for Franklin and Eleanor Roosevelt and the Kennedy family. Indeed, Hillary Rodham Clinton became a symbol of discomfiting changes in American families.

CONTRACT WITH AMERICA AND THE ELECTION OF 1996

Conservative political ideology and personal animosity against the Clintons were part of an extraordinary off-year election in 1994, in which voters defeated dozens of incumbents and gave Republicans control of Congress. For most of 1995, the new Speaker of the House, Newt Gingrich of Georgia, dominated political headlines as he pushed the **Contract with America**, the official Republican campaign platform for the 1994 elections, which called for a revolutionary reduction in federal responsibilities.

Clinton laid low and let the new Congress attack environmental protections, propose cuts in federal benefits for the elderly, and try to slice the capital-gains tax to help the rich. As Congress and president battled over the budget, congressional Republicans forced the federal government to shut down for more than three weeks between November 1995 and January 1996. Democrats painted Gingrich and his congressional allies as a radical fringe who wanted to gut core values and programs that most Americans wanted to protect.

After the budget confrontations, 1996 brought a series of measures to reward work—a centrist position acceptable to most Americans. The minimum wage increased.

Neoliberal   Advocate or participant in the effort to reshape the Democratic party for the 1990s around a policy emphasizing economic growth and competitiveness in the world economy.

Contract with America   Platform proposing a sweeping reduction in the role and activities of the federal government on which many Republican candidates ran for Congress in 1994.

Hillary Rodham Clinton's mastery of policy details seemed to some critics to be inappropiate for a first lady, but it helped her be an effective senator from New York beginning in 2001.

SIPA Press

WHERE TO LEARN MORE

★ Oklahoma City National Memorial Center Museum, Oklahoma City, OK
www.oklahomacitynationalmemorial.org

Temporary Assistance for Needy Families (TANF) Federal program, utilizing work requirements for and time limits on benefits, created in 1996 to replace earlier welfare programs to aid families and children.

Congress made pension programs easier for employers to create and made health insurance portable when workers changed jobs. Clinton signed bi-partisan legislation to "end welfare as we know it." The new program of **Temporary Assistance to Needy Families (TANF)** replaced Aid to Families with Dependent Children (AFDC). Aid recipients had to seek work or be enrolled in schooling, and there was a time limit on assistance. By 2001, the number of public-assistance recipients had declined 58 percent from its 1994 high, but there are doubts that many of the former recipients have found jobs adequate to support their families.

Clinton's reelection in 1996 was a virtual replay of 1992. His opponent, Robert Dole, represented an earlier political generation. The Republican party was uncertain whether to stress free markets or morality. The party tried to paper over its uneasy mix of traditional probusiness and socially moderate country-club Republicans, radical proponents of unregulated markets, and religious conservatives affiliated with the Cristian Coalition. The Republicans thus displayed many of the internal fractures that characterized American society as a whole.

Because the nation was prosperous and at peace, and because Clinton had claimed the political center, Clinton became the first Democratic president to be elected to a second term since Franklin Roosevelt. The Clinton-Gore ticket easily won the Northeast, the industrial Midwest, and the Far West; Hispanic voters alienated by anti-immigrant rhetoric from the Republicans helped Clinton also take usually Republican Florida and Arizona.

The election confirmed that voters liked the pragmatic center. They wanted to continue the reduction of the federal role in domestic affairs that began in the 1980s without damaging social insurance programs.

THE DANGERS OF EVERYDAY LIFE

Part of the background for the sometimes vicious politics of the mid-1990s was a sense of individual insecurity and fear of violence that coexisted with an economy that was booming in some sectors but still leaving many Americans behind. The solutions, however, seemed inadequate. Neither the liberal response of tighter gun controls or the conservative response of harsher and mandatory prison terms could prevent irrational actions.

Headlines and news flashes proclaimed terrifying random acts of violence. In April 1999, two high-school students in Littleton, Colorado took rifles and pipe bombs into Columbine High School to kill twelve classmates, a teacher, and themselves.

The greatest losses of life came in Waco, Texas, and in Oklahoma City. On April 19, 1993, federal agents raided the fortified compound of the Branch Davidian cult outside Waco after a fifty-one day siege. A fire, probably set from inside, killed more than eighty people. On the second anniversary of the Waco raid, Timothy McVeigh detonated a truck packed with explosives in front of the federal office building in downtown Oklahoma City. The blast killed 169 people, presumably as revenge against what McVeigh considered an oppressive government.

The Brady Handgun Violence Prevention Act, passed in 1994, set up a waiting period and background checks for purchases of firearms. But gun control was political dynamite. Americans have drastically differing understandings of the Second Amendment, which states: "A well regulated militia, being necessary to the security of a free State, the right of the people to keep and bear arms, shall not be infringed." The National Rifle Association argued that the amendment establishes an absolute individual right. Until the 1980s, in contrast, federal courts consistently interpreted the amendment to apply to citizen service in a government-organized militia, and federal courts have yet to strike down any gun control law for violating the Second Amendment.

Conservatives, including many gun-ownership absolutists, put their faith in strict law enforcement as the best route to public security. Many states adopted "three strike" measures that drastically increased penalties for individuals convicted of a third crime. One result was an explosive growth of the prison industry. States diverted funds from education and health care to build and staff more prisons. The number of people serving sentences of a year or longer in state and federal prisons grew from 316,000 in 1980 to 1,305,000 in 1999.

The war on drugs, begun in the 1980s, was the biggest contributor to the prison boom. Aggressive enforcement of domestic laws against drug possession or sales filled American prison cells and fell most heavily on minorities. In Connecticut, for example, minority offenders arrested on drug charges were nine times more likely than white offenders to end up in jail.

In fact, crime fell steadily after peaking in 1991. The rate of violent crime (murder, rape, robbery, aggravated assault) fell by 31 percent from 1991 to 1999, including a 37 percent drop in number of murders. The rate of major property crimes (burglary, larceny-theft, and motor vehicle theft) fell by 27 percent over the same period. Easing fears and escalating costs caused some states to soften sentencing laws.

MORALITY AND PARTISANSHIP

If the economy was the fundamental news of the later 1990s, Bill Clinton's personal life was the hot news. In 1998 and 1999, the United States was riveted by revelations about the president's sex life, doubts about his integrity, and debates about his fitness for high office. Years of rumors, and law suits, culminated in 1999 in the nation's second presidential impeachment trial.

Clinton's problems began in 1994 with the appointment of a special prosecutor to investigate possible fraud in the **Whitewater** development, an Arkansas land promotion in which Bill and Hillary Clinton had invested in the 1980s. The probe by Kenneth Starr, the independent counsel, however, expanded into a wide-ranging investigation that eventually encompassed the sexual behavior of the president. Meanwhile, Paula Jones had brought a lawsuit claiming sexual harassment by then-governor Clinton while she was a state worker in Arkansas. The investigation of Whitewater brought convictions of several friends and former associates of the Clintons, but no evidence pointing directly at either Bill or Hillary Clinton themselves.

The legal landscape changed in January 1998, when allegations surfaced about an affair between the president and Monica Lewinsky, a former White House intern. Lewinsky admitted to the relationship privately and then to Starr's staff after the president had denied it in a sworn deposition for the Paula Jones case. This opened Clinton to charges of perjury and obstruction of justice. Although a federal judge dismissed Jones's suit in April, the continued unfolding of the Lewinsky affair treated the nation to a barrage of personal details about Bill Clinton. The affair certainly revealed deep flaws in Clinton's character and showed his willingness to shade the truth. Newspaper, radio talk shows, and politicians debated whether such flaws were relevant to his ability to perform his Constitutional duties.

In the fall of 1998, the Republican leaders who controlled Congress decided that Clinton's statements and misstatements justified the Constitutional process of impeachment. In December, the Republican majority on the House Judiciary Committee recommended four articles of impeachment, or specific charges against the president, to the House of Representatives. By a partisan vote, the full House

Whitewater Arkansas real estate development in which Bill and Hillary Clinton were investors; several fraud convictions resulted from investigations into Whitewater, but evidence was not found that the Clinton's were involved in wrongdoing.

OVERVIEW

PRESIDENTIAL IMPEACHMENT

Andrew Johnson, 1868	Charges:	Failure to comply with Tenure of Office Act, requiring Congressional approval to fire cabinet members.
	Political Lineup:	Radical Republicans against Johnson; Democrats and moderate Republicans for him.
	Actions:	Tried and acquitted by Senate.
	Underlying Issues:	Johnson's opposition to Republican plans for reconstruction of southern states after the Civil War.
Richard Nixon, 1974	Charges:	Obstruction of justice in Watergate investigation; abuse of power of federal agencies for political purposes; refusal to recognize Congressional subpoena.
	Political Lineup:	Democrats and many Republicans against Nixon.
	Actions:	Charges approved by House committee; Nixon resigned before action by the full House of Representatives.
	Underlying Issues:	Nixon's construction of a secret government and his efforts to undermine integrity of national elections.
Bill Clinton, 1999	Charges:	Perjury and obstruction of justice in the investigation of sexual misconduct allegations by Paula Jones.
	Political Lineup:	Conservative Republicans against Clinton; Democrats and some moderate Republicans for him.
	Actions:	Tried and acquitted by Senate.
	Underlying Issues:	Republican frustration with Clinton's ability to block their agenda; deep concern about Clinton's character and moral fitness for presidency.

approved two of the charges and forwarded them to the Senate. The formal trial of the charges by the Senate began in January 1999 and ended on February 12. Moderate Republicans joined Democrats to assure that the Senate would fall far short of the two-thirds majority required for conviction and removal from office. Article 1, charging that the president had perjured himself, failed by a vote of 45 to 55. Article 2, charging that he had obstructed justice, failed by a vote of 50 to 50.

Why did Congressional Republicans pursue impeachment to the bitter end? It was clear that most Americans disapproved of Clinton's conduct but did not think that merited removal from office. The 1998 election, which reduced the Republican majority in the House and resulted in the resignation of Newt Gingrich, confirmed the opinion polls. At the same time, 25 to 30 percent of Americans remained convinced that Clinton's presence in the White House demeaned the nation. In other words, although impeachment was certainly motivated by politics, it was also another battle in America's culture wars.

A NEW ECONOMY?

WHAT IMPACT did information technologies have on the economy in the 1990s?

By the year 2000 the American economy had changed. More than ever, it was a global economy. And, unlike any time in the past, it was an economy that depended on electronic computing to manage and transmit vast quantities of data. The impacts of the electronic revolution are still being absorbed into the structures and routines of everyday life.

THE PROSPEROUS 1990S

From 1992 through 2000, Americans enjoyed nine years of continuous economic expansion. Unemployment dropped from 7.2 percent in 1992 to 4.0 percent at the start of 2000 as American businesses created more than 12 million new jobs. Key states like California experienced new growth driven by high-tech industries, entertainment, and foreign trade. The stock market soared; rising demand for shares in established blue-chip companies and new **Internet** firms swelled the value of individual portfolios, IRA accounts, and pension funds. The rate of home-ownership rose after declining for fifteen years. The proportion of Americans in poverty dropped to 12 percent in 1999, and the gap between rich and poor began to narrow (slightly) for the first time in two decades.

The economic boom was great news for the federal budget. Perennial deficits formed into surpluses for 1998, 1999, and 2000. Both political parties anticipated a growing surplus for the next decade and debated whether to offer massive tax cuts, buy down the national debt, or shore up Social Security and Medicare.

By the end of the decade the productivity of U.S. manufacturing workers was increasing more than 4 percent per year, the highest rate in a generation. Part of the gain was the payoff from the painful business restructuring and downsizing of the 1970s and 1980s. Another cause was improvements in efficiency from the full incorporation of personal computers and electronic communication into everyday life and business practice.

THE SERVICE ECONOMY

At the beginning of the twenty-first century, the United States was an economy of services. The service sector includes everyone not directly involved in producing and processing physical products, and by the 1990s, it included more than 70 percent of American jobs.

Service jobs vary greatly. At the bottom of the scale are minimum-wage jobs held mostly by women, immigrants, and the young such as cleaning people, child-care workers, hospital orderlies, and fast-food workers. In contrast, many of the best new jobs are in information industries. Teaching, research, government, advertising, mass communications, and professional consulting depend on producing and manipulating information. These fields add to national wealth by creating and applying new ideas rather than by supplying standardized products and services.

Another growth industry was health care. Spending on medical and health services amounted to 12 percent of the gross domestic product in 1990, up from 5 percent in 1960. The need to share this huge expense fairly was the motivation for Medicare and Medicaid in the 1960s and the search for a national health insurance program in the 1990s.

THE HIGH-TECH SECTOR

The epitome of the "sunrise" economy was electronics, which grew hand-in-glove with the defense budget. The first computers in the 1940s were derived in part from wartime code-breaking efforts. In the 1950s, IBM got half its revenues from air defense computers and guidance systems for B-52 bombers.

Invention of the microprocessor in 1971 kicked the industry into high gear. The farmlands of Santa Clara County, California, became a "silicon landscape" of neat one-story factories and research campuses. In 1950, the county had 800 factory workers. In 1980, it had 264,000 manufacturing workers and 3,000 electronics firms. Related hardware and microchip factories spread the industry throughout the West, creating "silicon prairies," "silicon forests," and "silicon deserts" to complement California's original **Silicon Valley**.

QUICK REVIEW

Boom Times
- U.S. enjoyed nine years of economic expansion between 1992 and 2000.
- Unemployment fell to 4.0 percent in 2000.
- The economic boom resulted in increased government revenues.

Internet   The system of interconnected computers and servers that allows the exchange of email, posting of Web sites, and other means of instant communication.

Silicon Valley   The region of California between San Jose and San Francisco that holds the nation's greatest concentration of electronics firms.

• AMERICAN VIEWS •

CREATING AND WORKING IN THE NEW ECONOMY

*ike many other American industries, the boom-
ing information technology sector that employed
millions of workers by the 1990s started with a few
key ideas and innovators. Bill Gates and Paul
Allen, the founders of software giant Microsoft Corporation,
talk about their early encounters with computers as high school
students and the origins of Allen's idea of a "wired world" in
the early 1970s. Following their interview a worker reflects on
the high-tech industry at the end of the 1990s.*

WHAT DO the experiences suggest about the pace of
technological innovation and industrial change? How do
high-tech workers cope with the pace of change in their
industry, and what are the implications for their jobs?

Bill Gates, Paul Allen, and the Seeds of the Personal
Computer Revolution

GATES:

*Our friendship started [in high school] after the mothers' club
paid to put a computer terminal in the school in 1968. The
notion was that, of course, the teachers would figure out this
computer thing and then teach it to the students. But that
didn't happen. It was the other way around. There was a
group of students who kind of went nuts.*

ALLEN:

*The teletype room was full of rolled-up paper-tape programs
and manuals and everything else. Between classes, or when-*
*ever any of us hard-core computer types had a spare period,
we would congregate there.*

GATES:

*We were always scrounging free computer time. One year a
student's mother arranged for us to go downtown to a new
commercial center. We didn't have to pay for the time as long
as we could find bugs in their system and report them. . . .*

ALLEN:

*At the end of every school day, a bunch of us would take our
little leather satchel briefcases and ride the bus downtown to
the computer center. Bill and I were the guys that stayed the
latest, and afterward we'd eat pizza at this hippie place across
the street. . . .*

GATES:

*The event that started everything for us business-wise was
when Paul found an article in 1971 in an electronics magazine. . . . about Intel's 4004 chip, which was the world's first
microprocessor. Paul comes up and says "Whoa" and explains that this microprocessor thing's only going to get better
and better. . . .*

ALLEN:

*I remember having pizza at Shakey's in Vancouver, Washing-
ton, in 1973, and talking about the fact that eventually
everyone is going to be online and have access to newspapers*

The computer industry generated an accompanying software industry as a
major component of information technology employment (see American Views,
"Creating and Working in the New Economy"). Every computer needed a com-
plexly coded operating system, word-processing programs, spreadsheet programs,
file-reading programs, Internet browsers, and, of course, games. Seattle-based
Microsoft parlayed an alliance with IBM into a dominant position that eventually
triggered federal antitrust action. Other software firms rose and fell with innovative and then outmoded programs. Software writing skills also spawned a new
world of multimedia entertainment.

and stuff and wouldn't people be willing to pay for information on a computer terminal.

Source: "Bill Gates and Paul Allen Talk," *Fortune*, 132, October 2, 1995, pp 69–72. Copyright © 1995 *Fortune* reprinted by permission.

Susie Johnson, Computer Chip Layout Designer

I design the layout of computer chips for Cirrus Logic in Austin, Texas. We're what they call a "chip solutions company." . . . [Laughs] Right now, we're laying out audio chips that go into computers and improve the sound of the speakers. I saw a demo of them recently. They had a regular PC with those regular little speakers and it sounded very weak. Then they put our chip in there, and the speakers sounded like this huge stereo. It was pretty wild.

My job is I'm given a schematic of the chip by the engineers, and it's basically just a bunch of symbols-triangles and rectangles with lines going in and out of them. Each symbol represents a device on the chip that hooks up to something else, and each of these little devices is designed to perform some function electronically. . . . I translate this technical information into the way the chip will actually look—how all this information will be contained in this tiny space. I draw it out using a computer program. It's mostly an automated process. In the past. I'd draw the devices by hand, but the chips I'm working on now are too complicated for that. . . .

I did lots of different jobs before—I was a waitress and I worked in a bunch of stores. . . . So I was wanting to change. . . . I certainly didn't think that I could do this, but one night I came into work with my ex-husband and he let me do some simple layout, and I thought, this is really cool, I want to try it. So I took a couple of classes at Austin Community College—an electrical design class and an integrated circuit layout class—so I'd understand a little more of the theory angle. . . . I've been doing this for three years. I have no plans to stop. I love it. . . .

There is some art to it. You could take one of these audio chips and give it to five different layout people and it would probably come back five different ways, you know? It's not all automated. Different people will put different things next to each other.

The way I think of it is I'm making little tiny highways for electrons. Some people say it's like New York City on a postage stamp. And it is! I mean, there are so many devices that I have to put into a tiny space. The one I was working on last week had over a hundred thousand. . . .

Sometimes there's problems that the computer catches and can't fix. I'm not sure why that happens, but it's the toughest part of the job. The computer will tell you what area of the chip the problem's in, but you have to go within that area yourself and find the problem and correct it. Like if something is too close to something else, then it needs to be moved over. . . . I think it's kind of fun. You have to figure it out, you have to be a detective. . . .

Source: John Bowe, Marisa Bowe, and Sabin Streeter, *Gig: Americans Talk about Their Jobs at the Turn of the Millenium* (New York: Crown Publishers, 2000), pp. 86–88, 305–308.

Personal computers and consumer electronics became part of everyday life in the 1990s. In 2000, 45 percent of adults reported that they had Internet access at home or work, up from around 14 percent in 1996. Children aged 10–14 used computers more frequently than any other age group, and nine out of ten could access the Internet at home or at school.

The electronics boom was part of a larger growth of "high-technology" industries. If "high tech" is applied to industries that devote a substantial portion of their income to research and development, it also covers chemicals, synthetic materials, cosmetics, aircraft and space satellites, drugs, measuring instruments, and

S.V. Marshall High School students Shawn Harris (left), 17, and Michael Clark, 17, join other Mississippi teens in building more than 125 new high-speed multimedia computers during a Computer Blitz Build at Jackson State University e-Center.

Barbara Gauntt/The Clarion-Ledger

QUICK REVIEW

Cable Television, the Internet, and Cell Phones

◆ Cable television reflected the fragmentation of American society and the increasing dependence on instant communication.

◆ The World Wide Web expanded dramatically in the 1990s.

◆ Cell phone subscribers reached 86 million by 2000.

World Wide Web   A part of the Internet designed to allow easier navigation of the network through the use of graphical user interfaces and hypertext links between different addresses.

many other products. Pharmaceuticals, medical imaging and diagnosis, bioengineering, and genetic engineering were all areas of rapid advance in the 1990s with momentum for the future.

AN INSTANT SOCIETY

On June 1, 1980, CNN Cable News Network gave television viewers their first chance to watch news coverage twenty-four hours a day. A decade later, CNN had hundreds of millions of viewers in more than seventy-five countries.

Fourteen months after CNN went on the air, another new cable channel, MTV: Music Television, started broadcasting round-the-clock music videos. It then created a new form of popular art and advertising, aimed at viewers aged 18 to 34.

CNN, MTV, and the rest of cable television reflected both the fragmentation of American society in the 1980s and 1990s and the increasing dependence on instant communication. As late as 1980, ordinary Americans had few shared choices for learning about their nation and world: virtually identical newscasts on NBC, CBS, and ABC and similar stories in *Time* and *Newsweek*. Fifteen years later, they had learned to surf through dozens of cable channels in search of specialized programs and were beginning to explore the Internet. Hundreds of magazines for niche markets had replaced the general-circulation periodicals of the postwar generation. Vast quantities of information were more easily available, but much of it was packaged for a subdivided marketplace of specialized consumers.

The electronic society in the 1990s also learned to communicate by email and to look up information on the **World Wide Web**. No longer did messages need the delays of the postal system or the costs of long-distance telephone calls. Students could avoid inconvenient trips to the library because information was so much quicker to search on the Web. The United States was increasingly a society that depended on instant information and expected instant results.

The Internet grew out of concerns about defense and national security. Its first form in 1969 was ARPANet (for Advanced Research Projects Administration, part of the Defense Department), intended to be a communication system to survive nuclear attack. As the Internet evolved to connected universities and national weapons laboratories, the Pentagon gave up control in 1984. The World Wide Web, created in 1991, expanded the Internet's uses by allowing organizations and companies to create Web sites that placed information only a few clicks away from wired consumers. The equally rapid expansion of bandwidth and modem capacities allowed Web pages filled with pictures and graphics to replace the text-only sites of the 1980s. By the start of the new century, Web surfers could find vast quantities of material, from Paris hotel rates to pornography, from song lyrics to stock prices. Although many of the dot-com companies crashed in 2001, they can be viewed as extensions of ongoing trends in retailing and services. Americans in 2000 spent 48 cents on meals out for every 52 cents spent on food to eat at home, paying for the convenience of quick meals without preparation and clean up time. Automatic-teller machines had become a necessity. Americans expected to be able to pull cash from their bank accounts 168 hours a week rather than finding a bank open perhaps 30 hours a week.

Mobile telephones or "cell phones" were part of the same instant society. The 5 million cell phone subscribers of 1990 had exploded to 86 million before the end of the decade.

IN THE WORLD MARKET

Instant access to business and financial information accelerated the globalizing of the American economy. With the help of national policy and booming economies overseas, the value of American imports and exports more than doubled, from 7 percent of the gross domestic product in 1965 to 16 percent in 1990. Americans in the 1970s began to worry about a "colonial" status, in which the United States exported food and raw materials and imported manufactured goods. By the 1980s, foreign economic competitiveness and trade deficits, especially with Japan, became issues of national concern.

The effects of international competition were more complex than "Japan-bashers" acknowledged. Mass-production industries, such as textiles and aluminum, suffered from cheaper and sometimes higher-quality imports, but many specialized industries and services such as Houston's oil equipment and exploration firms thrived. Globalization also created new regional winners and losers. In 1982, the United States began to do more business with Pacific nations than with Europe.

More recent steps to expand the global reach of the American economy were the **North American Free Trade Agreement (NAFTA)** in 1993 and a new world wide General Agreement on Tariffs and Trade (GATT) approved in 1994. Negotiated by Republican George H. W. Bush and pushed through Congress in 1993 by Democrat Bill Clinton, NAFTA combined 25 million Canadians, 90 million Mexicans, and 250 million U.S. consumers in a single "common market" similar to that of western Europe. GATT cut tariffs among 100 nations. NAFTA may have been a holdover from the Bush years, but it matched Clinton's ideas about reforming the American economy.

It was, however, a hard pill for many Democrats to swallow. Support was strongest from professional businesses and industries that sought foreign customers, including agriculture and electronics. Opponents included organized labor, communities already hit by industrial shutdowns, and environmentalists worried about industrial pollution in Mexico.

The **World Trade Organization (WTO)** which replaced GATT in 1996, became the unexpected target of a global protest movement. Thousands of protesters converged on its meetings in Geneva, Switzerland, Seattle, and Genoa, Italy. They were convinced that the WTO is a tool of transnational corporations that tramples on local labor and environmental protections in the name of "free trade" and benefits only the wealthy nations and their businesses. WTO defenders argued that open trade raised net production in the world economy and thereby made more wealth available for developing nations.

North American Free Trade Agreement (NAFTA) Agreement reached in 1993 by Canada, Mexico, and the United States to substantially reduce barriers to trade.

World Trade Organization (WTO) International organization that sets standards and practices for global trade, and the focus of international protests over world economic policy in the late 1990s.

BROADENING DEMOCRACY

Closely related to the changes in the American economy were the changing composition of the American people and the continued emergence of new participants in American government. In both the Clinton and George W. Bush administrations, the prominence of women and minorities in the cabinet and national government followed years of growing success in cities and states.

HOW DID the makeup of the American population change in the 1990s?

AMERICANS IN 2000

The federal census for the year 2000 found 281,400,000 Americans in the 50 states, District of Columbia, and Puerto Rico. The increase from 1990 was 13.2 percent, or 32,700,000, the largest ten-year population rise in U.S. history.

TABLE 31.1

States with Highest Proportions of Minority Residents in 2000 (percent of total population)

Hispanic	
New Mexico	42%
California	32
Texas	32
Arizona	35
Nevada	20
Asian and Pacific Islander	
Hawaii	51%
California	11
Washington	6
New Jersey	6
New York	6
Black	
Mississippi	36%
Louisiana	33
South Carolina	30
Georgia	29
Maryland	28
American Indian	
Alaska	16%
New Mexico	10
South Dakota	8
Oklahoma	8
Montana	6

One-third of all Americans lived in four states: California, Texas, New York, and Florida. Their regulations and consumer preferences conditioned national markets for products ranging from automobiles to textbooks.

No state lost populations, but the West grew the fastest. The super boom states were Nevada (66 percent growth), Arizona (40 percent), Colorado (31 percent), Utah (30 percent), and Idaho (29 percent).

In contrast, rural counties continued to empty out in Appalachia and across the Great Plains as fewer Americans were needed for mining and farming or for the small towns associated with those industries.

Another important trend was increasing ethnic and racial diversity (Table 3.1). Hispanics were the fastest-growing group in the American population. Indeed, the number of Hispanics in 2000 (35.2 million) matched the number of African Americans. Both Asians and Hispanics who had been in the United States for some time showed substantial economic success. Non-Hispanic whites are now a minority in California, the District of Columbia, Hawaii, and New Mexico. Over the coming decades, the effects of ethnic change will be apparent in schools, the workplace, popular culture, and politics.

WOMEN FROM THE GRASS ROOTS TO CONGRESS

The increasing prominence of women and family issues in national politics was a steady, quiet revolution that bore fruit in the 1990s, when the number of women in Congress more than doubled. In 1981, President Reagan had appointed Sandra Day O'Connor to be the first woman on the United States Supreme Court. In 1984, Walter Mondale chose Geraldine Ferraro as his vice presidential candidate. In 1993 Clinton appointed the second woman to the Supreme Court, Ruth Bader Ginsburg. Clinton appointee Janet Reno was the first woman to serve as Attorney General and Madeleine K. Albright, the first to serve as Secretary of State. In 2001, George W. Bush named Condoleezza Rice as his National Security Advisor.

Political gains for women at the national level reflected their importance in grass-roots politics. The spreading suburbs of postwar America were "frontiers" that required concerted action to solve immediate needs such as adequate schools and decent parks. They offered numerous opportunities for women to engage in civic work, learn political skills, and run for local office. Moreover, new cities and suburbs had fewer established political institutions, such as political machines and strong parties; their politics were open to energetic women.

Important support and training grounds are the League of Women Voters, which does nonpartisan studies of basic issues, and the National Women's Political Caucus, designed to support women candidates of both parties.

In 1991, the nomination of Judge Clarence Thomas, an African American, to the U.S. Supreme Court ensured that everyone knew that the terms of American politics were changing. His conservative positions on social and civil-rights issues, made Thomas a controversial nominee. Controversy

deepened when law professor Anita Hill accused Thomas of harassing her sexually while she had served on his staff at the U.S. Civil Rights Commission. Critics tried to discredit Hill with vicious attacks on her character, but failed to dispute her story. The public was left with Hill's unproved allegations and Thomas's equally unproved denials. The Senate confirmed Thomas to the Supreme Court.

Hill's badgering by skeptical senators angered millions of women. In the shadow of the hearings, women made impressive gains in the 1992 election, when the number of women in the U.S. Senate jumped from two to six (and grew further to nine Democrats and four Republicans after November 2000, including Hillary Rodham Clinton from New York).

Since the 1980s, voting patterns have shown a widening gender gap. Women in the 1990s identified with the Democratic party and voted for its candidates at a higher rate than men. This gender gap has helped keep Democrats competitive and dampened the nation's conservative swing.

MINORITIES AT THE BALLOT BOX

The changing makeup of the American populace also helped black and Latino candidates for public office to increased success. After the racial violence of the 1960s, many black people had turned to local politics to gain control of their own communities. The first black mayors of major twentieth-century cities included Carl Stokes in Cleveland in 1967 and Tom Bradley in Los Angeles in 1973. By 1983, three of the nation's four largest cities had black mayors. In 1989, Virginia made Douglas Wilder the first black state governor since Reconstruction.

As leadership opportunities for African Americans have increased in recent decades, they have gained positions of influence in a growing range of activities. In the field of foreign policy, for example, President George W. Bush chose Colin Powell as Secretary of State and Condolezza Rice as National Security Advisor. Here Powell (2nd from left) and Rice (right) observe a White House meeting between Bush and United Nations Secretary General Kofi Annan.

© AFP/Corbis Photo by Stephen Jaffe

MAP EXPLORATION

To explore an interactive version of this map, go to **http://www.prenhall.com/goldfield2/map31.2**

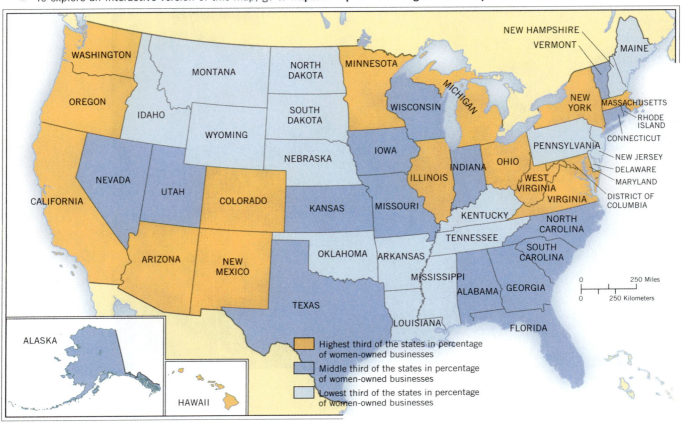

Highest third of the states in percentage of women-owned businesses

Middle third of the states in percentage of women-owned businesses

Lowest third of the states in percentage of women-owned businesses

MAP 31–2

Women as Business Owners, 1997   Some parts of the nation are more inviting to women-owned businesses than are others. The western and Great Lakes states, with histories of innovative politics, stand out as supportive of business opportunities for women.

U.S. Census Bureau, 1997 Economic Census

WHICH region of the country had the lowest percentage of women-owned businesses in 1997?

Most mid-sized cities had stopped electing city councils by wards or districts during the first half of the twentieth century. In the 1970s, minority leaders and community activists realized that a return to district voting could convert neighborhood segregation from a liability to a political resource. As amended in 1975, the federal Voting Rights Act allowed minorities to use the federal courts to challenge at-large voting systems that diluted the impact of their votes. African Americans and Mexican Americans used the act to reestablish city council districts in the late 1970s and early 1980s in city after city across the South and Southwest.

Young Hispanic and African-American politicians such as Henry Cisneros in San Antonio, Federico Peña in Denver, Dennis Archer in Detroit and Andrew Young in Atlanta, won elections, on positive platforms of growth and equity and mended fences with business leaders. Meanwhile, Washington state elected a Chinese American as governor, and Hawaii elected Japanese-American, native Hawaiian, and Filipino-American governors.

At the national level, minorities gradually increased their representation in Congress. Ben Nighthorse Campbell of Colorado, a Cheyenne, brought a Native American voice to the U.S. Senate in 1992. The number of African Americans in the House of Representatives topped forty after 1992, while the number of Latino members rose to 22 by 2003.

RIGHTS AND OPPORTUNITIES

The increasing presence of Latinos and African Americans in public life highlighted a set of troublesome debates that replayed many of the questions that European immigration had raised at the beginning of the twentieth Century.

One issue has been the economic impact of illegal immigration. Advocates of tight borders assert that illegal immigrants take jobs away from legal residents and eat up public assistance. Many studies, however, find that illegal immigrants fill jobs that nobody else wants. Over the long run, high employment levels among immigrants mean that their tax contributions more than pay for their use of welfare, food stamps, and unemployment benefits, which illegal immigrants are often afraid to claim. Nevertheless, high immigration can strain local government budgets. Partly for this reason, 60 percent of California voters approved **Proposition 187** in 1994, cutting off access to state-funded public education and health care for illegal immigrants. The mostly white supporters of the measure said that it was about following the rules; Hispanic opponents saw it as racism.

A symbolic issue was the degree to which American institutions should accommodate non-English speakers. Twenty-six states declared English their official language. California voters in 1998 banned bilingual public education, a system under which children whose first language was Spanish or another "immigrant" tongue were taught for several years in that language before shifting to English-language classrooms. Advocates of bilingual education claimed that it eased the transition into American society, while opponents said that it blocked immigrant children from fully assimilating into American life.

A more encompassing issue was a set of policies that originated in the 1960s as **affirmative action**. The initial goal was to require businesses that received federal contracts to "take affirmative action to ensure that employees are treated without regard for their race, creed, color, or national origin." By the 1970s, many states and cities had adopted similar policies for hiring their own employees and choosing contractors and extended affirmative action to women as well as minorities. Colleges and universities used affirmative action policies to recruit faculty and admit students.

As these efforts spread, the initial goal of nondiscrimination evolved into expectations and requirements for active ("affirmative") efforts to achieve greater diversity. Government agencies began to set aside a small percentages of contracts for woman-owned or minority-owned firms. Cities worked to hire more minority police officers and fire fighters. Colleges made special efforts to attract minority students. The landmark court case about affirmative action was *University of California v. Bakke* (1978). Allan Bakke, an unsuccessful applicant to the medical school at the University of California at Davis, argued that the university by reserving 16 of 100 places in its entering class for minority students, had engaged in reverse discrimination against white applicants. The U.S. Supreme Court ordered Bakke admitted because the only basis for his rejection had been race, but the Court also stated that race or ethnicity could legally be one of several factors considered in university admissions as long as a specific number of places were not reserved for minorities.

In 1996, California voters approved a ballot measure to eliminate state-sponsored affirmative action. One effect was to prohibit state-funded schools from using race or ethnicity as a factor in deciding which applicants to admit. In the same year, the Supreme Court let stand a lower-court ruling in *Hopwood* v. *Texas*, that had forbidden the University of Texas to consider race in admission decisions.

QUICK REVIEW

Divisive Issues
- The proper response to illegal immigration.
- Degree of accommodation of non-English speakers in U.S. schools.
- Affirmative action.

Proposition 187   California legislation adopted by popular vote in California in 1994, which cuts off state-funded health and education benefits to undocumented or illegal immigrants.

Affirmative action   A set of policies to open opportunities in business and education for members of minority groups and women by allowing race and sex to be factors included in decisions to hire, award contracts, or admit students to higher education programs.

University of California v. *Bakke*
U.S. Supreme Court case in 1978 that allowed race to be used as one of several factors in college and university admission decisions but made rigid quotas unacceptable.

The number of black freshmen in the University Texas dropped by half in 1997 and the number of black and Hispanic first-year law students by two-thirds. The results were similar at the University of California at Berkeley.

Affirmative action is a lightning rod for disagreements about American society. The goal of diversity seems to conflict with the fundamental American value of individual opportunity. Most Americans believe that individual merit and qualifications should be the sole basis for getting into school or getting a job, and that SAT scores and civil-service exams can measure those qualifications. Others argue that the merit system is severely flawed and that affirmative action helps to level the field. Nevertheless, many minorities worry that affirmative action suggests that they received jobs or contracts by racial preference rather than merit.

EDGING INTO A NEW CENTURY

On the evening of November 7, 2000, CBS-TV made a mistake that journalists dread. Relying on questions put to a sample of voters after they cast their ballots in the presidential contest between Albert Gore Jr. and George W. Bush, the CBS newsroom first projected that Gore would win Florida and likely the election, then reversed itself and called the election for Bush, only to find that it would be weeks before the votes in several pivotal states, including Florida, could be certified.

The inability to predict the outcome in 2000 was an indication of the degree to which Americans were split down the middle in their political preferences and their visions for the future. The United States entered the twenty-first century both divided and balanced, with extremes of opinion revolving around a center of basic goals and values.

THE ELECTION OF 2000

On November 8, 2000, the day after their national election, Americans woke up to the news that neither Republican George W. Bush nor Democrat Albert Gore Jr., had secured a majority of votes in the electoral college. Although Gore held a lead in the popular vote (about 340,000 votes out of more than 100 million cast), both candidates needed a majority in Florida to secure its electoral votes and the White House. After protracted protests and an on-again off-again recount in key counties, the U.S. Supreme Court ordered a halt to recounting on December 12 by the politically charged margin of 5 to 4. The result made Bush the winner in Florida by a few hundred votes and the winner nationwide by 271 electoral votes to 267.

It is difficult to know who "really" won Florida. African-American voters, who strongly favored Gore, were turned away in disproportionate numbers because of technical challenges to their registration. In one county, a poorly designed ballot probably caused several thousand mistaken votes for a minor candidate rather than Gore. Overseas absentee ballots, likely to favor Bush, were counted despite their frequent failure to meet the criteria for legitimate votes. But recounts by newspaper reporters came to different conclusions about who might have won, depending on what criteria were used to accept or reject disputed punch card ballots.

The election showed a nation that was paradoxically divided around a strong center. Gore appealed especially to residents of large cities, to women, to African

WHAT WERE the policies of George W. Bush during his first two years in office?

QUICK REVIEW

Election Controversy
- Al Gore secured a majority of the popular vote.
- Both sides needed Florida's contested electoral votes to secure election.
- The U.S. Supreme Court voted 5–4 to end the recount in Florida, making George W. Bush the new president.

Americans, and to families struggling to make it economically. Bush appealed to people from small towns, to men, and to members of households who had benefited the most from the prosperity of the Clinton era. These divisions had marked the two parties since the 1930s, and their persistence was a reminder of the nation's diversity of opinions and values. The nation also divided regionally, with Gore strong in the Northeast, upper Midwest, and Pacific Coast, Bush in the South, Ohio Valley, Great Plains, and Rocky Mountain states.

Both Bush and Gore targeted their campaigns at middle Americans. Each offered to cut taxes, reduce the federal government, and protect Social Security. Voters also shaved the Republican control of Congress to razor-thin margins, further undermining any chance of radical change in either a conservative or a liberal direction. To those on the political left and right, it looked like a formula for paralysis; for most Americans, it looked like stability.

REAGANOMICS REVISITED

Nevertheless, the Bush administration tilted domestic policy abruptly to the right. It decided it had a mandate for change and acted boldly to implement its goals. Following the example of Ronald Reagan, Bush made massive tax cuts

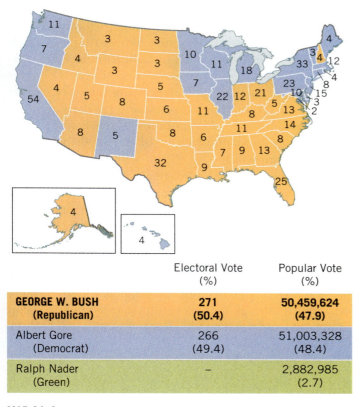

	Electoral Vote (%)	Popular Vote (%)
GEORGE W. BUSH (Republican)	**271 (50.4)**	**50,459,624 (47.9)**
Albert Gore (Democrat)	266 (49.4)	51,003,328 (48.4)
Ralph Nader (Green)	–	2,882,985 (2.7)

MAP 31–3

The Election of 2000 In the nation's closest presidential election, Democrat Al Gore was most successful in the Northeast and Far West, while George W. Bush swept the South and won most of the Great Plains states. Green Party candidate Ralph Nader took most of his votes from Gore, and, in a twist of irony, helped to swing the election to Bush.

WHAT DO the 2000 election results reveal about the divisions that separate Americans today?

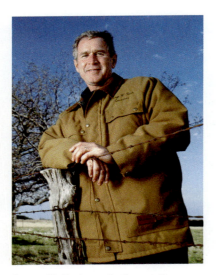

George W. Bush awaits the results of the 2000 Presidential Election recount at his ranch in Texas. The controversial Florida recount was part of the closest election in U.S. history, finally granting Bush the presidency one month after election day.

Corbis/Bettmann

the centerpiece of his first months in office. By starting with proposals for ten-year cuts so large that two generations of federal programs were threatened, Bush and congressional Republicans forced the Democrats to "compromise" on reductions far higher than the economy could probably support. The resulting cuts to income taxes and estate taxes were projected to total $1,350 billion over the decade, with one-third of the benefits going to families earning more than $200,000. By 2003, officials were forecasting a budget deficit of at least $300 billion for the coming year, undoing the fiscal discipline of the Clinton administration. Nevertheless, the administration seemed likely to achieve its goal of making the tax cuts permanent after the 2002 elections confirmed a Republican majority in Congress.

The Bush team also moved to deregulate the economy. It opened many of the environmental and business regulations of the last two decades to reconsideration—from arsenic standards in drinking water to protections for wetlands to the pollution controls required of electric utilities. In many cases, the administration proposed to rely on the market through voluntary compliance and incentives to replace regulations. Vice President Dick Cheney developed a new production-oriented energy policy in consultation with energy companies but not with environmental or consumer groups. The administration failed to secure congressional approval for oil drilling in the Arctic National Wildlife Refuge in the far north of Alaska but crafted development-friendly policies for other federal lands. Collapse of the energy-trading company Enron in a hailstorm of deceptive accounting and shady market manipulations to create an energy crisis in California in early 2000 slowed the push to deregulate. In turn, Enron proved to be the first of many companies that had to restate earnings in 2002, depressing the stock market and raising questions about the ethics of big business and business accounting practices. Stock market declines and the evaporation of retirement savings for many workers raised doubts about the solidity of the 1990s boom and helped to hold down economic growth.

Education policy, a centerpiece of Bush's image as an innovator from his service as governor of Texas, was another legislative front. Tough battles with Congress resulted in compromise legislation, reminiscent of the 1990s, that included national testing standards, as Bush wanted, balanced by more federal funding. More important for both education and religion was the narrow decision by the Supreme Court in Zelman v. Simmons-Harris (2002) to uphold the use of taxpayer-funded assistance, or vouchers, to help students attend religious schools. By declaring that both religious and secular institutions can compete for government money as long as it is channeled through individuals who decided how to spend it, the court continued a two-decade trend to narrow the constitutional prohibition on the "establishment of religion."

DOWNSIZED DIPLOMACY

Conservatives had long criticized subordinating U.S. authority and freedom of action to international agreements. The new Bush administration repeatedly adopted unilateral or bilateral policies in preference to the complexities of negotiations with an entire range of nations.

In his first eighteen months, Bush opted out of a series of treaties and negotiations on global issues. The goal in each case was to reduce restrictions on U.S. business and the military. The administration undercut efforts to implement the Convention on Biological Warfare. It refused to sign on to efforts to reduce the international trade in armaments, declined to acknowledge a new International Criminal Court to try war criminals, and ignored an international compact on the rights of women. Most prominently, it refused to accept the Kyoto Agreement, aimed at combating the threat of massive environmental change through global warming resulting from the carbon dioxide released by fossil fuels, dismissing a growing scientific consensus on the problem.

Bush also ended the 1972 treaty that had limited the deployment of antimissile defenses by the United States and Russia. In its place he revived Ronald Reagan's idea of a Strategic Defense Initiative with proposals for new but unproven technologies to protect the United States against nuclear attacks by "rogue states." This argument was supported in 2002 by North Korea's revelation that it was pursuing a nuclear weapons program, even though it had agreed not to do so in 1994. A new U.S. policy that explicitly claimed the right to act militarily to preempt potential threats confirmed the go-it-alone approach.

PARADOXES OF POWER

The United States in the twenty-first century faced the paradox of power: The enormous economic, military, and technological capacity, that allowed it to impose its will on other nations could not prevent anti-American actions by enraged individuals.

In the 1990s, the U.S. economy had surged while Japan stagnated, Europe marked time, and Russia verged on economic collapse. The American military budget exceeded the total military spending of the next dozen nations.

But the United States remained vulnerable. Terrorist attacks by Islamic radicals killed nineteen American soldiers at military housing in Saudi Arabia in 1996 and seventeen sailors on the destroyer *Cole* while in port in the Arab nation of Yemen in 2000. Bombs at the U.S. embassies in Kenya and Tanzania in 1998 killed more than 200 people. These bombings followed the detonation of explosives in the basement garage of the World Trade Center in New York in February 1993. Terrorism remained a constant threat—realized in an appalling manner on September 11, 2001.

After September 11, there were reports of information-gathering failures by the FBI and CIA, to be investigated by a commission appointed by President Bush at the end of 2002. However, it is always easier to read the warnings after an event has occurred than to pick out the essential data before the unexpected happens—something as true about the attack on Pearl Harbor, for example, as about the attack of 9/11.

SECURITY AND CONFLICT

On September 12, President George W. Bush called the Pentagon and World Trade Center attacks "acts of war." Three days later, Congress passed a Joint Resolution that gave the president sweeping powers "to use all necessary and appropriate force against those nations, organizations, or persons he determines planned, authorized, committed, or aided the terrorist attacks that occurred on September 11, 2001."

HOW DID 9/11 affect American views on security and foreign affairs?

FROM THEN TO NOW
Loyalty in 2001 and 1917

In mid-October of 2001, Congress completed work on anti-terrorism legislation that President George W. Bush and Attorney General John Ashcroft had demanded in the aftermath of the September 11 tragedy. The Patriot Act gave federal authorities substantial new capacity to conduct criminal investigations, in most provisions for the next three to five years. These included the power to request "roving" wiretaps of individuals rather than single telephones; to obtain nationwide search warrants; to tap information in computerized records; and to detain foreigners without filing charges for up to a week.

These measures raised a number of concerns about the protection of civil liberties, as noted by the several dozen members of Congress who voted against the act. In historical perspective, however, it is comparatively restrained. Congress deliberated for several weeks rather than instantly ratifying the administration's request. And it seemed as if some history lessons had sunk in, for numerous lawmakers and commentators raised the painful memory of the unnecessary internment of Japanese Americans during World War II.

Perhaps the most useful historical comparison—and contrast—is not World War II but World War I. (see Chapter 23). When Americans plunged into war in April 1917, the nation's political and economic leaders took the occasion to muffle dissent in the name of unity. Congress rushed through an Espionage Act that set prison terms for obstructing the war effort and quickly became a tool for squashing dissenting voices. The Sedition Act of 1918 was even broader, establishing penalties for speaking or writing against the draft, bond sales, or war production.

Federal authorities in the Justice Department cooperated with the private, reactionary American Protective League and with tens of thousands of local councils of defense. Neighbors spied on each other and reported suspicious conversations. The "loyalty" efforts targeted African Americans and Asian Americans as well as German Americans. The Post Office censored mail. Schools stopped teaching German, and immigrants spoke the language at their peril. Workers who failed to buy war bonds were fired. Loyalty became an excuse for crushing working class organizing. Socialist Party leader Eugene Debs was put in jail for noting, accurately, that it was now hard to exercise free speech. Authorities and their allies raided labor union offices and used the war emergency as an excuse for violent strike breaking.

The anti-radical vigilantism of 1917–18 segued into the Red Scare of 1919–20, when federal and local authorities targeted immigrants and labor organizers as potential revolutionaries. The Wilson administration kept wartime political prisoners in jail and arrested thousands more before the nation got tired of fighting off a revolution that never came.

In contrast to the 1910s, Americans in 2001 and 2002 were careful on the homefront. The leaders and supporters of the War on Terrorism have reacted to dissenting voices, particularly those from a pacifist tradition, with caustic remarks rather than repression. Censorship to date consists of careful management of the news and stonewalling of requests under the Freedom of Information Act rather than direct censorship of speech and the press. Violations of civil liberties have affected individuals rather than entire groups. Ethnic profiling has resulted in heightened suspicion and surveillance of Muslims, selective enforcement of immigration laws on visitors from twenty Muslim nations, and detention of several hundred U.S. residents of middle eastern origin, rather than incarceration of entire ethnic groups. Because a number of the detainees have been held without formal charges for periods of many months, a close analogy is the suspension of the writ of habeas corpus by President Lincoln during the Civil War rather than the wholesale constriction of freedom during World War I.

The different reactions can be linked to the far greater sense of national identity at the start of the twenty-first century than early in the twentieth century. Americans in the twenty-first century worry about the challenges of racial and ethnic variety and the stresses of immigration, but mass media and easy travel have helped to promote a shared sense of "being American." There are small fringe groups that advocate or practice violent preservation of a "white nation," but the middle and upper classes do not fear immigration or working class revolution in the way that was common a hundred years ago. Despite a number of individual hate crimes, the formal effort to recognize the Americanness of most of the nation's six million Muslims and Arab Americans stands in contrast to the demonizing of Japanese-Americans in the 1940s and discrimination against German-Americans in 1917–1918. Through the second half of the twentieth century, Americans seem to have learned at least something about tolerance, diversity, and the value of civil liberties.

The government response in the United States was a hodge-podge of security measures and arrests. Air travelers found endless lines and stringent new screening procedures, watched over by army reservists called to duty by the president. Members of Congress and journalists received letters containing potentially deadly anthrax spores, heightening fears of biological warfare (the source of the letters is still a mystery). Federal agents detained more than one thousand terrorist suspects, mostly men from the Middle East, releasing some but holding hundreds without charges, evidence, or legal counsel. President Bush also declared that "enemy combatants" could be tried by special military tribunals, although domestic and international protest caused the administration to agree to more legal safeguards than originally planned. Congress passed the **Patriot Act** in late October. The legislation tries to bring surveillance and information gathering into the electronic age.

In November 2002, Congress approved a massive reorganization of the federal government to improve security at home. The new Department of Homeland Security with 170,000 employees is the second-largest federal agency, after the Defense Department, but it leaves unsolved the problem of an ineffective FBI and CIA.

In the months after 9/11, the military response overseas focused on Afghanistan, where the ruling Taliban regime was harboring Bin-Laden. Afghanistan had been wracked by civil war since it had been invaded by the Soviet Union in 1979. The Taliban, who came to power after Soviet withdrawal and civil war, were repressive rulers with few international friends. American bombing attacks on Taliban forces began in early October 2001, and opposition groups within Afghanistan threw the Taliban out of power by December. Bin-Laden, however, escaped, leaving the U.S. with an uncertain commitment to rebuild a stable Afghanistan. The Al-Qaeda network and its sympathizer remained active around the world.

Patriot Act   Federal legislation adopted in 2001, in response to the terrorist attacks of September 11, intended to facilitate antiterror actions by federal law enforcement and intelligence agencies.

The overthrow of the Taliban regime in Afghanistan reopened many opportunities for women, including access to education as called for in Muslim scriptures. These young women are among 600 who were studying at the Cheva school for girls in Kabul by December 2002.

AP/Wilde World Photos

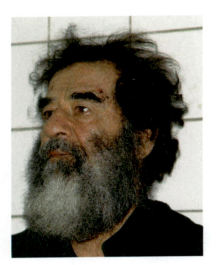

Saddam Hussein upon capture by U.S. troops in Iraq in December 2003.

Corbis/Bettmann

IRAQ AND CONFLICTS IN THE MIDDLE EAST

Even while the United States was intervening in Afghanistan, the administration was expanding its attention to other nations. George Bush named North Korea, Iran, and Iraq as an "axis of evil" for supporting terrorism and bearing weapons of mass destruction focused on Iraq. After the first Gulf War, Iraq had grudgingly accepted a United Nations requirement that it eliminate such weapons but had gradually made U.N. inspections impossible. Such resistance caused Bush to make the overthrow of Iraq's ruthless dictator, Saddam Hussein, the center of foreign policy. In effect, he declared one small, and possibly dangerous, nation to be the greatest menace that the United States faced. In the meantime, North Korea created a further crisis by actively pursuing its atomic weapons program with the threat of additional war.

In addition to the direct fallout from the first Gulf War, U.S. support of Israel in its worsening of relations with Arab Palestinians in territories occupied by Israel since 1967 also increased tensions in the Middle East. The United States has consistently backed Israel since the 1960s. The cornerstones of American policy have been the full endorsement of Israel's right to exist with secure borders and agreement on the right of Palestinians to a national state—in effect, a policy of coexistence. The United States had helped to broker an Israel-Egypt peace agreement in 1977 and agreements pointing toward an independent Palestinian state in the 1990s, but hardline Israeli governments have repeatedly taken advantage of U.S. support.

In 2001–2002, the United States watched from the sidelines as the Israeli-Palestinian agreements for transition to a Palestinian state fell apart. Palestinian extremists and suicide bombers and an Israeli government that favored military responses locked each other into a downward spiral that turned anti-Israel demonstrations into civil war. As a result, many Arabs regard the United States as an enemy of Arab nations and peoples, despite formal U.S. policy. The deep and seemingly unsolvable Israel-Palestinian conflict helps to explain anti-American terrorism among Arabs and other Muslims.

In the spring and summer of 2002, the administration began preparations for a second war in the Persian Gulf. On October 10, Congress authorized preemptive military action against Iraq. However, the prospect of war dismayed key allies, such as France and Germany. Together with Russia and China, they refused to support a war without U.N. backing and demanded that Bush allow more time for U.N. inspectors to search out and destroy any Iraqi weapons of mass destruction. Nonetheless, despite these objections and massive peace demonstrations in cities in the United States and around the world, American and British forces invaded Iraq in March 2003 and occupied Baghdad within two weeks, toppling Saddam's government. The United States was now faced with the possibility of a long-term occupation of Iraq and the difficult problems of rebuilding the country and trying to establish a democratic and pro-Western regime there.

CONCLUSION

If there was a dominant theme that ran through the changes and challenges of the 1990s and early 2000s, it was interconnection. The Internet, email, and cell phones brought instant communication. The national economy was more and more deeply engaged with the rest of the world through trade, investment, travel, and immigration. Corporate mismanagement affected far more people than before because of pensions and savings invested in the stock market.

The nation's growing diversity—closely connected to its internationalized economy—was reflected in the political gains of African Americans and Hispanics, as well as women. The same diversity fueled battles over affirmative action and language politics. It underlay the effort to increase security against terrorism without endangering the civil liberties of Muslim Americans.

Despite what some might have wished, Americans also found that they could not always isolate the nation from the world's problems and conflicts. The Clinton administration joined international peacekeeping efforts in Bosnia and Kosovo. The Bush administration adopted a "go it alone" policy.

The events of September 11 sparked a renewed sense of national unity, at least in the short run. There were inspiring acts of heroism and an outpouring of volunteers and contributions for rescue and relief efforts. However, the question that remained was whether Americans could sustain a new sense of unity and inclusiveness under the pressures of economic uncertainty, threats of terrorism, and war.

SUMMARY

Politics of the Center In 1992 voters ranked the economy as their first concern, and Bill Clinton hammered at this in his campaign messages. His elections in 1992 and 1996 showed a move toward the political center; Clinton emerged as a neoliberal. Conservative political ideology and animosity toward the Clintons dominated the headlines; the Contract with America, the budget battle that shut down the federal government, Whitewater, the Clinton scandals, and impeachment filled the political headlines. Domestic terrorism (Waco, Oklahoma City, and Columbine) also grabbed the national spotlight. In foreign affairs, the United States became involved in a multinational effort to restore peace in Bosnia and Kosovo.

A New Economy? At the end of the millennium, America had a new worry, the "Y2K" problem, that did not materialize. Americans enjoyed nine years of continuous economic expansion; services became the new underpinning of the economy; and an instant society based on twenty-four hour access gave people immediate satisfaction. The American economy also expanded internationally. The controversial North American Free Trade Act went into effect and protestors took on the World Trade Organization in the streets of Seattle which demonstrated part of a larger worldwide debate over free trade and the role of transnational corporations.

Broadening Democracy The changing composition of the American people is related to the changes in the economy. The growing West, the concentration of one-third of the population in four states, the largest ten-year population increase in history, and racial and ethnic diversity, are all significance trends. As women have become more influential in national politics, so have minorities; both have contributed to a political rebalancing. Questions about equal rights and equal opportunities (Proposition 187, bilingual education, and affirmative action) have become part of the American dialogue.

REVIEW QUESTIONS

1. Was the American political system more polarized and divided in 1992 than in 1980? How did religiously conservative and liberal Americans differ over foreign relations and economic policy? What was the gender gap in national politics in the 1990s? Why were Republicans unable to appeal to most black and Hispanic voters in 1992?

2. What were Bill Clinton's major policy accomplishments? Do these represent "liberal," "moderate," or "conservative" positions?

3. How was a conservative political trend evident in the 1990s?

4. What issues were involved in Clinton's impeachment? How does the impeachment compare with the challenges to presidents Andrew Johnson and Richard Nixon?

5. How did the American economy change in the 1990s? What has been the impact of the computer revolution?

6. What new directions did George W. Bush estabilish for U.S. domestic and foreign policy?

7. How did the terrorist attacks of September 11, 2001 change life inside the United States?

KEY TERMS

Affirmative action   (p. 837)
Bosnia   (p. 824)
Contract with America
(p. 825)
Internet   (p. 829)
Kosovo   (p. 824)
Neoliberal   (p. 825)

North American Free Trade Agreement (NAFTA)   (p. 833)
Patriot Act   (p. 843)
Proposition 187   (p. 837)
Silicon Valley   (p. 829)
Temporary Assistance for Needy Families (TANF)   (p. 826)

University of California vs. *Bakke*
(p. 837)
Whitewater   (p. 827)
World Trade Organization (WTO)   (p. 833)
World Wide Web   (p. 832)

WHERE TO LEARN MORE

Oklahoma City National Memorial Center Museum, Oklahoma City, OK. Exhibits about the federal building bombing and its impacts on the community. **www.oklahomacitynationalmemorial.org**

U.S. Census Bureau. Explore the demographic composition of the United States through the use of statistics concerning such topics as age, population distribution, income, education, and race. **http://www.census.gov/**

Computer History Museum. Trace the evolution of computers from 1945 through the present day with one of the largest collections of artifacts, photographs, documents, and film found anywhere in the world. **http://www.computerhistory.org**

Clinton Presidential Center. Showcases the legacy of the Clinton years and functions as the first virtual presidential library. The William J. Clinton Presidential Center in Little Rock, Arkansas opens November 2004. **http://www.clintonpresidentialcenter.com**

Republican Contract with America. Read the full text document of the official Republican campaign platform for the 1994 election. **http://www.house.gov/house/Contract/CONTRACT.html**

 For additional study resources for this chapter, go to: **www.prenhall.com/goldfield/chapter31**

APPENDIX

THE DECLARATION OF INDEPENDENCE

When in the course of human events it becomes necessary for one people to dissolve the political bands which have connected them with another and to assume, among the powers of the earth, the separate and equal station to which the laws of nature and of nature's God entitle them, a decent respect to the opinions of mankind requires that they should declare the causes which impel them to the separation.

We hold these truths to be self-evident, that all men are created equal; that they are endowed by their Creator with certain unalienable rights; that among these are life, liberty, and the pursuit of happiness. That, to secure these rights, governments are instituted among men, deriving their just powers from the consent of the governed; that, whenever any form of government becomes destructive of these ends, it is the right of the people to alter or to abolish it, and to institute a new government, laying its foundation on such principles, and organizing its powers in such form, as to them shall seem most likely to effect their safety and happiness. Prudence, indeed, will dictate that governments long established should not be changed for light and transient causes; and, accordingly, all experience hath shown that mankind are more disposed to suffer, while evils are sufferable, than to right themselves by abolishing the forms to which they are accustomed. But when a long train of abuses and usurpations, pursuing invariably the same object, evinces a design to reduce them under absolute despotism, it is their right, it is their duty, to throw off such government and to provide new guards for their future security. Such has been the patient sufferance of these colonies, and such is now the necessity which constrains them to alter their former systems of government. The history of the present King of Great Britain is a history of repeated injuries and usurpations, all having, in direct object, the establishment of an absolute tyranny over these States. To prove this, let facts be submitted to a candid world:

He has refused his assent to laws the most wholesome and necessary for the public good.

He has forbidden his governors to pass laws of immediate and pressing importance, unless suspended in their operation till his assent should be obtained; and, when so suspended, he has utterly neglected to attend to them.

He has refused to pass other laws for the accommodation of large districts of people, unless those people would relinquish the right of representation in the legislature, a right inestimable to them and formidable to tyrants only.

He has called together legislative bodies at places unusual, uncomfortable, and distant from the depository of their public records, for the sole purpose of fatiguing them into compliance with his measures.

He has dissolved representative houses, repeatedly for opposing, with manly firmness, his invasions on the rights of the people.

He has refused, for a long time after such dissolutions, to cause others to be elected; whereby the legislative powers, incapable of annihilation, have returned to the people at large for their exercise; the state remaining, in the meantime, exposed to all the danger of invasion from without and convulsions within.

He has endeavored to prevent the population of these States; for that purpose, obstructing the laws for naturalization of foreigners, refusing to pass others to encourage their migration hither, and raising the conditions of new appropriations of lands.

He has obstructed the administration of justice by refusing his assent to laws for establishing judiciary powers.

He has made judges dependent on his will alone for the tenure of their offices and the amount and payment of their salaries.

He has erected a multitude of new offices and sent hither swarms of officers to harass our people and eat out their substance.

He has kept among us, in time of peace, standing armies, without the consent of our legislatures.

He has affected to render the military independent of, and superior to, the civil power.

He has combined with others to subject us to a jurisdiction foreign to our Constitution and unacknowledged by our laws, giving his assent to their acts of pretended legislation—

For quartering large bodies of armed troops among us;

For protecting them by mock trial, from punishment for any murders which they should commit on the inhabitants of these States;

For cutting off our trade with all parts of the world;

For imposing taxes on us without our consent;

For depriving us, in many cases, of the benefit of trial by jury;

For transporting us beyond seas to be tried for pretended offences;

For abolishing the free system of English laws in a neighboring province, establishing therein an arbitrary government, and enlarging its boundaries, so as to render it at once an example and fit instrument for introducing the same absolute rule into these colonies;

For taking away our charters, abolishing our most valuable laws, and altering, fundamentally, the powers of our governments.

For suspending our own legislatures and declaring themselves invested with power to legislate for us in all cases whatsoever.

He has abdicated government here by declaring us out of his protection and waging war against us.

He has plundered our seas, ravaged our coasts, burnt our towns, and destroyed the lives of our people.

He is, at this time, transporting large armies of foreign mercenaries to complete the works of death, desolation, and tyranny already begun with circumstances of cruelty and perfidy scarcely paralleled in the most barbarous ages, and totally unworthy the head of a civilized nation.

He has constrained our fellow citizens, taken captive on the high seas, to bear arms against their country, to become the executioners of their friends and brethren, or to fall themselves by their hands.

He has excited domestic insurrections amongst us and has endeavored to bring on the inhabitants of our frontiers, the merciless Indian savages, whose known rule of warfare is an undistinguished destruction of all ages, sexes, and conditions.

In every stage of these oppressions, we have petitioned for redress in the most humble terms; our repeated petitions have been answered only by repeated injury. A prince whose character is thus marked by every act which may define a tyrant is unfit to be the ruler of a free people.

Nor have we been wanting in attention to our British brethren. We have warned them, from time to time, of attempts made by their legislature to extend an unwarrantable jurisdiction over us. We have reminded them of the circumstances of our emigration and settlement here. We have appealed to their native justice and magnanimity, and

we have conjured them, by the ties of our common kindred, to disavow these usurpations, which would inevitably interrupt our connections and correspondence. They, too, have been deaf to the voice of justice and consanguinity. We must, therefore, acquiesce in the necessity which denounces our separation, and hold them, as we hold the rest of mankind, enemies in war, in peace, friends.

We, therefore, the representatives of the United States of America, in general Congress assembled, appealing to the Supreme Judge of the world for the rectitude of our intentions, do, in the name and by the authority of the good people of these colonies, solemnly publish and declare, that these united colonies are, and of right ought to be, free and independent states: that they are absolved from all allegiance to the British Crown, and that all political connection between them and the state of Great Britain is, and ought to be, totally dissolved; and that, as free and independent states, they have full power to levy war, conclude peace, contract alliances, establish commerce, and to do all other acts and things which independent states may of right do. And, for the support of this declaration, with a firm reliance on the protection of Divine Providence, we mutually pledge to each other our lives, our fortunes, and our sacred honor.

THE ARTICLES OF CONFEDERATION AND PERPETUAL UNION*

Between the states of New Hampshire, Massachusetts-bay Rhode Island and Providence Plantations, Connecticut, New York, New Jersey, Pennsylvania, Delaware, Maryland, Virginia, North Carolina, South Carolina, and Georgia.

ARTICLE 1

The Stile of this Confederacy shall be "The United States of America."

ARTICLE 2

Each state retains its sovereignty, freedom, and independence, and every power, jurisdiction, and right, which is not by this Confederation expressly delegated to the United States, in Congress assembled.

ARTICLE 3

The said States hereby severally enter into a firm league of friendship with each other, for their common defense, the security of their liberties, and their mutual and general welfare, binding themselves to assist each other, against all force offered to, or attacks made upon them, or any of them, on account of religion, sovereignty, trade, or any other pretense whatever.

ARTICLE 4

The better to secure and perpetuate mutual friendship and intercourse among the people of the different States in this Union, the free inhabitants of each of these States, paupers, vagabonds, and fugitives from justice excepted, shall be entitled to all privileges and immunities of free citizens in the several States; and the people of each State shall have free ingress and regress to and from any other State, and shall

enjoy therein all the privileges of trade and commerce, subject to the same duties, impositions, and restrictions as the inhabitants thereof respectively, provided that such restrictions shall not extend so far as to prevent the removal of property imported into any State, to any other State of which the owner is an inhabitant; provided also that no imposition, duties or restriction shall be laid by any State, on the property of the United States, or either of them.

If any person guilty of, or charged with, treason, felony, or other high misdemeanor in any State, shall flee from justice, and be found in any of the United States, he shall, upon demand of the Governor or executive power of the State from which he fled, be delivered up and removed to the State having jurisdiction of his offense.

Full faith and credit shall be given in each of these States to the records, acts, and judicial proceedings of the courts and magistrates of every other State.

ARTICLE 5

For the most convenient management of the general interests of the United States, delegates shall be annually appointed in such manner as the legislatures of each State shall direct, to meet in Congress on the first Monday in November, in every year, with a power reserved to each State to recall its delegates, or any of them, at any time within the year, and to send others in their stead for the remainder of the year.

No State shall be represented in Congress by less than two, nor by more than seven members; and no person shall be capable of being a delegate for more than three years in any term of six years; nor shall any person, being a delegate,

---

*Agreed to in Congress November 15, 1777; ratified March 1781.

be capable of holding any office under the United States, for which he, or another for his benefit, receives any salary, fees or emolument of any kind.

Each State shall maintain its own delegates in a meeting of the States, and while they act as members of the committee of the States.

In determining questions in the United States in Congress assembled, each State shall have one vote.

Freedom of speech and debate in Congress shall not be impeached or questioned in any court or place out of Congress, and the members of Congress shall be protected in their persons from arrests or imprisonments, during the time of their going to and from, and attendence on Congress, except for treason, felony, or breach of the peace.

ARTICLE 6

No State, without the consent of the United States in Congress assembled, shall send any embassy to, or receive any embassy from, or enter into any conference, agreement, alliance or treaty with any King, Prince or State; nor shall any person holding any office of profit or trust under the United States, or any of them, accept any present, emolument, office or title of any kind whatever from any King, Prince or foreign State; nor shall the United States in Congress assembled, or any of them, grant any title of nobility.

No two or more States shall enter into any treaty, confederation or alliance whatever between them, without the consent of the United States in Congress assembled, specifying accurately the purposes for which the same is to be entered into, and how long it shall continue.

No State shall lay any imposts or duties, which may interfere with any stipulations in treaties, entered into by the United States in Congress assembled, with any King, Prince or State, in pursuance of any treaties already proposed by Congress, to the courts of France and Spain.

No vessel of war shall be kept up in time of peace by any State, except such number only, as shall be deemed necessary by the United States in Congress assembled, for the defense of such State, or its trade; nor shall any body of forces be kept up by any State in time of peace, except such number only, as in the judgement of the United States in Congress assembled, shall be deemed requisite to garrison the forts necessary for the defense of such State; but every State shall always keep up a well-regulated and disciplined militia, sufficiently armed and accoutered, and shall provide and constantly have ready for use, in public stores, a due number of filed pieces and tents, and a proper quantity of arms, ammunition and camp equipage.

No State shall engage in any war without the consent of the United States in Congress assembled, unless such State be actually invaded by enemies, or shall have received certain advice of a resolution being formed by some nation of Indians to invade such State, and the danger is so imminent as not to admit of a delay, till the United States in Congress assembled can be consulted; nor shall any State grant commissions to any ships or vessels of war, nor letters of marque or reprisal, except it be after a declaration of war by the United States in Congress assembled, and then only against the Kingdom or State and the subjects thereof, against which war has been so declared, and under such regulations as shall be established by the United States in Congress assem-

bled, unless such State be infested by pirates, in which case vessels of war may be fitted out for that occasion, and kept so long as the danger shall continue, or until the United States in Congress assembled shall determine otherwise.

ARTICLE 7

When land forces are raised by any State for the common defense, all officers of or under the rank of colonel, shall be appointed by the legislature of each State respectively, by whom such forces shall be raised, or in such manner as such State shall direct, and all vacancies shall be filled up by the State which first made the appointment.

ARTICLE 8

All charges of war, and all other expenses that shall be incurred for the common defense or general welfare, and allowed by the United States in Congress assembled, shall be defrayed out of a common treasury, which shall be supplied by the several States in proportion to the value of all land within each State, granted to or surveyed for any person, as such land and the buildings and improvements thereon shall be estimated according to such mode as the United States in Congress assembled, shall from time to time direct and appoint.

The taxes for paying that proportion shall be laid and levied by the authority and direction of the legislatures of the several States within the time agreed upon by the United States in Congress assembled.

ARTICLE 9

The United States in Congress assembled, shall have the sole and exclusive right and power of determining on peace and war, except in the cases mentioned in the sixth article; of sending and receiving ambassadors; entering into treaties and alliances, provided that no treaty of commerce shall be made whereby the legislative power of the respective States shall be restrained from imposing such imposts and duties on foreigners, as their own people are subjected to, or from prohibiting the exportation or importation of any species of goods or commodities whatsoever; of establishing rules for deciding in all cases, what captures on land or water shall be legal, and in what manner prizes taken by land or naval forces in the service of the United States shall be divided or appropriated; of granting letters of marque and reprisal in times of peace; appointing courts for the trial of piracies and felonies committed on the high seas and establishing courts for receiving and determining finally appeals in all cases of captures, provided that no member of Congress shall be appointed a judge of any of the said courts.

The United States in Congress assembled shall also be the last resort on appeal in all disputes and differences now subsisting or that hereafter may arise between two or more States concerning boundary, jurisdiction or any other causes whatever; which authority shall always be exercised in the manner following. Whenever the legislative or executive authority or lawful agent of any State in controversy with another shall present a petition to Congress stating the matter in question and praying for a hearing, notice thereof shall be given by order of Congress to the legislative or executive authority of the other State in controversy, and a day assigned for the appearance of the parties by their lawful agents, who shall then be directed to appoint by joint consent, commissioners or judges to constitute a court for hearing and determining the matter in question: but if they cannot agree, Congress shall name three persons out of each of the United States, and from the list of such persons each party shall alternately strike out one, the petitioners beginning, until the number shall be reduced to thirteen; and from that number not less than seven, nor more than nine names as Congress shall direct, shall in the presence of Congress be drawn out by lot, and the persons whose names shall be so drawn or any five of them, shall be commissioners or judges, to hear and finally determine the controversy, so always as a major part of the judges who shall hear the cause shall agree in the determination: and if either party shall neglect to attend at the day appointed, without showing reasons, which Congress shall judge sufficient, or being present shall refuse to strike, the Congress shall proceed to nominate three persons out of each State, and the secretary of Congress shall strike in behalf of such party absent or refusing; and the judgement and sentence of the court to be appointed, in the manner before prescribed, shall be final and conclusive; and if any of the parties shall refuse to submit to the authority of such court, or to appear or defend their claim or cause, the court shall nevertheless proceed to pronounce sentence, or judgement, which shall in like manner be final and decisive, the judgement or sentence and other proceedings being in either case transmitted to Congress, and lodged among the acts of Congress for the security of the parties concerned: provided that every commissioner, before he sits in judgement, shall take an oath to be administered by one of the judges of the supreme or superior court of the State, where the cause shall be tried, "well and truly to hear and determine the matter in question, according to the best of his judgement, without favor, affection or hope of reward:" provided also, that no State shall be deprived of territory for the benefit of the United States.

All controversies concerning the private right of soil claimed under different grants of two or more States, whose jurisdictions as they may respect such lands, and the States which passed such grants are adjusted, the said grants or either of them being at the same time claimed to have originated antecedent to such settlement of jurisdiction, shall on the petition of either party to the Congress of the United States, be finally determined as near as may be in the same manner as is before prescribed for deciding disputes respecting territorial jurisdiction between different States.

The United States in Congress assembled shall also have the sole and exclusive right and power of regulating the alloy and value of coin struck by their own authority, or by that of the respective States; fixing the standards of weights and measures throughout the United States; regulating the trade and managing all affairs with the Indians not members of any of the States; provided that the legislative right of any State within its own limits be not infringed or violated; establishing or regulating post offices from one State to another, throughout all the United States, and exacting such postage on the papers passing through the same as may be requisite to defray the expenses of the said office; appointing all officers of the land forces in the service of the United States, excepting regimental officers; appointing all the officers of the naval forces, and commissioning all officers whatever in the service of the United States; making rules for the government and regulation of the said land and naval forces, and directing their operations.

The United States in Congress assembled shall have authority to appoint a committee, to sit in the recess of Congress, to be denominated "A Committee of the States," and to consist of one delegate from each State; and to appoint such other committees and civil officers as may be necessary for managing the general affairs of the United States under their direction; to appoint one of their members to preside, provided that no person be allowed to serve in the office of president more than one year in any term of three years; to ascertain the necessary sums of money to be raised for the service of the United States, and to appropriate and apply the same for defraying the public expenses; to borrow money, or emit bills on the credit of the United States, transmitting every half year to the respective States an account of the sums of money so borrowed or emitted; to build and equip a navy; to agree upon the number of land forces, and to make requisitions from each State for its quota, in proportion to the number of white inhabitants in such State; which requisition shall be binding, and thereupon the legislature of each State shall appoint the regimental officers, raise the men and cloath, arm and equip them in a soldierlike manner, at the expense of the United States; and the officers and men so cloathed, armed and equipped shall march to the place appointed, and within the time agreed on by the United States in Congress assembled; but if the United States in Congress assembled shall, on consideration of circumstances judge proper that any State should not raise men, or should raise a smaller number of men than the quota thereof, such extra number shall be raised, officered, cloathed, armed and equipped in the same manner as the quota of each State, unless the legislature of such State shall judge that such extra number cannot be safely spared out in the same, in which case they shall raise, officer, cloath, arm and equip as many of such extra number as they judge can be safely spared. And the officers and men so cloathed, armed, and equipped, shall march to the place appointed, and within the time agreed on by the United States in Congress assembled.

The United States in Congress assembled shall never engage in a war, nor grant letters of marque or reprisal in time of peace, nor enter into any treaties or alliances, nor coin money, nor regulate the value thereof, nor ascertain the sums and expenses necessary for the defense and welfare of the United States, or any of them, nor emit bills, nor borrow money on the credit of the United States, nor appropriate money, nor agree upon the number of vessels of war, to be built or purchased, or the number of land or sea forces to be raised, nor appoint a commander in chief of the army or navy, unless nine States assent to the same: nor shall a question on any other point, except for adjourning from day to day be determined, unless by the votes of the majority of the United States in Congress assembled.

The Congress of the United States shall have power to adjourn to any time within the year, and to any place within the United States, so that no period of adjournment be for a longer duration than the space of six months, and shall publish the journal of their proceedings monthly, except such parts thereof relating to treaties, alliances or military operations, as in their judgement require secrecy; and the yeas and nays of the delegates of each State on any question shall be entered on the journal, when it is desired by any delegates of a State, or any of them, at his or their request shall be furnished with a transcript of the said journal, except such parts as are above excepted, to lay before the legislatures of the several States.

ARTICLE 10

The Committee of the States, or any nine of them, shall be authorized to execute, in the recess of Congress, such of the powers of Congress as the United States in Congress assembled, by the consent of the nine States, shall from time to time think expedient to vest them with; provided that no power be delegated to the said Committee, for the exercise of which, by the Articles of Confederation, the voice of nine States in the Congress of the United States assembled is requisite.

ARTICLE 11

Canada acceding to this confederation, and adjoining in the measures of the United States, shall be admitted into, and entitled to all the advantages of this Union; but no other colony shall be admitted into the same, unless such admission be agreed to by nine States.

ARTICLE 12

All bills of credit emitted, monies borrowed, and debts contracted by, or under the authority of Congress, before the assembling of the United States, in pursuance of the present confederation, shall be deemed and considered as a charge against the United States, for payment and satisfaction whereof the said United States, and the public faith are hereby solemnly pledged.

ARTICLE 13

Every State shall abide by the determination of the United States in Congress assembled, on all questions which by this confederation are submitted to them. And the Articles of this Confederation shall be inviolably observed by every State, and the Union shall be perpetual; nor shall any alteration at any time hereafter be made in any of them; unless such alteration be agreed to in a Congress of the United States, and be afterwards confirmed by the legislatures of every State.

These articles shall be proposed to the legislatures of all the United States, to be considered, and if approved of by them, they are advised to authorize their delegates to ratify the same in the Congress of the United States; which being done, the same shall become conclusive.

THE CONSTITUTION OF THE UNITED STATES OF AMERICA

We the people of the United States, in order to form a more perfect union, establish justice, insure domestic tranquillity, provide for the common defense, promote the general welfare, and secure the blessings of liberty to ourselves and our posterity, do ordain and establish this Constitution for the United States of America.

ARTICLE I

SECTION 1.   All legislative powers herein granted shall be vested in a Congress of the United States, which shall consist of a Senate and House of Representatives.

SECTION 2.   1. The House of Representatives shall be composed of members chosen every second year by the people of the several States, and the electors in each State shall have the qualifications requisite for electors of the most numerous branch of the State legislature.

2. No person shall be a representative who shall not have attained to the age of twenty-five years, and been seven years a citizen of the United States, and who shall not, when elected, be an inhabitant of that State in which he shall be chosen.

3. Representatives and direct taxes[1] shall be apportioned among the several States which may be included within this Union, according to their respective numbers, which shall be determined by adding to the whole number of free persons, including those bound to service for a term of years, and excluding Indians not taxed, three fifths of all other persons.[2] The actual enumeration shall be made within three years after the first meeting of the Congress of the United States, and within every subsequent term of ten years, in such manner as they shall by law direct. The number of representatives shall

not exceed one for every thirty thousand, but each State shall have at least one representative; and until such enumeration shall be made, the State of New Hampshire shall be entitled to choose three, Massachusetts eight, Rhode Island and Providence Plantations one, Connecticut five, New York six, New Jersey four, Pennsylvania eight, Delaware one, Maryland six, Virginia ten, North Carolina five, South Carolina five, and Georgia three.

4. When vacancies happen in the representation from any State, the executive authority thereof shall issue writs of election to fill such vacancies.

5. The House of Representatives shall choose their speaker and other officers; and shall have the sole power of impeachment.

SECTION 3.   1. The Senate of the United States shall be composed of two senators from each State, chosen by the legislature thereof,[3] for six years; and each senator shall have one vote.

2. Immediately after they shall be assembled in consequence of the first election, they shall be divided as equally as may be into three classes. The seats of the senators of the first class shall be vacated at the expiration of the second year, of the second class at the expiration of the fourth year, and of the third class at the expiration of the sixth year, so that one third may be chosen every second year; and if vacancies happen by resignation, or otherwise, during the recess of the legislature of any State, the executive thereof may make temporary appointments until the next meeting of the legislature, which shall then fill such vacancies.[4]

3. No person shall be a senator who shall not have attained to the age of thirty years, and been nine years a citizen of the

---

[1]See the Sixteenth Amendment.
[2]See the Fourteenth Amendment.

[3]See the Seventeenth Amendment.
[4]See the Seventeenth Amendment.

United States, and who shall not, when elected, be an inhabitant of that State for which he shall be chosen.

4. The Vice President of the United States shall be President of the Senate, but shall have no vote, unless they be equally divided.

5. The Senate shall choose their other officers, and also a president pro tempore, in the absence of the Vice President, or when he shall exercise the office of the President of the United States.

6. The Senate shall have the sole power to try all impeachments. When sitting for that purpose, they shall be on oath or affirmation. When the President of the United States is tried, the chief justice shall preside: and no person shall be convicted without the concurrence of two thirds of the members present.

7. Judgment in cases of impeachment shall not extend further than to removal from office, and disqualification to hold and enjoy any office of honor, trust or profit under the United States: but the party convicted shall nevertheless be liable and subject to indictment, trial, judgment and punishment, according to law.

SECTION 4. 1. The times, places, and manner of holding elections for senators and representatives, shall be prescribed in each State by the legislature thereof; but the Congress may at any time by law make or alter such regulations, except as to the places of choosing senators.

2. The Congress shall assemble at least once in every year, and such meeting shall be on the first Monday in December, unless they shall by law appoint a different day.

SECTION 5. 1. Each House shall be the judge of the elections, returns and qualifications of its own members, and a majority of each shall constitute a quorum to do business; but a smaller number may adjourn from day to day, and may be authorized to compel the attendance of absent members, in such manner, and under such penalties as each House may provide.

2. Each House may determine the rules of its proceedings, punish its members for disorderly behavior, and, with the concurrence of two thirds, expel a member.

3. Each House shall keep a journal of its proceedings, and from time to time publish the same, excepting such parts as may in their judgment require secrecy; and the yeas and nays of the members of either House on any question shall, at the desire of one fifth of those present, be entered on the journal.

4. Neither House, during the session of Congress, shall, without the consent of the other, adjourn for more than three days, nor to any other place than that in which the two Houses shall be sitting.

SECTION 6. 1. The senators and representatives shall receive a compensation for their services, to be ascertained by law, and paid out of the Treasury of the United States. They shall in all cases, except treason, felony, and breach of the peace, be privileged from arrest during their attendance at the session of their respective Houses, and in going to and returning from the same; and for any speech or debate in either House, they shall not be questioned in any other place.

2. No senator or representative shall, during the time for which he was elected, be appointed to any civil office under the authority of the United States, which shall have been cre-

ated, or the emoluments whereof shall have been increased, during such time; and no person holding any office under the United States shall be a member of either House during his continuance in office.

SECTION 7. 1. All bills for raising revenue shall originate in the House of Representatives; but the Senate may propose or concur with amendments as on other bills.

2. Every bill which shall have passed the House of Representatives and the Senate, shall, before it become a law, be presented to the President of the United States; If he approves he shall sign it, but if not he shall return it, with his objections, to that House in which it shall have originated, who shall enter the objections at large on their journal, and proceed to reconsider it. If after such reconsideration two thirds of that House shall agree to pass the bill, it shall be sent, together with the objections, to the other House, by which it shall likewise be reconsidered, and if approved by two thirds of that House, it shall become a law. But in all such cases the votes of both Houses shall be determined by yeas and nays, and the names of the persons voting for and against the bill shall be entered on the journal of each House respectively. If any bill shall not be returned by the President within ten days (Sundays excepted) after it shall have been presented to him, the same shall be a law, in like manner as if he had signed it, unless the Congress by their adjournment prevent its return, in which case it shall not be a law.

3. Every order, resolution, or vote to which the concurrence of the Senate and the House of Representatives may be necessary (except on a question of adjournment) shall be presented to the President of the United States; and before the same shall take effect, shall be approved by him, or being disapproved by him, shall be repassed by two thirds of the Senate and House of Representatives, according to the rules and limitations prescribed in the case of a bill.

SECTION 8. 1. The Congress shall have the power

1. To lay and collect taxes, duties, imposts, and excises, to pay the debts and provide for the common defense and general welfare of the United States; but all duties, imposts, and excises shall be uniform throughout the United States.

2. To borrow money on the credit of the United States;

3. To regulate commerce with foreign nations, and among the several States, and with the Indian tribes;

4. To establish a uniform rule of naturalization, and uniform laws on the subject of bankruptcies throughout the United States;

5. To coin money, regulate the value thereof, and of foreign coin, and fix the standard of weights and measures;

6. To provide for the punishment of counterfeiting the securities and current coin of the United States;

7. To establish post offices and post roads;

8. To promote the progress of science and useful arts, by securing for limited times to authors and inventors the exclusive right to their respective writings and discoveries;

9. To constitute tribunals inferior to the Supreme Court;

10. To define and punish piracies and felonies committed on the high seas, and offenses against the law of nations;

11. To declare war, grant letters of marque and reprisal, and make rules concerning captures on land and water;

12. To raise and support armies, but no appropriation of money to that use shall be for a longer term than two years;

13. To provide and maintain a navy;

14. To make rules for the government and regulation of the land and naval forces;

15. To provide for calling forth the militia to execute the laws of the Union, suppress insurrections and repel invasions;

16. To provide for organizing, arming, and disciplining the militia, and for governing such part of them as may be employed in the service of the United States, reserving to the States respectively, the appointment of the officers, and the authority of training the militia according to the discipline prescribed by Congress;

17. To exercise exclusive legislation in all cases whatsoever, over such district (not exceeding ten miles square) as may, by cession of particular States, and the acceptance of Congress, become the seat of the government of the United States, and to exercise like authority over all places purchased by the consent of the legislature of the State in which the same shall be, for the erection of forts, magazines, arsenals, dockyards, and other needful buildings; and

18. To make all laws which shall be necessary and proper for carrying into execution the foregoing powers, and all other powers vested by this Constitution in the government of the United States, or any department or officer thereof.

SECTION 9. 1. The migration or importation of such persons as any of the States now existing shall think proper to admit, shall not be prohibited by the Congress prior to the year one thousand eight hundred and eight, but a tax or duty may be imposed on such importation, not exceeding ten dollars for each person.

2. The privilege of the writ of habeas corpus shall not be suspended, unless when in cases of rebellion or invasion the public safety may require it.

3. No bill of attainder or ex post facto law shall be passed.

4. No capitation, or other direct, tax shall be laid, unless in proportion to the census or enumeration hereinbefore directed to be taken.[5]

5. No tax or duty shall be laid on articles exported from any State.

6. No preference shall be given by any regulation of commerce or revenue to the ports of one State over those of another: nor shall vessels bound to, or from, one State be obliged to enter, clear, or pay duties in another.

7. No money shall be drawn from the treasury, but in consequence of appropriations made by law; and a regular statement and account of the receipts and expenditures of all public money shall be published from time to time.

8. No title of nobility shall be granted by the United States: and no person holding any office of profit or trust under them, shall, without the consent of the Congress, accept of any present, emolument, office, or title, of any kind whatever, from any king, prince, or foreign State.

SECTION 10. 1 No State shall enter into any treaty, alliance, or confederation; grant letters of marque and reprisal; coin money; emit bills of credit; make any thing but gold and silver coin a tender in payment of debts; pass any bill of attainder, ex post facto law, or law impairing the obligation of contracts, or grant, any title of nobility.

2. No State shall, without the consent of the Congress, lay any imposts or duties on imports or exports, except what may be absolutely necessary for executing its inspection laws: and the net produce of all duties and imposts laid by any State on imports or exports, shall be for the use of the treasury of the United States; and all such laws shall be subject to the revision and control of the Congress.

3. No State shall, without the consent of the Congress, lay any duty of tonnage, keep troops, or ships of war in time of peace, enter into any agreement or compact with another State, or with a foreign power, or engage in war, unless actually invaded, or in such imminent danger as will not admit of delay.

ARTICLE II

SECTION 1. 1. The executive power shall be vested in a President of the United States of America. He shall hold his office during the term of four years, and, together with the Vice President, chosen for the same term, be elected, as follows:

2. Each State shall appoint, in such manner as the legislature thereof may direct, a number of electors, equal to the whole number of senators and representatives to which the State may be entitled in the Congress: but no senator or representative, or person holding any office of trust or profit under the United States, shall be appointed an elector.

The electors shall meet in their respective States, and vote by ballot for two persons, of whom one at least shall not be an inhabitant of the same State with themselves. And they shall make a list of all the persons voted for, and of the number of votes for each; which list they shall sign and certify, and transmit sealed to the seat of the government of the United States, directed to the president of the Senate. The president of the Senate shall, in the presence of the Senate and House of Representatives, open all the certificates, and the votes shall then be counted. The person having the greatest number of votes shall be the President, if such number be a majority of the whole number of electors appointed; and if there be more than one who have such majority, and have an equal number of votes, then the House of Representatives shall immediately choose by ballot one of them for President; and if no person have a majority, then from the five highest on the list the said House shall in like manner choose the President. But in choosing the President, the votes shall be taken by States, the representation from each State having one vote; a quorum for this purpose shall consist of a member or members from two thirds of the States, and a majority of all the States shall be necessary to a choice. In every case after the choice of the President, the person having the greatest number of votes of the electors shall be the Vice President. But if there should remain two or more who have equal votes, the Senate shall choose from them by ballot the Vice President.[6]

3. The Congress may determine the time of choosing the electors, and the day on which they shall give their votes; which day shall be the same throughout the United States.

4. No person except a natural born citizen, or a citizen of the United States, at the time of the adoption of this Constitution, shall be eligible to the office of President; neither shall any person be eligible to the office who shall not have attained to the

---

[5]See the Sixteenth Amendment.

[6]Superseded by the Twelfth Amendment.

age of thirty-five years, and been fourteen years a resident within the United States.

5. In case of the removal of the President from office, or of his death, resignation, or inability to discharge the powers and duties of the said office, the same shall devolve on the Vice President, and the congress may by law provide for the case of removal, death, resignation or inability, both of the President and Vice President, declaring what officer shall then act as President, and such officer shall act accordingly until the disability be removed, or a President shall be elected.

6. The President shall, at stated times, receive for his services a compensation which shall neither be increased nor diminished during the period for which he shall have been elected, and he shall not receive within that period any other emolument from the United States, or any of them.

7. Before he enter on the execution of his office, he shall take the following oath or affirmation:—"I do solemnly swear (or affirm) that I will faithfully execute the office of President of the United States, and will to the best of my ability, preserve, protect and defend the Constitution of the United States."

SECTION 2.   1. The President shall be commander in chief of the army and navy of the United States, and of the militia of the several States, when called into the actual service of the United States; he may require the opinion in writing, of the principal officer in each of the executive departments, upon any subject relating to the duties of their respective offices, and he shall have power to grant reprieves and pardons for offenses against the United States, except in cases of impeachment.

2. He shall have power, by and with the advice and consent of the Senate, to make treaties, provided two thirds of the senators present concur; and he shall nominate, and by and with the advice and consent of the Senate, shall appoint ambassadors, other public ministers and consuls, judges of the Supreme Court, and all other officers of the United States, whose appointments are not herein otherwise provided for, and which shall be established by law; but the Congress may by law vest the appointment of such inferior officers, as they think proper, in the President alone, in the courts of laws, or in the heads of departments.

3. The President shall have power to fill up all vacancies that may happen during the recess of the Senate, by granting commissions which shall expire at the end of their next session.

SECTION 3.   He shall from time to time give to the Congress information of the state of the Union, and recommend to their consideration such measures as he shall judge necessary and expedient; he may, on extraordinary occasions, convene both Houses, or either of them, and in case of disagreement between them with respect to the time of adjournment, he may adjourn them to such time as he shall think proper; he shall receive ambassadors and other public ministers; he shall take care that the laws be faithfully executed, and shall commission all the officers of the United States.

SECTION 4.   The President, Vice President, and all civil officers of the United States, shall be removed from office on impeachment for, and conviction of, treason, bribery, or other high crimes and misdemeanors.

ARTICLE III

SECTION 1. The judicial power of the United States shall be vested in one Supreme Court, and in such inferior courts as the Congress may from time to time ordain and establish. The judges, both of the Supreme and inferior courts, shall hold their offices during good behavior, and shall, at stated times, receive for their services, a compensation, which shall not be diminished during their continuance in office.

SECTION 2.   1. The judicial power shall extend to all cases, in law and equity, arising under this Constitution, the laws of the United States, and treaties made, or which shall be made, under their authority;—to all cases of admiralty and maritime jurisdiction;—to controversies to which the United States shall be a party;[7]—to controversies between two or more States;—between a State and citizens of another State;—between citizens of different States;—between citizens of the same State claiming lands under grants of different States, and between a State, or the citizens thereof, and foreign States, citizens or subjects.

2. In all cases affecting ambassadors, other public ministers and consuls, and those in which a State shall be party, the Supreme Court shall have original jurisdiction. In all the other cases before mentioned, the Supreme Court shall have appellate jurisdiction, both as to law and fact, with such exceptions, and under such regulations as the Congress shall make.

3. The trial of all crimes, except in cases of impeachment, shall be by jury; and such trial shall be held in the State where the said crimes shall have been committed; but when not committed within any State, the trial shall be such place or places as the congress may by law have directed.

SECTION 3.   1. Treason against the United States shall consist only in levying war against them, or in adhering to their enemies, giving them aid and comfort. No person shall be convicted of treason unless on the testimony of two witnesses to the same overt act, or on confession in open court.

2. The Congress shall have power to declare the punishment of treason, but no attainder of treason shall work corruption of blood, or forfeiture except during the life of the person attained.

ARTICLE IV

SECTION 1. Full faith and credit shall be given in each State to the public acts, records, and judicial proceedings of every other State. And the Congress may by general laws prescribe the manner in which such acts, records and proceedings shall be proved, and the effect thereof.

SECTION 2.   1. The citizens of each State shall be entitled to all privileges and immunities of citizens in the several States.[8]

2. A person charged in any State with treason, felony, or other crime, who shall flee from justice, and be found in another State, shall on demand of the executive authority of the State from which he fled, be delivered up to be removed to the State having jurisdiction of the crime.

3. No person held to service or labor in one State under the laws thereof, escaping into another, shall, in consequence of any law or regulation therein, be discharged from

---

[7]See the Eleventh Amendment.
[8]See the Fourteenth Amendment, Sec. 1.

such service or labor, but shall be delivered up on claim of the party to whom such service or labor may be due.[9]

SECTION 3. 1. New States may be admitted by the Congress into this Union; but no new State shall be formed or erected within the jurisdiction of any other State, nor any State be formed by the junction of two or more States, or parts of States, without the consent of the legislatures of the States concerned as well as of the Congress.

2. The Congress shall have power to dispose of and make all needful rules and regulations respecting the territory or other property belonging to the United States; and nothing in this Constitution shall be so construed as to prejudice any claims of the United States, or of any particular State.

SECTION 4. The United States shall guarantee to every State in this Union a republican form of government, and shall protect each of them against invasion; and on application of the legislature, or of the executive (when the legislature cannot be convened) against domestic violence.

ARTICLE V

The Congress, whenever two thirds of both Houses shall deem it necessary, shall propose amendments to this Constitution, or, on the application of the legislatures of two thirds of the several States, shall call a convention for proposing amendments, which in either case shall be valid to all intents and purposes, as part of this Constitution, when ratified by the legislatures of three fourths of the several States, or by conventions in three fourths thereof, as the one or the other mode of ratification may be proposed by the Congress; Provided that no amendment which may be made prior to the year one thousand eight hundred and eight shall in any manner affect the first and fourth clauses in the ninth section of the first article; and that no State, without its consent, shall be deprived of its equal suffrage in the Senate.

ARTICLE VI

1. All debts contracted and engagements entered into, before the adoption of this Constitution, shall be as valid against the United States under this Constitution, as under the Confederation.[10]

2. This Constitution, and the laws of the United States which shall be made in pursuance thereof; and all treaties made, or which shall be made, under the authority of the United States, shall be the supreme law of the land; and the judges in every State shall be bound thereby, any thing in the Constitution or laws of any State to the contrary notwithstanding.

3. The senators and representatives before mentioned, and the members of the several State legislatures, and all executive and judicial officers, both of the United States and of the several States, shall be bound by oath or affirmation to support this Constitution; but no religious test shall ever be required as a qualification to any office or public trust under the United States.

ARTICLE VII

The ratification of the conventions of nine States shall be sufficient for the establishment of this Constitution between the States so ratifying the same.

Done in Convention by the unanimous consent of the States present the seventeenth day of September in the year of our Lord one thousand seven hundred and eighty-seven, and of the independence of the United States of America the twelfth. In witness whereof we have hereunto subscribed our names.

[Signatories' names omitted]

Articles in addition to, and amendment of, the Constitution of the United States of America, proposed by Congress, and ratified by the legislatures of the several States, pursuant to the fifth article of the original Constitution.

Amendment I

[First ten amendments ratified December 15, 1791]
Congress shall make no law respecting an establishment of religion, or prohibiting the free exercise thereof; or abridging the freedom of speech, or of the press; or the right of the people peaceably to assemble, and to petition the government for a redress of grievances.

Amendment II

A well regulated militia, being necessary to the security of a free State, the right of the people to keep and bear arms, shall not be infringed.

Amendment III

No soldier shall, in time of peace be quartered in any house, without the consent of the owner, nor in time of war, but in a manner to be prescribed by law.

Amendment IV

The right of the people to be secure in their persons, houses, papers, and effects, against unreasonable searches and seizures, shall not be violated, and no warrants shall issue, but upon probable cause, supported by oath or affirmation, and particularly describing the place to be searched, and the persons or things to be seized.

Amendment V

No person shall be held to answer for a capital or otherwise infamous crime, unless on a presentment or indictment of a grand jury, except in cases arising in the land or naval forces, or in the militia, when in actual service in time of war or public danger; nor shall any person be subject for the same offense to be twice put in jeopardy of life or limb; nor shall be compelled in any criminal case to be a witness against himself, nor be deprived of life, liberty, or property, without due process of law; nor shall private property be taken for public use, without just compensation.

Amendment VI

In all criminal prosecutions, the accused shall enjoy the right to a speedy and public trial, by an impartial jury of the State and district wherein the crime shall have been committed, which district shall have been previously ascertained by law, and to be informed of the nature and cause of the accusation; to be confronted with the witnesses against him; to have compulsory process for obtaining witnesses in his favor, and to have the assistance of counsel for his defense.

[9]See the Thirteenth Amendment.
[10]See the Fourteenth Amendment, Sec. 4.

Amendment VII

In suits at common law, where the value in controversy shall exceed twenty dollars, the right of trial by jury shall be preserved, and no fact tried by a jury shall be otherwise reexamined in any court of the United States, than according to the rules of the common law.

Amendment VIII

Excessive bail shall not be required, nor excessive fines imposed, nor cruel and unusual punishments inflicted.

Amendment IX

The enumeration in the Constitution of certain rights shall not be construed to deny or disparage others retained by the people.

Amendment X

The powers not delegated to the United States by the Constitution, nor prohibited by it to the States, are reserved to the States respectively, or to the people.

Amendment XI [January 8, 1798]

The judicial power of the United States shall not be construed to extend to any suit in law or equity, commended or prosecuted against one of the United States by citizens of another State, or by citizens or subjects of any foreign State.

Amendment XII [September 25, 1804]

The electors shall meet in their respective States, and vote by ballot for President and Vice President, one of whom, at least, shall not be an inhabitant of the same State with themselves; they shall name in their ballots the person voted for as President, and in distinct ballots the person voted for as Vice President, and they shall make distinct lists of all persons voted for as President and of all persons voted for as Vice President, and of the number of votes for each, which lists they shall sign and certify, and transmit sealed to the seat of the government of the United States, directed to the President of the Senate;—The President of the Senate shall, in the presence of the Senate and House of Representatives, open all the certificates and the votes shall then be counted;—The person having the greatest number of votes for President, shall be the President, if such number be a majority of the whole number of electors appointed; and if no person have such majority, then from the persons having the highest numbers not exceeding three on the list of those voted for as President, the House of Representatives shall choose immediately, by ballot, the President. But in choosing the President, the votes shall be taken by States, the representation from each State having one vote; a quorum for this purpose shall consist of a member or members from two thirds of the States, and a majority of all the States shall be necessary to a choice. And if the House of Representatives shall not choose a President whenever the right of choice shall devolve upon them, before the fourth day of March next following, then the Vice President shall act as President, as in the case of the death or other constitutional disability of the President. The person having the greatest number of votes as Vice President shall be the Vice President, if such number be a majority of the whole number of electors appointed, and if no person have a majority, then from the

two highest numbers on the list, the Senate shall choose the Vice President; a quorum for the purpose shall consist of two thirds of the whole number of Senators, and a majority of the whole number shall be necessary to a choice. But no person constitutionally ineligible to the office of President shall be eligible to that of Vice President of the United States.

Amendment XIII [December 18, 1865]

SECTION 1. Neither slavery nor involuntary servitude, except as a punishment for crime whereof the party shall have been duly convicted, shall exist within the United States, or any place subject to their jurisdiction.

SECTION 2. Congress shall have power to enforce this article by appropriate legislation.

Amendment XIV [July 28, 1868]

SECTION 1. All persons born or naturalized in the United States, and subject to the jurisdiction thereof, are citizens of the United States and of the State wherein they reside. No State shall make or enforce any law which shall abridge the privileges or immunities of citizens of the United States; nor shall any State deprive any person of life, liberty, or property, without due process of law; nor deny to any person within its jurisdiction the equal protection of the laws.

SECTION 2. Representatives shall be apportioned among the several States according to their respective numbers, counting the whole number of persons in each State, excluding Indians not taxed. But when the right to vote at any election for the choice of electors for President and Vice President of the United States, representatives in Congress, the executive and judicial officers of a State, or the members of the legislature thereof, is denied to any of the male inhabitants of such State, being twenty-one years of age, and citizens of the United States, or in any way abridged, except for participating in rebellion, or other crime, the basis of representation there shall be reduced in the proportion which the number of such male citizens shall bear to the whole number of male citizens twenty-one years of age in such State.

SECTION 3. No person shall be a senator or representative in Congress, or elector of President and Vice President, or hold any office, civil or military, under the United States, or under any State, who having previously taken an oath, as a member of Congress, or as an officer of the United States, or as a member of any State legislature, or as an executive or judicial officer of any State, to support the Constitution of the United States, shall have engaged in insurrection or rebellion against the same, or given aid or comfort to the enemies thereof. But Congress may by a vote of two thirds of each House, remove such disability.

SECTION 4. The validity of the public debt of the United States, authorized by law, including debts incurred for payment of pensions and bounties for services in suppressing insurrection or rebellion; shall not be questioned. But neither the United States nor any State shall assume or pay any debt or obligation incurred in aid of insurrection or rebellion against the United States, or any claim for the loss or emancipation of any slave; but all such debts, obligations, and claims shall be held illegal and void.

SECTION 5. The Congress shall have the power to enforce, by appropriate legislation, the provisions of this article.

Amendment XV [March 30, 1870]
SECTION 1. The right of citizens of the United States to vote shall not be denied or abridged by the United States or by any State on account of race, color, or previous condition of servitude.

SECTION 2. The Congress shall have power to enforce this article by appropriate legislation.

Amendment XVI [February 25, 1913]
The Congress shall have power to lay and collect taxes on incomes, from whatever source derived, without apportionment among the several States, and without regard to any census or enumeration.

Amendment XVII [May 31, 1913]
The Senate of the United States shall be composed of two senators from each State, elected by the people thereof, for six years; and each senator shall have one vote. The electors in each State shall have the qualifications requisite for electors of the most numerous branch of the State legislature.

When vacancies happen in the representation of any State in the Senate, the executive authority of such State shall issue writs of election to fill such vacancies: Provided, That the legislature of any State may empower the executive thereof to make temporary appointments until the people fill the vacancies by election as the legislature may direct.

This amendment shall not be so construed as to affect the election or term of any senator chosen before it becomes valid as part of the Constitution.

Amendment XVIII11 [January 29, 1919]
After one year from the ratification of this article, the manufacture, sale, or transportation of intoxicating liquors within, the importation thereof into, or the exportation thereof from the United States and all territory subject to the jurisdiction thereof for beverage purposes is thereby prohibited.

The Congress and the several States shall have concurrent power to enforce this article by appropriate legislation.

This article shall be inoperative unless it shall have been ratified as an amendment to the Constitution by the legislatures of the several States, as provided in the constitution, within seven years from the date of the submission hereof to the States by Congress.

Amendment XIX [August 26, 1920]
The right of citizens of the United States to vote shall not be denied or abridged by the United States or by any State on account of sex.

Congress shall have the power to enforce this article by appropriate legislation.

Amendment XX [January 23, 1933]
SECTION 1. The terms of the President and Vice President shall end at noon on the 20th day of January and the terms of Senators and Representatives at noon on the 3d day of January, of the years in which such terms would have ended if this article had not been ratified; and the terms of their successors shall then begin.

SECTION 2. The Congress shall assemble at least once in every year, and such meeting shall begin at noon on the 3d day of January, unless they shall by law appoint a different day.

SECTION 3. If, at the time fixed for the beginning of the term of President, the President-elect shall have died, the Vice President-elect shall become President. If a President shall not have been chosen before the time fixed for the beginning of his term, or if the President-elect shall have failed to qualify, then the Vice President-elect shall act as President until a President shall have qualified; and the Congress may by law provide for the case wherein neither a President-elect nor a Vice President-elect shall have qualified, declaring who shall then act as President, or the manner in which one who is to act shall be selected, and such person shall act accordingly until a President or Vice President shall have qualified.

SECTION 4. The Congress may by law provide for the case of the death of any of the persons from whom, the House of Representatives may choose a President whenever the right of choice shall have devolved upon them, and for the case of the death of any of the persons from whom the Senate may choose a Vice President whenever the right of choice shall have devolved upon them.

SECTION 5. Sections 1 and 2 shall take effect on the 15th day of October following the ratification of this article.

SECTION 6. This article shall be inoperative unless it shall have been ratified as an amendment to the Constitution by the legislatures of three-fourths of the several States within seven years from the date of its submission.

Amendment XXI [December 5, 1933]
SECTION 1. The Eighteenth Article of amendment to the Constitution of the United States is hereby repealed.

SECTION 2. The transportation or importation into any State, Territory, or possession of the United States for delivery or use therein of intoxicating liquors in violation of the laws thereof, is hereby prohibited.

SECTION 3. This article shall be inoperative unless it shall have been ratified as an amendment to the Constitution by conventions in the several States, as provided in the Constitution, within seven years from the date of the submission thereof to the States by the Congress.

Amendment XXII [March 1, 1951]
No person shall be elected to the office of the President more than twice, and no person who has held the office of President, or acted as President, for more than two years of a term to which some other person was elected President shall be elected to the office of the President more than once.

But this article shall not apply to any person holding the office of President when this article was proposed by the Congress, and shall not prevent any person who may be holding the office of President, or acting as President, during the term within which this article becomes operative from holding the office of President or acting as President during the remainder of such term.

This article shall be inoperative unless it shall have been ratified as an amendment to the Constitution by the legislatures of three-fourths of the several States within seven years from the date of its submission to the States by the Congress.

Amendment XXIII [March 29, 1961]

SECTION 1.   The District constituting the seat of Government of the United States shall appoint in such manner as the Congress may direct.

A number of electors of President and Vice President equal to the whole number of Senators and Representatives in Congress to which the District would be entitled if it were a State, but in no event more than the least populous State; they shall be in addition to those appointed by the States, but they shall be considered, for the purposes of the election of President and Vice President, to be electors appointed by a State; and they shall meet in the District and perform such duties as provided by the twelfth article of amendment.

SECTION 2.   The Congress shall have power to enforce this article by appropriate legislation.

Amendment XXIV [January 23, 1964]

SECTION 1.   The right of citizens of the United States to vote in any primary or other election for President or Vice President, for electors for President or Vice President, or for Senator or Representative in Congress, shall not be denied or abridged by the United States or any State by reason of failure to pay any poll tax or other tax.

SECTION 2.   The Congress shall have power to enforce this article by appropriate legislation.

Amendment XXV [February 10, 1967]

SECTION 1.   In case of the removal of the President from office or of his death or resignation, the Vice President shall become President.

SECTION 2.   Whenever there is a vacancy in the office of the Vice President, the President shall nominate a Vice President who shall take office upon confirmation by a majority of both Houses of Congress.

SECTION 3.   Whenever the President transmits to the President pro tempore of the Senate and the Speaker of the House of Representatives his written declaration that he is unable to discharge the powers and duties of his office, and until he transmits to them a written declaration to the contrary, such powers and duties shall be discharged by the Vice President as Acting President.

SECTION 4.   Whenever the Vice President and a majority of either the principal officers of the executive departments or of such other body as Congress may by law provide, transmit

to the President pro tempore of the Senate and the Speaker of the House of Representatives their written declaration that the President is unable to discharge the powers and duties of his office, the Vice President shall immediately assume the powers and duties of the office as Acting President.

Thereafter, when the President transmits to the President pro tempore of the Senate and the Speaker of the House of Representatives his written declaration that no inability exists, he shall resume the powers and duties of his office unless the Vice President and a majority of either the principal officers of the executive departments or of such other body as Congress may by law provide, transmit within four days to the President pro tempore of the Senate and the Speaker of the House of Representatives their written declaration that the President is unable to discharge the powers and duties of his office. Thereupon Congress shall decide the issue, assembling within forty-eight hours for that purpose if not in session. If the Congress, within twenty-one days after receipt of the latter written declaration, or, if Congress is not in session, within twenty-one days after Congress is required to assemble, determines by two-thirds vote of both Houses that the President is unable to discharge the powers and duties of his office, the Vice President shall continue to discharge the same as Acting President; otherwise, the President shall resume the powers and duties of his office.

Amendment XXVI [June 30, 1971]

SECTION 1.   The right of citizens of the United States who are eighteen years of age or older to vote shall not be denied or abridged by the United States or by any State on account of age.

SECTION 2.   The Congress shall have power to enforce this article by appropriate legislation.

Amendment XXVII[12] [May 7, 1992]

No law, varying the compensation for services of the Senators and Representatives, shall take effect until an election of Representatives shall have intervened.

---

[12]James Madison proposed this amendment in 1789 together with the ten amendments that were adopted as the Bill of Rights, but it failed to win ratification at the time. Congress, however, had set no deadline for its ratification, and over the years—particularly in the 1980s and 1990s—many states voted to add it to the Constitution. With the ratification of Michigan in 1992 it passed the threshold of 3/4ths of the states required for adoption, but because the process took more than 200 years, its validity remains in doubt.

PRESIDENTIAL ELECTIONS   (CONTINUED)

Year	Number of States	Candidates	Party	Popular Vote*	Electoral Vote†	Percentage of Popular Vote
1789	11	GEORGE WASHINGTON	No party designations		69	
		John Adams			34	
		Other Candidates			35	
1792	15	GEORGE WASHINGTON	No party designations		132	
		John Adams			77	
		George Clinton			50	
		Other Candidates			5	
1796	16	JOHN ADAMS	Federalist		71	
		Thomas Jefferson	Democratic-Republican		68	
		Thomas Pinckney	Federalist		59	
		Aaron Burr	Democratic-Republican		30	
		Other Candidates			48	
1800	16	THOMAS JEFFERSON	Democratic-Republican		73	
		Aaron Burr	Democratic-Republican		73	
		John Adams	Federalist		65	
		Charles C. Pinckney	Federalist		64	
		John Jay	Federalist		1	
1804	17	THOMAS JEFFERSON	Democratic-Republican		162	
		Charles C. Pinckney	Federalist		14	
1808	17	JAMES MADISON	Democratic-Republican		122	
		Charles C. Pinckney	Federalist		47	
		George Clinton	Democratic-Republican		6	
1812	18	JAMES MADISON	Democratic-Republican		128	
		DeWitt Clinton	Federalist		89	
1816	19	JAMES MONROE	Democratic-Republican		183	
		Rufus King	Federalist		34	
1820	24	JAMES MONROE	Democratic-Republican		231	
		John Quincy Adams	Independent-Republican		1	
1824	24	JOHN QUINCY ADAMS	Democratic-Republican	108,740	84	30.5
		Andrew Jackson	Democratic-Republican	153,544	99	43.1
		William H. Crawford	Democratic-Republican	46,618	41	13.1
		Henry Clay	Democratic-Republican	47,136	37	13.2
1828	24	ANDREW JACKSON	Democrat	647,286	178	56.0
		John Quincy Adams	National Republican	508,064	83	44.0
1832	24	ANDREW JACKSON	Democrat	687,502	219	55.0
		Henry Clay	National Republican	530,189	49	42.4
		William Wirt	Anti-Masonic	33,108	7	2.6
		John Floyd	National Republican		11	

* Percentage of popular vote given for any election year may not total 100 percent because candidates receiving less than 1 percent of the popular vote have been omitted.

† Prior to the passage of the Twelfth Amendment in 1904, the electoral college voted for two presidential candidates; the runner-up became Vice-President. Data from Historical Statistics of the United States, Colonial Times to 1957 (1961), pp. 682–683, and The World Almanac.

PRESIDENTIAL ELECTIONS   (CONTINUED)

Year	Number of States	Candidates	Party	Popular Vote	Electoral Vote	Percentage of Popular Vote
1836	26	MARTIN VAN BUREN	Democrat	765,483	170	50.9
		William H. Harrison	Whig		73	
		Hugh L. White	Whig		26	
		Daniel Webster	Whig	739,795	14	49.1
		W. P. Mangum	Whig		11	
1840	26	WILLIAM H. HARRISON	Whig	1,274,624	234	53.1
		Martin Van Buren	Democrat	1,127,781	60	46.9
1844	26	JAMES K. POLK	Democrat	1,338,464	170	49.6
		Henry Clay	Whig	1,300,097	105	48.1
		James G. Birney	Liberty	62,300		2.3
1848	30	ZACHARY TAYLOR	Whig	1,360,967	163	47.4
		Lewis Cass	Democrat	1,222,342	127	42.5
		Martin Van Buren	Free Soil	291,263		10.1
1852	31	FRANKLIN PIERCE	Democrat	1,601,117	254	50.9
		Winfield Scott	Whig	1,385,453	42	44.1
		John P. Hale	Free Soil	155,825		5.0
1856	31	JAMES BUCHANAN	Democrat	1,832,955	174	45.3
		John C. Frémont	Republican	1,339,932	114	33.1
		Millard Fillmore	American ("Know Nothing")	871,731	8	21.6
1860	33	ABRAHAM LINCOLN	Republican	1,865,593	180	39.8
		Stephen A. Douglas	Democrat	1,382,713	12	29.5
		John C. Breckinridge	Democrat	848,356	72	18.1
		John Bell	Constitutional Union	592,906	39	12.6
1864	36	ABRAHAM LINCOLN	Republican	2,206,938	212	55.0
		George B. McClellan	Democrat	1,803,787	21	45.0
1868	37	ULYSSES S. GRANT	Republican	3,013,421	214	52.7
		Horatio Seymour	Democrat	2,706,829	80	47.3
1872	37	ULYSSES S. GRANT	Republican	3,596,745	286	55.6
		Horace Greeley	Democrat	2,843,446	*	43.9
1876	38	RUTHERFORD B. HAYES	Republican	4,036,572	185	48.0
		Samuel J. Tilden	Democrat	4,284,020	184	51.0
1880	38	JAMES A. GARFIELD	Republican	4,453,295	214	48.5
		Winfield S. Hancock	Democrat	4,414,082	155	48.1
		James B. Weaver	Greenback-Labor	308,578		3.4
1884	38	GROVER CLEVELAND	Democrat	4,879,507	219	48.5
		James G. Blaine	Republican	4,850,293	182	48.2
		Benjamin F. Butler	Greenback-Labor	175,370		1.8
		John P. St. John	Prohibition	150,369		1.5
1888	38	BENJAMIN HARRISON	Republican	5,447,129	233	47.9
		Grover Cleveland	Democrat	5,537,857	168	48.6
		Clinton B. Fisk	Prohibition	249,506		2.2
		Anson J. Streeter	Union Labor	146,935		1.3

Because of the death of Greeley, Democratic electors scattered their votes.

PRESIDENTIAL ELECTIONS (CONTINUED)

Year	Number of States	Candidates	Party	Popular Vote	Electoral Vote	Percentage of Popular Vote
1892	44	GROVER CLEVELAND	Democrat	5,555,426	277	46.1
		Benjamin Harrison	Republican	5,182,690	145	43.0
		James B. Weaver	People's	1,029,846	22	8.5
		John Bidwell	Prohibition	264,133		2.2
1896	45	WILLIAM MCKINLEY	Republican	7,102,246	271	51.1
		William J. Bryan	Democrat	6,492,559	176	47.7
1900	45	WILLIAM MCKINLEY	Republican	7,218,491	292	51.7
		William J. Bryan	Democrat; Populist	6,356,734	155	45.5
		John C. Woolley	Prohibition	208,914		1.5
1904	45	THEODORE ROOSEVELT	Republican	7,628,461	336	57.4
		Alton B. Parker	Democrat	5,084,223	140	37.6
		Eugene V. Debs	Socialist	402,283		3.0
		Silas C. Swallow	Prohibition	258,536		1.9
1908	46	WILLIAM H. TAFT	Republican	7,675,320	321	51.6
		William J. Bryan	Democrat	6,412,294	162	43.1
		Eugene V. Debs	Socialist	420,793		2.8
		Eugene W. Chafin	Prohibition	253,840		1.7
1912	48	WOODROW WILSON	Democrat	6,296,547	435	41.9
		Theodore Roosevelt	Progressive	4,118,571	88	27.4
		William H. Taft	Republican	3,486,720	8	23.2
		Eugene V. Debs	Socialist	900,672		6.0
		Eugene W. Chafin	Prohibition	206,275		1.4
1916	48	WOODROW WILSON	Democrat	9,127,695	277	49.4
		Charles E. Hughes	Republican	8,533,507	254	46.2
		A. L. Benson	Socialist	585,113		3.2
		J. Frank Hanly	Prohibition	220,506		1.2
1920	48	WARREN G. HARDING	Republican	16,143,407	404	60.4
		James M. Cox	Democrat	9,130,328	127	34.2
		Eugene V. Debs	Socialist	919,799		3.4
		P. P. Christensen	Farmer-Labor	265,411		1.0
1924	48	CALVIN COOLIDGE	Republican	15,718,211	382	54.0
		John W. Davis	Democrat	8,385,283	136	28.8
		Robert M. La Follette	Progressive	4,831,289	13	16.6
1928	48	HERBERT C. HOOVER	Republican	21,391,993	444	58.2
		Alfred E. Smith	Democrat	15,016,169	87	40.9
1932	48	FRANKLIN D. ROOSEVELT	Democrat	22,809,638	472	57.4
		Herbert C. Hoover	Republican	15,758,901	59	39.7
		Norman Thomas	Socialist	881,951		2.2
1936	48	FRANKLIN D. ROOSEVELT	Democrat	27,752,869	523	60.8
		Alfred M. Landon	Republican	16,674,665	8	36.5
		William Lemke	Union	882,479		1.9
1940	48	FRANKLIN D. ROOSEVELT	Democrat	27,307,819	449	54.8
		Wendell L. Willkie	Republican	22,321,018	82	44.8

PRESIDENTIAL ELECTIONS (CONTINUED)

Year	Number of States	Candidates	Party	Popular Vote	Electoral Vote	Percentage of Popular Vote
1944	48	FRANKLIN D. ROOSEVELT	Democrat	25,606,585	432	53.5
		Thomas E. Dewey	Republican	22,014,745	99	46.0
1948	48	HARRY S. TRUMAN	Democrat	24,105,812	303	49.5
		Thomas E. Dewey	Republican	21,970,065	189	45.1
		J. Strom Thurmond	States' Rights	1,169,063	39	2.4
		Henry A. Wallace	Progressive	1,157,172		2.4
1952	48	DWIGHT D. EISENHOWER	Republican	33,936,234	442	55.1
		Adlai E. Stevenson	Democrat	27,314,992	89	44.4
1956	48	DWIGHT D. EISENHOWER	Republican	35,590,472	457*	57.6
		Adlai E. Stevenson	Democrat	26,022,752	73	42.1
1960	50	JOHN F. KENNEDY	Democrat	34,227,096	303†	49.9
		Richard M. Nixon	Republican	34,108,546	219	49.6
1964	50	LYNDON B. JOHNSON	Democrat	42,676,220	486	61.3
		Barry M. Goldwater	Republican	26,860,314	52	38.5
1968	50	RICHARD M. NIXON	Republican	31,785,480	301	43.4
		Hubert H. Humphrey	Democrat	31,275,165	191	42.7
		George C. Wallace	American Independent	9,906,473	46	13.5
1972	50	RICHARD M. NIXON‡	Republican	47,165,234	520	60.6
		George S. McGovern	Democrat	29,168,110	17	37.5
1976	50	JIMMY CARTER	Democrat	40,828,929	297	50.1
		Gerald R. Ford	Republican	39,148,940	240	47.9
		Eugene McCarthy	Independent	739,256		
1980	50	RONALD REAGAN	Republican	43,201,220	489	50.9
		Jimmy Carter	Democrat	34,913,332	49	41.2
		John B. Anderson	Independent	5,581,379		
1984	50	RONALD REAGAN	Republican	53,428,357	525	59.0
		Walter F. Mondale	Democrat	36,930,923	13	41.0
1988	50	GEORGE BUSH	Republican	48,901,046	426	53.4
		Michael Dukakis	Democrat	41,809,030	111	45.6
1992	50	BILL CLINTON	Democrat	43,728,275	370	43.2
		George Bush	Republican	38,167,416	168	37.7
		H. Ross Perot	United We Stand, America	19,237,247		19.0
1996	50	BILL CLINTON	Democrat	45,590,703	379	49.0
		Robert Dole	Republican	37,816,307	159	41.0
		H. Ross Perot	Reform	7,866,284		8.0
2000	50	GEORGE W. BUSH	Republican	50,459,624	271	47.9
		Albert Gore, Jr.	Democrat	51,003,328	266	49.4
		Ralph Nader	Green	2,882,985		2.7

*Walter B. Jones received 1 electoral vote.

†Harry F. Byrd received 15 electoral votes.

‡Resigned August 9, 1974: Vice President Gerald R. Ford became President.

SUPREME COURT JUSTICES

Name*	Years on Court	Appointing President
JOHN JAY	1789–1795	Washington
James Wilson	1789–1798	Washington
John Rutledge	1790–1791	Washington
William Cushing	1790–1810	Washington
John Blair	1790–1796	Washington
James Iredell	1790–1799	Washington
Thomas Jefferson	1792–1793	Washington
William Paterson	1793–1806	Washington
JOHN RUTLEDGE†	1795	Washington
Samuel Chase	1796–1811	Washington
OLIVER ELLSWORTH	1796–1800	Washington
Bushrod Washington	1799–1829	J. Adams
Alfred Moore	1800–1804	J. Adams
JOHN MARSHALL	1801–1835	J. Adams
William Johnson	1804–1834	Jefferson
Brockholst Livingston	1807–1823	Jefferson
Thomas Todd	1807–1826	Jefferson
Gabriel Duvall	1811–1835	Madison
Joseph Story	1812–1845	Madison
Smith Thompson	1823–1843	Monroe
Robert Trimble	1826–1828	J. Q. Adams
John McLean	1830–1861	Jackson
Henry Baldwin	1830–1844	Jackson
James M. Wayne	1835–1867	Jackson
ROGER B. TANEY	1836–1864	Jackson
Philip P. Barbour	1836–1841	Jackson
John Cartron	1837–1865	Van Buren
John McKinley	1838–1852	Van Buren
Peter V. Daniel	1842–1860	Van Buren
Samuel Nelson	1845–1872	Tyler
Levi Woodbury	1845–1851	Polk
Robert C. Grier	1846–1870	Polk
Benjamin R. Curtis	1851–1857	Fillmore
John A. Campbell	1853–1861	Pierce
Nathan Clifford	1858–1881	Buchanan
Noah H. Swayne	1862–1881	Lincoln
Samuel F. Miller	1862–1890	Lincoln
David Davis	1862–1877	Lincoln
Stephen J. Field	1863–1897	Lincoln
SALMON P. CHASE	1864–1873	Lincoln
William Strong	1870–1880	Grant
Joseph P. Bradley	1870–1892	Grant
Ward Hunt	1873–1882	Grant
MORRISON R. WAITE	1874–1888	Grant
John M. Harlan	1877–1911	Hayes
William B. Woods	1881–1887	Hayes
Stanley Matthews	1881–1889	Garfield
Horace Gray	1882–1902	Arthur
Samuel Blatchford	1882–1893	Arthur

SUPREME COURT JUSTICES   (CONTINUED)

Name*	Years on Court	Appointing President
Lucious Q. C. Lamar	1888–1893	Cleveland
MELVILLE W. FULLER	1888–1910	Cleveland
David J. Brewer	1890–1910	B. Harrison
Henry B. Brown	1891–1906	B. Harrison
George Shiras, Jr.	1892–1903	B. Harrison
Howell E. Jackson	1893–1895	B. Harrison
Edward D. White	1894–1910	Cleveland
Rufus W. Peckham	1896–1909	Cleveland
Joseph McKenna	1898–1925	McKinley
Oliver W. Holmes	1902–1932	T. Roosevelt
William R. Day	1903–1922	T. Roosevelt
William H. Moody	1906–1910	T. Roosevelt
Horace H. Lurton	1910–1914	Taft
Charles E. Hughes	1910–1916	Taft
EDWARD D. WHITE	1910–1921	Taft
Willis Van Devanter	1911–1937	Taft
Joseph R. Lamar	1911–1916	Taft
Mahlon Pitney	1912–1922	Taft
James C. McReynolds	1914–1941	Wilson
Louis D. Brandeis	1916–1939	Wilson
John H. Clarke	1916–1922	Wilson
WILLIAM H. TAFT	1921–1930	Harding
George Sutherland	1922–1938	Harding
Pierce Butler	1923–1939	Harding
Edward T. Sanford	1923–1930	Harding
Harlan F. Stone	1925–1941	Coolidge
CHARLES E. HUGHES	1930–1941	Hoover
Owen J. Roberts	1930–1945	Hoover
Benjamin N. Cardozo	1932–1938	Hoover
Hugo L. Black	1937–1971	F. Roosevelt
Stanley F. Reed	1938–1957	F. Roosevelt
Felix Frankfurter	1939–1962	F. Roosevelt
William O. Douglas	1939–1975	F. Roosevelt
Frank Murphy	1940–1949	F. Roosevelt
HARLAN F. STONE	1941–1946	F. Roosevelt
James F. Brynes	1941–1942	F. Roosevelt
Robert H. Jackson	1941–1954	F. Roosevelt
Wiley B. Rutledge	1943–1949	F. Roosevelt
Harold H. Burton	1945–1958	Truman
FREDERICK M. VINSON	1946–1953	Truman
Tom C. Clark	1949–1967	Truman
Sherman Minton	1949–1956	Truman
EARL WARREN	1953–1969	Eisenhower
John Marshall Harlan	1955–1971	Eisenhower
William J. Brennan, Jr.	1956–1990	Eisenhower
Charles E. Whittaker	1957–1962	Eisenhower
Potter Stewart	1958–1981	Eisenhower
Byron R. White	1962–1993	Kennedy
Arthur J. Goldberg	1962–1965	Kennedy

SUPREME COURT JUSTICES   (CONTINUED)

Name*	Years on Court	Appointing President
Abe Fortas	1965–1970	L. Johnson
Thurgood Marshall	1967–1991	L. Johnson
WARREN E. BURGER	1969–1986	Nixon
Harry A. Blackmun	1970–1994	Nixon
Lewis F. Powell, Jr.	1971–1987	Nixon
William H. Rehnquist	1971–1986	Nixon
John Paul Stevens	1975–	Ford
Sandra Day O'Connor	1981–	Reagan
WILLIAM H. REHNQUIJST	1986–	Reagan
Antonin Scalia	1986–	Reagan
Anthony Kennedy	1988–	Reagan
David Souter	1990–	Bush
Clarence Thomas	1991–	Bush
Ruth Bader Ginsburg	1993–	Clinton
Stephen Breyer	1994–	Clinton

* Capital letters designate Chief Justices
† Never confirmed by the Senate as Chief Justice

ADMISSION OF STATES INTO THE UNION

State	Date of Admission	State	Date of Admission
1. Delaware	December 7, 1787	26. Michigan	January 26, 1837
2. Pennsylvania	December 12, 1787	27. Florida	March 3, 1845
3. New Jersey	December 18, 1787	28. Texas	December 29, 1845
4. Georgia	January 2, 1788	29. Iowa	December 28, 1846
5. Connecticut	January 9, 1788	30. Wisconsin	May 29, 1848
6. Massachusetts	February 6, 1788	31. California	September 9, 1850
7. Maryland	April 28, 1788	32. Minnesota	May 11, 1858
8. South Carolina	May 23, 1788	33. Oregon	February 14, 1859
9. New Hampshire	June 21, 1788	34. Kansas	January 29, 1861
10. Virginia	June 25, 1788	35. West Virginia	June 20, 1863
11. New York	July 26, 1788	36. Nevada	October 31, 1864
12. North Carolina	November 21, 1789	37. Nebraska	March 1, 1867
13. Rhode Island	May 29, 1790	38. Colorado	August 1, 1876
14. Vermont	March 4, 1791	39. North Dakota	November 2, 1889
15. Kentucky	June 1, 1792	40. South Dakota	November 2, 1889
16. Tennessee	June 1, 1796	41. Montana	November 8, 1889
17. Ohio	March 1, 1803	42. Washington	November 11, 1889
18. Louisiana	April 30, 1812	43. Idaho	July 3, 1890
19. Indiana	December 11, 1816	44. Wyoming	July 10, 1890
20. Mississippi	December 10, 1817	45. Utah	January 4, 1896
21. Illinois	December 3, 1818	46. Oklahoma	November 16, 1907
22. Alabama	December 14, 1819	47. New Mexico	January 6, 1912
23. Maine	March 15, 1820	48. Arizona	February 14, 1912
24. Missouri	August 10, 1821	49. Alaska	January 3, 1959
25. Arkansas	June 15, 1836	50. Hawaii	August 21, 1959

DEMOGRAPHICS OF THE UNITED STATES

POPULATION GROWTH

Year	Population	Percent Increase
1630	4,600	
1640	26,600	478.3
1650	50,400	90.8
1660	75,100	49.0
1670	111,900	49.0
1680	151,500	35.4
1690	210,400	38.9
1700	250,900	19.2
1710	331,700	32.2
1720	466,200	40.5
1730	629,400	35.0
1740	905,600	43.9
1750	1,170,800	29.3
1760	1,593,600	36.1
1770	2,148,100	34.8
1780	2,780,400	29.4
1790	3,929,214	41.3
1800	5,308,483	35.1
1810	7,239,881	36.4
1820	9,638,453	33.1
1830	12,866,020	33.5
1840	17,069,453	32.7
1850	23,191,876	35.9
1860	31,443,321	35.6
1870	39,818,449	26.6
1880	50,155,783	26.0
1890	62,947,714	25.5
1900	75,994,575	20.7
1910	91,972,266	21.0
1920	105,710,620	14.9
1930	122,775,046	16.1
1940	131,669,275	7.2
1950	151,325,798	14.5
1960	179,323,175	18.5
1970	203,302,031	13.4
1980	226,542,199	11.4
1990	248,718,301	9.8
2000	281,421,906	13.1

Source: *Historical Statistics of the United States* (1975); *Statistical Abstract by the United States* (2001).
Note: Figures for 1630–1780 include British colonies within limits of present United States only; Native American population included only in 1930 and thereafter.

WORK FORCE

Year	Total Number Workers (1000s)	Farmers as % of Total	Women as % of Total	% Workers in Unions
1810	2,330	84	(NA)	(NA)
1840	5,660	75	(NA)	(NA)
1860	11,110	53	(NA)	(NA)
1870	12,506	53	15	(NA)
1880	17,392	52	15	(NA)
1890	23,318	43	17	(NA)
1900	29,073	40	18	3
1910	38,167	31	21	6
1920	41,614	26	21	12
1930	48,830	22	22	7
1940	53,011	17	24	27
1950	59,643	12	28	25
1960	69,877	8	32	26
1970	82,049	4	37	25
1980	106,940	3	43	23
1990	125,840	3	45	16
2000	140,863	2	47	12

Source: *Historical Statistics of the United States* (1975); *Statistical Abstract of the United States* (2001).

VITAL STATISTICS (IN THOUSANDS)

Year	Births	Deaths	Marriages	Divorces
1800	55	(NA)	(NA)	(NA)
1810	54.3	(NA)	(NA)	(NA)
1820	55.2	(NA)	(NA)	(NA)
1830	51.4	(NA)	(NA)	(NA)
1840	51.8	(NA)	(NA)	(NA)
1850	43.3	(NA)	(NA)	(NA)
1860	44.3	(NA)	(NA)	(NA)
1870	38.3	(NA)	9.6 (1867)	0.3 (1867)
1880	39.8	(NA)	9.1 (1875)	0.3 (1875)
1890	31.5	(NA)	9.0	0.5
1900	32.3	17.2	9.3	0.7
1910	30.1	14.7	10.3	0.9
1920	27.7	13.0	12.0	1.6
1930	21.3	11.3	9.2	1.6
1940	19.4	10.8	12.1	2.0
1950	24.1	9.6	11.1	2.6
1960	23.7	9.5	8.5	2.2
1970	18.4	9.5	10.6	3.5
1980	15.9	8.8	10.6	5.2
1990	16.7	8.6	9.8	4.7
1997	14.6	8.6	8.9	4.3

Source: *Historical Statistics of the United States* (1975); *Statistical Abstract of the United States* (1999).

RACIAL COMPOSITION OF THE POPULATION

(IN THOUSANDS)

Year	White	Black	Indian	Hispanic	Asian/Pacific Islander
1790	3,172	757	(NA)	(NA)	(NA)
1800	4,306	1,002	(NA)	(NA)	(NA)
1820	7,867	1,772	(NA)	(NA)	(NA)
1840	14,196	2,874	(NA)	(NA)	(NA)
1860	26,923	4,442	(NA)	(NA)	(NA)
1880	43,403	6,581	(NA)	(NA)	(NA)
1900	66,809	8,834	(NA)	(NA)	(NA)
1910	81,732	9,828	(NA)	(NA)	(NA)
1920	94,821	10,463	(NA)	(NA)	(NA)
1930	110,287	11,891	(NA)	(NA)	(NA)
1940	118,215	12,866	(NA)	(NA)	(NA)
1950	134,942	15,042	(NA)	(NA)	(NA)
1960	158,832	18,872	(NA)	(NA)	(NA)
1970	178,098	22,581	(NA)	(NA)	(NA)
1980	194,713	26,683	1,420	14,609	3,729
1990	208,727	30,511	2,065	22,372	2,462
2000	211,461	34,658	2,476	35,306	10,642

Source: U.S. Bureau of the Census, U.S. *Census of Population: 1940*, vol. II, part 1, and vol. IV, part 1; *1950*, vol. II, part 1; *1960*, vol. I, part 1; *1970*, vol. I, part B; and *Current Population Reports*, P25-1095 and P25-1104; *Statistical Abstract of the United States* (2001).

THE ECONOMY AND FEDERAL SPENDING

Year	Gross National Product (GNP) (in billions)	Foreign Trade (in millions) Exports	Imports	Balance of Trade	Federal Budget (in billions)	Federal Surplus/Deficit (in billions)	Federal Debt (in billions)
1790	(NA)	$ 20	$ 23	$ −3	$ 0.004	$ +0.00015	$ 0.076
1800	(NA)	71	91	−20	0.011	+0.0006	0.083
1810	(NA)	67	85	−18	0.008	+0.0012	0.053
1820	(NA)	70	74	−4	0.018	−0.0004	0.091
1830	(NA)	74	71	+3	0.015	+0.100	0.049
1840	(NA)	132	107	+25	0.024	−0.005	0.004
1850	(NA)	152	178	−26	0.040	+0.004	0.064
1860	(NA)	400	362	−38	0.063	−0.01	0.065
1870	$ 7.4	451	462	−11	0.310	+0.10	2.4
1880	11.2	853	761	+92	0.268	+0.07	2.1
1890	13.1	910	823	+87	0.318	+0.09	1.2
1900	18.7	1,499	930	+569	0.521	+0.05	1.2
1910	35.3	1,919	1,646	+273	0.694	−0.02	1.1
1920	91.5	8,664	5,784	+2,880	6.357	+0.3	24.3
1930	90.7	4,013	3,500	+513	3.320	+0.7	16.3
1940	100.0	4,030	7,433	−3,403	9.6	−2.7	43.0
1950	286.5	10,816	9,125	+1,691	43.1	−2.2	257.4
1960	506.5	19,600	15,046	+4,556	92.2	+0.3	286.3
1970	992.7	42,700	40,189	+2,511	195.6	−2.8	371.0
1980	2,631.7	220,783	244,871	+24,088	590.9	−73.8	907.7
1990	5,524.5	394,030	494,042	−101,012	1,251.8	−220.5	3,233.3
2000	9,958.7	1,068,397	1,438,086	−369,689	1,788.8	+236.4	5,629.0

Source: *U.S. Office of Management and Budget, Budget of the United States Government, annual; Statistical Abstract of the United States,* 2001.

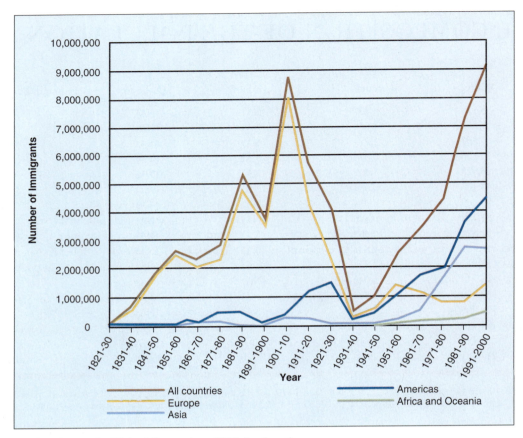

Immigration to the United States since 1820, by decade
Source: *Statistical Yearbook of the Immigration and Naturalization Service,* 2001.

GLOSSARY

Acquired Immune Deficiency Syndrome (AIDS) A complex of deadly pathologies resulting from infection with the human immunodeficiency virus (HIV).

Act for Religious Toleration The first law in America to call for freedom of worship for all Christians.

Actual Representation The practice whereby elected representatives normally reside in their districts and are directly responsive to local interests.

Affirmative action A set of policies to open opportunities in business and education for members of minority groups and women by allowing race and sex to be factors included in decisions to hire, award contracts, or admit students to higher education programs.

Age of Enlightenment Major intellectual movement occurring in Western Europe in the late seventeenth and early eighteenth centuries.

Agricultural Wheel One of several farmer organizations that emerged in the South during the 1880s. It sought federal legislation to deal with credit and currency issues.

Alamo Franciscan mission at San Antonio, Texas that was the site in 1836 of a siege and massacre of Texans by Mexican troops.

Albany Plan of Union Plan put forward in 1754 calling for an intercolonial union to manage defense and Indian affairs. The plan was rejected by participants at the Albany Congress.

Albany Regency The tightly disciplined state political machine built by Martin Van Buren in New York.

Alien and Sedition Acts Collective name given to four acts passed by Congress in 1798 that curtailed freedom of speech and the liberty of foreigners resident in the United States.

Alliance for Progress Program of economic aid to Latin America during the Kennedy administration.

Allies In World War I, Britain, France, Russia, and other belligerent nations fighting against the Central Powers but not including the United States.

American Anti-Slavery Society The first national organization of abolitionists, founded in 1833.

American Colonization Society Organization, founded in 1817 by antislavery reformers, that called for gradual emancipation and the removal of freed blacks to Africa.

American Federation of Labor (AFL) Union formed in 1886 that organized skilled workers along craft lines and emphasized a few workplace issues rather than a broad social program.

American Indian Movement (AIM) Group of Native-American political activists who used confrontations with the federal government to publicize their case for Indian rights.

American System of Manufacturing A technique of production pioneered in the United States in the first half of the nineteenth century that relied on precision manufacturing with the use of interchangeable parts.

American System The program of government subsidies favored by Henry Clay and his followers to promote American economic growth and protect domestic manufacturers from foreign competition.

Americans with Disabilities Act Legislation in 1992 that banned discrimination against physically handicapped persons in employment, transportation, and public accommodations.

Anarchists Persons who believe that all government interferes with individual liberty and should be abolished by whatever means necessary.

Anglican Of or belonging to the Church of England, a Protestant denomination.

Anglo-American Accords Series of agreements reached in the British-American Conventions of 1818 that fixed the western boundary between the United States and Canada, allowed for joint occupation of Oregon, and restored American fishing rights.

Annapolis Convention Conference of state delegates at Annapolis, Maryland, that issued a call in September 1786 for a convention to meet at Philadelphia to consider fundamental changes.

Antifederalists Opponents of the Constitution in the debate over its ratification.

Anti-Masons Third party formed in 1827 in opposition to the presumed power and influence of the Masonic order.

Appeal to the Colored Citizens of the World Written by David Walker, a published insistence that "America is more our country, than it is the whites'—we have enriched it with our blood and tears."

Articles of Confederation Written document setting up the loose confederation of states that comprised the first national government of the United States.

Atlanta Compromise Booker T. Washington's policy accepting segregation and disenfranchisement for African Americans in exchange for white assistance in education and job training.

Atlantic Charter Statement of common principles and war aims developed by President Franklin Roosevelt and British Prime Minister Winston Churchill at a meeting in August 1941.

Australian ballot Secret voting and the use of official ballots rather than party tickets.

Axis Powers The opponents of the United States and its allies in World War II.

Aztecs A warrior people who dominated the Valley of Mexico from 1100–1521.

Bacon's Rebellion Violent conflict in Virginia (1675–1676), beginning with settler attacks on Indians but culminating in a rebellion led by Nathaniel Bacon against Virginia's government.

Baker v. Carr U.S. Supreme Court decision in 1962 that allowed federal courts to review the appointment of state legislative districts and established the principle that such districts should have roughly equal populations ("one person, one vote").

Bank War The political struggle between President Andrew Jackson and the supporters of the Second Bank of the United States.

Battle of New Orleans Decisive American War of 1812 victory over British troops in January 1815 that ended any British hopes of gaining control of the lower Mississippi River Valley.

Battle of Put-in-Bay American naval victory on Lake Erie in September 1813 in the War of 1812 that denied the British strategic control over the Great Lakes.

Battle of the Atlantic The long struggle between German submarines and the British and U.S. navies in the North Atlantic from 1940 to 1943.

Battle of the Little Bighorn Battle in which Colonel George A. Custer and the Seventh Cavalry were defeated by the Sioux and Cheyennes under Sitting Bull and Crazy Horse in Montana in 1876.

Battles of Lexington and Concord The first two battles of the American Revolution which resulted in a total of 273 British soldiers dead, wounded, and missing and nearly one hundred Americans dead, wounded, and missing.

Bay of Pigs Site in Cuba of an unsuccessful landing by fourteen hundred anti-Castro Cuban refugees in April 1961.

Beaver Wars Series of bloody conflicts, occurring between 1640s and 1680s, during which the Iroquois fought the French for control of the fur trade in the east and the Great Lakes region.

Benevolent empire Network of reform associations affiliated with Protestant churches in the early nineteenth century dedicated to the restoration of moral order.

Berlin blockade Three-hundred-day Soviet blockade of land access to United States, British, and French occupation zones in Berlin, 1948–1949.

Berlin Wall Wall erected by East Germany in 1961 that isolated West Berlin from the surrounding areas in Communist-controlled East Berlin and East Germany.

Bill of Rights A written summary of inalienable rights and liberties.

Black codes Laws passed by states and municipalities denying many rights of citizenship to free black people before the Civil War.

Black Hawk's War Short 1832 war in which federal troops and Illinois militia units defeated the Sauk and Fox Indians led by Black Hawk.

Black Panthers Political and social movement among black Americans, founded in Oakland, California, in 1966 and emphasizing black economic and political power.

Black Power Philosophy emerging after 1965 that real economic and political gains for African Americans could come only through self-help, self-determination, and organizing for direct political influence.

"Bleeding Kansas" Violence between pro- and antislavery forces in Kansas Territory after the passage of the Kansas-Nebraska Act in 1854.

Blitzkrieg German war tactic in World War II ("lightning war") involving the concentration of air and armored firepower to punch and exploit holes in opposing defensive lines.

Bolshevik Member of the Communist movement in Russia that established the Soviet government after the 1917 Russian Revolution.

Bonus Army Unemployed veterans of World War I gathering in Washington in 1932 demanding payment of service bonuses not due until 1945.

Bosnia A nation in southeast Europe that split off from Yugoslavia and became the site of bitter civil and religious war, requiring NATO and U.S. intervention in the 1990s.

Boston Massacre After months of increasing friction between townspeople and the British troops stationed in the city, on March 5, 1770, British troops fired on American civilians in Boston.

Boston Tea Party Incident that occurred on December 16, 1773, in which Bostonians, disguised as Indians, destroyed £9,000 worth of tea belonging to the British East India Company in order to prevent payment of the duty on it.

British Constitution The principles, procedures, and precedents that governed the operation of the British government.

Brook Farm A utopian community and experimental farm established in 1841 near Boston.

Brown v. Board of Education of Topeka Supreme Court decision in 1954 that declared that "separate but equal" schools for children of different races violated the Constitution.

Bureau of Reclamation Federal agency established in 1902 providing public funds for irrigation projects in arid regions.

Cahokia One of the largest urban centers created by Mississippian peoples, containing 30,000 residents in 1250.

Californios Californians of Spanish descent.

Camp David Agreement Agreement to reduce points of conflict between Israel and Egypt, hammered out in 1977 with the help of U.S. President Jimmy Carter.

Carpetbaggers Northern transplants to the South, many of whom were Union soldiers who stayed in the South after the war.

Central Intelligence Agency (CIA) Agency established in 1947 that coordinates the gathering and evaluation of military and economic information on other nations.

Central Powers Germany and its World War I allies in Austria, Turkey, and Bulgaria.

Chain migration Process common to many immigrant groups whereby one family member brings over other family members, who in turn bring other relatives and friends and occasionally entire villages.

Charles River Bridge* v. *Warren Bridge Supreme Court decision of 1837 that promised economic competition by ruling that the broader rights of the community took precedence over any presumed right of monopoly granted in a corporate charter.

Cherokee War Conflict (1759–1761) on the southern frontier between the Cherokee Indians and colonists from Virginia southward.

***Chesapeake* incident** Attack in 1807 by the British ship *Leopard* on the American ship *Chesapeake* in American territorial waters.

Chisholm Trail The route followed by Texas cattle raisers driving their herds north to markets at Kansas railheads.

Church of Jesus Christ of Latter-day Saints (Mormon Church) Church founded in 1830 by Joseph Smith and based on the revelations in a sacred book he called the Book of Mormon.

Civil Rights Act of 1964 Federal legislation that outlawed discrimination in public accommodations and employment on the basis of race, skin color, sex, religion, or national origin.

Claims clubs Groups of local settlers on the nineteenth-century frontier who banded together to prevent the price of their land claims from being bid up by outsiders at public land auctions.

Coercive Acts Legislation passed by Parliament in 1774; included the Boston Port Act, the Massachusetts Government Act, the Administration of Justice Act, and the Quartering Act of 1774.

Cold War The political and economic confrontation between the Soviet Union and the United States that dominated world affairs from 1946 to 1989.

Collective Bargaining Representatives of a union negotiating with management on behalf of all members.

Colored Farmer's Alliance An organization of Southern black farmers formed in Texas in 1886 in response to the Southern Farmer's Alliance, which did not accept black people as members.

Columbian Exchange The transatlantic exchange of plants, animals, and diseases that occurred after the first European contact with the Americas.

Committee of Safety Any of the extralegal committees that directed the revolutionary movement and carried on the functions of government at the local level in the period between the breakdown of royal authority and the establishment of regular governments.

Committee on Public Information (CPI) Government agency during World War I that sought to shape public opinion in support of the war effort through newspapers, pamphlets, speeches, films, and other media.

Committees of Correspondence Committees formed in Massachusetts and other colonies in the pre-Revolutionary period to keep Americans informed about British measures that would affect the colonies.

Communism A social structure based on the common ownership of property.

Compromise of 1850 The four-step compromise which admitted California as a free state, allowed the residents of the New Mexico and Utah territories to decide the slavery issue for themselves, ended the slave trade in the District of Columbia, and passed a new fugitive slave law to enforce the constitutional provision stating that a slave escaping into a free state shall be delivered back to the owner.

Compromise of 1877 The Congressional settling of the 1876 election which installed Republican Rutherford B. Hayes in the White House and gave Democrats control of all state governments in the South.

Conciliatory Proposition Plan whereby Parliament would "forbear" taxation of Americans in colonies whose assemblies imposed taxes considered satisfactory by the British government.

Confederate States of America Nation proclaimed in Montgomery, Alabama, in February 1861, after the seven states of the Lower South seceded from the United States.

Confiscation Act Second confiscation law passed by Congress, ordering the seizure of land from disloyal Southerners and the emancipation of their slaves.

Congress of Industrial Organizations An alliance of industrial unions that spurred the 1930s organizational drive among the mass-production industries.

Congress of Racial Equality (CORE) Civil rights group formed in 1942 and committed to nonviolent civil disobedience.

Congressional Reconstruction Name given to the period 1867–1870 when the Republican-dominated Congress controlled Reconstruction era policy.

Conservation The efficient management and use of natural resources, such as forests, grasslands, and rivers, as opposed to preservation or controlled exploitation.

Constitution of the United States The written document providing for a new central government of the United States.

Constitutional Convention Convention that met in Philadelphia in 1787 and drafted the Constitution of the United States.

Constitutional Union Party National party formed in 1860, mainly by former Whigs, that emphasized allegiance to the Union and strict enforcement of all national legislation.

Continental Army The regular or professional army authorized by the Second Continental Congress and commanded by General George Washington during the Revolutionary War.

Continental Association Agreement, adopted by the First Continental Congress in 1774 in response to the Coercive Acts to cut off trade with Britain until the objectionable measures were repealed.

Contract Theory of Government The belief that government is established by human beings to protect certain rights—such as life, liberty, and property—that are theirs by natural, divinely sanctioned law and that when government protects these rights, people are obligated to obey it.

Contract with America Platform proposing a sweeping reduction in the role and activities of the federal government on which many Republican candidates ran for Congress in 1994.

Copper-heads A term Republicans applied to Northern war dissenters and those suspected of aiding the Confederate cause during the Civil War.

Council of Economic Advisers Board of three professional economists established in 1946 to advise the president on economic policy.

Counterculture Various alternatives to mainstream values and behaviors that became popular in the 1960s, including experimentation with psychedelic drugs, communal living, a return to the land, Asian religions, and experimental art.

Country (Real Whig) Ideology Strain of thought (focusing on the threat to personal liberty and the taxation of property holders) first appearing in England in the late seventeenth century in response to the growth of governmental power and a national debt.

Coureur de Bois French for "woods runner," an independent fur trader in New France.

Covenant A contract with God, binding settlers to meet their religious obligations in return for God's favor.

Coxey's Army A protest march of unemployed workers, led by Populist businessman Jacob Coxey, demanding inflation and a public works program during the depression of the 1890s.

Cult of domesticity The belief that women, by virtue of their sex, should stay home as the moral guardians of family life.

Currency Act Law passed by Parliament in 1764 to prevent the colonies from issuing legal tender paper money.

Dartmouth College v. Woodward Supreme Court decision of 1819 that prohibited states from interfering with the privileges granted to a private corporation.

Dawes Act An 1887 law terminating tribal ownership of land and allotting some parcels of land to individual Indians with the remainder opened for white settlement.

D-Day June 6, 1944, the day of the first paratroop drops and amphibious landings on the coast of Normandy, France, in the first stage of Operation OVERLORD during World War II.

Declaration of Independence The document by which the Second Continental Congress announced and justified its decision to renounce the colonies' allegiance to the British government.

Declaration of London Statement drafted by an international conference in 1909 to clarify international law and specify the rights of neutral nations.

Declaration of Rights and Grievances Resolves asserting that the Stamp Act and other taxes imposed on the colonists without their consent were unconstitutional.

Declaration of Sentiments The resolutions passed at the Seneca Falls Convention in 1848 calling for full female equality, including the right to vote.

Deism Religious orientation that rejects divine revelation and holds that the workings of nature alone reveal God's design for the universe.

Democratic Party Political party formed in the 1820s under the leadership of Andrew Jackson; favored states' rights and a limited role for the federal government.

Denmark Vesey's Conspiracy The most carefully devised slave revolt in which rebels planned to seize control of Charleston in 1822 and escape to freedom in Haiti, a free black republic, but they were betrayed by other slaves, and seventy-five conspirators were executed.

Deregulation Reduction or removal of government regulations and encouragement of direct competition in many important industries and economic sectors.

Détente (French for "easing of tension") Used to describe the new U.S. relations with China and the Soviet Union in 1972.

Disnfranchisement The use of legal means to bar individuals or groups from voting.

Dixiecrats States' Rights Democrats.

Dollar diplomacy The U.S. policy of using private investment in other nations to promote American diplomatic goals and business interests.

Dominion of New England James II's failed plan of 1686 to combine eight northern colonies into a single large province, to be governed by a royal appointee with no elective assembly.

Dred Scott Decision Supreme Court ruling, in a lawsuit brought by Dred Scott, a slave demanding his freedom based on his residence in a free state, that slaves could not be U.S. citizens and that Congress had no jurisdiction over slavery in the territories.

Eastern Front The area of military operations in World War II located east of Germany in eastern Europe and the Soviet Union.

Economic Recovery and Tax Act of 1981 (ERTA) A major revision of the federal income tax system.

Emancipation Proclamation Decree announced by President Abraham Lincoln in September 1862 and formally issued on January 1, 1863, freeing slaves in all Confederate states still in rebellion.

Embargo Act of 1807 Act passed by Congress in 1807 prohibiting American ships from leaving for any foreign port.

Empresarios Agents who received a land grant from the Spanish or Mexican government in return for organizing settlements.

Encomienda In the Spanish colonies, the grant to a Spanish settler of a certain number of Indian subjects, who would pay him tribute in goods and labor.

Enumerated Products Items produced in the colonies and enumerated in acts of Parliament that could be legally shipped from the colony of origin only to specified locations.

Environmental Protection Agency (EPA) Federal agency created in 1970 to oversee environmental monitoring and cleanup programs.

Era of Good Feelings The period from 1817 to 1823 in which the disappearance of the Federalists enabled the Republicans to govern in a spirit of seemingly nonpartisan harmony.

Espionage Act Law whose vague prohibition against obstructing the nation's war effort was used to crush dissent and criticism during World War I.

Fair Employment Practices Committee (FEPC) Federal agency established in 1941 to curb racial discrimination in war production jobs and government employment.

Farmers' Alliance A broad mass movement in the rural South and West during the late nineteenth century, encompassing several organizations and demanding economic and political reforms.

Fascist Government A government subscribing to a philosophy of dictatorship that merges the interests of the state, armed forces, and big business.

Federal Deposit Insurance Corporation (FDIC) Government agency that guarantees bank deposits, thereby protecting both depositors and banks.

Federal Highway Act of 1956 Measure that provided federal funding to build a nationwide system of interstate and defense highways.

Federal Reserve Act The 1913 law that revised banking and currency by extending limited government regulation through the creation of the Federal Reserve System.

Federal Trade Commission Government agency established in 1914 to provide regulatory oversight of business activity.

Federalism The sharing of powers between the national government and the states.

Federalists Supporters of the Constitution who favored its ratification.

Field Order No. 15 Order by General William T. Sherman in January 1865 to set aside abandoned land along the southern Atlantic coast for forty-acre grants to freedmen, rescinded by President Andrew Johnson later that year.

Fifteenth Amendment Passed by Congress in 1869, guaranteed the right of American men to vote, regardless of race.

Fireside Chats Speeches broadcast nationally over the radio in which President Franklin D. Roosevelt explained complex issues and programs in plain language, as though his listeners were gathered around the fireside with him.

First Continental Congress Meeting of delegates from most of the colonies held in 1774 in response to the Coercive Acts. The Congress endorsed the Suffolk Resolves, adopted the Declaration of Rights and Grievances, and agreed to establish the Continental Association.

First Persian Gulf War War (1991) between Iraq and a U.S.-led coalition that followed Iraq's invasion of Kuwait and resulted in the expulsion of Iraqi forces from that country.

Fletcher v. *Peck* Supreme Court decision of 1810 that overturned a state law by ruling that it violated a legal contract.

Fort Sumter A fort located in Charleston, South Carolina, where President Lincoln attempted to provision federal troops in 1861, triggering a hostile response from onshore Confederate forces, opening the Civil War.

Fourteenth Amendment Passed by Congress in 1866, guaranteed every citizen equality before the law by prohibiting states from violating the civil rights of their citizens, thus outlawing the black codes.

Frame of Government William Penn's constitution for Pennsylvania which included a provision allowing for religious freedom.

Franco-American Accord of 1800 Settlement reached with France that brought an end to the Quasi-War and released the United Sates from its 1778 alliance with France.

Free Silver Philosophy that the government should expand the money supply by purchasing and coining all the silver offered to it.

Free Speech Movement (FSM) Student movement at the University of California, Berkeley, formed in 1964 to protest limitations on political activities on campus.

Freedmen's Bureau Agency established by Congress in March 1865 to provide social, educational, and economic services, advice, and protection to former slaves and destitute whites; lasted seven years.

Freedom Summer Voter registration effort in rural Mississippi organized by black and white civil rights workers in 1964.

French and Indian War The last of the Anglo-French colonial wars (1754–1763) and the first in which fighting began in North America. The war ended with France's defeat.

Fugitive Slave Act Law, part of the Compromise of 1850, that required the authorities in the North to assist Southern slave catchers and return runaway slaves to their owners.

Fundamental Constitutions of Carolina A complex plan for organizing the colony of Carolina, drafted in 1669 by Anthony Ashley Cooper and John Locke.

Gabriel Prosser's Rebellion Slave revolt that failed when Gabriel Prosser, a slave preacher and blacksmith, organized a thousand slaves for an attack on Richmond, Virginia, in 1800.

Gag Rule A procedural device whereby antislavery petitions were automatically tabled in Congress with no discussion.

Gang System The organization and supervision of slave field hands into working teams on Southern plantations.

Gentlemen's Agreement A diplomatic agreement in 1907 between Japan and the United States curtailing but not abolishing Japanese immigration.

GI Bill of Rights Legislation in June 1944 that eased the return of veterans into American society by providing educational and employment benefits.

Gibbons v. *Ogden* Supreme Court decision of 1824 involving coastal commerce that overturned a steamboat monopoly granted by the state of New York on the grounds that only Congress had the authority to regulate interstate commerce.

Gilded Age Term applied to late-nineteenth-century America that refers to the shallow display and worship of wealth characteristic of that period.

Glasnost Russian for "openness" applied to Mikhail Gorbachev's encouragement of new ideas and easing of political repression in the Soviet Union.

Glorious Revolution Bloodless revolt that occurred in England in 1688 when parliamentary leaders invited William of Orange, a Protestant, to assume the English throne.

Gospel of Wealth Thesis that hard work and perseverance lead to wealth, implying that poverty is a character flaw.

Grand Settlement of 1701 Separate peace treaties negotiated by Iroquois diplomats at Montreal and Albany that marked the beginning of Iroquois neutrality in conflicts between the French and the British in North America.

Grandfather Clause Rule that required potential voters to demonstrate that their grandfathers had been eligible to vote; used in some Southern states after 1890 to limit the black electorate.

Grange The National Grange of the Patrons of Husbandry, a national organization of farm owners formed after the Civil War.

Granger Laws State laws enacted in the Midwest in the 1870s that regulated rates charged by railroads, grain elevator operators, and other middlemen.

Great Awakening Tremendous religious revival in colonial America striking first in the Middle Colonies and New England in the 1740s and then spreading to the southern colonies.

Great Compromise Plan proposed at the 1787 Constitutional Convention for creating a national bicameral legislature in which all states would be equally represented in the Senate and proportionally represented in the House.

Great Depression The nation's worst economic crisis, extending through the 1930s, producing unprecedented bank failures, unemployment, and industrial and agricultural collapse.

Great Migration The mass movement of African Americans from the rural South to the urban North.

Great Migration The mass movement of African Americans from the rural South to the urban North, spurred especially by new job opportunities during World War I and the 1920s.

Great Society Theme of Lyndon Johnson's administration, focusing on poverty, education, and civil rights.

Great Uprising Unsuccessful railroad strike of 1877 to protest wage cuts and the use of federal troops against strikers; the first nationwide work stoppage in American history.

Greater East Asia Co-Prosperity Sphere Japanese nationalists believed that Japan should expel the French, British, Dutch,

and Americans from Asia and create this sphere in which Japan would give the orders and other Asian peoples would comply.

Greenback Party A third party of the 1870s and 1880s that garnered temporary support by advocating currency inflation to expand the economy and assist debtors.

Gulf of Tonkin Resolution Request to Congress from President Lyndon Johnson in response to North Vietnamese torpedo boat attacks in which he sought authorization for "all necessary measures" to protect American forces and stop further aggression.

Halfway Covenant Plan adopted in 1662 by New England clergy to deal with the problem of declining church membership, allowing children of baptized parents to be baptized whether or not their parents had experienced conversion.

Harlem Renaissance A new African-American cultural awareness that flourished in literature, art, and music in the 1920s.

Headright System Instituted by the Virginia Company in 1616, this system gave fifty acres to anyone who paid his own way to Virginia and an additional fifty for each person (or "head") he brought with him.

Helsinki Accords Agreement in 1975 among NATO and Warsaw Pact members that recognized European national boundaries as set after World War II and included guarantees of human rights.

Holocaust The systematic murder of millions of European Jews and others deemed undesirable by Nazi Germany.

Homestead Act Law passed by Congress in May 1862 providing homesteads with 160 acres of free land in exchange for improving the land within five years of the grant.

Hoovervilles Shantytowns, sarcastically named after President Hoover, in which unemployed and homeless people lived in makeshift shacks, tents, and boxes.

Horizontal Integration The merger of competitors in the same industry.

House Committee on Un-American Activities (HUAC) Originally intended to ferret out pro-Fascists, it later investigated "un-American propaganda" that attacked constitutional government.

House of Burgesses The legislature of colonial Virginia. First organized in 1619, it was the first institution of representative government in the English colonies.

Hull House Chicago settlement house that became part of a broader neighborhood revitalization project led by Jane Addams.

Immigration and Nationality Act of 1965 Federal legislation that replaced the national quota system for immigration with new limits for each hemisphere.

Imperialism The policy and practice of exploiting nations and peoples for the benefit of an imperial power either directly through military occupation and colonial rule or indirectly through economic domination of resources and markets.

Indentured servants Individuals who contracted to serve a master for a period of four to seven years in return for payment of the servant's passage to America.

Independent Treasury System Fiscal arrangement first instituted by President Martin Van Buren in which the federal government kept its money in regional vaults and transacted its business in hard money.

Indian Removal Act President Andrew Jackson's measure that allowed state officials to override federal protection of Native Americans.

Initiative Procedure by which citizens can introduce a subject for legislation, usually through a petition signed by a specific number of voters.

Intermediate Nuclear Force Agreement (INF) Disarmament agreement between the United States and the Soviet Union under which an entire class of missiles would be removed and destroyed and on-site inspections would be permitted.

International Monetary Fund International organization established in 1945 to assist nations in maintaining stable currencies.

Internet The system of interconnected computers and servers that allows the exchange of email, posting of Web sites, and other means of instant communication.

Interstate Commerce Act The 1887 law that expanded federal power over business by prohibiting pooling and discriminatory rates by railroads and establishing the first federal regulatory agency, the Interstate Commerce Commission.

Intolerable Acts American term for the Coercive Acts and the Quebec Act.

Irreconcilables Group of U.S. senators adamantly opposed to ratification of the Treaty of Versailles after World War I.

Island Hopping The Pacific campaigns of 1944 that were the American naval versions of the *Blitzkrieg*.

Jay's Treaty Treaty with Britain negotiated in 1794 in which the United States made major concessions to avert a war over the British seizure of American ships.

Jazz Age The 1920s, so called for the popular music of the day as a symbol of the many changes taking place in the mass culture.

Jim Crow Laws Segregation laws that became widespread in the South during the 1890s.

John Brown's Raid New England abolitionist John Brown's ill-fated attempt to free Virginia's slaves with a raid on the federal arsenal at Harper's Ferry, Virginia, in 1859.

Joint-stock company Business enterprise in which a group of stockholders pooled their money to engage in trade or to fund colonizing expeditions.

Judicial Review A power implied in the Constitution that gives federal courts the right to review and determine the constitutionality of acts passed by Congress and state legislatures.

Judiciary Act of 1789 Act of Congress that implemented the judiciary clause of the Constitution by establishing the Supreme Court and a system of lower federal courts.

Kansas-Nebraska Act Law passed in 1854 creating the Kansas and Nebraska Territories but leaving the question of slavery open to residents, thereby repealing the Missouri Compromise.

King George's War The third Anglo-French war in North America (1744–1748), part of the European conflict known as the War of the Austrian Succession.

King Phillip's War Conflict in New England (1675–1676) between Wampanoags, Narragansetts, and other Indian peoples against English settlers; sparked by English encroachments on native lands.

King William's War The first Anglo-French conflict in North America (1689–1697), the American phase of Europe's War of the League of Augsburg.

Knights of Labor Labor union founded in 1869 that included skilled and unskilled workers irrespective of race or gender.

Know-Nothing Party Anti-immigrant party formed from the wreckage of the Whig Party and some disaffected Northern democrats in 1854.

Korean War Pacific war started on June 25, 1950, when North Korea, helped by Soviet equipment and Chinese training, attacked South Korea.

Kosovo Province of Yugoslavia where the United States and NATO intervened militarily in 1999 to protect ethnic Albanians from expulsion.

Ku Klux Klan Perhaps the most prominent of the vigilante groups that terrorized black people in the South during Reconstruction era, founded by the Confederate veterans in 1866.

Land Grant College Act Law passed by Congress in July 1862 awarding proceeds from the sale of public lands to the states for the establishment of agricultural and mechanical colleges.

Land Ordinance of 1785 Act passed by Congress under the Articles of Confederation that created the grid system of surveys by which all subsequent public land was made available for sale.

League of Nations International organization created by the Versailles Treaty after World War I to ensure world stability.

League of Women Voters League formed in 1920 advocating for women's rights, among them the right for women to serve on juries and equal pay laws.

Lecompton Constitution Proslavery draft written in 1857 by Kansas territorial delegates elected under questionable circumstances; it was rejected by two governors, supported by President Buchanan, and decisively defeated by Congress.

Levittown   Suburban Long Island community of postwar rental houses built by William Levitt for veterans of World War II.

Liberty Bonds   Interest-bearing certificates sold by the U.S. government to finance the American World War I effort.

Liberty party   The first antislavery political party, formed in 1840.

Limited Test Ban Treaty   Treaty, signed by the United States, Britain, and the Soviet Union, outlawing nuclear testing in the atmosphere, in outer space, and under water.

Lincoln-Douglas Debates   Series of debates in the 1858 Illinois senatorial campaign during which Douglas and Lincoln staked out their differing opinions on the issue of slavery.

Lost Cause   The phrase many white Southerners applied to their Civil War defeat. They viewed the war as a noble cause but only a temporary setback in the South's ultimate vindication.

Lynching   Execution, usually by a mob, without trial.

Mahanism   The ideas advanced by Alfred Thayer Mahan, stressing U.S. naval, economic, and territorial expansion.

Manhattan Project   The effort, using the code name Manhattan Engineer District, to develop an atomic bomb under the management of the U.S. Army Corps of Engineers during World War II.

Manifest Destiny   Doctrine, first expressed in 1845, that the expansion of white Americans across the continent was inevitable and ordained by God.

Marbury v. *Madison*   Supreme Court decision of 1803 that created the precedent of judicial review by ruling as unconstitutional part of the Judiciary Act of 1789.

Marshall Plan   Secretary of State George C. Marshall's European Recovery Plan of June 5, 1947, committing the United States to help in the rebuilding of post-World War II Europe.

McCarthyism   Anti-Communist attitudes and actions associated with Senator Joe McCarthy in the early 1950s, including smear tactics and innuendo.

Medicaid   Supplementary medical insurance for the poor, financed through the federal government; program created in 1965.

Medicare   Basic medical insurance for the elderly, financed through the federal government; program created in 1965.

Mercantilism   Economic system whereby the government intervenes in the economy for the purpose of increasing national wealth.

Mexican Cession of 1848   The addition of half a million square miles to the United States as a result of victory in the 1846 war between the United States and Mexico.

Middle Passage   The voyage between West Africa and the New World slave colonies.

Minute Men   Special companies of militia formed in Massachusetts and elsewhere beginning in late 1744.

Missouri Compromise   Sectional compromise in Congress in 1820 that admitted Missouri to the Union as a slave state and Maine as a free state and prohibited slavery in the northern Louisiana Purchase territory.

Model Cities Program   Effort to target federal funds to upgrade public services and economic opportunity in specifically defined urban neighborhoods between 1966 and 1974.

Monroe Doctrine   Declaration by President James Monroe in 1823 that the Western Hemisphere was to be closed off to further European colonization and that the United States would not interfere in the internal affairs of European nations.

Monroe Doctrine   In December 1823, Monroe declared to Congress that Americans "are henceforth not to be considered as subjects for future colonization by any European power."

Muckraking   Journalism exposing economic, social, and political evils, so named by Theodore Roosevelt for its "raking the muck" of American society.

Mugwumps   Elitist and conservative reformers who favored sound money and limited government and opposed tariffs and the spoils system.

Multinational corporations   Firms with direct investments, branches, factories, and offices in a number of countries.

Nat Turner's Rebellion   Uprising of slaves in Southampton County, Virginia, in the summer of 1831 led by Nat Turner that resulted in the death of fifty-five white people.

Nation of Islam   Religious movement among black Americans that emphasizes self-sufficiency, self-help, and separation from white society.

National Aeronautics and Space Administration (NASA)   Federal agency created in 1958 to manage American space flights and exploration.

National American Woman Suffrage Association   The organization, formed in 1890, that coordinated the ultimately successful campaign to achieve women's right to vote.

National Association for the Advancement of Colored People (NAACP)   Interracial organization co-founded by W. E. B. DuBois in 1910 dedicated to restoring African-American political and social rights.

National Origins Act of 1924   Law sharply restricting immigration on the basis of immigrants' national origins and discriminating against southern and eastern Europeans and Asians.

National Security Council Paper 68 (NSC-68)   Policy statement that committed the United States to a military approach to the Cold War.

National Security Council   The formal policymaking body for national defense and foreign relations, created in 1947 and consisting of the president, the secretary of defense, the secretary of state, and others appointed by the president.

Nationalists   Group of leaders in the 1780s who spearheaded the drive to replace the Articles of Confederation with a stronger central government.

Nativism   Favoring the interests and culture of native-born inhabitants over those of immigrants.

Nativist Organizations Joined by American-born artisans in the 1840s which sought to curb mass immigration from Europe and limit the political rights of Catholic immigrants.

Natural Rights Political philosophy that maintains that individuals have an inherent right, found in nature and preceding any government or written law, to life and liberty.

Neoliberal Advocate or participant in the effort to reshape the Democratic party for the 1990s around a policy emphasizing economic growth and competitiveness in the world economy.

New Deal The economic and political policies of the Roosevelt administration in the 1930s.

New Federalism President Richard Nixon's policy to shift responsibilities of government programs from the federal level to the states.

New Freedom Woodrow Wilson's 1912 program for limited government intervention in the economy to restore competition by curtailing the restrictive influences of trusts and protective tariffs, thereby providing opportunities for individual achievement.

New Frontier John F. Kennedy's domestic and foreign policy initiatives, designed to reinvigorate sense of national purpose and energy.

New Harmony Short-lived utopian community established in Indiana in 1825, based on the socialist ideas of Robert Owen, a wealthy Scottish manufacturer.

New Jersey Plan Proposal of the New Jersey delegation for a strengthened national government in which all states would have an equal representation in a unicameral legislature.

New Lights People who experienced conversion during the revivals of the Great Awakening.

New Nationalism Theodore Roosevelt's 1912 program calling for a strong national government to foster, regulate, and protect business, industry, workers, and consumers.

Niagara Movement African-Ameri-can group organized in 1905 to promote racial integration, civil and political rights, and equal access to economic opportunity.

Nineteenth Amendment Constitutional revision that in 1920 established women citizens' right to vote.

Nisei U.S. citizens born of immigrant Japanese parents.

Nixon Doctrine President Nixon's new American policy (1969) toward Asia in which the United States would honor treaty commitments but would gradually disengage and expect Asian nations to handle military defense on their own.

Nonimportation Movement A tactical means of putting economic pressure on Britain by refusing to buy its exports to the colonies.

North American Free Trade Agreement (NAFTA) Agreement reached in 1993 by Canada, Mexico, and the United States to substantially reduce barriers to trade.

North Atlantic Treaty Organization (NATO) Organization of ten European countries, Canada, and the United States whom together formed a mutual defense pact in April, 1949.

Northwest Ordinance of 1787 Legislation that prohibited slavery in the Northwest Territories and provided the model for the incorporation of future territories into the union as co-equal states.

Nullification A constitutional doctrine holding that a state has a legal right to declare a national law null and void within its borders.

Nullification Crisis Sectional crisis in the early 1830s in which a states' rights party in South Carolina attempted to nullify federal law.

Office of Economic Opportunity (OEO) Federal agency that coordinated many programs of the War on Poverty between 1964 and 1975.

Olive Branch Petition adopted by the Second Continental Congress as a last effort of peace that avowed America's loyalty to George III and requested that he protect them from further aggressions.

Omaha Platform The 1892 platform of the Populist party repudiating laissez-faire and demanding economic and political reforms to aid distressed farmers and workers.

Oneida Community Utopian community established in upstate New York in 1848 by John Humphrey Noyes and his followers.

Open Door American policy of seeking equal trade and investment opportunities in foreign nations or regions.

Open shop Factory of business employing workers whether or not they are union members; in practice, such a business usually refuses to hire union members and follows antiunion policies.

Operation Desert Storm Code name for the successful offensive against Iraq by the United States and its allies in the Persian Gulf War (1991).

Operation OVERLORD U.S. and British invasion of France in June 1944 during World War II.

Oregon Trail Overland trail of more than two thousand miles that carried American settlers from the Midwest to new settlements in Oregon, California, and Utah.

Organization of Petroleum Exporting Countries (OPEC) Cartel of oil-producing nations in Asia, Africa, and Latin America that gained substantial power over the world economy in the mid- to late-1970s by controlling the production and price of oil.

Panic of 1857 Banking crisis that caused a credit crunch in the North; it was less severe in the South, where high cotton prices spurred a quick recovery.

Pan-Indian Resistance Movement Movement calling for the political and cultural unification of Indian tribes in the late eighteenth and early nineteenth centuries.

Parson's Cause Series of developments (1758–1763) that began when the Virginia legislature modified the salaries of Anglican clergymen, who complained to the crown and sued to recover damages. British authorities responded by imposing additional restrictions on the legislature. Virginians, who saw this as a threat, reacted by strongly reasserting local autonomy.

Patriot Act   Federal legislation adopted in 2001, in response to the terrorist attacks of September 11, intended to facilitate antiterror actions by federal law enforcement and intelligence agencies.

Peace of Paris   Treaties signed in 1783 by Great Britain, the United States, France, Spain, and the Netherlands that ended the Revolutionary War.

Pendelton Civil Service Act   A law of 1883 that reformed the spoils system by prohibiting government workers from making political contributions and creating the Civil Service Commission to oversee their appointment on the basis of merit rather than politics.

Pentagon Papers   Classified Defense Department documents on the history of the United States' involvement in Vietnam, prepared in 1968 and leaked to the press in 1971.

Pequot War   Conflict between English settlers and Pequot Indians over control of land and trade in eastern Connecticut.

Perestroika   Russian for "restructuring," applied to Mikhail Gorbachev's efforts to make the Soviet economic and political systems more modern, flexible, and innovative.

Pilgrims   Settlers of Plymouth Colony, who viewed themselves as spiritual wanderers.

Platt Amendment   A stipulation the United States had inserted into the Cuban constitution in 1901 restricting Cuban autonomy and authorizing U.S. intervention and naval bases.

Plessy v. Ferguson   Supreme Court decision holding that Louisiana's railroad segregation law did not violate the Constitution as long as the railroads or the state provided equal accommodations.

Pogroms   Government-directed attacks against Jewish citizens, property, and villages in tsarist Russia beginning in the 1880s; a primary reason for Russian Jewish migration to the United States.

Poll Taxes   Taxes imposed on voters as a requirement for voting.

Pontiac's Rebellion   Indian uprising (1763–1766) led by Pontiac of the Ottawas and Neolin of the Delawares.

Popular Sovereignty   A solution to the slavery crisis suggested by Michigan senator Lewis Cass by which territorial residents, not Congress, would decide slavery's fate.

Populist Party   A major third party of the 1890s formed on the basis of the Southern Farmer's Alliance and other reform organizations.

Populist Party   A major third party of the 1890s, formed on the basis of the Southern Farmers' Alliance and other organizations, mounting electoral challenges against Democrats in the South and the Republicans in the West.

Potsdam Declaration   Statement issued by the United States during a meeting of U.S. President Harry Truman, British Prime Minister Winston Churchill, and So-

viet Premier Joseph Stalin in which the United States declared its intention to democratize the Japanese political system and reintroduce Japan into the international community.

Predestination   The belief that God decided at the moment of Creation which humans would achieve salvation.

Preparedness   Military buildup in preparation for possible U.S. participation in World War I.

Proclamation Line   Boundary, decreed as part of the Proclamation of 1763, that limited British settlements to the eastern side of the Appalachian Mountains.

Proclamation of 1763   Royal proclamation setting the boundary known as the Proclamation Line.

Progressive Era   An era in the United States (roughly between 1900 and 1917) in which important movements challenged traditional relationships and attitudes.

Prohibition   A ban on the production, sale, and consumption of liquor, achieved temporarily through state laws and the Eighteenth Amendment.

Prohibition Party   A venerable third party still in existence that has persistently campaigned for the abolition of alcohol but has also introduced many important reform ideas into American politics.

Proposition 187   California legislation adopted by popular vote in California in 1994, which cuts off state-funded health and education benefits to undocumented or illegal immigrants.

Proprietary Colony   A colony created when the English monarch granted a huge tract of land to an individual or group of individuals, who became "lords proprietor."

Protestant Fundamentalists   Religious conservatives who believe in the literal accuracy and divine inspiration of the Bible.

Protestants   All European supporters of religious reform under Charles V's Holy Roman Empire.

Pueblo Revolt   Rebellion in 1680 of Pueblo Indians in New Mexico against their Spanish overlords, sparked by religious conflict and excessive Spanish demands for tribute.

Puritans   Individuals who believed that Queen Elizabeth's reforms of the Church of England had not gone far enough in improving the church. Puritans led the settlement of Massachusetts Bay Colony.

Putting-out System   System of manufacturing in which merchants furnished households with raw materials for processing by family members.

Quakers   Members of the Society of Friends, a radical religious group that arose in the mid-seventeenth century. Quakers rejected formal theology, focusing instead on the Holy Spirit that dwelt within them.

Quartering Acts   Acts of Parliament requiring colonial legislatures to provide supplies and quarters for the troops stationed in America.

Quasi-War   Undeclared naval war of 1797 to 1800 between the United States and France.

Quebec Act Law passed by Parliament in 1774 that provided an appointed government for Canada, enlarged the boundaries of Quebec, and confirmed the privileges of the Catholic Church.

Queen Anne's War American phase (1702–1713) of Europe's War of the Spanish Succession.

Radical Republicans A shifting group of Republican congressmen, usually a substantial minority, who favored the abolition of slavery from the beginning of the Civil War and later advocated harsh treatment of the defeated South.

Recall The process of removing an official from office by popular vote, usually after using petitions to call for such a vote.

Reconquista The long struggle (ending in 1492) during which Spanish Christians reconquered the Iberian peninsula from Muslim occupiers.

Red Scare Post-World War I public hysteria over Bolshevik influence in the United States directed against labor activism, radical dissenters, and some ethnic groups.

Redemptioner Similar to an indentured servant, except that a redemptioner signed a labor contract in America rather than in Europe.

Redlining The withholding of home purchase loans and insurance coverage from inner-city older neighborhoods by federal housing agencies and private industry.

Referendum Submission of a law, proposed or already in effect, to a direct popular vote for approval or rejection.

Reformation Martin Luther's challenge to the Catholic Church, initiated in 1517, calling for a return to what he understood to be the purer practices and beliefs of the early church.

Regulators Vigilante groups active in the 1760s and 1770s in the western parts of North and South Carolina. The South Carolina Regulators attempted to rid the area of outlaws; the North Carolina Regulators were more concerned with high taxes and court costs.

Repartimiento In the Spanish colonies, the assignment of Indian workers to labor on public works projects.

Republican (Jeffersonian) Party Party headed by Thomas Jefferson that formed in opposition to the financial and diplomatic policies of the Federalist party; favored limiting the powers of the national government and placing the interests of farmers over those of financial and commercial groups.

Republican Party Party that emerged in the 1850s in the aftermath of the bitter controversy over the Kansas-Nebraska Act, consisting of former Whigs, some Northern Democrats, and many Know-Nothings.

Republicanism A complex, changing body of ideas, values, and assumptions, closely related to country ideology, that influenced American political behavior during the eighteenth and nineteenth centuries.

Rescate Procedure by which Spanish colonists would pay ransom to free Indians captured by rival natives.

Reservationists Group of U.S. senators favoring approval of the Treaty of Versailles, after amending it to incorporate their reservations.

Roe **v.** *Wade* U.S. Supreme Court decision (1973) that disallowed state laws prohibiting abortion during the first three months (trimester) of pregnancy and established guidelines for abortion in the second and third trimesters.

Roosevelt Corollary President Theodore Roosevelt's policy asserting U.S. authority to intervene in the affairs of Latin American nations; an expansion of the Monroe Doctrine.

Rush-Bagot Agreement Treaty of 1817 between the United States and Britain that effectively demilitarized the Great Lakes by sharply limiting the number of ships each power could station on them.

Sabbatarian Movement Reform organization founded in 1828 by Congregationalist and Presbyterian ministers that lobbied for an end to the delivery of mail on Sundays and other Sabbath violations.

"Sack of Lawrence" Vandalism and arson committed by a group of proslavery men in Lawrence, the free-state capital of Kansas Territory.

Sagebrush Rebellion Political movement in the Western states in the early 1980s that called for easing of regulations on the economic issue of federal lands and the transfer of some or all of those lands to state ownership.

SALT (Strategic Arms Limitation Treaty) Treaty signed in 1972 by the United States and the Soviet Union to slow the nuclear arms race.

Sand Creek Massacre The near annihilation in 1864 of Black Kettle's Cheyenne band by Colorado troops under Colonel John Chivington's orders to "kill and scalp all, big and little."

Santa Fe Trail The 900-mile trail opened by American merchants for trading purposes following Mexico's liberalization of the formerly restrictive trading policies of Spain.

Scalawags Southern whites, mainly small landowning farmers and well-off merchants and planters, who supported the Southern Republican party during Reconstruction.

Search and Destroy U.S. military tactic in South Vietnam, using small detachments to locate enemy units and then massive air, artillery, and ground forces to destroy them.

Second Bank of the United States A national bank chartered by Congress in 1816 with extensive regulatory powers over currency and credit.

Second Great Awakening Series of religious revivals in the first half of the nineteenth century characterized by great emotionalism in large public meetings.

Second Party System The national two-party competition between Democrats and Whigs from the 1830s through the early 1850s.

Second Treaty of Fort Laramie The treaty acknowledging U.S. defeat in the Great Sioux War in 1868 and supposedly guaranteeing the Sioux perpetual land and hunting rights in South Dakota, Wyoming, and Montana.

Securities and Exchange Commission (SEC) Federal agency with authority to regulate trading practices in stocks and bonds.

Sedition Act Broad law restricting criticism of America's involvement in World War I or its government, flag, military, taxes, or officials.

Segregation A system of racial control that separated the races, initially by custom but increasingly by law during and after Reconstruction.

Selective Service Act of 1917 The law establishing the military draft for World War I.

Selective Service System Federal agency that coordinated military conscription before and during the Vietnam War.

Self-determination The right of a people or a nation to decide on its own political allegiance or form of government without external influence.

Seneca Falls Convention The first convention for women's equality in legal rights, held in upstate New York in 1848.

Separatists Members of an offshoot branch of Puritanism. Separatists believed that the Church of England was too corrupt to be reformed and hence were convinced they must "separate" from it to save their souls.

Seventeenth Amendment Constitutional change that in 1913 established the direct popular election of U.S. senators.

Shakers The followers of Mother Ann Lee, who preached a religion of strict celibacy and communal living.

Sharecropping Labor system that evolved during and after Reconstruction whereby landowners furnished laborers with a house, farm animals, and tools and advanced credit in exchange for a share of the laborers' crop.

Shays's Rebellion An armed movement of debt-ridden farmers in western Massachusetts in the winter of 1786–1787. The rebellion created a crisis atmosphere.

Sheppard-Towner Maternity and Infancy Act The first federal social welfare law, passed in 1921, providing federal funds for infant and maternity care.

Sherman Antitrust Act The first federal antitrust measure, passed in 1890; sought to promote economic competition by prohibiting business combinations in restraint of trade or commerce.

Silicon Valley The region of California including San Jose and San Francisco that holds the nation's greatest concentration of electronics firms.

Sixteenth Amendment Constitutional revision that in 1913 authorized a federal income tax.

***Slaughterhouse* Cases** Group of cases resulting in one sweeping decision by the U.S. Supreme Court in 1873 that contradicted the intent of the Fourteenth Amendment by decreeing that most citizenship rights remained under state, not federal, control.

Slave Codes A series of laws passed mainly in the Southern colonies in the late seventeenth and early eighteenth centuries to defend the status of slaves and codify the denial of basic civil rights to them.

Social Darwinism The application of Charles Darwin's theory of biological evolution to society, holding that the fittest and wealthiest survive, the weak and the poor perish, and government action is unable to alter this "natural" process.

Social Gospel Movement Movement created by reform-minded Protestant ministers seeking to introduce religious ethics into industrial relations and appealing to churches to meet their social responsibilities.

Socialism Political and economic theory advocating that land, natural resources, and the chief industries should be owned by the community as a whole.

Solid South The one-party (Democratic) political system that dominated the South from the 1890s to the 1950s.

Sons of Liberty Secret organizations in the colonies formed to oppose the Stamp Act.

Sound Money Misleading slogan that referred to a conservative policy of restricting the money supply and adhering to the gold standard.

Southeast Asia Treaty Organization (SEATO) Mutual defense alliance signed in 1954 by the United States, Britain, France, Thailand, Pakistan, the Philippines, Australia, and New Zealand.

Southern Christian Leadership Conference (SCLC) Black civil rights organization founded in 1957 by Martin Luther King Jr., and other clergy.

Southern Farmer's Alliance The largest of several organizations that formed in the post-Reconstruction South to advance the interests of beleaguered small farmers.

Southern Homestead Act Largely unsuccessful law passed in 1866 that gave black people preferential access to public lands in five southern states.

Southern Manifesto A document signed by 101 members of Congress from Southern states in 1956 that argued that the Supreme Court's decision in *Brown* v. *Board of Education of Topeka* itself contradicted the Constitution.

Southwest Ordinance of 1790 Legislation passed by Congress that set up a government with no prohibition on slavery in U.S. territory south of the Ohio River.

Specie Circular Proclamation issued by President Andrew Jackson in 1836 stipulating that only gold or silver could be used as payment for public land.

Spheres of Influence Regions dominated and controlled by an outside power.

Spoils System The awarding of government jobs to party loyalists.

Stamp Act Congress October 1765 meeting of delegates sent by nine colonies, held in New York City, that adopted the Declaration of Rights and Grievances and petitioned against the Stamp Act.

Stamp Act Law passed by Parliament in 1765 to raise revenue in America by requiring taxed, stamped paper for legal documents, publications, and playing cards.

States' Rights Favoring the rights of individual states over rights claimed by the national government.

Stonewall Rebellion   On June 27, 1969, patrons fought back when police raided the gay Stonewall Inn in New York.

Stono Rebellion   Uprising in 1739 of South Carolina slaves against whites; inspired in part by Spanish officials' promise of freedom for American slaves who escaped to Florida.

Strategic Defense Initiative (SDI)   President Reagan's program, announced in 1983, to defend the United States against nuclear missile attack with untested weapons systems and sophisticated technologies.

Student Nonviolent Coordinating Committee (SNCC)   Black civil rights organization founded in 1960 and drawing heavily on younger activists and college students.

Students for a Democratic Society (SDS)   The leading student organization of the New Left of the early and mid-1960s.

Subtreasury Plan   A program promoted by the Southern Farmer's Alliance in response to low cotton prices and tight credit. Farmers would store their crop in a warehouse until prices rose, in the meantime borrowing up to 80 percent of the value of the stored crops from the government at a low interest rate.

Suffolk Resolves   Militant resolves adopted in 1774 in response to the Coercive Acts by representatives from the towns in Suffolk County, Massachusetts, including Boston.

Suffrage   The right to vote in a political election.

Sugar Act   Law passed in 1764 to raise revenue in the American colonies. It lowered the duty from 6 pence to 3 pence per gallon on foreign molasses imported into the colonies and increased the restrictions on colonial commerce.

Sunbelt   The states of the American South and Southwest.

***Sussex* Pledge**   Germany's pledge during World War I not to sink merchant ships without warning, on the condition that Britain also observe recognized rules of international laws.

Swann* v. *Charlotte-Mecklenburg Board of Education   U.S. Supreme Court decision in 1971 that upheld cross-city busing to achieve the racial integration of public schools.

Sweatshops   Small, poorly ventilated shops or apartments crammed with workers, often family members, who pieced together garments.

Taft-Hartley Act   Federal legislation of 1947 that substantially limited the tools available to labor unions in labor-management disputes.

Taos Revolt   Uprising of Pueblo Indians in New Mexico that broke out in January 1847 over the imposition of American rule during the Mexican War; the revolt was crushed within a few weeks.

Tariff Act of 1789   Apart from a few selected industries, this first tariff passed by Congress was intended to raise revenue and not protect American manufacturers from foreign competition.

Tea Act of 1773   Act of Parliament that permitted the East India Company to sell through agents in America without paying the duty customarily collected in Britain, thus reducing the retail price.

Tejanos   Persons of Spanish or Mexican descent born in Texas.

Teller Amendment   A congressional resolution adopted in 1898 renouncing any American intention to annex Cuba.

Temperance   Reform movement originating in the 1820s that sought to eliminate the consumption of alcohol.

Temporary Assistance for Needy Families (TANF)   Federal program, utilizing work requirements for and time limits on benefits, created in 1996 to replace earlier welfare programs to aid families and children.

Tenements   Four- to six-story residential dwellings, once common in New York, built on tiny lots without regard to providing ventilation or light.

Tennessee Valley Authority (TVA)   Federal regional planning agency established to promote conservation, produce electric power, and encourage economic development in seven southern states.

Thirteenth Amendment   Constitutional amendment ratified in 1865 that freed all slaves throughout the United States.

Tonnage Act of 1789   Duty levied on the tonnage of incoming ships to U.S. ports; tax was higher on foreign-owned ships to favor American shippers.

Tories   A derisive term applied to Loyalists in America who supported the king and Parliament just before and during the American Revolution.

Townshend Duty Act   Act of Parliament, passed in 1767, imposing duties on colonial tea, lead, paint, paper, and glass.

Trail of Tears   The forced march in 1838 of the Cherokee Indians from their homelands in Georgia to the Indian Territory in the West.

Transcendentalism   A philosophical and literary movement centered on an idealistic belief in the divinity of individuals and nature.

Trans-Continental Treaty of 1819   Treaty between the United States and Spain in which Spain ceded Florida to the United States, surrendered all claims to the Pacific Northwest, and agreed to a boundary between the Louisiana Purchase territory and the Spanish Southwest.

Transportation Revolution   Dramatic improvements in transportation that stimulated economic growth after 1815 by expanding the range of travel and reducing the time and cost of moving goods and people.

Treaty of Ghent   Treaty signed in December 1814 between the United States and Britain that ended the War of 1812.

Treaty of Greenville   Treaty of 1795 in which Native Americans in the Old Northwest were forced to cede most of the present state of Ohio to the United States.

Treaty of Lancaster   Negotiation in 1744 whereby Iroquois chiefs sold Virginia land speculators the right to trade at the Forks of the Ohio.

Treaty of Paris   The formal end to British hostilities against France and Spain in February 1763.

Treaty of San Lorenzo (Pickney's Treaty)   Treaty with Spain in 1795 in which Spain recognized the 31st parallel as the boundary between the United States and Spanish Florida.

Treaty of Tordesillas   Treaty negotiated by the pope in 1494 to resolve the territorial claims of Spain and Portugal.

Treaty of Versailles   The treaty ending World War I and creating the League of Nations.

Truman Doctrine   President Harry Truman's statement in 1947 that the United States should assist other nations that were facing external pressure or internal revolution.

Underground Railroad   Support system set up by antislavery groups in the Upper South and the North to assist fugitive slaves in escaping the South.

Underwood-Simmons Tariff Act   The 1913 reform law that lowered tariff rates and levied the first regular federal income tax.

Union Leagues   Republican party organizations in Northern cities that became an important organizing device among freedmen in Southern cities after 1865.

United States v. Cruikshank   Supreme Court ruling of 1876 that overturned the convictions of some of those responsible for the Colfax Massacre, ruling that the Enforcement Act applied only to violations of black rights by states, not individuals.

University of California v. Bakke   U.S. Supreme Court case in 1978 that allowed race to be used as one of several factors in college and university admission decisions but made rigid quotas unacceptable.

Valley Forge   Area of Pennsylvania approximately 20 miles northwest of Philadelphia where General George Washington's Continental troops were quartered from December 1777 to June 1778 while British forces occupied Philadelphia during the Revolutionary War.

Vertical Integration   The consolidation of numerous production functions, from the extraction of the raw materials to the distribution and marketing of the finished products, under the direction of one firm.

Viet Cong   Communist rebels in South Vietnam who fought the pro-American government established in South Vietnam in 1954.

Virginia Plan   Proposal calling for a national legislature in which the states would be represented according to population.

Virtual Representation   The notion that parliamentary members represented the interests of the nation as a whole, not those of the particular district that elected them.

Volstead Act   The 1920 law defining the liquor forbidden under the Eighteenth Amendment and giving enforcement responsibilities to the Prohibition Bureau of the Department of the Treasury.

Voting Rights Act   Legislation in 1965 that overturned a variety of practices by which states systematically denied voter registration to minorities.

Waltham System   During the industrialization of the early nineteenth century, the recruitment of unmarried young women for employment in factories.

War Hawks   Members of Congress, predominantly from the South and West, who aggressively pushed for a war against Britain after their election in 1810.

War Industries Board (WIB)   The federal agency that reorganized industry for maximum efficiency and productivity during World War I.

War of 1812   War fought between the United States and Britain from June 1812 to January 1815 largely over British restrictions on American shipping.

War on Poverty   Set of programs introduced by Lyndon Johnson between 1963 and 1966 designed to break the cycle of poverty by providing funds for job training, community development, nutrition, and supplementary education.

Watergate   A complex scandal involving attempts to cover up illegal actions taken by administration officials and leading to the resignation of President Richard Nixon in 1974.

Webster-Ashburton Treaty   Treaty signed by the United States and Britain in 1842 that settled a boundary dispute between Maine and Canada.

Welfare Capitalism   A paternalistic system of labor relations emphasizing management responsibility for employee well-being.

Whig Party   Political party, formed in the mid-1830s in opposition to the Jacksonian Democrats, that favored a strong role for the national government for promoting economic growth.

Whigs   The name used by advocates of colonial resistance to British measures during the 1760s and 1770s.

Whiskey Rebellion   Armed uprising in 1794 by farmers in western Pennsylvania who attempted to prevent the collection of the excise tax on whiskey.

Whitewater   Arkansas real estate development in which Bill and Hillary Clinton were investors; several fraud convictions resulted from investigations into Whitewater, but evidence was not found that the Clinton's were involved in wrongdoing.

Wilmot Proviso   The amendment offered by Pennsylvania Democrat David Wilmot in 1846 which stipulated that "as an express and fundamental condition to the acquisition of any territory from the Republic of Mexico . . . neither slavery nor involuntary servitude shall ever exist in any part of said territory."

Wobblies   Popular name for the members of the Industrial Workers of the World (IWW).

Women's Christian Temperance Union (WCTU)   Women's organization whose members visited schools to educate children about the evils of alcohol, addressed prisoners, and blanketed men's meetings with literature.

World Bank   Designed to revive postwar international trade, it drew on the resources of member nations to make economic development loans to governments for such projects as new dams or agricultural modernization.

World Trade Organization (WTO)   International organization that sets standards and practices for global trade, and the focus of international protests over world economic policy in the late 1990s.

World Wide Web   A part of the Internet designed to allow easier navigation of the network through the use of graphical user interfaces and hypertext links between different addresses.

Wounded Knee Massacre The U.S. Army's brutal winter massacre in 1890 of at least two hundred Sioux men, women, and children as part of the government's assault on the tribe's Ghost Dance religion.

Writs of Assistance Documents issued by a court of law that gave British officials in America the power to search for smuggled goods whenever they wished.

XYZ Affair Diplomatic incident in 1798 in which Americans were outraged by the demand of the French for a bribe as a condition for negotiating with American diplomats.

Yalta Conference Meeting of U.S. President Franklin Roosevelt, British Prime Minister Winston Churchill, and Soviet Premier Joseph Stalin held in February 1945 to plan the final stages of World War II and postwar arrangements.

Yellow press A deliberately sensational journalism of scandal and exposure designed to attract an urban mass audience and increase advertising revenues.

Yellow-dog Contracts Employment agreements binding workers not to join a union.

CREDITS

Chapter 19 Image Key: A. Lynton Gardiner, Dorling Kindersley Media Library; B. The Granger Collection, New York; C. Dave King ©, Dorling Kindersley Media Library; D. Dorling Kindersley Media Library; E. Library of Congress; F. Chinese mining laborers, Idaho, 76-119.2/A, Idaho State Historical Society. G. Library of Congress.

Chapter 20 Image Key: A. Picture Research Consultants. B. Courtesy of the Library of Congress. C. The Granger Collection, New York. D. The Granger Collection, New York. E. Corbis/Bettmann; F. Corbis/Bettmann; G. the Granger Collection, New York. H. Courtesy of the Library of Congress; I. Courtesy of the Library of Congress; J. Culver Pictures, Inc. K. Corbis/Bettmann; I. Courtesy of the Library of Congress.

Chapter 21 Image Key: A. Corbis/Bettmann; B. the Granger Collection, New York; C. the Granger Collection, New York; D. Corbis/Bettmann; E. Indiana Historical Society, A70. F. Kheel Center, Cornell University, Ithaca, NY 14853-3901. G. Corbis/Bettmann; H. the Granger Collection, New York; I. The Granger Collection, New York.

Chapter 22 Image Key: A. Corbis/Bettmann; B. Corbis/Bettmann; C. The Granger Collection, New York; D. Corbis/Bettmann; E. Courtesy of Library of Congress; F. Jonathan Potter, Dorling Kindersley Media Library; G. Corbis/Bettmann; H. The Granger Collection, New York. I. © Stock Montage, 2004. J. Theodore Roosevelt Collection, Harvard College Library.

Chapter 23 Image Key: A. Getty Images Inc.-Hulton Archive Photos; B. Corbis/Bettmann; C. Corbis/Bettmann; D. Richard Ward, Dorling Kindersley Media Library; E. the Granger Collection, New York; F. National Archives and Records Administration. G. Corbis/Bettmann.

Chapter 24 Image Key: A. Getty Images Inc.-Hulton Archive Photos; B. Corbis/Bettmann; C. Getty Images–Photodisc. D. C. Squared Studios, Getty Images, Inc. Photodisc. E. Wisconsin Historical Society/WHi-5020; F. Prentice Hall Higher Education; G. Stock Montage, Inc./Historical Pictures Collection. H. By permission of Campbell Soup Company. I. Courtesy W. A. Swift Photograph Collection, Archives and Special Collections, Ball State University.

Chapter 25 Image Key: A. Corbis/Bettmann; B. Corbis/Bettmann; C. SuperStock, Inc.; D. Corbis/Bettmann; E. Getty Images, Inc.-Photodisc. F. Brown Brothers; G. National Archives and Records Administration; H.

Corbis/Bettmann; I. The Granger Collection/© Estate Of Ben Shahn/Licensed By Vaga, New York, NY. J. Isaac Soyer, "Employment Agency". Oil on canvas, 34 1/2″ × 45″. The Whitney Museum of American Art.

Chapter 26 Image Key: A. Andy Crawford, Dorling Kindersley Media Library; B. Corbis/Bettmann; C. Andy Crawford, Dorling Kindersley Media Library; D. The Granger Collection, New York; E. Getty Images Inc.-Hulton Archive Photos; F. Corbis/Bettmann; G. Prentice Hall Higher Education; H. Rieger Communications, Inc. I. Corbis/Bettmann; J. The Granger Collection, New York.

Chapter 27 Image Key: A. Corbis/Bettmann; B. Getty Images/Time Life Pictures; C. Corbis/Bettmann; D. Getty Images Inc.-Hulton Archive Photos E. Corbis/Bettmann; F. AP/Wide World Photos; G. Getty Images/Time Life Pictures; H. National Archives and Records Administration; I. Corbis/Bettmann.

Chapter 28 Image Key: A. Corbis/Bettmann; B. Getty Images Inc.-Hulton Archive Photos; C. Dorling Kindersley Media Library; D. Getty Images, Inc.-Photodisc. E. Bernard Hoffman/Life Magazine/©1950 TimePix; F. Sondak, Getty Images, Inc.–Taxi; G. Ralph Crane, Getty Images/Time Life Pictures. H. AP/Wide World Photos; I. AP/Wide World Photos.

Chapter 29 Image Key: A. © Royalty-Free/CORBIS; B. © Royalty-Free/CORBIS C. ©John Paul Filo/Hulton/Archive; D. George Meany Memorial Archives; E. Corbis/Bettmann; F. AP/Wide World Photos; G. Philip Jones Griffith, Magnum Photos, Inc., H. AP/Wide World Photos; I. Wally McNamee, Corbis/Bettmann.

Chapter 30 Image key: A. Telepress Syndicate Agency, Corbis/Bettmann; B. Ron Edmonds, Corbis/Bettmann; C. Corbis/Bettmann; D. Dorling Kindersley Media Library; E. AP/Wide World Photos; F. Denis Paquin, Corbis/Bettmann; G. Jose L. Pelaez, Corbis/Stock Market; H. Joe Marquette, AP/Wide World Photos.

Chapter 31 Image Key: A. Doug Kanter, SIPA Press; B. Author supplied; C. Dorling Kindersley Media Library D. Dorling Kindersley Media Library; E. Dorling Kindersley Media Library; F. Dorling Kindersley Media Library; G. Dorling Kindersley Media Library; H. Ira Wyman, Corbis/Sygma; I. Barbara Gauntt/The Clarion-Ledger; J. Prentice Hall Higher Education; K. Stephen Crowley, New York Times Pictures.

INDEX

U.S. HISTORY DOCUMENTS CD-ROM

Over 300 Primary Source Documents

SINGLE PC LICENSE AGREEMENT AND LIMITED WARRANTY

READ THIS LICENSE CAREFULLY BEFORE OPENING THIS PACKAGE. BY OPENING THIS PACKAGE, YOU ARE AGREEING TO THE TERMS AND CONDITIONS OF THIS LICENSE. IF YOU DO NOT AGREE, DO NOT OPEN THE PACKAGE. PROMPTLY RETURN THE UNOPENED PACKAGE AND ALL ACCOMPANYING ITEMS TO THE PLACE YOU OBTAINED THEM.

1. GRANT OF LICENSE AND OWNERSHIP: THE ENCLOSED COMPUTER PROGRAMS <<AND DATA>> ("SOFTWARE") ARE LICENSED, NOT SOLD, TO YOU BY PEARSON EDUCATION, INC. PUBLISHING AS PEARSON PRENTICE HALL ("WE" OR THE "COMPANY") AND IN CONSIDERATION OF YOUR PURCHASE OR ADOPTION OF THE ACCOMPANYING COMPANY TEXTBOOKS AND/OR OTHER MATERIALS, AND YOUR AGREEMENT TO THESE TERMS. WE RESERVE ANY RIGHTS NOT GRANTED TO YOU. YOU OWN ONLY THE DISK(S) BUT WE AND/OR OUR LICENSORS OWN THE SOFTWARE ITSELF. THIS LICENSE ALLOWS YOU TO USE AND DISPLAY YOUR COPY OF THE SOFTWARE ON A SINGLE COMPUTER (I.E., WITH A SINGLE CPU) AT A SINGLE LOCATION FOR ACADEMIC USE ONLY, SO LONG AS YOU COMPLY WITH THE TERMS OF THIS AGREEMENT. YOU MAY MAKE ONE COPY FOR BACK UP, OR TRANSFER YOUR COPY TO ANOTHER CPU, PROVIDED THAT THE SOFTWARE IS USABLE ON ONLY ONE COMPUTER.

2. RESTRICTIONS: YOU MAY NOT TRANSFER OR DISTRIBUTE THE SOFTWARE OR DOCUMENTATION TO ANYONE ELSE. EXCEPT FOR BACKUP, YOU MAY NOT COPY THE DOCUMENTATION OR THE SOFTWARE. YOU MAY NOT NETWORK THE SOFTWARE OR OTHERWISE USE IT ON MORE THAN ONE COMPUTER OR COMPUTER TERMINAL AT THE SAME TIME. YOU MAY NOT REVERSE ENGINEER, DISASSEMBLE, DECOMPILE, MODIFY, ADAPT, TRANSLATE, OR CREATE DERIVATIVE WORKS BASED ON THE SOFTWARE OR THE DOCUMENTATION. YOU MAY BE HELD LEGALLY RESPONSIBLE FOR ANY COPYING OR COPYRIGHT INFRINGEMENT THAT IS CAUSED BY YOUR FAILURE TO ABIDE BY THE TERMS OF THESE RESTRICTIONS.

3. TERMINATION: THIS LICENSE IS EFFECTIVE UNTIL TERMINATED. THIS LICENSE WILL TERMINATE AUTOMATICALLY WITHOUT NOTICE FROM THE COMPANY IF YOU FAIL TO COMPLY WITH ANY PROVISIONS OR LIMITATIONS OF THIS LICENSE. UPON TERMINATION, YOU SHALL DESTROY THE DOCUMENTATION AND ALL COPIES OF THE SOFTWARE. ALL PROVISIONS OF THIS AGREEMENT AS TO LIMITATION AND DISCLAIMER OF WARRANTIES, LIMITATION OF LIABILITY, REMEDIES OR DAMAGES, AND OUR OWNERSHIP RIGHTS SHALL SURVIVE TERMINATION.

4. LIMITED WARRANTY AND DISCLAIMER OF WARRANTY: COMPANY WARRANTS THAT FOR A PERIOD OF 60 DAYS FROM THE DATE YOU PURCHASE THIS SOFTWARE (OR PURCHASE OR ADOPT THE ACCOMPANYING TEXTBOOK), THE SOFTWARE, WHEN PROPERLY INSTALLED AND USED IN ACCORDANCE WITH THE DOCUMENTATION, WILL OPERATE IN SUBSTANTIAL CONFORMITY WITH THE DESCRIPTION OF THE SOFTWARE SET FORTH IN THE DOCUMENTATION, AND THAT FOR A PERIOD OF 30 DAYS THE DISK(S) ON WHICH THE SOFTWARE IS DELIVERED SHALL BE FREE FROM DEFECTS IN MATERIALS AND WORKMANSHIP UNDER NORMAL USE. THE COMPANY DOES NOT WARRANT THAT THE SOFTWARE WILL MEET YOUR REQUIREMENTS OR THAT THE OPERATION OF THE SOFTWARE WILL BE UNINTERRUPTED OR ERROR-FREE. YOUR ONLY REMEDY AND THE COMPANY'S ONLY OBLIGATION UNDER THESE LIMITED WARRANTIES IS, AT THE COMPANY'S OPTION, RETURN OF THE DISK FOR A REFUND OF ANY AMOUNTS PAID FOR IT BY YOU OR REPLACEMENT OF THE DISK. THIS LIMITED WARRANTY IS THE ONLY WARRANTY PROVIDED BY THE COMPANY AND ITS LICENSORS, AND THE COMPANY AND ITS LICENSORS DISCLAIM ALL OTHER WARRANTIES, EXPRESS OR IMPLIED, INCLUDING WITHOUT LIMITATION, THE IMPLIED WARRANTIES OF MERCHANTABILITY AND FITNESS FOR A PARTICULAR PURPOSE. THE COMPANY DOES NOT WARRANT, GUARANTEE OR MAKE ANY REPRESENTATION REGARDING THE ACCURACY, RELIABILITY, CURRENTNESS, USE, OR RESULTS OF USE, OF THE SOFTWARE.

5. LIMITATION OF REMEDIES AND DAMAGES: IN NO EVENT, SHALL THE COMPANY OR ITS EMPLOYEES, AGENTS, LICENSORS, OR CONTRACTORS BE LIABLE FOR ANY INCIDENTAL, INDIRECT, SPECIAL, OR CONSEQUENTIAL DAMAGES ARISING OUT OF OR IN CONNECTION WITH THIS LICENSE OR THE SOFTWARE, INCLUDING FOR LOSS OF USE, LOSS OF DATA, LOSS OF INCOME OR PROFIT, OR OTHER LOSSES, SUSTAINED AS A RESULT OF INJURY TO ANY PERSON, OR LOSS OF OR DAMAGE TO PROPERTY, OR CLAIMS OF THIRD PARTIES, EVEN IF THE COMPANY OR AN AUTHORIZED REPRESENTATIVE OF THE COMPANY HAS BEEN ADVISED OF THE POSSIBILITY OF SUCH DAMAGES. IN NO EVENT SHALL THE LIABILITY OF THE COMPANY FOR DAMAGES WITH RESPECT TO THE SOFTWARE EXCEED THE AMOUNTS ACTUALLY PAID BY YOU, IF ANY, FOR THE SOFTWARE OR THE ACCOMPANYING TEXTBOOK. BECAUSE SOME JURISDICTIONS DO NOT ALLOW THE LIMITATION OF LIABILITY IN CERTAIN CIRCUMSTANCES, THE ABOVE LIMITATIONS MAY NOT ALWAYS APPLY TO YOU.

6. GENERAL: THIS AGREEMENT SHALL BE CONSTRUED IN ACCORDANCE WITH THE LAWS OF THE UNITED STATES OF AMERICA AND THE STATE OF NEW YORK, APPLICABLE TO CONTRACTS MADE IN NEW YORK, EXCLUDING THE STATE'S LAWS AND POLICIES ON CONFLICTS OF LAW, AND SHALL BENEFIT THE COMPANY, ITS AFFILIATES AND ASSIGNEES. THIS AGREEMENT IS THE COMPLETE AND EXCLUSIVE STATEMENT OF THE AGREEMENT BETWEEN YOU AND THE COMPANY AND SUPERSEDES ALL PROPOSALS OR PRIOR AGREEMENTS, ORAL, OR WRITTEN, AND ANY OTHER COMMUNICATIONS BETWEEN YOU AND THE COMPANY OR ANY REPRESENTATIVE OF THE COMPANY RELATING TO THE SUBJECT MATTER OF THIS AGREEMENT. IF YOU ARE A U.S. GOVERNMENT USER, THIS SOFTWARE IS LICENSED WITH "RESTRICTED RIGHTS" AS SET FORTH IN SUBPARAGRAPHS (A)-(D) OF THE COMMERCIAL COMPUTER-RESTRICTED RIGHTS CLAUSE AT FAR 52.227-19 OR IN SUBPARAGRAPHS (C)(1)(II) OF THE RIGHTS IN TECHNICAL DATA AND COMPUTER SOFTWARE CLAUSE AT DFARS 252.227-7013, AND SIMILAR CLAUSES, AS APPLICABLE.

SHOULD YOU HAVE ANY QUESTIONS CONCERNING THIS AGREEMENT OR IF YOU WISH TO CONTACT THE COMPANY FOR ANY REASON, PLEASE CONTACT IN WRITING: LEGAL DEPARTMENT, PRENTICE HALL, 1 LAKE STREET, UPPER SADDLE RIVER, NJ 07450 OR CALL PEARSON EDUCATION PRODUCT SUPPORT AT 1-800-677-6337.